D1398220

ARTIFICIAL INTELLIGENCE

A Knowledge-Based Approach

PWS-KENT Series in Computer Science

Borse, *FORTRAN 77 for Engineers*
Borse, *FORTRAN 77 and Numerical Methods for Engineers*
Brainerd, *FORTRAN 77 Fundamentals and Style*
Firebaugh, *Artificial Intelligence: A Knowledge-Based Approach*
Giarratano and Riley, *Expert Systems: Principles and Programming*
Goldberg, *PASCAL*
Hennefeld, *Using BASIC: An Introduction to Computer Programming,* Third Edition
Hennefeld, *Using Microsoft and IBM BASIC: An Introduction to Computer Programming*
Hennefeld, *Using Turbo PASCAL: 3.0, 4.0, and 5.0*
Kapps and Stafford, *Assembly Language for the PDP-11: RT-RSX-UNIX,* Second Edition
Korsh, *Data Structures, Algorithms and Program Style*
Korsh and Garrett, *Data Structures, Algorithms and Program Style Using C*
Lane and Mooney, *A Practical Approach to Operating Systems*
Lane, *Data Communications Software Design*
Payne, *Advanced Structured BASIC: File Processing with the IBM-PC*
Payne, *Structured Basic for the IBM-PC with Business Applications*
Popkin, *Advanced Structured COBOL,* Second Edition
Popkin, *Comprehensive Structured COBOL,* Third Edition
Popkin, *Introductory Structured COBOL Programming,* Second Edition
Radford and Haigh, *Turbo PASCAL for the IBM-PC*
Riley, *A Second Course in Turbo PASCAL*
Riley, *Data Abstraction and Structure: An Introduction To CS II*
Riley, *Programming Using Turbo PASCAL*
Riley, *Using MODULA-2*
Riley, *Using PASCAL: An Introduction To CS I*
Rojiani, *Programming in BASIC for Engineers*
Rood, *Logic and Structured Design for Computer Programmers*
Runnion, *Structured Programming in Assembly Language*
Skvarcius, *Problem Solving Using PASCAL: Algorithm Development and Programming Concepts*
Smith, *Design and Analysis of Algorithms*
Weinman, *FORTRAN for Scientists and Engineers*
Weinman, *VAX FORTRAN*
Worthington, *C Programming*

ARTIFICIAL INTELLIGENCE

A Knowledge-Based Approach

Morris W. Firebaugh

University of Wisconsin - Parkside

PWS-KENT PUBLISHING COMPANY

BOSTON

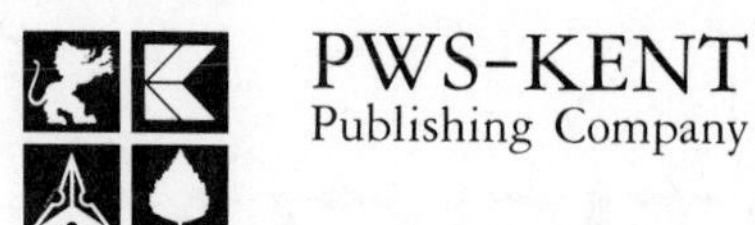

20 Park Plaza
Boston, Massachusetts 02116

CREDITS:

Cover Design: Ken Russo
Cover Computer Graphics: Morris W. Firebaugh

PWS-KENT Publishing Company is a division of Wadsworth, Inc.

Library of Congress Cataloging-in-Publication Data

Firebaugh, Morris W.
Artificial intelligence.

Includes index.
1. Artificial intelligence. I. Title.
Q335.F56 1988 006.3 87-36806
ISBN 0-87835-325-9

Printed in the United States of America
89 90 91 92 93 — 10 9 8 7 6 5 4 3 2

DEDICATION

To
Joyce, Steven, and Susan

for their love and patience
as this book grew from dream to reality.

CONTENTS

PREFACE

This book was written as a text for my class in Artificial Intelligence at the University of Wisconsin – Parkside. This is a course for upper level undergraduates and assumes programming skill in at least one high level language and some familiarity with data structure concepts. The book is designed to provide a broad and comprehensive survey of the field of artificial intelligence with particular emphasis on the role of knowledge in the design of intelligent systems.

Objectives of this text

The primary objective of the text is to introduce students to the major ideas of artificial intelligence so that they will understand and be able to implement AI concepts in their own programming. A thorough study of the material in this text will provide the student with at least a conceptual introduction to all the major areas of AI and a working knowledge of many of the more practical and applied areas. Since AI is rapidly coming out of the laboratory into the marketplace, I believe it is important to stress the role of knowledge engineering in the design of practical, knowledge-based systems.

Features of the text which help in meeting these goals include:

- A comprehensive and detailed discussion of ***expert systems***, including step-by-step instructions for building actual rule-based systems.

- An in-depth discussion of ***robotics*** from an AI perspective, with suggestions on the role of knowledge in the implementation of robotic systems.

- Identification of several of the bottlenecks to the implementation of useful AI systems and a focus on ***machine learning*** as the solution of the knowledge acquisition problem.

- A comprehensive survey of ***parallel machine architectures***, with particular emphasis on ***neural networks*** as a promising alternative to traditional, symbol-based representations of knowledge.

- An introduction to AI ***programming languages***, with a survey of several AI languages and an emphasis on both LISP and Prolog.

This text is, in fact, the first to integrate applied areas such as expert systems, robotics, and pattern recognition into the more traditional AI context and to trace the connection from early "toy systems" to these useful practical applications. It is also the first AI text to recognize the limitations of traditional symbol-oriented paradigms for knowledge representation and to suggest alternatives such as biologically-inspired neural networks for certain classes of AI problems.

Artificial intelligence as a discipline is characterized by a unique feature distinguishing it from almost all other disciplines. That is that almost all of the founders of the discipline are still living and many are still productive in AI research. As in all fields of science, AI is not simply a static body of facts and theories, but rather a dynamic collage of ideas and interactions between very human beings. Since I believe that important AI concepts can best be understood and interpreted in the human context in which they evolved, I have attempted to present material in this text within this human context. This is the basis for the historical presentation with frequent reference to the leading AI researchers in a given area and chapter heading photographs of representative authorities in each field. As a student I found it much easier to associate significant scientific contributions with particular faces, and I trust my students will find this a valuable learning tool as well.

Organization of courses using this text

There are at least four distinct modes in which this text may be used for courses in artificial intelligence and/or expert systems. From the least intensive to the most intensive, these modes may be classified as:

- ***A short course on expert systems*** — Chapters 10—13 provide a basis for a short course on expert systems. Chapter 10 describes production systems which are the most commonly used representation for expert systems, Chapter 11 surveys five benchmark expert systems which established the field, Chapter 12 provides architectural principles and considerations in the design of expert systems, and Chapter 13 examines knowledge engineering tools and presents a step-by-step example of building a simple expert system. It is recommended that the instructor for such a short course augment the text by purchasing one of the many fine, inexpensive expert system shells available for the IBM PC and Macintosh computers.

- ***A survey of artificial intelligence course*** — By skipping Chapter 2 and Appendix A on AI programming, the text would serve for a lower-level, one-semester survey course in artificial intelligence. The instructor may skip the programming examples in LISP and Prolog and assign concept related discussion questions at the end of each chapter.

• ***A one-semester introduction to artificial intelligence course*** — Including the language chapter and Appendix A the instructor can offer an intensive, one-semester introduction to artificial intelligence at the upper level undergraduate or introductory graduate level. It is recommended that programming assignments be done in LISP and/or Prolog and that the text be augmented by at least the language manuals for the dialect(s) selected. We have also found it useful to specify a one-credit module in *Languages of AI* to serve as a corequisite course for this mode of instruction. This frees the instructor to concentrate on important conceptual aspects while the language details are relegated to the language course.

• ***A two-semester artificial intelligence sequence*** — By integrating instruction in AI languages with the text material, the instructor should find the book adequate for a two-semester sequence in artificial intelligence. In this mode of instruction, it is recommended that this text be augmented by one or more of the excellent introductory level language texts now available. This mode allows a more relaxed pace with a deeper exploration of the material through assignment of the more difficult exercises and project work including the design and construction of expert systems.

Through my own experience as student and instructor I have found the most effective learning takes place by doing. Included at the end of each chapter are problems and programs which are intended to illustrate the important concepts presented in the chapter. These exercises are designed to make the material more meaningful and range in difficulty from simple to quite challenging. Students are encouraged to implement assigned programs in either of the two main languages of artificial intelligence, LISP or Prolog. The course instructor will provide instruction and language manuals for the dialects available on your particular computer system.

Some observations on the AI environment

It is the author's firm conviction that technological and institutional forces are rapidly converging to create an environment in which many of the past promises of artificial intelligence can be realized. Primary among these forces are two trends which promise to reshape our thinking about AI in particular and computer science in general. First is the trend towards ever more powerful microcomputers with megabytes of RAM, gigabyte optical disks, and clock rates of twenty megahertz or more. These machines provide tools of greater capability than the largest mainframe computers available to AI researchers during the first 25 years of investigation. Second is the trend toward new computer architectures which much more closely resemble the massively parallel architecture of the brain. Implementations of parallel architectures are now emerging in the form of digital connection machines and analog neural networks with capabilities for pattern recognition and machine learning previously impossible on von Neumann machines.

Such improvements in hardware make possible improved software, operating systems, and computing paradigms which greatly increase the rate at which new ideas may be tested and implemented. Graphically oriented "desk top" operating systems have improved the naturalness and ease with which knowledge engineering concepts may be investigated. The integrated-software capabilities now available on microcomputers are ideally suited for relating and organizing the variety of knowledge recognized as essential for successful knowledge-based expert systems. Successes of neural networks in such applications as content-addressable memories suggest alternate solutions to previously intractable AI problems.

The institutional phenomenon of computer networking in combination with advances in hardware and software provides a new environment from which artificial intelligence may emerge. Local area networks, national networks, information services, and data banks already provide a wealth of information. New techniques are sorely needed for integrating this information and extracting meaningful knowledge for both human consumption and for the education of intelligent systems.

What will be the impact of a network of a million or more powerful work-stations, each with access to virtually unlimited information? If small networks of totally unintelligent neurons exhibit computational capability suggestive of intelligence what might we expect from large networks of reasonably intelligent processors? The implications of these questions have only begun to be explored, and artificial intelligence will provide the tools for the search and the discipline for harnessing the emerging intelligence. Our hope in writing this book is that we might inspire students with both the excitement of the quest for artificial intelligence and an understanding of how to put it to use for human welfare.

Acknowledgements

I wish to thank a number of my colleagues for their contributions at various stages of preparing this manuscript. These include Ben Greenebaum, Bill Moy, George Perdikaris, and Bob Maleske from UW-Parkside, Dale Snider from UW-Milwaukee, Larry Travis, Leonard Uhr, and Bob Lorentz of UW-Madison, and Yong Auh and Ram Bhatia from Unico, Inc. I greatly appreciate the incisive comments of Yong Auh, from whom I learned a great deal, and his considerable effort in preparing the LISP appendix. I also wish to thank my student Susan Stever for her conscientious proofreading of the manuscript and my son and colleague Steven Firebaugh for careful reading of the text, helpful comments, and considerable effort in the indexing process. I owe a great debt to Theodora Gottstein for her patient and thorough editorial work, and my AI students for their forbearance and contributions in debugging the manuscript over the years.

I am also indebted to the UW-Parkside Committee on Research and Creative Activities, the Urban Corridor Consortium, and the Engineering Science Division for continued support of our Distinguished AI Lecturer Series. Campus visits by Roger Schank of Yale University, Larry Wos of Argonne National Laboratory, Ryszard Michalski of the University of Illinois, and Donald Michie of the Turing Institute of Scotland were of great benefit to our students as well as significant contributions to the book. In particular, the thoughtful comments of Professor Michie and his efforts in writing the Foreword are greatly appreciated. I also enjoyed my visit to Stanford University and the opportunity for brief conversations with Nils Nilsson and John McCarthy on their research. I also greatly appreciate the cooperation of the AI researchers who provided photographs and resumes for the chapter headings. And last, I must thank Tom Walker and Margorie Schlaikjer of Boyd and Fraser; Tom for his enthusiasm and forbearance toward this writing project and Marjorie for her hard work and support which finally made it happen.

UW-Parkside
January, 1988

Morris W. Firebaugh

FOREWORD

by

Donald Michie

The growth in recent years of Artificial Intelligence has been without historical precedent, as also the diversity of impact on human activities. These developments call for a new generation of professional people trained to think in fresh ways. Scientists, philosophers, mathematicians, educationists, engineers, managers, and medical, legal, financial and other specialists — our children will depend on these people to forge from the white heat of innovation a great betterment for human society. We cannot yet fully make out the shape of the coming Knowledge Revolution. But we know that it will be unlike anything seen on earth before.

It is unfortunately typical of white heat to be surrounded by not a little steam, smoke and noise. In the battle, many a hard pressed field commander would trade a wagonload of ammunition for a reliable sketch-map, good binoculars and a compass. In today's battle of the classroom, hard pressed AI instructors will give heart-felt welcome to Morris Firebaugh's book. It is what for a long time they have been waiting for.

Students and teachers of the subject have lately had their difficulties compounded by a rising tumult of books about AI. Opportunist offerings for the most part, they have tended to swamp from sight the few texts of quality and substance. Dr. Firebaugh's *Artificial Intelligence: A Knowledge-Based Approach* is one of these very few. It is at the same time different from the others. Rather than aiming to impart in-depth instruction in a few narrowly selected topics, as did the earlier tutorial masterpieces of MIT's Patrick Winston or of the Edinburgh group under Bundy's editorship, Morris Firebaugh's brilliantly motivated sketch-map takes survey of the entire field. Yet, being intended for use as an introductory text, it demands no more from the reader (apart from normal alertness) than that he should have written a few computer programs in at least one high-level programming language.

A reader who wishes to take off for closer study of any particular chapter's special topic finds himself amply equipped with reading list and evaluative signposts. I particularly noted that the author has built his text by successive refinement in systematic class-testing. To create a superior tutorial product, there is in fact no other way. A practical outcome is that each chapter ends with twenty or so sample "problems and programs" — a windfall of potential "take-home assignments"!

To his 700+ page construction, Dr. Firebaugh has brought skills of apt illustration and anecdotage to lighten the rigors of technical exposition, together with a rare grasp of the interplay of social issues and personality in the birth of a new discipline. I suspect that whoever reads *Artificial Intelligence: A Knowledge-Based Approach* will succumb to the spell. For him or her there will be no turning back.

There is a voyage of which the poet Tennyson speaks:

> *"... To follow knowledge like a sinking star*
> *Beyond the utmost bounds of human thought."*

I wish fair winds and fortune to Morris Firebaugh's ship, and to all who sail with her.

The Turing Institute
January, 1988

Donald Michie

Chapter 1

CAN MACHINES THINK?

(PHOTO: KING'S COLLEGE LIBRARY, CAMBRIDGE)

Alan M. Turing (1912-1954) was an outstanding British mathematician who contributed significantly to pure mathematics, cryptography, theory of computability, and practical computer design. He did his university study at Cambridge University. His seminal 1937 paper on Computable Numbers defined the conceptual *Universal Turing Machine*, the theoretical prototype for subsequent digital computers. His cryptanalysis work at Bletchley Park was instrumental in breaking the German *Enigma* code during World War II. His acquaintance with the war-time Colossi computers and his post-war work on the ACE computer convinced Turing that computers would eventually achieve the ability to think. He proposed the widely accepted "Turing Test" for machine intelligence.

1: CAN MACHINES THINK?

1.1 INTRODUCTION

The field of artificial intelligence is one of the most fascinating and challenging areas of computer science. It has raised some of the most profound questions about the very nature of humankind and what distinguishes humans from other creatures, both animate and inanimate. Intelligence is the one characteristic almost universally agreed upon as setting humans apart from (and above?) other creatures. Any suggestion that it may be possible to create non-human intelligence is bound to stimulate strong reactions. The central question at the heart of this issue is: **Can Machines Think?**

The declared goal of artificial intelligence research is to teach machines to "think", that is, to display those characteristics usually associated with human intelligence. The answer to the question *Can Machines Think?* is pivotal to the discipline of artificial intelligence. In asking this question, however, one should be prepared to face the fact that the answer may not be a neat "Yes" or "No" but rather a highly qualified "... to a certain extent under special conditions". This should not be a surprise in light of our everyday experience that intelligence in both humans and other animals is not a binary function but rather a continuum. Some people are smarter than other people, and there are examples of household pets where the dog is far smarter than the cat in some ways. If machines can think, it should not be a surprise that some computer systems are smarter than others or that some systems may be intelligent in some areas while moronic in others.

The "Imitation Game" proposed by Alan Turing provides a relatively objective, unambiguous restatement of the question *Can Machines Think?* in operational language. This classic definition of artificial intelligence with which this chapter opens has stood up well under the test of time. Next several criticisms of machine intelligence are proposed and addressed by Turing himself. These contrary opinions still characterize most of the present day doubts as to the feasibility of AI. Some of the characteristics of the discipline of artificial intelligence are outlined next, followed by a brief discussion of issues raised by research in AI. The chapter concludes with a summary of the history of AI research and representative contributions of the founders of this new science.

1.2 TURING'S IMITATION GAME

Alan M. Turing was a brilliant British mathematician (1912-1954) who began his career by rediscovering the Central Limit Theorem as a student of Sir Arthur Eddington in the early 1930s. In 1937 Turing wrote the seminal paper on Computable Numbers in which he invented the concept of a universal machine to prove that certain classes of problems are unsolvable. During World War II he played a key role in deciphering the German military encoding machine, the Enigma, which allowed the Allies to monitor critical German war plans. By the end of the war he successfully completed the Delilah project for enciphering voice messages into white noise.[1]

Following the war, Turing designed the Automatic Computing Engine (ACE), named in honor of his countryman of a century earlier, Charles Babbage, who had designed the Analytical Engine. Turing also wrote a chess-playing program, later implemented on the Manchester University computer, which qualified as the first program capable of playing a complete chess game.

Turing's success in inventing the conceptual universal computer and his practical experience in building real code-breaking computers led him to pose the key questions and formulate the research program for artificial intelligence. The central questions which he raised continue to perplex and stimulate inquiring minds: Is there thought without experience? Is there mind without communication? Is there language without living? Is there intelligence without life? These are all variations on the fundamental theme issue of AI: *Can machines think?*

Turing set himself the task of addressing the question with a direct and unambiguous operational test. His paper[2] "Computing Machinery and Intelligence" provides a beautifully simple operational test of artificial intelligence which continues to clarify discussion of this elusive concept.

To avoid semantic arguments over definitions of words such as "machines" and "think", Turing proposed playing what he called the *imitation game.* The first stage of the game is played between three people as shown in Figure 1-1. The interrogator uses his "natural intelligence" to distinguish between the man who tries to fool him and the woman who tries to convince him that she is the woman.

In the second stage, the man is replaced by a computer programmed to attempt to fool the interrogator just as the man did in the first stage. It would naturally be programmed to make occasional errors, slow up its response to numerical questions, and say "I don't know" in much the same way a person would.

Figure 1-1 Phase I of Turing's Imitation Game The interrogator tries to determine which is the man and which is the woman by questioning each. The rules of the game require the man to try to fool the interrogator and the woman to try to convince him that she is the woman. Queries are made through a neutral medium such as a remote terminal, and each party is isolated in a separate room to eliminate any visual or audible clues.

If the computer can fool the interrogator as often as the man did, the computer has demonstrated that "machines can think". Paraphrased in terms of intelligence, Turing's test may be stated: "If conversation with a computer is indistinguishable from that with a human, the computer is displaying intelligence." In other words, if you can't tell the difference between a person ("natural intelligence") and a machine ("artificial intelligence"), they must be the same. Turing's test has a number of transparent advantages over more complex definitions of intelligence.

• It frees the computer from any anthropomorphic (human-like) characteristics other than mental by communicating by terminals.

Figure 1-2 Phase II of Turing's Imitation Game Now the man is replaced by a computer and the game resumes. If the computer can deceive the interrogator as often as the man did, we say the computer is displaying intelligence.

• The test itself is quite robust, that is, independent of the details of the experiment. For instance, the test is frequently phrased in terms of a single stage game with the interrogator guessing between human and machine.

• By restricting the computer to "electronic computer" or "digital computer" Turing constrained the machine operations to symbol processing by finite state machines. This is an operational equivalent of the *Physical Symbol System Hypothesis,* a central tenent of classical AI research.

Turing's own statement of beliefs on the outcome of playing the imitation game is quite perceptive and goes, in part:

> *"I believe that in about fifty years' time it will be possible to program computers, with a storage capacity of about* 10^9 *to make them play the imitation game so well that an average interrogator will not have more than 70 percent chance of making the right identification after five minutes of questioning."*

[It is not clear whether 10^9 refers to bits, bytes, or words. He goes on to say:]

> *"Nevertheless, I believe that at the end of the century the use of words and general educated opinion will have altered so much that one will be able to speak of machines thinking without expecting to be contradicted. I believe further that no useful purpose is served by concealing these beliefs."*

Turing's projection on storage capacity is remarkably accurate from the perspective of 35 years, with an error of only 15 years if we interpret his prediction to specify a gigabyte of disk storage capacity which is routinely available. Furthermore, most of us both use and frequently hear expressions such as "Now the computer is thinking about it". That aspect of Turing's prediction has already proven accurate.

1.3 CONTRARY OPINION

It is not at all surprising that such opinions aroused intense opposition during Turing's time. This opposition continues even today. Turing was notoriously nonconformist, but he was sensitive enough to anticipate the arguments raised against his position. He succinctly presents each argument against artificial intelligence and then does his best to refute it. Below is a summary of Turing's discussion of contrary views.

1. *THE THEOLOGICAL OBJECTION* — "Thinking is a function of man's immortal soul." Turing refutes the above argument by noting: "It appears to me that the argument quoted above implies a serious restriction of the omnipotence of the Almighty". That is, could God have not given a soul to an elephant or a machine had he wanted to?

2. *THE "HEADS IN THE SAND" OBJECTION* — "The consequences of machines thinking would be too dreadful. Let us hope and believe that they cannot do so." Turing notes that this objection " ... is likely to be quite strong in intellectual people, since they value the power of thinking more highly than others ...", but then dismisses it as insufficiently substantial to require refutation.

3. *THE MATHEMATICAL OBJECTION* — (Gödel's Theorem) "... in any sufficiently powerful logical system, statements can be formulated which can neither be proved nor disproved within the system, unless possibly the system itself is inconsistent." Turing acknowledges the validity of this argument, noting that he himself had published similar results. He then observes that there is no proof that the human intellect does not suffer the same limitations and concludes, "We too often give wrong answers to questions ourselves to be justified in being very pleased at such evidence of fallibility on the part of the machines".

4. *THE ARGUMENT FROM CONSCIOUSNESS* — "Not until a machine can write a sonnet or compose a concerto because of thoughts and emotions felt, and not be a chance fall of symbols, could we agree that machine equals brain — that is, not only write it but know that it had written it." This argument leads to the classical solipsist position that the only way to know how a person thinks is to be that person. Rather than get into the endless circular arguments into which such a position leads, Turing notes that "... it is usual to have the polite convention that everyone thinks".

5. *ARGUMENTS FROM VARIOUS DISABILITIES* — "I grant you that you can make a machine do all the things you have mentioned, but you will never be able to make one to do X" where X is the ability to "...be kind, resourceful, beautiful, friendly, ... like ice cream..." Turing refutes this argument by correctly observing that "Many of these limitations are associated with the very small storage capacity of most machines." Perhaps it is significant that increased memory capacity has added the feature we call "user **friendliness**" to modern operating systems.

6. *LADY LOVELACE'S OBJECTION* — "The Analytical Engine has no pretensions to *originate* anything. It can do *whatever we know how to order it* to perform". Another version of this objection states: "Machines never do anything really new" or can never "take us by surprise". Turing says: "Machines take me by surprise with great frequency". Most of us who program certainly share this experience.

7. *ARGUMENTS FROM CONTINUITY OF THE NERVOUS SYSTEM* — "The nervous system is certainly not a discrete state machine." Since small errors in the size of an impulse striking a neuron may make a large difference in the size of the outgoing impulse one cannot expect to mimic the behavior of the nervous system with a discrete state system. Turing fails to offer a convincing rebuttal to this argument, but we should note that present day computers can simulate the behavior of non-linear, analog devices for which the transformation is known, to almost any desired accuracy by standard computational procedures. This argument, however, is the central tenet of those working in the field of neural network research as the basis for the validity of their approach.

8. *THE ARGUMENT FROM INFORMALITY OF BEHAVIOR* — "It is not possible to produce a set of rules purporting to describe what a man should do in every conceivable set of circumstances." For instance, if a red light means "stop" and a green light means "go", what would a computer do when faced with a simultaneous red and green light due to a fault in the system? This is a tough argument to refute, but Turing suggests that we can experimentally determine the "laws of behavior" (as opposed to the "rules of conduct") which may be able to resolve such dilemmas.

9. *THE ARGUMENT FROM EXTRASENSORY PERCEPTION* — Here Turing cites four manifestations of extrasensory perception: telepathy, clairvoyance, precognition, and psychokinesis and pathetically notes, "How we should like to discredit them! Unfortunately the statistical evidence, at least for telepathy, is overwhelming." Here at last Turing has blundered in interpreting telepathy as a valid phenomenon. The "overwhelming statistical evidence" has evaporated like the morning mist exposed to the harsh sunlight of full disclosure and independent confirmation. It is tempting to criticize Turing for not having the courage of his convictions, but one might also note that all great scientists have had at least one *faux pas*. Maxwell refers to the "luminiferous ether" to carry his light waves, Einstein did not accept many of the fundamental concepts of quantum mechanics ("God does not play dice with the Universe!"), and Enrico Fermi observed both the neutron and nuclear fission but failed to discover them.

Turing's discussion of "contrary views" has been presented in brief detail because even today most objections to the concept of artificial intelligence fall into one of these categories. Turing's response may help sharpen our own thinking on many of the fundamental philosophical issues raised by artificial intelligence.

1.4 AI AS A DISCIPLINE

The field of artificial intelligence is gradually and painfully emerging as a science. The reasons for the birth pains are not difficult to understand: uncertainty as to what constitutes the subject matter, uncertainty on the goals of AI research, and uncertainty on the most effective approaches. From this point of view the discipline more closely resembles psychology or the social sciences than it does the "hard sciences" such as mathematics and physics.

Since each AI researcher's mental model of the mind helped shape his/her definition of the discipline, there were nearly as many schools of thought in the early days of AI as there were researchers. This has led to many sharp confrontations and controversies within this discipline as compared to the hard sciences in which "the truth" has a relatively objective existence determined unambiguously by experiment.

THE FLIP SIDES OF AI

A helpful concept in understanding some of the confusion within the field is to classify AI researchers by a "means vs ends" test. If the "end" of AI research is defined as the principle object of study and the "means" is defined as the primary tool or model used to assist in the study, then AI research generally falls into one of the following two categories:

- *Mind as object and machine as tool.* This school of thought includes many cognitive psychologists and linguists who view understanding the behavior of the human mind as the goal and computers as simply computational tools for testing models of the mind.

- *Computer as object and mind as model.* This school views the design of more intelligent machines as the goal of AI and the behavior of the human mind as a frequently helpful model for simulating intelligence.

These "flip sides" of AI research are clearly inconsistent and have resulted in some rancorous debate within the AI community. However, it is inaccurate to classify all AI researchers as falling cleanly into either one of these two schools. A number of the most prominent AI workers started their careers in one of the camps and later moved into the other. In principle, this diversity should be a source of strength to the AI enterprise — advances in understanding the human mind provides richer models to draw upon for advanced concepts in computer architecture and new algorithms and data structure concepts may shed light on particular mental functions.

AN INTERDISCIPLINARY SCIENCE

By the very nature of the subject area, AI is an interdisciplinary science. It attracts and draws heavily on the academic areas of philosophy, linguistics, psychology, mathematics, physics, electrical engineering, and computer science. Yet AI cannot be considered to be a branch of any of these fields. This interdisciplinary nature is at once both a source of strength and a weakness of the discipline.

The source of strength is the strong integrative role of AI in recognizing promising new concepts discovered in each contributing discipline and bringing them to the attention of other AI researchers. One example of this cross fertilization is the contribution of holography from the discipline of physics to the study of memory. In a hologram, a whole three-dimensional scene is captured and distributed over a whole piece of film. If the film is cut in half, the complete scene is still contained on each of the halves. Similarly, certain aspects of memory seem to be distributed throughout the brain — portions of the brain can be removed without particular memories being lost.

Another example in which the model of the brain has provided useful concepts for computer science is in parallel processing. The brain is vastly superior to any computer in such pattern recognition tasks as vision and continuous speech recognition in spite of the fact that the brain's "clock cycles" are typically milliseconds long compared to the microsecond → picosecond cycles of computers. How can a biological machine which runs so much slower outperform a high speed silicon machine? The answer lies in parallel processing. In fact, it is fairly easy to show that technology is approaching the limits of classical serial computers (von Neumann machines) set by the finite speed of signal propagation. The brain's slow but incredibly complex parallel processing architecture has provided the model for the next generation of computer architecture which will overcome the limits of serial machines.

The same diversity which generates the interdisciplinary strength of AI is also one of its weaknesses. Numerous studies have shown that any enterprise operates most efficiently and productively when its participants share common language, values, and perspectives. The wide variation in background and "epistemological framework" has been identified as one of the greatest obstacles to effective communication within the AI community.[3] While other disciplines may offer criticism of their colleagues with polite but well understood code words such as "somewhat incomplete" or "potentially misleading", AI reseachers have been known to criticize their colleagues' papers and curricula as "junk" and "scandalous." Until AI matures into a more unified discipline in which at least certain values are shared and differences of methodology are accepted and respected, these noisy disputes will continue. Such disagreements may make the discipline exciting, but it is not clear that they improve its productivity.

1.5 ISSUES IN AI

In addition to the somewhat boisterous and fractious history of the AI discipline, there are several additional issues which should be mentioned here. Subsequent discussion in the book will illuminate and help resolve some of the issues — others are by their very nature essentially intractable.

THE ISSUE OF DEFINITION

Each worker in the field of AI has his/her own definition of AI which seems to best express the goals and methods of his/her research. These range from machine-oriented perspectives:

> *Artificial Intelligence is the study of ideas that enable computers to be intelligent.*[4]

to strongly mind-oriented viewpoints:

> *Artificial Intelligence is the study of mental faculties through the use of computational models.*[5]

Some definitions strive for a comprehensive definition:

> *Artificial Intelligence is the ability of a human-made machine (an automaton) to emulate or simulate human methods for the deductive and inductive acquisition and application of knowledge and reason.*[6]

The definition preferred by the author and credited to Professor Marvin Minsky of MIT captures both the brevity of the first definition while maintaining the generality of the original Turing test:

> *Artificial intelligence is the science of making machines do things that would require intelligence if done by men.*[7]

A final observation on the definition of AI — the actual subject area is a moving target. As a frontier science, AI is concerned with the difficult, unsolved problems of machine intelligence. Once a problem is clarified or solved by AI researchers it moves out of the domain of AI and into the domain of standard computer science. Thus, game playing and theorem proving programs, which were at the cutting edge of AI research in the 1950s and 60s, are no longer the dominant areas they once were. The frontier has moved on to the even more difficult areas of common sense reasoning, vision, and models of memory and learning.

THE OVER-PROMISES ISSUE

The problem of over-promising has been a recurring one for the field of AI. Early expectations for automatic natural language translation failed to materialize. A 1957 prediction by Herbert Simon, one of the founders of AI, that a machine would be world chess champion within ten years has still not been fulfilled. After each successful small-scale AI experiment was announced, the press (and even sometimes the investigators themselves) could not resist the temptation to extrapolate with the optimistic prediction, "This experiment proves that we are on the verge of a new era when computers will be able to ... ." The failure of AI to produce the extrapolated products has led to disillusionment, and, in some instances, severe damage to a whole national research program. In citing the "grandiose aims" which AI had failed to reach, Sir James Lighthill recommended phasing out Great Britain's entire AI research program in 1973.

More recently the problem has reappeared in the form of exaggerated claims for AI features on otherwise unexceptional commercial data base and personality analysis programs. While AI may have contributed concepts which have been incorporated into these programs, it is doubtful whether the programs themselves can justify the AI label. The industry may be risking further backlash against AI if these programs do not perform at a significantly higher level than their non-AI counterparts.[8]

THE PHILOSOPHICAL ISSUE

At the very heart of the AI research program is the great empiricist tradition of Western science. This tradition dates from the time of Aristotle and holds that, since the mind is a physical system and since the behavior of physical systems may be explained in principle through adequate experimental investigation, the behavior of the mind is understandable in principle. An important element in empiricism is reductionism. The reductionist position is that the complex behavior of the mind may in principle be reduced to simpler rules and laws which may be complex but which can be investigated and understood. The paradigm for this tradition was the success in understanding the physical universe through systematic discovery and application of the laws of physics.

The implications of the reductionist philosophy of mind are many, profound and, to some, disturbing. The concept of *mind as machine* raises serious questions on the uniqueness of humanity, concepts of free will and creativity, and personal and social responsibility. It challenges some of the most sacred tenets of both religion and the humanist tradition.

One philosopher who has sensed this threat and responded by trying to discredit AI is Hubert L. Dreyfus of the University of California at Berkeley. In his book, *What Computers Can't Do,* he cites the difficulties and unfulfilled promises of AI as evidence that the whole reductionist philosophy is false.[9] Critics of AI enjoy Dreyfus' jabs at AI researchers and find his conclusions based on gestalt psychology reassuring. The AI community has, not surprisingly, generally rejected Dreyfus' attack on AI as intemperate in tone, misleading or false in detail, and fundamentally flawed in philosophy.

In order to understand the strong reaction by the AI community one must understand the implications of Dreyfus' criticism. In a more recent article, Dreyfus says:

> *"Great artists have always sensed the truth, stubbornly denied by both philosophers and technologists, that the basis of human intelligence cannot be isolated and explicitly understood."*

and again, quoting Yeats:

> *"Man can embody the truth, but he cannot know it."*[10]

It is primarily this rejection of the empirical/reductionist philosophy which upsets AI researchers. If Dreyfus is right, the whole AI enterprise is fundamentally flawed. Time will clearly resolve this argument, and in the meantime the author suggests the much more constructive outlook voiced by Donald Michie, Chief Scientist of the Turing Institute in Scotland:

> *It is a mistake to take up too much time asking, "Can computers think?" "Can they be really creative?" For all practical purposes they can. The best course for us is to leave the philosophers in their dark room and get on with using the creative computer to the full.*[11]

The converse of the *mind as machine* issue is the *machine as mind* issue. That is, assuming machines attain increasing intelligence, at what point do they achieve other human attributes such as consciousness, emotions, and personhood? And once consciousness and personhood are attained, to what civil rights are such artificial persons entitled? These and other fascinating ethical issues are now under serious discussion by scholars of AI.[12]

THE MILITARY EMPHASIS ISSUE

A continuing concern to some within the AI community and to many outside is the military connection. The Advanced Research Projects Agency (ARPA) has been the primary source of federal support for AI research in the United States from the very beginning of the field. The causes of the concern can be summarized as:

- The *ethics* of researching better and more efficient ways of killing people. Much of the research is on "smart" munitions, intelligent submersibles, and more recently, on space weapons.

- The *diversion of brain-power* from more important domestic priorities. If the enormous resources now dedicated to basically unproductive military research could be redirected to improving the productivity of our domestic industry, our economy would be strengthened. While the U.S. concentrates on defense, our competitors (particularly Japan) are concentrating on improved productivity.

- The *risk of censorship and loss of academic freedom.* It is only natural to expect that the Department of Defense would fund only projects that have potential for contribution to the national defense. There have been AI projects which looked promising from the academic point of view but which lost their ARPA funding because of lack of military potential.

- The *skewing of research from theory to product.* The military is naturally interested in *products* of AI which can be used in weapons systems. Many in the AI community feel, however, that the most important priority for AI research should be the development of *sturdy theories* of knowledge representation, memory, and learning. These objectives are clearly incompatible and run the risk of an unhealthy skewing of the direction of AI research.

1.6 CAST OF CHARACTERS

The field of artificial intelligence was founded by several generations of researchers, many of whom are equally as fascinating as was Turing. While space does not permit listing all contributors, some of the most important representatives from each generation are presented next.

FIRST GENERATION: PRE-1950

Warren McCulloch majored in philosophy and went on to get his medical degree from Columbia University. As an undergraduate he stated what turned out to be a lifetime quest:[13] "... there is one question I would like to answer — What is a number, that a man may know it, and a man that he may know a number?" He began his research on epilepsy, head injuries, and the central nervous system. As Director of the Laboratory for Basic Research in the Department of Psychiatry at the University of Illinois he made his major contribution, the neural net model of the brain.[14]

The neural net model was described in his famous paper, "A Logical Calculus of the Ideas Immanent in Nervous Activity" which he and an eighteen year old mathematician, Walter Pitts, published in 1943. Their model consisted of a network of synapses and neurons which they postulated behaved in binary fashion, that is, either firing or not firing. They showed that their neural net model was essentially equivalent to the Turing machine, and the Princeton mathematician, John von Neumann, used it to teach the theory of computing machines. This model, with considerable refinements, continues to serve as the corner stone of research on neural network computers.

The neural net model stimulated considerable theoretical and experimental investigation in attempts to model the behavior of the brain in the laboratory. However, later experiments showed that the model was fundamentally flawed in its assumption that neurons behaved strictly digitally — neurons, in fact, are highly non-linear devices which exhibit both digital and analog characteristics. McCulloch himself said in 1965, "Facts have often compelled me to change my mind...", and the early neural net model of the brain reproduced only the most trivial behavior. In more recent neural network models, such as those of John Hopfield, have produced much more impressive results. These are discussed in detail in the last chapter.

The third "founding father" of computer science which made the science of artificial intelligence possible was the brilliant Hungarian-born mathematician, John von Neumann. In 1930 von Neumann moved to Princeton University to lecture in mathematical physics, and he spent the rest of his career there. He was a cohort and colleague of Alan Turing, and they visited each other during World War II. He also played a key role in the war, serving as consultant to the Manhattan atomic bomb project.[15]

From the experience of calculating the propagation of shock waves on desk calculators von Neumann became acutely aware of the need for improved machines for numerical calculations. He became an advisor to the ENIAC (Electronic Numerical Integrator and Calculator) project of the Moore School of the University of Pennsylvania. He also helped develop the design of the EDVAC (Electronic Discrete Variable Calculator), an early "stored program" machine. For this work he is frequently credited with inventing the idea of the stored program, although he never laid claim to this invention and it apparently was part of the design of the Analytical Engine which was designed 100 years earlier.

While von Neumann's contributions to the development of the computer were brilliant and indisputable, his contribution to AI is less significant. He was greatly influenced by the neural network model of McCulloch and Pitts in his design of the EDVAC, but he never made the leap that Turing took of concluding that machines might someday have the ability to think. However, some of the anthropomorphic terms such as "memory" which von Neumann coined are still with us today and probably stem from the McCulloch influence.

The final first generation patriarch of AI we will mention is Claude Shannon, an MIT graduate who joined Bell Telephone Laboratories in 1941. His master's thesis work had drawn the connection between the switching operations of electromagnetic relays and the Boolean algebra on which modern digital logic is based.[16] He had also written seminal papers on communication theory in which channel capacity, signal, and noise were defined precisely in terms of information content.

Shannon shared Alan Turing's conviction on the possibility of machines thinking. He and Turing shared many animated discussions during a short visit Turing made to Bell Labs. Turing once commented: "Shannon wants to feed not just *data* to a Brain, but *cultural* things! He wants to play *music* to it!"

Shannon published an article "A Chess-Playing Machine" in *Scientific American* in 1950 in which he pointed out that a typical chess game involved about 10^{120} possible moves. Even if the newly invented computer could examine one move per microsecond it would require 10^{95} years to make its first move. In his paper "Computers and Automata" published three years later, Shannon raised a number of provocative questions which AI researchers have been addressing ever since. These include: Can a self-repairing machine be built that will locate and repair faults in its own components? Can a digital computer be programmed to program itself? Using hierarchical concepts, can a computer be programmed to learn?

SECOND GENERATION: 1950-1970

The second generation of AI researchers started with high hopes and expectations in the 1950s, but by 1970 few of these expectations had materialized. This early optimism is illustrated by the rationale for the Dartmouth College study funded by the Rockefeller Foundation in 1956 which stated: "The study is to proceed on the basis of the conjecture that every aspect of learning or any other feature of intelligence can in principle be so precisely described that a machine can be made to simulate it." However, by the end of this period J. Lighthill of Cambridge University reported in a study funded by the British government : "... in no part of the field have the discoveries made so far produced the major impact that was promised."

Some significant milestones were reached in this period, and some of the most prominent contributors and their contributions will be mentioned briefly. Many of these contributions will be discussed later in the book under particular topic headings. One interesting observation at this time is the following: many of the second generation researchers had been students or colleagues of scientists mentioned in the first generation section, and many of the third generation contributors were students of the second generation researchers.

One of the organizers of the Dartmouth Conference was John McCarthy, then assistant professor of mathematics at Dartmouth. He is credited with originating the term "artificial intelligence" and is the author of LISP, the original language of artificial intelligence research. He is presently a professor at Stanford University.

A second organizer of the Dartmouth Conference was Marvin Minsky, then at Harvard University and presently professor at MIT. He has written widely on AI and is generally considered one of the leading spokesmen for the discipline. His theory of "frames" was a major contribution in the area of knowledge representation. Many of his students have also made significant contributions to the field.

One of the most significant AI programs of this period was the *Logic Theorist* by Allen Newell, Herbert Simon, and J. C. Shaw then at the RAND Corporation. The Logic Theorist was able to prove 38 of the first 52 theorems of Chapter 2 of Whitehead and Russell's *Principia Mathematica.* Its proof of Theorem 2.85 is, in fact, shorter and more elegant than that given in *Principia Mathematica.* Newell and Simon later expanded their work into the problem solving program, the *General Problem Solver.*

One of Herbert Simon's students at Carnegie-Mellon University was Edward Feigenbaum, who has subsequently become one of the most articulate spokesmen for the field of artificial intelligence. While his Ph.D. degree was in psychology he is the author of the DENDRAL program, one of the first and most successful expert systems. Along with Pamela McCorduck he also wrote *THE FIFTH GENERATION - Artificial Intelligence and Japan's Computer Challenge to the World,* a book which has done much to stimulate United States interest in the field of AI.[17]

A final major contributor during this period is Seymour Papert, a South African who began his career as a mathematician and studied under child psychologist Jean Piaget. Papert became acquainted with Edward Feigenbaum in London, and Warren McCulloch invited him to come to MIT where Papert subsequently worked with Marvin Minsky. He is author of LOGO, a high-level AI language designed especially for teaching children concepts of logical thinking. He is also author of *MINDSTORMS,* an important book on the use of computers in education.[18]

The second generation researchers mentioned here illustrate the range and nature of AI work performed during this period, but the list certainly does not include all significant contributions. This period can perhaps best be characterized by the following two observations: (i) many approaches to AI were tried and proven unsuccessful, and (ii) these second generation researchers trained many excellent students together with whom they were to score many successes. Some of these successes are sketched in the next section.

THE THIRD GENERATION: 1970-PRESENT

The realization that computers could display "intelligent behavior" if the domain in which they operated were sufficiently restricted is perhaps the most significant discovery during this period. This concept, combined with a shift to "knowledge-based" reasoning, enabled third generation AI workers to make some very impressive progress in designing intelligent machines.

There are too many contributions in the ongoing research in AI to mention them all, but some of the major players along with the name of the system they helped develop are presented next. Each of these systems is discussed in greater detail later in the book.

Terry Winograd wrote one of the most successful programs, SHRDLU, for the manipulations of blocks and objects on the very restricted domain of a table top. Bertram Raphael of Stanford Research Institute built one of the first robots, SHAKEY, to respond to human instructions. Nils Nilsson and Richard Fikes developed STRIPS, a program to achieve goals by the use of plans and a sequence of operators. Daniel Bobrow of MIT wrote the program, STUDENT, for solving simple algebraic word problems. David Slate and Larry Atkin of Northwestern University wrote a number of chess playing programs, one of which, CHESS 4.5 played nearly even with one of the world's chess experts. Raj Reddy of Carnegie-Mellon University created the HEARSAY system which could "understand" human speech with better than 90% accuracy. Roger Schank and Robert Abelson of Yale University introduced the concept of SCRIPTS in an attempt to model human "common sense" behavior in routine situations. Edward Shortliffe of Stanford University wrote the MYCIN expert system for diagnosing infectious diseases. Richard O. Duda of SRI International wrote PROSPECTOR, a geological analysis program which has successfully discovered a molybdenum deposit.

PROBLEMS AND PROGRAMS

1-1. Discuss the Turing test for artificial intelligence. In your discussion you should: (i) justify the validity of the Turing test, or (ii) criticize the Turing test.

1-2. Turing's original imitation game test specified two phases: (i) interrogator, man, and woman, and (ii) interrogator, machine, and woman. Yet, it is frequently cited in terms of an interrogator guessing between human and machine. How might the validity of the test be effected by switching to this single phase test?

1-3. Rank the nine contrary opinions suggested by Turing in order of importance, with the most significant objections first. Which do you believe will pose serious problems in the design of an intelligent machine?

1-4. Which do you see as the primary object of AI research: the human mind or an intelligent machine? Give some convincing arguments to support your position.

1-5. Using the references listed below, identify four leading researchers in each of the two AI schools: (i) mind is object, and (ii) machine is object.

1-6. Discuss contributions which cognitive psychology has made which have contributed to improvement in the performance of computers.

1-7. Discuss another contribution not mentioned in the text which computer architecture or algorithms have made to understanding the behavior of the mind.

1-8. How would you improve the definition of AI suggested by Professor Minsky?

1-9. Survey some popular computer magazines (*BYTE, Infoworld, PC World, Mac World*) for advertisements of products claiming AI capabilities. Discuss the product application and whether or not you feel the AI label is justified.

1-10. Gestalt psychology maintains that "The whole is greater than the sum of its parts", and Professor Dreyfus uses this argument to claim that the mind will never even be understood, let alone simulated by AI. Write a critique of this position, documenting your position.

1-11. Reductionist philosophy maintains that the behavior of any physical system such as the brain may be reduced to a set of laws, perhaps complex, which we may discover with enough patience and hard work. Write a critique of this position, documenting your position.

1-12. Which of the concerns discussed in the text related to military support of AI research do you see as the most serious, and what policy revisions would you suggest to minimize the risks voiced in this concern?

1-13. Discuss the differences between the dictionary definitions of "simulate" and "emulate" as they relate to AI.

REFERENCES AND FOOTNOTES

1 Hodges, Andrew, *Alan Turing — The Enigma,* Simon and Schuster, New York, NY (1983)

2 Turing, Alan M., "Computing Machinery and Intelligence," *Mind,* Vol LIX, No. 236 (1950). Reprinted in: Hofstadter, Douglas R. and Dennett, Daniel C., *THE MIND'S I* , Bantam Books, New York, NY (1981) pp. 53—68

3 Hall, Rogers P. and Kibler, Dennis F., "Differing Methodological Perspectives in Artificial Intelligence Research", *The AI Magazine,* p. 166—178, Fall, (1985)

4 Winston, Patrick Henry, *Artificial Intelligence,* Second Edition, p. 1, Addison-Wesley Publishing Company, Reading, MA (1984)

5 Charniak, Eugene and McDermott, Drew, *Introduction to Artificial Intelligence,* p. 6, Addison-Wesley Publishing Company, Reading, MA (1985)

6 Bock, Peter, "The Emergence of Artificial Intelligence: Learning to Learn", *The AI Magazine,* pp. 180—190, Fall (1985)

7 Boden, Margaret A., *Artificial Intelligence and Natural Man,* Basic Books, Inc., p. 4, New York, NY (1977)

8 McDermott, Drew, Waldrop, M. Mitchell, Schank, Roger, Chandrasekaran, B, and McDermott, John, "The Dark Ages of AI: A Panel Discussion at AAAI-84", *AI Magazine* **6**, No. 3, pp. 122—134, Fall (1985)

9 Dreyfus, Hubert L., *What Computers Can't Do: A Critique of Artificial Reason,* Harper and Row, New York, NY (1972)

10 Dreyfus, Hubert L., "From Micro-Worlds to Knowledge Representation", in *Mind Design,* John Haugeland (Ed), The MIT Press, Cambridge, MA (1985)

11 Michie, Donald and Johnston, Rory, *The Knowledge Machine,* William Morrow and Company, New York, NY (1985)

12 LaChat, Michael R., "Artificial Intelligence and Ethics: An Exercise in the Moral Imagination", *The AI Magazine* **7**, No. 2., pp. 70—79, Summer (1986)

13 McCorduck, Pamela, *MACHINES WHO THINK* , W. H. Freeman and Company, San Francisco, CA (1979) p. 72

14 McCulloch and Pitts, W., "A Logical Calculus of the Ideas Immanent in Nervous Activity", *Bull. Math.Biophys.* **5**, 115 (1943)

15 Shurkin, Joel, *ENGINES OF THE MIND,* W. W. Norton & Co., New York, NY (1984) pp. 173—208

16 McCorduck, *Op Cit,* p. 100

17 Feigenbaum, Edward A. and McCorduck, Pamela, *THE FIFTH GENERATION — Artificial Intelligence and Japan's Computer Challenge to the World,* Addison-Wesley, Reading, MA (1983)

18 Papert, Seymour, *MINDSTORMS — Children, Computers, and Powerful Ideas,* Basic Books, Inc., New York, NY (1980)

Chapter 2

LANGUAGES OF AI

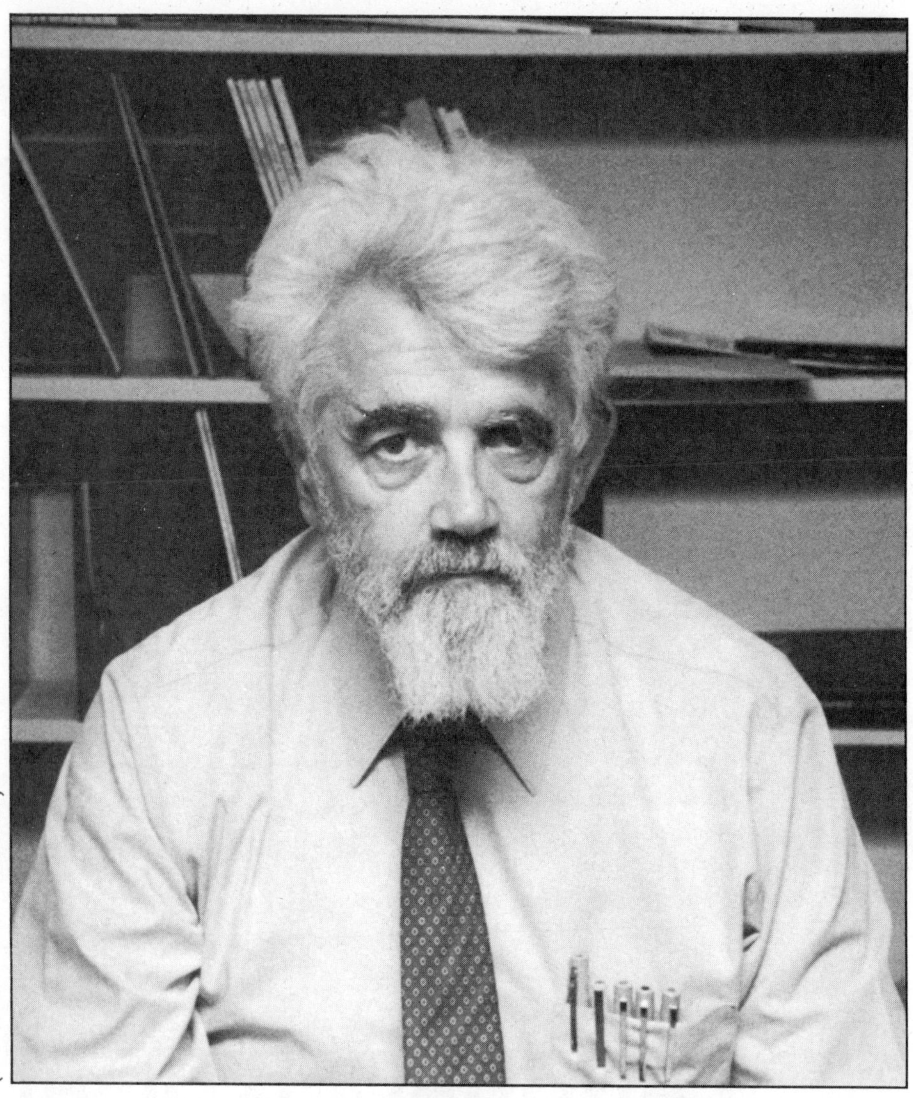

(PHOTO: CAROLYN CADDES)

John McCarthy is Professor of Computer Science at Stanford University. He earned his B.S. in mathematics from California Institute of Technology and his Ph.D. from Princeton University. His research interests include formalization of common sense knowledge and nonmonotonic reasoning. He invented the LISP language and developed the concept of time-sharing in the late fifties and early sixties. He was one of the organizers of the 1956 Dartmouth Conference from which emerged the new science of artificial intelligence. McCarthy is credited with giving the discipline the name "artificial intelligence." He has served as President of the American Association of Artificial Intelligence and received the A. M. Turing Award of the ACM.

2: LANGUAGES OF AI

2.1 INTRODUCTION

As we have seen in the previous chapter, the computer plays the key role in artificial intelligence research, either as the direct object of research or as a capable tool for modeling the cognitive processes under study. An impressive arsenal of application and programming languages has emerged to facilitate solving the problems investigated in such research. While the AI community may differ significantly as to the most effective approaches for simulating artificial intelligence, there is a common thread linking all traditional AI research efforts. This theme can be summarized as:

> ***Physical symbol systems* are essential for representing knowledge in both mind and machine.**

A brief discussion of this concept will help students understand the nature of AI languages.

THE PHYSICAL SYMBOL SYSTEM HYPOTHESIS

One of the first features that strikes new students of AI languages is how different they are from the more traditional high-level languages such as BASIC, FORTRAN, and Pascal. The root of this distinction lies in a fundamental hypothesis of artificial intelligence research — *The Physical Symbol System Hypothesis.*[1] This hypothesis, suggested by Alan Turing's work, was formally proposed by Allen Newell and Herbert Simon. They demonstrated that it was a logical extension of the reductionist, empirical tradition of natural science. In defining a physical symbol system, they state:

> *A physical symbol system consists of a set of entities, called symbols, which are physical patterns that can occur as components of another type of entity called an expression (or symbol structure). Thus a symbol structure is composed of a number of instances (or tokens) of symbols related in some physical way (such as one token being next to another). At any instant of time the system will contain a collection of these symbol structures. Besides*

these structures, the system also contains a collection of processes that operate on expressions to produce other expressions: processes of creation, modification, reproduction, and destruction. A physical symbol system is a machine that produces through time an evolving collection of symbol structures. Such a system exists in a world of objects wider than just these symbolic expressions themselves.

After clarifying some other concepts and comments on the mathematical basis for their hypothesis, they state it as

The Physical Symbol System Hypothesis: *A physical symbol system has the necessary and sufficient means for general intelligent action.*

It is apparent that this very strong hypothesis provides the philosophical basis for the traditional AI research program. It also helps explain why computer languages based on this hypothesis are heavily oriented towards abstract symbol manipulation. It is also interesting to note that the physical symbol system hypothesis and the modern digital computer share the common feature of operating with discrete "states of mind". This is in contrast with the non-symbolic, analog operation of neural networks such as the brain and computers based on neural network models.

CHARACTERISTICS OF AI LANGUAGES

The physical symbol system hypothesis helps explain several features of most AI languages which distinguish them from conventional high-level languages. These characteristics are:

- *Symbol vs data based* — Conventional languages typically consist of a fixed program with variable data which, in many cases such as Pascal, is rigorously typed. Symbol-based AI languages, on the other hand, are much more fluid in their organization. The sharp distinction between program and data also frequently disappears in AI languages.

- *Descriptive vs procedural* — Conventional languages are generally procedure-oriented with languages such as Pascal and MODULA-2 making a highly structured approach a conscious design goal. AI languages, on the other hand, are more concerned with stating relationships between symbols which are generally more amorphous and dynamic. Thus, conventional languages may be classified as sequential, procedural, or imperative whereas AI languages are described by terms such as relational, functional, declarative, or descriptive.

• *A supportive system environment* — AI languages have pioneered concepts for improving the programming environment, including such innovations as interactive time-sharing, powerful debuggers and trace options, friendly editors, bit-mapped graphics, and techniques from object-oriented programming. Many of these concepts which were invented to meet the needs of AI research have subsequently "trickled down" to become standard features of conventional computing environments.

SUMMARY OF LANGUAGES

Most languages which have been developed for AI can be classified as dialects of one of the following:

- LISP — The premier language of AI research in the United States.

- Prolog — The language selected for Japan's Fifth Generation Project and widely used throughout Europe

- Object-Oriented Languages

- Expert System Shells

Several major languages of AI are surveyed below. LISP is introduced in sufficient detail that students will get a good feeling for the language and its capabilities. A more detailed introduction with numerous examples is presented in Appendix A. These introductions in combination with any one of several excellent introductory level LISP texts should provide a good background for students interested in AI programming. Recommended LISP texts include Daniel Friedman's *The Little LISPer*,[2] David Touretzky's *LISP — A Gentle Introduction to Symbolic Computation*,[3] Rodney Brooks' *Programming in COMMON LISP*,[4] Robert Wilensky's *COMMON LISPcraft*,[5] and *LISP* Second Edition by Patrick Winston and Berthold Horn.[6] An excellent introduction to computer science using the Scheme dialect of LISP is presented in *Structure and Interpretation of Computer Programs* by Harold Abelson, Gerald Sussman, and Julie Sussman.[7]

The second major AI language we examine is Prolog. Prolog is used widely in Europe and Japan and is rapidly gaining converts in the United States as powerful new dialects appear. Several examples and an introduction to the syntax of Prolog are presented. For additional examples and the complete syntax, students are referred to *Program-*

ming in Prolog by Clocksin and Mellish,[8] *The Art of Prolog* by Sterling and Shapiro,[9] and *Prolog* by Garavaglia.[10] Finally, we survey some of the most important features of two other AI languages, Smalltalk and POP-11. Expert system shells are discussed in Chapters 11 — 13.

2.2 LISP — LIST PROCESSOR

LISP is the second oldest surviving high-level language in computer science (only FORTRAN predates it). It was written by John McCarthy in 1958—60 in order to represent recursive functions on the computer.[11] It is a dynamic language of exceptional power and flexibility and has become the standard language in the United States for solving problems of artificial intelligence. LISP has a number of features which satisfy the requirements for an AI language as outlined in the introduction and which distinguish it from procedural languages. Some of the more distinctive features are highlighted below.

LISP FEATURES

- LISP is highly *extensible* and *flexible* — Very complex extended LISPs may be written in LISP using more elementary LISP functions. The "bare bones" primitive set of functions which any LISP interpreter or compiler must contain includes *CAR, CDR, CONS, ATOM,* and the equality test, *EQ,* along with the forms *COND* for conditional expressions and *LAMBDA* for defining functions. This extensibility of LISP makes it an ideal tool for writing applications programs and even implementations of other languages such as Prolog, but it has also led to the problem of the proliferation of LISP dialects.

- LISP is a *recursive* language — LISP functions may be defined in terms of themselves. Although some procedural languages such as Pascal support recursion, it is an integral part of LISP programming style. Consider the following LISP function for calculation of n!:

```
-> (define  (factorial  n)
       (cond ((=?  n  1)  1)
             (t  (*  n  (factorial  (-  n  1))))))
```

Typing in this function "teaches" the LISP system the definition of n! and at any later time this newly defined function is available for evaluation. For instance, if we type (we use "->" as the LISP prompt and italics for program output):

```
-> (factorial 10)
```

the computer responds with

```
3628800
```

Note the economy of code made possible by recursion.

- LISP has a highly *symbol-oriented data structure* — The basic data structures are *atoms* and *lists*. Lists are objects composed of other lists and/or *atoms* which are the primitive, indivisible data type. Lists in LISP are also known as *s-expressions* or "symbolic expressions." The unique feature of LISP is that programs, functions, and data are all represented by lists. This gives LISP programs the capability of operating on other programs as if they were data. This, in turn, leads to the remarkable property that LISP programs can modify themselves and even write other LISP programs!

- LISP is an *interactive language* — AI researchers at MIT were the first to recognize the need for an interactive programming environment and helped develop the Project MAC time-sharing system which supported LISP. Since then LISP has been routinely available as an interpreter on mainframe and minicomputers. More recently, compact implementations of LISP have become available on microcomputers in both interpreter and compiler format.

- LISP provides automatic *dynamic storage allocation* — Since a LISP program is a dynamic collection of shrinking and growing lists, the problem of storage allocation can be quite complex. However, modern LISP systems provide for automatic storage allocation with "garbage collection" to reclaim memory no longer needed by the program. Thus the programmer is relieved of responsibility for estimating the dimensions of the program's data structures which procedural language programs require.

- LISP is an ideal *metalanguage* — *Meta* is Greek for *about*, so a metalanguage is a language for talking about language. The language to be talked about may be natural language, another computer language, or LISP itself. The metalanguage characteristic of LISP is evident from the fact that a number of other languages such as Prolog have been written in LISP.

ELEMENTARY LISP SYNTAX

Next we present an overview of the syntax of LISP list structure and some of the functions available for manipulating these lists. The dialect selected is Scheme, an elegant and concise version of LISP developed by Guy Steele Jr. and Gerald Sussman at MIT. Scheme incorporates features of ALGOL as well as LISP and is available as **MacScheme** for the Macintosh and **PC Scheme** for the IBM-PC. Both follow the standard defined in the *Revised Revised Report on Scheme.*[12] Guy Steele Jr. subsequently chaired the committee that defined the standards for COMMON LISP, so it is not surprising that COMMON LISP inherited many Scheme concepts.[13]

Atoms

The smallest indivisible element of LISP syntax is called an *atom.* Scheme supports several kinds of atoms including numbers, characters, symbols, strings, and vectors. Examples of *numerical atoms* include:

```
5        -300        +31000        3.14159        1.234E+250
```

Characters in Scheme syntax are designated by a '#\' preceding the character and permit use of non-printing control characters. Examples include:

```
#\a         ;ASCII lower-case a
#\A         ;ASCII upper-case A
#\(         ;ASCII parenthesis as a character
#\backspace ;ASCII backspace command
#\return    ;ASCII carriage return command
#\rubout    ;ASCII delete command
#\tab       ;ASCII tab command
```

Symbols are identifiers made from any combination of letters, numbers, and special characters (except those identified as special LISP characters below). Case is ignored in Scheme. Examples of *symbolic* or literal atoms include:

```
X      Steven      T      NIL     foo    This-is-a-long-symbol
```

LISP *strings* closely resemble strings of procedural languages and include any sequence of characters enclosed within double quotes, ("):

```
"This is a string!"   "So is this."   "City, State, and Zip"
```

The final atomic data structure we will discuss is the *vector.* A vector is a data structure with an arbitrary number of components. Its structure resembles a list, defined below, prefixed by a "#". An example is:

```
#(a b c d e f)
```

Examples of illegal atoms include:

```
)      (34   25   35)     This sentence has spaces
```

The first is illegal because it is a special LISP character; the second is a list rather than a symbol; and the third contains spaces, the *delimiter* used by LISP. LISP symbols may contain such special characters as +, *, and ? but may not contain the following special LISP characters: \ |) ( ] [} { " ; # ' ' , @ and **blank.**

There are two special atoms which LISP programmers encounter frequently. The first of these is the atom indicating "true" or "non-zero". This is the atom "t" which Scheme refers to as `#!TRUE`. For example, after evaluating the following predicate (a predicate asks a question about data):

```
-> (=?  5  5)
```

LISP responds

```
#!TRUE
```

That is, LISP has indicated that "It is true that 5 = 5." What if we asked LISP whether 4 = 5? We would do this with the code:

```
-> (=?  4  5)
```

We might expect that the answer would be "f" or `#!FALSE`, but instead we read:

```
()
```

This is the second special symbol, referred to as NIL, and, in fact, if we ask LISP:

```
-> (equal?  nil  ())
```

it replies

```
#!TRUE
```

Note that we have used a different equality query for the numerical comparison and the special symbol comparison. Scheme provides several equivalence predicates, including:

```
eq?          ;compares symbols  (most restrictive)
=?  or  =    ;compares numbers
eqv?         ;compares symbols or numbers
```

```
equal?      ;compares lists, vectors, and arrays
```

NIL carries a very heavy load in the LISP language.

• *NIL is an atom.* We can verify this with the LISP predicate, ATOM:

```
-> (atom?  nil)
```

and find

```
#!TRUE
```

• *NIL is a list.* NIL happens to be the empty or "NULL" list. We can verify this assertion by asking LISP if NIL is the NULL list:

```
-> (null?  nil)
```

and LISP responds:

```
#!TRUE
```

• *NIL is equivalent to "false" in testing predicates and conditions.* Thus if we ask the question, "Is a list containing two NULL lists empty?", we find:

```
-> (null?  '(()  ()))

()
```

That is, the answer is "false". A list cannot be empty if it contains two atoms (recall that ( ) is an atom). The evaluation blocking "'" is discussed below.

One final feature of atoms should be mentioned, and that concerns *evaluation*. As we will see when we study expressions, procedures specify how symbols are evaluated. However, numbers and the two symbols "t" and "( )" evaluate to themselves.

Lists

It appears that a few lists have crept into our discussion of atoms, so it is time that we consider lists a bit more formally. In keeping with the recursive spirit of LISP, we define:

A list is a possibly empty delimited list of expressions bracketed by parentheses.

The delimiter is the *blank*. Expressions may be either atoms or lists. Examples of some valid LISP lists are:

```
(sort!   #(1  2  3  4  5)  <?)

(Joe  (loves  Susie))

(sqrt  95)

((The  delimiter)  is  (the  blank))
```

There is no limit in theory on the level of nesting of lists within lists. The syntax of the *let* command, for instance, requires three levels of list nesting:

```
-> (define help "LISP comments start with a semicolon, ;")
help
-> (let  ((prompt  help))  (display  prompt))
```

The define command initializes the identifier help to the value of the string. In the *let* command, the symbol prompt is bound to the value of help, and the final list in the let command displays the string:

```
LISP comments start with a semicolon, ;
```

Symbolic-Expressions

You may have noticed that many of the lists presented so far seem to have the sentence-like structure:

```
-> (function   arg1  arg2  ...)
```

This form is known as the Cambridge Polish notation for function representation. The objective of the LISP interpreter is to evaluate this symbolic expression (also known as "s-expression" or simply, "expression"). The argument list may itself be composed of expressions, so again we recognize a recursive definition. The order of the evaluation logically must be from the innermost nested arguments outward, although on the same level of nesting, the order of evaluation is unspecified. If the order of evaluation is important, for instance in cases with I/O, a left → right order may be forced by a *begin* command or a *sequence* command.

The model of a LISP interpreter is the simple sequence:

READ-EVALUATE-PRINT

Regular LISP functions all follow this REP rule (the only exceptions are the so-called special functions). There may be instances where the user may wish to pass on a list as an unevaluated expression. LISP provides the *quote* special function to allow for this possibility. If we type in the simple list, for instance,

```
-> (a  b  c  d  e)
```

LISP will respond with the error message:

```
Variable not defined in the lexical environment
E
```

Using *quote,* however, we can return this list as a literal, unevaluated expression:

```
-> (quote  (a  b  c  d  e))
(A  B  C  D  E)
```

This evaluation blocking function is used so frequently that most LISP systems, including Scheme, provide a short hand version using the single quote, " ' " without the associated bounding parentheses. For example:

```
-> '(Comments start with a ";".)
(Comments start with a ";".)
```

The great power of LISP lies in the richness of the functions available for processing arguments and the ease with which new required functions may be generated. Below we illustrate several categories of functions available in LISP:

- *Numerical arithmetic* —

```
-> (+  5  10  15)         ; Performs addition
30

-> (-  20  27)            ; Performs subtraction
-7

-> (*  1  2  3  4  5)    ; Performs multiplication
120

-> (/  75  5)             ; Performs division
15

-> (abs  -7)              ; Takes absolute value
7
```

- *Transcendental Functions* —

```
-> (exp  1)               ; Exponential function, base e
2.71828182845905
```

```
-> (expt  3  5)           ; Exponentiation function
243

-> (sqrt  144)            ; Square root function
12.

-> (cos  (/  3.141592654  4)) ; Cosine function
0.707106781114031
```

- *Relational Predicates* —

```
-> (=  8  9)              ; Equality test
()

-> (<=  18  24)           ; Less than or equal test
#!TRUE

-> (>  100  144)          ; Greater than test
()

-> (max 45 64 125 17)     ; Maximum function
125

-> (min 45 64 125 17)     ; Minimum function
17
```

- *List manipulation* —

```
-> (car '(one two three))     ; returns the first
ONE                          ;element of a non-null list

-> (cdr '(one two three))     ; complements the car
(TWO THREE)                  ; function, returning the
                             ; remainder of the list

-> (cons 'a '(b c d))        ; inverse function to the
(A  B  C  D)                 ; car  +  cdr operations,
                             ; called constructor fcn

-> (append '(John loves)      ; concatenates lists,
        '(Mary))             ; takes any number of
(JOHN  LOVES  MARY)          ; arguments

-> (list '(a b) '(c d))      ; makes a new list built
((A B)  (C D))               ; from its arguments

-> (reverse '(1 2 3 4))      ; reverses order of
(4  3  2  1)                 ; argument list

-> (length '(a b c d e));    computes length of
5                            ; list
```

Control Structures

LISP provides the same or equivalent control structures as any other high-level language. These structures are called *special forms,* and several of the most important ones are summarized below:

<IF> Special Form

```
(if <cond> <conseq> <alternative>)
```

where

`<cond>`	is a condition to be evaluated
`<conseq>`	is evaluated and returned if `cond` =`t`
`<alternative>`	is evaluated and returned if `cond` =`()`

For instance,

```
(if (>? 5 10) 'continue 'stop)
```

yields

STOP

Note that the LISP *IF* behaves precisely like the *IF-THEN-ELSE* of Pascal.

<COND> Special Form

```
(cond <clause1> <clause2> ...)
```

where

`<clause1>`	= (`<pred>` `<expr>` ...)
`<pred>`	is a predicate expression
`<expr>`	is evaluated if the predicate is not nil

This condition test steps through the clauses until it finds one with a true predicate. Upon finding a true predicate it evaluates the associated expression list, returning the last expression evaluated as the value for the condition test. For example, the following comparison of numbers:

```
(cond ((<? 80386 68030) 'less_than)
      ((>? 80386 68030) 'greater_than)
      (else 'is_equal))
```

produces the output:

GREATER_THAN

Note that the *COND* special form is equivalent to the Pascal *IF ... ELSE IF* structure.

<DO> Special Form

```
(do   ((<var1>   <init1>   <step1>   ...)
      (<test>   <expr1>   ...)
      <stmt1>   ...)
```

where

`<var1>`	identifier which serves as counter
`<init1>`	expression evaluated as initial value of **var1**
`<step1>`	expression evaluated as next value of **var1**
`<test>`	expression evaluated first for each iteration: if **test** evaluates to **()**, then all **stmts** evaluated if **test** evaluates to **t**, then iteration is terminated **expri** evaluated in order DO returns the value of the last **expri**

An example of the use of this iterative special form to print out the first five integers and return the value of the square of the sixth is shown:

```
-> (do  ((i  1  (+  i  1)))
        ((> i  5)  (*  i  i))
        (display  i)
        (display  "  "))
```

yields

1 2 3 4 5 36

Both **init1** and **step1** are optional parameters; if they are missing **var1** is not updated and, rather than looping, the DO structure performs as an IF structure. The key distinction between DO in LISP and in conventional languages is that the LISP DO allows multiple iteration variables each with its own increment control. A FORTRAN DO is essentially a subset of the LISP DO structure.

Other LISP Structures and Functions

There are a great many other structures and functions supported by LISP which space does not allow us to introduce here. These include the MACRO special form, iterative MAPPING functions, a variety of function definition structures, and commands for file management and I/O. Interested students should work their way through one of many good tutorial reference works while seated before a computer running LISP.

LISP EXAMPLES

To give you a better feeling of what can be done in LISP we present several short examples.

Example 1: Pythagorean Theorem

The Pythagorean Theorem says that the hypotenuse, c, of a right triangle with short sides a and b is given by $c = \sqrt{a^2 + b^2}$. We define the function **pythag** to calculate c, given a and b, as follows:

```
-> (define (pythag a b)
       (sqrt (+ (* a a) (* b b))))
```

The function is invoked by the call:

```
-> (pythag 3 4)
```

and returns:

```
5.
```

Example 2: Convert Fahrenheit to Celsius Temperatures

The standard conversion equation from Fahrenheit temperature F° to Celsius temperature C° is given by:

$$C^\circ = (5/9)*(F^\circ - 32)$$

The LISP code implementing this conversion equation is:

```
-> (define (F->C f)
       (/ (* 5 (- f 32)) 9))
```

Invocation by the call:

```
-> (F->C 212)
```

yields the expected result

```
100
```

Example 3: Fibonacci Sequence

The Fibonacci sequence is an interesting mathematical series generated by the recursive definition:

Fibonacci(0) = 0
Fibonacci(1) = 1
...
Fibonacci(n) = Fibonacci(n—1) + Fibonacci(n—2)

This generates the sequence of numbers: 0, 1, 1, 2, 3, 5, 8, 13, 21, 34, 55, ... in which any given element is the sum of the preceding two elements.

The recursive definition of the Fibonacci sequence is captured by the following recursively defined LISP function (although it is computationally much less efficient than an iterative algorithm):

```
-> (define (fibonacci  n)
       (cond ((=? n 0) 0)
             ((=? n 1) 1)
             (else (+ (fibonacci (- n 1))
                      (fibonacci (- n 2)))))))
```

For instance, typing:

```
-> (fibonacci  10)
```

produces the response:

```
55.
```

To generate a list of terms from the series, we can embed the Fibonacci function in a DO loop:

```
-> (define (FibSeries)
       (do ((i 0 (1+ i)))
             ((= i 12) 'done)
                  (display (fibonacci i))
                  (newline)))
```

Entering

```
-> (FibSeries)
```

produces the Fibonacci sequence:

```
0
1
1
2
3
5
```

```
8
13
21
34
55
89
DONE
```

Example 4: Search and Replace

We have all gotten junk mail which appeared to be personalized by numerous instances of our name and/or home town. The substitution of one word for another is also a valuable function on word processors. Below we define a recursive substitution function capable of performing these functions.[14]

```
-> (define (subst new old data)
      (if (atom? data)
            data
      (cons (if (equal? old (car data))
                  new
                  (subst new old (car data)))
                  (subst new old (cdr data)))))
```

Upon receiving the input:

```
->  (Subst  'Bennet  'dummy
      '((Dear Mr/Ms dummy)
      (You may already have won one million dollars)
      (Yes you Mr/Ms dummy could already be rich!)))
```

the substitution program produces:

```
((Dear Mr/Ms Bennet)
(You may already have won one million dollars)
(Yes you Mr/Ms Bennet could already be rich!))
```

which, except for the parentheses, looks depressingly familiar!

Example 5: List of Atoms

The final example illustrates the flexibility and extensibility of the LISP language. We have already demonstrated the intrinsic predicate, *ATOM?*, which tells whether or not a LISP structure is an atom. Suppose we have need of a predicate which will tell us whether or not a list is composed solely of atoms. Examination of the Scheme language reference manual indicates that such an atomic list function is missing. In general, however, it is a relatively straightforward task to construct the required functions from more primitive intrinsic or user-defined functions. Friedman proposes calling the atomic list predicate *LAT?* (for "List of Atoms"), and the function is given simply by the following recursive definition:[15]

```
-> (define (lat? l)
       (cond
             ((null? l) t)
             ((atom? (car l)) (lat? (cdr l)))
             (t nil)))
```

Testing this newly defined predicate yields:

```
-> (lat? '(a b c d e))
#!TRUE

-> (lat? '(a b c d (e f)))
()
```

This is consistent with the first list being composed purely of atoms while the second list contains another *list* in addition to several atoms.

2.3 DIALECTS OF LISP

The very flexibility and extensibility discussed under the "Features of LISP" section has spurred the development of numerous LISP dialects and prevented, until recently, the emergence of a LISP standard. While this splintering of the language can be interpreted as a sign of growth and vitality within the discipline, it has had the detrimental side effect of making programs developed under one dialect unintelligible to other dialects. This has proved to be a serious handicap for sharing of programs and techniques, and has forced many "wheels to be re-invented."

Recognition of these problems led to the development of COMMON LISP by a huge team of over 60 participants representing every major AI research institution. The effort was coordinated by Guy L. Steele, Jr., of Carnegie-Mellon University, and his book *COMMON LISP — The Language* has become the *de facto* definition of what is becoming the accepted standard LISP. Some of the major dialects and their relationship to COMMON LISP are shown in Figure 2-1.

MACLISP developed at MIT is a direct descendant of John McCarthy's LISP 1.5. It is a very fast, flexible language designed to run on the PDP-10 and PDP-20 series of machines and has had considerable influence on the development of other LISPs.

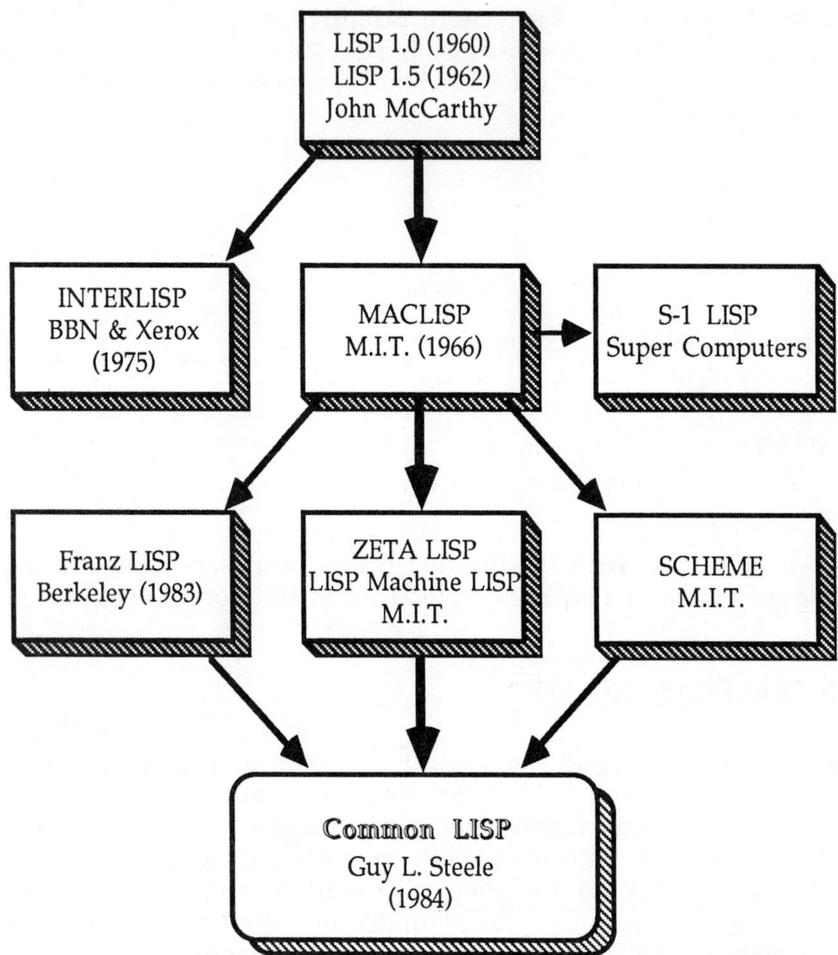

Figure 2-1 **The LISP Family Tree** Some of the major LISP dialects are shown in approximate historical order. The arrows indicate which dialects influenced the development of other dialects. COMMON LISP was designed by a committee coordinated by Guy L. Steele to provide a standard, portable, stable language which incorporates the expressiveness and power of other major dialects.

ZETALISP is an enhanced version of MIT's LISP-Machine LISP. It provides a sophisticated development environment and supports object-oriented programming and extensible data structures. ZETALISP, along with MACLISP and SCHEME, was influential in the development of COMMON LISP.

SCHEME is a very compact and flexible "clean" version of LISP developed at MIT by Guy L. Steele and Gerald J. Sussman for use in teaching computer concepts. Compiled versions of Scheme running on major brand microcomputers run as fast as do some interpreted LISPs on large minicomputers.

INTERLISP was developed by Bolt Beranek and Newman of Cambridge, MA, and by Xerox Palo Alto Research Center (PARC) in California. It was designed for exploratory programming and provides excellent support and documentation.

Franz LISP was developed at the University of California at Berkeley to provide MACLISP for the VAX family of computers in order to support the MACSYMA mathematics expert system. It runs under the UNIX operating system.

COMMON LISP is a new dialect of LISP similar to MACLISP and ZETALISP and influenced by SCHEME and INTERLISP. The objectives for developing the new language were:

- *Commonality* — COMMON LISP attempted to provide a standard for other LISPs to follow as they continued their evolution.

- *Portability* — COMMON LISP intentionally excludes features that cannot be implemented easily on a broad class of machines.

- *Consistency* — COMMON LISP explicitly requires the interpreter and compiler versions to impose identical semantics, a feature missing on other LISPs.

- *Efficiency* — Some optimizing compilers in COMMON LISP provide code as efficient for numerical computation as compiled FORTRAN.

- *Expressiveness* — COMMON LISP has incorporated the best features from other LISPs and excluded their less useful ones.

- *Compatibility* — COMMON LISP attempts to be compatible with ZETALISP, MACLISP, and INTERLISP in that order.

- *Stability* — It is intended that COMMON LISP will change only slowly and with due deliberation. Extensions will be added only after careful examination and experimentation.

2.4 PROLOG — PROGRAMMING IN LOGIC

If LISP is the "native language" of AI research in the United States, then Prolog is the "foreign language." Prolog was written by a team headed by Alain Colmerauer[16] of Marseilles, France, during 1970 — 1972, and a very fast version was implemented on the DEC-10 computer at the University of Edinburgh, Scotland, by David Warren and his group in 1979. Prolog has been used to write large AI applications programs at the University of Edinburgh, the New University of Lisbon, Portugal, and by Hungarian researchers for developing industrial applications. In 1981 Prolog was selected by the Japanese government as the principal language for Japan's Fifth Generation Computer Systems project.[17]

Prolog has been implemented on a variety of computers ranging from the DEC VAX down to the British Acorn educational computer. There are several dialects available for the IBM-PC family including Prolog-86,[18] Micro-Prolog,[19] Turbo Prolog,[20] and Prolog-1. An excellent introduction to the language including a tutorial and numerous examples is presented in *Programming in Prolog* by W. F. Clocksin and C. S. Mellish which was cited earlier. The dialect used for the present discussion is Prolog-86, a subset of DEC-10 Prolog which is compatible with essentially all the examples from Clocksin and Mellish.

FEATURES OF PROLOG

• *Prolog is a declarative language.* Facts and relationships about the system under investigation are encoded by making this information part of the knowledge base of the system. The user can then query the system for information either explicitly stated in the knowledge base or which is implied from this information. In this sense Prolog resembles a data base/query system.

• *Prolog uses the language of predicate calculus.* In predicate calculus, objects are represented by terms which may have one of the following forms:

> ♦ *A constant symbol* representing a concept or single individual. A constant symbol is equivalent to a Prolog atom, and examples include **greek, alberta,** and **peace** (note lower case convention for constants).
>
> ♦ *A variable symbol* which may represent different individuals at different times. Variables must be introduced along with quantifiers as shown below. Examples of Prolog variables are **X,**

Woman, and **Roman** (note upper case convention for variables).

♦ *A compound term* which resembles the symbolic-expression in LISP. A compound term consists of a *function symbol* in conjunction with an ordered set of terms as its *arguments*. The function symbol represents how the function depends on the arguments. Thus, the Prolog syntax for the relationship (predicate) "John likes Pat" takes the form:

```
likes(john,pat).
```

After building this data base, a query of the form:

```
likes(john,pat)?
```

will elicit the response

```
** yes
```

while the query

```
likes(john,ellen)?
```

will generate a

```
** no
```

since this fact has not yet been entered into the data base. The Prolog "no" should be interpreted as "not known".

• *Prolog handles lists and recursion naturally.* A very useful, recursively defined predicate is **member(A,L)?** which answers the question, *"Is A a member of list L?"* If we have a list L defined as:

L = [a, b, c, d, ...]

then we may write

L = [Head | Tail]

where

Head = a	(the first element of the list)
Tail = [b, c, d, ...]	(the remainder of the list)

A is defined to be a member of list L if it satisfies either of the following two rules:

♦ A is a member of list L if A is the first element of L.

♦ If A is not the first element of L, then A is a member of L if and only if A is a member of the tail of the list L.

These two rules may be encoded recursively in Prolog by the statements:

```
member(A,[A|_]).
member(A,[_|Tail]) :- member(A,Tail).
```

Note that the "_" symbol signifies "this variable matches anything". Once this recursive function has been defined, we may ask:

```
member(cat,[the,cat,sat,on,the,hat])?
```

and Prolog answers

```
** yes
```

but if we ask:

```
member(8,[1,2,3,4,5])?
```

Prolog says

```
** no
```

• *Prolog provides for very efficient coding for problems requiring inference.* That is, to solve the logical inference problem:

All humans are mortal.
Socrates is a human.

Is Socrates mortal?

can easily be encoded in Prolog as

```
mortal(X) :- human(X).
human(socrates).

mortal(socrates)?
```

to which Prolog responds:

```
** yes
```

Note that nowhere have we stated explicitly that Socrates is mortal, but that it is implicit from the rule relating humans and mortality and the fact about Socrates. This inference takes only three lines of Prolog but several pages of code in conventional procedural languages.

• *Prolog has some serious disadvantages compared to LISP*. These include:

- ♦ LISP in general has better I/O features than does Prolog.

- ♦ Prolog in general does not support graphics. An exception is the recently released Turbo Prolog.

- ♦ The order in which rules are entered greatly effects the efficiency of Prolog. The order of LISP functions has minimal effect on LISP efficiency.

• *Prolog and LISP may be used together.* Certain AI applications are more naturally programmed in LISP and others in Prolog. A hybrid system which mixes and merges the two languages may provide the optimum configuration. There are two modes in which this combination may be implemented. The first is the use of "externals" from within both languages. Presently many LISP systems support the call to external routines which may be written in Prolog. Several Prologs support this feature as well. The second solution is to use Prolog written in LISP. Since several Prologs have been written in LISP, this provides a natural solution to the problem of merging languages.

SYNTAX OF PROLOG

The general structure of Prolog programs can be summarized by the following four statement types:

1. *Facts* are declared describing object and their relationships.

2. *Rules* governing the objects and their relationships are then defined.

3. *Questions* are then asked about the objects and their relationships.

4. *Commands* are available at any time for system operations.

Facts:

Facts are represented in the Prolog data base by predicate clauses of the form:

```
likes(john, mary).
```

Note that the *punctuation key* indicating a fact is the *period*. This clause represents the fact that **John likes Mary**. Because "john" and "mary" are Prolog atoms they are written in lower case. The predicates may be user-defined such as **likes, is_grandfather_of, elephant**, and **loves_to_mountain_climb**. Examples of built-in predicates provided by Prolog include: the test for an uninstantiated variable, **var**; the test for an atom, **atom**; the equality test "="; and **length** for determining the length of a list.

Rules:

A Prolog rule is a general statement about objects and their relationships. It is represented by the general statement form:

```
X :- Y.
```

which may be interpreted in English as **X is true if Y is true**. X is defined as the *head* of the rule and Y is the *body*. Note that the punctuation key is the combination symbol *colon plus hyphen* and is pronounced "if". The Y predicate may be of compound form including logical connectives such as **and** "," and **or** " ; ". Thus the Prolog rule:

```
A :-  B,
      C,
      (D;E).
```

means

A is true IF
B is true, AND
C is true, AND
(either D OR E) is true.

Note that the variables in *rules* are capitalized since they represent general truths, not specific instances as do Prolog *facts*. Consider the following rule and associated database of facts:

```
mammal(X) :- has_hair(X),
             warm_blooded(X).
```

```
has_hair(dog).
has_hair(caterpillar).
warm_blooded(robin).
warm_blooded(dog).
```

When we request a list of all mammals

```
mammal(X)?
```

we get

```
X = dog
```

Questions:

Once the data base is established by entering the appropriate facts and rules, the user queries the system by the use of Prolog *questions.* For instance, assume that our data base consisted of one fact and one rule:

```
professor (mr_jones).
poor (Person) :- professor(Person).
```

We ask, *"Is Mr. Jones poor?"* by the question:

```
poor(mr_jones)?
```

and Prolog responds:

```
** yes
```

Note that the punctuation key for questions is the *question mark* and the syntax of the question is the same as for Prolog facts and rules. Note also one of the most powerful features of Prolog, the built-in "inference engine". That is, we have never explicitly told the system that Mr. Jones is poor. The system inferred this logical conclusion based on the two propositions: ***Mr. Jones is a professor*** and ***All professors are poor.***

If we added another fact to the database:

```
professor(mr_smith).
```

and asked such questions as

```
poor(X)?
```

Prolog-86 would respond

```
X = mr_jones
```

```
X = mr_smith
```

That is, the question asks, *"What are all instances of X for which X is poor?*, and Prolog lists the only two poor people it knows as *Mr. Jones* and *Mr. Smith*. It would give the same list of answers to the question:

```
professor(X)?
```

Commands:

These are imperatives denoted by the punctuation key *exclamation point* which tell Prolog to take some action. Examples of Prolog-86 commands include:

```
dir ('a:')!                 % directory of drive a:
load('a:mwf1.pro')!         % load a file from  a:
listing!                    % list current data base
save 'testfile.pro'!        % save current data base
exit!                       % exit Prolog.
```

Note that the "%" symbol denotes a *comment* in Prolog.

ARITHMETIC IN PROLOG

Prolog-86 can work with integers in the range from —32,268 to 32,767 and provides the following arithmetic functions:

```
X is 35 + 40?               %  Addition
X = 75

X is 35 - 40?               %  Subtraction
X = -5

X is 35*40?                 %  Multiplication
X = 1400

X is 35/40?                 %  Integer divide
X = 0

X is 40 mod 35?             %  Modulo operator
X = 5

X is 4 ^ 5?                 %  Exponentiation
X = 1024

X is 7 /\ 4?                %  Bit-wise AND
X = 4

X = 7 \/ 4?                 %  Bit-wise OR
X = 7
```

LOGICAL CONNECTIVES

The following logical connectives are available in Prolog for comparing atoms and numbers:

```
75 = 75?                    % Equality test
** yes

45 /= 35?                   % Inequality test
** yes

45 < 35?                    % Less than
** no

45 > 35?                    % Greater than
** yes

45 <= 35?                   % Less than or equal
** no

45 >= 35?                   % Greater than,equal
** yes
```

THE "CUT" IN PROLOG

As the student may have guessed from several of the previous examples, Prolog performs its amazing feats of inference by a process known as *backtracking*, a sequence of substitution which continues until the truth or falsehood of a proposition is established or all instances of a variable are determined. In the jargon of Prolog, this is called *satisfying a goal* or causing a goal to *fail*. It is easy to show that there are many instances when this automatic backtracking may lead to unpleasant or disastrous results. To handle these cases, the special operator "cut" is introduced. The symbol for cut is "!".

Consider for example the output generated by the following query:

```
member(a,[a,b,a,c,a,d])?
** yes
** yes
** yes
```

Since we are only concerned whether **a** is a member of the list rather than how many times **a** appears in the list, we can use the cut to write a more appropriate predicate to answer this specific question. This is done as follows:

```
member_one(X, [X|_]) :- !.
member_one(X, [_|Y]) :- member_one(X,Y).
```

Now, once the cut is encountered as a goal, it succeeds and subsequent backtracking does not produce additional solutions. This produces a better behaved function, yielding:

```
member_one(a, [a,b,a,c,a,d])?
** yes
```

and

```
member_one(X, [c,b,a])?
X = c
```

ADDITIONAL PROLOG EXAMPLES

Below are listed two examples which illustrate the use of Prolog programming for both numeric and symbolic information processing.

Example 1: Celsius to Fahrenheit Conversion

A Prolog procedure to convert Celsius to Fahrenheit can be written as:

```
Cel_to_Fahren(C,F)  :-  F  is 9*C/5 + 32.
```

We know the boiling point of water is 100 C°, and we can compute the equivalent Fahrenheit temperature by asking:

```
Cel_to_Fahren(100,F)?
```

and Prolog will respond:

```
F = 212
```

Example 2: Symbolic Differentiation

Differential calculus is very much concerned with symbolic differentiation. The following equations specify the rules for carrying out differentiation for most elementary expressions.

dc/dx = 0
dx/dx = 1
d(—u)/dx = —du/dx
d(u + v)/dx = du/dx + dv/dx
d(u — v)/dx = du/dx — dv/dx
d(u * v)/dx = u * dv/dx + v * du/dx
d(u/v)/dx = (v * du/dx — u * dv/dx)/(v^2)

d(u^c)/dx = c * (u^(c—1)) * du/dx
d(e^u)/dx = (e^u) * du/dx
d(sin u)/dx = (cos u) * du/dx
d(cos u)/dx = (—sin u) * du/dx
d(ln u)/dx = (1/u) * du/dx

These may be expressed by the Prolog rules shown below. Note the use of recursion and of the cut operator to terminate backtracking when the trivial goals, dx/dx = 1 and dc/dx = 0 are successful.

```
d(-U,X,-DU) :-
        !,
        d(U,X,DU).
d(U+V,X,DU+DV) :-
        !,
        d(U,X,DU),
        d(V,X,DV).
d(U-V,X,DU-DV) :-
        !,
        d(U,X,DU),
        d(V, X,  DV).
d(U*V,X,U*DV+V*DU) :-
        !,
        d(U,X,DU),
        d(V,X,DV).
d(U/V,X,(V*DU-U*DV)/V^2) :-
        !,
        d(U,X,DU),
        d(V,X,DV).
d(U^N,X,N*(U^N1)*DU) :-
        integer(N),!,
        N1 is N-1,
        d(U,X,DU).
d(e^U,X,(e^U)*DU) :-
        !,
        d(U,X,DU).
d(sin(U),X,DU*cos(U)) :-
        !,
        d(U,X,DU).
d(cos(U),X,-DU*sin(U)) :-
        !,
        d(U,X,DU).
d(ln(U),X,DU/U) :-
        !,
        d(U,X,DU).
d(X,X,1) :- !.
d(C,X,0) :- !.
```

Applying these rules for the differentiation of some arbitrary expressions yields:

```
d(a*e^x^2,x,X)?
X = a*(e^x^2*(2*x^1*1)) + e^x^2*0

d(a*x^3+b*x^2+c*x+d,x,X)?
```

```
X = a*(3*x^2*1)+x^3*0+(b*(2*x^1*1)+x^2*0 +
(c*1+x*0)+0

d(cos(x)^2+sin(x)^2,x,X)?
X = 2*cos(x)^1*(-1*sin(x))+2*sin(x)^1*(1*cos(x))
```

This segment of Prolog code is capable of carrying out most standard symbolic differentiation. Although the output expressions may not be completely simplified, they are technically correct. Another set of Prolog rules could readily be written to simplify the output.

2.5 SMALLTALK

Smalltalk was developed by Alan Kay and Dan Ingalls of the Learning Research Group at Xerox Palo Alto Research Center (PARC) in the early 1970s. Smalltalk introduced the concept of "object-oriented" programming and traces its roots back to LISP, Sketchpad, and Simula. It was designed for workstations such as the Xerox 1100 series, the Tektronix 4400 series, and Sun workstations and is also available for powerful microcomputers such as the Apple Macintosh and IBM PC AT. Smalltalk introduced the concept of the desktop metaphor as a elegant and integrated operating environment, including overlapping windows and pull-down menus, which was successfully commercialized by Apple with its LISA/Macintosh series and which has been widely emulated on most other modern workstations and microcomputers. Smalltalk-80 is a well-documented version of the language described by a series of books appearing in 1983.[21] Excellent summaries of Smalltalk and object-oriented languages are presented in special issues of *BYTE Magazine*.[22]

CHARACTERISTICS OF OBJECT-ORIENTED LANGUAGES

There are a number of features of object-oriented languages such as Smalltalk which distinguish them from standard procedural languages and make them particularly appropriate for large applications such as AI research requires. These advantages have resulted in the development of several object-oriented languages in addition to Smalltalk, including Object Pascal, Object Logo, Objective-C, C++ and Neon. A summary of object-oriented features include:

- **Information Hiding** — The scope of the data contained within each object is local to the object itself, and only the methods local to the object can manipulate it. This helps ensure reliability and modifiablilty of the software system by reducing interdependencies between components. The only communications with the outside world available to the object is through sending and receiving messages. Therefore the information present in the object is safely hidden from interference by other objects in the program.

- **Data Abstraction** — The methodology of isolating the part of a program that deals with *how an object is represented* from that part which deals with *how an object is used* is called *data abstraction*. The programmer may wish to define an abstract data type representing complex numbers or 3-dimensional vectors along with the set of procedures to access and manipulate the data. Since the abstract data type and associated methods are localized to the object, data abstraction provides for flexibility and modularity in program design.

- **Dynamic Binding** — Dynamic binding means that free variables in a procedure get their values from the environment from which the procedure is called rather than from the environment in which the procedure is defined. With lexical or static binding, on the other hand, values are bound to free variables only within the scope of the procedure definition. Dynamic binding is important to object-oriented programming because it allows for addition of new classes of objects (data types) without having to completely revise the program. In object-oriented programming, the new data type carries with it the appropriate method for printing, for instance, so that the same message selector, **print**, will work before and after the addition of the new data type.

- **Inheritance** — As discussed in the previous section, inheritance through the use of class structure improves the efficiency of creating objects and assigning them appropriate attributes common to the class. Coupled with dynamic binding, inheritance permits code to be reused which also improves programming efficiency.

These features give object-oriented programming significant advantages in the production and maintenance of complex software systems. There are a few disadvantages of object-oriented languages, however. These include:

- They tend to be somewhat *less efficient* than conventional languages. A message-send, for instance, takes about 1.75 times as long as a standard function call. In addition, the run-time cost of dynamic binding is greater than that for static binding.

• Implementation of object-oriented languages is *more complex* than comparable procedure-oriented languages because the higher level of abstraction provided by object-oriented languages leaves a greater "semantic gap" between their syntax and machine language.

• Programmers must learn an *extensive class library* before becoming proficient in an object-oriented language. This requires a high level of documentation and good development tools such as editors, browsers, and debuggers.

FEATURES OF SMALLTALK-80

Some of the distinguishing features of Smalltalk-80 are presented briefly here. We begin by defining some of the basic elements of the language and how these elements interact.

• **Object** — The standard definition of *object* is *a package of information and descriptions of its manipulation.* Another definition states that an object is a package of data and procedures that belong together.[23] The only elements of Smalltalk which are not objects are *message selectors* (defined below), comments, and punctuation characters. While conventional languages cleanly distinguish data from the procedures that operate on it, a Smalltalk object consists of both the knowledge-base and procedures which operate on it.

• **Message** — Sending a *message* is the Smalltalk equivalent of invoking a procedure or operator in conventional language. Computation is performed by sending messages to objects. The message includes a *message selector* (procedure name) and its operands. The result of sending a message to an object is to generate another object as the answer or value. The Smalltalk equivalent of the LISP *read-evaluate-print* cycle is the *specify-object, send-it-message, receive-resulting-object* cycle.

• **Method** — The Smalltalk *method* is the equivalent of the body of a conventional language subroutine or procedure. It is a description of the sequence of actions to be taken when a message is received by an object. It consists of three parts:

- ♦ a message pattern (procedure name containing a selector)
- ♦ temporary variable names
- ♦ list of expressions.

Smalltalk punctuation requires separating these three parts by vertical bars (|) and separating expressions by a period (.).

• **Class** — The class is the fundamental Smalltalk data structure describing one or more similar objects. A new object is described (by creating its class) before it is actually constructed. This is done by creating a *basic class template,* a framework with slots which are filled in to create the object. The slot names include the following quantities:

- class name
- instance variable names
- methods

By filling the slots for a particular object with its characteristic set of *instance variables* we create an *instance* of the object.

• **Inheritance** — The Smalltalk class structure provides the feature of *inheritance,* a very efficient scheme for knowledge representation in which objects share all the attributes of their class and all classes of which they are subclasses. Class structure relationships may be:

- **Subclass** — A class of objects which is a specialization of the general class
- **Superclass** — A class of objects created to generalize a group of classes
- **Metaclass** — A class that describes a class as an object. The single instance of the class is itself a class.

• **Method Dictionary** — The method dictionary contains pairs of selectors and methods. When a message is sent to an object, the method dictionary for that class is scanned for the appropriate method to execute. A method dictionary is included in every class description.

Example of a Smalltalk-80 Program

Although the control paradigm of Smalltalk is markedly different from conventional languages, the code does not appear radically different. Below we list one solution to the Towers of Hanoi puzzle[24] in Smalltalk-80 although the recursive solution presented does not emphasize object-oriented style[25].

```
moveTower: height from: fromPin to: toPin using: usingPin
      "Recursive procedure to move the disk at a height from one
      pin to another pin using a third pin"
      (height>0) ifTrue:[
      self moveTower: (height-1) from: fromPin to:usingPin
      using:toPin.
      self moveDisk: fromPin to: toPin.
      self moveTower: (height-1) from: usingPin to:toPin
      using:fromPin]

moveDisk: fromPin to: toPin
      "Move disk from a pin to another pin.  Print the results in
      the transcript window"
      Transcript cr.
      Transcript show: (fromPin printString,'->',toPin
      printString).
```

Then, typing the following command:

```
(Object new) moveTower: 3 from: 1 to: 3 using:2.
```

followed by selecting **do it** from the menu, results in:

```
1  ->  3
1  ->  2
3  ->  2
1  ->  3
2  ->  1
2  ->  3
1  ->  3
```

which is the correct solution.

2.6 POP-11

POP-11 is a powerful general purpose programming language designed originally by Robin Popplestone of Edinburgh University.[26] Developed as a tool for artificial intelligence research and teaching, its use has spread to graphics, image processing, expert system design, and VLSI circuit design. It is the core language of POPLOG, an integrated, interactive software development environment which includes LISP, Prolog, and a series of incremental compilers and editors. POPLOG provides an environment in which programs written in Pascal, FORTRAN, C, and POP-11 can be integrated and linked dynamically.

POP-11 resembles LISP in its sophistication but has a richer, more redundant syntax. This makes it a better teaching language than LISP. It encourages writing well-structured, clear programs in the style of Pascal with modular, testable parts. Program editing, documentation, compilation, linking, and testing all use the same process which speeds up program development time. Because of the large environment it provides, POPLOG requires minicomputers or workstations with one or more megabytes of memory.

FEATURES OF POP-11

Syntax

The syntax of POP-11 falls into two general categories:

- *Expressions* referring to objects
- *Imperatives* referring to actions.

The objects defined in POP-11 include, among other, simple data types such as numbers, words, strings, and lists. Imperatives result in POP-11 actions which may create objects, compare, search, store, and print out objects. For example, a simple imperative to add two numbers is written as:

```
25 + 75 =>  ;;;This is the print arrow.
```

and POP-11 responds

```
** 100
```

To assign a variable, Grade, a value, we would write:

```
92 -> Grade;
```

Note the Pascal-like semicolon usage and the reversal of the the usual algorithmic language assignment arrow direction. Comments are indicated by three semicolons on a single line or multi-line comments enclosed by /* ... */.

Variable and constant declarations also closely resemble Pascal, but without the strict typing Pascal requires. To declare x,y, and z as objects, we write:

```
vars  x, y, z;
```

Constants may be declared and assigned a single value only:

```
constant City;
'Racine' -> City;
```

Lists are assigned, using the [...] list delimiters as:

```
vars List1;
[a b c d e f] -> List1;
```

Procedure definitions resemble those of LISP without the parentheses:

```
define cute(anything);
     anything =>  anything =>
enddefine;
```

which can be invoked to yield:

```
cute( [ Happy Birthday to You ] );

** [ Happy Birthday to You ]
** [ Happy Birthday to You ]
```

Stack Operation

While all languages make use of a stack for keeping track of such things as calls to procedures, POP-11 gives the programmer direct access to a "user stack". The stack performs as a push-down array with the first element on being the last off. We can, for instance, assign x, y, and z the values 10, 20, and 30 respectively with the multiple assignment statement:

```
10, 20, 30 -> z  ->y  -> x;
```

To interchange the value of two variables on the stack, we type:

```
x,  y  ->  x  ->  y;
```

which is more efficient than the three-way rotation required in other languages. Stack manipulation is very straightforward.

```
vars  y;
25, 50, 75; ;;;put three numbers on stack
-> x;       ;;;pull the top one off and assign to x
=>          ;;;print the stack
** 25, 50   ;;;first two numbers are left on stack
```

There are several intrinsic functions provided by POP-11 for manipulating the stack. These include:

```
StackLength()    ;;;counts # of items, n, on stack, puts n on top
Erase            ;;;removes one item from the top of the stack
Erasenum(n)      ;;;erases n items from the stack
ClearStack       ;;;removes everything from the stack
Subscr_stack(n)  ;;;returns or updates the nth item on the stack
```

Program control, Iteration and Recursion

POP-11 supports essentially all standard conditionals and control of flow structures. The general form of some of these structures are shown next:

```
if <condition> then <action1> else <action2> endif

until <condition> do <action> enduntil

while <condition> do <action> endwhile

repeat <expression> times <action> endrepeat

for <x> in <list> do <action> endfor
```

In addition to these standard forms, there are several variations that provide efficient program control for almost any conceivable application.

To illustrate recursion and show some typical POP-11 code, we revisit the **member** procedure:

```
define member(item, List);
      if List = [ ]  then
            false
      elseif item = hd(List)  then   ;;;head function
            true
      else
            member(item, tL(List))   ;;;tail function
      endif
enddefine;
```

Note the natural syntax which resembles Pascal in form and LISP and Prolog in capability.

Pattern Matching

As we will see throughout the book, pattern matching is one of the most important tasks in many artificial intelligence applications. POP-11 provides very natural and powerful pattern matching procedures. The pattern matcher follows the general syntax:

```
<List>   matches   <pattern>
```

Consider, for example, the list defined by:

```
[a  b  c  d  e]  -> x;
```

We could use the member procedure defined above to verify that both a and c were present in the list. However, we would know nothing of their relative positions within the list. POP-11 allows testing for particular patterns as follows:

```
x matches [==a==c==] => ;;;does c follow a anywhere in x?
** <true>

x matches [==ac==] =>   ;;;does the pattern ac exist in x?
** <false>
```

The double equal symbol "==" corresponds to a wild card including the NIL list.

The double length arrow procedure "-->" provides an even more useful pattern matcher, particularly for applications in natural language processing. Consider the following code:

```
vars  first, second, rest;
[GIGO means Garbage In Garbage Out]-->[?first ?second ??rest];
```

which gives:

```
first  =>
** [ GIGO ]

second  =>
** [ means ]

rest  =>
** [ Garbage In Garbage Out ]
```

POP-11 provides many other features which make it an excellent language for AI research and teaching. Space does not permit a complete summary, but the segments of code presented above should give an indication of the natural syntax and power of the language.

In conclusion, we have surveyed four of the major languages available for investigations in artificial intelligence. Other languages have come and gone during the quarter century history of AI, but these four have survived and continue to win converts. In later chapters we will examine several special purpose languages designed for building expert systems.

PROBLEMS AND PROGRAMS

2-1. The Physical Symbol System Hypothesis makes a very strong statement for the reductionist position as the basis of artificial intelligence. Discuss case studies from the history of science which provide support for this hypothesis.

2-2. The Physical Symbol System Hypothesis makes a very strong statement for the reductionist position as the basis of artificial intelligence. Discuss evidence from the fine arts and/or (gestalt) psychology which may cast doubt on this hypothesis.

2-3. What characteristics of LISP do you believe most likely caused the proliferation of LISP dialects? What advantages and disadvantages do you see for the newly emerging standard, COMMON LISP?

2-4. Pascal is the paradigm of a procedural language, and Prolog is the ideal model of a declarative language. List as many features as you can which distinguish these two languages and the effects of these differences on the effectiveness of each language for its intended purpose.

2-5. The motivation for John McCarthy to write LISP was to implement Alonzo Church's recursive function theory on the IBM 704. Write a brief paper summarizing the salient features of recursive function theory.

2-6. A *metalanguage* is a language useful for the study and analysis of other languages. What features of LISP make it an effective metalanguage?

2-7. Write a LISP function to return the **fourth element** of a list (if it exists) and NIL otherwise.

2-8. Write a recursive LISP function to compute the **Fibonacci sequence** up to the nth term. Run the program for large enough values of n so that the computation takes a measurable amount of time. Measure the time required for each subsequent term in the series and interpret your measurements in terms of your recursive definition.

2-9. The "quote" was described as an "evaluation blocker". What does this mean and why is an evaluation blocker necessary ?

2-10. Write a LISP function **length** to calculate the length of an arbitrary list.

2-11. Write a LISP function **reverse1** to reverse the order of a LISP list.

Check it out against the intrinsic LISP **reverse**.

2-12. Write a LISP function **append1** to append one LISP list to another. Check it out against the intrinsic LISP **append**.

2-13. LISP is sometimes described as the "assembly language" of artificial intelligence while Prolog is the "high-level language." Discuss as many features as you can in support of this statement.

2-14. Write a Prolog program to convert from Fahrenheit to Celsius temperature using a single Prolog rule, and check the program out for 0 F°, 32 F°, and 212 F°.

2-15. Write a Prolog program to solve the "logical syllogism" expressed by:

> *Mozart was an excellent pianist.*
> *Excellent pianists are musicians.*
>
> *Was Mozart a musician?*

2-16. Write the Prolog rules corresponding to the following statements:

> *John likes anyone who likes wine and food.*
>
> *John likes any female who likes wine.*
>
> *X is a sister of Y if X is a female, X has mother M and father F, and Y has the same mother and father as X does.*

2-17. Write a Prolog database of employee records for a small, 10-person company. The format to be used is:

> employee(name,salary_in_$K,years_employed,sex,job_title,college_degree)

Use the database and Prolog queries to generate five reports such as:

> *List all employees who have worked more than 5 years and earn over $45K.*

2-18. Estimate the size of program and effort involved in writing the database query program in problem 2-17 in a procedural language such as Pascal.

2-19. It has been noted that object-oriented languages seem more natural to novices than to professional programmers on their first exposure. What features of Smalltalk would give credibility to this statement?

2-20. Find one or more journal reviews of POP-11 and/or the POPLOG environment and write a short paper presenting their relative advantages and disadvantages.

REFERENCES AND FOOTNOTES

1 Newell, Allen and Simon, Herbert A., "Computer Science as Empirical Inquiry: Symbols and Search," *Communications of the Association for Computing Machinery* **19**, pp. 113—126, March (1976)

2 Friedman, Daniel P. and Felleisen, Matthias, *The Little LISPer*, Second Edition, SRA, Inc., Chicago, IL (1985)

3 Touretzky, David S., *LISP — A Gentle Introduction,* Harper and Row, New York, NY (1984)

4 Brooks, Rodney A., *Programming in Common LISP,* John Wiley & Sons, Inc., Sommerset, NJ (1985)

5 Wilensky, Robert, *Common LISPcraft,* W. W. Norton & Company, New York, NY (1986)

6 Winston, Patrick Henry and Horn, Berthold Klaus Paul, *LISP,* Second Edition, Addison-Wesley, Reading, MA (1984)

7 Abelson, Harold and Sussman, Gerald Jay with Sussman, Julie, *Structure and Interpretation of Computer Programs,* The MIT Press, Cambridge, MA (1985)

8 Clocksin, W. F. and Mellish, C. S., *Programming in PROLOG,* Second Edition, Springer-Verlag, Berlin (1984)

9 Sterling, Leon and Shapiro, Ehud, *The Art of Prolog,* The MIT Press, Cambridge, MA (1986)

10 Garavaglia, Susan, *Prolog,* Harper & Row, New York, NY (1987)

11 McCarthy, J., Abrahams, P. W., Edwards, D. J., Hart, T. P., and Levin, M. I., *LISP 1.5 Programmer's Manual,* Second Edition, The MIT Press, Cambridge, MA (1965)

12 Clinger, W. (ed), *The Revised Revised Report on Scheme,* MIT AI Memo No. 848, August (1985)

13 Steele, Jr., Guy L., *Common LISP - The Language,* Digital Press, Burlington, MA (1984)

14 Wilensky, Robert, *Op cit,* p. 99

15 Friedman, Daniel P. and Felleisen, Matthias, *Op cit,* p. 15

16 Colmerauer, Alain, "PROLOG IN 10 FIGURES", *Communications of the ACM* **28**, pp. 1296—1310, December (1985)

17 For an excellent summary article, see Ernie Tello's "The Languages of AI Research", *PC Magazine,* pp. 173—189, April 16 (1985)

18 *PROLOG-86™ User's Guide and Reference Manual,* MIRCO-AI, P. O. Box 91, Rheem Valley, CA 94570

19 de Saram, Hugh, *Programming in Micro-PROLOG,* John Wiley & Sons, Inc., Sommerset, NJ (1985)

20 *Turbo PROLOG — The Natural Language of Artificial Intelligence,* Borland International, Inc., 4585 Scotts Valley Drive, Scotts Valey, CA 95066 (1986)

21 Goldberg, Adele and Robson, David, *Smalltalk-80: The Language and Its Implementation,* Addison-Wesley, Reading MA (1983). See also Goldberg, Adele, *Smalltalk-80: The Interactive Programming Environment,* Addison-Wesley, Reading, MA (1984), and Krasner, Glenn, *Smalltalk-80: Bits of History, Words of Advice,* Addison-Wesley, Reading, MA (1983).

22 BTYE Special Issue on Smalltalk, *BYTE* **6**, No. 8, August, 1981 and BYTE Special Issue on Object-Oriented Languages, *BYTE* **11**, No. 8, August, 1986

23 Kaehler, Ted and Patterson, Dave, *A Taste of Smalltalk,* p. 11, W.

W. Norton & Company, New York, NY (1986)

24 See Chapter 3, Section 3.2 for a more detailed description of this puzzle.

25 Kaehler, Ted and Patterson, Dave, *Op Cit.*, p. 7

26 Barrett, Rosalind, Ramsay, Allan, and Sloman, Aaron, *POP-11 - A practical language for Artificial Intelligence,* Halsted Press/John Wiley & Sons, New York, NY (1985)

Chapter 3

BASIC SEARCH TECHNIQUES

(PHOTO: COURTESY OF MARVIN MINSKY)

Marvin Minsky is Donner Professor of Science in the Department of Electrical Engineering and Computer Science at MIT. He received his B. A. in mathematics from Harvard University and his Ph.D. from Princeton. With his colleague John McCarthy, he organized the 1956 Dartmouth Conference at which AI as a discipline was born. With McCarthy he created MIT's Artificial Intelligence Laboratory and served as its director for many years. His theory of frames has proven to be a valuable technique for knowledge representation. His book *Semantic Information Processing* contains much seminal work, and his most recent book is *The Society of Mind*. Minsky is considered to be one of the leading researchers and spokesmen in the field of AI.

3: BASIC SEARCH TECHNIQUES

3.1 INTRODUCTION

Many of the tasks of AI can be phrased in terms of a search for the solution to the problem at hand. Basic search techniques provide the key to many historically important accomplishments in the area of artificial intelligence. These include applications in such areas as:

- Board games and puzzles (Tic-tac-toe, chess, Towers of Hanoi)
- Scheduling and routing problems (Traveling salesman problem)
- Language parsing and interpretation (Search for structure and meaning)
- Logic programming (Search for facts and implications)
- Computer vision and pattern recognition
- Rule-based expert systems.

Since the concept of the search for solutions in *state space* is central to both AI as well as other areas of computer science we will explore some of the most effective techniques of searching. These techniques also provide a background which will prove valuable for the discussion of general problem solving presented in Chapter 6.

An important property of most of the significant search problems studied in artificial intelligence is that they suffer from the *combinatorial explosion*. That is, the number of states which must be searched generally grows very rapidly with the size and complexity of the system studied. If the size of the system is specified by some parameter **n**, the number of possible states typically goes as 2^{n} or **n!**. This is what is meant by the combinatorial explosion.

Various strategies for effective search have emerged from the fields of mathematics and computer science over the years. These range from totally uninformed search methods with no knowledge of the domain being searched (also known as *weak methods*) to well-informed techniques in which knowledge of the domain is used effectively to speed the search. The principle contribution of artificial intelligence to the science of searching is the concept of knowledge-based *heuristics* for constraining and directing search. In the next chapter the concept of heuristics will be examined in greater detail. For the present we define a heuristic as a knowledge-based, search-limiting rule-of-thumb or strategy which yields solutions most of the time but is not guaranteed to do so. The importance of heuristics was strongly emphasized by George Polya in his book *How To Solve It.*[1]

We begin the discussion by rephrasing several of the classical problems of artificial intelligence in terms of a search for a solution. An important concept from game theory suggests that a successful game winning strategy must incorporate an efficient search for the optimum path down the branches of the game tree. In board games the critical factor is to design effective heuristics to limit the search so that real computers can look ahead the maximum number of levels or *plies* in the game in a finite amount of time. The programmer's job in board games is to guide the computer's search using any heuristics which prove effective.

3.2 CLASSIC PROBLEMS

There is a long and honorable tradition of testing AI concepts against a battery of favorite problems. In this chapter we introduce several intriguing problems including:

- The Airline Booking Problem
- The Towers of Hanoi
- The 15-Puzzle
- The Traveling Salesman Problem

These examples illustrate an interesting characteristic of problems — they fall into two classes: algorithmically solvable and heuristically solvable. They also demonstrate important aspects of searching for solutions in problem space, including:

- The search for an optimal knowledge representation scheme
- The search for effective solution algorithms
- The search for efficient heuristics.

Some problems such as the airline booking problem yield elegant iterative solution algorithms once an appropriate representation scheme is identified. Others such as the Towers of Hanoi are most readily solved by identifying a natural recursive algorithm for their solution. As with many recursive solutions, however, a deceptively simple algorithm may yield a solution which soon bogs down even the largest computer as the initial problem size grows. The second class of problems illustrated by the 15-Puzzle and the traveling salesman problem have no direct, simple algorithmic solution due to the combinatorial explosion in the number of states which must be examined. In such cases, effective heuristic search becomes the optimum strategy for obtaining an exact or acceptable solution.

In phrasing problem solving strategy in game tree language, the starting point of the game is called the root or initial state of the game tree, e.g. a blank tic-tac-toe sheet. A number of final states called terminal nodes or goal states are possible corresponding to a win or loss (three X's or O's in line for tic-tac-toe) or a draw. The game strategy for either player is to search for an effective path from the initial state to a desired winning state through a series of intermediate problem states. Any strategy which reduces the distance between player A's present state and a winning state is considered an acceptable move. The optimum move is generally that which minimizes the remaining distance between the chosen state and the winning state. This rather intuitive heuristic for selecting the path between starting and goal state was developed by Newell and Simon as the basis for their General Problem Solver program and generally goes under the name of *means-ends analysis*.

THE AIRLINE BOOKING PROBLEM

The airline booking problem illustrates the key role which a good knowledge representation system plays in solving complex problems. The first step in the search for a problem solution should be a careful search for an effective knowledge representation scheme. The optimum representation can easily make the difference in an order of magnitude in the size of code and time required for solution. Frequently the appropriate knowledge representation system will itself suggest the optimum algorithm for solution.

The problem may be described as follows: given a flight schedule describing the direct flights between cities as shown in Figure 3-1, can one get from city A to city B by a direct flight or will a 1 stop (2-leg) or a 2 stop (3-leg) flight or more be required? This problem differs fundamentally from the traveling salesman problem described below because it can be represented by a logical function rather than the numerical mileage representation required for the second part of the salesman problem. This allows an elegant algorithmic solution of the problem in terms of what we call an "adjacency matrix", A.

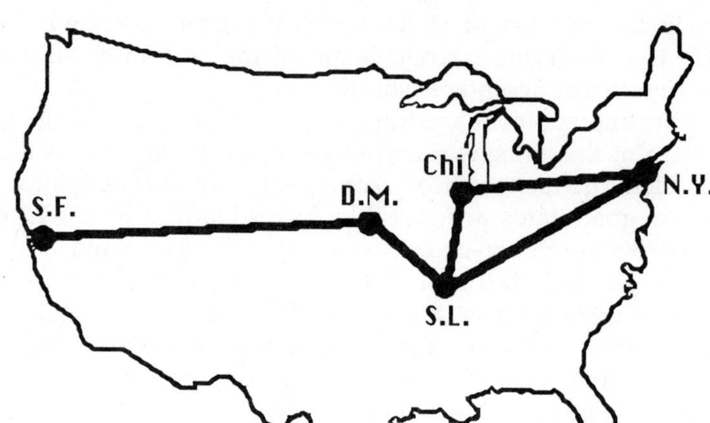

Figure 3-1 The Airline Booking Problem The question is: Is there an N-leg path between cities A and B? The adjacency matrix representation provides a direct algorithmic solution to the problem without resorting to heuristic search techniques.

Using graph theory, we can define each of the cities as nodes and each of the direct flight routes as edges. The adjacency matrix A has elements a_{ij} defined as follows:

$a_{ij} = 1$ if an edge connects node i and j
$a_{ij} = 0$ if no edge connects i and j

For the particular graph shown in Figure 3-1, we would have a 5 × 5 adjacency matrix, A, identical to the flight schedule:

	S.F.	D.M.	S.L.	Chi	N.Y.
S.F.	0	1	0	0	0
D.M.	1	0	1	0	0
S.L.	0	1	0	1	1
Chi	0	0	1	0	1
N.Y.	0	0	1	1	0

Element 4,3 of the adjacency matrix A is $a_{43} = 1$ since there is a direct flight from Chicago to St. Louis, and $a_{52} = 0$ since there is no direct flight from Des Moines to New York.

To answer the question: *Is there a 1-stop (2-leg) path between cities A and B?* we may compute the second order adjacency matrix, A^2 defined as

$$A^2 = A \wedge A$$

with element a_{ij}^2 given by

$$a_{ij}^2 = a_{i1} \wedge a_{1j} \vee a_{i2} \wedge a_{2j} \vee \dots \vee a_{in} \wedge a_{nj}$$

$$= \bigvee_{k=1}^{n} a_{ik} \wedge a_{kj}$$

where

n = the size of A = the number of nodes in graph
$\wedge$ = the logical "AND" operation
$\vee$ = the logical "OR" operation

Element a_{13}^2 of this matrix will be 1 indicating there is a 2-leg flight between San Francisco and St. Louis since there is a 1-leg (direct) flight from San Francisco to Des Moines AND a 1-leg flight from Des Moines to St. Louis.

All 3-leg paths are indicated by the third order adjacency matrix, A^3, given by:

$$A^3 = A^2 \wedge A$$

and so on.

Such matrices may be rapidly evaluated by matrix multiplication techniques and readily provide answers to the N-leg problem in terms of the Nth order adjacency matrix. The first order adjacency matrix is useful for answering the first question associated with the traveling salesman problem — Does a round trip tour linking all cities by direct flight exist? This is what is known as the Hamilton cycle question.

The key to the solution of the airline booking problem lies in selecting the appropriate knowledge representation system and associated operators. Unfortunately for the field of artificial intelligence, most problems of interest do not lend themselves easily to such simple and straightforward representations.

TOWERS OF HANOI

The Towers of Hanoi is another classic puzzle illustrated in Figure 3-2. The initial state and goal state are shown, and the rules allow the movement of only one disk at a time and require an additional constraint that the disks must always be in order of ascending size. Human players generally master such puzzles by a trial and error search. After some blind searching for simple 1, 2, and 3 disk configuration solutions, an elegant recursive algorithm becomes evident for the solution of the arbitrary n-disk Towers of Hanoi problem. This recursive algorithm may be summarized as:

1. *Move n-1 disks from source to auxiliary post.*
2. *Move nth disk from source to destination post.*
3. *Move n-1 disks from auxiliary to destination post.*

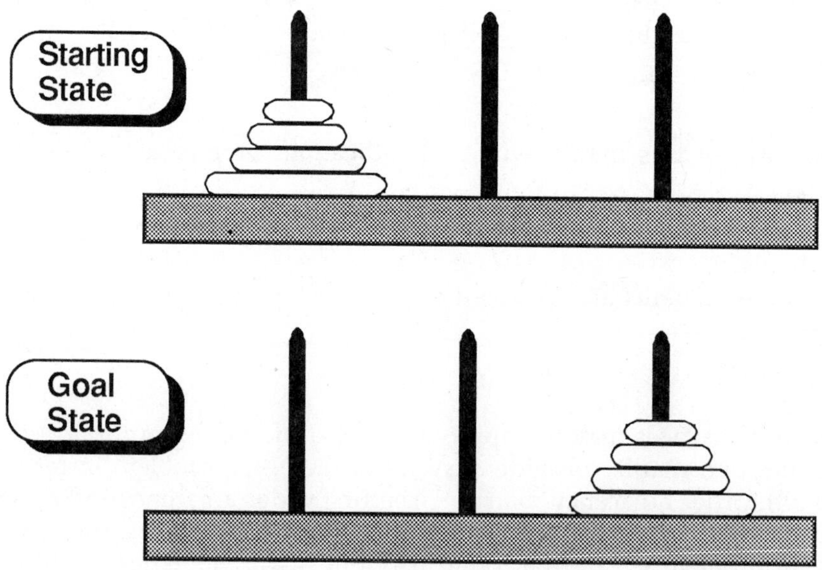

Figure 3-2 The Towers of Hanoi Puzzle The object of the puzzle is to transfer all disks from the left hand post (source) to the right hand post (destination), keeping the same order. The auxiliary post is used for intermediate storage, but at no time may a larger disk rest above a smaller disk. A search soon demonstrates a recursive algorithm for the process.

It is apparent that the key to the solution of the Towers of Hanoi puzzle is success in the search for an effective algorithm. The knowledge representation requirements for this puzzle are minimal, requiring only procedural specification for the movement of disks. Since the recursive definition of the solution is the only efficient one, we simply have to live with the fact that the number of steps required explodes rapidly as the number of disks increases. No heuristics have been proposed for improving the efficiency of this completely constrained disk transfer algorithm.

LISP SOLUTION TO THE TOWERS OF HANOI PUZZLE

The recursive solution algorithm is readily coded in LISP as:

```
->(define (Hanoi n source aux dest)
          (cond ((=  n 0) nil)
                (t (Hanoi (- n 1) source dest aux)
                   (move source dest)
                   (Hanoi (- n 1) aux source dest))))
->(define (move s d)
          (display "Move disk from ")
          (display s)
          (display "  to  ")
          (display d)
          (newline))
```

where the **source** is the left post, the **dest** is the right post, and **aux** is an auxiliary post which may be used for intermediate storage. Invoking Hanoi for a 3-disk initial state yields:

```
->(Hanoi 3 'A 'B 'C)
Move disk from A  to  C
Move disk from A  to  B
Move disk from C  to  B
Move disk from A  to  C
Move disk from B  to  A
Move disk from B  to  C
Move disk from A  to  C
()
```

which is the correct recursive solution.

THE 15-PUZZLE

Most research in AI deals with problems which do not lend themselves to simple knowledge representation systems or elegant algorithms such as the ones just presented. Many AI problems require searching through many intermediate problem states for the desired goal state. The "15-Puzzle" shown below nicely illustrates the search for the goal state through a large number of intermediate problem states. In addition, the puzzle demonstrates the concept of *heuristic search* as the player quickly learns to apply means-ends analysis.

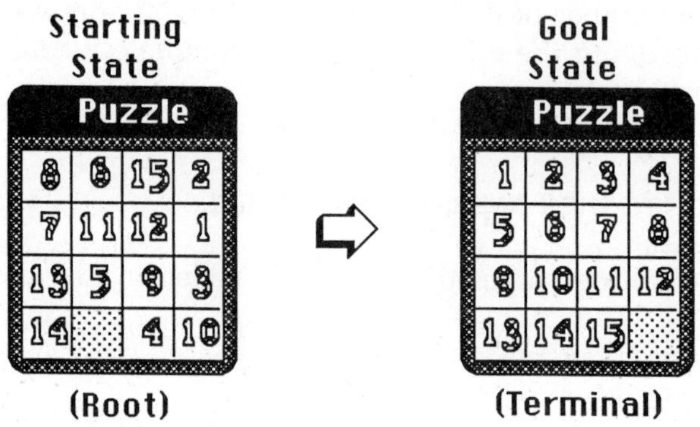

Figure 3-3 Typical game puzzle with random starting state and ordered goal state. Numbers may be shifted one space at a time to transform the initial state into the desired final state. The heuristic suggested by means-ends analysis works well for beginning and intermediate levels of the puzzle but often gets trapped in a loop near the end game.

The desired final state is defined as the *goal state* of an ordered board. Since there are over 20 trillion (16!) possible board combinations it is impossible to specify a unique algorithm for reaching the goal state shown. However, means-ends analysis suggests the following heuristic:

1. *Repeat until goal state reached*
   - 1.1 *Select the lowest out-of-position number as target.*
   - 1.2 *Move other out-of-position numbers aside to position target*

This simple heuristic works well until the final stages of the puzzle when unproductive looping may occur. At this point one must move "in-place" numbers in order to achieve the solution. The situation illustrates the important concept of *back-tracking* to recover an acceptable intermediate problem state after a series of moves has lead to an unproductive dead-end.

TRAVELING SALESMAN PROBLEM

One of the classic problems in graph theory which still has no closed analytic, algorithmic solution is the traveling salesman problem illustrated in Figure 3-4. The problem may be stated as follows: given a road map showing the direct path between every pair of cities, what is the optimum route such that a salesman will visit every city only once and return home while keeping his or her mileage to a minimum. Surprising as it seems, there is no analytic expression in terms of the city coordinates for computing such an optimum route, and the most obvious computational algorithm is to *generate-and-test* all possible solutions and select the minimum distance.

The combinatorial explosion makes this approach extremely time consuming for realistic problems. For instance, a 30-city problem requires examination of more than 10^{30} routes. Several heuristics have been developed to reduce the search space so that a near optimal route can be selected. Not only is this problem of considerable theoretical interest, but it also has a very significant practical interest to such institutions as the Post Office, UPS, and any company with sizable sales and field representative force.

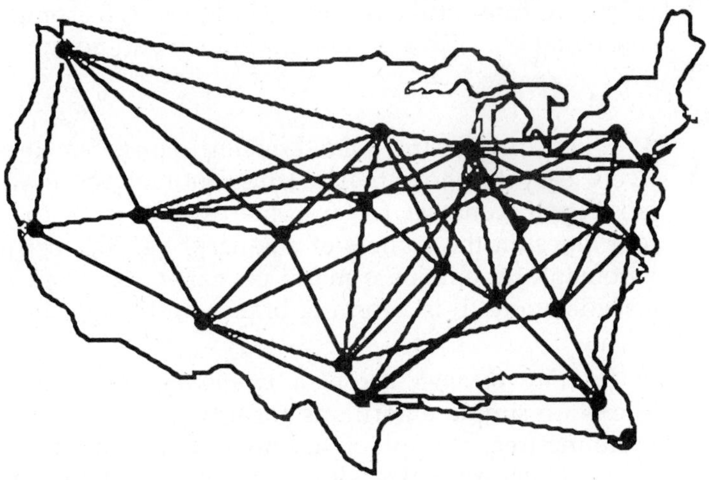

Figure 3-4 Traveling Salesman Problem Given the location of cities on a map with every city directly connected to every other city (not all routes shown), what is the minimum distance route by which the salesman can make a round trip but visit every city only once? This problem which has great practical as well as theoretical significance has never been solved analytically, although efficient search heuristics have produced routes very close to optimal.

The traveling salesman problem can be decomposed into two sub-problems:

- *Does a route exist which connects every city on the tour?* This problem, when phrased in terms of a complete round trip visiting each city once and returning to the starting city, is known as the Hamilton cycle problem.[2]

- *Which route minimizes the total distance?* There is no solution to this problem except exhaustive search with a generate-and-test algorithm. There are several heuristics which help to reduce the search space, however. These include, among others:

  ♦ *Pruning of paths which exceed the present minimum* — An obvious heuristic for pruning the search tree is to eliminate alternative routes to a given level which have a larger distance than the minimum achieved to date. That is, if we can get from San Francisco to Chicago with 10 intermediate stops by route A by traveling 2300 miles while a 10 city route B between the same two cities takes 2700 miles, we can automatically exclude route B from further consideration. This is called a branch-and-bound heuristic.

  ♦ *Eliminating routes with crossing paths* — It is relatively easy to show that a true minimal route will not cross itself (consider for example two alternate routes for four cities on the corners of a square). This heuristic will automatically eliminate many partial routes from further consideration. It is a form of branch-and-bound heuristic.

  ♦ *Pruning through use of a minimum spanning tree* — There are simple algorithms for constructing a minimum spanning tree, a graph of city nodes connected by a set of edges which minimizes some weight associated with the edges. In this case the weight is equal to the distance between the nodes. The minimum spanning tree is, in effect, the road map connecting all cities in the graph which minimizes the total length of highway. Following the map of the minimum spanning tree itself does not satisfy the rules of the traveling salesman problem because of the backtracking that would be necessary. However, the following algorithm can be shown to be within a factor of two of the best solution of the traveling salesman problem:

1. Begin at node x
2. Visit each son of x, returning to x after each visit, in a recursive fashion

This tour clearly costs a distance of twice that of the minimum spanning tree, but it also visits many nodes more than once. It can be converted into a simple salesman tour by simply deleting all but the first visit to each city. The net effect of such deletions will be to shorten the tour.

Even with clever heuristics such as those above, the traveling salesman problem is a time-consuming task on standard, sequential von Neumann computers. However, new architectures incorporating models of neural networks have already produced near-optimal solutions of this problem. We return to the discussion of new computer architectures in the last chapter.

3.3 GRAPHS AND GOAL TREES

To demonstrate several of the standard search techniques and illustrate some of their features, consider the graph shown in Figure 3-5. The term *graph* is used in its modern mathematical sense of denoting a set of *nodes* connected by *arcs* or lines. When the abstract concept of a graph is used to represent a real situation with arcs of length proportional to distance, we call it a *map*. In this variation of the map traversal problem, the traveler wants to get from starting point S to goal G in the minimum distance but has no *a priori* knowledge of the terrain (map). The problem may be divided into two logical stages:

- Find *any* path from S to G
- Find the *optimal* path from S to G

To illustrate two alternate strategies in carrying out the search for the goal, G, we may represent this graph by the tree structure shown in Figure 3-6. A *tree* is a graph with a starting or *root* node, intermediate problem states which are *sons* of the root or other problem states, and *terminal states* or *leaves*.

The first search strategy is called *depth first search* and the second is called *breadth first search.*

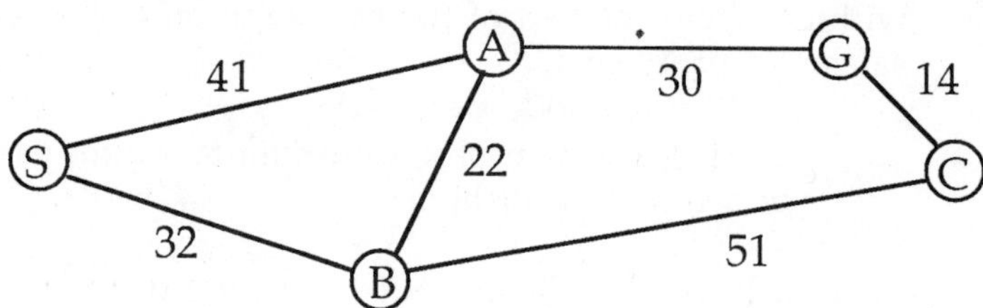

Figure 3-5 Map Traversal Problem The problem is to find a route from starting state S to goal state G which covers the minimum total distance. The nodes may be cities with the numbers indicating the distance between each pair. The first step is to design a search procedure to identify ANY route between S and G.

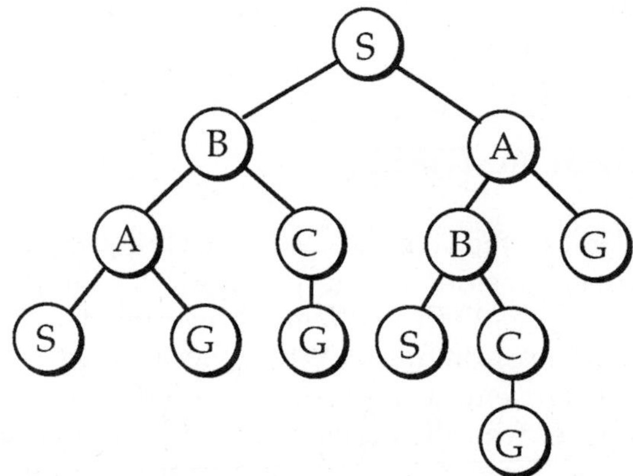

Figure 3-6 Tree representing the search for a path from S to G It is assumed that the investigator is conducting a "blind" search, that is there is no road map or sign posts in one city pointing to the next. The investigator does note, however, that the return to S represents an unproductive "dead-end" and produces a terminal failure node which prevents the search from falling into an infinite loop.

Let us consider properties of depth first and breadth first search in more detail.

3.4 DEPTH-FIRST SEARCH

In depth-first search, the search is conducted from the starting node as far as it can be carried until either a "dead-end" or the goal is encountered. At each node some arbitrary rule (e.g. "take the left-most fork") is used to direct the search. If a dead end is encountered, the search is backed up one level, and the next left-most branch is taken. This operation is called *backtracking*. The basic technique applied to the Figure 3-6 tree is shown in Figure 3-7.

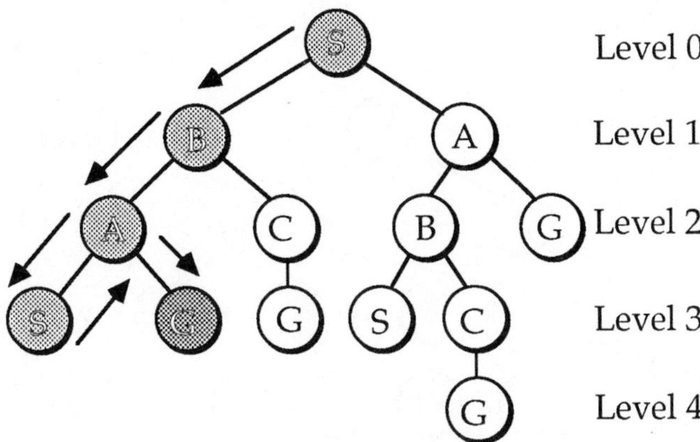

Figure 3-7 A Depth-First Search The search proceeds straight down the goal tree until a failure or goal node is encountered. Upon failure, the search backtracks to the previous branch to continue on down the tree. Note that this problem was solved after examining the 4 shaded nodes and traversing 5 branches.

For certain trees with a high average number of levels required before the goal is reached, the depth-first strategy provides an efficient "race for the goal" by avoiding a large number of unproductive intermediate states. However, it turns into a very inefficient technique when the tree has a complex branch structure with the goal state attainable in some of the upper levels. In such cases, the depth-first search may easily "shoot on by" the goal state as happened in Figure 3-7 (see goal state in level 2) and waste considerable time searching unproductive lower portions of the tree before back-tracking to the goal state. A totally informed, knowledge-based search such as would be possible using a road map would have allowed the goal state to be reached by a 2 node/2 branch path. However, with total knowledge the path is completely defined and no search is necessary. Notice how the addition of knowledge converts the map traversal problem from a blind search to an algorithm for getting from source to goal.

3.5 BREADTH-FIRST SEARCH

An alternative strategy illustrated in Figure 3-8 is called *breadth-first search.* Breadth-first is a form of exhaustive search in which each of the nodes is systematically explored at each level of the search until the goal state is attained.

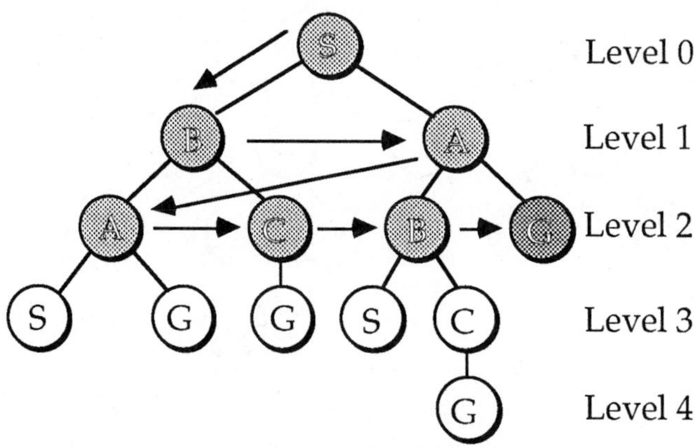

Figure 3-8 Breadth-First Search The algorithm requires that all nodes at a given level be evaluated for a possible goal state before proceeding on to the next level as indicated by the arrows. Although the goal state is the 6th state examined, the breadth-first search requires traversal of between 11 and 14 branch segments, depending on what knowledge is recorded, to reach the goal.

While the breadth-first technique appears to be a more conservative approach which avoids the problem of racing by goal states at shallow levels, this method also has its problems. Chief among these is the combinatorial explosion mentioned earlier which becomes particularly troublesome for "bushy" trees with a high branching multiplicity. The number of nodes N over which the search must be conducted grows as:

$$N = b^n$$

where

b = Number of branches at each node
n = Number of levels of decision tree

In the case of chess, for example, b is the order of 35 and n is approximately 100 which leads to the staggering number of possible nodes requiring evaluation:

$$N = (35)^{100} = 2.5 \times 10^{154}$$

It is clear that the combinatorial explosion prevents exhaustive breadth-first searches for trees of high branching multiplicity .

It is also clear that knowledge and logistics of a practical search play important roles in the efficiency of breadth-first searches. Consider a real traveler carrying out a "blind" depth-first search for goal city G. S/he would, in fact have to traverse the 5 nodes shown in Figure 3-7 before reaching the destination. How would the same traveler conduct a breadth-first search for the same goal, assuming the same blind search? The logic of breadth-first searching would determine the following branch traversals: Level 1 — SB, BS, SA, AS; Level 2 — SB, BA, AB, BC, CB, BA (short cut), AG. Thus, even taking the short-cut which the searcher recorded from his earlier trips, this partially-informed breadth-first search must traverse 11 branches. This search sequence has made use of the knowledge that node B and node A are connected so that returning to node B in level 1 is equivalent to continuing the search from the third node in level 2. Without using this information, a systematic breadth-first search would require a 14 branch search back through source node S which would give an even higher odometer reading.

It is interesting to compare depth-first searching strategy for the map traversal problem to that of board games such as chess. That is, in board games successive nodes may be examined sequentially as indicated in Figure 3-8 with no penalty in wasted miles due to physical backtracking. The nearest analogy for the traveler searching for city G would be if s/he hired two drivers in city S with radio-equipped cars to sequentially explore nodes A and B and report back the results. If node B had been the goal, driver B would have reported back and the second driver would not have been sent to node A. After reaching nodes B and A and reporting failure, each of the two drivers would hire additional drivers to explore the branches of nodes B and A in sequence. The first driver from node B would explore node A and report failure. Similarly, the second driver from node B would reach node C while the first driver from node A would rediscover node B, and both would report failure. However, the second driver from node A would reach the goal G and report success and the search would halt. Thus, through proper logistics and communication the goal could, in fact, be located by traversing 6 branches instead of the 11 — 14 required if no communication occured (but the project manager might still have to transport the two drivers stranded in nodes B and C to the goal).

STATE EVALUATION FUNCTION

In Figure 3.6 the goal state, G, appears four times because there are four possible paths on Figure 3-5 for reaching it. In terms of satisfying the existence criteria these four paths are completely equivalent, that is, each leads from the source to the goal. However, from a mileage or cost point of view they differ markedly. This suggests that for solving the second aspect of the map traversal problem there is a need for some measure of cost associated with each node of the tree structure of Figure 3-6 which indicates the mileage necessary for reaching this node. The term used for such a cost estimation function is the *state evaluation function*. In the case of the map traversal problem this function will obviously be the total number of miles from the source to this node. For instance, node A in Level 1 in Figure 3-6 would have an evaluation function of 41 miles, whereas node A in Level 2 would have an evaluation function of 54 miles (SB(32) + BA(22)). In the case of board games, the evaluation function provides some measure of the "goodness" of the board position for that state of the game. In all cases, such state evaluation functions provide the basis for the development and application of heuristics to guide the search.

3.6 HILL-CLIMBING HEURISTIC

Both of the techniques considered above, depth-first and breadth-first search, may be classified as *blind* or *uninformed* searches since the order in which nodes were selected was unaffected by information concerning the goal state or the unexplored region between the explored states and the goal state. The search was conducted by the systematic application of simple rules such as "always take the left-most path leading away from this node" (depth-first) or "evaluate all possible nodes at this level before proceeding to the next level" (breadth-first). Information was accumulated, of course, for purposes of documenting the actual path from starting state to goal state and avoiding loops.

Blind search should be distinguished from *directed* or *informed* search in which knowledge of the unexplored region including information on the goal state is used to guide the search. The only characteristic the evaluation function can have in blind search is that of a binary function; 0 if the present state is not the goal state and 1 if it is. So the blind searches discussed so far essentially ignore information which may, in fact, be available in the vicinity of the node under evaluation or for the problem as a whole.

Hill-climbing techniques, although basically uninformed on the features of the unexplored region, do make use of *local knowledge* about the particular node. Local knowledge is frequently available in the form of the gradient (slope) of the evaluation function in the immediate vicinity of the node. The name of this heuristic itself indicates the intuitive human analogy to problem solving. Two examples illustrate the basic ideas:[3]

- A single team of mountain climbers equipped with only an altimeter and compass (no topological maps) find themselves in heavy fog on the side of a mountain. What is the optimum strategy to reach the summit?

- Your television set is flickering badly, very fuzzy, and displaying terrible colors. There are 4 controls exposed. What is the optimum strategy for getting a good picture?

One solution to the first problem would be to walk 100 feet to the north and note the change in altimeter reading. Then return to the starting point and repeat the process, walking 100 feet to the east. From this information and a little trigonometry (assuming no violent local fluctuations such as cliffs or chasms), we could compute the direction for a maximum ascent of the mountain in that area (also known as the direction of the maximum gradient). After a few hundred feet the process would be repeated until, eventually, any direction we stepped off in would lead to a reduced elevation. Such a point is, by definition, the (local) summit.

From experience we know that an effective technique for tuning the badly out-of-tune television is to start with an arbitrarily selected control and twist it through its whole range, stopping when the picture is sharpest, even though this may still be a pretty bad picture. Then we go on to the second control and repeat the process. This technique is repeated for the third and fourth controls. After one cycle of the 4-knob tuning, the process is repeated until an acceptable picture is obtained. Note that, because of the continuous nature of the parameters being examined, we have searched an infinite number but still not all of the states available in the process.

So hill-climbing, by making use of knowledge about the local terrain, provides a very useful and effective heuristic for eliminating much of the unproductive search space. It is a variety of depth-first search in which the search is guided by a local evaluation function. Although formally in the class of *uninformed* search (it doesn't know where the summit is) it does make use of knowledge of the characteristics of a summit: *it is always higher if you are not there* and *all paths lead down if you are.*

Risks of Mountain Climbing

Just as real mountain climbers have problems with false summits and getting lost in the fog, so hill-climbing heuristics may run into a number of problems. Most of these problems may be easily understood in terms of their topological analogs.

• *The false summit problem* also known as the *foothills* problem — This is one of the most serious problems facing both mountain climbers and hill-climbing heuristics, particularly in jumbled terrain. The fundamental problem is that a false summit satisfies locally all the characteristics of the real summit, so that the heuristic is fundamentally defeated. Real climbers can survey the area (on a clear day), observe the higher summit, issue some expletives, climb down (backtrack), and capture the real summit. The best analogy for hill climbing heuristics is to systematically or randomly sample the terrain (problem space) to assure that the search has produced the real summit. If a higher elevation is generated by the sampling procedure, the hill-climbing heuristic is repeated using the new elevation as a starting point until the final summit is reached.

• *The ridge problem* — Once a ridge is attained, it is entirely possible that marching off in the north direction and then marching off in the east direction could easily both produce a loss of elevation if, for example, the ridge runs northwest to southeast. The ridge problem is particularly severe if the ridge is very steep on its sides and very gradual in its elevation gain. The maximum gradient algorithm tends to result in a path with violent oscillations across the ridge and very little elevation gain along it. This problem can be contained by decreasing the step size to operate within the region of the local maximum of the ridge. Careful interpretation of such data indicates the presence and direction of the ridge which can be followed successfully to the summit.

• *The plateau or mesa problem* — The hill-climbing heuristic works best for gradual, well-behaved, single-valued functions. Discontinuities on topographic maps give real mountain climbers great difficulty, and they give hill-climbing heuristics great difficulty as well. In unfriendly terrain it is entirely possible that this heuristic may, in fact, fail. This is a risk we take with all heuristics, but the benefits from the successful behavior of the hill-climbing heuristic in well behaved terrain outweigh its occasional failure. It is often a valuable heuristic for starting a search and ending a search in combination with sampling heuristics for resolving the false summit, ridge, and mesa problems.

3.7 THE BEST-FIRST HEURISTIC

This heuristic combines some of the advantages of such depth-first techniques as hill-climbing with the best features of breadth-first search. This procedure, also known as ordered depth-first search, always expands the most promising successor of the nodes evaluated to date. By computing the evaluation function, **f***, sometimes called a *cost function,* we evaluate the "promise" of the present node. The cost function may be any linear or higher order function of the parameters of the search tree. For example, interpreting the cost function as the miles between cities, it becomes straightforward to attack such problems as the traveling salesman problem.

The basic algorithm for the best-first search was published by Nilsson in 1971.[4] Starting at state S, a series of successor nodes is generated and **f*** is evaluated for each. The state showing the most promise is again expanded, and **f*** is evaluated on its successor nodes. For example, in the map traversal problem of Figure 3-5, our goal is to minimize the number of miles the traveling salesman must travel. We select the level 1 node to which to move based on the value of **f*** of each of these nodes. In such cases the optimum node (node showing the most promise) is that with the lowest **f***, regardless of the level at which that node has been evaluated. The evaluation function **f*** may be based on such parameters as the accumulated length of path from starting point to that node, the estimated distance from the given node to the goal, and linear combinations of such parameters. As a cost function, the lower **f*** is, the more promise a node shows.

To use the mountain climbing analogy one more time, the evaluation function might be defined in terms of the elevation, **a**, and gradient, **g**, and arbitrary normalization constants, c_1 and c_2, as:

$$f^* = \frac{c_1}{(a + c_2 g)} \tag{3.1}$$

and the object of the expedition is to climb the tallest peak of the range. This would be carried out by radio equipped teams in much the same way as the radio equipped drivers conducted the breadth-first search in the previous discussion. Teams reaching false summits (**g** = 0) would show lower promise (higher **f***) than those at lower elevation on higher peaks (**a** smaller but **g** larger). Whenever this happened, the team showing the most promise would move on up. It is clear that this best-first heuristic combines the race-for-the-goal feature of depth-first search with the evaluation-of-promising-alternatives feature of breadth-first search.

To handle general graphs in which a given node can have more than one predecessor, Nilsson proposed the following algorithm:

1. Put the start node S on a list, called OPEN, of unexpanded nodes. Calculate f*(S) and associate its value with node S.

2. If OPEN is empty, exit with failure; no solution exists.

3. Select from OPEN a node i at which **f*** is minimum. If several nodes qualify, choose a goal node if there is one; otherwise choose among them arbitrarily.

4. Remove node i from OPEN and place it on a list called CLOSED of expanded nodes.

5. If i is a goal node, exit with success; a solution has been found.

6. Expand node i, creating nodes for all its successors. For every successor node j of i:
   - 6.1 Calculate **f***(j).
   - 6.2 If j is neither in list OPEN nor in list CLOSED, then add it to OPEN, with its **f*** value. Attach a pointer from j back to its predecessor i (in order to trace back a solution path once a goal node is found).
   - 6.3 If j was already on either OPEN or CLOSED, compare the **f*** value just calculated for j with the value previously associated with node j. If the new value is lower, then
     - 6.3.1 Substitute it for the old value.
     - 6.3.2 Point j back to i instead of to its previous predecessor.
     - 6.3.3 If node j was on the CLOSED list, move it back to OPEN.

7. Go to (2).

CONSIDERATIONS ON THE CHOICE OF f*

It is clear that the success of any best-first search depends on the choice of the heuristic function **f***. In fact, the best-first search reverts to a breadth-first search if the evaluation function for node i, **f***(i), is just the level of node i. It turns into a depth-first search if **f***(i) is the inverse or the negative of the level of node i. From practical considerations such as that encountered in a real traveling salesman problem, the **f*** function should contain information on the distance already traveled and possibly an estimate of the remaining distance to the goal node (thus turning the search into an informed search). Solving the problem will involve some compromise between finding the optimum solution through exhaustive search and finding a satisfactory solution while minimizing the search effort.

Three levels in this spectrum have been identified as:[5]

1) If minimizing the search effort is the primary consideration, then any successful solution is an acceptable solution. There may, in fact, be only one solution in which case the **f*** yielding the minimum effort is optimal.

2) This category of search attempts to minimize some combination of search cost and search effort. The traveling salesman problem falls into this category as a practical matter, since a near optimal solution after a reasonable search effort is generally acceptable. The cost function may reflect both the distance traveled and the number of nodes searched.

3) Assuming the state space contains multiple solutions, the object is to identify the optimal solution. Hart, Nilsson, and Raphael proposed what they called the A* search as an optimal search for an optimal solution.[6]

THE A* ALGORITHM

Under certain well-defined conditions this heuristic is guaranteed to find the minimum cost path between starting point and goal state, if such a path exists, while generating the fewest number of nodes in the process. This somewhat startling result is obtained, not surprisingly, by adding knowledge to the **f*** evaluation function. It is now redefined for node n as:

$$\mathbf{f^*(n)} = \mathbf{g(n)} + \mathbf{h^*(n)}$$

where

> **g**(n) is the true measure of cost of getting from the starting point to the present node (e.g. calculated from the actual distance)
>
> **h***(n) is an estimator of the minimum cost from the present node n to the goal. This function should be non-negative and never overestimate the cost of reaching the goal node.

While the **g** function may be determined exactly for each path from S to n, the **h*** function is much less certain and is the carrier of heuristic information. If **h*** = 0 for all nodes, the search reverts back to a best-first search. If **h***(n) overestimates the cost of reaching the goal from state n, some acceptable nodes are eliminated from the OPEN list and the final path may not be the optimum one.

The A* heuristic, by using knowledge about the goal state to help guide the search, is the most informed search technique considered so far. Although the A* heuristic assures a minimal cost path in terms of the total distance the salesman must travel, it does not reveal anything about the computing effort necessary in order to evaluate **h*** or the number of nodes which must be evaluated to find the optimal path. Therefore, it is not necessarily the method of choice for this class of problems.

3.8 AND/OR TREES

Up to this point only graphs which can be represented as OR trees as indicated in Figure 3-6 have been considered. This type of tree can be identified by the fact that at each node the search must select one *OR* another path to the next level. The final goal is one or more terminal states which may be reached by one or more distinct paths through the OR tree.

In the more general concept of problem solving it is useful to consider AND trees as a representation in a problem reduction language. This is a graphical representation of the general concept of "top-down design" or "modular programming" in which the guiding principle is to break a difficult problem or goal down into a number of sub-problems or sub-goals, each of which is simpler and easier to solve than the original problem. The solution of the original problem, A, is then accomplished by the solution of all sub-problems at level 1, i.e. the solution of A is equivalent to the solution of B AND C as shown in Figure 3-9. In the spirit of top-down design, each of sub-problems B and C may themselves be reduced to even simpler sub-problems as shown. The important point here is that in an AND tree, ALL nodes at a given level must be solved for a solution to the original problem.

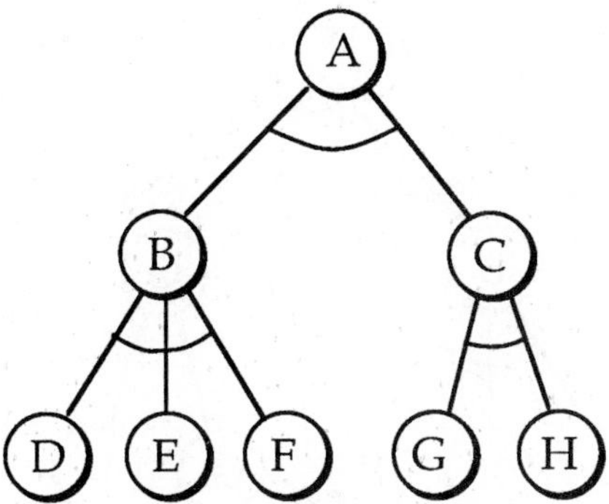

Figure 3-9 AND Tree for Problem Reduction The original problem A may be solved by breaking it up into problems B AND C and solving both. Problem B may be solved, in turn, by solving D AND E AND F and so on. This representation is also known as a goal tree in which the sub-goals at lower levels are solved in order to reach the goal of A.

Another characteristic which distinguishes AND and OR trees is the direction of motion of information flow through the tree. In an OR tree using forward chaining, we start at the initial state and progress downward, expanding and evaluating nodes as we search for the goal state hiding at some lower level in the tree. In an AND tree, on the other hand, while control information travels from the top down, the partial solutions are carried out at the lowest levels first, and the results must be combined and reprocessed by higher level functions until the answer to the problem finally emerges at the top node.

Real life problem solving generally involves some combination of AND and OR trees. There are frequently several alternative methods of problem solution (paths on an OR tree), but at each stage of the chosen solution, problems may be encountered which require resolution into problem segments, all of which must be solved in order to proceed with the overall solution. This type of problem is represented by AND/OR trees such as that shown in Figure 3-10.

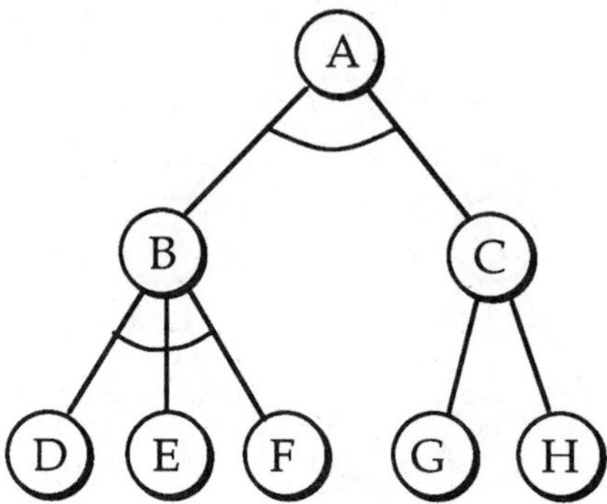

Figure 3-10 AND/OR Tree for real problems Most actual problems admit to alternate paths to solution. Here, to solve A, both B and C must be solved. However C can be solved by solving either G or H (OR Tree).

As one would expect from the previous discussion, information in AND/OR trees moves in both directions — upward in local AND branches and downward as the overall control strategy progresses from the initial state to the final state. Special heuristics such as the AO* described by Nilsson have been developed for expanding and evaluating nodes on AND/OR trees.[7]

In summary, we have presented some of the major techniques in carrying out searches under a range of knowledge availability. These techniques are used widely throughout AI research and will be used throughout the rest of the book. In particular, the next chapter on game playing will put many of the concepts studied in this chapter to immediate use.

PROBLEMS AND PROGRAMS

3-1. Compute, if possible, or look up in the references, if not, the following:

- The number of possible board configurations in tic-tac-toe
- The actual number of possible tic-tac-toe games, taking into account games identical under $\pm 90^\circ$ and mirror rotations
- The number of possible checker board configurations
- The number of possible chess board configurations

- The number of punch configurations possible on a 12 row × 80 column "Hollerith" punch card

Compare these numbers to Sir Arthur Eddington's estimate of $2 \times 136 \times 2^{256}$ particles in the universe.[8]

3-2. The number of states for Problem A goes as N^5 and for Problem B it goes as 2^N where N is some measure of problem size. Using appropriate logarithmic scales, plot the number of states which must be searched for each of these problems as a function of N and note the point(s) for which they are equal.

3-3. The 15-Puzzle is available on popular microcomputers if you do not already have a mechanical model. Play the game a number of times using the following three heuristics and discuss your results:

a) Your own intuitive heuristics
b) The heuristics suggested in the text
c) An improved heuristic you propose based on your experience above

3-4. Write a program to solve the Towers of Hanoi puzzle recursively and use it to analyze the 5-disk problem.

3-5. Program the airline booking problem in Prolog, entering the flight schedule as facts in the data base and the higher-order adjacency matrices as rules. Ask the system to answer several 1-, 2-, and 3-leg flight questions, e.g. "Is there a 2-leg flight from Chicago to San Francisco?"

3-6. One effective heuristic for solving the traveling salesman problem is the *nearest neighbor algorithm* which can be specified as follows:

1. Select a starting city at random
2. Repeat until all cities visited
    - 2.1 Check distance to all remaining un-visited cities
    - 2.2 Select next city with minimum distance from present city
    - 2.3 Move to selected city

Implement the nearest city algorithm in LISP or Prolog and test on a small model.

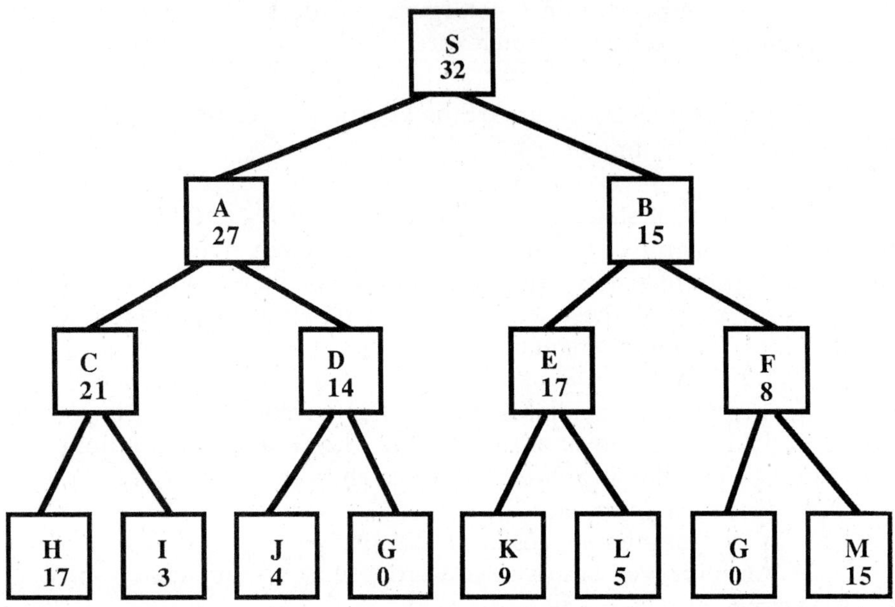

Figure 3-11 Search Tree with Evaluation Function Values Note the two goal states, G, among the terminal nodes.

3-7. Using the search tree in Figure 3-11, trace the search (sequence of nodes) which would be conducted using:

a) Depth-first search
b) Breadth-first search
c) Best-first heuristic

3-8. Suggest procedures for generating reasonable evaluation functions for the following problems:

a) The 15-Puzzle
b) The traveling salesman
c) Tic-tac-toe
d) Chess

3-9. *Beam search* is a type of breadth-first search using the f* evaluation function in which only the *n* best nodes at each level are expanded, where **n** is some small, user-defined number. What would be the relative advantage of beam search over depth-first and breadth-first search?

3-10. Write a LISP program to perform the following operations:

a) Create a small (4-5 entries) telephone directory with the format

(NAME NUMBER)

b) Invert the order of the original directory

c) Given the name as input, return the number as output.

3-11. Discuss the problems caused by ridges for the hill climbing heuristic. Sketch a topographic map for an imaginary ridge and the path of ascent if only the maximum gradient function is used. Outline an algorithm for overcoming these problems.

3-12. Consider the three search techniques: Depth-First, Breadth-First, and Hill Climbing. Write a short (1-2 page) description of 3 distinct search problems, each of which you would solve by one of these methods, and indicate the features of the problems and the search techniques which led to your choice.

3-13. Consider the following puzzle: Suppose two diagonally opposite corner squares are removed from a standard 8 by 8 square chessboard. Can 31 rectangular dominoes, each the size of exactly two squares, be so placed as to cover precisely the remaining board? Estimate the search space required for the two techniques:

a) Blind trial-and-error

b) Consideration of board color — each domino must cover 1 red and 1 black square.

3-14. How does the best-first algorithm introduced in the text differ from the A* algorithm? Why is the A* algorithm called a heuristic approach?

3-15. Clearly an optimal search strategy involves trade-offs between blindly searching vast problem spaces on one hand and computationally complex, time-consuming evaluation function calculations on the other. Discuss strategies for selecting the best balance between blind search and function evaluation and describe two applications, one which favors emphasis on blind search and one in which a detailed evaluation function would be more efficient.

3-16. Write down an evaluation function, **f***, for an A* search for the solution to the 15-puzzle. Parameters you may wish to consider include the number of tiles in correct position and the "distance" (in tile spaces) of displaced tiles from their correct position.

3-17. Write a LISP or Prolog algorithm for solution of the 15-puzzle or the 8-puzzle (3×3 version) using the A* heuristic to guide your search.

3-18. Discuss the similarities and differences between the hill-climbing algorithm and various best-first algorithms. What role does knowledge play in each?

3-19. What information must be retained at each node as it is expanded during the A* search in order to obtain a solution?

3-20. Describe two realistic search problems which are best described by AND/OR trees. Discuss the flow of information throughout the tree for each case.

REFERENCES AND FOOTNOTES

[1] Polya, George, *How to Solve It,* Princeton University Press, Princeton, NJ (1945, 1973)

[2] Sedgewick, Robert, *Algorithms,* p. 514, Addison-Wesley Publishing Company, Reading, MA (1984)

[3] Winston, Patrick Henry, *Artificial Intelligence,* Second Edition, Addison-Wesley, Reading, MA (1984)

[4] Nilsson N. J., *Problem-solving Methods in Artificial Intelligence,* McGraw-Hill Book Company, New York, NY (1971)

[5] Feigenbaum, Edward A., Barr, Avron, and Cohen, Paul R. (Eds), *The Handbook of Artificial Intelligence,*Vol. 1—3, HeurisTech Press/William Kaufmann, Inc., Stanford, CA (1981—82)

[6] Hart, P. E., Nilsson, N. J., and Raphael, B., "A Formal Basis for the Heuristic Determination of Minimum Cost Paths", *IEEE Transactions on SSC,* **SSC-4**, pp. 100—107, (1968)

[7] Nilsson, Nils J., *Principles of Artificial Intelligence,* pp. 103—109, Tioga Publishing Co., Palo Alto, CA (1980)

[8] Eddington, Sir Arthur Stanley, "The Constants of Nature", in *The World of Mathematics,* James R. Newman (ed), pp. 1069—1093, Simon and Schuster, New York, NY (1956)

Chapter 4

GAME PLAYING

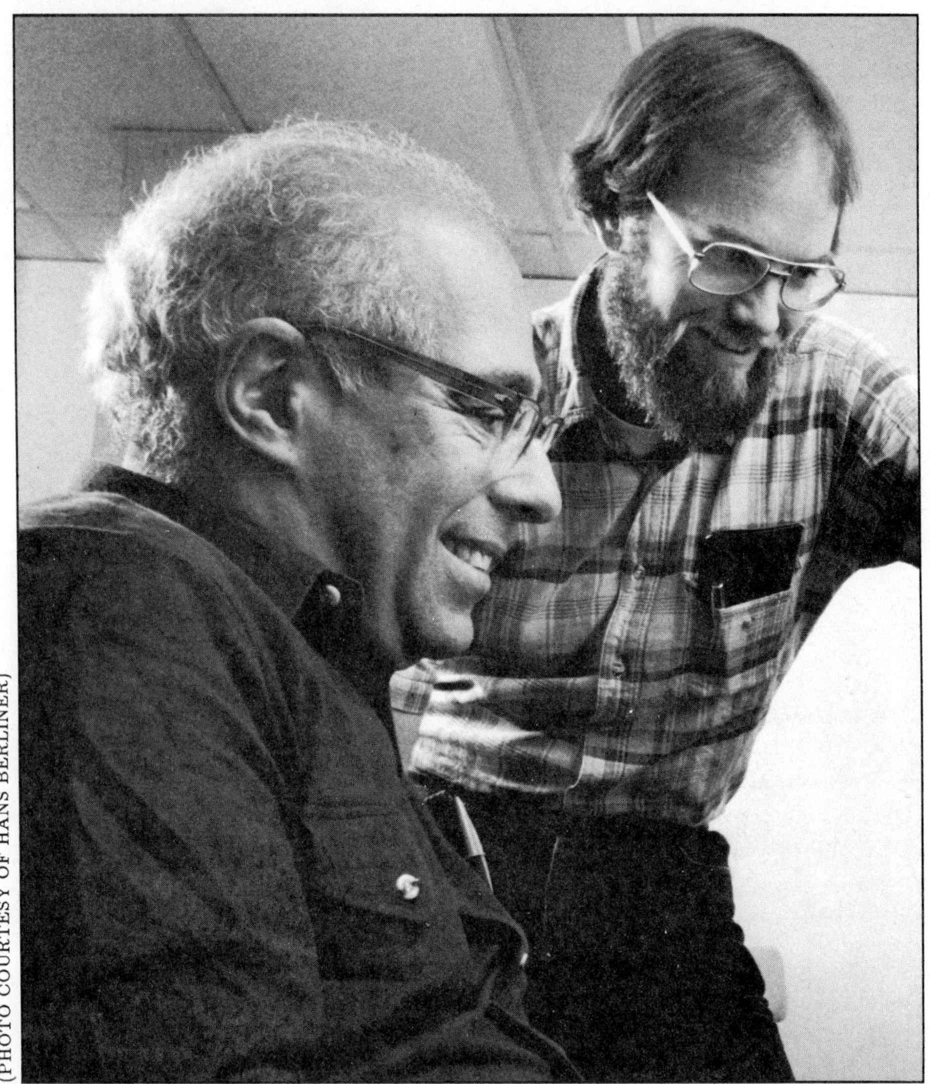

(PHOTO COURTESY OF HANS BERLINER)

Hans J. Berliner is Senior Research Computer Scientist in the Computer Science Department of Carnegie-Mellon University. He holds a B. A. in psychology from George Washington University and a Ph.D. in computer science from CMU. His research interests include representation of knowledge for large domains and learning structures, usually in a game-playing or puzzle environment. He has held the World Correspondence Chess Championship, and his program *BKG 9.8* beat the World Backgammon Champion by a score of 7–1. With Carl Ebeling he developed the chess machine *Hitech* which ranks in the top 1/2% of all registered chess players in the U.S.

4: GAME PLAYING

4.1 INTRODUCTION

Game playing is one of the most fascinating human pastimes. This fascination stems from several characteristics of games: they simulate real life (generally without the risks of real life), they symbolize our conflicts and aggressive tendencies (without the high price to health and happiness which indulging in these tendencies would involve), and they provide intellectual challenge and stimulation. Because successful play of board games such as checkers and chess requires purely intellectual activity, these games have attracted AI researchers from the very beginning. As a result, computers can now play all of the time-honored games such as tic-tac-toe, backgammon, checkers, and chess. Computers have also spawned a whole new industry of computer-based adventure games which are rapidly developing a large following of avid and even rabid fans.

It is interesting to speculate on the evolutionary basis of the instinct for game playing. Its roots most likely lie in the improvement of the survival probability of those participating. Game playing is not a uniquely human phenomenon. This is evident to anyone who has observed otters playing, puppies rough-housing, and martins soaring. Games themselves have a remarkable longevity. Pamela McCorduck has noted that present day London school children play games which date back to the time of Nero.[1] Even the fascination of computer scientists with games has a long tradition. Sir Charles Babbage, the brilliant British mathematician who invented the Analytical Engine, wrote papers on the knight's move in chess and on games of chance. He and his associate, Lady Augusta Ada Lovelace, considered building a tic-tac-toe playing automata machine for raising funds at carnivals. Lady Lovelace, who was a compulsive gambler, hoped to use one of Babbage's computing schemes to improve her betting odds on the horses.[2]

Recent improvements in computer graphics, voice, and sound I/O have greatly enhanced the capabilities of computers for playing games and emulating real life situations. This capability has not been lost on the new breed of "war gamers", both amateur and professional. A very significant segment of the Pentagon's strategic planning is performed by war gaming techniques. The author has even half seriously suggested that for a fraction of the cost of the Strategic Defense Initiative, every military commander could be provided with a computer loaded with the most sophisticated war games and tied directly with their Russian counterparts. Hopefully, the risk of global war would decline as they gradually came under the spell of the computer based war games. From direct observation at war gaming conferences such as GENCON, the war gamers national convention, it is apparent that the dangers and triumphs of the imaginary world of the war gamer play a far more significant role in many of the participant's lives than do the concerns of the real world.

4.2 THE NEED FOR HEURISTICS

Two of the important conclusions of early AI work on traditional board games were:

- The value of restricting the domain of the problem
- The need for the introduction of heuristics to aid in the solution.

The formal rules for board games such as checkers are relatively few and are clearly specified. Thus the need for broader based logical inference systems for solving general problems was avoided, and the game designers could work on a very specific problem: maximizing the computer's chances of winning.

Secondly, the combinatorial explosion arising from all possible board games forces the game program's author to adopt heuristics in order to reduce the search space which the computer must examine. Arthur Samuel has calculated the number of checkers games as 10^{40}, and other estimates[3] give the number of possible checkers plays (nodes in the game tree) to be 10^{78}. Claude Shannon has calculated the number of chess plays to be 10^{120}, and the number of possible plays is 10^{761} in the game GO.[4] Even in lowly tic-tac-toe, since the first player has 9 possible board positions, the second has 8, and so on, one might naively expect that there are 9! = 362,880 possible complete games. However, the four-fold symmetry of tic-tac-toe reduces the first play to 3 unique positions (corner, side, or center), a bi-lateral symmetry appears after two moves, and the average game takes about 6 plays rather than the 9 allowed. These symmetries and realities reduce the number of actual games substantially. Thus exhaustive searches are impossible except for the very simplest games such as tic-tac-toe, and even in this case, the use of heuristics is advisable for making the program run at a reasonable speed.

Heuristics play a very important role in many AI programming efforts, and therefore we examine the concept in more detail. As an adjective, heuristic means "Helping to discover or learn; guiding or furthering investigation".[5] Various AI researchers have offered the following definitions of heuristics and heuristic programming:

> **Newell, Shaw, and Simon (1957):** "A process that MAY solve a given problem, but offers no guarantees of doing so, is called a heuristic for that problem".
>
> **Marvin Minsky (1961):** A heuristic is " . . . any method or trick used to improve the efficiency of a problem-solving program ...", and that heuristic methods are "... related to improving problem-solving performance".
>
> **Feigenbaum and Feldman (1963):** "A heuristic (heuristic rule, heuristic method) is a rule of thumb, strategy, trick, simplification, or any other kind of device which drastically limits search for solutions in large problem spaces. Heuristics do not guarantee optimal solutions; in fact, they do not guarantee any solution at all; all that can be said for a useful heuristic is that it offers solutions which are good enough most of the time".
>
> **Judea Pearl (1984):** "It is the nature of good heuristics both that they provide a simple means of indicating which among several courses of action is to be preferred, and that they are not necessarily guaranteed to identify the most effective course of action, but do so sufficiently often. ... It is often said that heuristic methods are unpredictable; they work wonders *most* of the time, but may fail miserably *some* of the time".

It is clear, then, that heuristic programming differs significantly from algorithmic programming even though heuristic programs themselves must be expressed in algorithmic form. Straight algorithms ("A well-defined set of steps used to solve a problem") fail us in the face of the tremendous search spaces and variability of conditions encountered in typical AI applications.

This chapter will review some of the major contributions to the art of teaching computers to play games and the present level of success for several of the major board games. Then, game trees expressed in terms of graph theory are discussed, and the chapter is concluded with several heuristics for pruning the game trees to manageable size. These will include the *minimax* formalism and the *alpha-beta cutoff* heuristic.

4.3 HISTORY OF AI IN GAME PLAYING

CHECKERS

Although both Alan Turing and Claude Shannon made significant contributions to the theory of chess playing by computer, one of the first really competent computer game players was the checkers (draughts) program of Arthur Samuel. Samuel first became interested in writing a program to play checkers in 1947 while a professor of electrical engineering at the University of Illinois. He was an expert on vacuum tubes and hoped to build a "quick and dirty" computer which would win at checkers. This success would, he hoped, attract financial support for a project to build an even bigger computer.

Samuel convinced the dean to come up with over $100,000. However, it was still not enough to build the checkers playing computer. He next tried to buy a computer from Mauchly and Eckert of ENIAC fame and even talked with John von Neumann in his attempt to obtain a computer. Eventually, Samuel's interest in computers led him to IBM where he continued to follow his hobby of building a checkers playing program. By 1963 he had produced a reasonably competent checkers player which had the additional feature of learning from experience. Samuel's program finally reached a level of master capable of beating its author. IBM, rather than cheering this accomplishment, found it somewhat embarrassing because of sensitivity to fears that Samuel's program proved that computers are capable of taking over the world.

Two Duke University researchers, Eric Jensen and Tom Truscott, have since written a master-level checkers player which they claim is the tenth strongest checkers player in the world.[6]

BACKGAMMON

In backgammon, computers have fared better, even though it is a game with incomplete information (dice must be rolled). Hans Berliner's program, BKG 9.8, decisively won its match with Luigi Villa, the world backgammon champion. The program was implemented on Carnegie-Mellon University's PDP-10 and relayed to the match site in Monte Carlo by satellite. Berliner, a student of Newell and Simon, has subsequently taken up the challenge of designing a successful chess program.

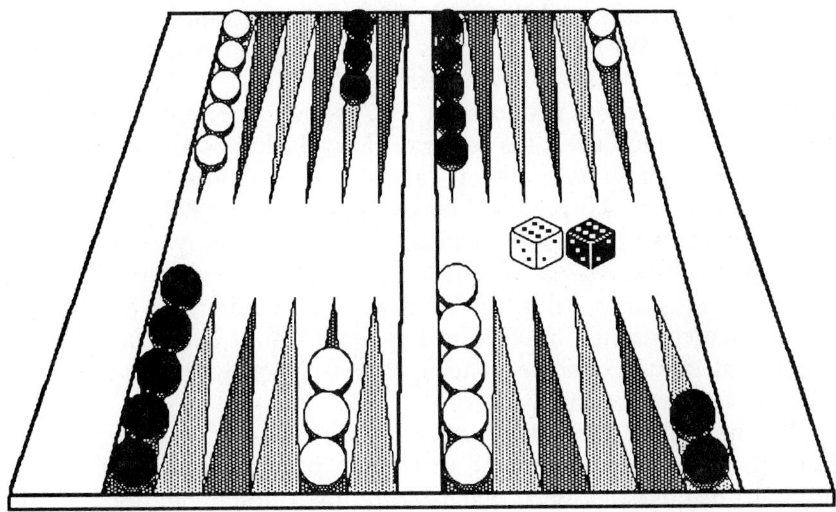

Figure 4-1 Backgammon Board - This ancient game inspired many later games such as parchesi. Each player puts 15 *men* or checkers on the board as shown. The side of the board with two men on one point is called the *inner table.* The other side of the board is the *outer table.* The object of the game is to move the men from point to point until they are all on the *home table* (the half of the inner table nearest the player) and then remove the men from the table in order. Each player throws two dice to determine the number of moves. The first player to remove all his men wins.

CHESS

Alex Bernstein was a chess aficionado first and later took up the challenge of implementing a chess playing program on the computer. This is in contrast to Samuel's experience with checkers in which he began the program before he had any real knowledge of the game. Bernstein was an avid chess player in both high school and college where his love of the game interfered with his studies. After spending time at Columbia University he went to work for IBM where he made his real contribution to building an intelligent chess program.

Bernstein went about the task very systematically, studying such works as **My System** by the Russian chess master, Aron Nimzowitsch, and the periodical *Modern Chess Openings.* By using an evaluation function based on pieces, board position, and "greens area", and heuristics for discarding less than optimal moves, Bernstein was able to produce a program which played "... a sort of respectable beginner's game" by 1959. About the same time, Newell, Shaw, and Simon introduced the concept of "goal-directed" move generation, but apparently neither their program nor Bernstein's ever won a chess game.[7]

One of AI founder Marvin Minsky's students at M.I.T., Richard Greenblatt, wrote a chess program in 1967, somewhat against the advice of his professor. However, his program MacHack was the first to compete in a chess tournament, and it earned a U. S. Chess Federation rating of 1400-1450, ranking as a Class C player. In 1974 the program KAISSA by Adelson-Velskiy, Arlazarov, and Donskoy of the Soviet Union won the first world computer chess championship. By 1976, David Slate and Larry Atkin of Northwestern University had written CHESS 4.5 which earned a USCF rating of 2070 and could beat Class B players. It also succeeded in beating the Soviet program in a 1977 international conference in Toronto.

The next Slate and Atkin program, CHESS 4.7, was the first program to achieve an Expert rating in human play, ranking at 2160. Although this is just below a Master ranking (which begins at 2200), CHESS 4.7 lost the famous challenge match to international chess master, David Levy. In 1968 Levy had wagered 500£ that no machine would beat him in chess within the next 10 years. The wager aroused intense interest in both the AI and chess communities, and both John McCarthy and Seymour Papert helped raise the bet to 1250£. Although Levy won the match $3\frac{1}{2}$— $1\frac{1}{2}$, George Koltanowski, the commentator for the match, reported:

> *"Too bad, but I am now definitely convinced that it will not take another ten years before the computer will be ready for participation in international tournaments with Grandmasters."*

In the early 1980s, computer chess was dominated by the Cray Blitz program implemented on a $14 million Cray X-MP/48 in Mendota Heights, Minnesota. The Cray Blitz compiled an enviable record of no losses to other computers for a period of 4 years prior to the 1985 ACM sponsored North American Computer Chess Championship. Although the Cray Blitz appeared invincible to other computer chess programs, it was still not playing at the level of top human players. In a $5000 re-match against this new computer challenger, David Levy again won handily.[8] In the best-of-four match held at Brunel University near London he defeated the Cray Blitz 4-0.

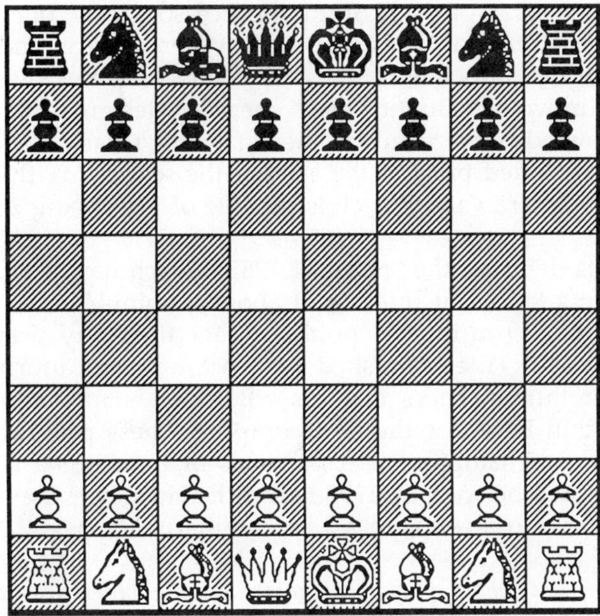

Figure 4-2 Chess Board from the game SARGON III Although powerful programs now play at the international chess master level, the best human grand masters still have a slight edge over the machine.

An interesting reversal in the trend in computer chess appeared in 1985. The trend for over 20 years had been towards implementation of programs on larger and larger main frame computers. The strategy was to use the power available only on such machines to maximize the number of "look-ahead" moves examined for each play. The Cray Blitz, for instance, scans 100,000 moves per second. In October, 1985, the Cray Blitz lost twice to much smaller, special purpose machines using parallel architectures. In the ACM North American Computer Chess Championship held in Denver, a new program, Hitech won the tournament with a 4-0 record. In round 1, it beat LACHEX, a Los Alamos Scientific Laboratory program running on a Cray-1. In round 2, Hitech defeated PHOENIX from the University of Alberta running on several multiplexed VAX's. In round 3, it beat the eventual runner-up system, Bebe, a special purpose, bit-slice machine from Chicago. In the final round, Hitech defeated the Cray Blitz. Bebe also defeated the Cray Blitz and ended up with a 3-1 record.[9]

Hitech is the product of a 3 year development effort of a Carnegie-Mellon University team headed by Hans Berliner. The Hitech system consists of a $20,000 Sun minicomputer together with a special purpose move generator called the "Searcher". The Searcher is a bread-box-size array of 64 VLSI microprocessors, each one of which is assigned to one square of the chessboard. When a piece lands on a particular square, the associated microprocessor computes the likely outcomes of the move. Evaluation uses specially designed hardware and compiled knowledge prepared by the software "Oracle" of the system which is down-loaded prior to the start of the search. With this special purpose parallel hardware, Hitech is capable of processing 200,000 positions/second.

Since its debut in the spring of 1985, Hitech has been moving up the USCF rating ladder at the rate of about 8 points/game. By 1988 it had reached a 2559 rating, 50 points higher than any previous computer. In late 1985 Hitech finished first in a ten-team tournament that included four human chess masters. Berliner is now aiming at the $100,000 Fredkin Prize for the first computer chess program to defeat the human world champion. He estimates that there is a 50-50 chance that the prize will be won by 1990. Even David Levy, the hero for the human side of the contest, agrees with Berliner, and says:

> *"In the past, chess players came to laugh. Next year they will be coming to watch. Soon they'll be coming to learn."*[10]

A final note is in order on the popularity and availability of chess-playing computer programs. It is not necessary to have access to a $14 million Cray mainframe or even a $20,000 Sun work station to play chess against a computer. High quality chess programs are now available for all major brands of microcomputers. One of these, SARGON III, costs less than $50 and recently beat a human chess master rated at 2209. SARGON III includes a library of 68,000 opening moves and won the 1984 *PC World* microcomputer chess tournament.

GO

Another interesting case study in the changing trend in computer game playing is the game GO. GO is an ancient game from China which became the major intellectual "national game" of Japan. It is a game more profound than chess and is taught as a required course in the Japanese military colleges.

The GO board is ruled with 19 parallel lines each way. A standard set of 181 black stones and 180 white stones may be placed at the 361 intersections of the ruled lines, although the game rarely goes that far. The goal of the game is the control of the larger territory consisting of vacant points on which the opponent does not dare play for fear of losing stones. No stone is moved once placed unless it becomes a prisoner of the opponent. The final score is the number of vacant points a player controls, minus the number of prisoners the player has lost.

Bruce Wilcox of Bolt, Beranek and Newman, Incorporated has designed the world's strongest computer GO program. The first version of his program took 7 person-years, 8K lines of LISP code, and 3 Mb of memory on an IBM mainframe. Because of the $2000 cost of playing each GO game, Wilcox decided to re-code his program on a smaller machine. The second version, called **NEMESIS...The GO Master™** required 1 person-year, 13.5 K lines of C code, and 146 Kb of memory on an IBM-PC. The microcomputer and mainframe versions play GO at a similar strength and by similar means.[11]

This brief history has summarized the status of several of the more important board games and indicated the role which these games has played in the development of artificial intelligence. Since board games such as checkers and chess are considered representative examples of the highest forms of intellectual activity, it is not surprising that they have attracted the attention and efforts of AI researchers from the very beginning. The success of computer games in these areas has been considered by both layman and expert alike as a significant test of machine intelligence. The primary contributions of the research in game theory to AI has been the recognition of the important role which heuristics plays in any application involving sizable domains to search. Finally, research on game theory has contributed even more to our appreciation of the wonders and mystery of the human brain, since even the most brilliant and articulate checkers and chess experts seem unable to identify and quantify their remarkable ability to play at the level of champions.

4.4 GAME TREES AND GRAPH THEORY

Most efforts to program the computer to play board games are based on a graph theory approach using game trees. Game trees are simply a mathematical (graph theoretic) approach to describing what happens when two players compete in a game with multiple options at each stage of the game. Most board games (with the exception of GO) follow the fundamental procedure common to games such as tic-tac-toe, checkers, and chess. The fundamental difference between these games is the average multiplicity of choices available from each state and the number of levels or *ply* through which the game can go before it ends in win, draw, or lose states (*terminal nodes*). The general concept of a game tree is illustrated in Figure 4-3.

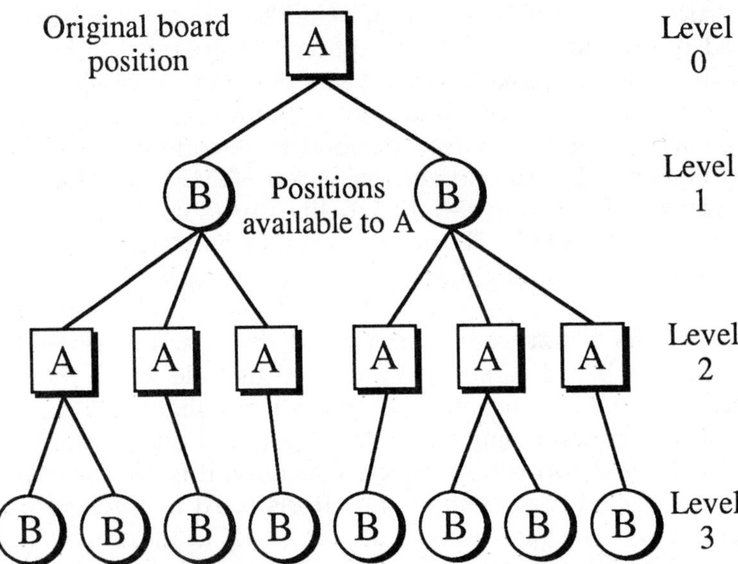

Figure 4-3 Game Tree showing 4 levels, starting with level 0 in which player A has two options. In both states of level 1, player B has 3 options and in level 2 player A has either 1 or 2 options. The options available to player B in level 3 are not shown. This figure is also said to show 3 "ply" of play.

The three basic operations which can be performed on game trees in the process of designing a game playing program are the following:

- Generation
- Evaluation
- Pruning

Generation

The two methods available for generation are variations of the breadth-first and depth-first searches presented in the previous chapter. In breadth first generation, all possible states at level 1 are generated before proceeding to level 2, at which point all possible game states are generated before proceeding to level 3, and so on. In depth first generation, the game rules are applied to generate all states along the left side of the graph, for instance, until a terminal node or some predetermined number of ply is reached. Then the generator backs up until it reaches the next left-most branch and follows that to its terminal node or ply limit, and so on.

Both of these methods are applicable in practice to only the simplest possible games and totally impractical for complex games such as chess unless restrictions are placed on the number of ply searched. For such complex games, the generator runs ahead to some predetermined level or follows certain branches to various levels depending on the particular heuristic in effect. The game tree terminates in one of three states: **A Wins, B Wins,** or **Draw** for most board games, and these terminal nodes are sometimes called *leaves* of the game tree. An example of a very small portion of the terminal node structure is shown in Figure 4-4.

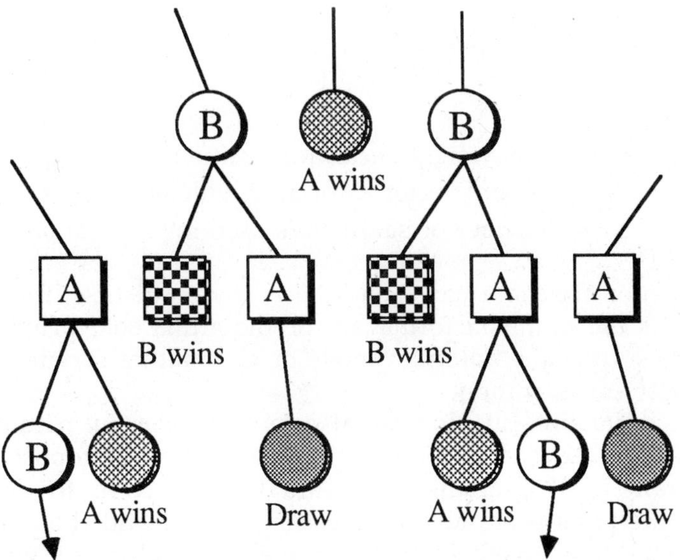

Figure 4-4 A small section of the game tree showing the terminal states allowed: A Wins, B Wins, or Draw. Such terminal nodes or leaves occur throughout the game tree and may be reached early if one of the players is much more skillful than the other.

EVALUATION

While the generation operation is strictly determined by the "rules of the game" and hence may be algorithmic in nature, the evaluation operation is much more subjective and becomes the point at which the game program author tries to incorporate the skill and tricks of clever play into the program, generally in heuristic form. If the game is sufficiently simple that all nodes can be generated then the optimum strategy for player A, for example, is to examine which terminal nodes lead to a win and make those forward moves from level 0 which maximize his chances of reaching a winning node. However, for complex games it is simply impossible to generate, much less evaluate, all possible nodes.

This leads, then, to the concept of the *static evaluation function,* the game tree equivalent of the evaluation function for the search tree nodes of Chapter 3. This function estimates the *present value* to chess player A of the particular node in question, say node j, in terms of such parameters as "material" (a numerical value assigned to each piece on the board), king safety, center control, and pawn structure. Generally, the function is a linear polynomial of the form:

$$f_j = C_j \cdot Y_j = \sum_{i=1}^{N} c_{ji}\, y_{ij} \qquad (4.1)$$

where

C_j = $1 \times N$ weight vector for position j
Y_j = Column vector associated with system parameters
N = Number of parameters used for evaluation

This evaluation function may then be used by heuristics discussed below such as the minimax formalism or the alpha-beta pruning technique for selecting the optimum move or eliminating certain branches from further consideration.

The evaluation function can also serve as a useful parameter for heuristics to guide machine learning. Arthur Samuel proposed letting the program itself evaluate the evaluation function to determine which of the parameters are the most significant and then adjust its weight accordingly. Such techniques are also useful in studying correlations between parameters which may be represented by quadratic terms in the weighting polynomial. By such cross terms, the interactions between various parameters are taken into account. The program adapts to a player's style and improves the quality of its game as time goes on. These characteristics suggest human abilities in "learning", and we consider both machine learning and Samuel's checkers player in greater detail in the Machine Learning chapter.

PRUNING

The evaluation function can be interpreted as one of the most efficient ways of adding knowledge of game strategy to the program in order to prune the game tree back to a manageable size. The adversarial nature of games also supplies constraints which significantly prune the game tree. We turn to this topic next.

4.5 MINIMAX PROCEDURE

The heuristic search techniques discussed in the last chapter are not directly applicable to the search for a winning strategy in board games. The basic difficulty is that there is not a single searcher for the path from source to goal state. Rather, games involve two players determined to defeat each other. This fundamentally alters the nature of the search which must be conducted. The first step is to incorporate this adversarial relationship into the search procedure. By combining the results of the static evaluation function with two fairly obvious heuristic rules, we obtain the *minimax procedure* first clearly stated by Claude Shannon in 1949.[12] The two heuristic rules state:

- When A has the option to move, she will always choose the alternative which leads to the MAXIMUM benefit to her, that is, she will move to the subsequent state with the largest value of f_j.

- When B has the option to move, he will always choose the alternative which leads to the MINIMUM benefit for player A, that is he will move to the subsequent state with the smallest value of f_j.

Examples of each of these moves are shown in Figures 4-5 and 4-6. In these examples, the static evaluation function produces a normalized number on the range $0 \leq f_j \leq 1$ which is proportional to the value of the node to player A. A "1" would guarantee player A a win and a "0" means a win for player B.

Note several features of the minimax procedure. First, it assumes a *perfect* opponent, that is, that player B never makes a bad move from his point of view. Second, the larger the number of look-ahead ply, the more information can be brought to bear in evaluating the current move. In the extreme case of a very simple game in which an exhaustive search is possible, all nodes are evaluated, and the win/loss/draw information can be propagated back up the tree to indicate precisely the optimum move for player A.

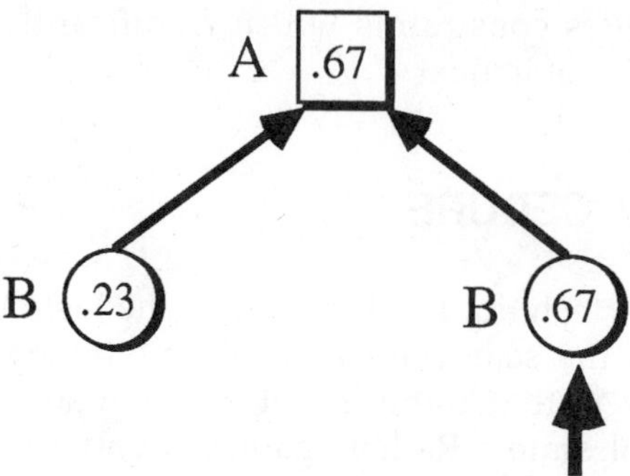

Figure 4-5 The minimax procedure applied to the first move by player A. If, after one or more ply (levels of play), the two moves open to player A evaluate to .23 and .67, her wisest move is to the .67 position since it will **maximize** her advantage. Since the minimax procedure specifies that she choose the move with the highest value, this value propagates upward, giving a value of .67 to her starting position.

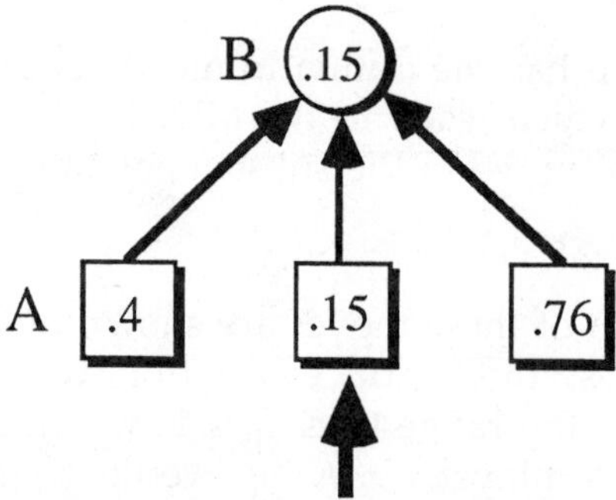

Figure 4-6 The minimax procedure applied to a subsequent move by player B. In calculating her subsequent moves, player A must assume that B will choose the alternative indicated which will **minimize** the value of the board position to player A.

NEGMAX PROCEDURE

An elegant simplification of the minimax formalism was introduced by Donald Knuth and R. W. Moore in 1975. This is the *negmax procedure* which uses the same function to evaluate each node in backing up from the successor nodes.[13] Assume the evaluation function for the jth terminal node in a complete tree given as:

$$
\begin{aligned}
f_j &= -1 && \text{for loss} \\
f_j &= 0 && \text{for draw} \\
f_j &= +1 && \text{for win}
\end{aligned}
\qquad (4.2)
$$

The negmax evaluation function, F(j), may then be written:

$$F(j) = f_j \qquad \text{for terminal nodes}$$

$$F(j) = \text{MAX}\{-F(i_1), -F(i_2), \ldots, -F(i_n)\} \qquad (4.3)$$
$$\text{for successor states } i_1 \rightarrow i_n$$

The formalism states that the best move for either player is that which maximizes F(j). This is illustrated in the simple win/loss/draw game tree shown in Figure 4-7.

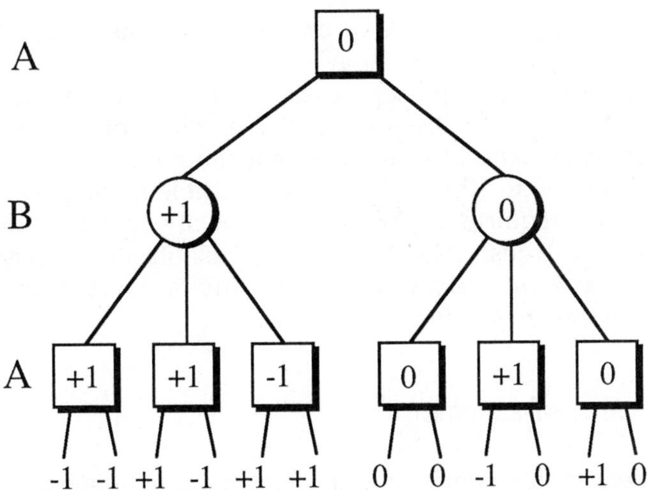

Figure 4-7 A game tree illustrating the negmax formalism of Knuth and Moore By simply selecting the move which maximizes the negative of the successor positions' evaluation function, the negmax formalism implements the minimax heuristic.

4.6 PRUNING THE GAME TREE

The minimax and negmax procedures specify how static evaluation function information from lower levels of the game tree should be propagated upward through the game tree in order to select the optimum move. The minimax (negmax) procedures themselves are heuristic only in the sense that they select the optimum move based on the heuristic function, f_j. The minimax procedure by itself does not prune away any of the search space of the game tree. A number of heuristics are available for additional pruning of the game tree to permit a reasonable number of ply to be searched in a reasonable time.

PLAUSIBLE MOVE GENERATOR

Certain moves are unproductive or dangerous because they obviously lead away from engagement or to an immediate loss of a piece with no hope of trapping the other player. These moves can be avoided by the substitution of a *plausible move generator* in place of the legal move generator. If, for instance, the average branching from a node in chess could be cut from 30 to 10 by means of a plausible move generator, the number of nodes requiring evaluation in a 6 ply search could be cut from 729 million to just 1 million. The plausible move generator is equivalent to a *beam search* in which only a limited number of promising nodes are expanded at each ply.

ALPHA-BETA CUTOFF HEURISTIC

The alpha-beta cutoff heuristic is a form of branch-and-bound technique in which logic applied to the minimax search is used to prune the game tree.[14] The idea can be stated as: *If, as a result of evaluating certain nodes of the game tree, it is obvious that the play will not proceed down certain branches then don't perform any more searching or evaluation down those unproductive branches.* In Figure 4-8 we show the application of the alpha cutoff and in Figure 4-9 the application of the beta cutoff.

Note how the value of alpha will assume the largest of the minimum values generated from expanding successive B nodes at a given level (ply). Once a successor node from any B node at that level is evaluated as less than alpha, that node and all its successors may be pruned.

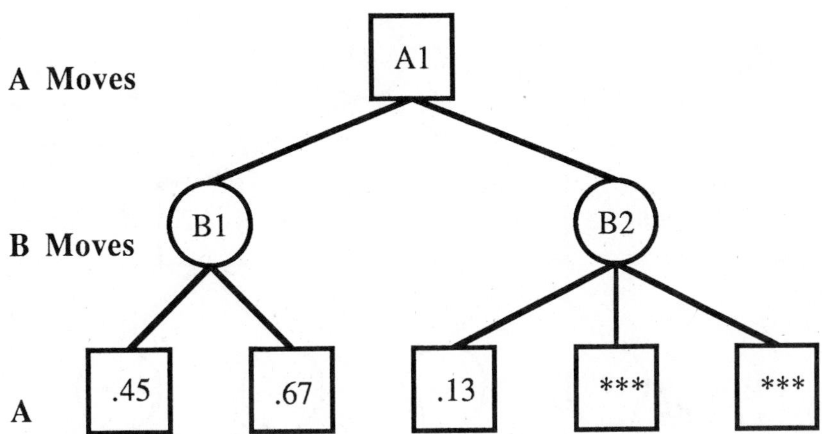

Figure 4-8 Pruning by ALPHA cutoff heuristic Note that as the minimax search evaluates nodes in ply 2 (bottom level as shown), it can stop once the $f_j = .13$ node is computed. The argument is that B1 will select .45 if A1 selects move B1. (Alpha is set to 0.45 by the expansion of the B1 nodes.) If A1 selects move B2, B2 will select the node evaluating to .13 or smaller. Therefore, A1 must select move B1 independently of the *** node values. Therefore, these nodes and their successors may be pruned from the game tree.

A similar branch-and-bound argument may be used to generate the beta cutoff by examining nodes resulting from expanding nodes in an A ply. Note that in Figure 4-9, beta will be set to a value of .35. Any additional A nodes in ply 1 which have any successors evaluating to more than .35 will automatically be pruned from the game tree by the beta cutoff.

The use of alpha-beta pruning can greatly narrow the search and offer the opportunity of searching much more deeply (more ply) into the game tree with the same number of evaluations. As a result, this heuristic is almost universally applied, at least as an outer limit on the width of the search. It is also clear, after a little thought, that alpha is a bound which continues to get larger as higher values of the evaluation function are found at a given level. The higher the value of alpha, the more branches of the tree can be eliminated from the search. The general statement is that alpha is the largest of the minimum values of f_j for the sons of Bn. Similarly, the value of beta will decrease as more nodes are opened at the 2-ply level of Figure 4-9. The general statement is that beta will be the smallest of the maximum values of f_j for the sons of a given An.

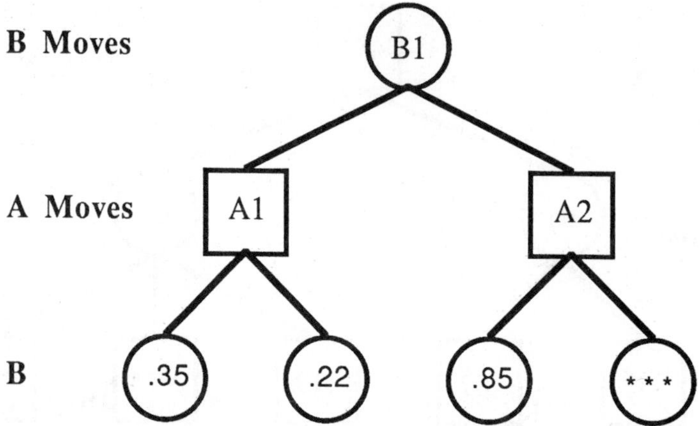

Figure 4-9 Pruning by the BETA cutoff heuristic It is clear that A would select the 0.35 node if node A1 was reached and at least .85 if A2 were reached. Therefore, B1 will choose to move to A1, and A2 and all its successor nodes may be pruned from the game tree. Beta is set to 0.35 in this portion of the search.

ALPHA-BETA CUTOFF EXAMPLE

Consider the following 3-ply game tree which has been completely evaluated with the minimax procedure.

The first step in applying the alpha-beta heuristic is to evaluate the B-A-B structures in the lowest three ply (Ply 1,2,3) for each family (sons and grandsons) of Bn at ply 1. Beta is set equal to 47 after evaluating nodes (47, 9). Since no smaller maximum occurs in the leftmost 6 nodes, no further ratchetting downwards of beta occurs in this set, but nodes (25, 3) are eliminated without evaluation. As the evaluations proceeds into the (19—66) series of nodes, beta is set to 43 after evaluating nodes (19, 43). No ratchetting of beta occurs, and nodes (28, 66) are eliminated. Within the series (63—45), beta starts at 63 after nodes (63, 13) and ratchets downward to 23 after node (23), thus eliminating node (26). In the series (16—55), beta starts at 16 after nodes (16, 8) and eliminates evaluation of node (55).

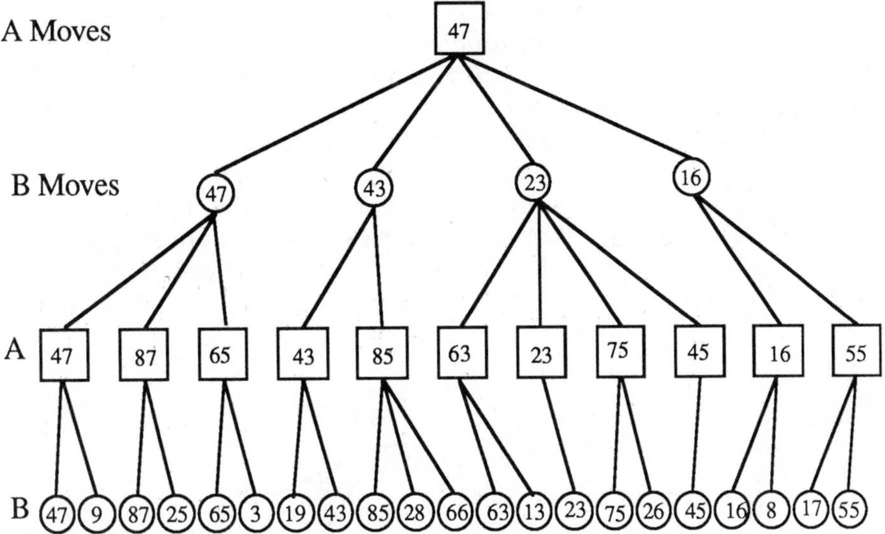

Figure 4-10 Original game tree after minimax procedure

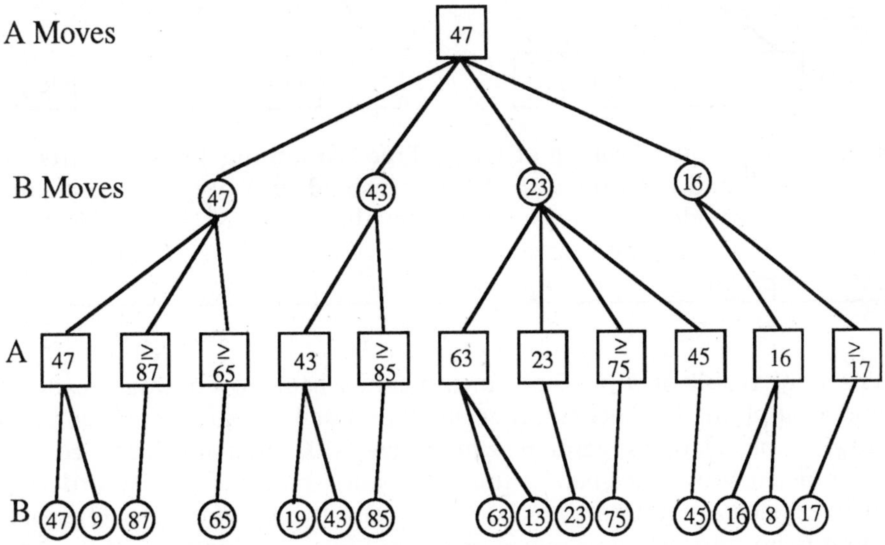

Figure 4-11 Result of Beta Pruning in the lower three ply. Six of the 21 3-ply nodes are eliminated from the search and evaluation process by the beta pruning heuristic. Note the "≥" signs resulting from reduced information available at the A_n nodes at ply 3. This uncertainty in no way effects the final result of the pruned search.

Finally, assume we had opened the game tree down only two plies and had computed the evaluation function f_j to give the A_n shown in ply 2 of Figure 4-10. Let's see what pruning the alpha cut-off would provide. After nodes (47, 87, 65) are evaluated, alpha is set to 47, and no further ratchetting of alpha occurs (since no larger minimum of sons of B_n occurs). After opening node 43 in ply 2, the alpha cutoff of 47 tells us to propagate "≤ 43" upward to B_n and thereby eliminating the node which would evaluate to (85). Similarly, after evaluating nodes (63, 23) we can propagate "≤ 23" up to B_n, and so on. The results are shown in Figure 4-12.

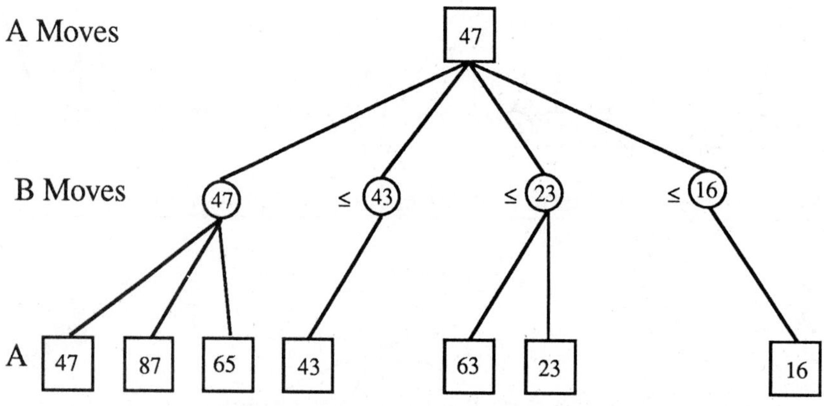

Figure 4-12 Alpha Pruning of Game Tree Assuming the game tree of Figure 4-10 had been opened at 2 ply instead of 3 ply, alpha pruning eliminates 4 nodes which would have evaluated to (85, 75, 45, 55). After the left three nodes are evaluated, alpha is set to 47 and does not ratchet upward in this example.

The final result of alpha-beta pruning has been to eliminate 6 of 21 nodes (applying the beta cutoff at ply 3) or 4 of 11 nodes (applying alpha cutoff at ply 2). of the game tree in Figure 4-10. It should be noted that the efficiency of alpha-beta pruning depends critically on the ordering of the nodes at the lower levels of the tree. In the worst possible case, there is no improvement over normal minimax evaluation. It the best possible case, the number of nodes requiring evaluation is $2\sqrt{N}$ where N is the number of nodes in the normal minimax tree.

The alpha-beta cutoff algorithm was first introduced in Greenblatt's chess program MacHack. It has been an important tool in essentially all significant chess and checkers programs since then.

4.7 QUIESCENT HEURISTICS AND THE HORIZON EFFECT

The minimax and alpha-beta heuristics presented so far implicitly assumed a fixed level in which breadth-first search is conducted. The computing power of a particular machine may restrict the search to 6 ply, for instance. This sets a *horizon* for the search 6 levels below the present game state. The problem is: some of the moves in ply 4 and 5 may indicate that a critical move (e.g. check) is "just over the horizon". Other game states at ply 3, 4, and 5 may indicate a very stable or *quiescent* board condition. It would seem wise, in such situations, to extend the search several ply further in the active region of the game tree. If time constraints permit a limited number of node evaluations, the search should be cut back in depth in those regions of the game tree showing little activity. Quiescent heuristics provide a measure of such activity and help guide the search deeper along critical paths. Such quiescent heuristics are a variation of the best-first heuristic discussed in Chapter 3.

Many other heuristics have been developed to prune the game tree in order to improve the depth of search and quality of machine play. These include techniques for ranking the nodes at a given level by their promise and using this priority to follow the most promising nodes to a deeper level. By simply not evaluating nodes below bad moves, much of the game tree is eliminated. By including the level of play in the evaluation function a node priority scheme can generate a *tapered search* which very effectively cuts back the region of the tree to be searched.

In conclusion, teaching machines to play games has taught us a great deal about the nature of search and effective heuristics in dealing with exponentially growing problems. Game playing was one of the earliest testing grounds for machine intelligence and continues to be an exciting area for applying new hardware and algorithms. Perhaps the most promising developments for rapid improvement in the level of machine play are in the area of parallel architecture machines. The success of Hans Berliner's Hitech chess machines indicates that we will continue to see progress in the performance of game playing machines.

PROBLEMS AND PROGRAMS

4-1. From your own personal experience, describe three examples of animals playing. In your description please discuss:

- Specific modes of play
- "Emotions" apparently displayed, e.g. curiosity, rage, love, and so on
- Evidence of "self awareness", i.e. their tail, shadow, and so on
- Interpretation of their play in terms of instinct for survival training.

4-2. Clearly state your own definition of *heuristic*, and carefully distinguish how heuristics differ from conventional algorithms.

4-3. From your knowledge of checkers, write down a reasonable *static board evaluator function*, f_j, and justify your choice for each parameter.

4-4. Along with a person (yourself or some other) knowledgeable in the game, locate a computer version of backgammon or checkers, play several games, document one of the games at least partially with screen dumps, and write a brief critique on the level of sophistication of the game.

4-5. Assume your chess program is capable of evaluating 200,000 nodes/second. How many ply could your program look ahead in the allotted time of three minutes, assuming an effective branching ratio of 20 from each node in chess?

4-6. Along with a person knowledgeable in the game, play SARGON III (or an equivalent chess program) at three different levels of play and evaluate the program.

4-7. Write a brief paper on the design, operation, characteristics, and performance of Carnegie-Mellon University's chess program, Hitech.

4-8. The minimax procedure assumes "perfect" play on the part of both players A and B. Assume you are writing a computer game in which the computer will be player A, but you find most of the opponents B do NOT play perfectly, but rather frequently overlook good opportunities to hurt your position. What changes would you make in the minimax algorithm to take advantage of this weak play of player B?

4-9. What are the advantages of the negmax procedure over the minimax procedure?

4-10. Write down some *plausible move generating heuristics* for both tic-tac-toe and checkers.

4-11. Sketch the game tree from Figure 4-10 with all nodes unevaluated except the bottom level (ply 3). Evaluate them by copying in the list in **reverse order** , i.e. 55, 17, 8, 16,... going from left to right. Before proceeding further, try the following questions:

a) Will minimax yield a different set of static board evaluations in ply 2?

b) Will the set differ in ply 1 and 0?

c) Will the alpha-beta heuristic discard the same number of nodes as in Figure 4-11 and Figure 4-12?

4-12. Using the game tree produced in Problem 4-11, carefully apply the alpha-beta cutoff procedure on ply 3 using the minimax procedure. Do NOT minimax the whole game tree before applying alpha-beta cutoff, and evaluate the minimum possible number of nodes. You may need inequalities to describe some of the nodes.

4-13. Now minimax the game tree produced in Problem 4-11 and reapply the alpha-beta heuristic. Are there any differences from your results in Problem 4-12? How does the pruned game tree from Problem 4-13 differ from that shown in Figure 4-12? Did minimaxing produce the same final evaluation function for the 0 ply node in this problem as given in Figure 4-10?

4-14. Suggest a useful *quiescent heuristic* for the game of checkers.

4-15. Given the tic-tac-toe board state after 6 levels of play as shown below, develop the complete remaining possible game tree, evaluate the terminal nodes with the following static functions: f = + 1 (win for X), f = 0 (draw for X), f = -1 (win for 0), and propagate the function back to the initial game state using the minimax heuristic.

0	X	0
	X	
	0	X

4-16. Write a program using Pascal, LISP, or Prolog to play **tic-tac-toe**. Clearly define your choice of board representation, evaluation function, and pruning heuristics before you begin coding.

4-17. Using some of the ideas in the Quiescent Heuristics section and the principle of best-first search discussed in the previous chapter, develop an algorithm for a best-first checkers player.

4-18. Discuss the role which machine learning might play in improving the quality of play by machines. What particular parameters do you think would be most critical to the learning process?

4-19. Traditional von Neumann serial machines soon reach a limit in the number of plies they can reach during allotted playing time. Discuss how a machine built with parallel architecture is more naturally suited for many board games.

FOOTNOTES AND REFERENCES

[1] McCorduck, Pamela, *Machines Who Think*, W. H. Freeman and Company, San Francisco, CA (1979)

[2] Shurkin,Joel, *Engines of the Mind,* W. W. Norton & Company, New York, NY (1984)

[3] Jackson, Jr., Philip C., *Introduction to Artificial Intelligence,* Second Edition, p. 125, Dover Publications, Inc. New York, NY (1985)

[4] Zobrist, A., "A Model of Visual Organization for the Game GO", *SJCC* **34**, pp. 103—112 (1969)

[5] *The American Heritage Dictionary of the English Language,* William Morris (ed), Houghton Mifflin Company, Boston, MA (1973)

[6] Krutch, John, *Experiments in Artificial Intelligence for Small Computers,* Howard. W. Sams & Co. , Indianapolis, IN (1981)

[7] Feigenbaum, Edward A., Barr, Avron, and Cohen, Paul R. (eds), *The Handbook of Artificial Intelligence* Vol. 1—3, p 106, HeurisTech Press/William Kaufmann, Inc., Stanford, CA, (1981-82)

8 Forsyth, Richard and Naylor, Chris, *The Hitch-Hiker's Guide to Artificial Intelligence*, p. 178, Chapman and Hall/Methuen, London (1985)

9 Berliner, Hans, "Hitech wins North American Computer Chess Championship", *AI Magazine* **6**, p. 30, Winter (1986)

10 *TIME Magazine*, p. 88, October 29, (1985)

11 Wilcox, Bruce, "Reflections on Building Two GO Programs", *SIGART Newsletter* **94**, pp. 29—43, October (1985)

12 Pearl, Judea, *HEURISTICS: Intelligent Search Strategies for Computer Problem Solving*, Addison-Wesley, Reading, MA (1984)

13 Feigenbaum, *et al*, Op Cit, pp. 86—87

14 Rich, Elaine, *Artificial Intelligence*, McGraw-Hill Series in Artificial Intelligence, New York, NY (1983)

Chapter 5

AUTOMATED REASONING

(PHOTO COURTESY OF UNIVERSITY OF WISCONSIN, PARKSIDE)

Dr. Larry Wos is Senior Mathematician at Argonne National Laboratory. He earned his Ph.D. in mathematics from the University of Illinois — Urbana in group theory and is one of the founders of the field of automated reasoning. His automated reasoning program, *AURA*, has solved many of the interesting puzzles of artificial intelligence and answered significant questions in ternary Boolean algebra, finite semi-groups, and equivalential calculus. Dr. Wos is editor of *The Journal of Automated Reasoning* and with his Argonne colleagues has written the book, *Automated Reasoning — Introduction and Applications*. He recently won the American Mathematical Society's First Prize for current achievements in automatic theorem proving.

5: AUTOMATED REASONING

5.1 INTRODUCTION

Study of the previous chapters shows that search techniques become more efficient as more knowledge is added to the process. The addition of a static evaluation function, for example, incorporated the knowledge of human experts on board position and game strategy. The minimax rules incorporated the strategy that informed game players use in competing against each other. Using the minimax rules and some elementary logic, it was possible to significantly prune the game tree through application of the alpha-beta cutoff. In each case, performance of the automated game player was significantly enhanced as more knowledge was incorporated in the program.

As our study of artificial intelligence continues, it should become apparent that progress in solving the problems of AI has closely paralleled the development of tools and techniques for manipulating knowledge. From the earliest days AI researchers recognized that the rules of inference of formal logic provided one of the strongest tools in the knowledge processing toolkit. The purpose of this chapter is to summarize the elements of formal logic and to show how the reasoning process may be automated for solving many classical and practical problems of AI.

Logic may be considered the study of the rules of inference. Inference is the means by which we reason from given knowledge to new knowledge. Early AI researchers hoped that they could provide the computer with fundamental postulates and rules of inference and then stand aside while the computer marched bravely forward, deducing or inferring truth about the universe from a carefully constructed and reasonably complete set of basic hypotheses. While this hope soon proved to be false, it did become clear that any moderately general artificial intelligence system must include inference rules for sifting and applying available knowledge to the problem at hand. Without such rules of logic, many problems would degenerate into exhaustive searches which would defeat even the most capable computer system.

Another very important role of logic is in representing knowledge itself and providing a formalism for extracting the implications of that knowledge.[1] As we will see in this chapter, propositional calculus and predicate calculus provide a language for representing knowledge and reaching inferences based on that information. Because symbolic logic is one of the most complete and powerful formalisms for reasoning ever developed, it is natural that a continuing goal of AI research has been to incorporate rules of inference into computer systems and thereby automate the reasoning process.

One final observation may be relevant at this point. The trend in evolutionary development of all systems is from simplicity to complexity, and the history of the study of such systems indicates a tendency to move from the specific to the more abstract. As more complex systems are studied, whether they are biological or electronic, more abstract concepts are required to understand and cope with this complexity. Formal rules of logic which are outlined below provide the tools for constructing and applying the necessary abstract concepts.

5.2 TYPES OF LOGIC

Although the lines of distinction may not always be as clean as one might hope, we can distinguish between the following three types of logical inferences: deduction, induction, and abduction. A formal definition of each type is given as:

- **DEDUCTION** — "The process of reasoning in which a conclusion follows necessarily from the stated premises; inference by reasoning from the general to the specific."[2] For instance, from the two statements that *All cats are felines* and *Bootsy is a cat*, I can deduce that *Bootsy is a feline.*

- **INDUCTION** — "A principle of reasoning to a conclusion about all members of a class from examination of only a few members of the class; broadly, reasoning from the particular to the general."[2] For example, if I notice that *All Siamese cats at the 1986 cat show had blue eyes*, and *All Siamese cats at the 1987 cat show had blue eyes*, and *All Siamese cats at the 1988 cat show had blue eyes*, I would logically infer that *All Siamese cats have blue eyes.* This may or may not be true, but it provides a useful generalization.

- **ABDUCTION** — This is a form of deductive logic which provides only a "plausible inference." For instance, if I read *Smoking causes lung cancer* and *Frank died of lung cancer*, I may infer that *Frank was a smoker.* Again, this may or may not be true. Using statistics and probability theory, abduction may yield the most probable inference among many possible inferences.[3]

Notice that these three types of logic are ranked in order of the confidence one can place in the new knowledge inferred from the given knowledge. That is, new knowledge based on deductive reasoning is always true if the assumptions are true, new knowledge based on many cases is generally true as long as the systems studied are well-behaved, and an inference based on abduction may be plausible but should carry an associated confidence factor to indicate the likelihood it is correct.

In general it is much easier to implement rules of deduction than to use induction for deriving general truths from a data base of particular facts. One successful system based on generalization was the METADENDRAL program of Feigenbaum which was designed to detect general patterns or laws relating the wealth of chemical data available in the DENDRAL database and heuristics.[4] It did, in fact, succeed in detecting relationships which had been overlooked by its human creators.

DEDUCTION

The starting point for deductive reasoning is a set of *propositions* (sometimes called *postulates*) and associated *axioms* and *definitions*. One of the postulates of geometry, for instance, would be: "Through 2 points 1 and only 1 straight line can be drawn." Axioms are more or less self-evident propositions such as: "Two things equal to the same thing are equal to each other." Finally, the characteristics of certain objects must be defined, as for instance: "A line has length, but not breadth."

Starting with such a set of postulates, axioms, and definitions, Euclid was able to prove 465 geometric propositions as the logical consequence of the input assumptions. It is possible to prove additional *theorems* based on these postulates. Theorems have the following characteristics:

- The theorem must contain nothing that cannot be proven.

- The theorem must be implied entirely by propositions other than itself (i.e., recursive proofs are not allowed).

- It must contain no assumptions not contained in the postulates.

- Two theorems deduced from the same set of postulates cannot be contradictory.

One of the basic rules of inference of deductive logic is the *modus ponens* rule. A formal English statement of this rule is: *If X is true and if X being true implies Y is true, then Y is true.*

INDUCTION

Lord Bertrand Russell, British mathematician and philosopher, observed that there are three ways for arriving at the validity of general propositions:

- Tautologies
- Complete enumeration
- Induction

Tautologies are self-evident truths which, for example, might even have definitions incorporated within the proposition. Examples include: "All circles are round" and "Essential things are necessary". Because of their redundant nature, they contain little information and are not particularly useful tools for artificial intelligence.

Complete enumeration is a somewhat more useful tool. One way, for example, of determining how many opening moves there are in tic-tac-toe is to simply count them. It becomes even more useful when combined with certain propositions or rules and has provided the basis, for instance, for the proof of the four-color theorem in map design. The four-color theorem states that four colors are sufficient to color any flat, two-dimensional map of an arbitrary number of states in such a fashion that no adjacent two states have the same color. The four-color theorem was long thought to be true, but has only recently been proven with the help of a computer to carry out the enumeration.

The *method of induction*, even in human reasoning, is hard to describe since it operates at a high level of abstraction closely related to pattern recognition. It is easier to illustrate with an example than to specify an algorithmic procedure. Consider the series:

$$1 = 1^2$$

$$1 + 3 = 2^2$$

$$1 + 3 + 5 = 3^2$$

$$1 + 3 + 5 + 7 = 4^2$$

and, by *induction*,

$$\sum \text{(n successive odd integers)} = n^2$$

The cognitive process of detecting a general pattern in the particular equations is called inductive reasoning or scientific induction.

A more formal English statement of the induction process may be written:

> *For a set of objects, X = {a,b,c,d,...}, if property P is true for a, and if P is true for b, and if P is true for c, ... then P is true for all X.*

ABDUCTION

Abduction is a heuristic for making plausible inferences. The inferences of deductive logic are always correct; that is, they are logical consequences of the basic postulates and axioms. The inferences drawn from scientific induction are correct to the extent that nature is orderly and mathematical functions well behaved. Abduction, on the other hand is heuristic in the sense that it provides a plausible conclusion consistent with available information, but one which may, in fact, be wrong.

To illustrate how abduction works, consider the following logical system consisting of a general rule and a specific proposition:

1) All successful, entrepreneurial industrialists are rich persons.

2) Sally Smith is a rich person.

If this was the only information available, a plausible inference would be that *Sally Smith was a successful, entrepreneurial industrialist.* This conclusion could also be false since there are other roads to riches such as inheritance, the lottery, and the Reader's Digest Sweepstakes. If we had a table of the income distribution of wealthy persons along with their personal histories, we could refine our abduction inference with the probability of the inference being true.

A formal English statement of the abduction heuristic says:

> *If Y is true and X implies Y, then X is true.*

But since P, Q, and R may also imply Y is true, inference made with the abduction heuristic will fail in the case of P, Q, or R leading to the truth of Y.

5.3 LOGIC AS THE GRAMMAR OF REASON

Logic is sometimes called the "grammar of reason".[5] As such it has its own syntax and logical rules. First, consider some of the standard syntax of propositional calculus. The basic element of propositional calculus is the *proposition*. A proposition is a simple statement which may have a *truth value* of TRUE or FALSE. Propositions may be generated, manipulated, and related through the logical functions also known as *sentential connectives*, AND, OR, NOT, IMPLIES, and EQUIVALENT, whose symbols are:

AND	$\wedge$ or $\cap$ or $*$
OR	$\vee$ or $\cup$ or $+$
NOT	$\neg$ or $\sim$ or $\overline{}$ (overstrike)
IMPLIES	$\rightarrow$ or $\supset$
EQUIVALENT	$\equiv$ or $\leftrightarrow$

The syntax of propositional calculus resembles that of natural language interpretation. For instance, if X and Y are each logical propositions, then the logical quantity $(X \wedge Y)$ is TRUE if X is TRUE *and* Y is TRUE.

BOOLEAN ALGEBRA

In his 1854 article "An Investigation of the Laws of Thought," George Boole proposed the formalism which is now called Boolean Algebra. One can think of these laws of Boolean algebra as the formal grammar of propositional calculus. One of the most fruitful applications of Boolean algebra has been to digital electronics since the binary states of digital logic are naturally represented by a logical **0** (FALSE) or logical **1** (TRUE). These laws are summarized below in terms of the Boolean variables, **A, B,** and **C** and logical states **0**, and **1**:

<u>AND Laws</u>

$$\mathbf{A} \wedge \mathbf{0} = \mathbf{0}$$
$$\mathbf{A} \wedge \mathbf{1} = \mathbf{A}$$
$$\mathbf{A} \wedge \mathbf{A} = \mathbf{A}$$

$$A \wedge \neg A = 0$$

OR Laws

$$A \vee 0 = A$$
$$A \vee 1 = 1$$
$$A \vee A = A$$
$$A \vee \neg A = 1$$

NOT Laws

$$A \wedge \neg A = 0$$
$$A \vee \neg A = 1$$
$$\neg(\neg A) = A$$

Commutative Laws

$$A \wedge B = B \wedge A$$
$$A \vee B = B \vee A$$

Associative Laws

$$A \wedge (B \wedge C) = (A \wedge B) \wedge C$$
$$A \vee (B \vee C) = (A \vee B) \vee C$$

Distributive Laws

$$A \wedge (B \vee C) = (A \wedge B) \vee (A \wedge C)$$
$$A \vee (B \wedge C) = (A \vee B) \wedge (A \vee C)$$

Absorptive Laws

$$A \vee (A \wedge B) = A$$
$$A \wedge (A \vee B) = A$$

DeMorgan's Laws

$$\neg(A \wedge B) = \neg A \vee \neg B$$
$$\neg(A \vee B) = \neg A \wedge \neg B$$

These laws of Boolean algebra are extremely useful in solving digital design problems. For instance, in transistor-transistor-logic

(TTL) the basic logic element is the NAND gate (NOT AND). To build an OR gate from NAND gates, DeMorgan's law may be used with three NAND gates as shown in Figure 5-1.

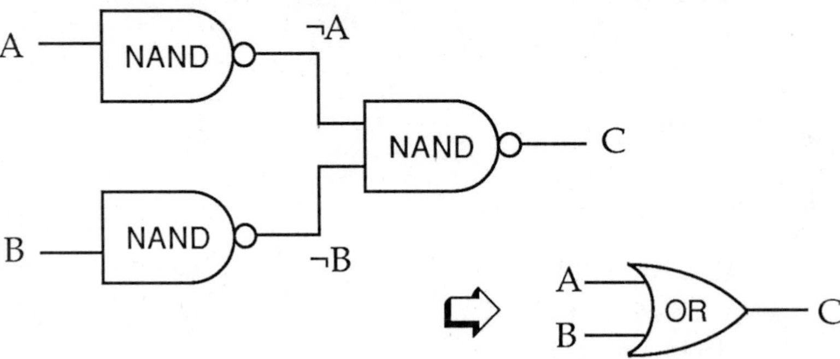

Figure 5-1 Synthesis of OR gate from NAND gates C in the top diagram is given as C = ¬(¬A ∧ ¬B) which, by DeMorgan's law is (¬¬A ∨ ¬¬B) = (A ∨ B) which is the desired function. A 1-input NAND assumes all other inputs are logical 1s and therefore acts like a NOT gate.

An exclusive OR (XOR) may then be easily constructed from inverting, AND, and OR gates as shown in Figure 5-2.

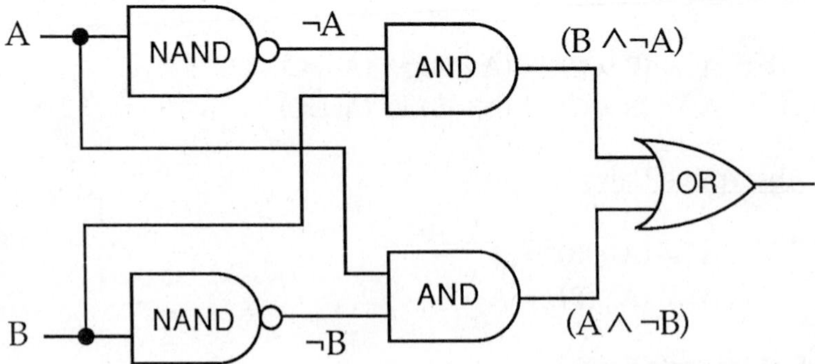

Figure 5-2 Synthesis of Exclusive OR (XOR) from primitive gates The OR gate may be synthesized from NAND gates as in Figure 5-1, and the AND gate may be synthesized from NAND gates by inverting a NAND gate. NAND gates may be substituted for both the AND and OR gates to produce a circuit with the identical XOR output.

Such elementary arithmetic circuits as the *half-adder* are simply a combination of an AND gate and an XOR gate as shown in Figure 5-3.

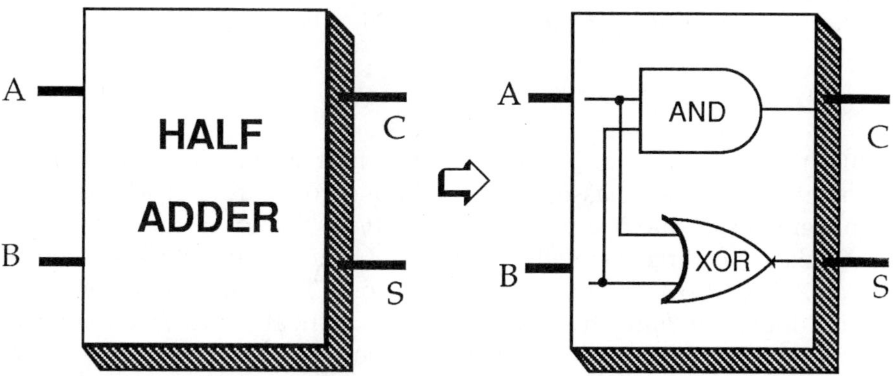

Figure 5-3 Half-Adder Circuit synthesized from primitive gates. C is a *carry* produced if both A and B are 1, and S is the *sum* produced if A or B but not both is a 1 (XOR). A full-adder (with additional carry-in signal) may be constructed from two half-adders and an OR gate.

These examples illustrate instances of a very important fact: given the laws of Boolean algebra and enough NAND gates, one can build the world's largest digital computer (although it may not be the world's fastest!). It also illustrates the very important fact that logic is valuable because of the useful structures one can build using it. All of the operations of the most complex computer may be reduced to the extremely elementary operation of NAND gates.

This particularly useful application of Boolean algebra to binary digital logic is a special case of Boole's more general algebra of classes. Boole's goal was to symbolize, systematize, and generalize the concepts of logic which had been invented by the Greeks. In so doing, he laid the foundation for propositional calculus ("... I purpose to establish the Calculus of Logic...").[6] He also made an observation that will be reconsidered in Chapter 7, "The theory of Logic is thus intimately connected with that of Language." Let us look a little deeper into Boolean algebra.

5.4 BOOLEAN ALGEBRA OF CLASSES

First, consider the concept of *class*. A class is defined as "a group of all objects obeying the algebra of the class." The class of all elements is called the *universe class*, U = 1. The class containing no elements is called the *null class* (note the resemblance to the *nil list* in the LISP language). Any combination of elements from the U = 1 class is also a class. From the definition of the *order of the class*, n, as the number of elements in the universe class, it can be shown that the number of classes contained in the universe class is N, where:

$$N = 2^n$$

Thus, the null class, 0, has n = 0; the first order (n=1) class has 1 element, X, and two classes, 0 and 1; the second order (n=2) class has two elements, X and Y and four classes, 0, X, Y, and 1; the third order (n=3) class has three elements, X, Y, and Z and contains 8 classes, 0, X, Y, Z, (X+Y), (X+Z), (Y+Z), and 1, and so on. The binary digit or *bit* of digital logic falls into the first order class with the two discrete states represented by the two classes, 0 and 1, contained in the universe class.

Many of the laws of Boolean algebra cited earlier for the particular first order class of digital logic have more general expressions in the algebra of classes and may be illustrated by Venn diagrams.[7] For this more general representation two new symbols are introduced:

$\subset$ ⇒ "is contained in"
iff ⇒ "if and only if"

The various regions in the Venn diagram shown in Figure 5-4 illustrate several of the basic Boolean operations. The black area represents the *intersection* of class a *and* b, also known as (a ∧ b). The intermediate grey shaded area plus the black area is the *union*, (a ∨ b), of class a and class b, that is, the region in which the object is either in class a *or* class b. The lightest shaded area is the region outside of both a and b, that is, the region *not* in a and *not* in b. This statement can be rephrased in a completely equivalent fashion as the region belonging to neither a nor b which can be expressed as *not* (a ∨ b). This equivalent statement is an English version of DeMorgan's law, $(\neg a \wedge \neg b) = \neg(a \vee b)$.

Before the postulates of the Boolean algebra of classes are listed, we need to define "equality". We say that class a = class b if and only if (iff) class a $\subset$ class b and class b $\subset$ class a.

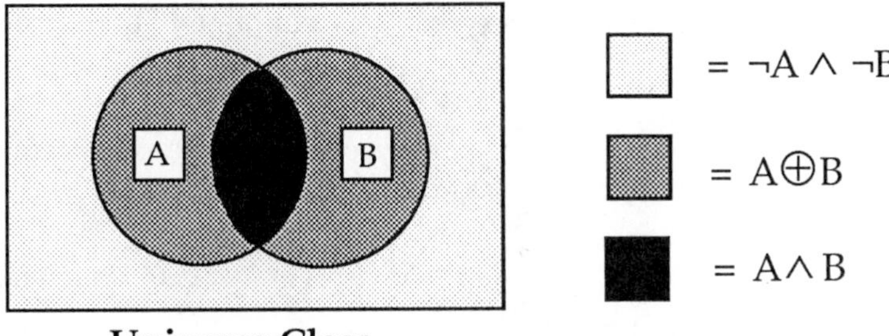

Figure 5-4 Venn Diagram illustrating several Boolean operations. The black region is clearly in A *and* B (A ∧ B), the grey region is in A and not B or in B and not A ((A ∧ ¬B) ∨ (B ∧ ¬A)). This is what is meant by *exclusive OR,* (A⊕B). The light grey region demonstrates a word proof of DeMorgan's law: the region that is neither A *nor* B (¬(A∨B)) is the region that is not A and not B(¬A ∧ ¬B).

POSTULATES OF BOOLEAN ALGEBRA

Next the postulates of Boolean algebra are listed and several of them illustrated with Venn diagrams shown in Figure 5-5.

1. **a ⊂ a** That is, "every class contains itself."

2. **If a ⊂ b and b ⊂ c then a ⊂ c** That is, "every class contains the subclasses of its subclasses." See Figure 5-5-(1).

3. **a ⊂ b ∧ c iff a ⊂ b and a ⊂ c** That is, "a is contained in the intersection of b and c if and only if a is contained in b and a is contained in c." This defines the "product of classes" and is illustrated in Figure 5-5-(2).

4. **a ∨ b ⊂ c iff a ⊂ c and b ⊂ c** That is, "the union of a and b is contained in c if and only if a is contained in c and b is contained in c." See Figure 5-5-(3).

5. **(a ∨ b) ∧ (a ∨ c) ⊂ a ∨ (b ∧ c)** This is the distributive property of classes. See Figure 5-5-(4).

6. **0 ⊂ a** That is, "every class contains the null class."

7. $\mathbf{a \subset 1}$ That is, "every class is contained in the universal class."

8. $\mathbf{a \wedge \neg a \subset 0}$ That is, "every class and its complement are mutually exclusive."

9. $\mathbf{1 \subset a \vee \neg a}$ That is, "the universe class consists of all elements in a and in (NOT a)."

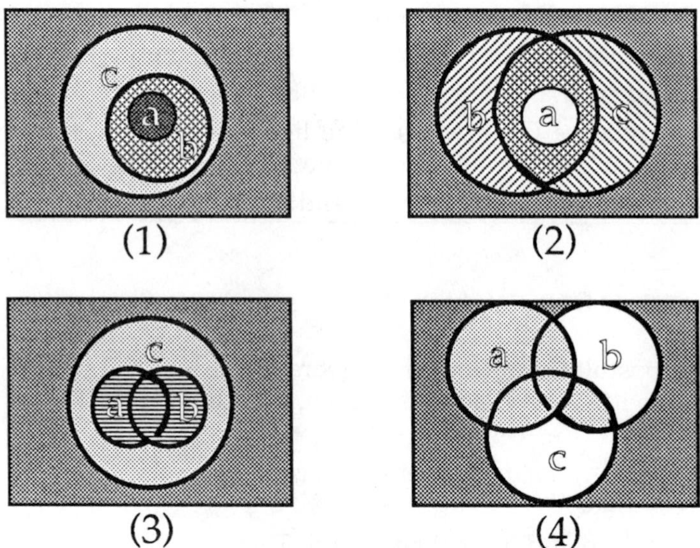

Figure 5-5 Venn Diagrams for Boolean Algebra Postulates Diagram (1) corresponds to postulate 2, diagram (2) illustrates postulate 3, diagram (3) illustrates postulate 4, and diagram (4) corresponds to postulate 5.

From these postulates it is possible to prove additional theorems of Boolean algebra, such as:

- $\mathbf{a \subset a \wedge a}$
- $\mathbf{a \wedge a \subset a}$
- $\mathbf{a \vee a \subset a}$
- $\mathbf{a \subset a \vee a}$
- $\mathbf{\neg(a \vee b) \subset \neg a \wedge \neg b}$ ⇒ (DeMorgan's law)

5.5 PROPOSITIONAL CALCULUS

The real value of formal logic to the field of artificial intelligence lies in the generality of the propositions which may be expressed. In the digital logic examples discussed above we assume that the elements such as A and B each have logical values of 0 or 1 corresponding to the logically FALSE or TRUE condition. However, in propositional logic, the propositions may be *any* statement which can be evaluated as TRUE or FALSE. All of the laws of Boolean algebra apply to the propositions. Examples of a few propositions (which happen to have value TRUE) illustrate the range of application of propositional logic:

- Mozart was a composer.
- A composer is a writer of music.
- A dog is an animal.
- The density of 1-ethyl-2-nitro-benzene is 1.126 g/ml.
- The site of the culture is blood.
- Igneous rocks in the region have porphyritic texture.

It is clear that deductive logic applied to the above set of propositions would enable an automated reasoning system to answer the question *Was Mozart a writer of music?* even though this proposition was not explicitly stated. This is an example of Boolean postulate 2 — Mozart belonged to the class of *composers* and the class of composer is contained in the class of *writers of music*. Therefore Mozart was a writer of music.

Consider the following three (not necessarily true) propositions:

p = Computer system X successfully passed the Turing Test.
$(p \rightarrow q)$ = Successfully passing the Turing Test implies that machines can think.
q = Machines can think.

The logical relationship between these three propositions is one of the most useful formal rules of inference, the rule previously introduced as *modus ponens* :

$$(p \wedge (p \rightarrow q)) \rightarrow q$$

This can be easily understood in terms of its English equivalent: If passing the Turing Test implies that a machine can think AND a certain computer passed the Turing Test then the implication is that machines can think. While neither proposition has, in fact, been proven true, the logical implication of proving both propositions true is inescapable. The rule of *modus ponens* has proven to be very valuable in the reduction of complex sets of logical statements. It is called the "$\rightarrow$" elimination rule.

Propositional logic provides a clean, well-defined test bed for automating the inference process. Much of what we know about geometry was proven by Euclid using propositional logic. It is natural that AI researchers would turn their attention to this area early in the history of AI. We now turn to one of the first successful programs to emerge from AI research.

THE LOGIC THEORIST

One of the first milestones in all of artificial intelligence research was the automatic theorem proving program, The Logic Theorist of Allen Newell, Herbert Simon, and J. C. Shaw. Pamela McCorduck gives a most fascinating account of the birth of this theorem proving program:[8]

> *"... and Herb Simon was able to walk into his mathematical modeling class in January 1956, and declare that over the Christmas holidays he and Allen Newell had invented a thinking machine."*

The Logic Theorist was implemented on the RAND Corporation Johnniac computer by programmer Cliff Shaw working in collaboration with Newell and Simon at Carnegie-Mellon University. It was written in IPL-I (Information Processing Language I), an early, somewhat awkward list-processing language. By limiting the problem domain of interest to the proof of theorems in propositional calculus, Newell and Simon were able to create a successful program using very primitive hardware and software.

The problem Newell and Simon assigned themselves was to use propositional calculus to prove theorems from Russell and Whitehead's *Principia Mathematica*. Starting with the five axioms:

1. $(p \vee p) \rightarrow p$
2. $p \rightarrow (q \vee p)$
3. $(p \vee q) \rightarrow (q \vee p)$
4. $[p \vee (q \vee r)] \rightarrow [q \vee (p \vee r)]$
5. $(p \rightarrow q) \rightarrow [(r \vee p) \rightarrow (r \vee q)]$

the Logic Theorist was able to prove

2.01 $(p \rightarrow \neg p) \rightarrow \neg p$
2.45 $\neg(p \vee q) \rightarrow \neg p$
2.31 $[p \vee (q \vee r)] \rightarrow [(p \vee q) \vee r]$.

By combining already proven theorems with the basic axioms, the Logic Theorist was able to prove 38 of the first 52 theorems in sequence in Chapter 2 of *Principia Mathematica*. In fact, the Logic Theorist discovered a more elegant proof of Theorem 2.85 than the original by Russell and Whitehead. When Simon informed Bertrand Russell of this new proof, Russell was delighted!

The Logic Theorist used *working backwards* (backward chaining) as its basic heuristic algorithm. Starting with X as the theorem to be proved, it used three operators to transform X into one of the basic axioms:[9]

- **Detachment**: In order to prove X, find an axiom or theorem of the form $A \rightarrow X$ and transform the problem to the problem of proving A.

- **Forward Chaining**: In order to prove X where X has the form $A \rightarrow C$, find an axiom or theorem of the form $A \rightarrow B$ and transform the problem to the problem of proving $B \rightarrow C$.

- **Backward Chaining**: In order to prove X where X has the form $A \rightarrow C$, find an axiom or theorem of the form $B \rightarrow C$ and transform the problem to the problem of proving $A \rightarrow B$.

These operators were combined with the "→" replacement rule and a substitution test to determine when X had been reduced to an axiom. The basic algorithm used in the Logic Theorist was a blind, breadth-first, state-space search using backward reasoning weakly guided by choice of operator heuristics.

The Logic Theorist did fail on certain theorems, such as those requiring AND/OR trees in which the problem X was reduced to several sub-problems, each of which had to be successfully solved to solve X. However, it can with some justification claim the distinction of being the first program to produce significant results in the new field of artificial intelligence. The Logic Theorist also demonstrated the essential role of heuristics in guiding search in complex search spaces.

LIMITATIONS OF PROPOSITIONAL LOGIC

Propositions stating chemical, medical, and geological information suggest the possibility of creating enormous data bases containing "all the known facts" about these disciplines. By combining these propositions with propositions concerning their relationships, one should in principle be able to create *expert systems* for analyzing physical systems in terms of input information. Successful expert systems do indeed exist but in general do not use propositional calculus for the representation of information. The fundamental problem lies in a combinatorial explosion — in this case explosion of the number of deductions possible from a set of input propositions. This number tends to grow exponentially with the number of propositions, thereby making this representation of information impractical for all but the simplest data bases.

You may have also noticed that propositional logic is built on static propositions which require one statement to establish each proposition. Missing are concepts for general class variables, existential quantifiers, and functional relationships.

5.6 PREDICATE CALCULUS

Predicate calculus is an extension and generalization of propositional calculus which provides more power and efficiency for making logical inferences. Propositional logic deals only with the truth value of complete statements and does not consider relationships or dependencies between objects. First-order predicate calculus introduces the following concepts:[10]

- **Use of Predicates with Arguments** — "Statements about individuals, both by themselves and in relation to other individuals, are called *predicates*. A predicate is applied to a specific number of arguments and has a value of either TRUE or FALSE when individuals are used as the arguments."[11] Thus the predicate *IS-A-COMPOSER* is TRUE when applied to the arguments *MOZART* and *HAYDN* but FALSE when applied to *COLUMBUS*. LISP and Prolog provide many intrinsic predicate functions such as **equal?**, **atom?**, and **member?**. These predicate functions answer the questions of whether two elements are equal, whether an element is an atom, and whether an element is a member of a list, respectively.

The general form for expressing predicates is:

Predicate(Arguments)

and examples include:

Is-a-composer(Mozart)
Is-a-composer(Haydn)
Explorer(Columbus)
On(red-box,blue-box)

These statements in the language of predicate calculus are called *well-formed formulas* (wffs) or *expressions* of the language.

• **Use of Variables and Quantifiers** — General statements about classes of objects may be made by introducing two quantifiers:

$\forall \Rightarrow$ "for all ..." (universal quantifier)

and

$\exists \Rightarrow$ "there exists" (existential quantifier).

Thus, the general predicate, "All mammals are warm blooded" may be expressed in predicate calculus as:

$$\forall\ X.\text{Mammal}(X) \rightarrow \text{Warm blooded}(X)$$

which may be translated, "For all individuals X, if X belongs to the mammal class, then X is warm blooded."

• **Functions of Variables** — The extension of the concept of variables includes the capability of functional relationships. This permits quite general statements to be made, for instance:

"For all earth satellites, there exists a point y on the satellite that is closest to the earth."

which is a translation of the predicate:

$$\forall(x)\text{SATELLITE}(x) \rightarrow \exists(y)\ (\text{CLOSEST}(y,\text{earth}) \wedge \text{ON}(y,x))$$

Predicate calculus extends the rules of propositional calculus with the concepts of predicates, quantification, and inference rules for quantifiers. It is clear that predicate calculus has a great advantage over propositional calculus in its power of expression. This capability has made predicate calculus an essential technique in specific fields of AI such as automatic theorem proving.

SYNTAX OF PREDICATE CALCULUS

Next we summarize some of the nomenclature and syntax of predicate calculus.

- ***Symbols*** — The symbols from which symbolic logic gets its name come in several varieties, including:

  - Variable symbols ⇒ x,y,z,...
  - Function symbols ⇒ f,g,h,...
  - Predicate symbols ⇒ P,Q,R,...
  - Logic symbols ⇒ $\forall, \exists, \neg, \wedge, \vee, \rightarrow$
  - Punctuation symbols ⇒ " , ", "(", and ")".

- ***Universe*** — The domain of discourse, D, corresponding to the set of objects represented by logical variables.

- ***Terms*** — Variables are terms and f(T) is a term, where f is a function and T is a sequence of n terms.

- ***Atomic formula*** — P(T) is an atomic formula, where P is a predicate and T is a sequence of n terms.

- ***Literals*** — Atomic formulas and negated atomic formulas.

- ***Well-formed formulas (wffs)*** — Literals are wffs and wffs connected or quantified by logic symbols are also wffs.

- ***Sentence*** — A wff in which all variables are within the scope of corresponding quantifiers.

- ***Clause*** — A wff consisting of a literal or a disjunction of literals (literals connected by ORs).

A *system* in first-order predicate calculus consists of a set of sentences, S, which express a mathematical theory or represent a physical system. The system builder has complete freedom in selecting predicates and building expressions to represent the problem s/he is trying to solve. If all of the expressions of the system have the value TRUE then we say that the logical system S represents a *model* of the mathematical or physical system under study. Any formulas which are logically implied by system S are said to be *theorems* of S.

Several rules of inference have been developed for extracting new knowledge from the knowledge contained in the system. This new knowledge is in the form of new formulas and sentences which are logically implied by the original set S. Among others, these rules include:[12]

- **Expansion Rule** — If U and V are formulas and U is logically implied by S, then ∨(U,V) is also logically implied.

- **Contraction Rule** — If ∧(U,V) is logically implied by S, then U is also implied.

- **Associative Rule** — If ∨(U,∨(W,V)) is logically implied by S, then ∨(∨(U,V),W) and ∨(U,V,W) are logically implied. The inverse is also true.

- **Cut Rule** — If ∨(U,V) and U→W are logically implied by S, then ∨(W,V) is also implied.

New knowledge is generated by proving new theorems in the language of predicate calculus. Inference rules such as those shown above and the resolution principle discussed below provide the tools for proving new theorems.

5.7 AUTOMATIC THEOREM PROVING

Ever since the days of the Logic Theorist, automatic theorem proving has attracted the interest of AI researchers. Theorem proving continues to provide the most general technique for applying logic to real-world problems. The *method of resolution* is the most widely used method for automatic theorem proving. This method is the basic algorithm used in the Prolog language and the AURA automated reasoning tool.

METHOD OF RESOLUTION

The operation of the resolution rule may be illustrated by the following example. Suppose one of the axioms of our original system is of the form Q∨R ("Q is true or R is true") and a second is of the form ¬R∨P ("either R is not true or P is true"). Since all axioms must be true if S is a consistent model, these two axioms are associated with a logical AND, and may be represented by:

$$\begin{array}{ll} & Q \vee R \\ & \underline{\neg R \vee P} \\ \text{giving} & Q \vee P \end{array}$$

since $R \wedge \neg R = 0$

That is, the R terms have been "resolved out" of the reduced set of axioms, leaving only Q∨P as the *resolvent*.

The resolution principle relies on the fact that, for purposes of proving the *satisfiability* of the model, the substitution:

$$(Q \vee R) \wedge (\neg R \vee P) \rightarrow Q \vee P$$

is admissible even though, as my students have pointed out, the RHS is not logically equivalent to the LHS. A simple truth table demonstrates that the RHS is more generally true than the LHS. Thus, it may be substituted for the LHS and still preserve the satisfiability of the original set of clauses.

The essential question to be answered by theorem provers is whether proposition P is implied by the set of axioms, S, of the logical system. The basic concept in the method of resolution is that of *refutation*.[13] The approach is to express the negation of P., denoted by ¬P, as an additional proposition to form an extended set of axioms, and then to prove that ¬P is FALSE. If that can be shown, then P must be TRUE. The algorithm is summarized by the following four steps:

1) Assume that ¬P is TRUE
2) Show that the basic axioms together with ¬P lead to a contradiction
3) Conclude that, since the axioms are correct, ¬P must be FALSE
4) Since ¬P is FALSE, P must be TRUE.

This algorithm is known as the *unification procedure* for implementation of the inference rule known as the *binary resolution principle.*

In order to carry out the analysis, it is necessary to convert both the basic axioms and the theorem P (or rather ¬P) into what is called *conjunctive normal form* or *clause form* as shown below:

$$(\forall x_1)(\forall x_2)\ldots(\forall x_n)[C_1 \wedge C_2 \wedge \ldots \wedge C_m]$$

where

C_i $(1 \leq i \leq m)$ are clauses
$x_1, x_2, \ldots x_n$ are variables appearing in clauses.

It is an interesting result that any sentence in predicate logic can be written in this form. There is a well-defined 6 stage algorithm for this process which has itself been implemented in the Prolog language.[14] A summary of the steps to convert a wff into clausal form is shown:[15]

1. Change $P \rightarrow Q$ into $\neg P \vee Q$, and $A \equiv B$ into $(\neg A \vee B) \wedge (\neg B \vee A)$.

2. Standardize variables. For instance, the x in $(\forall x)[\neg P(x) \vee (\exists x) Q(x)]$ associated with the $\forall$ and the $\exists$ are different variables, so the sentence should be rewritten as $(\forall x)[\neg P(x) \vee (\exists y) Q(y)]$.

3. Restrict the range of negation. For instance, convert $\neg(\forall x)[P \wedge \neg(Q \wedge R)]$ into $(\exists x)[\neg P \vee (Q \wedge R)]$.

4. Eliminate existential quantifiers. The axiom $(\forall x)(\exists y)P(x,y)$ is equivalent to the functional representation, $(\forall x)P(x,f(x))$. This is called the Skolem function.

5. Relocate the universal quantifiers to the front of the clause. For instance, substitute $(\forall x)(\forall y)[P(x) \vee \neg Q(y)]$ for $(\forall x)[P(x) \vee (\forall y) \neg Q(y)]$.

6. Rewrite the sentence in conjunctive normal form. The AND would be distributed with respect to the OR. For instance, $(U \wedge V) \vee (V \wedge W)$ would be redistributed as $(U \vee V) \wedge (V \vee W) \wedge V \wedge (U \vee W)$.

With the axioms of the system in clause form, it is a relatively straight-forward process to apply the resolution principle repeatedly until the system is shown to be consistent (original P is FALSE) or inconsistent (original P is TRUE).

Example

Consider the following set of axioms for which we wish to prove the theorem that *P is TRUE* (it is implied only if R AND Q are true). Shown also is the equivalent clause form of each.

Axiom #	Axiom	Axiom in Clause Form
1	R	R
2	$(R \wedge Q) \rightarrow P$	$\neg R \vee \neg Q \vee P$
3	$(S \vee T) \rightarrow Q$	$\neg S \vee Q$
		$\neg T \vee Q$
4	T	T

Next we add the negation of the theorem to the list:

5	$\neg P$	$\neg P$

and begin the reduction process, looking for a contradiction. We begin by resolving the clause involving the negation of the theorem (which must contain the inconsistency if there is one) against the first axiom containing its symbols, (2):

$$\begin{array}{ll} \neg R \vee \neg Q \vee P & (2) \\ \underline{\neg P \qquad\qquad} & (5) \\ \neg R \vee \neg Q & (6) \end{array}$$

Now resolve resolvent (6) against an axiom containing one of its symbols:

$$\begin{array}{ll} \neg R \vee \neg Q & (6) \\ \underline{R \qquad\qquad} & (1) \\ \qquad \neg Q & (7) \end{array}$$

Next resolve (7) against the second clause of axiom (3):

$$\begin{array}{ll} \neg T \vee Q & (3) \\ \underline{\neg Q \qquad} & (7) \\ \neg T & (8) \end{array}$$

Finally, resolve (8) against the only remaining axiom containing its symbols:

$$\begin{array}{ll} T & (4) \\ \underline{\neg T} & (8) \\ (\square) & = \text{empty clause} \end{array}$$

The last resolvent is the empty clause indicating a contradiction in the extended set of axioms. That is, there are no conditions under which the basic axioms can be TRUE at the same time that P is FALSE. Since the axioms are assumed to be TRUE, the inference by refutation is that P is TRUE.

The propositional calculus example used here is one of the simplest possible examples which still illustrates some of the important features of theorem proving by the method of resolution. Theorem proving in predicate calculus systems requires procedures for transforming the existential quantifiers into clausal form. These involve operations known as the *unification algorithm* and the introduction of *Skolem functions* with arguments which preserve the information represented by predicate calculus quantifiers.

OTHER THEOREM PROVERS

Because theorem proving is the optimum strategy for applying logic in such areas as database/query systems and logic-based languages, a great deal of AI research has been devoted to the subject. A number of other theorem-proving systems have emerged from this research.

The *nonresolution* theorem prover is designed to emulate the reasoning of human theorem-provers. For this reason it is also known as a *natural-deduction* theorem prover. One disadvantage of the resolution method is that because of the clausal form of the axioms, the operation of the theorem prover is difficult to follow in practice. By operating in a natural-deduction mode, nonresolution solvers overcome this problem and allow the user to follow the progress of the solver and interact with it when it runs into difficulty. Nonresolution solvers generally use a backward-chaining technique involving substitution in an attempt to transform the theorem to be proven into a form consistent with the original axioms. One successful nonresolution system is IMPLY by Bledsoe.[16]

The *Boyer-Moore Theorem Prover* (BMTP) is based on recursive function theory and application of rewrite rules to the basic axioms.[17] The BMTP considers axioms and theorems to be functions which have values of TRUE or FALSE. A theorem is proved by recursively rewriting the formula until the value of the theorem is TRUE. The process is assisted by the introduction of rewrite lemmas intuitively selected by the user. If the theorem prover fails, the user may introduce additional lemmas to help the computer in its proof. A unique feature of the BMTP is that it can prove theorems by induction.

Through the use of sophisticated heuristics, the BMTP has become one of the most powerful theorem provers available.

5.8 SUCCESSFUL AUTOMATED REASONING SYSTEMS

Predicate calculus provides the structure for representing knowledge in the language of logic, and theorem proving algorithms such as the resolution principle provide the mechanisms for extracting new knowledge implied by the original system. The reader must have anticipated by now that by embedding the predicate calculus formalism and theorem prover in a supportive programming environment and supplying an appropriate control mechanism for performing the equivalent of the LISP read-evaluate-print cycle, we would have a useful language for automated reasoning. We summarize next two of the more successful attempts at producing a language for automated reasoning.

PROLOG REVISITED

Prolog was designed to provide a practical implementation of the language of predicate calculus. The Prolog programming environment provides the mechanism for entering the database of knowledge in terms of facts and relationships between those facts. Once the database is established, the Prolog language serves as database/query system providing answers to the user's queries. The user asks questions of the system by restating with question marks the facts or predicates s/he used in building the system. This query becomes the goal, the theorem which Prolog attempts to prove.

Some of the main features of Prolog include:

- Prolog uses ***resolution theorem proving*** as its basic algorithm for solution.

- Prolog rewrites and stores its database in the form of ***Horn clauses,*** a disjunction of literals with at most one positive literal.

- Prolog uses a ***depth-first strategy*** in searching for a match between the goal and the clauses contained in the database.

- Prolog is a ***declarative*** rather than procedural language.

Is PROLOG a true logic programming language?

A language implementation of logic programming must include meta-logical and extra-logical features such as I/O handling, fast arithmetic, an interpreter scheduling policy, and infinite loop avoidance.[18] Among these extra-logical features provided by Prolog are:

- A ***stack scheduling policy*** to search the Horn clause list from left to right. Thus, the order in which clauses are entered will effect the efficiency of running the program.

- ***Communication predicates*** — Prolog provides the predicates *read(X)?* and *write(X)?* to communicate terms to and from the system. These are necessary for a practical implementation but have no strict logical analog.

- ***The CUT Control*** — The "cut" (!) provides a useful predicate in controlling the backtracking chain of logical inferences. This increases program efficiency in avoiding unproductive substitution and infinite loops. Judicious use of the NOT connective can greatly reduce the need for the extra-logical cut.

- ***Dynamic database modification*** — Prolog provides predicates such as *assert* and *retract* for adding and removing clauses from the database. These extensions provide much greater programming flexibility but deviate from the concept of a static, logical system of given axioms.

So, while there are significant deviations between Prolog and pure logic programming, the consensus of those who have studied the language is that Prolog is a very good first approximation to pure logic programming. The essential elements of logic programming have survived the implementation, and several of the extra-logical features actually improve the power and flexibility of the language. For instance, the assert and retract predicates are helpful in solving the problem of *nonmonotonic reasoning*. In monotonic logic, the axioms are invariant even though new information may indicate that certain axioms must be false. Nonmonotonic reasoning provides for updating the set of axioms to reflect the best available information. Clearly, predicates such as *assert* and *retract* are essential to nonmonotonic logic.

AURA - AUTOMATED REASONING ASSISTANT

AURA, the Automated Reasoning Assistant, is a program developed by a joint group from Northern Illinois University and Argonne National Laboratory under the direction of Dr. Larry Wos of Argonne. An excellent introduction to the topic of automated reasoning and its implementation in AURA is given in *AUTOMATED REASONING — Introduction and Applications* by Wos, Overbeek, Lusk, and Boyle.[19] Wos, who gave automated reasoning its name, defines it as:

> *Automated reasoning is concerned with the discovery, formulation, and implementation of concepts and procedures that permit the computer to be used as a reasoning assistant.*[20]

AURA is a very powerful and versatile automated reasoning program which has solved many interesting problems ranging from the Missionaries and Cannibals puzzle to open questions in equivalential calculus. AURA consists of more than 40,000 lines of IBM assembly code and more than 20,000 lines of PL/I. Two other automated reasoning programs, LMA (Logic Machine Architecture) and ITP (Interactive Theorem Prover), have been written by the same group in Pascal and are available on a variety of machines with one or more megabytes of memory.

Features of AURA

• *Modes of operation* — The authors of these automated reasoning programs suggest the following three modes of operation:

1. **Batch** — Submit the problem and disappear, hoping the program will have found a solution by the time you return.

2. **Interactive** — You can sit at the terminal and carry on a dialog with the system in a mode similar to a LISP or Prolog session.

3. **Graduate assistant** — You submit a problem to it with strict constraints on the processing time and amount of new information to be found.

• *Language* — The language selected in which to represent the problems posed to the automated reasoning programs is a "clause language" very closely related to the first-order predicate calculus. Predicate terms closely resemble those of Prolog. The language uses the conjunctive normal form, i.e. all statements are assumed to be separated by AND and all literals of a statement are separated by OR. The only other acceptable operator is the NOT.

• ***Theorem proving algorithm*** — As do most automatic theorem provers, the AURA family of programs uses proof by refutation. The theorem to be proven is assumed to be false and the program unifies the false proposition with clauses in the database by the resolution principle until a contradiction is discovered.

• ***Set of support strategy*** — This strategy was introduced by Wos to help the program avoid many fruitless paths of investigation. This strategy asks the user to pick certain key input clauses from which the program can begin reasoning and treats the remaining clauses as auxiliary information. This effectively weights the clauses by their value in reaching a solution rapidly and provides a means by which to incorporate the user's knowledge and intuition.

• ***Subsumption*** — This feature enables a reasoning program to prefer general information to specific information. When the program is presented with two statements, one of which is a trivial corollary of the other, the program retains the theorem and discards the trivial corollary. Subsumption increases the efficiency of the program and enhances its effectiveness in finding proofs.

• ***Demodulation*** — This is a simplification process for rewriting complex expression in a reduced or canonical form. For example, 0 + x is rewritten as x, – (–x) is rewritten as x, and xy + xz is rewritten as x(y+z). The demodulation process is a most valuable and often necessary feature for solving problems.

Successes of AURA

The AURA series of programs has tackled and successfully solved a remarkably wide range of hard problems. Three distinct problem areas and the particular problems solved are summarized.

1. Puzzles

• *Missionaries and Cannibals* — Can the missionaries and cannibals safely cross the river even though the boat is quite small, and even though they do not share the same outlook on life?

• *Dominoes and Checkerboard* — Can the checkerboard be covered with dominoes even though certain squares are missing?

• *Billiard Ball and Balance Scale* — Can you find the odd ball in three weighings?

2. Digital Electronics and Program Validation

• *Circuit Design* — Given specifications for a circuit and components that can be used to design it, design a circuit fulfilling the requirements.

• *Circuit Validation* — Given the design of a circuit and the specifications it supposedly meets, prove that the design is correct.

• *Program Validation* — Given a program and its expected properties, prove that the properties hold, or find a counter-example establishing the existence of a bug.

3. Open Questions in Mathematics

• *Ternary Boolean Algebra* — Are any of the five axioms independent of the remaining four?

(1) f(f(v,w,x),y,f(v,w,z))=f(v,w,f(x,y,z))
(2) f(y,x,x)=x
(3) f(x,y g(y))=x
(4) f(x,x,y)=x
(5) f(g(y),y,x)=x

• *Equivalential Calculus* — Are any of the following seven formulas strong enough to serve as a single axiom for the equivalential calculus?

(1) XJL = E(x,E(y,E(E(E(z,y),x),z)))
...
(7) XHN = E(x,E(E(y,z),E(E(z,x),y)))

- *Finite Semigroups* — Does there exist a finite semigroup admitting a non-trivial antiautomorphism but admitting no non-trivial involutions?

Is Automated Reasoning the Future Wave of AI?

The performance of the AURA class of programs is truly impressive, and a number of ideas which Wos has introduced to improve the performance of automated reasoning programs are very significant contributions. However, success in each of these problem areas did not come easily. Some indication of the difficulty involved in solving problems with AURA is given by Wos' admonition:

> " ... *Despite the power and richness of the language, the presentation of a problem to an automated reasoning program is an art.*
>
> *In addition to the representation problem, there are closely related problems of choosing the appropriate rules of reasoning and of choosing the strategies to control the rules. Good choices of representation, inference rule, and strategy are extremely interconnected.* ...
>
> "... *Even with the various successes and the current activities, we must again say that the use of an automated reasoning program is at present an art.*"[21]

PROBLEMS AND PROGRAMS

5-1. Logic has proven valuable to AI not only for providing a formalism for reasoning, but also as a knowledge representation system. Explain how logic may be used to represent knowledge. The analogy with Prolog may help.

5-2. Set up starting hypotheses and make an appropriate logical inference for three different "real life" situations, one each for the three logic types of deduction, induction, and abduction.

5-3. Is the Law of Mathematical Induction a formalism for inductive or deductive reasoning? Explain.

5-4. The claim is made that inferences made by scientific induction are trustworthy as long as "nature is orderly and mathematical functions well behaved." What does this mean and what exceptions to this qualifier have occurred in natural science?

5-5. Abduction is frequently used in medical diagnostic expert systems. Discuss whether such systems would be forward or backward chaining and how probabilities might enter in to the diagnosis.

5-6. Prove DeMorgan's law by a word proof by interpreting the LHS of the second statement of the theorem as the NOR operation.

5-7. Using the second statement of DeMorgan's law as proved, prove the first statement of DeMorgan's law. (Hint: re-define variables and use the NOT laws.)

5-8. Write down the Boolean expression for the two-input exclusive OR (XOR) shown in Figure 5-2 and prove that the circuit shown will implement the operation.

5-9. Sketch Figure 5-2 with NAND implementations of the AND and OR gates. How can your diagram be simplified? (Hint: use the third line of the NOT laws.)

5-10. Work out the truth table for a half-adder and show that the two gates indicated in Figure 5-3 will perform the required operations.

5-11. Work out the truth table for a full adder which adds two bits, A and B, with a carry in, C_{n-1}, and produces a sum, S_n, and carry out, C_n. Design a full adder circuit using two half adders plus an OR gate.

5-12. List the elements and specify the classes of the fourth order (n=4) Boolean class.

5-13. Using appropriate color shading on the Venn diagram in Figure 5-5 (d), prove Postulate 5 of Boolean algebra.

5-14. Use Prolog syntax to rewrite the six propositions indicated by bullets in section 5.5.

5-15. Generate three unique situations each containing two propositions, p and q, and use *modus ponens* to infer the truth value of q for each.

5-16. What can be done in propositional calculus which can't be in predicate calculus? What can be done in predicate calculus which can't be in propositional calculus?

5-17. Rewrite the following relationships in the syntax of predicate calculus:

John is a good student.
All good students have high grades.
All students with high grades are bright or work hard.
For all objects, there exists properties of mass, volume, and color.

5-18. The truth table for "implies" (→) is given by:

p	q	p → q
T	T	T
T	F	F
F	T	T
F	F	T

Give word proofs for all four lines and cite a confirming example of each.

5-19. What was the significance of the announcement of the Logic Theorist at the 1956 Dartmouth Conference? How was it received by the AI community?

5-20. In the example listed in the Method of Resolution discussion, rewrite the axioms with the $\wedge$ and $\vee$ symbols of axioms 2 and 3 interchanged. Work out the clause form of the axioms and use the resolution technique to try to prove the theorem, *Q is TRUE*.

5-21. Discuss the similarities and differences between Prolog and AURA. Which is easier to use and why? Which is more powerful as a reasoning tool and why?

FOOTNOTES AND REFERENCES

1 Moore, Robert C., "The Role of Logic in Artificial Intelligence," *Technical Note: 335*, SRI International, Menlo Park, CA (1984)

2 *The American Heritage Dictionary of the English Language*, Houghton Mifflin Company, Boston, MA (1973)

3 Charniak, Eugene and McDermott, Drew, *Introduction to Artificial Intelligence*, p. 457, Addison-Wesley, Reading, MA (1985)

4 Feigenbaum, Edward A., Barr, Avron, and Cohen, Paul R. (eds), *The Handbook of Artificial Intelligence*,Vol.2, HeurisTech Press/William Kaufmann, Inc., Stanford, CA (1981—82)

5 Glorioso, Robert M. and Osorio, F. C. Colon, *Engineering Intelligent Systems: Concepts, Theory, and Applications*, Digital Press, Bedford, MA (1980)

6 Boole, George, "Mathematical Analysis of Logic," *The World of Mathematics*, James R. Newman (ed), Simon and Schuster, New York, NY (1956)

7 Brennan, Joseph Gerard, *A Handbook of Logic*, Second Edition, Harper & Row, Publishers, New York, NY (1961)

8 McCorduck, Pamela, *Machines Who Think*, p. 145, W. H. Freeman and Company, San Francisco, CA (1979)

9 Feigenbaum, Edward A., *et al*, Op cit, p. 109—112

10 Mendelson, Elliott, *Introduction to Mathematical Logic*, Van Nostrand Reinhold Company, New York, NY (1964)

11 Feigenbaum, Edward A., *et al*, Op cit

12 Jackson, Jr., Philip C., *Introduction to Artificial Intelligence*, Second Edition, p. 221, Dover Publications, Inc., New York, NY (1985)

13 Robinson, J. A., "A Machine-Oriented Logic Based on the Resolution Principle," *Journal of the ACM* **12** (1), p. 23 (1965)

14 Clocksin, W. F. and Mellish, C. S., *Programming in PROLOG*, Second Edition, p. 237, Springer-Verlag, Berlin (1984)

15 Shirai, Yoshiaki and Tsujii, Jun-ichi, *Artificial Intelligence Concepts, Techniques, and Applications*, p. 79, John Wiley & Sons, New York, NY (1984)

16 Bledsoe, W. W., "Non-resolution Theorem Proving," *Artificial Intelligence* **9**, pp. 1—35 (1977)

17 Boyer, R. S. and Moore, J. S., *A Computational Logic,* Academic Press, New York, NY (1979)

18 Sterling, Leon and Shapiro, Ehud, *The Art of Prolog,* p. 93, The MIT Press, Cambridge, MA (1986)

19 Wos, Larry, Overbeek, Ross, Lusk, Ewing, and Boyle, Jim, *AUTOMATED REASONING — Introduction and Applications,* 482 pp., Prentice-Hall, Inc., Englewood Cliffs, NJ (1984)

20 Wos, L., "Automated Reasoning," *American Mathematical Monthly* **92** (2), p. 85—92, February (1985) *See also* Wos, Larry, "Achievements in Automated Reasoning," *SIAM News,* Computational Sciences, Part 1, July 4, 1984, and Part 2, September 4, 1984

21 Wos, L. *American Mathematical Monthly,* Op cit, p. 90

Chapter 6

PROBLEM SOLVING

(PHOTO: UPI/BETTMANN NEWSPHOTOS)

Herbert A. Simon is Distinguished Professor of Computer Science and Psychology at Carnegie-Mellon University. A native of Milwaukee, he is one of the founders of the science of AI. With his colleague Alan Newell, he introduced the concept of the *physical symbol system* and wrote several of the first working AI programs, including The Logic Theorist and the General Problem Solver. His books, *The Sciences of the Artificial* and *Administrative Behavior* are seminal works in these areas. His most recent book is *Scientific Discovery — Computational Explorations of the Creative Process.* His contributions were recognized by the 1978 Nobel Prize in Economics.

6: PROBLEM SOLVING

6.1 INTRODUCTION

Our study began with an operational definition of artificial intelligence and then surveyed various tools and techniques which AI researchers have found valuable in trying to solve problems which, if done by humans, require intelligence. Search techniques were shown to be essential items in the AI toolkit. From the discussion of game theory, it became apparent that the search spaces generated by the combinatorial explosion required additional heuristic information to prune away unproductive paths of the search tree. The rules of formal logic were presented as a concise and systematic formalism for inferring new knowledge from existing knowledge as well as a technique of representing knowledge itself.

The goal of this chapter is to integrate these topics and demonstrate their usefulness as tools for problem solving. This is an area we instinctively associate with intelligence,whether natural or artificial. After the struggle many of us went through with eighth grade word problems ("If Johnny had 3 times as many apples as Mary who sold 20% of hers at 15¢ apiece, how many ... "), our first reaction is that any computer system which can solve such problems can't be completely stupid (and, in fact, might even be useful to have as an assistant). In this chapter we discuss the progress AI research has made toward the goal of a machine capable of solving generalized problems, the limitations which this research has revealed, and several problem-solving programs which have been successful for more restrictive problem domains.

Many disciplines in the areas of social science, physical science, engineering, and mathematics assume a "problem solving" attitude towards their subject matter, and AI has been strongly influenced by the success of this approach. Now, in turn, AI is starting to contribute effective problem solving concepts to a number of the science and engineering disciplines. Perhaps the most important of these is the essential role of knowledge in problem solving. An elusive goal of AI research has been the development of a general purpose problem solver which could solve a wide range of problems with no special knowledge of the problem domain. This approach makes use of the so-called *weak methods* of solution such as blind search, hill climbing and means-ends analysis.[1] Allen Newell has proposed that such weak methods form the basis of operation of all intelligent systems, and this assumption has provided the inspiration for much of the research on general problem solvers. However, all weak methods dealing with more than trivial problems soon run into search spaces too large to handle without heuristics for limiting the search. It is the addition of task-dependent knowledge in the form of heuristic rules which allow weak methods to solve more complex problems in a finite amount of time. Even the strictly logic-based automated reasoning program AURA requires a "set of support strategy" by which the program user indicates which of the logic clauses are most important to solving the problem. This is a knowledge-based heuristic by which additional, problem-dependent knowledge can be introduced to facilitate a solution.

As mentioned earlier, the concept of a heuristic as an aid to problem solving was first introduced by George Polya in his 1945 Princeton University Press book, *How To Solve It.*[2] This delightful book contains a wealth of useful advice for college students struggling with mathematical difficulties, and it has had a considerable influence on several of the early AI researchers even though it was written before computers were available for implementing any of the heuristics Polya suggested. His students included both John von Neumann and Allen Newell, coauthor of the General Problem Solver.

In *How to Solve It* Polya outlines what he calls the "four phases" of problem solution. These include:

1. **Understand the problem** — That is, we must clearly answer the questions: What is the *Given*? What is the unknown or the *To Find*? What are the conditions or *constraints* within which the problem must be solved?

2. **Devise a plan** — The plan includes the calculations, computations, and constructions necessary in order to obtain the unknown. For AI programming this involves selecting the problem representation, solution algorithm, and applicable heuristics.

3. **Carry out the plan** — This involves what Polya calls filling in the details outlined by the plan and checking each step. In AI programming terms this includes both implementation in a programming language and proof of correctness.

4. **Look back** — Polya suggests that an important and instructive phase of problem solution involves reexamining the result and the path that led to it. This provides opportunity for detecting overlooked errors, fine tuning and optimizing the solution, and recognizing alternative solutions.

The largest section of Polya's small book is a "Short Dictionary of Heuristic." One of the heuristics Polya proposed was *working backwards.* Since this heuristic nicely illustrates the AI technique of *backward chaining,* we open the discussion of this chapter with a discussion of working backwards.

6.2 WORKING BACKWARDS

Consider the following tricky problem Polya proposed: *How can you bring up from the river exactly six quarts of water when you have only two containers, a four quart pail and a nine quart pail, to measure with?*

As the first step, Polya suggests the problem be clearly stated:

- What is given? (i.e. What is the starting state?)
- What is the unknown? (i.e. What is the goal state?)

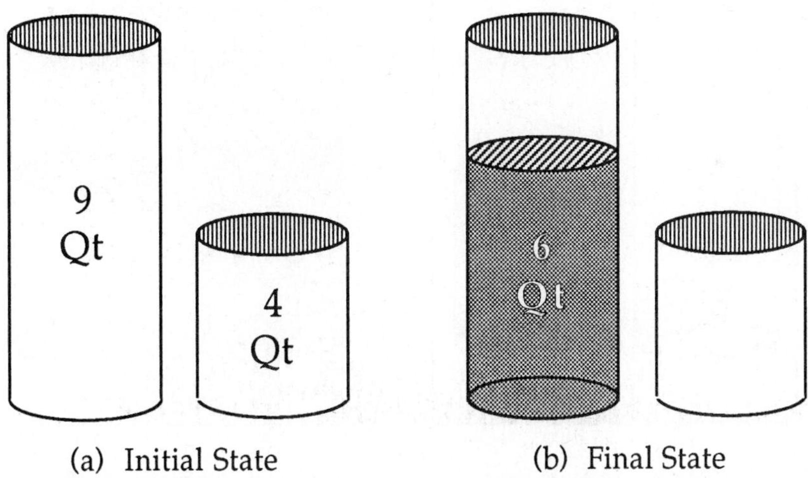

Figure 6-1 The 6-Quart Problem Given two pails of capacity 9 quart and 4 quart, how can we get exactly 6 quarts in a pail?

These two states are clearly stated by diagrams as shown in Figure 6-1 (a,b). One could begin with the two empty containers and begin a series of trial-and-error fillings and pourings in hopes of ending up with the required 6 quarts in the 9-quart pail, but it is not at all obvious what

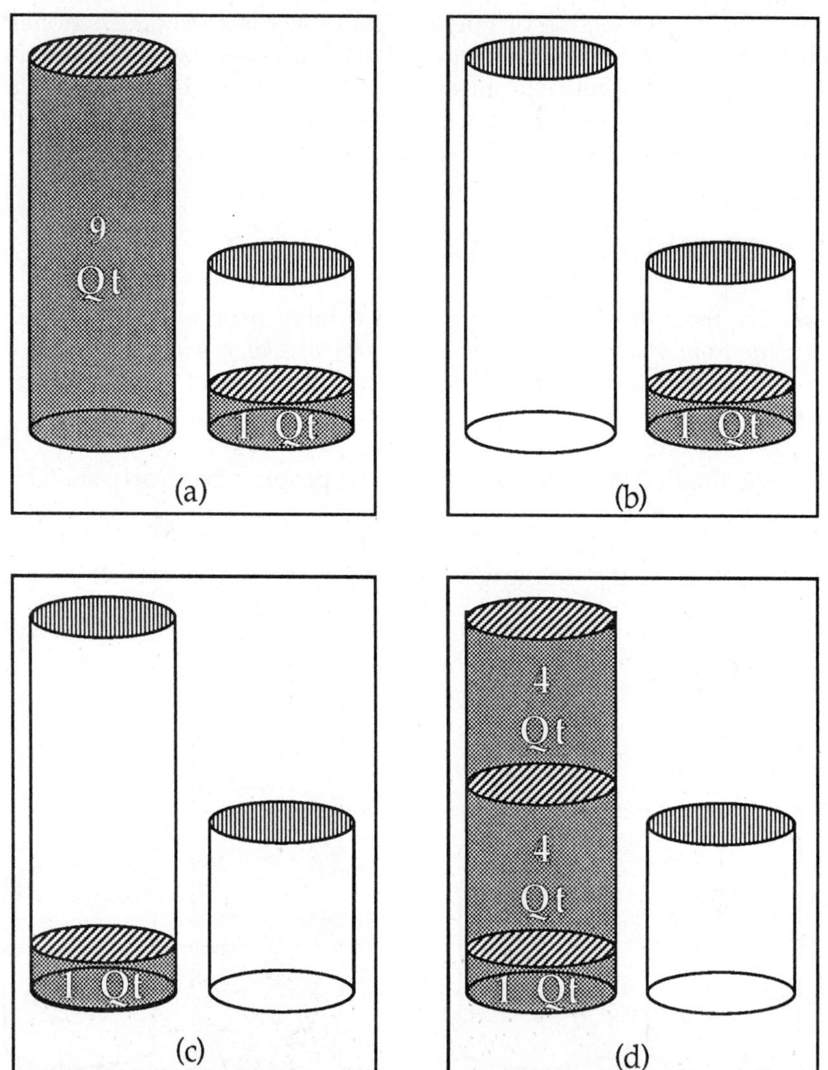

Figure 6-2 Working Backwards to solve 6-Quart Problem Path a, b, c, d takes us from the desired goal state to the initial state. To actually solve the problem, we would reverse this order.

heuristic would be optimal for guiding the forward search. However, Polya wisely observes that by starting with the goal state (Figure 6-1-b) and working backward, the solution is easily discovered.

The question is: What antecedent state leads to the desired goal state? Figure 6-2-a shows one possible combination. By pouring from a full 9-quart bucket into the 4-quart bucket which would start at 1 quart full, we would empty out exactly 3 quarts leaving the desired 6 quarts. Fine, but how do we get to the desired antecedent state, Figure 6-2-a? One possibility is from state Figure 6-2-b, by filling the empty 9-quart pail.

State 6-2-b can be reached from its antecedent, 6-2-c by pouring 1 quart from the 9-quart pail to the 4-quart pail. And state 6-2-c can be reached by filling the 9-quart pail and pouring off exactly 4 quarts twice. Thus, with 5 steps of working backwards (also known as backward chaining) we have gone from the desired final state to the given initial state. The actual solution would be accomplished by reversing the order of these operations.

Polya also made some amusing observations on **The traditional mathematics professor** which should be taken to heart by AI researchers and professors alike. When the traditional, absent-minded professor faces the blackboard with his back to the class, "He writes *a*, he says *b*, he means *c*; but it should be *d*." Some of the gems passed down from generation to generation include: "In order to solve this differential equation you look at it till a solution occurs to you." and "This principle is so perfectly general that no particular application of it is possible." Some of the general principles of AI published down through the years seem to share this feature.

6.3 GENERAL PROBLEM SOLVER

The success of the Logic Theorist prompted Newell, Simon, and Shaw to begin development of the General Problem Solver (GPS) in 1957. They were acutely aware of the limited domain in which the Logic Theorist operated, and Newell and Simon were both interested in the process of human problem solving. They studied the recorded "protocols" of human subjects thinking aloud as they solved puzzles and tried to codify the problem-solving techniques that emerged.[3] These techniques seemed to include:

- Means-ends analysis
- Planning
- Selective trial-and-error.

The objectives of the authors of GPS were two-fold: a) to develop an explicit, operational paradigm (model) for human problem solving, and b) to implement this model on the computer. The underlying consideration in the design of the GPS was to separate the general methods of problem solving from the task-specific data specifying the problem.[4]

In the research towards these goals, GPS made a number of important contributions to the progress of artificial intelligence. Perhaps the most significant of these is the concept of *means-ends analysis.*

MEANS-ENDS ANALYSIS

The fundamental idea of means-ends analysis is illustrated in Figure 6-3 which simply captures our intuitive problem solving behavior in more formal data structures such as *objects, operators, goals,* and the *task environment.* The goal of GPS is to transform, with the appropriate operator(s), the initial object into the desired object. There are obvious analogies between the initial object of GPS and the starting state of standard search techniques; the desired object of GPS and the goal state in searching; and the transformation operators of GPS with various search heuristics of the state-space search representation. GPS also exhibited some important differences and extensions to these concepts in an effort to introduce greater generality than traditional search techniques provided.

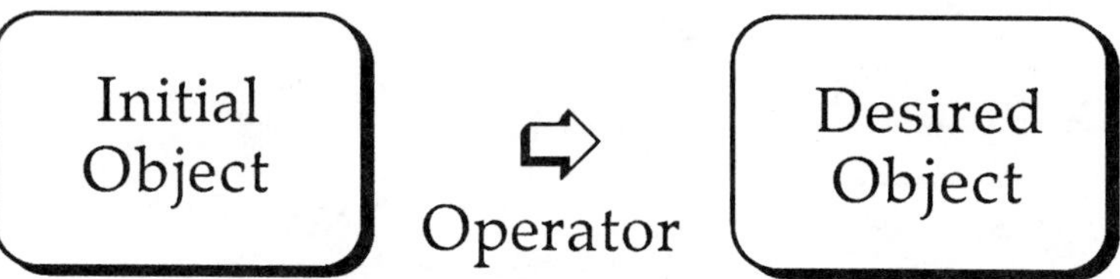

Figure 6-3 Means-Ends Analysis used in GPS Appropriate operators are selected to transform the initial object into the desired object in the situation-space of the problem.

This greater generality stems from several important novel ideas:

- The difference between the current object and the desired object can be classified by type and evaluated.

- Operators can be classified by the type of difference which may be reduced.

- If the operator can transform the present object into an object nearer the desired object, it is applied; otherwise, the object may be transformed into another object more appropriate for a given operator.

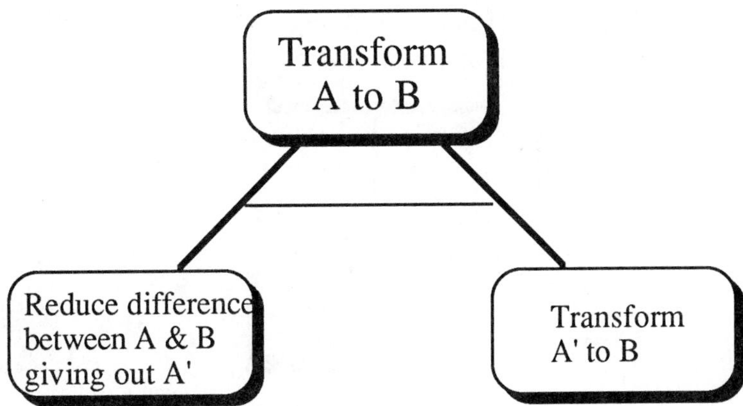

Figure 6-4 First Goal of GPS This AND graph involves sub-dividing the problem into an intermediate problem, A', and transforming that problem into the goal state, B. The recursive procedure stops when the primitive goal is reached, that is, when there is no difference between A' and B.

The basic data structure of GPS is the *goal* . The three primary goals are illustrated in Figures 6-4, 6-5, and 6-6 and are summarized below.

1. **Transform**: Transform object A into object B

2. **Reduce**: Reduce the difference between object A and object B by modifying object A.

3. **Apply**: Apply the operator Q to object A.

Thus, the general heuristic is to choose that goal which reduces the difference between the present object and the desired object. Almost by definition, this heuristic should provide a successful solution to the initial problem and clearly simulates our human processes of problem solving. It is not immune from the problems facing search techniques discussed earlier, such as the "false summit syndrome", but GPS does use several heuristics to prevent following false paths forever. These include:

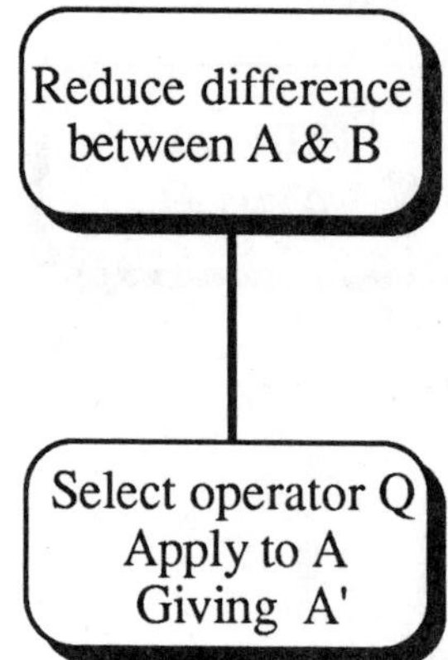

Figure 6-5 The *Reduce* Sub-Goal of GPS The goal of this operation is to reduce the difference between object A and object B by transforming object A into object A' nearer the goal B by means of a relevant operator Q.

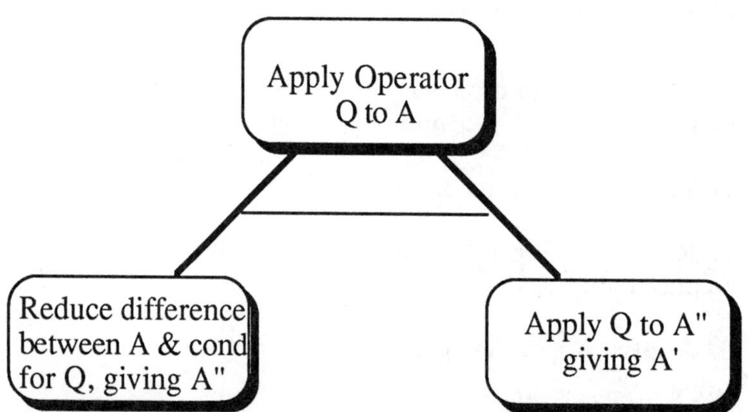

Figure 6-6 The *Apply* Sub-Goal of GPS This AND graph shows the goal of reducing the difference between object A and the preconditions required for operator Q, giving intermediate object A". Operator Q is then applied to A", transforming it into A' which is closer to the goal B.

1. Each goal should be easier than its parent goal.

2. Of a pair of AND nodes representing sub-goals generated by *transform* or *apply*, the second sub-goal attempted should be easier than the first.

3. A newly generated object should not be much larger (more difficult) than the objects occurring in the topmost goal.

4. Once a goal has been generated, the identical goal should not be generated again.

Let us look in more detail at how GPS would apply these ideas to solve one of the classic problems of AI.

EXAMPLE — MONKEY AND BANANA PROBLEM

We are given a room in which there is a hungry monkey, a bunch of bananas hanging from the ceiling, and a light-weight, movable box sitting in the corner. If the monkey were on top of the box directly beneath the bananas, he could reach them. Problem: How can the monkey get a banana?

To represent the problem for GPS we must specify the initial object (state), desired object (goal state), operators, the measurable differences between states, and a means-ends table relating operators to appropriate differences. The language of predicate calculus is convenient for this purpose. Note that operators may have preconditions and may result in changes to the present state which we represent as additions and deletions to a list of applicable predicates. Assuming the monkey is originally empty-handed at arbitrary position x, the box at position y, and the bananas hanging over position B, we may specify these as:[5]

Initial Object

AT(monkey,x)
AT(box,y)
EMPTY

Desired Object

HOLD(banana)

Operators

GOTO(z) — the monkey goes to position z
Precondition: none
Delete list: AT(monkey, x) where x is arbitrary
Add list: AT(monkey, z)

MOVE-BOX(w) — the monkey moves box to position w
Precondition: AT(monkey,x) $\wedge$ AT(box,x) — the monkey and the box are at the same place, x

Delete list: AT(monkey,x), AT(box,x)
Add list: AT(monkey,w), AT(box,w)

CLIMB — the monkey climbs on top of the box

Precondition: AT(monkey,x) $\wedge$ AT(box,x)
Delete list: AT(monkey,x)
Add list: ON(monkey,box)

GRASP(banana) — the monkey grasps the banana

Precondition: AT(box,B) $\wedge$ ON(monkey,box)
Delete list: EMPTY
Add list: HOLD(banana)

Differences

D_{xB} = difference between monkey position and desired object position
D_{yB} = difference between box position and banana position
D_{pB} = difference in state of the monkey's paw

Means-ends Table

Operators	*Differences*		
	D_{xB}	D_{yB}	D_{pB}
GOTO	X		
MOVE-BOX	X	X	
CLIMB	X		
GRASP			X

The last information we must specify before submitting the problem to GPS is the priority order of the differences. The ranking is in order of D_{pB}, D_{yB}, D_{xB} to reflect the fact that the state closest to the goal state is with the monkey on the box directly below the bananas and ready to grasp a banana. Reducing the distance between the monkey's paw and the banana would solve this trivial case.

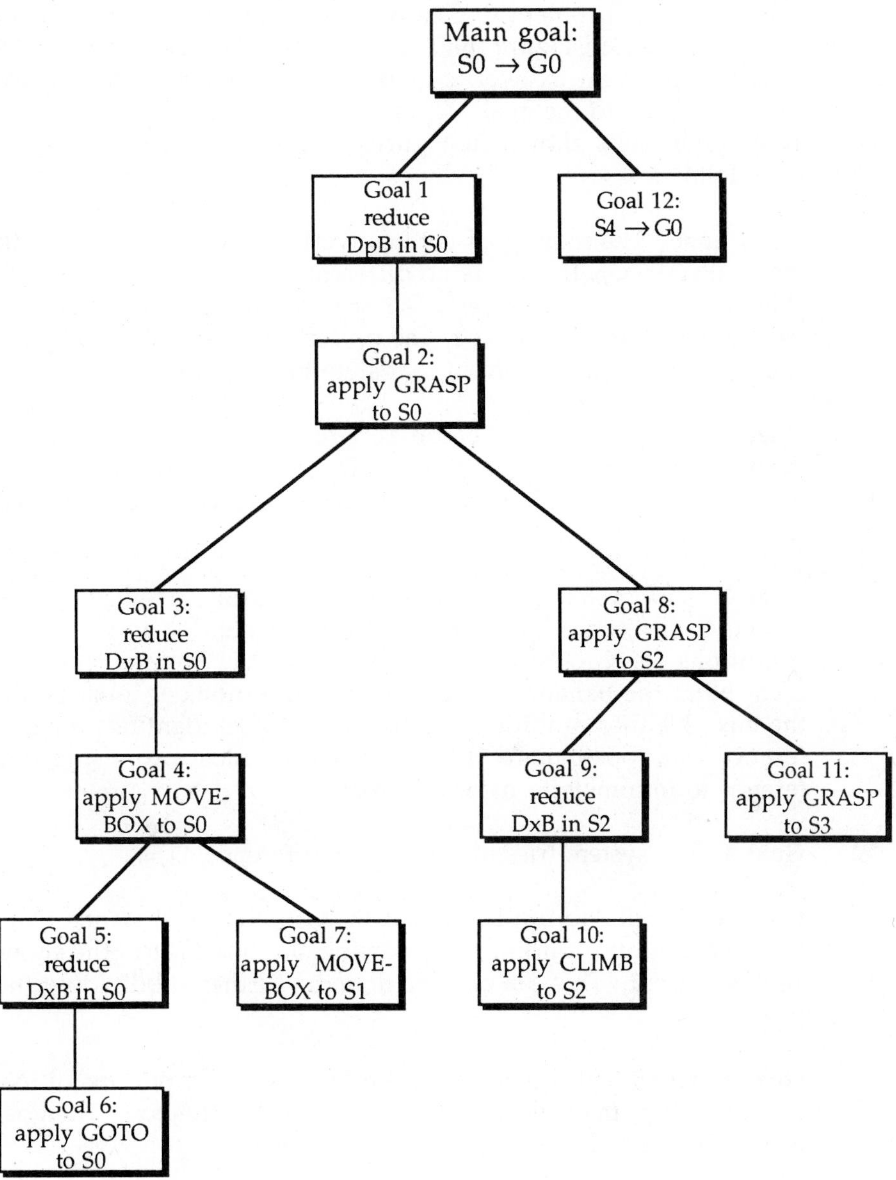

Figure 6-7 GPS Solution to Monkey-Banana Problem Note depth-first search for operator to convert initial state S0 → S1 and subsequent backtracking as conditions are met for other operators.

Submitting the problem to GPS will generate a series of problem reducing steps shown in Figure 6-7. Let us trace the operation of GPS as it solves the problem by working its way through the state space from the initial object to the goal. Figure 6-7 is a recursive combination of the basic operations shown in Figures 6-4, 6-5, and 6-6 which we interpret as follows:

Main goal: The main goal is to convert the initial state, S_0, into the goal state, G_0. If there is no difference, the problem is solved. Otherwise, as is the case here, GPS searches for a state which will reduce the difference between the present state and the goal state and then will transform from that state to the goal.

Goal 1: The first sub-goal becomes reducing the distance between the monkey paw and the banana, D_{pB}. The means-ends table indicates that the only operator available for achieving this goal is GRASP.

Goal 2: The system attempts to apply GRASP. However, GPS detects a difference between the present state, S_0, and the preconditions for GRASP. That is, to grasp the banana, the box must be at the banana position, B, and the monkey must be on the box. Neither condition is satisfied, but GPS identifies the difference D_{yB} (box-banana difference) as the most promising difference to minimize to meet this goal.

Goal 3: The system tries to reduce the difference, D_{yB}.

Goal 4: It tries to apply MOVE-BOX to reduce distance D_{yB}. However, the precondition on moving the box is that the monkey be present. This can only be done by further subdividing the problem.

Goal 5: GPS identifies the distance D_{xB} as the important difference to reduce in order to bring the monkey to the box. The goal is to reduce this distance.

Goal 6: The operator GOTO is applied to the monkey to move it to the box, thereby minimizing the distance between the monkey and box and satisfying the precondition for moving the box. This results in the new state, S_1.

Goal 7: We now backtrack through Goal 4 to Goal 7 which is to move the box from box position y to banana position, B. This is done by applying MOVE-BOX to state S_1, generating state S_2 with both monkey and box directly beneath the bananas.

Goal 8: Now backtracking takes us up through Goal 2 to Goal 8 where we try to apply GRASP again. Now the precondition AT(box,B) is satisfied, but the precondition ON(box,monkey) is still not.

Goal 9: Once again, GPS is called, now to reduce the vertical distance between the monkey and bananas. The means-end table indicates that the operator CLIMB is available for this task.

Goal 10: GPS applies CLIMB to state S_2 which results in a new state, S_3, with the monkey on top of the box.

Goal 11: Now backtracking through Goal 8 yields Goal 11 which is to apply GRASP. The preconditions for GRASP are now all met, and so it is applied to state S_3 to yield state S_4 in which the monkey has the banana in his paw.

Goal 12: Backtracking now takes us to Goal 12 in which a comparison of state S_4 with goal state G_0 indicates that the main goal has been achieved, that is, the monkey is grasping the banana in his paw.

6.4 CONTRIBUTIONS OF GPS

The example above illustrates a number of important contributions which the GPS program made to the world of AI research.

RECURSIVE PROGRAMMING

The GPS approach is intrinsically recursive in its operation. That is, after it "solves" each object by transforming it into the desired object or some new object closer to the desired object, it is faced with two choices: STOP because the desired object has been reached, or CALL GPS to solve the problem of reaching the desired object from the present object. This recursive procedure is most readily implemented in recursive languages such as LISP, Prolog, and Pascal.

PROBLEM REPRESENTATION AND EXTRAPOLATION

GPS was designed to separate the "data" from the "program". The goal of the authors of GPS was to write a problem solving program with an algorithm and heuristics which were independent of the particular problem under consideration. A particular problem would then be posed to the GPS in terms of the properly specified objects and operators, and GPS would then take over and solve the problem using its general transformation/reduction techniques. This approach was a huge conceptual leap beyond the Logic Theorist or any previous AI program.

The extrapolation from the success of the Logic Theorist, which operated in a limited domain, to the GPS which operated in a broader domain has an interesting analogy to the extrapolation made by Charles Babbage over a hundred years earlier. From his success in designing a prototype Difference Engine for solving polynomial equations of low order, Babbage extrapolated to the design of the Analytical Engine, a theoretical mechanical machine with essentially all of the features of the modern computer. GPS encountered some of the same extrapolation problems as did Babbage.

CYBERNETICS AND ADAPTIVE CONTROL

Cybernetics was the title of the seminal book by Norbert Weiner in 1948.[6] The term cybernetics stems from the Greek terms for "steersman" and was redefined by Weiner as the science of communication and control in machines or living organisms. It is frequently used it in connection with feedback and control theory.

The reason cybernetics is introduced at this point is that the GPS demonstrated the complex behavior typical of systems with built in feedback. By using the heuristic of well-informed, depth-first search, GPS often appeared to demonstrate keen intelligence in transforming from one object to the next. Herbert Simon has warned, however, that such complex behavior may often reflect more the characteristics of the problem space being explored than the complexity of the problem solving system. To illustrate the point, he cites the "parable of the ant", the apparently complex path of an ant through the pebbles on a beach.[7] The ant's tortuous path is more likely a result of implementing the simple goal "Return to anthill" in the presence of complex terrain than it is a demonstration of deep insight and decision making by the ant.

ACCOMPLISHMENTS OF GPS

As its name implies, GPS was written to solve problems of a general nature. It was designed to operate in a domain far broader than the propositional calculus of the Logic Theorist or the restricted domain of the chess or checkers board. To demonstrate the extent to which this objective was met we present a list of eleven non-trivial problems assigned to GPS and solved successfully. The work was part of the Ph.D. thesis of George Ernst who used a modified version called GPS-2-6.[8]

- **Missionaries and cannibals** — This famous problem introduced in the last chapter involves moving three missionaries and three cannibals from the left side of a river to the right side in a boat capable of carrying two persons. The constraint is that the cannibals must never outnumber missionaries for obvious reasons.

- **Symbolic integration** — GPS successfully evaluated the following integrals:

$$\int t \exp(t^2)\, dt$$

$$\int (\sin^2(ct) \cos(ct) + t^{-1})\, dt$$

- **Towers of Hanoi** — This classical puzzle involves transferring a number of disks from a source peg to a destination peg of a three-peg system with the constraint that the disks must preserve their descending order. A recursive solution was presented in Chapter 3. By the use of an optimal difference function, GPS was also able to solve the 4-disk problem without making a mistake.

- **Theorem proving using predicate calculus** — GPS proved the following theorem in the first order predicate calculus:

$$(\exists u)(\exists y)(\forall z)((P(u,y) \rightarrow (P(y,z) \wedge P(z,z))) \rightarrow$$
$$((P(u,y) \wedge Q(u,y)) \rightarrow (Q(u,z) \wedge Q(z,z))))$$

Interestingly, by posing the theorem in the formulation developed by Robinson, GPS automatically used the resolution principle for proving the theorem.

- **Father and sons task** — The task is to transport a father weighing 200 pounds and two sons each weighing 100 pounds across a river using a boat with a 200 pound capacity. While it appears that the task environment resembles the missionaries and cannibals problem, GPS required different objects, operators and differences in order to solve this problem.

- **Monkey task** — This problem used in the preceding example was invented by John McCarthy. The solution is an example of what is generally termed *common sense reasoning*, a feature which has been notoriously difficult to incorporate in computer programs of any type.

• **Three coins puzzle** — Three coins are sitting on a table with coin 1 and coin 3 showing tails and coin 2 showing heads. The problem is: How can all three coins be made to read the same in just three moves, each move of which requires two coins to be flipped. The three-move constraint was incorporated in the representation by defining the object to include a counter which registers the number of moves.

• **Parsing sentences** — Using a simple context-free grammar, GPS was able to parse the sentence:

Free variables cause confusion.

The role of grammars in artificial intelligence is considered in detail in Chapter 7.

• **Bridges of Konigsberg** — In the German town of Konigsberg a river contains two islands connected by seven bridges as shown in Figure 6-8. The problem is: What round-trip path leads from a starting point in town and crosses each bridge once and only once? The problem is interesting because *it has no solution,* a fact discovered by Euler in 1736 using topological arguments. GPS, of course, failed to solve the puzzle although it found a path containing six bridges. GPS was not able to prove that the problem had no solution since it did not have a representation of the topological information.

• **Polya's water jug problem** — This was a slight variation of the problem described in Figure 6-1. Means-ends analysis did not provide an effective heuristic for this problem, but GPS managed to stumble onto the solution. The difficulty was in the formulation of the difference function. A better difference function would make use of modular arithmetic.

• **Letter series completion** — This task is of the type used in aptitude tests in which the problem is : Given a series of letters, what are the next elements of the series? GPS was able to correctly complete the series:

B C B D B E __ __.

Note that this task involves recognition of a pattern and *inductive reasoning*. It was the only problem assigned to GPS which required inductive reasoning. The formulation of the problem was clumsy, but the solution demonstrated how problems can be solved by searching for a suitable description in a space of descriptions.

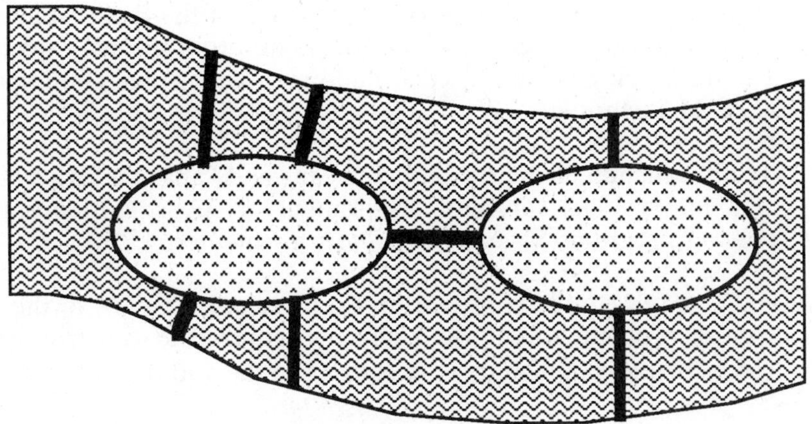

Figure 6-8 The Seven Bridges of Konigsberg Shown is a section of the Pregel River in Konigsberg with two islands connected by seven bridges. The problem is to find a round-trip path starting in town and traverse every bridge just once. Euler has proven that the problem has no solution.

LIMITATIONS OF GPS

With that impressive record of successful problem solving one might expect that GPS would be available on every machine with 64K or more of memory (the size of the machine used by Ernst). Why did its authors eventually recommend that GPS be laid to rest?

The two closely related difficulties which led to the demise of GPS can be summarized as:

- *The problem of representation*
- *The problem of generality*

As you read the list of problems which GPS successfully solved, the question probably came immediately to mind: How in the world would I represent problems as diverse as the missionary and cannibal problem, symbolic integration, and the bridges of Konigsberg? The answer was: With great difficulty!

The specific purpose of Ernst's thesis was to extend the generality of GPS while keeping its power constant. This involved extending the internal representation of GPS in such a way that its problem solving methods remained applicable while the domain of problems which could be represented was expanded. However, a very interesting effect became apparent in the process of generalizing the program: the more general it became, the less sensitive it became to the difference between the current object and the desired object. In fact, in the final version of GPS, it had even lost its initial capacity for doing propositional calculus.

Far from being a failure, GPS made significant contributions to the field of AI, including:

- Introduction of the concept of means-ends analysis as a useful tool for problem solving. A number of subsequent problem solving programs have made use of this method.

- "... a series of lessons that give a more perfect view of the nature of problem solving and what is required to construct processes that accomplish it ..." according to the authors of GPS.[9]

- A strong hint as to the most productive direction AI research should take on the issue of *general purpose* vs *narrowly restricted* problem domains. The success of AI applications such as expert systems, as we shall see later in the book, depends critically on restricting the domain of the problem solver to a limited region in which adequate knowledge is provided.

6.5 OTHER SUCCESSFUL PROBLEM SOLVERS

STUDENT

This program was the doctoral thesis of Daniel Bobrow of MIT and was designed to read and solve story problems at the high school algebra level. Consider the problem:

> *If the number of customers Tom gets is twice the square of 20% of the number of ads he runs, and the number of ads he runs is 45, what is the number of customers he gets?*

STUDENT used a clever linguistic pattern matching algorithm which interpreted questions in terms of basic formats such as:

- (HOW MANY * DO * HAVE)
- (WHAT IS *)
- (FIND *)
- (* IS MULTIPLIED BY *)

where the " * " is a dummy argument representing a string of arbitrary length.

The program was a LISP implementation based on the following four functions:

- **SEPARATE**: Separates each piece of information into the corresponding equation statements

- **TRANSLATE**: Convert the English equation statement into LISP

- **SOLVE**: Solves the LISP equations, working out from the most deeply nested equation

- **ANSWER**: Convert the LISP answer to English

In addition, in case SOLVE failed to do the job, a heuristic function REMEMBER was called to contribute such information as:

- (FEET IS THE PLURAL OF FOOT)
- (ONE FOOT EQUALS 12 INCHES)
- (DISTANCE EQUALS SPEED TIMES TIME)

STUDENT did an impressive job of parsing algebra word problems at the high school level, solving problems at least as fast as human could. However, it was possible to trick the program with ambiguous language.

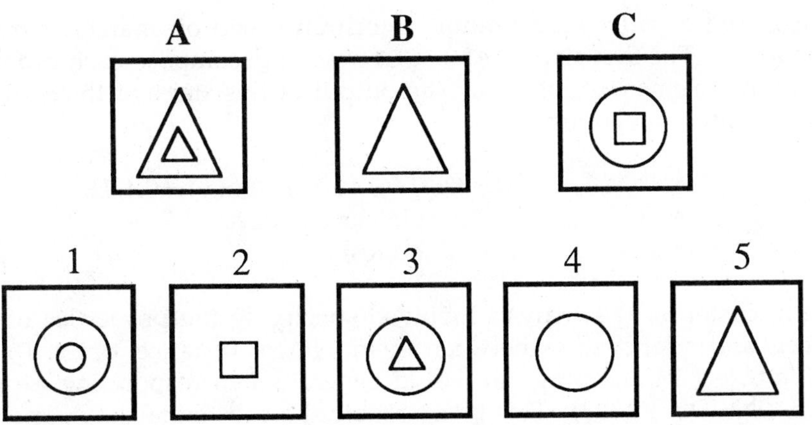

Figure 6-9 Geometric Analogy Problem "A is to B as C is to what?" This example taken from the 1942 *Psychological Test for College Freshmen* of the American Council on Education is typical of a "culture-free" problem given on IQ tests.

ANALOGY GEOMETRIC PROGRAM

Thomas Evans' Ph.D. thesis at MIT involved automating the process we usually call *reasoning by analogy*. His program called ANALOGY successfully solved geometric analogy problems of the type commonly found on IQ tests:[10]

Given the objects shown in Figure 6-9, A is to B as C is to what?

The motivation for selecting this problem for solution was three-fold:

- The problem required elaborate processing of complex line drawings, an intrinsically interesting problem and one which has considerable potential value for the analysis of other graphical data.

- The problem required explicit internal representations of both figures and transformations. It addition, it represented an interesting model of the human process of "reasoning by analogy".

- Problems of this sort are widely recognized as requiring considerable intelligence for their solution. As such they are typically used as general IQ tests for college admission and employment screening.

Evans used a pattern-recognition algorithm based on matching transformations. The first step of ANALOGY was to decompose each problem figure into elementary objects. The output of this stage of the analysis fell into three categories:

- DOT e.g., (DOT (0.4 . 0.8)) at (x,y) = 0.4,0.8
- SCC for "simple closed curve"
- REG for "all the rest"

The next step of the analysis involved specifying the properties of the objects and relationships between them. If, for instance, object P_2 lay inside object P_3, the program would generate a corresponding expression: (INSIDE P2 P3). This phase required a substantial set of analytic geometry routines for computing intersections of lines and curves, and tests for transformations such as scale changes, rotations, and reflections. The purpose of this phase was to determine what mapping carried objects A into objects B, and what mappings carried objects C into objects 1, 2, 3, 4, and 5.

The final phase involved generating rules which represented the mappings found in the preceding phase. The rules for (A → B) were then compared with the rules for (C → (list)) and if an exact match occurred for a particular element of the list, that was the answer. If no exact match occurred, the (A → B) rules were generalized until they did match one of the (C → (list)) set of rules. The generalization process involved a complex mechanism for manipulating rules and selecting those of greatest weight.

Evans program proved quite successful on this class of problems. He estimated that ANALOGY would correctly solve 15—20 such problems on a 30 problem test. This is approximately the same level of performance as that of an average high school student.

ANALOGY had the distinction of being the largest LISP program written to date (1964). In addition to developing a problem solving program which performed at a high level on the human IQ scale, Evans emphasized several concepts which have subsequently been recognized as important to AI research:

- LISP as a convenient and elegant language for writing and debugging complex programs.

- The importance of good internal representation of *objects* and *methods*. This principle has become the central theme of object-oriented programming.

- The central role of sophisticated pattern-recognition techniques for problem solving programs. We will return later to the study of pattern recognition.

STRIPS

Richard Fikes and Nils Nilsson designed STRIPS to guide a robot at the Stanford Research Institute in carrying out simple tasks.[11] The robot operated in a highly constrained world of rooms, doors, and boxes. The problems which STRIPS was assigned were of the type:

> *Go to ROOM3 and stack BLOCKB on BLOCKC and BLOCKA on BLOCKB.*

The heuristic employed is a combination of resolution-based theorem proving and the means-ends analysis described earlier.

STRIPS represents the world model by a set of well-formed formulas (wffs) expressed in predicate calculus. Given a goal state, G, the program tries to prove that G is satisfied by the current world model. If the current state is not G, then the difference between the two states is determined and a new world model reducing the difference is selected along with the relevant operator to generate the new world model.

Two important new concepts were introduced in STRIPS. The first is that of a *plan*, a sequence of operators to be used in reaching the goal. The second is the capacity for *learning*, by generalizing a set of plans and using the new plans over again. A later program, ABSTRIPS, even has the ability of deferring the details of its task solution until the main steps of the plan have been completed. This heuristic greatly pruned the search space of possible actions by the robot.

6.6 MATHEMATICS PROBLEM SOLVERS

SAINT AND SIN

Mathematics as perhaps the most problem-oriented of all disciplines has attracted some of the most sophisticated problem solving tools. One of the earliest efforts was SAINT, the 1961 Ph. D. thesis of James Slagle of MIT.[12] The domain on which SAINT operated was symbolic integration, a restricted domain with well-specified rules, many of which are recursively defined. Slagle selected LISP as the language in which to implement SAINT.

SAINT could handle the following elementary functions which were defined recursively:

- Constant functions
- The identity function
- The sum, product, and power elementary functions
- Trigonometric and logarithmic functions of the elementary functions, and their inverses.

SAINT was capable of performing symbolic integration at the college calculus level. On a performance test of 86 calculus problems (54 of which were from freshman level MIT calculus final exams), SAINT was able to solve 84 of the problems.

The next step toward developing a program with expert capabilities was the 1967 doctoral thesis of Joel Moses called SIN (for Symbolic INtegrator). According to its author, SIN was "capable of solving integration problems as difficult as ones found in the largest tables." [13]

MACSYMA

MACSYMA was one of the offspring of SAINT and SIN and has proven to be one of the most successful expert systems. In the Expert System section MACSYMA will be discussed in more detail. Here we summarize some of its features.

MACSYMA was designed in 1969 by Engleman, Martin, and Moses to assist mathematicians, scientists, and engineers in solving mathematical problems interactively. It is a knowledge-based system that can perform over 600 distinct operations such as differentiation, integration, solution of systems of equations, and matrix and vector operations.

MACSYMA is written in a combination of LISP and the MACSYMA programming language and contains more than 300,000 lines of code. It represents more than 100 person-years of development. MACSYMA runs on a number of mainframe and large minicomputers, including Digital Equipment Corporation's VAX and Honeywell Multics computer systems. It is currently available commercially from Symbolics, Inc., of Cambridge, MA.

SMP

Another powerful problem solver with features similar to MACSYMA is SMP (Symbolic Manipulation Program) from Inference Corporation of Culver City, CA. This system is written in "C" for efficient execution and runs on both IBM mainframe and VAX machines. It will eventually be implemented on M680X0 based microcomputers. Its capabilities include:

- Expansion and distribution of algebraic expressions
- Manipulation of polynomials and rational functions
- Solution of linear and certain non-linear equations
- Differentiation of any expression (numeric and symbolic)
- Integration of a wide class of expressions
- Evaluation of special functions (e.g., Bessel, Gamma, etc.)
- Performing matrix and tensor algebra
- Manipulation of both infinite and finite series, limits, and sums
- Numerical evaluation of any mathematical expression

muMATH

Users with more limited budgets or lesser needs may be interested in a remarkably capable microcomputer-based mathematical problem solver distributed by Microsoft, Inc. called muMATH. This interactive solver language has all the capabilities listed above for SMP, but with a more restricted range of most functions. It performs all numerical calculations in exact, infinite precision rational arithmetic. So, for instance, evaluation of the large number $10!^{10}$ yields:

```
39594086612242519324387557078266845
    776303882240000000000000000000000
```

To evaluate the symbolic expression:

$$\int (c\,x^2 + x\sin(x^2))\,dx$$

one enters the expression

```
INT (C*X^2  +  X*SIN(X^2),X);
```

and muMATH responds with

```
C*X^3/3  -  COS(X^2)/2
```

In addition to the interactive solver, muMATH, the system provides the parent language, **muSIMP** which has many of the features of LISP, including recursion.

The widespread availability of such symbolic problem solving languages should eventually have the same effect on symbolic mathematics analysis which the numeric languages had on data processing — a great reduction in the tedium and a greatly enhanced opportunity for exploring alternative solutions of difficult theoretical problems.

PROBLEMS AND PROGRAMS

6-1. Given a five gallon bucket and an eight gallon bucket, how can precisely two gallons be put into the five gallon bucket? Assume no level marking on the buckets and the presence of a nearby lake as a source and sink for water.

6-2. In Chapter 3 a number of search techniques were discussed, ranging from blind depth-first and breadth-first searches to the informed, optimal A* search. Which of these search techniques most closely resembles the means-ends analysis used in the GPS? Restate the search procedure you identify in the language of means-ends analysis (i.e., identify the objects, operators, and so on).

6-3. Re-interpret the hill-climbing search algorithm in terms of the GPS formalism. How might the GPS avoid some of the problems of hill-climbing such as the false summit, ridge, and mesa problems?

6-4. Compare the intellectual leap Charles Babbage made in jumping from the successful Difference Engine prototype to the Analytical Engine with the intellectual leap by Newell and Simon in jumping from the successful Logic Theorist to the General Problem Solver (GPS). What similarities are there and in what ways does the analogy break down?

6-5. The text implies that the control mechanism necessary for implementing the means-ends analysis of the GPS is equivalent to a feedback mechanism in traditional cybernetic systems. Write a brief justification of this assumption and use the feedback concept to describe and interpret the parable of the ant.

6-6. Write a LISP or Prolog program to solve the "Father and Sons" problem.

6-7. First work out a solution by hand to the "Three Coins Puzzle" and then write a program for a blind search solution in LISP or Prolog.

6-8. Ernst claims that the GPS was able to discover a 6-bridge solution to the Seven Bridges of Konigsberg problem. Sketch Figure 6-7, number the bridges, and trace out a 6-bridge solution.

6-9. Develop an effective representation for the Seven Bridges of Konigsberg problem and write a program using exhaustive search to find a solution which maximizes the number of bridges crossed once only.

6-10. Consider the problem of writing a program to perform inductive reasoning of the type discussed in the example of letter series completion. Specify and write a LISP program to test for suggestive letter patterns and extend the series.

6-11. A natural application of means-ends analysis is to the 15-puzzle. Specify how you would represent the problem, define the allowed operators, and indicate what measure you would use for the "distance to the goal."

6-12. Write and verify LISP functions to implement the data representation, operators, and difference calculations for the 15-puzzle described in problem 6-11.

6-13. Combine the functions developed in problem 6-12 into a LISP program to solve at least the initial moves of the 15-puzzle. Discuss the difficulties you encounter and propose backtracking procedures to resolve them.

6-14. GPS foundered on the shoal of generality. Discuss the proposition: *The generality gained with a general problem solver (weak methods) is paid for by increased difficulty in problem representation.*

6-15. Compare the algorithm used in GPS with that of STUDENT. Which is "more intelligent" as measured by comparison to human intellectual processes? From the information available in the text, which program do you believe would be easier to use in solving a high school algebra problem?

6-16. Consider the design of a geometric analogy program. Assuming only three kinds of shapes, triangles, squares, and circles, develop a representation for the features and transformations necessary for solving the analogy problem.

6-17. Using the representation scheme developed in 6-16, write a LISP or Prolog program to implement the geometric analogy algorithm.

6-18. Key in or load the Prolog symbolic differentiation program listed in Chapter 2 and use it to differentiate 10 expressions taken from a standard calculus text.

6-19. Using the Prolog program from Chapter 2 as a model, develop a symbolic integration program in Prolog for polynomial integration. Use the same recursive structure used in the Chapter 2 example.

6-20. Solve the following algebra and calculus problems using one of the commercial problem solving languages: muMATH, SMP, or MACSYMA.

a) Solve the following expression for x in terms of c:

$$x\,(3 + x^2) = 4\,x\,(1 + c^2) - x$$

b) Calculate the integral

$$\int (c\,x^2 + x \sin(x^2))\,dx$$

c) Calculate the truncated Taylor series expansion of $e^{\sin x}$ about the point x = 0 truncated to 6th order.

d) Use L'Hospital's rule to calculate

$$\lim_{x \to 0} \left[\frac{a^x - a^{\sin x}}{x^3} \right]$$

FOOTNOTES AND REFERENCES

1 Laird, John E. and Newell, Allen, "A Universal Weak Method: Summary of Results," *Proceedings of the Eighth International Joint Conference on Artificial Intelligence*, Vol. 2, pp. 771–773, 8–12 August, 1983

2 Polya, George, *How to Solve It,* Princeton University Press, Princeton, NJ (1945, 1973)

3 Newell, A. and Simon, H. A., *Human Problem Solving,* Prentice-Hall Book Company, Englewood Cliffs, NJ (1973)

4 Ernst, G. and Newell, A., *GPS: A Case Study in Generality and Problem Solving,* Academic Press, New York, NY (1969)

5 Shirai, Yoshiaki and Tsujii, Jun-ichi, *Artificial Intelligence — Concepts, Techniques, and Applications,* p. 72, John Wiley & Sons, New York, NY (1984)

6 Wiener, N., *Cybernetics*, John Wiley & Company, New York, NY (1948)

7 Simon, Herbert A., *The Science of the Artificial,* pp. 63–65, The MIT Press, Cambridge, MA (1969, 1981)

8 Ernst, George, W. and Newell, Allen, "Some issues of representation in a general problem solver," *Spring Joint Computer Conference* **30**, (1967). See also *Artificial Intelligence — The Information Technology Series,* O. Firschein (ed), pp. 31–48, ARIPS Press, Reston, VA (1984)

9 Ernst and Newell, (1969), *op cit*

10 Evans, T. G., "A Heuristic Program to Solve Geometric-Analogy Problems," *Spring Joint Computer Conference* **25**, (1964)

11 Fikes, R. E. and Nilsson, N. J., "STRIPS: A New Approach to the Application of Theorem Proving to Problem Solving," *Artificial Intelligence* **2**, pp. 189–208, (1972)

12 Slagle, J. R., "A Heuristic Program that Solves Symbolic Integration Problems in Freshman Calculus: Symbolic Automatic Integrator (SAINT)," *Report No. 5G-0001*, Lincoln Laboratory, MIT, Cambridge, MA (1961)

13 Feigenbaum, Edward A., Barr, Avron, and Cohen, Paul R. (eds), *The Handbook of Artificial Intelligence*, Vol.1–3, HeurisTech Press/-William Kaufmann, Inc., Stanford, CA (1981–82)

Chapter 7

COMPUTATIONAL LINGUISTICS

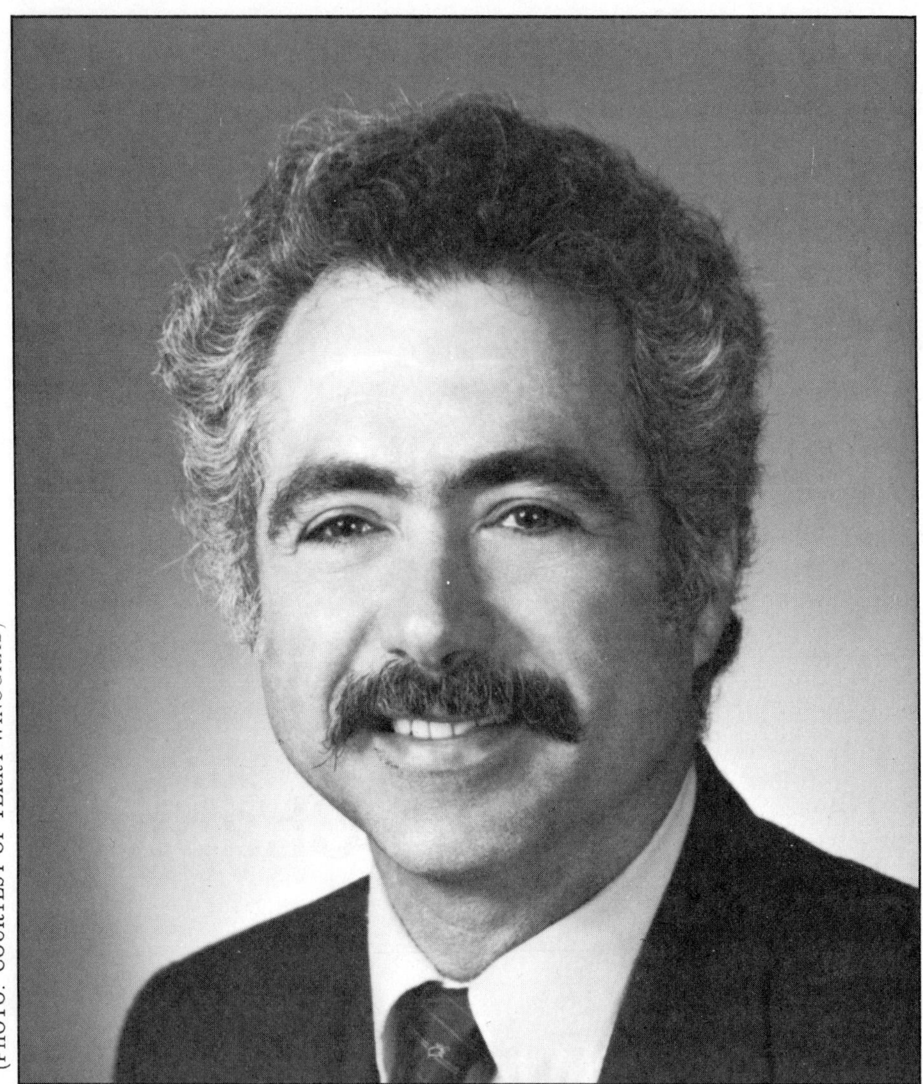

(PHOTO: COURTESY OF TERRY WINOGRAD)

Terry Winograd is Associate Professor of Computer Science and Linguistics at Stanford University. He received his B.S. from The Colorado College and his Ph.D. from MIT. He is best known for his work in AI and has written several books on computational linguistics including the influential *Understanding Natural Language* describing the blocks world of SHRDLU. His most recent book is the award winning *Understanding Computers and Cognition: A new Foundation for Design* which he coauthored with Fernando Flores. Winograd is a board member of the software workgroup, Action Technologies, and a founder and President of Computer Professionals for Social Responsibility.

7: COMPUTATIONAL LINGUISTICS

7.1 INTRODUCTION

We have been accumulating, chapter by chapter, the tools with which to build useful intelligent systems. These tools include basic search techniques, inference rules formalized by predicate calculus, and means-ends analysis. One remaining hurdle preventing us from putting these concepts to work in practical systems is the problem of communication between human and machine. This problem was recognized early in the history of AI research and has provided the impetus for many subsequent research efforts. It is particularly critical in the development of expert systems. Even the "world's leading expert", whether human or machine, is useless without the ability to communicate with human beings.

There are three elements to the human/computer communication problem: 1) understanding the computational mechanisms underlying the use of natural language, 2) communicating with the application program or expert system in a most natural and efficient format, and 3) encoding knowledge and human experience in a form appropriate for computer storage and manipulation. These three subjects often go under the headings of *computational linguistics, natural language processing* (NLP), and *knowledge representation* (KR), respectively, and are the subjects of the next three chapters. In this chapter we study some principles of computational linguistics. Computational linguistics is the science connecting linguistics with artificial intelligence, with significant overtones of psychology and philosophy. A central task of computational linguistics is extracting meaning from language in order to develop within the computer a deeper understanding of what it is reading. The question of understanding is a particular branch of the theory of the nature of knowledge called *epistemology*.[1]

One of the key tools available for research in computational linguistics is the theory of formal language. The theory of formal language has proven to be an important tool in many areas in addition to linguistics and artificial intelligence. Formal language methods have been applied productively in such diverse areas as:

- Pattern recognition in speech and visual scene analysis[2]

- Classification of plants using fractal geometry[3]
- Field and vector manipulation in finite element analysis.[4]

Computer languages themselves are classical examples of well defined formal languages. After sketching the nature of the difficulties in natural language understanding we outline the theory of formal language and its contributions to computational linguistics.

Success in natural language understanding, as in many hard areas of AI, has been slow in coming and achieved at great cost in thought and effort. It remains as the Holy Grail of AI research since success in creating a computer system which truly understands general human conversation and responds appropriately would pass anyone's test for artificial intelligence. Apart from the philosophical implications of such success, the practical applications are breathtaking. Consider, for example:

- **Removal of the language barrier to machines** — The percentage of the population using computers has historically been directly proportional to their ease of use. When machine language was the only channel of communication, an infinitesimal segment of society used computers. As computer languages improved in clarity and simplicity, more and more people used them. Now virtually everyone in the information industry who needs to can use at least a word processor or spread sheet, particularly on machines with transparent operating systems provided by a windows environment. When natural language interfaces are perfected, the last remaining psychological barrier should disappear, and computing machines will become accessible to everyone.

- **Removal of the language barrier between people** — The goal of *natural language translation* was one of the first attempted by AI researchers, and failure to reach it proved to be one of AI's greatest disappointments. Significant progress has been made since the early failures, but we are still incapable of general machine translation. Success in machine understanding of natural language will, by definition, solve the natural language translation goal.

- **Remove the "knowledge bottleneck"** — As we have frequently noted, knowledge is the basis for intelligent behavior of systems. The problem of getting knowledge into machines in a representation which allows the computer to understand it has been described as the "knowledge bottleneck." It remains as one of the chief hurdles in building expert systems. If the natural language understanding problem were solved, computers could in effect "read books" and collect and organize knowledge in much the same way humans do. This would not only solve the knowledge bottle-neck problem, but it would also provide the basis for machine learning, another of the great unsolved problems of AI.

7.2 UNDERSTANDING — THE PROBLEM

A perennial goal of AI research has been to write a computer program which understands what we say when we tell it things in English. Consider the following impressive segment of human (italics)/ computer (bold) dialog:

I took the dog for a walk this morning.
I understand.
It was raining, so I brought my umbrella.
I understand.

So far so good. However, the next segment offers a clue that all may not be well with our friendly, understanding computer program:

What did I do this morning?
I understand.

A truly intelligent system would have replied:

You took the dog for a walk.

In fact, the "understanding" but totally non-intelligent program which carried on this dialog may be written in LISP as:

```
(while (not (null? (read)))
      (display "I understand")
            (newline))
```

Clearly, it is much easier to write a program to carry on a dialog than it is to write a program which understands what is being said.

The problem of understanding natural language is not relieved any by the ambiguities and idiosyncrasies of the language. Consider the statement:

Time flies like an arrow.

Of course, we all know what this means — a little homily on the passing of time, or could it be a statement of the second law of thermodynamics that time reversal invariance does not hold for macroscopic systems? Or could it be an instruction to the physics class which up till now had been timing arrows? Or maybe it indicates the favorite menu item of a particular type of fly (cf. "Fruit flies like a banana").

Once the computer can interpret the various and sundry meanings of the statement above, we could pose even more complex statements of strange syntax, hyperbole, twisted epigrams, and oxymorons:[5]

- *Throw mama from the train a kiss.*
- *I'm just dying to find out my score on the last exam!*
- *Hell hath no fury like a bird in the hand.*
- *She was a little big and pretty ugly, but awful nice.*

and highly repetitive phrases like:

- *John, where Bill had had "had", had had "had had".*

In the face of the incredible complexity and ambiguity of natural languages, it is not surprising that the job of teaching computers to extract the correct meaning from a given English statement has not been easy.

What criteria could we use to determine if a program can, in fact, extract meaning from natural language? One convincing test proposed by Schank,[6] in the spirit of Turing's Imitation Game, is called the *Explanation Game.* This test states that any program with knowledge of a given situation (such as Winograd's block world in SHRDLU) which can give the right answer to questions concerning this world and *explain the reasoning which led to the answer* can be said to understand the situation. In fact, this characteristic of explanation capability is one of the features which distinguishes the more capable expert systems from the less capable ones. An equivalent test is the ability to paraphrase information which has been supplied to the computer. Any program which can paraphrase the information from a newspaper clipping, for example, without losing any of the information content can be said to understand the meaning of the article. Schank's group has produced a number of intelligent systems discussed later which can, among other things, successfully abstract newspaper clippings.

7.3 DEFINITIONS AND CLASSES OF UNDERSTANDING

A useful approach in any effort to teach computers to understand human communication is the study and mastery of the *grammar* of the language. According to Feigenbaum *et al*, "A grammar of a language is a scheme for specifying the sentences allowed in the language, indicating the syntactic rules for combining words into well-formed phrases and clauses."[7] As in any technical area, the study of grammar has generated its own peculiar terminology. Some terms are now defined.

Morphology — The study of form and structure of a word and its relationship to its roots and derived forms.

Parse — To break a sentence down into its component parts of speech with an explanation of the form, function, and syntactical relationship of each part. One can think of parsing as "picking apart" a sentence.

Lexical — Relating to the vocabulary, words, or morphemes (atoms) of a language. Derived from *lexicon*.

Syntax — The way in which words are put together to form phrases and sentences. The syntax of a grammar expresses the rules of the grammar.

Semantics — The study or science of meaning in language.

Pragmatics — The study of the use of language in context.

Ellipsis — The omission of a portion of a sentence necessary syntactically but for which the semantics are clear from context.

HENDRIX AND SACERDOTI CLASSIFICATION

Various classification schemes have been proposed to describe differing levels of sophistication of natural language processors. Hendrix and Sacerdoti propose three levels of sophistication of NLP systems based on the amount of knowledge of the outside world embedded in the system.[8] These three levels include:

Type A: No world-knowledge models

Type A language processors use only sentence syntax and semantics to analyze dialog. The upper end of the range involves compositional semantics in which the meaning of larger syntactic units is derived from the semantics of its component parts. Although these models do not benefit from knowledge of the world, they are particularly effective in applications to database query systems. An outstanding example of thus application is the LADDER naval database system discussed later.

At the lower end of this category are simple keyword or pattern matching algorithms which carry on the dialog with the human operator. This is the system used in Weizenbaum's ELIZA[9] which can hold what appears to be a reasonably "intelligent" conversation with the user. By any test of real understanding ELIZA fails badly. It is an intriguing program, however, which can at times show "real flashes of insight" by giving the illusion of understanding the context of a conversation and making associations which sometimes enhance the illusion of understanding. Type A processors like database query systems and ELIZA have no real knowledge of the world on which to perform logic and make deductions. Their only advantage over more sophisticated NLP systems is their simplicity and low cost in terms of development time and computer resources.

Type B: Systems that use explicit world models

Type B systems contain domain-specific knowledge usually in the form of semantic networks, frames, or scripts. This allows understanding of user input in terms of context and physical constraints. Such additional knowledge gives Type B systems a much higher level of performance by any measure of understanding. Two outstanding examples are Winograd's SHRDLU discussed later in this chapter and Cullingford's Script Applier Mechanism (SAM) which we examine in greater detail in the next chapter.

Knowledge in Type B systems consists of explicit models of the real objects being discussed, relationships among the objects, and explicit descriptions of the operations which can transform the objects and relationships. The price paid for this increased sophistication is much higher cost in system development and greater computer resources to handle the increased quantity of information and the greatly increased volume of inferences which can be drawn from the additional knowledge.

Type C: Systems that include human-world models

Computational linguistics research is gradually revealing the importance of beliefs, goals, and plans in effective communication between humans. These human characteristics act like filters through which the message must pass and be interpreted. The incorporation of such knowledge in NLP systems has become one of the most promising but difficult goals of AI research.

Hendrix and Sacerdoti illustrate the subtle nature of human communication with the following example. Grandma asks a young mother at Junior's birthday party, "When shall I light the candles?" Mother replies, in the presence of the children, "We'll have the cake as soon as the children wash their hands," from which Grandma deduces it will be about five minutes. How did Grandma reach this conclusion based on the conditional statement by Mother?

- The children want the cake.

- Mother's response to Grandma informs them that the only obstacle to eating cake is washing their hands.

- Knowing this, they will wash up promptly. This takes about five minutes.

Grandma knows that she should light the candles in five minutes because she knows the circumstances outlined above and she knows that Mother knows them and that Mother knows that Grandma knows.

A system with the levels of understanding illustrated by the Mother/Grandma dialog would be able to carry on conversation with humans which would be indistinguishable from strictly human dialog. No NLP system has yet been developed with this level of sophistication, but a number of research groups are studying elements of the problem. Some of the most impressive progress in incorporating social and emotional knowledge has emerged from the Yale group headed by Roger Schank.

SCHANK'S CLASSIFICATION OF UNDERSTANDING

Schank and Abelson[10] have shown that interpreting meaning from messages is much easier if the goals, beliefs, and expectations of the communicator is known. Such information provides the social and emotional context for interpreting input information and greatly improves the performance of the natural language system.

Schank's own classification system essentially starts with Type B above and refines the scheme into the following three classes briefly summarized as:[11]

1. Making sense

Input:	news from the UPI wire
Output:	a summary of the newspaper story

2. Cognitive understanding

Input:	A set of stories about airplane crashes, complete with knowledge structures about flight, airplanes,

and the circumstances of air travel

Output: Highly informed conclusions about what may have caused a recent crash

3. Complete empathy

Input: Remarks about a personal problem

Output: Thoughts that indicate that the person to whom you are talking appreciates your situation and can help you by explaining his/her similar experiences.

Schank indicates that systems now exist which operate at the level of **Making Sense** and that we are well into the **Cognitive Understanding** phase. The **Complete Empathy** level of understanding may never be reached by machines simply because of the structural differences between humans and machines. It is difficult to visualize a machine offering "advice to the lovelorn", particularly from personal experience!

7.4 TYPES OF GRAMMAR

Next we present the outline of several grammars which have been proposed for interpreting language and extracting meaning from it. We start with the most formal, mathematical grammar and subsequently introduce more knowledge-based grammars. In order to more effectively parse input sentences it is useful to understand the process by which sentences may be generated. The theory of formal language specifies the mathematical "machine" which can generate all sentences of a language.

CHOMSKY'S THEORY OF FORMAL LANGUAGE

The seminal work in the systematic and mathematical study of language syntax was done by MIT linguist Noam Chomsky in 1957.[12] Chomsky defines a formal language as a *set of strings* composed of a *vocabulary of symbol* according to *rules of grammar*. The set of strings correspond to the set of all possible sentences and may be infinite in number. The vocabulary of symbols corresponds to a finite alphabet or lexicon of words. The four rules of grammar are defined as:

1. Syntactic categories serving as *variables* or *non-terminal symbols* are defined. Examples of syntactic variables include <VERB>, <NOUN>, <ADJECTIVE>, and <PREPOSITION>.

2. Natural language words from the vocabulary are considered *terminal symbols* and are concatenated (strung together) to form sentences according to rewrite rules.

3. The relationships between particular strings of terminal and non-terminal symbols are specified by *rewrite rules* or *productions*. Examples of productions are:

<SENTENCE> ⇒ <NOUN PHRASE> <VERB PHRASE>
<NOUN PHRASE> ⇒ the <NOUN>
<NOUN> ⇒ student
<NOUN> ⇒ engineer
<VERB PHRASE> ⇒ studies

Note that variables are enclosed in <...>, and terminal symbols are lower case.

4. The start symbol, S, or <SENTENCE> is distinguished from the productions and causes the generation of all possible sentences according to the productions specified in (3). This set of sentences is called the *language generated by the grammar.* The simple grammar outlined here would generate the sentences:

The student studies
The engineer studies

following the rewrite rules to substitute words for phrases as follows:

<SENTENCE>
<NOUN PHRASE> <VERB PHRASE>
The <NOUN> <VERB PHRASE>
The student <VERB PHRASE>
The student studies.

Note how application of each production gradually converts the abstract representation of a sentence into a concrete instance of an English sentence. The grammar acts as a machine which "cranks out" all possible sentences allowed by the rewrite rules.

This may seem like rather unexciting stuff, but note the following very valuable contributions Chomsky's theory of formal language made to computational linguistics. First, the grammar specifies precisely how all possible sentences are formed from a given vocabulary and set of productions. Second, by reversing the process, the rules for parsing sentences into their syntactic categories is completely specified. Parsing algorithms are the first phase of essentially all NLP systems.

Chomsky was able to show that his formal theory could generate four types of grammars. If the grammar is defined as the quadruplet:

(VN, VT, P, S)

where

V = vocabulary
N = non-terminal symbols from the vocabulary
T = terminal symbols from the vocabulary
P = productions of the form $X \Rightarrow Y$
S = the start symbol

then the four types have the following characteristics:

Type 0: Recursively Enumerable Language — This type has no restrictions on the form of the productions and consequently is too general to be useful. However, sentences generated by Type 0 grammar will be recognized by a Turing machine, the generalized conceptual computer which laid the groundwork for present day machines.[13]

Type 1: Context-Sensitive Language — In this type of grammar rewrite rules of the form $X \Rightarrow Y$ are restricted by the rule that the right hand side, Y, must contain as many or more symbols than the left hand side, X. The allowed productions are of the form:

$$u\,X\,v \Rightarrow u\,Y\,v$$

where

X = single non-terminal symbol
u,v = arbitrary strings including the null string
Y = non-empty string over vocabulary V

This form of production (rewrite rule) is equivalent to saying, "X can be replaced by Y in the context u,v." Consider for example, the grammar:

$S \Rightarrow aSBC$
$S \Rightarrow aBC$
$CB \Rightarrow BC$
$aB \Rightarrow ab$
$bB \Rightarrow bb$

bC ⇒ bc
cC ⇒ cc

where	S	= Start symbol
	A, B, C	= Variables
	a, b, c	= terminal symbols

To derive one of the sentences generated by this grammar, we substitute according to the rewrite rules:

S
aSBC
aaBCBC
aaBBCC
aabBCC
aabbCC
aabbcC
aabbcc

It is easily shown that this particular grammar generates strings of the pattern *abc, aabbcc, aaabbbccc, …* .

Type 2: Context-Free Language — In *context-free* grammars the left-hand side must contain only a single non-terminal symbol. Context-free means that each word in the language occurs in accordance with rules which are not dependent on the context in which the words are used. This grammar most closely represents natural language. Using the particular productions:

S ⇒ a S b
S ⇒ a b

sentences of the form ab, aabb, aaabbb, and so on are generated.

To see how a context-free grammar can generate natural language sentences, consider the following rewrite rules:

<SENTENCE> ⇒ <NOUN PHRASE> <VERB PHRASE>
<NOUN PHRASE> ⇒ <DETERMINER> <NOUN>
<NOUN PHRASE> ⇒ <NOUN>
<VERB PHRASE> ⇒ <VERB> <NOUN PHRASE>
<DETERMINER> ⇒ the
<NOUN> ⇒ wolves
<NOUN> ⇒ mice
<VERB> ⇒ eat

Sentence structure as well as the generation of sentences is explicitly presented by writing down the *derivation tree* or generating the *parse tree*:

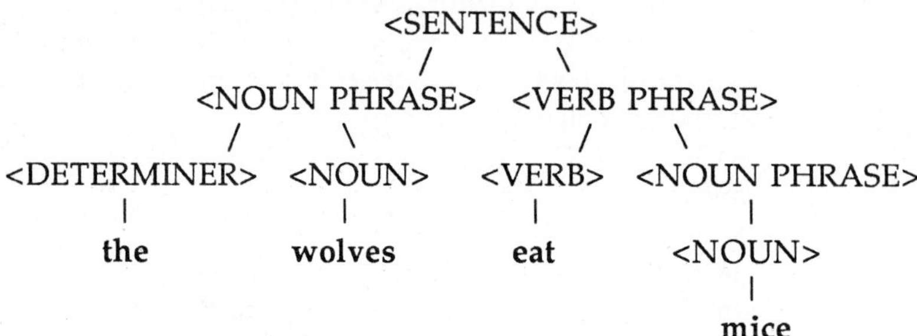

So this context-free grammar has generated the sentence:

The wolves eat mice.

Unfortunately, this grammar also generates the sentence:

The mice eat wolves.

Although the second sentence is probably unrealistic semantically, it is completely legal syntactically. This illustrates an important point in computational linguistics: ***syntax is concerned only with structure and not with meaning.***

In the next section a Prolog program is presented for automating the generation of all possible sentences.

Type 3: Regular Language — This class of language is also called a *finite-state grammar* and generates sentences according to the productions:

$$X \Rightarrow aY$$

$$X \Rightarrow a$$

where

X, Y = single variables
a = single terminal.

For instance, a regular grammar to generate an arbitrary string of binary digits is given by:

$$S \Rightarrow 0S$$

$$S \Rightarrow 1S$$

$$S \Rightarrow 0$$

S ⇒ 1

Note that as we move from Type 0 to Type 3 languages we move from more general to more restrictive grammars. That is, every regular grammar is context-free, every context-free grammar can generate context-sensitive sentences, and every context-sensitive grammar is of Type 0 since anything goes in this unrestricted type. The more restrictive the rewrite rules, the simpler become the languages generated.

LIMITATIONS OF FORMAL LANGUAGE IN NLP

Context-free grammars are particularly useful in the design of programming languages and large segments of natural languages. However, Chomsky has shown that natural languages such as English cannot be completely represented by either general grammars or context-free grammars (Types 3 and 2, respectively). For instance, Types 2 and 3 cannot generate such constructions as *respectively*. Since each type is a subclass of the previous type, the question then is: Can English be described as the more general Class 1 language?

Although Chomsky did not answer this question, he did suggest that phrase-structure grammars such as Type 0 — 3 be rejected for interpreting natural language for the following reasons:

1. They make the interpretation of English unnecessarily clumsy and complex.

2. Sentences with different meaning are assigned identical structures, for instance:

   The cook is baking.
   The cake is baking.

3. These grammars provide no basis for identifying the similarity in meaning of the following sentences:

   Steve climbed a mountain.
   A mountain was climbed by Steve.
   Did Steve climb a mountain?
   What mountain did Steve climb?

The importance of the conclusion that *syntax alone is not sufficient for interpreting natural language* should be emphasized. That is, while grammar is essential for understanding natural language (i.e. a necessary condition), the rules of syntax do not provide adequate information for understanding language (i.e. syntax alone does not provide a sufficient condition).

There is an interesting analogy between the use of grammar for language interpretation and the use of logic for problem solving. That is, propositional logic may be adequate for solving logical problems in a limited, well-defined problem domain but fails in larger, more general real-world domains. Similarly, rules of syntax may be adequate for completely specifying both structure and meaning for restricted domains such as computer languages but fail in the larger domain of natural (human) languages.

A PROLOG LANGUAGE GENERATOR

It is a relatively straightforward process to implement the natural language generator presented in the discussion of context free grammar in one of the languages of AI. Here we present a Prolog program for specifying the grammar of a language and generating all allowed phrases of the language at any level from discrete words up to full sentences.

```
%Natural Language Generator Program
%Using the GRAMMAR specified in the
%phrase structure defined below,
%this program generates all possible
%elements, phrases, or sentences of the language.
%The general syntax used in calling the program is:
%        CONSTRUCT(structure,X)?
%
phrase(sentence, [noun_phrase, verb_phrase]).    %Define
phrase(noun_phrase, [determiner, noun]).         %sentence
phrase(determiner, [the]).
phrase(noun, [cat]).
phrase(noun, [hat]).
phrase(noun, [rat]).
phrase(verb_phrase,[tverb,noun_phrase])   %Transitive verb
phrase(verb_phrase,[iverb,prep_phrase])   %Intransitive verb
phrase(prep_phrase, [prep, noun_phrase])  %Preposition
phrase(prep, [on]).
phrase(prep, [under]).
phrase(iverb, [sat]).
phrase(tverb, [ate]).

composed_of([], []).                      %Grounding case
composed_of([P, ..Tail], Total) :-        %Recursive definition
   construct(P, Headparts),               %Finds the elements of
   composed_of(Tail, Tailparts),          %each list of parts of
   append(Headparts,Tailparts,Total)            %phrases and
                                                %concatenates
word(the).                                %List the VOCABULARY
word(cat).
word(sat).
word(on).
```

```
word(hat).
word(ate).
word(rat).
word(under).

construct(X,P) :-                    %Predicate to construct
    phrase(X,Elements),              %list P of words of grammar
    composed_of(Elements,P)          %from phrases which may be
construct(X,[X]) :- word(X).         %complex or simply words.
append([],L,L).                      %Need append to add
append([X,..L1],L2,[X,..L3]) :-      %words to list
    append(L1,L2,L3).
```

The grammar of the language is defined by the phrase and word terms. A phrase is defined in terms of other phrases or terminal words and represent variables or non-terminal symbols in the theory of formal language. The word terms represent terminal symbols. The three rules used to generate sentences from the language include:

`append(L1,L2,L3)` Appends list L1 to list L2 to create list L3.

`construct(Phrase,List)` Constructs a list of words specified by the phrase structure hierarchy. It calls **composed–of** to generate the words or subphrases of each phrase.

`composed_of(Elements,Phrase)`
Recursively appends words from the Elements list into the Phrase list to generate the output list.

We can use the program by calling CONSTRUCT to generate all possible phrases of the language. First let's list all nouns available:

```
:construct(noun,Nouns)?

Nouns = [cat]
Nouns = [hat]
Nouns = [rat]
```

Next we construct all well-formed prepositional phrases:

```
:construct(prep_phrase,PP)?

PP = [on, the, cat]
PP = [on, the, hat]
PP = [on, the, rat]
PP = [under, the, cat]
PP = [under, the, hat]
PP = [under, the, rat]
```

Next we examine all verb phrases, both transitive and intransitive, contained in the language:

```
: construct(verb_phrase,VP)?

VP = [ate, the, cat]
VP = [ate, the, hat]
VP = [ate, the, rat]
VP = [sat, on, the, cat]
VP = [sat, on, the, hat]
VP = [sat, on, the, rat]
VP = [sat, under, the, cat]
VP = [sat, under, the, hat]
VP = [sat, under, the, rat]
```

Finally, we put it all together by constructing all well-formed sentences generated by the language:

```
: construct(sentence,Sentence)?

Sentence = [the, cat, ate, the, cat]
Sentence = [the, cat, ate, the, hat]
Sentence = [the, cat, ate, the, rat]
Sentence = [the, cat, sat, on, the, cat]
Sentence = [the, cat, sat, on, the, hat]
Sentence = [the, cat, sat, on, the, rat]
Sentence = [the, cat, sat, under, the, cat]
Sentence = [the, cat, sat, under, the, hat]
Sentence = [the, cat, sat, under, the, rat]
Sentence = [the, hat, ate, the, cat]
Sentence = [the, hat, ate, the, hat]
```

etc..........., until, finally

```
Sentence = [the, hat, sat, under, the, cat]
Sentence = [the, hat, sat, under, the, hat]
Sentence = [the, hat, sat, under, the, rat]
Sentence = [the, rat, ate, the, cat]
Sentence = [the, rat, ate, the, hat]
Sentence = [the, rat, ate, the, rat]
Sentence = [the, rat, sat, on, the, cat]
Sentence = [the, rat, sat, on, the, hat]
Sentence = [the, rat, sat, on, the, rat]
Sentence = [the, rat, sat, under, the, cat]
Sentence = [the, rat, sat, under, the, hat]
Sentence = [the, rat, sat, under, the, rat]
```

This example illustrates several interesting features of grammars. One is that there are many syntactically correct sentences possible from a relatively small vocabulary. This suggests the exponential explosion of sentences possible in any language of realistic size. Secondly, although well-formed sentences are grammatically correct, many do not make sense semantically. The next section presents various attempts to integrate semantics with grammar.

7.5 EXTENDED GRAMMARS

The main theme of the language-generating grammars (and parsers built on inverting them) is that language can be analyzed by breaking it down into phrases and breaking the phrases down into phrases until the terminal leaves (words) appear which comprise the sentence. Thus these grammars are frequently referred to as *phrase-structure grammars*. While they have provided valuable insight into the structure of language and valuable tools for parsing natural language, they have proven inadequate for extracting meaning from the sentences analyzed. For automated systems to understand natural language they must have the capability of extracting the full and unambiguous meaning of input sentences. How can we bridge this gap between syntactical knowledge and semantic knowledge?

By induction based on several previous solutions to difficult problems presented earlier, you should at least suspect that the answer is: *by adding knowledge to the system!* If that was your response, you're right! Each of the grammars presented next extend the strictly phrase-structured grammars by incorporating additional knowledge — knowledge of a deeper structure of sentences, knowledge of the purpose of sentences, knowledge of the case of words, or even knowledge in the form of exhaustive enumeration of all possible meaning of a given sentence or phrase. These are the extensions to phrase-structure grammar which we summarize next.

TRANSFORMATIONAL GRAMMAR

In an attempt to overcome some of the limitations of the strictly phrase-structure grammars, Chomsky[14] proposed that language must be interpreted at two levels: the *surface structure* which may be analyzed and parsed with phrase-structure grammar, and the underlying structure *(deep structure)* in which the semantic information resides. The task of transformational grammar is to connect these two levels. Since the information content of the first two sentences concerning mountain climbing above are identical, transformational grammar should generate an identical deep structure to represent the two sentences. The idea of transformational grammar resembles the conversion of arbitrary predicate calculus expressions into the normal clause form.

In transformational grammar, transformations are introduced to properly transform between present and past tense and between singular and plural objects. Transformations are provided to transform between active and passive tenses of sentences. A dictionary (lexicon) is introduced for use with context-free grammar in parsing the surface structure, and transformation rules are defined for transforming from the surface structure to the deep structure.

Since several statements distinct in structure but identical in semantic content are mapped into the same deep structure, queries directed to the system are interpreted at the deep level and answered intelligently. In order to do this, transformational grammar must provide two additional elements missing in phrase-structure grammars:

- **Phonological component** — This element translates from the deep structure back to the surface structure to make the sentence sound correct.

- **Semantic component** — This element determines the meaning from the deep structure representation.

This basic approach for deriving meaning from transformational grammar is called *interpretive semantics.* Its basic assumption, that syntax and semantics can be cleanly distinguished, has been challenged by more recent work. The concept representing meaning through a deeper structure continues to inspire research, however. We will return to it in the next chapter under the topic of *conceptual dependency.*

SYSTEMIC GRAMMAR

One reason that phrase-structure grammar fails to extract meaning from syntax is the important role which social context plays in natural language interpretation. One of the first attempts to acknowledge the role of context in understanding was by Michael Halliday of the University of London in his systemic grammar.[15] The key concept in systemic grammar is the *function* or *purpose* of the language in question. The study of the functional context of language is now called *pragmatics.* Halliday defines three functions which every sentence generally serves:

- **Ideational Function** — This function provides the reader with the basic *idea* of what the sentence is trying to convey. Analyzing a sentence or clause in terms of its ideational function answers such questions as:

    - Who is the actor (object)?
    - What kind of process does the clause describe?
    - Are there other participants such as direct or indirect objects?

- Are time and place circumstances described?

The basic concept of the ideational function of a sentence and its elements is expanded and formalized by what are called *case grammars*.

- **Interpersonal Function** — The interpersonal function concerns the social context of the sentence. This context indicates the purpose or *mood* of the sentence such as asking a question, answering a question, making a request, or giving information. Punctuation specifying the mood of a sentence in written expression helps indicate the interpersonal function. Mood punctuation is a thoughtful feature of Prolog which makes it easy to learn and intuitive to use.

- **Textual Function** — This function indicates the coherence of the present sentence with knowledge of what has come before, the theme of the question or statement, and an indication of what is new and what is given. The given portion becomes the connection with what the listener already knows.

Halliday classifies his grammar by four categories:

1. **Units of language** — A hierarchical structure of sentence, clause, group, word, and morpheme.

2. **Structure of Units** — Each unit is made up of one or more units of lower rank which serve a particular role such as subject or predicator.

3. **Classification of Units** — Units are classified by the role to be filled at the next higher level such as verbal for the predicator and nominal for the subject.

4. **System** — A system is a list of available options for the speaker. Options to use certain clauses are constrained by the nature of the clause (dependent or independent) and by the choice of previous options. The system effectively provides the rules of syntax and is represented by a network structure.

By adding these pragmatics of the context of language, the meaning potential becomes much clearer and much ambiguity is removed. Systemic grammar's embedding of the purpose of sentence units within the grammar itself is called *generative semantics* and is distinct from the transformational grammar of Chomsky. It provided the basis for the dialog used by Terry Winograd in his highly successful block manipulation program, SHRDLU.

CASE GRAMMARS

Any former Latin students will recall the struggle with "endings" of nouns. These endings identified the *case* of the noun and included nominative, genitive, accusative, dative, and ablative. The contribution of these case endings was in helping the reader identify the function which the noun played within the sentence (the subject, the direct object, possession, and so on). Thus, the noun carried its own "tag" telling how it was to be used, and the matter of word order within the sentence became much less important. English contains remnants of case in the use of *I, me, mine, thine, thee, thy,* and *thou*.

The case for case was made again by C. Fillmore in an article with that name in 1968.[16] In this extension of transformational grammar, Fillmore proposed that noun phrases are always related to verbs in uniquely identified ways which indicate the "deep case" of the noun phrase. The following deep cases were proposed:

Agent — the instigator of the event

Counteragent — the force or resistance against which the action is carried out

Object — the entity that moves or changes or whose position or existence is in consideration

Result — the entity that comes into existence as a result of the action

Instrument — the stimulus or immediate physical cause of an event

Source — the place from which something moves

Goal — the place to which something moves

Experiencer — the entity which receives or accepts or experiences or undergoes the effect of an action.

Verbs were designated as having *case frames* which, for verbs such as *grow*, are defined as:

[(OBJECT) (INSTRUMENT) (AGENT)]

which means that the verb grow may or may not have an object, instruments, or agents. For instance:

Grass grows. [Intransitive use; no object or instrument]
Farmers grow corn. [Transitive use; no instrument]
Grass grows with sunlight. [Intransitive use; no agent]

The case frame of the verb serves as a *template* by which the sentence may be interpreted. Case frames for verbs resemble the predicates with associated argument lists in predicate calculus and Prolog. They may be represented by *semantic network* structure discussed in Chapter 9.

The case grammar can resolve certain ambiguities that have baffled previous grammars. Its contributions included:

1. By ordering cases, ambiguities as to which noun in a sentence was the subject were removed. The highest ranking case noun becomes the subject, for instance.

2. While sentences such as *The cook is baking* and *The cake is baking* are still both legitimate, nonsense sentences such as *The cook and the cake are baking* are avoided since *cook* and *cake* are of different cases, and different cases may not be conjoined.

3. The similarity but inverse nature of such verb pairs as *buy* and *sell* or *teach* and *learn* are distinguished by different case frames.

By applying rules of deep case, this grammar is able to recognize the equivalence of such statements as:

John opened the door
The door was opened by John

and give them the same representation. While this seems like a relatively minor triumph in natural language understanding, the effort necessary to achieve even this simple intuitive result illustrates the difficulty of extracting meaning from grammar.

SEMANTIC GRAMMARS

The final grammar we consider is the semantic grammar of Gary Hendrix used to build the natural language tool LIFER[17] and the database query system LADDER described by Hendrix and Sacerdoti.[18] Semantic grammar represents a three-pronged attack on the problem of natural language processing, and LIFER and LADDER demonstrate the success of the strategy. The three prongs include:

- **Restrict the domain** — LIFER is designed to provide a "natural language front-end" for a variety of applications such as information retrieval systems and database management systems. For a given system there is a relatively small set of objects such as <PERSON> and <SHIP> about which the system must be knowledgeable.

- **Integrate semantics into the syntax** — LIFER is designed as a performance program. That is, it carries out searches to answer questions posed in a natural language format. The user using LIFER to build a particular query system specifies the format of questions similar to that used in the program STUDENT. This restricts the range of sentences which the grammar can generate to a manageable set for which matching templates can be built. Secondly, the non-terminal symbols (called meta-symbols) are very narrowly defined to such semantically-based syntactic categories as <PERSON> and <ATTRIBUTE> instead of broad categories such as <NOUN>. Thus the semantics are intrinsic to the fine-grained syntax of the grammar. Finally, after the narrow categories are drawn, they are exhaustively enumerated. For example, the variable <PERSON> may be defined as:

  <PERSON> = the set[Tom, Dick, Harry]

  This feature again dramatically restricts the range of sentences with which the grammar must deal.

- **Excellent user interface** — To make life easier for the user both in designing the query system and in using it, LIFER provides a very friendly user interface. It includes features such as spelling correction, ellipsis, and paraphrase generation. These features are demonstrated in the dialog displayed below.

The formats for queries are designed by the system builder and are typically rewrite rules (production rules) as shown here with starting symbol <LTG> corresponding to <LIFER TOP GRAMMAR>:

<LTG> ⇒ WHAT IS THE <ATTRIBUTE> OF <PERSON> | e1

<LTG> ⇒ WHAT IS <PERSON> <ATTRIBUTE> | e2

<LTG> ⇒ HOW <ATTRIBUTE> IS <PERSON> | e3

The input question pattern is matched against these templates and if a match is found, the appropriate expression e1, e2, or e3 is evaluated. The expressions may, in principle, be as simple as:

(GETPROP 'PERSON 'ATTRIBUTE)

to print out the requested attribute or a complex search program that scans databases scattered throughout the country. Note how the three simple templates defined above can handle a wide range of questions such as:

What is the home-run record of Henry Aaron?
What is the cause of death of Alan Turing?
What is Mrs. Aquino's plurality?
What is Gary Hart's age?
How wealthy is Bill Gates?
How old is Steven Jobs?

To illustrate the capabilities of a database management system using semantic grammar as the front-end we next consider a dialog with LADDER. LADDER is the mnemonic for Language Access to Distributed Data with Error Recovery and was build by Hendrix and Sacerdoti at SRI International. It designed to query a large, distributed naval database containing information on 40,000 ships, each represented by a record of over one hundred fields. A sample dialog goes as follows, with queries in boldface and LADDER's response in regular type:

```
1-Give me the length of the Kenedy.
        spelling—>KENNEDY
PARSED!
Give the length of the ship KENNEDY JF
LEN  —  1072
2-width and draft
PARSED!
Trying Ellipsis:  GIVE ME WIDTH AND DRAFT OF THE KENEDY
Give the beam and draft of the ship KENNEDY JF
(BEAM 130  DFT 36)
3-Who is her commander?
PARSED!
Give the rank and name of the commander of the ship KENNEDY
JF
(RANK CAPT  NAME MOFFETT P)
4-What about the Fox?
PARSED!
Trying Ellipsis on:  THE FOX
       WHO IS THE FOX COMMANDER
Give the rank and name of the commander of the ship FOX
(RANK CAPT  NAME EVERETT J)
5-What U.S. merchant ships carrying vanadium ore
are within 500 miles of the Kimlow?
PARSED!
```

```
Give the position of and time at position for the ship
KIMLOW T
Give the name of merchant American ship S
   where the type of cargo on S is VNAD
         the great-circle distance from the position of S to
               15-33N,30-10W, is less than or equal to 500
SHIP  =  GREENVILLE VICTORY,  CRAIN ME,  TOTOR
```
6-How fast are the U.S. subs with lengths greater than 150 feet?

```
PARSED!
Give the maximum cruising speed for and name of American
ship S
   where the first character of the type of S is S
         the second character of the type S is S
         the length of S is greater than 150
```
[A long table relating the names and maximum cruising speeds of American submarines is printed.]

7-What French ships are at readiness status 1?

```
PARSED!
Give the name of French ship S
   where the state of readiness of S is 1
There is no French ship S
NONE
```

Note several interesting features of LADDER. First, it automatically corrects the spelling error in the first question and makes a note of the correction to the user. If no match between a query and the variables in the database occurs, LADDER calls the spelling checker to guess at the correct spelling. Secondly, LADDER correctly handles ellipsis in queries 2 and 4. If parsing fails (no template is found to match the query) and the spelling corrector fails, LADDER calls its elliptic processor to see if the question can be interpreted in terms of a previous context. It prints out the results of the elliptic processor so the user can verify that the truncated question was interpreted in the proper context. Finally, in query 7, LADDER prints the useful information that the database contains no French ships and thereby avoids the scandalous (and incorrect) conclusion that no French ships are in readiness condition.

The impressive performance of LADDER is a result of encoding semantic knowledge directly into its grammar and associated functions. Note that the feasibility of building semantic grammars depends on restricting the problem domain, in this case to a large, but manageable, database. However, database management systems suffer from weaknesses of their own. They are incapable of handling in a general way more difficult logical concepts such as disjunction, quantification, implication, causality, and possibility. LADDER's most significant linguistic deficiency is its limited notion of linguistic context. With the exception of the ellipsis examples shown it is incapable of treating queries in context. It interprets each input as if it were given in isolation.

7.6 CONCLUSIONS ON THE ROLE OF GRAMMAR

The reader has probably observed that improved performance in extracting meaning from language has been bought at the price of adding specific knowledge to the system. Phrase-based, context-free grammar provides a useful tool for parsing sentences but is inadequate for interpreting meaning. Each subsequent grammar we considered contained more information relating to the purpose of the language, the purpose of the speaker, or the specific semantic use of the words themselves. This leaves us with the uncomfortable feeling that there is another uncertainty principle at work here. This can perhaps best be stated as:

$$\text{GENERALITY} \times \text{USEFULNESS} = \text{Constant}$$

If, for instance, we choose to use a semantic grammar for writing a natural language interpreter it would be necessary to provide a list of all possible cases and uses for each word. The power and beauty of natural languages such as French and English is that words may be used in so many different ways and the resulting meanings are strongly influenced by the context in which words appear. This is part of the magic of poetry! The property list for each word of a semantic grammar would increase the size of the language by orders of magnitude and still fail to capture all the subtleties of the language.

7.7 EARLY APPLICATIONS PROGRAMS

Next we look in some detail at two programs that illustrate early approaches to computational linguistics. The first of these, ELIZA, uses only a simple pattern matching scheme for interpreting input sentences. The only semantics contained in ELIZA are based on simple pattern matching to emulate knowledgeable responses which give the illusion of understanding.

The second program, SHRDLU, contains an integration of a syntactic parser, semantic analysis programs, and a theorem-proving problem-solver. These two programs span the range of sophistication of the early attempts at natural language interpretation.

WEIZENBAUM'S ELIZA

One of the most interesting episodes in NLP research centers around this curious program, one of the very few early experiments which has survived and flourishes on a variety of computers in a variety of languages. ELIZA was written by Joseph Weizenbaum of MIT working in loose collaboration with a Stanford University psychiatrist, Kenneth Colby. ELIZA was written to simulate the conversation which a psychiatrist of the Carl Rogers school might carry on with a patient (the user).

Weizenbaum used pattern matching and some clever syntactic tricks to create the illusion of a sympathetic, understanding counselor. He explains how humans themselves often create this illusion of understanding in situations such as described by the cocktail party script:[19]

> *"I might say to you, 'Well, this is rather like the quantum mechanical something or other,' and you'll say, 'I understand.' Well, maybe you don't understand. Maybe you don't know anything about quantum mechanics except in the most rudimentary terms. You don't really see how it's quite like that. But you say, 'Okay, in this context and for the purposes of this conversation, I can say I understand.' You might even dig as deep as you can into your shallow pool of quantum-mechanical knowledge and say, 'Oh, you mean it's the Heisenberg Principle,' and that's really all you know. And I say, 'Yes, wonderful — you really do understand,' and all that sort of thing. That's necessary. It's not cheating."*

Let's see just how realistic this illusion can be. Below is listed an actual conversation carried on with a microcomputer implementation of ELIZA. The user speaks in italics and ELIZA in upper case:

HOW DO YOU DO. PLEASE TELL ME YOUR PROBLEM.

I want to learn how much Eliza knows.
WHAT WOULD IT MEAN TO YOU IF YOU GOT TO LEARN HOW MUCH ELIZA KNOWS?

I could better explain pattern matching to my class.
YOUR CLASS – THAT'S INTERESTING.

Yes, they want to know what intelligence really is.
YOU SEEM QUITE POSITIVE.

Can you help explain how you work?
YOU BELIEVE I CAN HELP EXPLAIN HOW I WORK, DON'T YOU?

If computers are smart, they should explain their thought processes.
DO COMPUTERS WORRY YOU?

No, I use them every day and have great fun.
WHY NOT?

```
That's what I say, why not?
WHY DO YOU ASK?

You were the one who asked.
WE WERE DISCUSSING YOU - NOT ME.

Do doctors just discuss sex and family?
DOES THAT HAVE ANYTHING TO DO WITH THE FACT THAT
YOUR CLASS?
```

After playing with ELIZA for a while, many of the word patterns for which it scans become apparent. For example, input containing "Yes" or "No" generally triggers responses about being positive or negative. One trick used in ELIZA often with rather devastating effect is to "remember" previous input and recall it several statements later in the context of "DOES THAT HAVE ANYTHING TO DO WITH THE FACT THAT ***". However, in this particular example this feature falls flat.

The impressive performance of ELIZA in creating an impression of understanding is due in large part to creating an illusion that it understands the context of the conversation and responds appropriately. While ELIZA is faking it, the strength of this illusion demonstrates the significance of context in human understanding.

Simple-minded though ELIZA is, the program has had a rather remarkable effect on a number of people, not the least of whom is Weizenbaum himself. McCorduck tells of the following incident in which a visitor from the Soviet Union sat down at a terminal in Polya Hall at Stanford University and played Colby's version of ELIZA called DOCTOR:

> *"And it was here that the conversation suddenly became intimate. Our visitor, an internationally respected computer scientist, who knew very well that there was a computer at the other end of the line and not a human being, nevertheless began to disclose his worries about his wife, his children, his distance — both geographical and emotional — from them. We watched in painful embarrassment, trying hard not to look, yet mesmerized all the same. Something about that impartial machine had evoked a response from the visitor that the norms of polite human conduct forbade. If a sophisticated computer scientist could be lured into participating in such a conversation so that he became nearly oblivious to the spectators about him, what effect might such a conversation machine have on a less sophisticated person? It was just such possibilities (and they were to happen: frantic people who telephoned Weizenbaum and pleaded with him for just a little time with ELIZA in order to straighten themselves out) that worried Weizenbaum and made him seek advice about publishing."*

Weizenbaum did publish in due course, making clear by the title of his paper that ELIZA was an experiment in human/machine communication rather than a therapeutic tool.[20] However, Colby beat Weizenbaum into print with a short note to the *Journal of Nervous and Mental Diseases* in which he stressed the therapeutic value of DOCTOR, his version of ELIZA. Disagreement over credit for authorship of the program as well as a fundamental disagreement over ELIZA's value as a therapeutic tool ended the collaboration between Weizenbaum and Colby. Weizenbaum discusses questions raised by such issues in much greater detail in his full length book.[21]

The issues raised in this dispute are very profound and are coming to the surface again with the release of personality analysis programs. Weizenbaum insists that programs such as ELIZA contain absolutely no intelligence and therefore cannot possibly be a valid tool for psychiatric care (and, as he says, he should know because he wrote it). Colby would take the operational view that, regardless of the author's intention, if the program helps people, then it helps people and, by definition, is helpful. His argument can be extended to claim that properly designed programs could provide psychiatric help for many citizens now unable to afford any kind of help.

So the unresolved issue remains: if ELIZA, by design or serendipity, provided what some of its users felt was valuable counseling, would not a modern system with expert input and proper design prove even more effective in delivering such a useful service? And if the answer to this question is "yes", ought we not be working as intensively developing such a system which could prevent death by suicide as we are, say, on an artificial heart for preventing death from heart failure. What, in fact, are the moral implications of taking the position that all such developments in artificial intelligence should be avoided? These are the kinds of questions which must be faced and resolved as computers continue their evolution into intelligent machines.

WINOGRAD'S SHRDLU

In spite of the difficulties in understanding natural language, there have been some signal successes in this area. One of the impressive accomplishments in this area is the doctoral thesis of Terry Winograd of MIT in 1972.[22] SHRDLU was written in LISP and a LISP-based language called MICROPLANNER. SHRDLU was able to achieve high-level performance by restricting the domain of interest to a table top populated with simple geometric objects such as colored blocks, pyramids, and boxes. The program graphically simulated a robot arm which followed instructions from the human operator given in natural language. (See Figure 7-1.)

By limiting the domain in which it operated and using a procedural representation, SHRDLU was able to integrate syntactic, semantic, and reasoning knowledge. It used a context-free, systemic grammar to parse sentences into noun phrases and verb phrases, <S> ⇒ <NP> <VP>. This is implemented in LISP as:

```
(PDEFINE SENTENCE
      (((PARSE NP) NIL FAIL)
      ((PARSE VP) FAIL FAIL RETURN)))

(PDEFINE NP
      (((PARSE DETERMINER) NIL FAIL)
      ((PARSE NOUN) RETURN FAIL)))

(PDEFINE VP
      (((PARSE VERB) NIL FAIL)
      ((ISQ H TRANSITIVE) NIL INTRANS)
      ((PARSE NP) RETURN  NIL)))
INTRANS
      ((ISQ H INTRANSITIVE) RETURN FAIL)))
```

To interpret the operator's commands, SHRDLU used the following sequence of subroutines:

- A *syntactic specialist,* called PROGRAMMAR, which performed the parsing described above and properly assigned various adverbs, modifiers, and auxiliaries.

- A *sentence specialist* which provided both syntactic and semantic information for the analysis. By using *semantic markers,* this specialist could eliminate semantically incorrect sentences such as *The table picks up blocks.*

- A *scenario specialist* which maintained the "world model" of the table top and could relate individual sentences to one another. This specialist handled the pronoun references and time order of all actions performed by the robot.

When the user instructed SHRDLU to place one block on top of another, MICROPLANNER would use the following code:

```
(THGOAL  (ON  ?X  ?Y)
      (OR (ON_TOP  ?X  ?Y)
          (AND     (CLEAR_TOP  ?X)
                   (CLEAR_TOP  ?Y)
                   (PUT_ON  ?X  ?Y))))
```

This program is a form of theorem proving which says that if X is not already on Y, then clear off X and clear off Y and put X on top of Y. It makes no distinction as to whether the condition is already satisfied or whether it will be satisfied in the second part of the procedure — in either case, X is on top of Y when the procedure is completed.

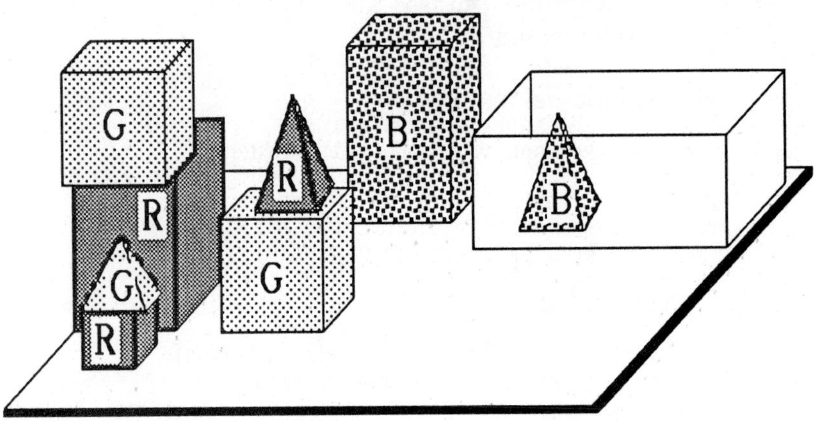

Figure 7-1 The Block World of SHRDLU The human operator can command a robot arm to move the red (R), green (G), and blue (B) objects on the table top using the English language.

Below we list some of the dialog between the human master (lower case), the robot (bold face), and commentary by Winograd (in italics):[23]

```
1. pick up a big red block.
O.K.
```

(The system answers "OK" when it carries out a command. In order to pick up the red block, it had to clear it off by finding a space for the green one and moving the green one away.)

```
2. grasp the pyramid.
I DON'T UNDERSTAND WHICH PYRAMID YOU MEAN.
```

(There are three pyramids in the scene, so the program does nothing.)

```
3. find a block which is taller than the one you are
holding and put it into the box.
```

(The system has to figure out what is meant by "one" and "it," as well as using deduction to decide which block it is holding.)

```
BY "IT", I ASSUME YOU MEAN THE BLOCK
WHICH IS TALLER THAN THE ONE I AM HOLDING.
```

(Printed out to keep us informed.)

```
O.K.
```

(The hand has to set down the red block to pick up the taller blue one.)

```
4.  what does the box contain?
THE BLUE PYRAMID AND THE BLUE BLOCK.

5.  what is the pyramid supported by?
```

(Earlier the system responded to "the pyramid" by saying "I don't understand which pyramid you mean." Now it assumes that we mean the one just mentioned.)

```
THE BOX.

6.  how many blocks are not in the box?
```

(Negatives such as "not" and "no" are handled whether they appear in clauses or noun groups (such as "no boxes").)

```
FOUR OF THEM.

7.  is at least one of them narrower than the one which I
told you to pick up?
```

(The phrase "at least one of them" must be analyzed to refer back to the previous question, and "the one which ..." must also refer to blocks. Noun groups can have complicated numbers such as "at least one", "more than three", "exactly seven", etc. The memory of past events is used to deduce which block is "the one which I told you to pick up". Notice the complicated syntactic structure in which "the one" is actually the object of a clause embedded two levels deeper.)

```
YES, THE RED CUBE.

17.  will you please stack up both of the red blocks and
either a green cube or a pyramid?
OK.
```

(Logical connectives such as "and", "or","either", etc. are handled in both the grammar and semantics. A command is executed even if it looks like a question. The command is carried out by the following series of steps: It puts a green cube on the large red block (note that it chooses the green cube with nothing on it), then removes the small pyramid from the little red cube, so that it can use that cube to complete the stack as specified, ...)

23. had you touched any pyramid before you put the green one on the little cube?
YES, THE GREEN ONE.

(The system deduces from its memory what event is being referred to and can relate other events to it in time. The analysis includes complex tenses or verb groups, and there are special facilities for keeping track of the various forms of irregular verbs like "have".)

```
24. when did you pick it up?
WHILE I WAS STACKING UP THE RED CUBE, A
LARGE RED BLOCK AND A LARGE GREEN CUBE.
```

(A time is described by naming the main goal which was being worked on.)

```
25. why?
```

(The system remembers immediately previous sentences to understand questions like this and the following ones.)

```
TO GET RID OF IT.
```

(By keeping track of selected parts of the original sub-goal tree, the system has some understanding of its own motives.)

```
26. why did you do that?
TO CLEAR OFF THE RED CUBE.
```

("That" refers to the action mentioned in the answer.)

```
27. why did you clear off that cube?
```

(Here, "that" means the one just referred to.)

```
TO PUT IT ON A LARGE GREEN CUBE.

28. why did you do that?
TO STACK UP THE RED CUBE, A LARGE RED
BLOCK AND A LARGE GREEN CUBE.

29. why did you do that?
BECAUSE YOU ASKED ME TO.
```

(It remembers what it did, not how the request was worded.)

As demonstrated by this dialog, SHRDLU performed at a remarkably high level and displayed many of the features we associate with reasoning, understanding, and intelligence. This program proved that by combining syntax with semantics and some useful heuristics, it is possible to build a program which responds intelligently to natural language commands. SHRDLU did, in fact, extract meaning from language and a good argument could be made that it passed Schank's Explanation Game test for understanding.

SHRDLU did have some limitations, however. These included:

- It was unable to remember what went wrong when failure occurred or to improve its performance in subsequent cases.

- It had trouble dealing with hypotheses.

- It had trouble handling words like *the* and *and*.

In spite of these weaknesses, SHRDLU was a benchmark program and showed the feasibility of designing responsive programs to operate within a limited domain using a natural language interface. As such it clarified many of the problems associated with natural language processing and suggested useful techniques for integrating semantic with syntactic functions.

In this chapter we have summarized the main ideas underlying computational linguistics. The theory of formal language has contributed greatly to our understanding of the structure of both human and computer languages, but the tools it provides are not yet capable of automating the semantic function of natural language processing. Several NLP techniques with semantic power have been developed for AI applications and are examined in greater detail in the next chapter.

PROBLEMS AND PROGRAMS

7-1. Concepts of syntactic analysis have proven useful in areas other than linguistics and natural language processing. Give examples of three other applications using a special grammar, and indicate the advantages obtained by this approach.

7-2. Write two context-free grammars to generate the sentence, "Time flies like an arrow", each representing a different meaning of this sentence.

7-3. Do you find Schank's Explanation Game a stronger or weaker test of AI than Turing's Imitation Game? Which test would ELIZA come closest to passing?

7-4. Sentences may be correct syntactically but not semantically, and they may be correct semantically but not pragmatically. Give examples of sentences which fall into each of these two categories and justify your assignments.

7-5. Extend the grammar presented in the Prolog example to include adjectival noun phrases (e.g. "the big, black, vicious cat") and recompute the number of possible sentences the grammar will now generate.

7-6. Compare the sentences:

The cook is baking
The cake is baking

using a syntactic and semantic analysis. What does this suggest as to the value of syntax alone in extracting meaning from natural language utterances? How would a case grammar resolve the differing semantics of the two sentences?

7-7. Write down two different parse trees for the following sentence:

I saw the Grand Canyon flying to San Francisco.

One of these makes sense and one nonsense. What semantic rules would you suggest to eliminate the nonsense interpretation?

7-8. After extensive discussion of Chomsky's formal grammars our conclusion was that none of the four grammars presented was a complete model of natural language. What contributions did Chomsky's grammars make to the field of AI?

7-9. Both transformational grammar and systemic grammar attempt to overcome the limitations of purely syntactical grammar by the addition of knowledge to the system. Describe the characteristics of the knowledge added in each case and suggest which you think would be most successful in developing a system which would understand human communication.

7-10. Case grammars and semantic grammars both improve the semantic understanding of sentences by the addition of knowledge. Describe the nature of the knowledge in each case. In what ways do the two grammars differ and in what ways do they resemble each other?

7-11. The LADDER natural language system achieved a high level of performance by extending the number of parts of speech to encompass the various ships, the properties of each, and operations of the fleet. Compare this approach to the experience of the GPS authors in extending the domain of its problems. What are the limitations of each approach?

7-12. Obtain a copy of ELIZA and run several pages of conversation with her. You should include reference to "computers", family ("mother, father," etc.), and even swear at her. What patterns do you observe?

7-13. How close would you say ELIZA comes to passing the Turing Test? What suggestions do you have for program revisions which would bring her closer to passing the test? Interpret your suggestions in terms of "adding knowledge to the system."

7-14. ELIZA apparently exerted a strong influence on a number of people who ran the program. Do you think a "New ELIZA" should be written using the best up-to-date psychiatric knowledge in order to provide low-cost "counselling" and help not available elsewhere?

7-15. Discuss the performance of SHRDLU with respect to Turing's Imitation Game and Schank's Explanation Game. What should be cited as its accomplishments and limitations?

7-16. Winograd observes the interesting problem of determining the correct time context with the following three sentences:

a) Many rich people made their fortunes during the depression.
b) Many rich people lost their fortunes during the depression.
c) Many rich people worked in restaurants during the depression.

Consider the question: "When were the people rich?" and justify your answer for each of the sentences.

7-17. Natural language parsers are available on many systems supporting LISP and Prolog. Find such a parser, make a listing, and interpret the functions of each program segment.

7-18. Select ten sentences from the text ranging from to trivial to complex, and submit them to a natural language parser. Based on the parsed results, evaluate the capability of the parser.

7-19. Write a LISP version of a natural language generator which will generate all grammatical phrases of the language from words to full sentences.

7-20. The "knowledge-bottleneck" term coined by Feigenbaum graphically describes the laborious hand-crafting required for building most knowledge-based systems. Assuming that progress in computational linguistics and NLP eventually removes the bottleneck and allows the knowledge acquisition process to become automated. Discuss what you consider to be the most important implication of the resulting rapid accumulation of machine knowledge.

REFERENCES AND FOOTNOTES

[1] McCarthy, J. "Epistemological problems of artificial intelligence," *IJCAI* **3**, pp. 1—11 (1977)

[2] Fu, K. S., *Syntactic Pattern Recognition and Applications*, Prentice-Hall, Inc., Englewood Cliffs, NJ (1982)

[3] Smith, Alva R., "Plants, Fractals, and Formal Languages", *Computer Graphics* **18**, pp. 1—10, July (1984)

[4] Lowther, D. A., *MagNet User's Manual*, Infolytica Corporation, Montreal, Canada (1985)

[5] Elliott, Steve, "Synapse Understanding vs Straight Silicon Logic," *The Club Mac News*, p. 8, February (1986)

[6] Schank, Roger C., *THE COGNITIVE COMPUTER — On Language, Learning, and Artificial Intelligence,* Addison-Wesley, Reading, MA (1984)

[7] Feigenbaum, Edward, Barr, Avron, and Cohen, Paul, (eds) *The Handbook of Artificial Intelligence* Vol. 1—3, p. 229, HeurisTech Press/William Kaufmann, Inc., Stanford, CA (1981-1982)

[8] Hendrix, G. G. and Sacerdoti, E. D., "Natural-Language Processing: The Field in Perspective," *BYTE*, September, pp. 304—352 (1981)

[9] Weizenbaum, J., "ELIZA — A Computer Program for the Study of Natural Language Communication between Man and Machine,"

CACM **9**, pp. 36—45 (1966)

10 Schank, R. C. and Abelson, R. P., *Scripts, Plans, Goals and Understanding,* Lawrence Erlbaum, Hillsdale, NJ (1977)

11 Schank, *Op. Cit.*, pp. 56—57

12 Chomsky, N., *Syntactic Structures,* The Hague: Mouton (1957)

13 Turing, A. M., "On Computable Numbers, with an Application to the Entscheidungs Problem," *Proceedings of the London Mathematical Society* **42**, pp. 230—265 (1937)

14 Chomsky, N., *Aspects of the Theory of Syntax,* MIT Press, Cambridge, MA (1965)

15 Halliday, M. A. K., "Categories of the Theory of Grammar," *Word* **17**, pp. 241—292 (1961)

16 Fillmore, C. "The Case for Case," in *Universals in Linguistic Theory,* E. Bach and R. Harms (eds), Holt, Rinehart, and Winston, New York, NY (1968)

17 Hendrix, G. G., "LIFER: A natural language interface facility," *SIGART Newsletter* **61**, pp. 25—26 (1977)

18 Hendrix, G. G. and Sacerdoti, E. D., *Op cit,* pp. 310—316

19 McCorduck, Pamela, *MACHINES WHO THINK* , W. H. Freeman and Company, San Francisco, CA (1979)

20 Weizenbaum, J., *Op. Cit.* (1966)

21 Weizenbaum, J., *Computer Power and Human Reason: From Judgement to Calculation,* Freeman & Co., San Francisco, CA (1976)

22 Winograd, Terry, *Understanding Natural Language,* Academic Press, New York, NY (1972)

23 Winograd, Terry, *Op cit* , (1972)

Chapter 8

NATURAL LANGUAGE PROCESSING

(PHOTO: COURTESY OF ROGER SCHANK)

Roger C. Schank is Professor of Computer Science and Psychology and head of the Artificial Intelligence Laboratory at Yale University. He did his undergraduate work at Carnegie-Mellon University and his doctoral work at the University of Texas in linguistics. He invented the concept of scripts for knowledge representation with Yale colleague Robert Abelson, and he developed the theory of conceptual dependency. He has written a number of books and directed graduate students in building NLP systems MARGIE, SAM, PAM, FRUMP, IPP, and CYRUS. Schank is considered one of the leading researchers in the field of natural language understanding.

8: NATURAL LANGUAGE PROCESSING

8.1 INTRODUCTION

In the previous chapter we introduced the concept of computational linguistics, the science concerned with the computational generation and analysis of language. Chomsky's theory of formal language provides a mathematical framework for studying the structure of natural language. By gaining a better understanding of how humans communicate, we gain insight on what is required to build machines with human-like communication skills. Conversely, the requirement for developing systematic syntactic analysis systems for computers has forced a deeper and more careful study of the structure of natural languages. However, as we discovered, syntactic correctness alone is generally inadequate for interpreting natural language sentences. Semantic knowledge must somehow be integrated in order to determine the meaning of the communication. This conclusion led to the development of the more knowledge-rich, extended grammars such as the semantic grammar used in LIFER.

In this chapter we broaden the discussion by defining a natural language processing system as any system which performs a useful operation on natural language input. At the simple lexical level, this definition includes powerful spelling checkers, many of which now contain lexicons of more than 100,000 words. At the syntactic level, style checkers are now available which check for double word usage, typographic errors, incorrect punctuation, capitalization, sexist/racist language, vague or overworked expressions, and weak constructions. Such NLP software provides authors with extremely valuable writing tools and sets the stage for what publisher David Bunnell has described as an "AI editor".[1] An AI editor, by understanding the context of word usage, could resolve errors in usage of *their*, *there*, and *they're*, for instance. As semantic knowledge becomes available, the AI editor would assist the writer with questions such as "What do you mean by ...?" and "Do you really want to include ...?". Several interesting and successful techniques for making such semantic knowledge available are the subjects of this chapter.

Before turning to these examples, a brief interpretation of the evolution of software systems is in order. The trend in computer software development can be characterized as a shift from the natural language of the computer (bits and bytes) to the natural languages of humans. In terms of programming languages this trend describes the history of the shift from machine language to assembly language, high-level languages, and finally special purpose languages (spreadsheets, data-base systems, and so on). In terms of operating systems, the evolution has been from bootstrap loaders through disk operating systems to icon and menu-driven operating systems using the desktop metaphor. The goal of modern operating systems should be to teach the computer to respond to intuitive human commands rather than force humans to learn opaque, arcane language such as that shown in Figure 8-1.

Alan Turing foresaw the resistance which traditional computing center "masters" would raise to the introduction of what we now call "user-friendly systems." In a talk to the London Mathematical Society he stated:[2]

> *"The masters are liable to get replaced because as soon as any technique becomes at all stereotyped it becomes possible to devise a system of instruction tables which will enable the electronic computer to do it for itself. It may happen however that the masters will refulse to do this. They may be unwilling to let their jobs be stolen from them in this way. In that case they would surround the whole of their work with mystery and make excuses, couched in well chosen gibberish, whenever any dangerous suggestions were made. I think that a reaction of this kind is a very real danger. ..."*

```
//UOX608 JOB (1,X60800S,2N01),'MAGSQN94 RUN',
//MSGLEVEL=(2,0),CLASS=N,MSGCLASS=S
/*ROUTE PRINT R15
//A EXEC TSMAGSQN,RUNNAME=HUGE,REGION.MAG=2800K,RESEQ=HUGE,
//USERID=UOX608,PLTNAME=HUGE,PROS=MAGSTA94,PROG=MAGNET94
//START.STEPLIB DD DSN=AOS1.GRP23.TLOAD1,DISP=SHR
//MAG.STEPLIB DD DSN=AOS1.GRP23.TLOAD1,DISP=SHR
//MAG.FT08F001 DD UNIT=SYSDA,SPACE=(18144,300)
//MAG.FT09F001 DD UNIT=SYSDA,SPACE=(18144,300)
//MAG.FT07F001 DDUNIT=SYSDA,DCB=(RECFM=FB,LRECL=1440,BLKSIZE=1440)
//SPACE=(1440,5000)
```

Figure 8-1 Example of Job Control Language This segment of JCL is listed directly from one of the author's finite element analysis runs on a mainframe computer. The difficulty of translating such language into English rivals that of natural language translation. The main difference is that this problem is self-inflicted.

The effects of this climb up the evolutionary ladder of computer development have included, among others:

- An increase in productivity by a factor of two or more for each major improvement in operating system and/or language.

- An increase in the number of users by at least a factor of two as each step up the ladder makes systems easier to use and more versatile.

- Computer assimilation of human-like qualities. Increased memory capacity and processor speed has shifted the burden of effective human/machine communication from humans to the machine.

In the early days of the automobile, drivers had to be amateur mechanics to start their cars and keep them running. The invention of the self-starter and dependable, "user-friendly" clutches and transmissions made driving an activity available to virtually everyone. The trend toward giving computers natural language capabilities will almost certainly serve the same function for computers.

Two primary functions which NLP systems are presently serving are the following:

- Providing lexical and syntactic analysis tools such as style and spelling checkers; concordance, index, and table of contents generators; and textual analysis programs for purposes such as verification of authorship. In general these applications require little or no semantic knowledge.

- Providing the communication interface or "front-end" for existing systems such as information retrieval and data-base management systems. These applications require semantic information to interpret what the user means by his/her request and possibly even what the requested information means.

Two more elusive goals of NLP are *speech recognition* and *machine translation*. Speech recognition will be discussed as an instance of pattern recognition in Chapter 14. Machine translation (MT) has been a tantalizing goal always just over the horizon since the earliest days of artificial intelligence. Because of the enormous practical benefits of an effective machine translator and the enormous complexity of the problems involved, it continues to attract AI researchers.

In this chapter we study how some of the concepts introduced in the last chapter have been extended to a number of NLP programs. First we discuss the problems of NLP in terms of *mappings* between the input language and the desired target language. Then a number of successful NLP programs, classified according to the following scheme, are presented:

- Simple pattern matching or "template" systems
- Syntactic parsers — augmented transition networks
- Conceptual dependency systems using semantic primitives
- Some commercially available systems are described in Appendix B.

Finally, we discuss one of the chief disappointments in AI — the failure to produce an effective natural language translator.

8.2 MAPPING REPRESENTATIONS

A very useful way of looking at problems of natural language processing is to represent them as a mapping from a source representation to a target representation. In general, the source will be an input request, command, or story and the target will be a parsed, interpreted, deep representation within the computer which conveys the meaning intended in the user request. The user's intentions are then interpreted as instructions or data on which to carry out the required operations.

Because of the complex nature of natural languages, any NLP system must deal with the following types of mappings which are concisely summarized by Elaine Rich as:[3]

- One-to-one
- Many-to-one
- One-to-many
- Many-to-many

One-to-one:

The unique mapping of the following information of the planet Venus:

> *Venus is the second planet from the sun with mean radius of 3,800 miles, orbit radius 67.2 million miles, and sidereal period of 224.7 days.*

might be represented in LISP as:

```
(VENUS '(PLANET   2)  '(R  38000)
     '(RO  67200000)  '(T  224.7))
```

or in Prolog as:

```
venus([planet(2), radius(3800),orbit(67200000),
period(224.7]).
```

It is clear that no other planet would generate this attribute list nor would Venus generate any other values for this attribute list.

Many-to-one:

A good natural language query system would interpret all the following requests:

> *Tell me all about the balance of trade deficit.*
>
> *I'd like to see all the stories on the balance of trade deficit.*
>
> *I am interested in the deficit in the trade balance.*

as:

```
(SEARCH_KEYWORDS  TRADE BALANCE DEFICIT).
```

One-to-many:

As we have seen, the old chestnut *Time flies like an arrow* can be tortured into at least the following three syntactically correct statements:

```
(Time   (flies)  (like an arrow))
   N       V       ADV Phrase

(Time    flies   (like an arrow))
V(imp)    N       ADV Phrase

((Time  flies)  like  (an arrow))
   ADJ    N       V    N Phrase
```

So the ambiguities of such words as "time" and "flies" leads to at least three distinct semantically valid mappings for this simple statement. Another simple statement leading to multiple interpretations (aircraft, wood-working tool, geometric figure) is:

They are flying planes.

Many-to-many:

Consider the sentence:

John saw the boy in the park with a telescope.

It is clear that there are a number of distinct semantic interpretations possible for this statement, and that for each of them there are a number of distinct syntactically correct sentences to say the same thing. This illustrates the very difficult many-to-many problem in mapping. It also illustrates why context is so important in determining meaning.

8.3 PATTERN MATCHING NLP SYSTEMS

First, two programs are discussed which use pattern matching for mapping natural language into a representation which could be interpreted by the computer in a meaningful way.

SIR

The basic algorithm used in Bertram Raphael's thesis work, SIR[4] (Semantic Information Retrieval) is a pattern matching scheme similar to that used in ELIZA, but SIR differs in a very significant way from ELIZA. The difference is that SIR saves and "understands" input information at a high enough level to allow it to make deductions from the input data. In this sense it closely resembles the semantic grammar approach of LIFER. SIR could understand a restricted subset of 24 patterns of the following type:

> * *is* *
> * *is part of* *
> *Is* * *?
> *How many* * *does* * *have?*
> *What is the* * *of* * ?

where the wild-card "*" symbols represent arbitrary nouns or noun phrases containing a noun plus such quantifiers as *a, the, every, each,* or a number. The basic logic used in SIR is the *hypothetical syllogism* which can be stated as: *If A is B and B is C, then A is C.* This enabled SIR (upper case) to make logical deductions from information provided by the user (lower case italics) as shown:

```
Max is an IBM 7094.
I UNDERSTAND.

An IBM 7094 is a computer.
I UNDERSTAND.

Is MAX a computer?
YES.
```

```
The boy is an MIT student.
I UNDERSTAND.

Every MIT student is a bright person.
I UNDERSTAND.

Is the boy a bright person?
YES.
```

Through the careful choice of patterns to match the most common forms of statement and query, SIR was able to achieve a very good performance with a minimum of analysis. It could even interact with the user to resolve ambiguities and expand its information base. However, since its performance was limited to dealing with the standard pattern subset, it cannot be considered to be a general NLP system.

STUDENT

This program was introduced as a successful problem solving system in Chapter 6 and is discussed here in terms of its NLP capability. Daniel Bobrow wrote STUDENT at MIT as his Ph.D. thesis which was published in 1968.[5] The complete set of templates used by STUDENT in solving high-school-algebra story problems are the following 12 patterns:

```
(WHAT ARE * AND *)
(WHAT IS *)
(HOW MANY *1 IS *)
(HOW MANY * DO * HAVE)
(HOW MANY * DOES * HAVE)
(FIND *)
(FIND * AND *)
(* IS MULTIPLIED BY *)
(* IS DIVIDED BY *)
(* IS *)
(* ((1/VERB) *1 *)
(* (*1/VERB) * AS MANY * AS * (*1/VERB) *)
```

where

`*` ⇒ a string of arbitrary length

`*1` ⇒ one word

`(*1/VERB)` ⇒ matching element must be dictionary verb

Although this set of templates appears very restricted, STUDENT could solve complex word problems such as the following:

If the number of customers Tom gets is twice the square of 20 per cent of the number of advertisements he runs, and the number of advertisements he runs is 45, what is the number of customers Tom gets?

STUDENT would reply:

```
(THE NUMBER OF CUSTOMERS TOM GETS IS 162)
```

The program scanned the problem statement for variable assignment indicated by the `(* IS *)`, then for algebraic operators, and finally for the answers required along with units. STUDENT then called a SOLVE routine with the set of equations and desired unknowns. To help resolve ambiguities or unknown information, it called on a special fact dictionary with information such as `(ONE FOOT EQUALS 12 INCHES)`.

STUDENT, using this very simple template matching system, was able to solve problems as fast as MIT graduate students could. A somewhat modified version of the program was found to be a good model for human problem solving.

8.4 SYNTACTIC PARSERS

It is legitimate to consider the template matching schemes described above as elementary parsing ("picking apart") algorithms in which semantic knowledge is embedded in the structure of the template. We next consider more general parsers, one of the most successful of which is the *augmented transition network* (ATN) approach of William Woods.[6] The ATN method of parsing sentences integrates many concepts from Chomsky's formal grammar theory with a matching process resembling a dynamic semantic network. Such parsing techniques may be considered as *recursive pattern matching* in which the string of words of the sentence are mapped onto a meaningful syntactic pattern.

We can understand the characteristics of an ATN by studying the progression from *finite-state transition diagrams* through *recursive transition networks* to *augmented transition networks.* Each level of this progression represents increased levels of incorporating options for semantic input into the formal syntactic structure of the parsing program. The goal of all this effort is to take an arbitrary input sentence and assign each word of the sentence its proper part of speech.

FINITE STATE TRANSITION DIAGRAMS

The starting point in studying ATNs is the finite-state transition diagram (FSTD) as shown in Figure 8-2. FSTD diagrams consist of a set of nodes and arcs connecting the nodes according to the following rules:

- All terminal symbols (words of the sentence) are represented as arcs.

- One state (or node) is defined as "S",the *START* state, and one subset of states as the *FINAL* state, "**".

- The FSTD specifies a (dynamic) *process* for operating on arbitrary sentences instead of a static relationship between words as in a semantic network. For this reason, an ATN is sometimes called a *machine*.

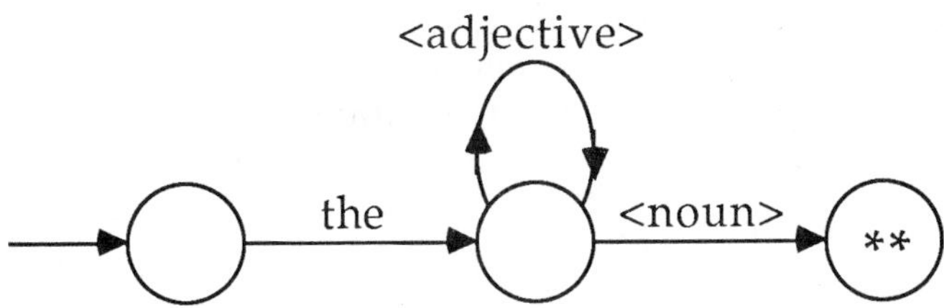

Figure 8-2 Finite-state Transition Diagram This FSTD can process any noun phrase starting with *the*, containing an arbitrary number of adjectives, and terminating with a noun. Note arc and node structure with all terminal symbols (words) on the arcs and the final node "**".

The FSTD processes the input sentence one word at a time, checking to see if the word matches the prescribed structure. If it matches, the word is placed on the appropriate arc and removed from the input sentence. When the FINAL state is reached with no words in the sentence left over, we say the FSTD has *accepted* the sentence; that is, we know that the sentence matches the syntactic structure specified by the FSTD.

The FSTD shown above will accept any sentence segment beginning with *the*, ending with a noun, and containing an arbitrary number of adjectives in between. For instance, *The big, hairy, black, male cat* would be accepted by this FSTD.

The main problem with the FSTD is that it can recognize only sentences written as a regular language (Type 3) which is the most restrictive of Chomsky's four categories of language. It cannot handle sentences from the more general context-free (Type 2) grammar.

RECURSIVE TRANSITION NETWORKS

To extend the capability of FSTDs to handle more general context-free language, a recursion mechanism was added to the FSTD and it became a *recursive transition network* (RTN). This extension is somewhat like adding a subroutine capability at each arc. Now, in addition to containing a terminal (word), an arc may contain the name of a sub-network to which control may be transferred to parse, for instance, a prepositional phrase. When the sub-network is finished, control returns to the subsequent node and processing continues. This subroutine structure is illustrated in Figure 8-3.

The capability for recursion gives the RTN a considerable advantage over its predecessor, the FSTD. There is no restriction on the level of hierarchy or recursion possible with RTNs. That is, a sub-network may call another sub-network which may, in turn, call another and so on. Recursion is supported by allowing a sub-network to call itself.

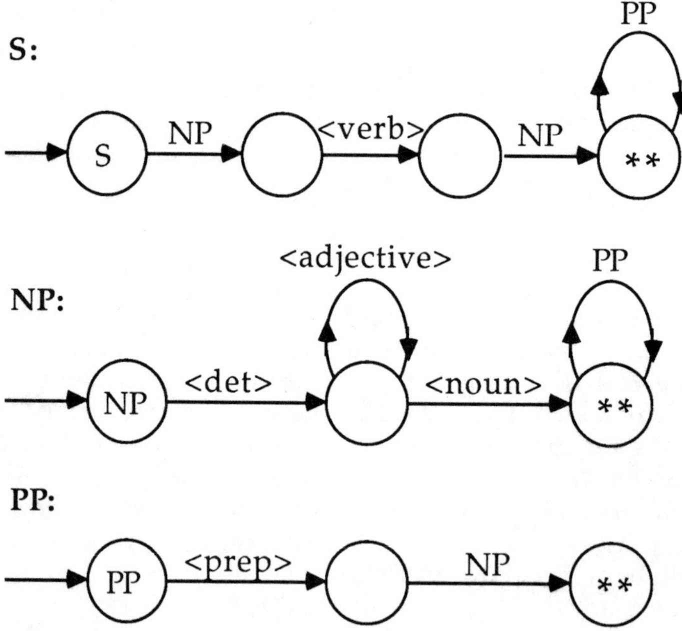

Figure 8-3 Recursive Transition Network (RTN) *S* signifies sentence, *NP* means noun phrase, *PP* means prepositional phrase, *det* signifies determiner, and *prep* means preposition. Note that arcs may now contain calls to sub-networks to any level and recursively (i.e. a network may call itself).

There is also no restriction on the number of sub-networks which may be called from a certain arc. Several sub-structures may be investigated simultaneously, and thus RTNs have the capability of parallel processing. Often, of course, many of the parallel sub-networks will fail to parse the phrase they are examining because it may not fit the structure specified by the RTN.

However, even context-free grammars cannot handle all English sentence structure. To extend the capabilities of syntactic parsers, the *augmented transition network* (ATN) was invented.

AUGMENTED TRANSITION NETWORK

By adding the following additional features to a RTN, it becomes an augmented transition network (ATN).

- Add a set of *registers* which store information such as partially formed derivation trees (a parsed sentence with words as leaves).

- Allow arcs to be *executed conditionally,* i.e. tests must be passed before the arc is taken.

- Attach certain *actions* to arcs, usually in the form of modifying the data structure returned.

As one might expect, these new features greatly expand the ability of ATNs to handle natural language. In fact, an ATN has the power of a Turing machine. This gives the ATN the ability to recognize any language that a computer can recognize. By incorporating the ability to make tests and specify actions (such as rearranging the structure of sentences while parsing them), ATNs have the ability to generate deep structures underlying the surface language.

Because of this great power and flexibility, ATNs have been used in a number of successful NLP programs. Two such programs are Bolt Beranek and Newman's HWIM (Hear What I Mean) speech recognition program to which we will return later and William Wood's LUNAR[7] program for information retrieval which we will consider below. About the only failure of the ATN technique is in correctly interpreting ungrammatical utterances which may, nonetheless, contain meaning.

A PROLOG SYNTACTIC PARSER

To illustrate the basic ideas of syntactic parsers and show how they can be implemented in an AI language, we next present a Prolog parser based on a simple, context-free grammar.[8] The basic algorithm used in parsing a list of words to determine if it matches the sentence structure specified by the grammar is shown in the first rule:

sentence(A, C) :- noun_phrase(A, B), verb_phrase(B, C).

This rule states that a sentence is composed of a noun phrase followed by a verb phrase. The arguments, A, B, and C are lists of words with the following interpretation:

- **First argument** → Input word list to the phrase parser.

- **Second argument** → List of surplus words left over after parsing. This output list becomes the input list for the following parser, if one exists, or the "answer" if there is no subsequent phrase parser. An answer of C = [ ] means that all words of the phrase have been parsed correctly, that is, the word list is a well-formed sentence. A non-null C contains words left over after parsing.

The phrase-structured grammar is hierarchical in structure with noun phrases, for example, composed of either a single noun, a modifier plus noun, or a modifier plus noun plus prepositional phrase.

```
%Context-free, Definite Clause Grammar Program
%
%A sentence is composed of a noun phrase
%followed by a verb phrase.
sentence(A, C) :-
    noun_phrase(A, B),
    verb_phrase(B, C).
%
%Rules for testing legal noun phrases.
noun_phrase(A, C) :- noun(A, C).
noun_phrase(A, D) :-
    mod(A, B),
    noun(B, C),
    prep_phrase(C, D).
noun_phrase(A, C) :-
    mod(A, B),
    noun(B, C).
%
%Rules for testing legal verb phrases.
verb_phrase(A, C) :-
    verb_form(A, B),
```

```
    noun_phrase(B, C).
verb_phrase(A, C) :-
    verb_form(A, B),
    prep_phrase(B, C).
verb_phrase(A, C) :- verb_form(A, C).
%
%Rules representing allowed  verb forms.
verb_form(A, C) :-
    aux(A, B),
    infin(B, C).
verb_form(A, C) :- verb(A, C).
%
%Rules specifying  structure of adjectival phrases.
adj_phrase(A, C) :- adj(A, C).
adj_phrase(A, C) :-
    adj(A, B),
    adj(B, C).
adj_phrase(A, D) :-
    adj(A, B),
    adj(B, C),
    adj(C, D).
%
%List of adjective terminal symbols.
adj([big, ..X], X).
adj([little, ..X], X).
adj([black, ..X], X).
%
%Definition of prepositional phrases.
prep_phrase(A, C) :-
    prep(A, B),
    noun_phrase(B, C).
%
%List of prepositions in the vocabulary.
prep([in, ..X], X).
prep([on, ..X], X).
prep([after, ..X], X).
prep([for, ..X], X).
%
%Definition of allowed modifiers.
mod(A, C) :- det(A, C).
mod(A, C) :- adj_phrase(A, C).
mod(A, C) :-
    det(A, B),
    adj_phrase(B, C).
%
%List of terminal infinitives.
infin([catch, ..X], X).
infin([scratch, ..X], X).
infin([run, ..X], X).
infin([eat, ..X], X).
%
%List of auxiliary terminal symbols.
aux([can, ..X], X).
aux([may, ..X], X).
%
%Definition of determiners of the language.
det([the, ..X], X).
det(A, C) :- poss_pron_adj(A, C).
```

```
%
%List of allowed possessive pronouns adjectives.
poss_pron_adj([my, ..X], X).
poss_pron_adj([your, ..X], X).
%
%List of vocabulary verbs.
verb([catches, ..X], X).
verb([scratches, ..X], X).
verb([runs, ..X], X).
verb([eats, ..X], X).
%
%List of vocabulary nouns.
noun([cat, ..X], X).
noun([mouse, ..X], X).
noun([dinner, ..X], X).
noun([dog, ..X], X).
```

Let's examine some of the components of the grammar to determine if it contains given words. To determine whether *dog* and *horse* are nouns of the vocabulary, we ask:

```
: noun([dog],Noun)?
Noun = []

:noun([horse],Noun)?
** no
```

This means that *dog* is an element of the language, since the list containing words not falling into slots of the syntax is empty, i.e. the null list. Prolog indicates by the *no* that horse is not a noun of the language.

To get a list of all nouns contained in the language, we query:

```
: noun(Noun,Extra)?
Noun = [cat, .._1]
Extra = _1
Noun = [mouse,.. _1]
Extra = _1
Noun = [dinner, .._1]
Extra = _1
Noun = [dog, .._1]
Extra = _1
```

This result specifies the nouns of the grammar as the heads of lists with arbitrary ("don't care") tails.

Next we check out a particular noun phrase to see if it can be parsed:

```
: noun_phrase([your,little,dog,barks],X)?
X = [barks]
```

This means that everything in the phrase can be parsed as a noun phrase except the word *barks*. When we parse the verb phrases shown, we get two answers:

```
: verb_phrase([may,catch,the,little,black,mouse],X)?
X = []
X = [the, little, black, mouse]

: verb_phrase([runs,after,dinner],X)?
X = []
X = [after, dinner]

: verb_phrase([runs,after,dinner,daily],X)?
X = [daily]
X = [after, dinner, daily]
```

This means, in the case of the middle phrase, that *runs after dinner* is a well-formed verb phrase, and that the word *runs* is also a verb phrase standing alone, in which case *after dinner* are the extra words which do not fit the syntax. This is consistent with the control strategy used in Prolog -86 of finding all possible solutions of the problem.

Finally, the sentence predicate is queried to determine if the given list is a syntactically correct sentence. If Prolog returns a null list, X = [ ], the answer is *yes*, the input list has matched the structure specified in the grammar of the program. If list X contains words, the interpretation is that the first part of the sentence parsed correctly with the words in X as stragglers. If the input list contains vocabulary words which are out of order or a foreign word in proper sequence, the parser will answer *no*.

```
: sentence([dog,runs],X)?
X = []

: sentence([the,cat,scratches,for,dinner],X)?
X = []
X = [for, dinner]

:
sentence([the,little,dog,may,catch,the,mouse,for,dinner],X)?
X = []
X = [for, dinner]
X = [the, mouse, for, dinner]

: sentence([my,dog,may,catch,the,big,mouse,for,your,cat],X)?
X = []
X = [for, your, cat]
X = [the, big, mouse, for, your, cat]

: sentence([the,mouse,squeaks],X)?
** no
```

So the first four sentences are correct as they stand (X = [ ]), and three of them have sub-structures which are also well-formed sentences. The last sentence fails the parser because *squeaks* is not a vocabulary word.

The reader should note that the parsing algorithm used in this program closely resembles that described for the FSTD described above.

The starting state **S** corresponds to the list of words comprising the input sentence, and the final state ** corresponds to the successfully parsed null list, X = [ ].

8.5 LUNAR

LUNAR was developed by William Woods of Bolt Beranek and Newman as a NLP program for retrieving and analyzing geological information obtained from the Apollo-11 mission to the moon. LUNAR used a query language based on predicate calculus, augmented transition networks for translation, and a dictionary of approximately 3,500 words. It was one of the first "real world" NLP programs (as opposed to previous "toy" programs) and could correctly understand and respond to queries such as:[9]

```
(WHAT IS THE AVERAGE CONCENTRATION OF ALUMINUM IN HIGH
ALKALI ROCKS?)

(WHAT SAMPLES CONTAIN P205?)

(GIVE ME THE MODAL ANALYSES OF P205 IN THOSE SAMPLES)

(GIVE ME EU DETERMINATIONS IN SAMPLES WHICH CONTAIN ILM)
```

The three steps used in processing these requests were:

- *Syntactic analysis* using an ATN parser and heuristic information to generate the most probable derivation tree.

- *Semantic interpretation* to produce a representation of the meaning in a formal query language.

- *Execution* of the query language expression on the database to generate the answer to the request.

As an example of the operation of the query language representation, consider the following request:

Request:

```
(DO ANY SAMPLES HAVE GREATER THAN 13 PERCENT ALUMINUM)
```

Query Language Translation after parsing:

```
(TEST (FOR SOME X1 / (SEQ SAMPLES):T;
      (CONTAIN X1
      (NPR* X2 / "AL203)
```

```
(GREATERTHAN 13 PCT))))
```

Response:

```
YES
```

While the domain of LUNAR was restricted to information on the geology and chemistry of moon rocks, the program did display an impressive ability for understanding a fairly broad range of English commands. The success of this program inspired work on the HWIM (Hear What I Mean) system of BBN. This speech understanding system applies the ATN approach at the phoneme level to interpret instructions spoken to the computer through a microphone.

8.6 CONCEPTUAL DEPENDENCY THEORY

In the next chapter we will study *frames* and *scripts* as knowledge representation schemes which take into account context and relationships. These techniques provide a useful formalism for representing more complex structures such as objects, scenes, and multiple-sentence stories. One of the key ideas of the script approach is to reduce a sentence or story to a set of *semantic primitives* using a formalism called *conceptual dependency theory.*

The emphasis in this theory of Schank and Abelson[10] is to shift the focus of NLP from the *form* (i.e. syntax) of a communication to its *content* (i.e. semantics). The goal of a CD "understander" is to convert sentences describing an event into a representation of the event itself as shown in Figure 8-4.

Consider how one would represent an event in CD theory. Every event has:

- An ACTOR
- An ACTION performed by that actor
- An OBJECT that the action is performed upon
- A DIRECTION in which that action is oriented.

By reducing the action taking place in CD theory to a set of simple primitives such as:

Action:

MOVE_BODY_PART	MOVE_OBJECT
EXPEL	INGEST
PROPEL	SPEAK

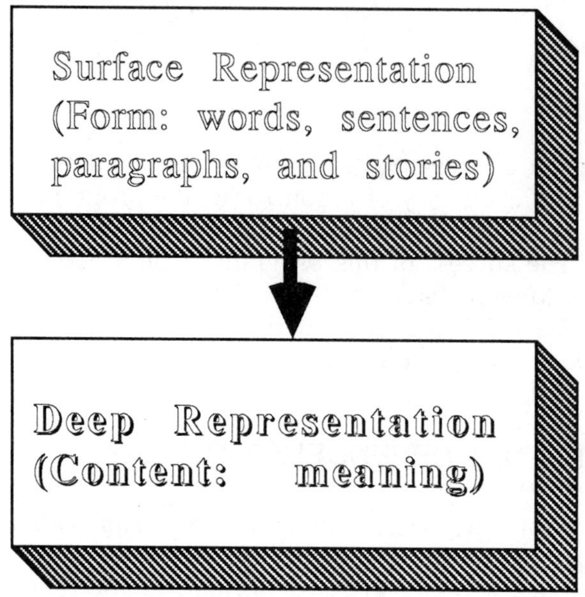

Figure 8-4 Role of Conceptual Dependency In the theory of conceptual dependency (CD) it is possible to transform the surface representation of a communication into a deep representation of its meaning. Different utterances conveying the same meaning should transform into the same deep representation.

Perception:

SEE	HEAR
SMELL	FEEL

Mental and Social Acts:

MOVE_CONCEPT	CONCLUDE
TRANSFER-POSSESSION	THINK_ABOUT

Schank and Abelson were able to represent the deeper semantic meaning present in input stories. Conceptual dependency theory could then be used to answer questions not specifically stated in the story, paraphrase the main ideas of the story, and even translate the paraphrased account into other natural languages. Several application programs which have emerged from conceptual dependency theory research are presented below in some detail.

The basic idea in conceptual dependency theory is that it should be possible to reduce any surface sentence into a deeper representation in terms of semantic primitives. The advantage is that such a system will automatically solve many of the mapping problems discussed earlier, that is, two distinct sentences with identical meaning should transform into the same representation in terms of semantic primitives. The semantic primitives of CD theory may be classified in terms of *primitive acts, primitive states,* and the *rules* relating them.[11] Some of these primitives with their abbreviations include:

Primitive Acts:

ATRANS — Transfer of an *abstract* relationship such as possession-changing actions.

MTRANS — Transfer of *mental* information between people or within a person.

PTRANS — Transfer of the *physical* location of an object.

PROPEL — Application of physical force to an object.

MBUILD — Construction of new conceptual (mental) structures from old, e.g. *deciding, inferring,* and *imagining* transform into MBUILDs.

The general syntax is:

(*act* <*arguments*>)

Primitive States — Examples:

PHYSICAL STATE — Leg PHYSICAL STATE(–10)
⇒The leg is broken.

MENTAL STATE — Sally MENTAL STATE(+10)
⇒ Sally is ecstatic.

HEALTH — Nancy HEALTH(–10)
⇒ Nancy is dead.

HAS — Indicates that a character owns something.

AT — Indicates where a character is.

KNOW — Indicates a character knows something.

GOAL — Indicates the goal of a character.

The general syntax is:

(state <arguments>)

Causality Rules:

1. Actions can cause state changes.
2. States can make certain actions possible.
3. States can prevent certain actions from occurring.
4. States (or acts) can cause mental events.
5. Mental events can cause actions.

Through the semantic implications of the semantic primitives, the CD method permits paraphrasing the input information and drawing inferences from it. As an example, consider the sentence below and its representation in CD theory and associated paraphrases and inferences:[12]

INPUT: John sold Mary a book.

INTERNAL REPRESENTATION:

```
ACTION:   ATRANS
ACTOR:    John
OBJECT:   book                  ACTION:   ATRANS
TO:       Mary   <------->      ACTOR:    Mary
FROM:     John                  OBJECT:   money
                                TO:       John
                                FROM:     Mary
```

OUTPUT:
Mary gave John some money and John gave her a book.

PARAPHRASES:
Mary bought John's book. Mary paid John for a book.

OUTPUT:
Mary has a book. John has money. Mary wanted John's book.

INFERENCES:

John didn't want the book anymore.
John had already read the book.
Mary will read the book.
John needed the money.

The CD representation permits this rather impressive performance by using semantic information about the word *sell.* It resolves the two-function verb *sell* into two instances of the one-function verb *give.* That is, the word sell as used in this sentence implies that John gives Mary the book and Mary gives John money.

The first program to emerge from the research on CD theory was MARGIE: Memory, Analysis, Response Generation in English (and also the name of Roger Schank's mother).

MARGIE

Schank, then at Stanford University, and his students combined a parser, a generator, and an inference engine in the program MARGIE (1973). The parser took an English sentence and converted it into the semantic primitive representation. The generator looked at the internal representation and returned valid English paraphrases of the statement. The inferencer, using 16 rules of inference, generated the implications of the statement in semantic primitive language and sent this to the generator which converted the inferences into English.

MARGIE could run in two modes: *paraphrase mode* or *inference mode.* Sample output from each are shown below:

INFERENCE MODE

INPUT: John told Mary that Bill wants a book.
OUTPUT1: A book about what?
OUTPUT2: Mary knows that Bill wants a book.
OUTPUT3: Bill wants to come to have a book.
OUTPUT4: Bill wants someone to cease to have a book.
OUTPUT5: Bill wants to read a book.

INPUT: John gave Mary an aspirin.
OUTPUT1: John believes that Mary wants an aspirin.
OUTPUT2: Mary is sick.
OUTPUT3: Mary wants to feel better.
OUTPUT4: Mary will ingest the aspirin.

PARAPHRASE MODE

INPUT: John advised Mary to drink the wine.
OUTPUT: John told Mary that drinking the wine would benefit her.

INPUT: John killed Mary by choking Mary.
OUTPUT1: John strangled Mary.
OUTPUT2: John choked Mary and she died because she could not breathe.
OUTPUT3: Mary died because she was unable to inhale some air and she was unable to inhale some air because John grabbed her neck.

Again, although the performance of MARGIE is impressive, it had its limitations. Two of the most serious were:

- It could process single sentences only.

- It demonstrated the problem of an "inference explosion." That is, inferences could be drawn from the original statement. And inferences could be drawn from the first generation inferences and so on, leading to a combinatorial explosion.

SAM

By 1974, Schank had moved to Yale University where he and Robert Abelson, Professor of Psychology, invented *scripts*. Scripts helped solve both of the problems with MARGIE mentioned above. A script provides the framework for integrating the individual sentences of a story. A script also helps reduce the explosion of inferences by providing a *context* for validating some inferences and eliminating many others. The program which first made use of these ideas was SAM (Script Applier Mechanism), the Ph.D. thesis work of Richard Cullingford.

The internal structure of SAM consisted of four parts:

- A *parser* to convert the story sentences to CD formalism. A modified version of MARGIE's parser was used.

- A modified version of MARGIE's *generator* to convert CD representations back into correct English.

- A *script applier* to check the consistency of the CD representation with that specified in the script.

- A *question-answerer* module.

Using automobile accident scripts, SAM was capable of reading, paraphrasing, translating, and answering questions on newspaper reports of accidents. Below is an excerpt from Schank.[13]

INPUT

```
Friday evening a car swerved off Route 69.  The vehicle
struck a tree.  The passenger, a New Jersey man, was killed.
David Hall, 27, was pronounced dead at the scene by Dr. Dana
Blanchard, medical examiner.  Frank Miller, 32, of 593 Foxon
Rd., the driver, was taken to Milford Hospital by Flanagan
Ambulance.  He was treated and released.  No charges were
made.  Patrolman Robert Onofrio investigated the accident.
```

ENGLISH SUMMARY

```
AN AUTOMOBILE HIT A TREE NEAR HIGHWAY 69 FOUR DAYS AGO.
DAVID HALL, AGE 27, RESIDENCE IN NEW JERSEY, THE PASSENGER,
DIED.  FRANK MILLER, AGE 32, RESIDENCE AT 593 FOXON ROAD IN
NEW HAVEN, CONNECTICUT, THE DRIVER, WAS SLIGHTLY INJURED.
THE POLICE DEPARTMENT DID NOT FILE CHARGES.
```

SPANISH SUMMARY

```
UN AUTO CHOCO CONTRA UN ARBOL CERCA DE LA CARRETERA 69 EL
VIERNES AL ANOCHECER.  DAVID HALL, DE 27 ANOS, QUE VIVIA EN
NEW JERSEY, EL PASAGERO, SE MURIO.  FRANK MILLER, DE 32
ANOS, QUE VIVIA EN 593 CALLE FOXON EN NEW HAVEN,
CONNECTICUT, EL CHOFER, QUEDO UN POCO HERIDO.  EL DEPARTA-
MENTO DE POLICIA NO ACUSO A NADIE.
```

QUESTION-ANSWERING OUTPUT

```
Q1:  Was anyone killed?
A1:  YES, DAVID HALL DIED.

Q2:  Was anyone hurt?
A2:  YES, FRANK MILLER WAS SLIGHTLY INJURED.

Q3:  Why was Miller hurt?
A3:  BECAUSE THE AUTOMOBILE HIT THE TREE.

Q4:  Did Miller go to the hospital?
A4:  YES, HE WAS IN THE MILFORD HOSPITAL.

Q5:  How did Miller get to the hospital?
A5:  THE FLANAGAN AMBULANCE COMPANY TOOK HIM TO THE MILFORD
     HOSPITAL.
```

The use of semantic primitives gave SAM the capability of paraphrasing the article in Chinese, Russian, and Dutch as well as English and Spanish as shown above. However, SAM worked for very restrictive scripts and had no knowledge of the plans and goals of the players in a story. The Yale group's efforts to address these problems culminated in the program, PAM.

PAM

PAM (Plan Applier Mechanism) by Robert Wilensky was a hybrid of the ideas from SAM and those from TALE-SPIN. In TALE-SPIN, Schank and his students gave the characters of a story certain goals and simulated human planning to meet those goals. The program was then turned loose and wrote its own stories.

PAM differed from SAM in using a different generator and special vocabulary to enhance the realism of its conversations. Also, since it had the goals and plans of each of its main actors available, PAM was able to narrate story summaries from various points of view. Several of these features are apparent in the following excerpt from a PAM dialog about a liquor store robbery.[14]

INPUT TEXT

```
John wanted money.  He got a gun and walked into a liquor
store.  He told the owner he wanted some money.  The owner
gave John the money and John left.
```

OUTPUT — STORY FROM JOHN'S POINT OF VIEW:

```
I needed to get some dough.  So I got myself this gun, and I
walked down to the liquor store.  I told the shopkeeper that
if he didn't let me have the money then I would shoot him.
So he handed it over.  Then I left.
```

OUTPUT — STORY FROM THE OWNER'S POINT OF VIEW:

```
I was minding the store when a man entered.  He threatened
me with a gun and demanded all the cash receipts.  Well, I
didn't want to get hurt, so I gave him the money.  Then he
escaped.
```

INPUT: `Why did John get a gun?`
OUTPUT: `Because John wanted to rob the liquor store.`

INPUT: `Why did John threaten the shopkeeper?`
OUTPUT: `Because John needed to get some money.`

INPUT: `Why did the shopkeeper give John the money?`
OUTPUT: `Because the shopkeeper didn't want to get hurt.`

INPUT: `Why did John leave?`
OUTPUT: `Because John didn't want to get caught.`

8.7 OTHER CD-BASED NLP PROGRAMS

The parsers, generators, and script appliers developed in the MARGIE, SAM, and PAM programs provided the tools and inspiration for numerous additional investigations. Among the more prominent of these were:

POLITICS — This doctoral work of Jaime Carbonell integrated the features of the previous programs so that beliefs, plans, goals, and inferences were continuously applied during the conversation rather than in separate stages as previously. The program was applied to analyzing international issues and could interpret events and advise from either a liberal or conservative point of view.

FRUMP — This was the acronym for Fast Reading, Understanding, and Memory Program and was the thesis work of Gerry DeJong. It was essentially a highly tuned and optimized version of POLITICS which was hooked up to the UPI news service. It rapidly read stories from the wire service and produced summaries of the stories in several languages. FRUMP was Schank's first attempt to build a commercial program.

IPP — This Integrated Partial Parser was an extension of FRUMP dedicated to the analysis of news stories on terrorism with the additional ability to learn from what it read. While FRUMP used only scripts, IPP used plans, goals, scripts, and had a memory.

BORIS — BORIS was a Better Organized Reasoning and Inference System which was the thesis work of Michael Dyer under the supervision of Professor Wendy Lehnert of Yale University. As Schank explains it, "We wanted also to see how we could improve our general story understanding capabilities by using a new set of memory structures we were devising, ones more suited to facilitate learning by cross-contextual understanding. We created a more fully integrated program that relied on a model of human beliefs and interactions that we could use in understanding little melodramas."

CYRUS — CYRUS stands for Computerized Yale Reasoning

and Understanding System. It was written by Janet Kolodner as part of her thesis work, and had some remarkable capabilities and accomplishments. It was the culmination of the previous series of CD-based programs and had the following features:

- It was an attempt to model the memory of a particular individual, the diplomat Cyrus Vance.

- It could learn, that is, continuously change on the basis of new experience.

- It continually reorganized itself to best reflect what it knew. This feature resembles the human capability of "self-awareness."

- It had the capability of "guessing" about events of which it had no direct knowledge.

To illustrate this last feature, CYRUS was asked if his wife had ever met Mrs. Begin. The program searched for social occasions to which it was likely that both Cyrus Vance and Prime Minister Begin had brought their wives. If such a case were found, it was likely that the wives had met. It did find such an occasion and answered: "YES, MOST RECENTLY AT A STATE DINNER IN ISRAEL IN JAN 1980." Both the program's guess and the assumptions on which it was based turned out to be correct.

MORRIS — This program is a Moral and Reminding Inference System written by Michael Dyer as an extension of his previous program, BORIS.[15] MORRIS is intended to read a story in depth and perform a careful analysis of the appropriateness of character actions. As a result of this analysis it extracts the *moral of the story* in terms of abstract planning advice, and uses this moral as an indexing structure for storage of the story in long-term episodic memory. Whenever a later story is read which can be analyzed in terms of the same planning advice, MORRIS is reminded of the prior story. The goal of MORRIS is the ability to express this advice in terms of an appropriate cultural saying or adage.

8.8 MACHINE TRANSLATION

One of the first applications of computers was by the British Colossus computer in deciphering the German military code produced by the Enigma machine during World War II. This feat, which played an important role in the outcome of the war, was essentially a translation of one language into another. The success of this effort in cryptanalysis led Warren Weaver to publish an important memorandum which inspired interest in natural language machine translation (MT).[16]

Weaver suggested three ideas which were to stimulate and guide the early researchers in MT:

1. When viewing 2N + 1 words of text through a window, the unique, correct translation of the word in the center of the window may be achieved by letting N become sufficiently large. This is the theory of statistical semantics derived from cryptography.

2. Translation was seen as a problem of cryptanalysis, an area which had been successfully "cracked." Weaver stated, "When I look at an article in Russian, I say, *This is really written in English, but it has been coded in some strange symbols. I will now proceed to decode."*

3. Translation from source language A to target language B is a two-step process. First we translate source A to a "universal language" known as *interlingua* which is equivalent to the "deep representation" discussed previously. Then we convert from interlingua to target language B.

The basic idea of translation was to read a Russian/English dictionary into the computer, along with rules of syntax, and then enter the text to be translated. The computer would look up each unknown Russian word, apply the syntax rules, and print out the translation.

This paradigm for MT was given additional credence by the results of a MT project at Georgetown University in 1954. Using six syntactic rules and a 250 word dictionary, the Georgetown project translated the following Russian sentences:[17]

The quality of crude oil is determined by calorie content.
The quality of saltpeter is determined by chemical methods.
TNT is produced from coal.
They obtain dynamite from nitroglycerine.

Soon large MT projects were established at MIT, Harvard, and the University of Pennsylvania; a journal of machine translation, MT, was founded; and by 1966 over $20 million had been spent on research into machine translation.

However, the research did not go well. The straight syntactical approach soon stumbled over at least three unresolved problems:

- No complete specification of English syntax exists.

- Referent ambiguities (e.g. "I hit the boy with the girl with long hair with a hammer with vengeance.")[18]

- Word ambiguity in both source and target languages.

After nine years of struggling with such problems, the linguist Yehoshua Bar-Hillel concluded that MT was impossible, citing the following pair of sentences in what is now known as the "Bar-Hillel paradox":

The pen is in the box.
The box is in the pen.

Note that the syntax of these two sentences is identical. Humans generally interpret the first sentence as meaning, *The writing instrument is in the box,* and the second as meaning, *The box is in the play-pen or in the pig-pen.* How can humans automatically make these interpretations which are most likely correct while the computer generally fails? The answer is the vast store of knowledge about the world and common sense reasoning which come as "second nature" to humans but which is virtually impossible to teach computers, or at least the computers of Bar-Hillel's day (1960). He dismissed the idea of encoding facts about pens and boxes into the data-base with the observation:

> *"What such a suggestion amounts to, if taken seriously, is the requirement that a translation machine should not only be supplied with a dictionary but also with a universal encyclopedia. This is surely utterly chimerical and hardly deserves any further discussion."*[19]

Because of such problems with ambiguities, MT researchers were forced to provide human *pre-editors* to attempt to disambiguate questionable words found by the computer in the source document and *post-editors* to scan the target document to select the correct word or phrase from an ambiguity list generated by the machine translator. By 1966, for example, a segment of an article on Russian space biology was translated by a MT program to read:

> **"Biological experiments, conducted on various/different cosmic aircraft, astrophysical researches of the cosmic space and flights of Soviet and American astronauts with the sufficient/rather persuasiveness showed/indicated/pointed, that momentary/transitory/short orbital flights of lower/below than radiation belts/regions/flanges of earth/land/soil in the absence of the raised/increased/heightened sun/sunny/solar activity with respect to radiation are/appear/arrive report safe/not-**

dangerous/secure."[20]

The human post-editor would scan such material, select the appropriate word from the "/" separated alternatives to resolve ambiguities, and convert the output to grammatical, comprehensible prose. To the great dismay of MT researchers, this whole process would often take more time and cost more money than hiring a competent human translator!

Because of disillusionment with the progress of MT, the National Research Council established the Automatic Language Processing Advisory Committee (ALPAC) to study the problems of MT. The committee report (The Pierce Report) issued in 1966 stated in part:

> *"'Machine Translation' presumably means going by algorithm from machine-readable source text to useful target text, without recourse to human translation or editing. In this context, there has been no machine translation of general scientific text, and none is in immediate prospect."*

This negative evaluation of the prospects of MT caused funding in the United States to be discontinued and effectively killed active research in the area.

However, since that time there have been a number of significant events which have improved the outlook for MT. Consider the following important contributions and advances which have occurred since the early days of MT.

Linguistics

- The publication of Noam Chomsky's *Syntactic Structure* in 1957
- New syntactic parsers such as Augmented Transition Networks
- New deep representations such as the conceptual dependency theory

Software

- Powerful list processing languages such as LISP
- Powerful logic programming languages such as Prolog
- New knowledge representation techniques such as production rules

- Very fast and flexible data-base retrieval systems

Hardware

- Machines of greater speed and capacity at 0.001–0.0001 the 1960's cost

- Machines with 100–1000 times the memory and disk storage capacity

- The Bar-Hillel chimera — a 500 megabyte optical disk-based encyclopedia for microcomputers at a cost of about $1 per megabyte

- Terabyte hard disks for larger computers at a cost of well below $\$10^6$.

As a result of these new conceptual and programming tools, interest in MT has revived. There are now active MT projects underway in Japan, Europe, and the United States. A summary of several of these projects including the languages being translated, the techniques used, and other implementation details was reported by Nirenburg.[21] A more detailed history of the development of MT was presented by Tucker.[22]

8.9 IS NLP THE WAVE OF THE FUTURE?

Our intuition tells us that there are a great many applications in which NLP will become the standard I/O technique, particularly in those cases where management personnel and other professionals with minimal computer literacy need direct access to information. Is it correct, then, to assume that almost all applications will eventually shift to NL interfaces? Not necessarily!

One of the main goals of adding intelligence to machines is to *communicate effectively*, but not necessarily in natural language. There are a number of applications for which alternative I/O protocols will prove more efficient than natural language processors. These include:

- Applications such as word processors and spread sheets with specialized command structure in which key- or menu-driven I/O is far faster and more natural.

- Sophisticated, object-driven graphical operating systems such as those in the Xerox Star, the Apple Macintosh, and Microsoft's WINDOWS™ which are icon oriented and most efficiently commanded by a pointing device such as a mouse.

- Any system requiring manual dexterity such as driving a car or playing a video game. Graphically oriented applications programs such as CAD/ CAM systems fall into this category.

Our conclusion is that NLP will play a very important role in future computer systems but not to the exclusion of more efficient communications techniques. NLP techniques will, however, most certainly eliminate the more obscure, arcane systems and job control languages as the burden of effective communication between humans and computers shifts towards more intelligent computer interfaces.

PROBLEMS AND PROGRAMS

8-1. Experience indicates that converting from machine language to assembly language (or from assembler to FORTRAN or Pascal) reduces the programming error rate by a factor of N where N may be as large as 10. Cite evidence for the actual value determined for N and interpret this result in terms of the shift to a more natural language.

8-2. Experience indicates that the average programmer produces N lines of documented, debugged code per day on the average, where N is some number less than 10. High-level language code is typically n_1 times as efficient as assembly code (i.e. a given job requires $1/n_1$ times as many lines of code), and Prolog is typically n_2 times as efficient as high-level language where n_1 and n_2 are in the range 4–10. Find evidence supporting these numbers and interpret your results in terms of the implications of NLP for programming productivity.

8-3. "User-friendly" is a term introduced to describe modern operating systems, but it applies equally well to innovations that turned the early "cranky" automobile into the transportation system for the masses. Write an comparative analysis of user-friendliness in automobiles and computers, indicating particular innovations and the effects on the widespread acceptance and use of each device.

8-4. Identify the most "user-unfriendly" computer operating system you can find on campus and compare it to the most user-friendly system of which you are aware. List several equivalent standard commands in each system and interpret in NLP terms.

8-5. Write two example sentences illustrating each of the following *source* → *target* mappings: one-to-one, one-to-many, many-to-one, and many-to-many.

8-6. Write all the interpretations you can possibly imagine which make sense for the sentence:

John saw the boy in the park with the telescope.

8-7. Interpret the early attempts at machine translation in terms of simple pattern matching.

8-8. Discussions of NLP programs using pattern matching usually cite ELIZA, SIR, and STUDENT although these programs range widely in their design and performance. Discuss the similarities and differences between these three programs in terms of their syntactic and semantic content.

8-9. Analyze the following sentences using the recursive transition network specified in Figure 8-3.

Steve loves Julie.

The absent-minded, middle-aged, flaky professor continued studying physics.

He skied the high, beautiful mountains of Colorado.

She hit the girl with the boy with long hair with a ball bat with vengeance.

8-10. The goal of conceptual dependency theory is a *language independent* deep representation of events. Compare this concept to that of the *interlingua* of machine translation.

8-11. The theory of conceptual dependency states that it is possible to transform the *sentences* describing an event into a *representation of the event itself.* Discuss the feasibility of this approach for machine understanding in light of cognitive theories that human thought is ultimately connected to language.

8-12. In conceptual dependency theory all actions are reduced to combinations of 10–15 *primitive acts.* Discuss the difference in performance this implies for the following two tasks assigned to a CD program:

- *Reading* the Great American Novel (paraphrasing it and answering questions about it), and

- *Writing* the Great American Novel (given the actors and plot in the appropriate deep representation).

8-13. Conceptual dependency theory is sometimes criticized as a "scruffy" approach to NLP compared to the "clean" syntactic approach, because of CD's operational, *ad hoc* techniques of building real-world experience into the computer. Do you feel this criticism is justified? If so, what do you feel is a better approach? If not, how do you feel CD theory might be extended to a broader range of situations?

8-14. Operational programs developed using CD theory display a remarkable range of "human" attributes such as ability to guess, ideology, and so on. Make a table of such human emotions and attributes, and indicate which programs discussed in the text exhibited them.

8-15. One interpretation for the failure of early efforts in MT is that AI researchers failed to distinguish between *formal language* and *natural language*. Discuss this distinction in light of the success of cryptanalysis and statistical semantics.

8-16. Bar-Hillel expressed amazement that no one had ever pointed out that in language understanding there is a world-modeling process going on in the mind of the listener. In what ways is this observation related to the basic hypothesis of conceptual dependency theory?

8-17. Assume your first job assignment on your new job as programmer for an AI firm designing MT software is to estimate the memory storage capacity of an optical disk required to resolve the Bar-Hillel paradox. That is, how many bytes would be required for an encyclopedia containing "the whole truth about everything"? Suggestions for steps in this analysis involve answering questions like:

- What things are there to classify?
- What classification scheme would I use for these things?
- Would existing encyclopedias and data-bases be adequate for providing such information?

8-18. Use articles from the trade literature to specify the storage capacity and costs of presently available mass storage devices (magnetic and optical disks) and the projections for future availability. What are the implications of this technology for a natural language translation encyclopedia?

8-19. Extend the Prolog parser presented in the text by expanding both the noun and verb list to 15 and the adjective, preposition, and infinitive lists to 10 each. Estimate how many well-formed sentences are now possible with the grammar and test it on several sample sentences.

8-20. Modify the Prolog parser to handle the grammar of the first grade reading class. Include imperatives and conjunctions such as:

Come, Spot, come!
See Dick and Jane run and play.

REFERENCES AND FOOTNOTES

[1] Bunnell, David, "Artificial Intelligence on the Desktop," *Publish!* **2**, pp. 11–14, March, (1987)

[2] Hodges, Andrew, *Alan Turing — The Enigma*, p. 357, Simon and Schuster, New York, NY (1983)

[3] Rich, Elaine, *Artificial Intelligence*, McGraw-Hill Series in Artificial Intelligence, pp. 297–301, New York, NY (1983)

[4] Raphael, B., "SIR: A Computer Program for Semantic Information Retrieval," in *Semantic Information Processing*, M. Minsky (ed), MIT Press, Cambridge, MA (1968)

[5] Bobrow, D. G., "Natural Language Input for a Computer Problem-solving System", in *Semantic Information Processing*, MIT Press, Cambridge, MA (1968)

[6] Woods, W. A., "Transition Network Grammars for Natural Language Analysis," *CACM* **13**, pp. 591–606 (1970)

[7] Woods, W. A., "Progress in Natural Language Understanding: An Application to Lunar Geology," *AFIPS Conference Proceedings* **42**, pp. 441–450, AFIPS Press Montvale, NJ (1973)

[8] Garavaglia, Susan, *PROLOG — Programming Techniques and*

Applications, pp. 251–257, Harper & Row, Publishers, Inc., New York, NY (1987)

9 Feigenbaum, Edward A., Barr, Avron, and Cohen, Paul R. (eds), *The Handbook of Artificial Intelligence* Vol.1–3, HeurisTech Press/-William Kaufmann, Inc., Stanford, CA (1981–82)

10 Schank, R. C. and Abelson, R. P., *Scripts, Plans, Goals, and Understanding,* Lawrence Erlbaum Associates, Publishers, Hillsdale, NJ (1977)

11 Feigenbaum, *Op Cit,* pp. 300–315

12 Schank, Roger C., *THE COGNITIVE COMPUTER — On Language, Learning, and Artificial Intelligence,* Addison-Wesley, Reading, MA (1984)

13 Schank, *Op Cit*, p. 145

14 Schank, *Op Cit*, p. 146

15 Dyer, Michael G., "Understanding Stories through Morals and Remindings," *Proceedings of the Eighth International Joint Conference on Artificial Intelligence,* pp. 75–77, August (1983)

16 Weaver, W., "Translation," in *Machine Translation of Languages,* Locke and Booth (eds), pp. 15–23, Technology Press, Wiley, New York, NY (1955)

17 Charniak, Eugene and McDermott, Drew, *Introduction to Artificial Intelligence,* p. 173, Addison-Wesley, Reading, MA (1985)

18 Andrew, A.M., *Artificial Intelligence,* Abacus Press, Cambridge, MA (1983)

19 Bar-Hillel, Yehoshua, "The Present Status of Automatic Translation of Languages", in *Advances in Computers* **1**, Academic Press, New York, NY (1960)

20 Pierce, John R., "Language and Machines: Computers in Translation and Linguistics," Publication 1416, National Academy of Sciences-/National Research Council, Washington, DC (1966)

21 Nirenburg, Sergie, "Special Section on Machine Translation of Natural Languages," *SIGART Newsletter* **92**, pp. 128–144, April (1985)

22 Tucker, Allen B., Jr., "A Perspective on Machine Translation: Theory and Practice," *Communications of the ACM* **27**, pp. 322–329, April (1984)

Chapter 9

KNOWLEDGE REPRESENTATION

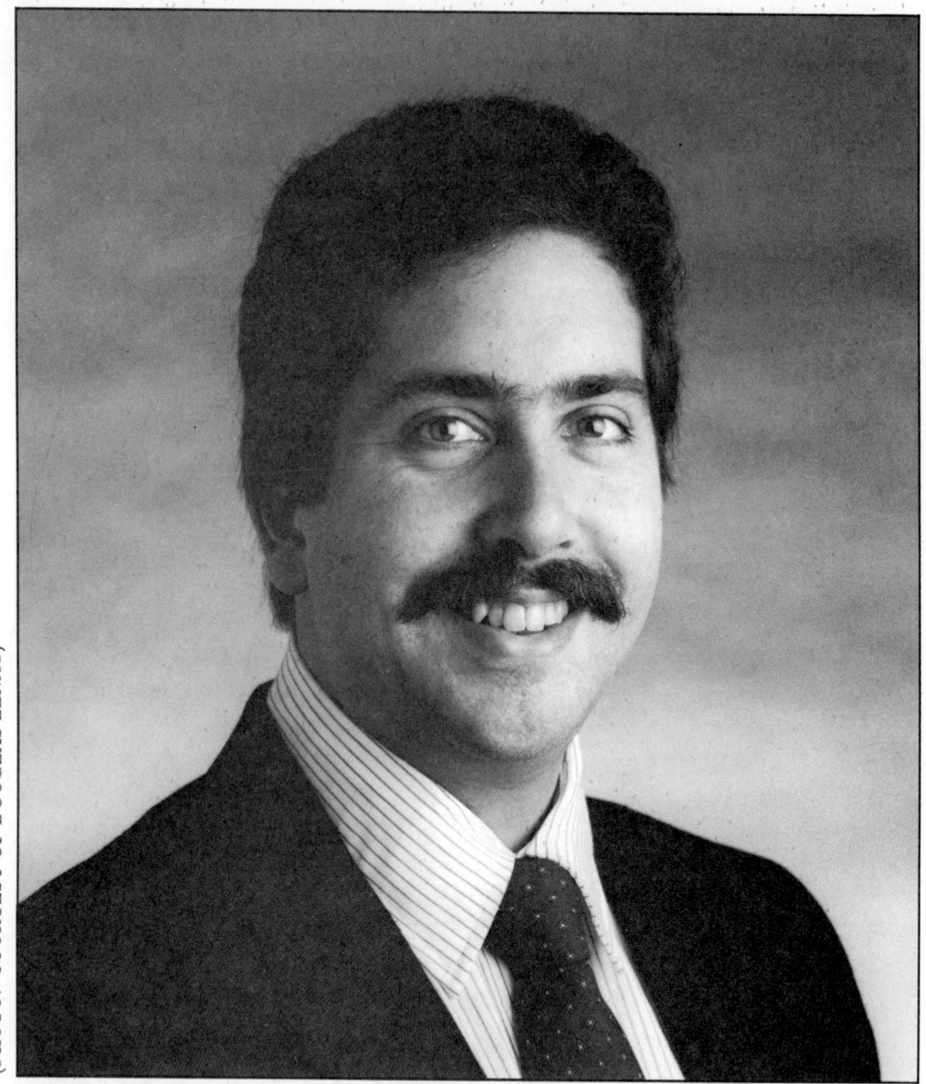

(PHOTO: COURTESY OF DOUGLAS LENAT)

Dr. Douglas B. Lenat is Principal Scientist in the Artificial Intelligence Project of the Microelectronics and Computer Technology Corporation (MCC) in Austin, Texas. He did his undergraduate work in Applied Mathematics and Physics at the University of Pennsylvania and his Ph.D. in Computer Science at Stanford. His research on the foundations of scientific discovery has been applied to elementary mathematics and more recently to VLSI design. He is editor of *Building Expert Systems* and is one of the founders of Teknowledge, Inc. Lenat's research at MCC involves building a large knowledge base of common sense, a step he believes essential to progress in AI. The project is expected to require two person-centuries of effort.

9: KNOWLEDGE REPRESENTATION

9.1 INTRODUCTION

We now address, head on, the problem which has been lurking under the surface in all of our discussion heretofore. That is the problem of how to represent the knowledge on which any intelligent system must be based. As our previous discussion has suggested, knowledge is more than simply data or information. Raw data, when refined, processed, or analyzed yields information which is useful in answering users queries. Upon further refinement, analysis, and the addition of heuristics, information may be converted into knowledge which is useful in problem solving and from which additional knowledge may be inferred. It should be noted that several techniques for representing knowledge have been introduced in previous chapters, including:

- *Lists,* and their manipulation in LISP
- *Predicate calculus,* and its implementation in Prolog[1]
- *Tree graphs* with search heuristics
- *Natural language* and semantic parsers.

Some psychologists believe that the limit of our thought is set by the expressiveness of our language. That is, how can we think something that we can't put into words? This concept helps explain the common association of a large vocabulary with profound thinking (a sometimes misleading connection!). It also explains why people with no formal training or skill in mathematics never make significant contributions to mathematics. You will never write the great French novel if you don't know French.

There is a close analogy between the expressiveness of natural language and that of computer languages. One could start by comparing machine language to the grunts and signs of pre-historic humans. Sign-language may not have been elegant, but it got the job done (or we all wouldn't be here). It was not the language of great literature, however, and fortunately natural language had improved by the time of William Shakespeare.

The analogy of the expressiveness of natural language can be extended to the representation of knowledge. This argument would hold that progress in AI research closely paralleled the development of more sophisticated schemes for representing knowledge. Relatively simple structures like search trees were adequate for representing knowledge about board games, and progress was made by increasing the sophistication of the search heuristics. More complex structures like propositional and predicate calculus allowed a broader range of problems to be addressed. In natural language understanding, progress was made by moving from the simplest grammars to more complex parsers such as the augmented transition networks. To deal with the complexity of problems such as natural language processing, more powerful computer languages have been developed. The appropriateness and expressiveness of various specialized computer languages are subjects of active AI research.[2]

Why do AI workers prefer the term *knowledge representation* rather than information representation or data base? The reason is that conventional data bases have traditionally represented simple data types such as numbers, strings, and Boolean values. AI research has indicated the need for much more complex information such as processes, procedures, actions, causality, time, motivations, goals, and common sense reasoning. To describe this broader category of information the term *knowledge* has been widely accepted.

In this chapter and the next chapter we present the following techniques which have proven effective for knowledge representation:

- Semantic Networks
- Frames and Scripts
- Production Systems.

However, before introducing these topics it is useful to consider what features a good knowledge representation system should include and some considerations on its design.

9.2 FEATURES OF KNOWLEDGE REPRESENTATION SCHEMES

Typically, knowledge representation (KR) systems combine the following two elements: data structures and interpretive procedures for using the knowledge embedded in the data structures. It is important to realize that both elements of the KR system are essential. Data structures without interpretive procedures are as useless as a dictionary without a reader or a spelling-checker lexicon without the spelling-checker program.

It is useful to consider a broad classification of the types of knowledge which must be represented by KR systems. Feigenbaum *et al* suggest the following categories for which knowledge must be accessible:[3]

Objects — Any system must have the ability to encode information about the properties of physical objects and concepts. This may be accomplished by simple statements such as *Hobbits have fuzzy-toes*, production rules such as **IF** (cloud_height = 3-8 km, cloud_structure = towering, cloud_top = anvil_shaped) **THEN** (cloud_type = cumulonimbus), or attribute lists (Mozart '((*Austrian Comp-oser*) (*Lived 1756-1791*) (*Wrote over 600 works*)).

Events — This category includes actions and events in the world. It generally specifies a time element and may indicate cause and effect relationships.

Performance — This category includes information on how to perform certain tasks. Examples: How to ride a bike; How to compose a sentence; How to prove a theorem. There is often a fine semantic difference between *performance* information and, for instance, the *object* called "algorithm for riding a bike."

Meta-Knowledge — Meta-knowledge is knowledge about the knowledge represented. It includes such issues as: extent and origin of knowledge, reliability of knowledge, relative importance of certain facts, and evaluation of our own performance as cognitive processors. In a rule-based system, for example, meta-knowledge can be represented by rules on which other rules take precedence and which rules must not be retracted.[4]

USES OF KNOWLEDGE

Another consideration in knowledge representation is the use of knowledge. The particular situation in which knowledge is used should influence the representation chosen. Applications range from database query systems and diagnostic uses of expert systems to object recognition for uses with robot systems. Three stages in the use of knowledge may be summarized:

Acquisition — Acquisition involves the integration of new information into the knowledge system. Knowledge acquisition can occur at two levels. The lower level is concerned with structuring facts in a data base. The higher level is concerned with relating information to previously stored information. This higher level more closely resembles the function we call *learning* in humans which integrates new information with existing knowledge structures.

Retrieval — This use of knowledge resembles the human function of *recall*. Retrieval requires sorting through a huge knowledge base for the particular facts or relationships required for the task at hand. Humans perform this complex function instinctively and very efficiently. AI systems have attempted to model this human behavior by using the concepts of *linking* and *lumping*. Linking extracts information explicitly used as well as that implied or deduced from the given information. Lumping groups component structures into a larger structure as needed for the problem.

Reasoning — Knowledge may be used for reasoning at several levels. One level is *formal reasoning* according to the rules of propositional calculus discussed in Chapter 5. Another kind of reasoning is procedural reasoning as represented by *production rules* discussed in the next chapter. Other forms of reasoning which come very naturally to humans but have been extremely difficult for machines are *reasoning by analogy* and *generalization and abstraction*. Since these forms of inductive reasoning occur at a higher conceptual level than deductive reasoning, progress in implementing induction systems on machines has been very slow.

OTHER CHARACTERISTICS OF KR SYSTEMS

It has been noted that there is no good theory of knowledge representation.[5] Some systems work well for certain applications and others work well for other applications. The actual process of representing external objects and events internally in the machine has been described as a *mapping* process by Bobrow.[6] The mapping process in conceptual dependency theory, for instance, is the process by which the deep representation is generated by the surface expressions of natural language. Several characteristics of knowledge representations systems are useful for describing the optimum system for a particular application and in designing the appropriate mapping of information into an internal representation.

Scope and Grain Size — The *scope* of a KR system is a measure of the domain from which knowledge is represented. The scope of the LADDER database, for instance, included ships of the United States navy and merchant marine. The resolution or detail with which knowledge is represented is call the *grain size*. Simplicity would suggest a grain size which is uniform across the objects and events being described such as those provided naturally by databases and spread sheets. Efficiency of resources and representation requires a grain size adapted to the details of the object represented and is most easily provided by flexible list-structured languages.

Modularity and Understandability — One of the canons of good "top-down" program design is modularity. This is also one of the highly desirable features exhibited by the production system scheme of knowledge representation presented in the next chapter. The idea, in theory, is that procedures of a program or new production rules are all independent of other procedures or productions rules and may be added or deleted without changing the structure of the system. In practice, however, many events are better represented in a context-dependent or procedural way. In many cases, the apparent improvement in understanding gained by the simplicity of the production rules is lost when they are applied by the control program.

Explicit vs Implicit Knowledge — Explicit knowledge is that knowledge to which the programmer and program have direct access and can manipulate. An example would be the information contained in a relational database. Implicit knowledge is that which is logically entailed in the system by, for instance, the process of deduction applied to a predicate calculus system. One advantage of explicit representation is that the knowledge is available for global use. In expert systems, for instance, an explicit production rule could be used for producing a particular diagnosis and again to justify its line of argument in a later stage. Implicit representations have the advantage of efficiency and "data compression" by appropriate classification schemes.

Declarative versus procedural representations — An important controversy in the development of AI systems concerns the relative effectiveness of declarative versus procedural representations of knowledge. Procedural knowledge is most readily represented by conventional languages or functional languages such as LISP. Declarative representations are most easily accomplished through the facts and rules of Prolog. The statements of predicate calculus are perfect examples of a declarative representation of knowledge.

The backers of declarative systems such as first order logic have noted that such systems have the advantages of flexibility, economy, certainty, and ability to prove theorems. Supporters of the procedural school (represented by Winograd's SHRDLU) claimed that their systems used direct inference, were easy to code, and operated understandably. Both schools have learned from the other, however, and modern systems often contain the best elements of each.

9.3 DESIGN CONSIDERATIONS FOR A KR SYSTEM

A little reflection on the systematics which humans have devised for representing knowledge efficiently provides valuable insight on designing KR systems for machines. All KR systems have at least some of the capabilities outlined below, and the number of capabilities is a fairly direct measure of the expressiveness and power of the KR system.

PROPERTY LISTS

To usefully represent an object, it is necessary to define properties of the object and attach property values. In SHRDLU these would include such properties as the color, size, shape, position, and relationship to the other objects of all blocks on the table. Because of the importance of property lists, LISP provides at least three intrinsic functions for manipulating property values:

- PUTPROP — adds a value to the property list of a symbol
- GETPROP — returns the value of a specific property from the list
- PROPLIST — returns the property list of a symbol

In Prolog, the functor notation provides a natural representation of properties and property values. For example:

```
block(block1,color(red),size(large),position(14,8),on(block2)).
```

An important predicate to indicate components of an object is the HAS relationship. For instance, an elephant represented in Prolog would certainly require at least the following property list:

```
elephant(size(huge),color(grey),has([legs(4),tail,trunk])).
```

HIERARCHICAL STRUCTURE

Humans have found that categorization of information provides efficient structures for refining information and organizing it as knowledge. Biological taxonomy, for example, provides a structure for organizing all plants of the plant kingdom into divisions, classes, subclasses, orders, families, genera, species, and varieties. The Prolog representation of the biological classification of *romaine lettuce* is given precisely as:

```
plant(division(vascular_plant),class(flowering_plant), sub-
class(dicotyledon),order(campanulatae),family
(composites),genus(lettuce),species(cultivated_lettuce),
variety(romaine_lettuce)).
```

The powerful idea here is that every plant on Earth may be classified within this hierarchical taxonomy by simply substituting the appropriate argument for each of the classifications. Can you imagine the utter confusion facing the biology student *without* such a classification system? (Please have the following 350,000 plants memorized for the quiz next Tuesday!)

A closely related advantage of classification hierarchy is the concept of *inheritance*. That is, once I identify *romaine lettuce* as a plant, it automatically inherits all characteristics of plants, e.g. it is alive, it can reproduce, and so on. Once I specify its class and subclass, I know it shares all the characteristics of the flowering plants and dicotyledons, respectively, without having to specify these in detail for each instance of the plant. Furthermore, if I am developing a florist's database, I can probably set the class of all plants to a default value of "flowering plant" and gain additional efficiency in my classification system. In many KR systems the hierarchy classification requires the ISA predicate, i.e.

```
isa(romaine_lettuce,cultivated_lettuce).
isa(dicotyledon,flowering_plant).
```

These predicates indicate an instance of a class in the first case and a subclass of a more general class in the second.

SEMANTIC POWER

The central idea in natural language processing was that a capable NLP system had to analyze not only the syntax but also the semantics of a given communication. A very suggestive definition of knowledge, in fact, incorporates the semantic aspect in the statement:

Knowledge is information in a meaningful context.

That is, the KR system must provide the mechanism by which meaning may be associated with the information represented. In a predicate calculus system, for example, meaning is associated with the symbols of the predicates themselves, and inference rules provide a means for deriving knowledge implicit in a given logical system.

To provide semantic power for deriving meaning from information a KR system should have the following features:

- It should *support a truth theory* — That is, if a given proposition in the KR structure is true, it should be possible to say how the world would be different if the proposition were not true; that is, the knowledge must have measurable consequences. This is equivalent to specifying what the proposition means.

- It should provide for *constraint satisfaction* — Constraints are the rules of the game or the boundary conditions within which a problem must be solved. In checkers, for instance, the pieces are constrained to move diagonally and in the forward direction. In digital circuit design, the fanout (the number of connections from a device output to other inputs) may be constrained to 10 or less.

- It should be able to cope with *incompleteness and uncertainty* — One of the key differences between KR systems in AI and the databases of conventional information systems is the quality of the information available to the system. As the science of difficult and/or impossible problems, AI frequently deals with knowledge which is incomplete, uncertain, inconsistent, or "fuzzy." Since the majority of real world problems are not completely "clean" and well-defined, KR systems should provide the means of representing fuzzy knowledge and extracting the maximum possible meaning from it.

- It should provide some capability for *common sense reasoning* — This has proven to be one of the most difficult areas of AI and that difficulty is apparent when attempting to formulate a KR system for representing the knowledge that is transparently obvious to most 3 year-old humans. SHRDLU, for example, was forced to include "semantic markers" to represent the common sense knowledge that "The table may not sit on the block" and "The block may not sit on the pyramid."

We next turn to three of the most successful approaches to building KR systems which incorporate many of the desirable features discussed above.

9.4 SEMANTIC NETWORKS

The concept of semantic networks was introduced in 1968 by Ross Quillian.[7] It was designed as a psychological model of human associative memory. All semantic networks are constructed from the two basic components:

- **NODES** representing objects, concepts, or situations. Nodes are indicated by boxes or circles.

- **ARCS** representing relationships between nodes. Arcs are indicated by arrows connecting the nodes.

EXAMPLE — TOLKIEN'S HOBBIT WORLD

The following examples, derived from Feigenbaum *et al,*[8] illustrate how knowledge may be represented and used in semantic networks. Assume we wish to represent the fact that *All Hobbits are Little-persons.*[9] We can create two nodes to represent *Hobbits* and *Little-persons* and connect them with the very useful arc or link called *isa* :

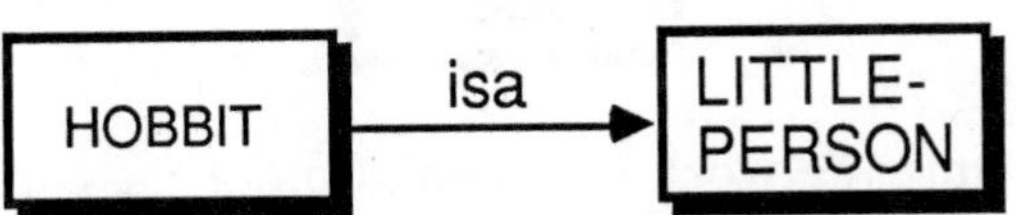

Figure 9-1 Semantic network representation of the statement "All Hobbits are Little-persons." Note the hierarchical classification system implicit — Hobbits are a subclass of the more general class of Little-persons which also includes the subclasses of elves and dwarves.

We can indicate that a particular Hobbit is named "Bilbo" by adding a node:

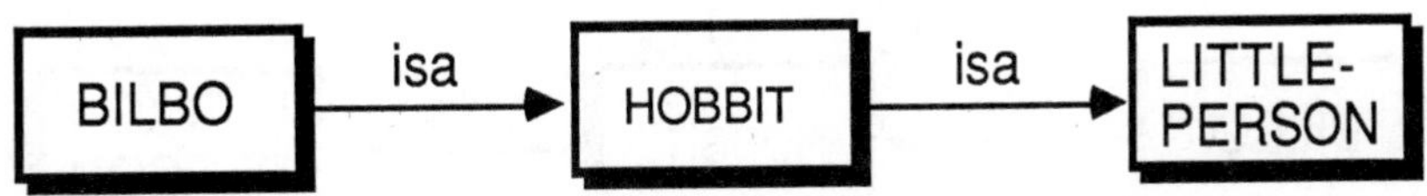

Figure 9-2 Semantic network representation of the fact that Bilbo is a particular Hobbit. Here Bilbo is an instantiation of the subclass of Hobbits rather than a sub-subclass. In grammar notation, Bilbo is a terminal symbol rather than a variable.

Now note that not only have we represented two facts: *Bilbo is a Hobbit,* and *Hobbits are Little-persons,* but also by following the *isa* links, we can deduce the new fact that *Bilbo is a Little-person.* This transitive property of semantic networks, called the *inheritance hierarchy,* makes deduction possible in a very natural way.

How could property values be assigned to objects within a semantic network? Suppose we want to represent the fact that *Hobbits have fuzzy-toes.* We could do it simply by adding the node *fuzzy-toes* connected by the arc as shown:

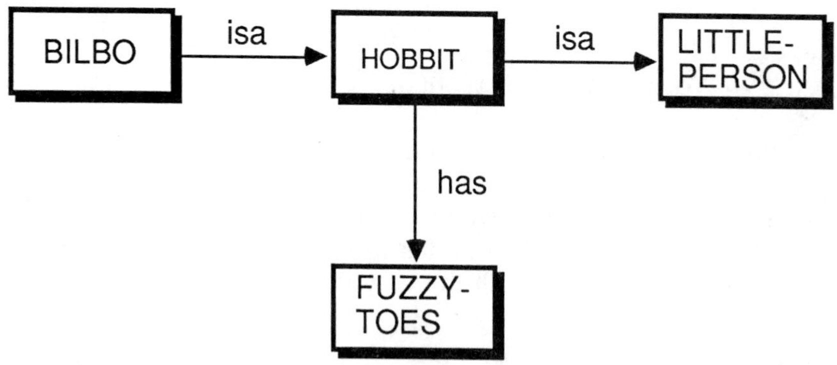

Figure 9-3 Semantic network representation of the curious feature that Hobbits have fuzzy toes.

Now we can make additional deductions from the network: *Some Little-persons have fuzzy-toes* and *Bilbo has fuzzy-toes.* This is called the *property inheritance* feature of semantic networks.

Since this network seems to be working pretty well, let's add the additional information that *Bilbo owns a magic ring.* Introducing a new link *owns* and one instance, MAGIC-RING, of the category, RING, produces the network in Figure 9-4.

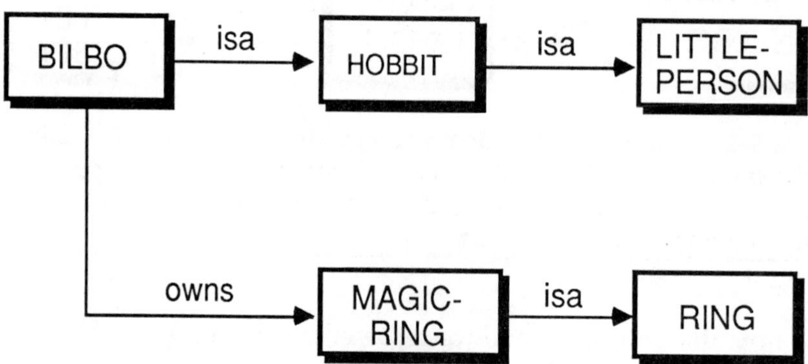

Figure 9-4 Semantic network representation of the fact that Bilbo owns a magic ring, a special instance of the class of rings.

That was easy enough and correctly represents the fact of ring ownership. However, if we want to tell part of the story or specify time dependent information in the *owns* arc we begin to have problems. This is due to the binary nature of the arc *owns*. Either Bilbo owns a magic ring or does not own a magic ring. To relate causal or sequential information, we need some analog of the five-place predicate specifying 2 *times, ownership process, owner,* and *ownee*.

The solution is found in the definition of a new structure called a *case frame* which defines a particular *situation,* in this case "ownership". Now, to specify the fact that *Bilbo owns a ring from the time he found it in Gollum's cave to the present,*we can add the case frame to our semantic network, yielding:

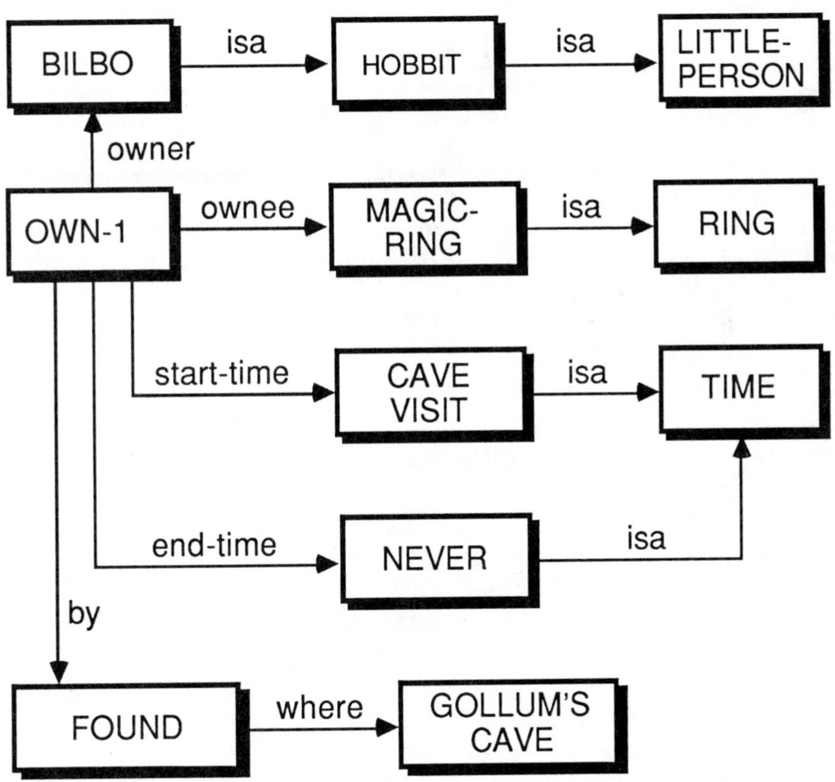

Figure 9-5 Semantic network representation using a case frame to represent time duration and the process by which ownership was achieved.

Here OWN-1 is one instance of ownership and inherits the properties of ownership specified by the arcs *owner, ownee, start-time, end-time* and *by* indicating the method of ownership.

Semantic networks are not without problems, however. Consider the following network to encode the information that *Hobbits are mythical creatures* and that *Mythical creatures are studied by literature students.*

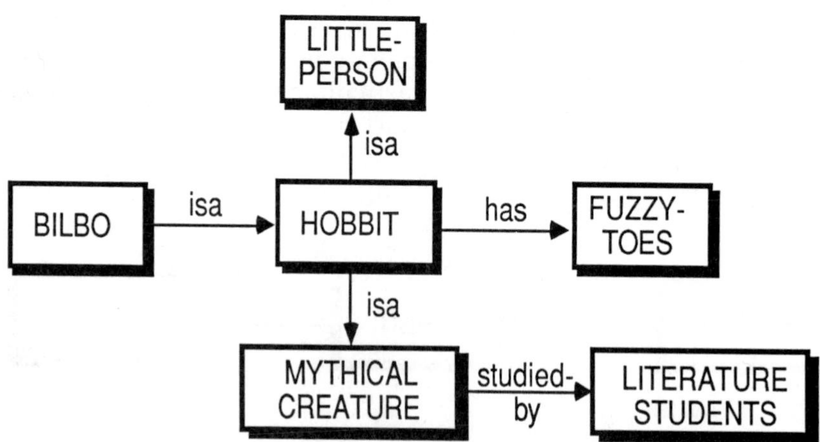

Figure 9-6 Semantic network representation of the knowledge that *Hobbits are mythical creatures* and *Mythical creatures are studied by literature students.*

This certainly represents the two sentences correctly. However, this particular network could also lead to false deductions through the inheritance properties. It implies that *Bilbo is studied by literature students* which may or may not be true, but probably isn't. The heart of the problem is the lack of a formalism for distinguishing between the *individual* (BILBO) and the *class* (HOBBIT) or what is sometimes called the *token/type* distinction.

One of the advantages of semantic networks is the simplicity with which logic can be performed to answer questions. A query to the system is rewritten in terms of a *network fragment,* and the semantic network is then searched for a pattern matching the query fragment. If a matching pattern is found, the answer to the query is "yes" and implications of the answer may be explored by following arcs away from the matching pattern.

Assume that the following question was posed to the system: *What does Bilbo own that he found?* This question may be reformulated into the network fragment:

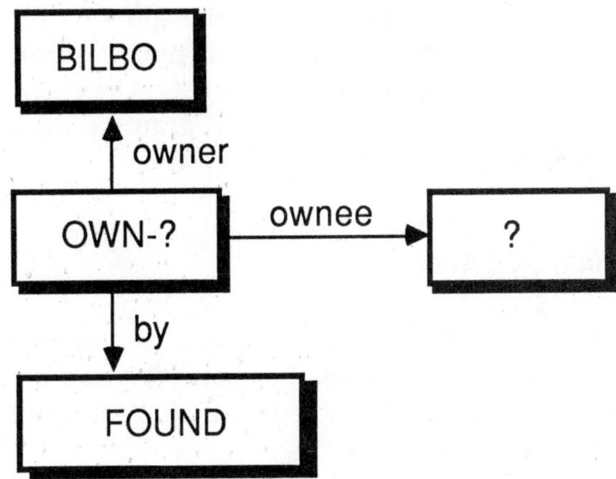

Figure 9-7 Semantic network representation using a network fragment to represent the question *What does Bilbo own that he found?*

Next the network would be searched for a structure matching that of the query. If, for instance, the following network statement was contained within the data base:

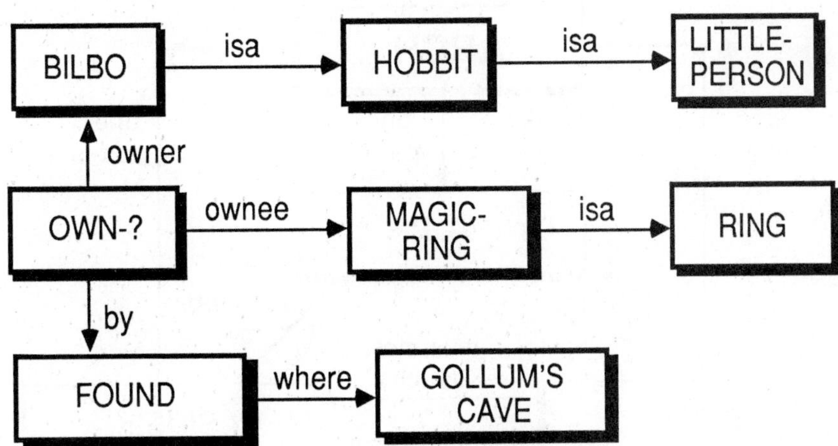

Figure 9-8 Semantic network representation of ownership property which may exist in the knowledge representation data base. If it does, the pattern match will be able to answer the question of Figure 9-7 and provide answers to related questions such as where Bilbo got to own the magic ring.

then the pattern matcher would detect the agreement and respond with: *Bilbo owns a magic ring.* With a bit more prompting, the program would indicate: *Bilbo owns a ring.* Using the inheritance characteristic of semantic networks, the program could even conclude that *The magic ring was found in Gollum's cave.*

EXAMPLE — WINSTON'S ARCH

More complex relationships may use semantic networks to clarify relationships. Patrick Winston uses the example of an arch to illustrate this point.[10] The relationship involved in the structure of an arch may be represented by the fact list:

```
(ARCH  ONE_PART_IS  SIDE1)
(ARCH  ONE_PART_IS  SIDE2)
(ARCH  ONE_PART_IS  TOP)
(TOP  MUST_BE_SUPPORTED_BY  SIDE1)
(TOP  MUST_BE_SUPPORTED_BY  SIDE2)
(SIDE1  MUST_NOT_TOUCH  SIDE2)
(SIDE2  MUST_NOT_TOUCH  SIDE1)
```

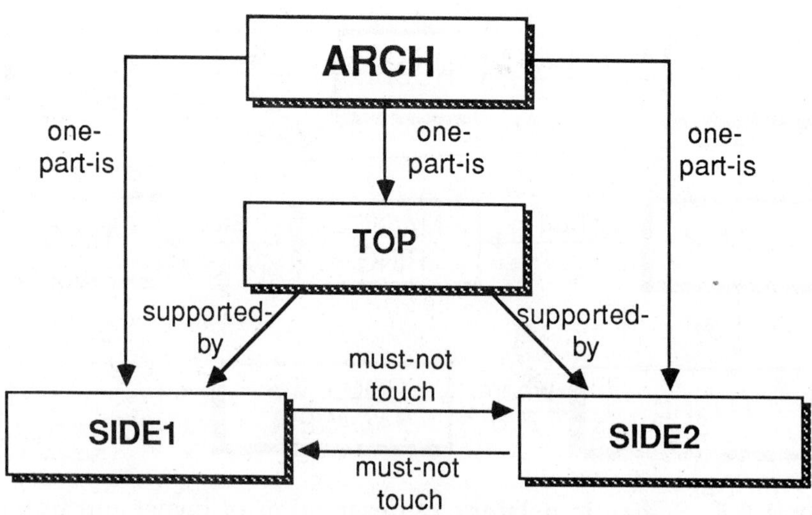

Figure 9-11 Semantic Network Representation of Arch Note that the relationships apparent in this network may be represented internally in terms of the LISP list shown above.

This knowledge may be diagrammed in a semantic network which represents the same information in a somewhat more transparent form shown in Figure 9-11.

The semantic network has proven to be a highly productive prototype for other knowledge representations systems. Among the successful early AI systems using this representation were SIR (discussed in the last chapter) by Bertram Raphael[11] and SCHOLAR by Jaime Carbonell.[12] In one application, the SIR program used semantic networks to store human anatomy information, and it could answer questions such as: *Is a finger part of a person?* SCHOLAR could answer questions on the geography of South America and could even give the student timely hints to assist in instruction.

More recently, a number of knowledge representation languages have appeared which incorporate the basic concepts of semantic networks. One of these is KL-ONE developed by Brachman and his colleagues at Bolt Beranek and Newman, Inc. KL-ONE allows the user to define a class of descriptive terms called *concepts* which it can classify and rank in order of comprehensiveness.[13]

9.5 MINSKY'S THEORY OF FRAMES

Representing Prototypical Situations

Both the theory of *frames* by Marvin Minsky[14] and *scripts* by Schank and Abelson[15] were attempts to represent knowledge in the context of which many ordinary events and objects appear. The two theories have many features in common, the central one of which is that many situations are "stereotypical" and provide a framework of expectations, goals, and plans which greatly assist both humans and machines in understanding what is going on. Thus we have the typical *dentist's office visit,* or the typical *child's birthday party,* or the typical *going to the restaurant script,* or the typical *car accident scenario.*

The fundamental validity of both theories is indicated by the set of mental images which just stating these four scenarios calls to mind. At the heart of both systems is *expectation-driven processing,* which is based on the human trait of associating complex contexts with each prototypical situation. The task of AI research is to construct corresponding contexts and trigger them in the appropriate problem environment.

Minsky describes a frame as a network of nodes and relations. The top levels of the frame represent attributes which are always true about the situation and so remain fixed. Lower levels of the frame have *terminals* or *slots* which must be filled by specific instances or data. Each terminal may specify conditions requiring smaller sub-frames. Collections of related frames may be linked to form frame-systems. Transformations between various frames may be triggered depending on information contained in slots. Improved efficiency is possible by specifying default values for slots in typical situations. These default values may be modified by the process of cancellation.

Consider the following frame for the generic *tree*:

TREE Frame

Specialization_of:	Plant
Number_of_trunks:	Integer (default → 1)
Style_of_bark:	Smooth, shingled,...
Leaf_mode:	Coniferous, deciduous
Leaf_shape:	Simple, lobed, compound,...

It is clear that these four slots tell us a great deal about the possible configurations of a common plant, the tree. By adding a few more slots such as trunk_color, tree_height, number_of_leaf_lobes, number_of_needles, and so on we could describe a particular tree to almost any degree of detail.

To describe a specific tree, such as the clump-birch in my back yard, I would fill the slots to read:

MY_TREE Frame

Specialization_of:	Tree
Number_of_trunks:	3
Style_of_bark:	Smooth
Leaf_mode:	Deciduous
Leaf_style:	Simple,toothed

Two immediate advantages of frames are suggested. One is that a number of different objects may share the same frame. Thus the frame for a given railway train may contain a slot for length and slots containing frames for engine, cars, and caboose. This frame may very easily be generalized sufficiently to describe the great majority of all railway trains in the world.

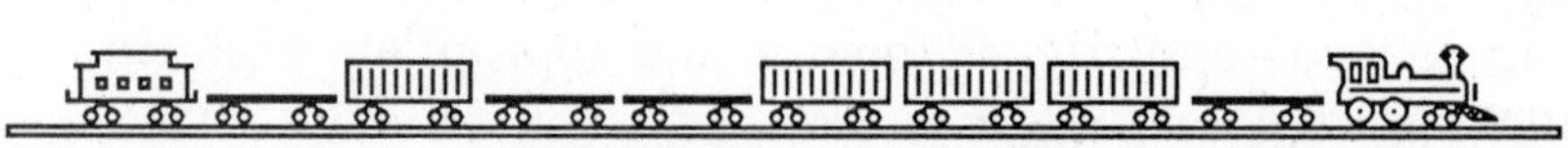

Figure 9-9 Physical situation to be represented by Train Frame Note that the car sub-frame would need at least two sub-frames, one for *cattle* and one for *flatbed*. The general train frame would contain additional car types giving it the capability of describing virtually all trains.

It is clear that the car frame will have several instances of the same type of car (here "flatbed" or "cattle") and so can share that frame. This assists in data compression. The car sub-frame might have the following slot structure:

RAILWAY_CAR Frame

Component_of:	Train frame
Car_type:	Flatbed
Empty_weight:	16 Ton
Length:	48 feet
No_Axles:	4
Contents:	Contents sub-frame

The second advantage suggested in this example is that frames provide a natural hierarchy through the sub-frame structure.[16] Thus, the frame for describing a room should have sub-frames for each wall, the ceiling, and floor. Each wall frame may contain sub-frames for picture, door, window, and so on. This hierarchical structure is illustrated in Figure 9-10.

How can information be represented explicitly in the frame representation? First, one can key in certain propositions using simple declarative grammar:

```
fear(goblins,gandalf).
has_temper(smaug,terrible).
```

Some facts may entail other facts:

FACT144	GANDALF ISA WIZARD
FACT028	FACT144 HAS_AGE MANY_YEARS
FACT765	FACT144 RESCUED DWARVES

and it is possible to represent facts about relationships:

RESPECT ISA RELATIONSHIP
ISA IS_USED OFTEN.

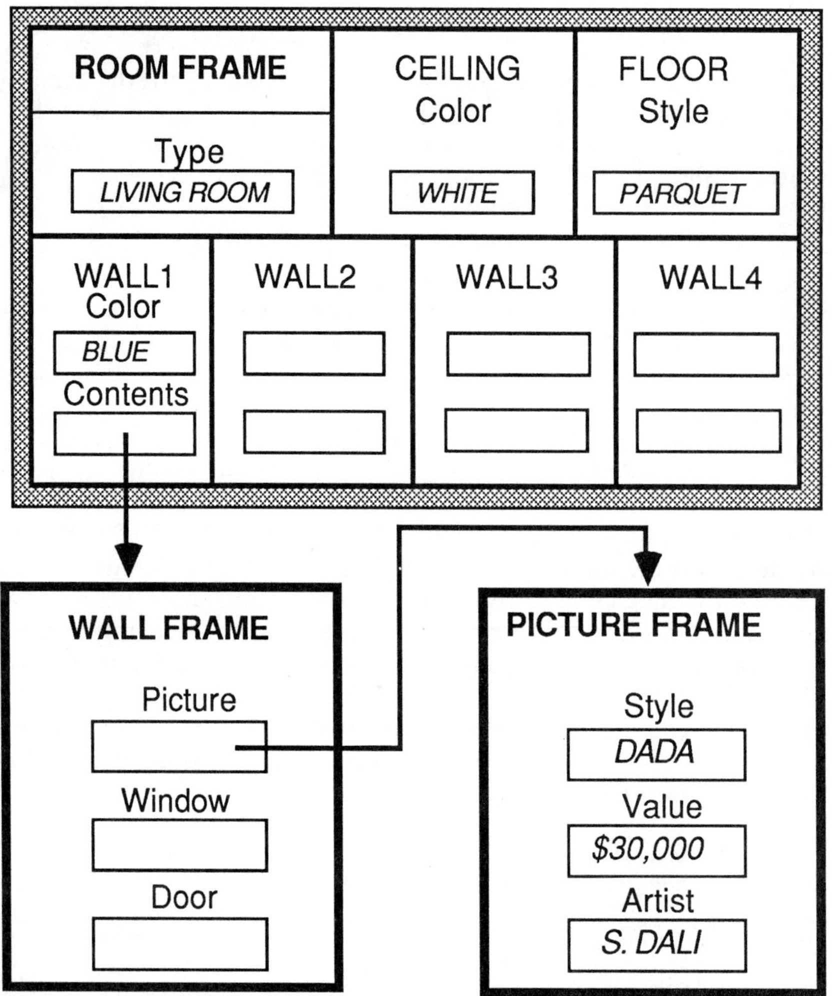

Figure 9-10 Frame Representation of a Room Note how each slot may contain another frame and the resulting hierarchy of frames. This sub-structure may be refined to represent very fine-grained detail.

There are several other characteristics of frames which make them particularly appealing as a knowledge representation scheme. These include:

- Default values may be supplied by the program and overwritten by the user as more information becomes available

- Frames lend themselves nicely to query systems. Once the appropriate frame is found it is straightforward to search the slots for information

- If new information casts doubt on the validity of a certain frame, the system can skip to a new, more appropriate frame.

- If more information is needed, an IF_NEEDED slot can be used to activate an attached procedure to fill in the slot. This concept of *procedural attachment* is closely related to the concept of *demons*.

DEMONS

Demons are procedures which are activated at any time during a program execution depending on conditions evaluated in the demon itself. Examples of demons used in conventional programming include error detection, default commands, and end of file detection (eof).

In programs using demons a list of demons is created and, as processing proceeds, all changes of state are recorded on a list. All demons in the demon list check the status list for each change against their network fragment. If a match is made, control immediately passes to the demon. This feature provides the key to self-modifying programs which, in turn, are essential for systems which can adapt to new situations and improve their performance with experience. Such dynamic behavior is one of the central ideas of machine learning.

CRITICISMS OF FRAMES

Although frame theory has contributed much to improving the capacity for knowledge representation, it also has its problems. Some of the strongest criticisms have been made by Brachman[17] who cites the following problems and ambiguities of frames:

- The concept of the prototypical case representations with default values which may be overridden "... makes one crucial type of representation impossible — that of composite descriptions whose meanings are functions of the structure and interrelation of their parts."

- If we allow for separate slots to accommodate all possible variations on the prototypical case, we lose all of the advantages of a case representation. That is, we may build a slot for *number_of_legs* to take care of the rare case of a three-legged elephant, but how do we handle the case of Clyde, the elephant who lost his trunk during the Punic wars?

• The *isa* relation may prove more a source of confusion than of clarification and distinction. Consider, for example the following semantic network statements about some mammals:

CLYDE ISA ELEPHANT ISA MAMMAL
PLATYPUS ISA MAMMAL

So even the concept of the typical mammal may not help much in this case since the platypus is the typical *atypical* mammal.

Brachman summarizes his criticisms in the following three ideas:

1. Frames are typically not very frame-like.

2. Definitions are more important than one might think.

3. Cancellation (of default properties) is more difficult than it looks.

9.6 SCRIPT THEORY OF SCHANK AND ABELSON

The concept of a *script* grew out of the work of Schank and Abelson at Yale University. The goal of this research was to develop cognitive understanding by computers. A script closely resembles a frame with additional information included about the expected *sequence of events* and the *goals* and *plans* of the actors involved. This is the representation which best illustrates the concept of expectation-driven processing, and the script approach has proven to be a valuable tool for building both knowledge and understanding into computer systems. Scripts have proven very effective for developing systems which pass the explanation game test for computer understanding of stories and newspaper accounts.

As was stated in the last chapter, one of the key ideas of the script approach is to reduce the story to a set of semantic primitives using the conceptual dependency theory formalism. By reducing the action taking place in a script to a set of simple primitives such as:

Action:

MOVE_BODY_PART	MOVE_OBJECT
EXPEL	INGEST
PROPEL	SPEAK

Perception:

SEE	HEAR
SMELL	FEEL

Mental and Social Acts:

MOVE_CONCEPT	CONCLUDE
TRANSFER_POSSESSION	THINK_ABOUT

Schank and Abelson were able to represent the deeper semantic meaning present in input stories. Conceptual dependency theory could then be used to answer questions not specifically stated in the story, paraphrase the main contents of the story, and even translate the paraphrased account into other natural languages.

GOING TO A RESTAURANT SCRIPT

Consider the *Going to a Restaurant* script, a favorite of many frame and script theorists, as described in Feigenbaum *et al.*[18] First we will establish the setting using the more or less static concept of a RESTAURANT FRAME and embed the procedure involved using the EAT_AT_RESTAURANT SCRIPT.

RESTAURANT FRAME

```
Specialization_of:    Business_establishment

Types:
    Range:            (Cafeteria, Seat_yourself,
                      Wait_to_be_seated)
    Default:          Wait_to_be_seated
    If_needed:        IF[plastic_orange_counter]
                          THEN[fast_food]
                      IF[stack_of_trays]
                          THEN[cafeteria]
                      IF[wait_for_waitress_sign
                          OR reservations made_sign]
                          THEN[wait_to_be_seated]
                      OTHERWISE  seat_yourself
Location:
    Range:            An ADDRESS
    If_needed:        (Look at the menu)

Name:
    If_needed:        (Look at the menu)

Food_style:
    Range:            (Burgers, Chinese, American,
```

Sea_food, French)
Default: American
If_added: (Update alternatives of restaurant)

Time_of_operation:
Range: A Time_of_day
Default: Open evenings except Mondays

Payment_form:
Range: (Cash, Credit-card, Check, Washing_dishes_Script)

Event_sequence:
Default: Eat_at_restaurant script

Alternatives:
Range: All restaurants with same Food_style
If_needed: (Find all restaurants with same Food_style)

You will note that the procedures embedded in the restaurant frame are specified in terms of scripts. Now lets look at the *Eat_at_Restaurant* script in more detail:

EAT_AT_RESTAURANT SCRIPT

Props: (Restaurant, Money, Food, Menu, Tables, Chairs)

Roles: (Hungry_persons, Wait_persons, Chef_persons)

Point_of_view:
Hungry_persons

Time_of_occurrence:
(Times_of_operation of restaurant)

Place_of_occurrence:
(Location of restaurant)

Event_sequence:
First: Enter_restaurant script
Then: IF[wait_to_be_seated_sign OR reservations]
THEN [get_maitre_d's_attention script]
Then: Please_be_seated script
Then: Order_food script
Then: Eat_food script UNLESS[long_wait]

	WHEN[exit_restaurant_angry script]
Then:	IF[food_quality was better than palatable]
	THEN [compliments_to_the_chef script]
Then:	Pay_for_it script
Finally:	Leave_restaurant script.

With a more complete extension of this background script, a script applier program such as SAM can read the following short story and respond intelligently to queries about what happened.[19]

Input Text:

```
JOHN WENT TO A RESTAURANT.  HE ORDERED A HOT DOG.  THE
WAITER SAID THEY DIDN'T HAVE ANY.  HE ASKED FOR A HAMBURGER.
WHEN THE HAMBURGER CAME, IT WAS BURNT.  HE LEFT THE RESTAU-
RANT.
```

Question—Answering Output:

```
Q1:  DID JOHN SIT DOWN IN THE RESTAURANT?
A1:  PROBABLY.

Q2:  DID JOHN ORDER A HOT DOG?
A2:  YES.

Q3:  DID JOHN EAT A HOT DOG?
A3:  NO, THE WAITER TOLD JOHN THE MANAGEMENT WAS UNABLE TO
      GIVE IT TO HIM.

Q4:  WHAT DID THE WAITER SERVE JOHN?
A4:  THE WAITER SERVED JOHN A HAMBURGER.

Q5:  WHY DIDN'T JOHN EAT THE HAMBURGER?
A5:  BECAUSE THE HAMBURGER WAS OVERDONE.

Q6:  DID JOHN PAY THE CHECK?
A6:  NO JOHN WAS ANGRY BECAUSE THE HAMBURGER WAS
      OVERDONE AND SO HE LEFT THE RESTAURANT.
```

Note how the context provided by the script allows SAM to make inferences about cause and effect relationships not given explicitly in the story and to reconstruct the probable sequence of events. SAM "fills in the blanks" in the story in much the same way a human experienced in restaurant visits would.

Several features of scripts should be noted. First, scripts provide a very natural way of representing "common sense information," a problem which has plagued AI systems from the beginning. Second, scripts also provide a hierarchical structure for representing information through the inclusion of subscripts within scripts. Finally, other knowledge representation structures such as production rules may be used in a natural way within the script formalism.

These features give scripts the following powerful capabilities:

- Scripts can predict events and answer questions about information not explicitly stated in the story line.

- Scripts provide a framework for integrating a set of observations into a coherent interpretation.

- Scripts provide a scheme for detecting unusual events.

Scripts have provided the basis for the development of a number of the previously discussed programs with capabilities for understanding stories, answering questions about the stories, and paraphrasing them. These include the program SAM (Script Applier Mechanism) and PAM (Plan Applier Mechanism) developed by Schank and Abelson and their students at Yale.

CRITICISMS OF SCRIPTS

By adding expectation-driven processing incorporating the goals and plans of the actors and the expected sequence of events, the concept of scripts has significantly improved the explanatory power available for knowledge representation. The script theory, however, is not without its critics. One of the sharpest criticisms of script theory is that of perennial AI critic, Hubert Dreyfus.[20] His criticisms of scripts focus primarily on the *ad hoc* nature of scripts.

Consider for example additional questions which might be asked the EAT_AT_RESTAURANT Script:

- When the waitress came to the table, did she wear clothes?

- Did she walk forward or backward?

- Did the customer eat his food with his mouth or his ear?

If the program answers "I don't know", we feel that all of its right answers were tricks or lucky guesses and that it has not understood anything of our every day restaurant behavior.

Dreyfus criticizes Schank's claim that "... the paths of a script are the possibilities that are extant in a situation" as insidiously misleading. He states:

> *"Either it means that the script accounts for the possibilities in the restaurant game defined by Schank, in which case it is true*

but uninteresting; or he is claiming that he can account for the possibilities in an everyday restaurant situation which is impressive but, by Schank's own admission, false."

In summary, we have presented two of the more successful systems for representing knowledge and using it to reach intelligent conclusions. In the next chapter we turn to a final technique for representing knowledge, the *production rule.* For those wishing to pursue the topic of knowledge representation in more detail, an excellent summary and reference list has been prepared by Hector Levesque.[21]

PROBLEMS AND PROGRAMS

9-1. Successful researchers in all fields of mathematics, science, and engineering are fluent in the language of their discipline. This fluency is generally achieved through formal education. Write a brief paper on an exception to this rule, that is, a major scientific contribution in a field in which the researcher had no formal training.

9-2. Discuss the analogy between the development of computer languages and the development of natural languages from pre-historic times to the present. What role does specialized "jargon" and "extensions" play in each?

9-3. In your study of data structures, you have become acquainted with vectors, arrays, linked lists, and files all of which are important for data base manipulation. In what ways do knowledge representation (KR) systems resemble databases and in what ways do they differ?

9-4. Interpret a spelling checker program as a KR system. Is it accurate to say that spelling checkers "learn"? What other stylistic or syntactic checks would be relatively easy to implement in a text screening program? Describe one such commercial style checker.

9-5. An issue which must be resolved in any KR system is the grain size of the knowledge represented. Two extremes are a uniform grain size for all objects and a totally object-dependent grain size. What are the arguments in favor of each position? Which computer languages would be most natural for each approach?

9-6. Meta-knowledge is knowledge about the knowledge represented in a KR system. Give some examples of meta-knowledge and the uses to which it is put.

9-7. Reasoning by analogy, generalization, and abstraction have all been very difficult areas in AI research. Discuss how problems of knowledge representation are related to the slow progress in these areas.

9-8. Common sense reasoning has proven to be a particularly difficult and intractable area of AI research. Interpret this difficulty in terms of the difficulty of representing common sense knowledge. What approach do you feel offers the most promise for solving this problem?

9-9. Successful expert systems and AI programs generally have been characterized by a very restricted domain or *scope*. What are the obstacles to merging such systems to expand the scope of the composite system until we eventually develop a very general, competent system?

9-10. Using Pascal as an example of procedural knowledge representation and Prolog as an example of declarative knowledge representation, compare the two representations in terms of efficiency, transparency, and ease of use. Discuss two different applications, one for which Pascal is best and one for which Prolog is best.

9-11. Write down the semantic network representation for the following statements:

> *Bilbo found a magic ring.*
> *Dwarfs and elves lived in the Misty Mountains.*
> *Smaug, the dragon, slept with one eye open and guarded the treasure.*

9-12. Show how the inheritance properties of semantic networks may lead to incorrect conclusions based on representations (show them) of the statements:

> *Bilbo is a Hobbit.*
> *Gollum eats Hobbits.*

9-13. Try to represent the story of *Goldilocks and the Three Bears* in terms of semantic networks. What limitations of the technique did you detect? Did you find yourself searching for primitive acts *a la* conceptual dependency theory?

9-14. Phrase three questions as semantic network fragments to query the representation constructed in Problem 9-13. What answers would a semantic network pattern matcher return to your questions?

9-15. Without thinking about either in depth, write down your immediate mental images and reactions to the phrases:

Child's birthday party script.
Motorcycle accident scenario.

Interpret your answers to this question in terms of the validity of the frames and scripts concept.

9-16. Construct a frame for describing the following objects:
a) Your own home
b) A newspaper account on a terrorist attack
c) A newspaper clipping on a motorcycle accident.

9-17. Bertram Raphael asks the question: *What properties do these chairs have in common?*[22]

Develop a frame representation for CHAIR adequate for describing each of these chairs and capable of distinguishing between them.

9-18. One problem with frames can be formulated in terms of an "uncertainty principle" stated as:

$$N \cdot C \geq \text{constant}$$

where
N = number of frames required to describe an object
C = complexity of frame, i.e. the number of slots

Verify this principle by reference to cases such as three-legged-elephant, elephant-without-a-trunk, and so on.

9-19. Write scripts for the following proto-typical real-life experiences:
a) Register-for-next-semester script
b) Visit-dentist-office script
c) Interview-for-first-job script.

9-20. Consider the criticisms of scripts discussed in the text. Can you re-cast this criticism in the form of an uncertainty principle? Do you consider the criticism valid? What changes or new features would you suggest for scripts to answer such criticism?

REFERENCES AND FOOTNOTES

[1] Dahl, Veronica, "Logic Programming as a Representation of Knowledge," *IEEE COMPUTER,* pp. 106–111, October (1983) This whole issue of IEEE COMPUTER is devoted to knowledge representation and is an excellent review of the subject.

[2] Mackinlay, Jock and Genesereth, Michael R., "Expressiveness of Languages," *Proceedings of the National Conference on Artificial Intelligence AAAI-84*, pp. 226–232, August (1984)

[3] Feigenbaum, Edward A., Barr, Avron, and Cohen, Paul R. (eds), *The Handbook of Artificial Intelligence,* Vol.1–3, HeurisTech Press/-William Kaufmann, Inc., Stanford, CA (1981–82)

[4] Lenat, D., Davis, R.,Doyle, J., Genesereth, M., Goldstein, R., and Schrobe, H., "Reasoning about Reasoning," in *Building Expert Systems,* Hayes-Roth, F., Waterman, D. A., and Lenat, D. B. (eds), pp. 219–239, Addison-Wesley Publishing Company, Reading, MA (1983)

[5] Feigenbaum, *Op Cit,* p. 147

[6] Bobrow, D. G. and Collins, A., (eds), *Representation and Understanding Studies in Cognitive Science,* Academic Press, New York, NY (1975)

[7] Quillian, M. R., "Semantic Memory," in *Semantic Information Processing,* Minsky, M., (ed), MIT Press, Cambridge, MA (1968)

[8] Feigenbaum, *Op Cit,* pp. 110–189

[9] For more information on these delightful creatures, see Tolkien, J.R.R., *The Hobbit,* Ballantine Books, New York, NY (1937, 1966)

[10] Winston, Patrick Henry, *Op Cit.* See also Second Edition, pp. 385–392

11 Raphael, B., "SIR: A Computer Program for Semantic Information Retrieval," in *Semantic Information Processing,* M. Minsky (ed), MIT Press, Cambridge, MA (1968)

12 Carbonell, J. R., "AI in CAI: An Artificial Intelligence Approach to Computer-Assisted Instruction," *IEEE Transactions on Man-Machine Systems,* MMS-11, pp. 190–202 (1970)

13 Schmolze, James G. and Lipkis, Thomas A., "Classification in the KL-ONE Knowledge Representation System," *Proceedings of the Eighth International Joint Conference on Artificial Intelligence,* pp. 330–332, August (1983)

14 Minsky, M., "A Framework for Representing Knowledge," in *The Psychology of Computer Vision,* Winston, P., (ed), pp. 211–277, McGraw-Hill, New York, NY (1975)

15 Schank, R. C., and Abelson, R. P., *Scripts, Plans, Goals, and Understanding,* Lawrence Erlbaum, Hillsdale, NJ (1977)

16 Winston, Patrick Henry, *Artificial Intelligence,* pp. 181–187, Addison-Wesley Publishing Company, Reading, MA (1977)

17 Brachman, Ronald J.," 'I Lied about the Trees'–Or, Defaults and Definitions in Knowledge Representation," *The AI Magazine* **6**, pp. 80–93, Fall (1985)

18 Feigenbaum, *Op Cit,* p. 217–219

19 Schank, Roger C. and Riesbeck, Christopher K., *Inside Computer Understanding: Five Programs Plus Miniatures,* p. 78, Lawrence Erlbaum Associates, Hillsdale, NJ (1981)

20 Dreyfus, Hubert L., "From Micro-Worlds to Knowledge Representation," in *Mind Design,* John Haugeland (ed), MIT Press, Cambridge, MA (1981)

21 Levesque, Hector, "Knowledge Representation and Reasoning," *Annual Review of Computer Science* **1**, pp. 255–287, Annual Reviews Inc., Palo Alto, CA (1986)

22 Raphael, Bertram, *The Thinking Computer — Mind Inside Matter,* p. 108, W. H. Freeman and Company, San Francisco, CA (1976)

Chapter 10

PRODUCTION SYSTEMS

(PHOTO: COURTESY OF ALLEN NEWELL)

Allen Newell is Professor of Computer Science and Psychology at Carnegie-Mellon University. He was a student of Polya at Stanford University where he received his B.S. in Physics, and he holds a Ph.D. in Industrial Administration from CMU. At the RAND Corporation he met Herbert Simon, and they began a long and productive collaboration. He wrote the list-processing language, *IPL,* and is coauthor of The Logic Theorist and the General Problem Solver. He has continued his study of cognitive psychology and recently proposed the *Power Law of Practice* and the *Chunking Theory of Learning*. Newell's current research activity is centered on SOAR, an architecture for intelligent problem solving and learning.

10: PRODUCTION SYSTEMS

10.1 INTRODUCTION

The distinction between artificial intelligence and expert systems reflects the distinction between theory and practice. While expert systems are the direct products of AI research, many AI researchers feel uncomfortable considering expert systems a branch of AI. The reason is that AI research deals with the unknown, the great unsolved problems of making machines intelligent. The design of expert systems, on the other hand, is becoming a well developed technology which is in the process of rapid commercialization. The key to the success of this new technology was the appropriate representation of knowledge. One of the most successful schemes for knowledge representation in expert systems has proven to be the *production system*.

The concept of production systems was introduced by Post[1] in 1943. The concept re-emerged in the context of natural language processing in the *rewrite rules* of Chomsky[2] in 1957. Production systems were proposed for modeling human problem-solving behavior by Newell and Simon[3] in 1972, and since then Alan Newell has been one of the chief proponents of the technique as a useful tool for AI. Production systems are frequently referred to as *inference systems, rule-based systems,* and in the case of human problem-solving behavior, simply *productions.*

Production systems play a number of important roles which we examine to a greater or lesser extent in this chapter. These include:

- *A powerful knowledge representation scheme.* Production systems represent not only knowledge but also action. The production system architecture, in fact, is equivalent in its generality to the universal Turing machine and has been identified as a "Newell machine."[4]

- *The bridge connecting AI research to expert systems.* Production systems provide a language in which the representation of expert knowledge is very natural. For this reason it is the knowledge representation system of choice for many expert systems.

- *A heuristic model for human behavior.* The study of human behavior protocols originally led Newell to formulate the concept of productions. This paradigm for human behavior has served a valuable heuristic function of stimulating further research. At the close of the chapter we examine some of the philosophical implications of human production systems.

10.2 DEFINITION OF PRODUCTION SYSTEMS

Knowledge in a production system may be represented by a set of rules of the form:

IF [*condition*] **THEN** [*action*]

along with a control system and database. The control system serves as rule interpreter and sequencer. The database acts as a context buffer in which to record the conditions evaluated by the rules and information on which the rules act. In addition to the *if-then* syntax, production rules are also frequently described as *condition-action, antecedent-consequent, pattern-action,* or *situation-response* pairs.

Examples of productions from everyday experience might include:

IF [driving 15 mph over limit AND
see flashing red light in rear-view mirror]
THEN [pull over AND stop]

IF [have head-ache AND sore throat AND runny nose]
THEN [take aspirin AND go to bed]

IF [barometer falling AND thunderheads to southwest]
THEN [head for a safe harbor]

Examples of a somewhat more analytical approach to classifying an object might start with rules such as:

IF [the category is a form OR a coloring OR a texture]
THEN [the object has an appearance]

IF [the category is an appearance OR an odor OR a tactile-quality]
THEN [the object has an external quality]

IF [the category is a size OR an external quality OR a mass OR a substance]
THEN [the object has a physical quality]
...

This natural, intuitive structure for representing knowledge has made production systems the preferred method for many expert systems, including the pioneering programs DENDRAL and MYCIN. Examples of production rules from these systems are shown below. In the next chapter we examine both expert systems in greater detail.

DENDRAL

IF [the spectrum of the molecule has two peaks at masses x_1 and x_2 such that
a) $x_1 + x_2 = M + 28$ AND
b) $x_1 - 28$ is a high peak AND
c) $x_2 - 28$ is a high peak AND
d) at least one of x_1 or x_2 is high]
THEN [the molecule contains a ketone group]

MYCIN

IF [a) the stain of the organism is gramneg AND
b) the morphology of the organism is rod AND
c) the patient is a compromised host]
THEN [there is suggestive evidence (.6) that the identity of the organism is pseudomonas]

From the similarity of the formulation of these production rules we note one of the first attractive features of the production system formalism: the clean separation of the program structure from the data. The three major elements in all productions systems include:

- A global database
- A set of production rules
- A control system.

Global Database — This is the main data structure of production systems. The database may range from a simple list or small matrix up to a complex, relational, indexed file structure. It is the basic structure on which the production rules operate. It is a dynamic structure, continually changing as a result of the operation of the production rules. The global database is also referred to as the *context, short-term memory buffer,* or *working memory.*

Production Rules — As indicated in the examples above, production rules have a condition part (IF) called the *left-hand side* and an action part (THEN) called the *right-hand side* . If the left-hand side, sometimes called the *condition* or *premise,* is satisfied by the database, the rule becomes *applicable* and subject to being *fired* by the control system. Note how production rules resemble the demons described in the previous chapter.

Control System — The control system is essentially an interpreter program to control the order in which the production rules are fired and resolve conflicts if more than one rule is applicable. The control system repeatedly applies rules to the database until a description of a goal state is produced. It then detects the occurrence of such a goal state and records the rules which have been applied to reach it for later reference.

The relationship between these three elements and the iterative nature of the operation of production systems is illustrated in Figure 10-1. The problem of reducing a real system to these three elements is called the *representation problem.* It is the central problem in the design of any production system. We illustrate the complete design and operation of a classification production system in the following example.

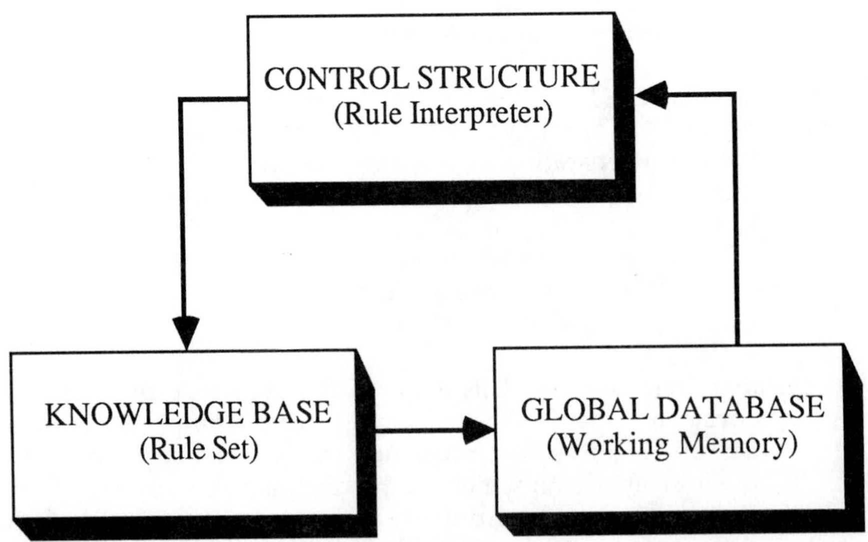

Figure 10-1 A Production System Production systems contain these three basic components which interact iteratively as indicated.

10.3 EXAMPLE — THE NATURALIST

Using a production rule system similar to that outlined in Feigenbaum *et al*[5] we can build a naturalist which can identify trees from a few clues such as leaf shape. For the global database we use a simple list, WM (working memory). The only two operations which the rule interpreter must provide is the query function to test if a identifying characteristic is on the WM list and an action function to put some characteristic on the list in response to a rule firing. These functions are called:

- ON_WM X — Tests if property X is in WM
- PUT_ON_WM X — Puts property X in WM.

The first step in creating the production system is to translate some elementary knowledge about tree characteristics into the form of production rules. This process generates representations such as the following set of rules:

Production Rules:

R1: **IF**[ON_WM loses_leaves]
THEN [PUT_ON_WM deciduous]

R2: **IF**[ON_WM keeps_leaves]
THEN [PUT_ON_WM evergreen]

R3: **IF**[ON_WM broad_leaf AND NOT ginko]
THEN [PUT_ON_WM angiosperm]

R4: **IF**[ON_WM needle_leaf]
THEN [PUT_ON_WM gymnosperm]

R5: **IF**[ON_WM one_seed_leaf]
THEN [PUT_ON_WM monocotyledon]

R6: **IF**[ON_WM two_seed_leaves]
THEN [PUT_ON_WM dicotyledon]

R7: **IF**[ON_WM monocotyledon OR ON_WM dicotyledon]
THEN [PUT_ON_WM angiosperm]

R8: **IF**[ON_WM cones]
THEN [PUT_ON_WM gymnosperm]

R9: **IF**[ON_WM two-needle OR ON_WM three_needle OR ON_WM 5-needle OR ON_WM clump_needle]
THEN [PUT_ON_WM needle_leaf]

R10: **IF**[ON_WM angiosperm AND ON_WM deciduous AND ON_WM serrated_leaf]
THEN [PUT_ON_WM sugar_maple]

R11: **IF**[ON_WM angiosperm AND ON_WM evergreen AND ON_WM serrated_leaf]
THEN [PUT_ON_WM American_holly]

R12: **IF**[ON_WM angiosperm AND ON_WM deciduous AND ON_WM compound_leaf]
THEN [PUT_ON_WM hickory]

R13: **IF**[ON_WM gymnosperm AND ON_WM evergreen AND ON_WM three_needle]
THEN [PUT_ON_WM Ponderosa_pine]

R14: **IF**[ON_WM gymnosperm AND ON_WM deciduous AND ON_WM clump_needle]
THEN [PUT_ON_WM tamarack]

R15: **IF**[ON_WM gymnosperm AND ON_WM evergreen AND ON_WM five_needle]
THEN [PUT_ON_WM white_pine]

Next we examine the interpreter, that is, the control system which will apply the above production rules in the appropriate order to accomplish the task of putting relevant characteristics of the tree in working memory and arriving at the best estimate for the tree type.

Control System:

1) Scan the production rules for those *active* or *applicable*, i.e. those whose IF condition evaluates to TRUE (do not fire them yet). This step generates a list of active rules (which might be the null list).

2) If more than one rule is active, then deactivate those rules which would duplicate characteristics already on the WM. This step prevents redundancy.

3) Fire the lowest numbered active production rule. If there are

no applicable rules, exit the loop. The best guess will be the top item on the WM list.

4) Turn the IF part of all production rules to FALSE and go to control statement (1). This provides an iterative loop structure.

Note the two clearly distinguished functions of the control system. The first is to examine the working memory (database) for the purpose of answering questions such as: Is this a deciduous tree? Finding rule R1 applicable (i.e. evaluating the left-hand-side as TRUE) would answer this question "yes". The second function is to add to our knowledge about the unknown tree by logical inference accomplished by the process of firing the applicable production rules. Thus, from information that the tree has leaves of a two-needle structure, the program can infer, using rules R9 and R4, that the tree is a gymnosperm. At any point in the analysis, the working memory may be examined to list the original data along with the new knowledge inferred from the data up to that point.

Note also that the control system provides an iterative solution to the problem by repeating the four-step program until no more applicable rules are found. The program then exits through step 3, and the answer is left at the top of the working memory list. The first phase of the iteration cycle performs *pattern-matching,* the second phase provides *conflict resolution,* and the third phase performs *action* .

During our walk in the woods some crisp, fall day we notice a beautiful, golden, coniferous tree whose needles appear in clumps and are falling off. These features are noted, and upon return to the office we call up THE NATURALIST and enter our observations as the following list:

WM = (*cones, clump_needle,loses_leaves*)

On iteration 1, the pattern-matching functions find rules R1, R8, and R9 active. Since none of these rules will put redundant information on the WM, the rule interpreter uses control system step 3 to fire R1, resulting in an addition to the database which now reads (latest addition in boldface):

WM = (***deciduous***,*cones, clump_needle,loses_leaves*)

Step 4 clears the applicability of all rules and returns to step 1 for the second iteration. On this scan we again find rules R1, R8, and R9 applicable. Now, however, step 2 deactivates rule R1 and step 3 fires the lowest remaining, active rule, namely R8. The database now reads:

WM = (***gymnosperm***,*deciduous,cones, clump_needle,*

loses_leaves)

Notice how relevant information is accumulating in working memory. The system should soon conclude the correct type of tree. In the third iteration we find that rules R1, R8, R9, and R14 are applicable. Rules R1 and R8 are ruled out as redundant, and rule R9 is fired, adding needle_leaf to the list:

WM = (***needle_leaf***,*gymnosperm*,*deciduous*,*cones*, *clump_needle*,*loses_leaves*)

In the fourth iteration, rules R1, R4, R8, R9, and R14 are active. The new addition to the list, R4, would add the characteristic *gymnosperm* to the list, had rule R8 not already done so, because all needle-bearing trees fall within the gymnosperm class. So the first four active rules on the list are redundant, and the only remaining active rule, R14, is fired. This puts the tree type *tamarack* on the WM list:

WM = (***tamarack***,*needle_leaf*,*gymnosperm*,*deciduous*,*cones*, *clump_needle*,*loses_leaves*)

Technically, the production system is not yet finished even though the correct answer is at the head of the WM list. In the fifth iteration the same five rules from the fourth iteration are applicable. However, all five now contribute redundant information. Therefore, the second clause of step 3 causes an exit. The conclusion of the production system is:

The beautiful, golden, "pine tree" losing its needles is a tamarack.

Notice that this simple, 15-rule production system is capable of identifying six types of trees, including a broad-leafed evergreen and a deciduous conifer. A biologist could certainly build a more efficient and accurate NATURALIST, but the example does illustrate many of the attractive features and some of the problems of production systems which we now examine in more detail.

10.4 ADVANTAGES OF PRODUCTION SYSTEMS

Some of the features of production systems which make them a particularly appealing form of knowledge representation for expert systems include:

Expressiveness and Intuitiveness — Experience in working with human experts indicates heavy repetition of the theme

"Well, in the case of so-and-so I usually do such-and-such." This theme maps quite naturally into the IF...THEN format of production rules. Production rules essentially tell us what to do in a given situation. Since many expert systems are organized in terms of advice on what to do, this property of production systems is particularly natural for representing knowledge.

Simplicity — The uniform structure of the IF...THEN syntax in rule-based systems provides an attractive simplicity for the representation of knowledge. This feature improves the readability of the production rules and the communication between various parts of a single program. Production rules, by their very syntax, tend to be self documenting.

Modularity and Modifiability — By their very nature, production rules encode discrete pieces of information which are generally unrelated to other production rules unless there is an explicit production rule relating them. Information can be treated as a collection of independent facts which may be added to or deleted from the system with essentially no deleterious "side effects". This modular feature of production systems allows for the incremental improvement and fine tuning of production systems with no degradation of performance. A simple, "skeletal" system can be rapidly developed and gradually "fleshed out" as more information becomes available.

Knowledge Intensive — Note that the three-part structure of rule interpreter/knowledge base/working memory provides a very effective separation of the knowledge base from the rule interpreter or *inference engine*. Thus, the inference engine can be general purpose and work equally effectively, in principle, on various knowledge bases. The knowledge base composed of production rules, in turn, is essentially "pure knowledge" since it need contain no control or programming information. Since each production rule is equivalent to a concise and unambiguous English sentence, the problem of semantics is solved by the very structure of the representation.

10.5 PROBLEMS WITH PRODUCTION SYSTEMS

While many features of production systems make them desirable for representing and reasoning with knowledge of real-world objects and situations they are not immune from the problems plaguing other AI systems. Among these problems are:[6]

Opacity — Although the individual production rules may be models of clarity, the combined operation and effect of the control program may be relatively opaque. That is, production systems may make it difficult to see the forest (overall strategy) because of the trees (the interaction between the rule interpreter and individual production rules). Again, this difficulty is rooted in the lack of hierarchy within the set of production rules, and a dynamic database which must be queried often to follow the operation of the analysis.

Inefficiency — As the example illustrated, several of the rules were tested and became active several times during execution even though it was apparent that they would never be fired. A more intelligent control strategy would reduce this problem. An even more effective approach would be an effective hierarchy which, for instance, would eliminate all broad_leaf tests when needle_leaf was indicted in the WM. Since production rules are basically "democratic" in their structure and contribution to the system, there are serious difficulties in creating any hierarchy among the rules. This implies exhaustive search through all the production rules for each cycle of the control program. Some systems, like EMYCIN, have successfully implemented a rule hierarchy to minimize this problem.

Inability to Learn — Simple rule-based systems do not have the ability to automatically modify or add to the rule base. These characteristics would be essential for any learning system. Human experts know when to "break the rules" in exceptional cases. Unless there is some provision for adding and modifying rules based on experience, the production system cannot learn.

10.6 TECHNIQUES OF CONFLICT RESOLUTION

In an ideal production system, all rules continually monitor the condition of the global database and fire instantaneously when their IF condition is true. In this picture, the set of production rules act like a set of demons discussed in the previous chapter. In practice, however, the control structure cycles through the set of rules checking to see which rules have their conditions satisfied, i.e. which are applicable. Since the firing of one rule may change the activation of other rules, the control structure allows only one rule to fire per cycle. If more than one rule is activated in a given cycle, the control structure must determine which rule to fire from this *conflict set* of active rules. This selection is called *conflict resolution.*

A number of methods for conflict resolution have been proposed, including:[7]

- Rank the rules in a list according to priority and fire the first activated rule, i.e. the rule with the *highest priority*. This, combined with redundancy avoidance, was the strategy used in the NATURALIST. Its virtue is its simplicity, and, by ordering the rules in the approximate order of their firing frequency, can be made a relatively efficient strategy.

- From the conflict set, fire the rule with the most strict condition. This is known as the *longest matching* strategy. Its advantage is that the discrimination power of a strict condition is greater than that of a more general condition. A rule with a strict condition effectively "injects more knowledge into the database" when it fires.

- Fire the *most recently used* rule of the conflict set. This strategy was ruled out by the rule interpreter in the NATURALIST but would be possible in a more realistic inference engine. Its advantage, interpreted in terms of search for a solution, is that it represents a depth-first search which follows the path of greatest activity in generating new knowledge in the database.

- Fire the rule from the conflict set with the *most recently used variable*. This strategy would have been possible in the NATURALIST as long as firing the rule did not contribute redundant information. Its advantage is similar to that of the previous strategy.

- Fire the rule *most recently added* to the set of rules. This is a strategy possible only for dynamic knowledge base systems in which the production rules themselves may be added, deleted, or modified during execution. This again would provide greater efficiency by enhancing depth-first search. Such systems, however, represent a much higher level of abstraction and complexity than the simple production system used in the NATURALIST.

- Compute an *execution time priority* and fire the rule with the highest priority. This priority may be some function of the above rankings and is similar to strategy underlying the state evaluation function discussed in the chapters on search and game theory.

- Simply fire *all applicable rules* of the conflict set. This strategy is equivalent to treating rules as demons and can lead to problems. For instance, firing the first applicable rule may change the condition on the second active rule from TRUE to FALSE. If the second rule fires anyway, it is acting on erroneous information. If, through feedback of the new status of the database, it does not fire, the strategy reduces to a cyclic firing of applicable rules which represents a departure from the stated strategy.

The intelligent design of conflict resolution strategies is one of the current areas of research in AI. The particular choice of strategy affects both the *sensitivity* of the production system (the ability to respond quickly to changes in the database) and its *stability* (the ability to carry out long sequences of actions).

10.7 APPLICABILITY OF PRODUCTION SYSTEMS

From the previous discussion it is not surprising that certain domains of knowledge are more appropriate for representation by production systems than others. These appropriate domains may be characterized as follows:

- Domains in which the structure of the knowledge resembles the structure of production rules. Clinical medicine is frequently cited as an example of such a knowledge domain consisting of many independent facts with no underlying theoretical structure such as that supporting domains like physics and mathematics. However, there is growing concern that the independence and modularity of rules may be illusory since it is difficult to predict the effect of adding extra rules on program behavior.

- Domains in which actions are required which are relatively independent of other actions and thereby naturally represented by the THEN part of independent production rules. A typical application with this characteristic is a medical patient-monitoring system. This is in contrast to domains with hierarchical systems with dependent sub-processes such as mechanical or electromagnetic finite element analysis programs.

- Domains in which knowledge itself is distinct from the application to which it will be put. The NATURALIST system above illustrates this separation — the taxonomy for tree identification can be developed quite independently from potential uses. This is in contrast to systems in which the process and the knowledge are inextricably related such as sailing, skiing, or dating.

Several other features have been incorporated into various production systems, all of which improve the performance of the system and in general enhance its "intelligence." One of the most important of these features is the *justification* or *explanation* capability of an expert system. This feature is particularly important in medicine where medical experts require detailed justification for any diagnosis, whether it issues from natural or artificial intelligence. This ability to trace the line of reasoning leading to a given conclusion is relatively easy to incorporate in the operation of production systems.

Another feature which has been built into certain production systems is that of *knowledge acquisition,* or in common jargon, *learning.* Systems with this feature can actually modify or add to their set of production rules based on past experience. By any reasonable definition, this qualifies as artificial or machine learning.

A final feature present in many production systems is the capability of dealing correctly with *inexact knowledge* and *probability.* Problems involving uncertainties or probabilistic reasoning are generally classified in the domain of *fuzzy logic* or *fuzzy reasoning.* This is a basic problem facing most areas of human endeavor — there may be no clean yes or no answer in a given situation, only a set of possible solutions with varying likelihoods of being correct. This is particularly true in such areas as medicine in which both human and machine diagnosis must be phrased in terms of probabilities. As the earlier example from MYCIN illustrates, production systems can incorporate uncertainty within the statement of the production rule and correctly propagate such uncertainties through to the final diagnosis.

10.8 PRODUCTION RULES FOR CELLULAR AUTOMATA

In the early 1950s John von Neumann became interested in a question of tremendous intellectual interest: Can a machine be made that can replicate itself? This is sometimes called the problem of *self-replicating automata.*[8] Von Neumann envisioned a robot type machine equipped with vision, following a program encoded in a Turing machine, and assembling a copy of itself from component parts. When it finished, there would be two machines capable of self-replication which would then set about assembling copies of themselves ....

Von Neumann realized that the technology of the day was not capable of actually constructing such a machine. The Los Alamos mathematician Stanislaw Ulam suggested to von Neumann that he construct an abstract model of the universe in which he could construct a hypothetical machine with which to test his self-replication hypothesis. Ulam had invented two-dimensional cellular patterns which obeyed a very simple "physics". Von Neumann was impressed by Ulam's cellular automata and decided they offered a promising test-bed for his ideas.[9]

Von Neumann constructed a checkerboard-type universe on each square of which one of 29 different game pieces could reside (one being the empty square). He was able to prove that under certain initial configurations the pattern could, in fact, reproduce itself. This was the proof of principle for which he was searching — a self-reproducing machine is possible in an abstract logical world governed by simple laws. He then argued that a self-replicating machine should, by extension, be possible in our world. There is a close analogy to the extension of Turing's universal machine to present day computers.

Many of von Neumann's ideas reappeared in the *Game of Life* written by John H. Conway in 1970.[10] The universe of LIFE is a checkerboard, each square of which may contain 0 or 1 cell. The starting pattern may be a random pattern selected by the computer or a particular pattern designed by the user. The game proceeds in generations, with the pattern of each succeeding generation determined by the pattern of the preceding generation and very simple (re)production rules based on N, the number of nearest neighbor cells. These rules of birth, life, and death are beautifully stated in terms of production rules.

PRODUCTION RULES FOR LIFE

Part of the fascination of the research on LIFE in exploring the effect of various sets of production rules on the resulting behavior of cell development. Although in principle the designer of the LIFE micro-universe can select any set of production s/he wants to, one set that has proved to yield particularly interesting cellular growth patters is given by:

R1: **IF** [N = 2]
THEN [cell maintains status quo]

R2: **IF** [N = 3]
THEN [cell is on (lives) in next generation]

R3: **IF** [N=0 OR N=1 OR N=4 OR N=5 OR N=6 OR N=7 OR N=8]
THEN [cell is off (dies) in next generation]

where

N = number of neighbors (range is 0 → 8)

The N = 0,1 cases of rule R3 can be anthropomorphically explained as the cell dying from loneliness while the N = 4,5,6,7,8 cases correspond to dying from overpopulation. Applying these simple production rules to simple initial states results in some remarkable patterns. Some are stable, some disappear, some oscillate, and some, in effect, explode.

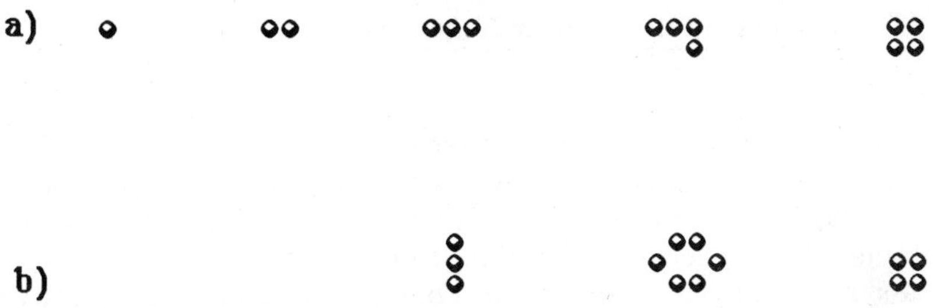

Figure 10-2 LIFE Patterns Line a) shows several patterns in generation 0 and line b) shows the same patterns in generation 3. Note how the two left-most have died out, the third pattern has become a "blinker" and the right-most two patterns are or have evolved into stable patterns.

One of the most fascinating aspects of the game of LIFE is its unpredictable nature. In the next figure we show the famous "R-Pentomino" in the first generation.

Figure 10-3 The R-Pentomino Configuration

After 20 generations it has evolved into the following pattern:

Figure 10-4 The R-Pentomino after 20 generations

Finally, after 1103 generations, the pattern stabilizes into Figure 10-5.

So what do cellular automata have to do with AI? First of all, the physics of the cellular automata universe is completely represented by a simple, elegant set of production rules. Secondly, LIFE demonstrates an important characteristic of complexity which appears over and over in AI research. This characteristic was symbolized by Simon's parable of the ant — very *complex* behavior can arise from the interaction of a *simple* system with a *complex* environment. Both LIFE and other simple production systems illustrate behavior even more surprising than Simon's ant, however. That is: very *complex* behavior can arise from the interaction of *simple* systems with *simple* environments. The R-pentomino, for instance, reaches a maximum population of 319 cells in generation 821, long before it stabilizes to a final population of 116 cells in generation 1103. In the process it produces the following LIFE standard configurations: 8 blocks, 6 gliders, 4 beehives, 4 blinkers, 1 boat, 1 loaf, and 1 ship.

How can this amazing complexity arise from a simple, R-shaped configuration of five cells? Information theory says that it is impossible to store the "genetic code" program for such complexity in just five bits. Similar surprising behavior can result from a relatively simple set of simple production rules interacting with a simple rule interpreter. Such complex behavior may help us understand another puzzle of the human condition — the matter of free will.

10.9 HUMAN PRODUCTIONS AND FREE WILL

From the earliest days of AI research there has been a lively interchange between those scientists trying to teach the computer to be more intelligent and those trying to understand the mechanisms of human intelligence. Each science has contributed greatly to progress in understanding in the other area. Production systems in human and machine illustrate this point. The concept of human productions raises some fascinating philosophical issues which we consider next.

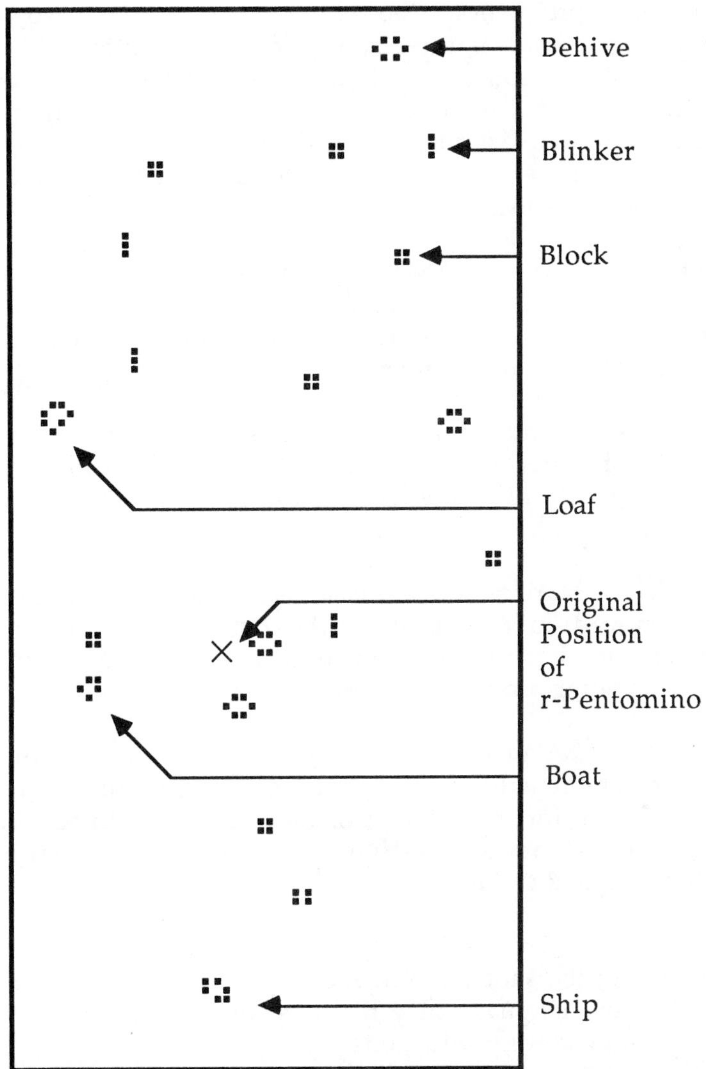

Figure 10-5 The R-Pentomino in stable equilibrium The ultimate stable unbounded condition is reached after 1103 generations. In the process, 6 *gliders* (patterns which "walk" across the screen) are generated which sail off to infinity. This figure is rotated +90° from Figure 10-4.

In the mid-1950s experiments were performed at the RAND corporation and by O. K. Moore of Yale University analyzing how human subjects solved problems. Tape recordings were made of humans "thinking aloud" and these *protocols* were, in the words of Alan Newell "fabulously interesting". They provided much of the insight which led Newell and Simon to write the GPS and develop the concept of string-modifying production rules in 1972.

In human productions, the role of the global database is played by short-term memory. Short-term memory may contain between five and nine symbolic concepts called *chunks* at any one time. Such chunks may be labeled **headache** or **Problem: Smokes cigarettes**. In one elementary model of such a human production system the right-hand-side parts of the rules contain the following actions which act on the information in short-term memory:

Write — A rule may write a new item to the top of the short-term memory list. Since short-term memory seems to hold ~7±2 items at any one time, the lowest priority item tends to be forgotten when this happens.

Note — A production rule can note an item already contained on the short-term memory list. This automatically moves the item to the front of the list and thereby prevents it from being forgotten soon.

Mark — Marking an item is similar to noting it except that it is not moved to the front of the list. This action prevents redundant activation of the production rules. ("My mind seems to keep going around in circles!")

Send — A production rule can send a message out to the environment which, for instance, can request additional information for the solution of the problem at hand. This may involve asking a question, looking up information in a reference, and so on.

Receive — The response to the send production is recorded on the top of the short-term memory list by the receive production. Vision and language play the most important roles in both the send and receive productions.

Using this simple model of human productions, psychologists try to interpret human problem-solving behavior in terms of a *problem-behavior graph* in which the subject moves from one *state of knowledge* to another hopefully closer to the problem goal.

IS THE MIND A MEAT MACHINE?

Marvin Minsky is fond of shocking his audiences by describing the operation of the mind as that of a "meat machine." The basic concept is that, though the mind is obviously awesome in its capability and complexity, it is nonetheless simply an electro-chemical machine carrying out the stimulus/response actions (productions) for which it has been programmed. This program is largely determined, the meat machine concept claims, by the genetic code of each individual.

This is a highly controversial concept because of its profound implications in almost all areas of human activity. Just to mention a few:

> **Artificial Intelligence** — If human intelligence is nothing more than the product of a biological "meat machine", it should be possible to decode its operation and eventually model it by a computing machine. This position holds that the main differences between natural and artificial intelligence stem from the differences between carbon-based and silicon-based systems.
>
> **Social and Political Science** — The "nature *vs* nurture" debate has raged for years between those who feel that nature in the form of the genetic code determines individual behavior and those who feel that nurture through the environment and early childhood experience heavily influences the future behavior of the person. The whole philosophy of many programs for social improvement is based on the importance of the nurture concept, whereas the meat machine model of the mind implies that human behavior is largely predetermined at birth.
>
> **Religion and Law** What role would religion play and what would be the responsibility of the individual under law if, in fact, the meat machine concept of the brain is correct? What is the meaning of moral responsibility, ethical behavior, and our intuitive concept of "ought" if, in fact, humans are all on a one-way railroad track fixed by their genetic code? Our highly cherished concept of "free will" appears to become a hostage of the meat machine concept.

These are just some of the fundamental questions raised by the concept of the human mind as a machine programmed by the genetic code. While questions raised by such models of the mind are disturbing, they are also enormously interesting, and these models have guided much of the research on artificial intelligence. Recent studies have shed new light on the "nature vs nurture" debate, and one of the most interesting is the "Twins Reunited" study of psychologist Thomas Bouchard of the University of Minnesota.[11]

TWINS REUNITED

The object of the twins reunited experiment at the University of Minnesota is to study identical twins which have been separated at or near birth and raised in two independent environments. Previous studies of identical twins had always assumed identical genetic heritage and nearly identical environments. However, studies of twins raised together must unravel that component of behavior resulting from pressures to differentiate the twins and encourage them to assert their individuality ("Bruce always wears blue and David wears red"). This may lead, for instance, to the development of a dominant and a submissive twin as both twins feel compelled to exaggerate the (externally imposed) differences. The University of Minnesota study environment removes this socially imposed differentiation, and at least one of the researchers on the project thinks that twins raised separately may actually have more in common than those raised together.

One of the problems of the experiment is how to reach statistically valid conclusions based on a very limited set of data (early results were based on 80 sets of twins). The experiment involved a week of intensive testing of all aspects of the twins medical histories, personality traits, and mental abilities determined by a battery of 15,000 questions. Data was collected on diet, smoking and exercise habits, electrocardiograms, EEG tests, chest X-rays, heart stress tests, and psychological and IQ tests to measure skills in vocabulary, spatial reasoning, numerical ability, and memory.

While the statistical problem has prevented many strong scientific conclusions, some of the coincidences uncovered in the study are indeed remarkable. One of the most astounding was the similarities of the "Jim twins". They had been adopted into separate working-class Ohio families at age four weeks and had not met until age 39. Their histories included these facts:

- Both had law enforcement training and worked part time as deputy sheriffs.

- Both vacationed in Florida and drove Chevrolets.

- Both had dogs named Toy; one had a son James Allan and the other a son named James Alan.

- Both married and divorced women named Linda and remarried women named Betty.

- In school, both liked math but not spelling.

- They both presently enjoy mechanical drawing and carpentry.
- They have identical pulse, blood pressure and sleep patterns.
- At the same age their weight suddenly increased 10 pounds.
- Both developed "mixed headache syndrome" at age 18.

Most of the IQ scores of the twins did not differ more than those of one person taken at two different times. What differences were detected were interpreted as reflecting large differences in education (see, environment is important!). The twins reunited even shared a tendency toward phobias and certain emotional problems. According to one of the project researchers "... the most important thing to come out of this study is a strong sense that vastly more of human behavior is genetically determined or influenced than we ever supposed."

CAN WE RESOLVE THE DILEMMA?

Our value as human beings seems so dependent on the concept of free will and the corresponding personal responsibility, and yet the success of any eventual artificially intelligent system seems to hinge on a mechanistic, deterministic view of mind and machine. Can productive AI researchers still believe in free will? While the real answer may, in fact, be "no", there are at least three arguments, one semantic, one from mathematics, and one from physics which allow us both free will and the hope of building intelligent machines.

The **semantic argument** says that it may be in the very nature of things that we demonstrate free will. That is, our genetic code may compel us to the kind of behavior to which we have attributed moral, ethical, and religious motivations in earlier times. The **mathematical argument** was presented by Alan Turing and is based on Gödel's Incompleteness Theorem which states: "All consistent axiomatic formulations of number theory include undecidable propositions." Loosely reinterpreted this may mean that even in a logically deterministic machine such as the brain or computer, indeterminate situations may occur which would require free will or the flip of a coin to resolve. The **physics argument** states that for sufficiently small dimensions, the Heisenberg uncertainty principle of quantum mechanics prevents strict determinism in predicting the outcome of a given situation. That is, on the atomic scale, the precise position and momentum of an electron cannot both be specified simultaneously. And since the behavior of electrons determines the behavior of atoms, and the behavior of atoms determines the behavior of molecules, and the behavior of molecules determines the properties of genes, and the property of genes... *Voila,* the free will hostage is rescued by quantum mechanics!

The student may sense that all three of these rationales seem a bit forced. Rather than grasping at these straws, one might consider the parable of the ant and the complexity of the R-pentomino to shed light on the mystery of free will. That is, we know that the amazingly complex behavior of the R-pentomino is determined by the interaction of this simple, five-celled "animal" with its environment consisting of a simple square grid and three almost trivial production rules. A naive observer, unaware of this deterministic situation, might well associate attributes such as purpose and free will with this behavior. Might not human attributes of purpose and free will also be explainable as the interaction of a much larger set of genetically determined production rules with a vastly more complex environment?

These are greatly oversimplified observations on very complex issues of the nature of man and machines. Since the feasibility of artificial intelligence and eventual understanding of human intelligence involves such issues, it is useful to introduce them here if only in outline form. The illumination and understanding of these issues will require many lifetimes of dedicated research.

PROBLEMS AND PROGRAMS

10-1. Until now you have probably considered the IF-THEN-ELSE structure available in most programming languages as simply a powerful construct for control of flow for sequential programming. In production systems, the same structure is interpreted as a knowledge representation scheme. Discuss these two interpretations of the IF-THEN-ELSE structure, and give an example from one of your recent procedural language programs of your use of IF-THEN-ELSE in which you can interpret its use as representing knowledge.

10-2. Discuss the proposition: *A production system using FIRE ALL conflict resolution is simply a* ***set of demons***. Under what circumstances may this be an appropriate control strategy? How can it lead to ambiguity and inconsistencies?

10-3. The Global Database illustrated in Figure 10-1 is sometimes called short-term memory to reflect its dynamic nature. Discuss how a production system database differs from databases frequently encountered in conventional database systems.

10-4. Write a LISP or Prolog program to implement THE NATURALIST example described in Section 10.3.

10-5. Which of the conflict resolution techniques discussed in section 10.6 does THE NATURALIST example of Section 10.3 use?

10-6. Note how the working memory list (WM) describing the unknown tree in Section 10.3 not only selects the correct object (tamarack) but also contains many of its attributes. How is the order and contents of WM dependent upon the order in which the production rules appear? Can you postulate a production system containing a given set of rules in which the answer depends upon the order in which the rules appear?

10-7. Three advantages listed for production rules as a scheme for knowledge representation are: intuitiveness, modularity, and knowledge intensive nature. Discuss each of these features briefly, and give examples from a set of production rules of your own invention illustrating each.

10-8. Why is *conflict resolution* necessary for production systems? List all possible problems you can imagine if conflict resolution was missing.

10-9. Production rule systems are usually selected for expert systems requiring heuristic rules-of-thumb, whereas other systems using automated reasoning are usually selected for systems involving clean logic and/or physical laws. Give examples of each type of system and discuss your rationale for selecting each.

10-10. An essential feature of expert systems, as we shall see in the following chapters, is the capacity for *justification* and *explanation* of the reasoning underlying the expert system's conclusion or advice. How might this capacity be incorporated into a production system? (Hint: An "audit trail" may be useful.)

10-11. One of the problems with production systems is the *opacity* of the line of reasoning leading to the conclusion. Discuss how a *clear* set of production rules and a *clear* control strategy can lead to an *opaque* system performance.

10-12. What technique of conflict resolution is employed on Conway's Game of LIFE? Is a control system necessary for firing the three production rules or do they act like a set of demons?

10-13. Play the Game of LIFE on a computer with graphics capability, and show the life cycle patterns for the blinker (three cells in a row), the beehive (4 cells in a row), and the T-Tetromino (a four-celled "T" with three cells in the top row).

10-14. Play the Game of LIFE on a computer with graphics capability, and show the life cycle patterns for the R-Pentomino, showing the resulting cellular pattern after 5, 10, 50, and 100 cycles. How can such complexity be encoded into this simple pattern? Do you see similarities and differences with the DNA encoding of genetic information?

10-15. Discuss the strengths and weaknesses of von Neumann's argument that his self-replicating cellular automata prove that self-replicating machines are possible in the real world.

10-16. What if von Neumann's results had indicated that it is impossible to build a cellular automaton that is self-replicating. Would that result rule out the possibility of building a self-replicating machine in the real, three-dimensional world? How does complexity and the problem of scaling from n to n+1 dimensions enter in?

10-17. Discuss the mind as "meat machine" concept in terms of the empirical/reductionist philosophy discussed in Chapter 1.

10-18. Discuss the proposition: *Shocking as the "mind as meat machine" concept is, the alternative is even worse.* What is the alternative?

10-19. Read the most recent analysis of the "Twins Reunited" you can find, and discuss the following issues:

- Identical twins raised together are artificially differentiated
- Identical twins raised separately are as identical as separate environments allow
- The role of *genetics* vs *environment* in the twins experiment.

10-20. Discuss the proposition: *The concept of free will is fundamentally inconsistent with empiricist tradition of mind as machine.*

10-21. Do you feel the concept of free will is important? Which of the three arguments supporting free will do you find most convincing and why? What other arguments have been proposed to support the concept of free will?

REFERENCES AND FOOTNOTES

1 Post, Emil, "Formal Reductions of the General Combinatorial Decision Problem," *American Journal of Mathematics* **65**, pp. 197–215 (1943)

2 Chomsky, Noam, *Syntactic Structures*, The Hague: Mouton (1957)

3 Newell, Allen and Simon, Herbert A., *Human Problem Solving*, Prentice-Hall, Englewood Cliffs, NJ (1972)

4 Haugeland, John, *Artificial Intelligence —The Very Idea,* The MIT Press, p. 157 (1985)

5 Feigenbaum, Edward A., Barr, Avron, and Cohen, Paul R. (eds), *The Handbook of Artificial Intelligence,*Vol.1–3, HeurisTech Press/-William Kaufmann, Inc., Stanford, CA (1981–82)

6 Jackson, Peter, *Introduction to Expert Systems,* pp. 29–47, Addison-Wesley Publishers, Workingham, England (1986)

7 Shirai, Yoshiaki and Tsuji, Jun-ichi, *Artificial Intelligence — Concepts, Techniques, and Applications*, John Wiley & Sons, New York, NY (1982)

8 von Neumann, John, "The General and Logical Theory of Automata," *The World of Mathematics*, James R. Newman (ed), pp. 2070–2-98, Simon & Schuster, New York, NY (1956)

9 Poundstone, William, *The Recursive Universe,* Contemporary Books, Inc. Chicago, IL (1985)

10 Gardner, Martin, *Wheels, Life, and Other Mathematical Amusements*, W. H. Freeman, New York, NY (1983)

11 Holden, Constance, "Twins Reunited," *Science 80*, pp. 55–59, November (1980)

Chapter 11

SURVEY OF EXPERT SYSTEMS

(PHOTO: CAROLYN CADDES)

Dr. Edward A. Feigenbaum is Professor of Computer Science at Stanford University and Scientific Director of the Stanford Heuristic Programming Project, a leading laboratory in knowledge engineering and expert systems. He was a student of Herbert Simon at Carnegie-Mellon University where he received both his B.S. and Ph.D.. Working with Joshua Lederberg, he wrote the DENDRAL program, the first expert system to perform at the level of a human expert. He is co-editor of the first AI book, *Computers and Thought* and, more recently, the encyclopedic *Handbook of Artificial Intelligence.* He and Pamela McCorduck wrote *The Fifth Generation.* He is co-founder of Teknowledge, Inc. and IntelliCorp, two firms in applied artificial intelligence.

11: SURVEY OF EXPERT SYSTEMS

11.1 INTRODUCTION

As we have suggested several times previously in this book, the most significant practical product to emerge from 30 years of AI research is the so-called *expert system*. Expert systems belong to a broader category of programs known as *knowledge-based systems*. Depending upon the level of performance of knowledge-based systems, they are also known as "automated advisors", "computerized assistants", "virtual consultants", or "expert systems". For purposes of the following discussion we adopt the very general definition of expert systems:[1]

> *"Expert systems are a class of computer programs that can advise, analyze, categorize, communicate, consult, design, diagnose, explain, explore, forecast, form concepts, identify, interpret, justify, learn, manage, monitor, plan, present, retrieve, schedule, test, and tutor. They address problems normally thought to require human specialists for their solution."*

This definition certainly can not be criticized as unduly restrictive. It does emphasize the wide range of capabilities which expert systems have demonstrated, although no single program has ever included all these features. Based solely on the human specialist criterion, this definition implies that several of the programs we have already studied may be considered expert systems as long as we do not require the system to include a justification feature. Examples from the field of logic include: The Logic Theorist, General Problem Solver (GPS), and the Automated Reasoning Assistant, AURA. Examples from games include the better backgammon, checkers, and GO programs and even microcomputer chess programs such as SARGON III.

The mathematics problem solvers such as MuMath, SMP, and MACSYMA also qualify under this definition as expert systems. However, such impressive natural language processors as SAM, PAM, and BORIS would not qualify since they can carry on intelligent conversations about particular subjects taken from everyday life but not ones requiring specialized knowledge. CYRUS, on the other hand, would qualify as an expert system since only such experts as the man himself, his relatives, and his biographers would know as much about Cyrus Vance as did the program.

To avoid the conclusion that essentially all of the AI systems we have discussed are expert systems, it is generally agreed that a system must have the capability of explaining or justifying its conclusions in order to qualify as an expert system. A system which can explain its reasoning process is said to demonstrate *meta-knowledge* (knowledge about its own knowledge). This higher level of abstraction is a useful criterion for distinguishing expert systems from other AI systems which perform at a high level.

Partly because of renewed interest in AI sparked by the Japanese Fifth Generation computer project[2] and the flurry of commercial products now coming on the market, the common impression is that expert systems are a relatively new phenomenon. This is far from the case. Some of the most impressive, powerful, and currently useful expert systems appeared in the mid-1960s. Two examples are Stanford University's DENDRAL project and MIT's MACSYMA, each of which have celebrated their 20th birthday. Through the years both have gained new capability and broadened the range of their application. We discuss these programs and three benchmark programs from the fields of geology, electronics, and medicine in some detail in this chapter. Finally, we summarize several expert systems from a variety of fields to illustrate the range of application of this new technology.

The key concept underlying the success of all expert systems is the importance of *knowledge.* Without an adequate knowledge base, an expert system is doomed to fail, regardless of the sophistication of the knowledge representation or inference engine it uses. The task of extracting knowledge from human experts and transmitting it to computers is defined as *knowledge engineering,* a term introduced by Professor Donald Michie of the University of Edinburgh in 1972.[3]

11.2 CHARACTERISTICS OF EXPERT SYSTEMS

With this background we can summarize some characteristics shared by almost all expert systems.

- The system performs at a level generally recognized as *equivalent to that of a human expert* or specialist in the field.

- The system is *highly domain specific,* that is, it knows a great deal about a narrow range of knowledge rather than something about everything.

- The system can *explain its reasoning,* that is, to provide a useful tool it must be able to justify its advice, analysis, or conclusions.

- If the information with which it is working is *probabilistic* or *fuzzy*, the system can correctly propagate uncertainties and provide a range of alternate solutions with associated likelihoods.

STRUCTURE OF EXPERT SYSTEMS

Most production rule based expert systems include the basic components related to each other as shown in Figure 11-1:

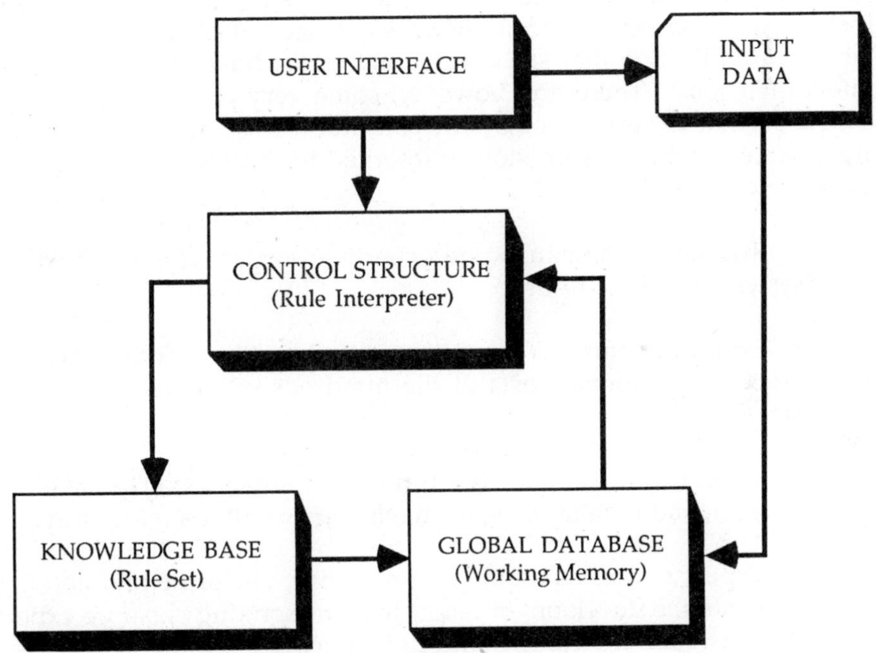

Figure 11-1 Components of an Expert System This structure is based on the production rule method of representing knowledge.

1) *A user interface.* This can range from simple menu-driven I/O to sophisticated natural language dialog and commands.

2) *A knowledge base.* This source of knowledge includes domain specific facts and heuristics useful for solving problems in the domain, generally structured in the form of production rules.

3) *A control structure.* This rule interpreter or inference engine applies the knowledge base information for solving the problem.

4) *A short term memory.* This working memory or global data base registers the current problem status and history of solution to date.

ARTIFICIAL *VS* HUMAN EXPERTS

It is always good, clean fun to gloat over the failures of computer systems like the banking system that deposits $1,000,000 rather than $10 to some lucky person's account, or the defense system which interprets a flock of geese crossing a full moon as a fleet of Russian missiles. There's no indication that such occasional errors have ever "cost computers their job." There are, however, some very convincing reasons to believe that expert systems will continue to assume a larger and larger share of what was previously reserved for human experts. These reasons include:

- Salaries for human experts continue to rise; costs for expert systems continue to drop.

- Expert systems can be replicated for pennies; human experts require educational costs in the hundreds of thousands of dollars.

- Expert systems can live forever; human experts develop, flourish, and then fade away, making errors all along the way.

- Expert systems should be cumulative; in principle, nothing prevents the development of systems integrating separate expert systems. An interesting question concerns possible synergistic effects of an integrated system.

Now let's consider some of the major expert systems in their approximate historical order.

11.3 DENDRAL — CHEMICAL ANALYSIS EXPERT SYSTEM

This benchmark expert system was developed by Edward Feigenbaum, one of the students in Herbert Simon's class when Simon announced his invention of a thinking machine in 1956. Feigenbaum, an undergraduate at the time, went on to finish his Ph.D. in cognitive psychology and in the process wrote EPAM (Elementary Perceiver and Memorizer). Simon was studying Greek at the time, and author Pamela McCorduck suggests that EPAM may have been named in honor of the Greek general and statesman, Epaminondas.[4]

EPAM was an experiment in cognitive psychology with the objective of teaching a machine to memorize nonsense syllables. Both Simon and Feigenbaum considered their work as research in behavioral science, and Feigenbaum defined the goal of EPAM as follows:[5]

> *"But the EPAM payoff was a good explanation of data, of psychological data. Could we come up with something that was cogent, clear, fairly simple, realized by a program, whose structure at least psychologists could understand, and that could explain a wide range of phenomena?"*

The answer to this challenge was "yes", and the discrimination net structure developed for EPAM is still in use today.

Following his degree from Carnegie-Mellon University, Feigenbaum spent a year as Fulbright Fellow in London where he met Seymour Papert. He then moved to Berkeley where he spent more time developing the EPAM concept with a former colleague, Julian Feldman. However, Feigenbaum had difficulty in getting his psychology colleagues at Berkeley to appreciate his work in computer modeling of human psychology, and he moved to his present position at Stanford University.

With his move to Stanford, Feigenbaum switched the emphasis of his research from trying to model the processes of the human brain to building a system to effectively perform the empirical induction process which characterizes much of science. The particular problem to which he was to devote a considerable portion of his life was suggested to him by a Stanford colleague, Joshua Lederberg, a Nobel prize winner in genetics who had devised a program called DENDRAL (short for dendritic algorithm) for enumerating all possible configurations of a set of atoms.

As Feigenbaum defines the problem:[6]

> *"It was a problem which had all the elements of classical empirical induction. Here's an array of data that comes from a physical instrument, the mass spectrograph. Here's a set of primitive constructs out of which to compose a hypothesis about what organic compound is being analyzed. Here's a legal-move generator for generating all possible hypotheses. The problem is to find good ones out of the set of all possible ones, since in the general case, you don't want to generate all possible hypotheses. How do you find the good ones? And how do you employ knowledge of the world of chemistry, mass spectrometry, to constrain the set of*

alternatives, steering away from large sets of unfruitful ones? That was the framework."

The product of this challenge was Heuristic DENDRAL which we refer to from here on as DENDRAL. As Feigenbaum indicates in the comments above, there is no scientific algorithm for mapping the mass spectrum of a compound into its molecular structure. This is where the skill, experience, and expertise of human experts come into play. The job for Feigenbaum was to incorporate the expertise of Lederberg into a computer program which could perform at a human expert level.

In the process of writing DENDRAL, Lederberg had to teach himself computing and Feigenbaum had to teach himself chemistry. One of the first problems identified in the project was what Feigenbaum has termed the "knowledge acquisition bottleneck", that is, how do you extract expert knowledge from humans and transfer it to computers? It became apparent that in addition to the many rules of chemistry, chemists use a vast body of heuristic knowledge based on experience and guessing.

The input data to DENDRAL typically consists of information on the compound under study of the following sort:

- The chemical formula, for instance, $C_8H_{16}O$.
- The mass spectrum like that shown in Figure 11-2.
- Nuclear magnetic resonance spectroscopy information.

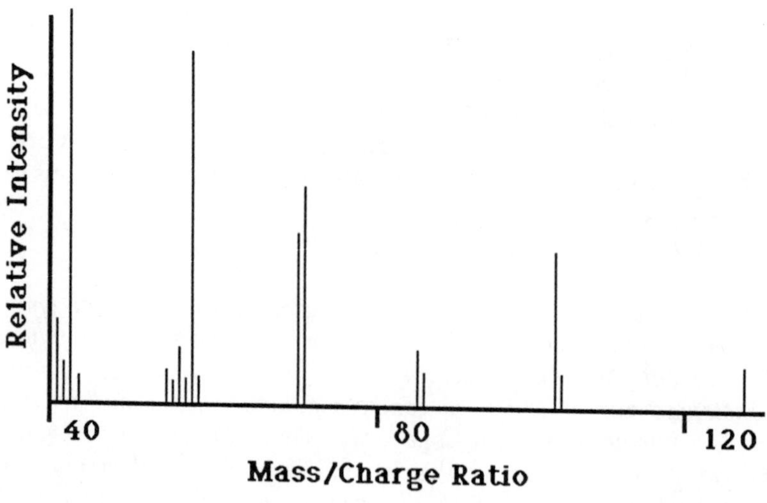

Figure 11-2 Typical mass spectrum for an organic compound

DENDRAL uses the following three steps for identifying the structure of the parent compound from an input formula, mass spectrometer, and magnetic resonance data:

1. PLAN — The planning portion of the program reduces the answer from the set of all possible configurations of atoms to that consistent with the constraints derived from the mass spectrum. The constraints are applied in two ways; the molecular fragments which *must* appear in the final structure and those which *must not* appear.

2. GENERATE — Using the constraints from (1), GENERATE generates all structures which contain the required atomic groups and not the excluded molecular fragments. The name of the generator of all such possible (or plausible) chemical graphs is called CONGEN (for constrained generator).

3. TEST — This section ranks the output of (2) according to the quality of the fit between the hypothesized mass structure and the experimental one.

As examples of the rules used by DENDRAL in sorting out the mass spectrometer information, consider the following:

Rule74:

```
IF     THE SPECTRUM FOR THE MOLECULE HAS TWO
       PEAKS AT MASSES X1 AND X2 SUCH THAT:
             X1 + X2  =  M + 28, AND
             X1 - 28  IS A HIGH PEAK, AND
             X2 - 28 IS A HIGH PEAK, AND
             AT LEAST ONE OF X1 OR X2 IS HIGH,

THEN   THE MOLECULE CONTAINS A KETONE GROUP.
```

Rule 75:

```
IF     THERE IS A HIGH PEAK AT MASS 71, AND
       THERE IS A HIGH PEAK AT MASS 43, AND
       THERE IS A HIGH PEAK AT MASS 86, AND
       THERE IS A HIGH PEAK AT MASS 58

THEN   THERE MUST BE AN  N-PROPYL-KETONE3 STRUCTURE.
```

As DENDRAL applies the constraints imposed by the chemical formula the mass spectrum information, and the rules stored in the knowledge base, the number of possible structures is reduced from the original 698 permitted by the formula $C_8H_{16}O$, first to about 40 ketone structures, and finally to the unique structure:[7]

$$
\begin{array}{c} \quad\quad\quad O \\ \quad\quad\quad \| \\ CH_3\text{-}CH_2\text{-}C\text{-}CH_2\text{-}CH_2\text{-}CH_2\text{-}CH_2\text{-}CH_3 \end{array}
$$

If DENDRAL cannot arrive at a unique identification of the chemical structure, it will list the most likely structures with an indication of their relative probability.

The most obvious contribution of DENDRAL is that it proved that computers could play the role of expert in certain restrictive domains. It performs at or above the level of a Ph.D. human chemist. The DENDRAL program itself was written largely in a dialect of LISP called INTERLISP, with some subroutines like CONGEN written in FORTRAN and SAIL. DENDRAL has proven to be so useful as an analysis tool that it is widely used by chemists throughout the United States and is marketed commercially.

Perhaps the most significant contribution of DENDRAL is that it marked an important "paradigm shift" in AI — a shift from appealing general purpose, knowledge-sparse, *weak methods* to domain-specific, *knowledge-rich techniques* in which knowledge is explicitly represented. The success of DENDRAL and other knowledge-based systems such as MACSYMA attest to the validity of this paradigm shift.

11.4 MACSYMA — MATHEMATICS EXPERT SYSTEM

MACSYMA was designed in 1968 by Carl Engleman, William Martin, and Joel Moses and provided the doctoral theses for Martin and Moses at MIT. It grew out of earlier work on symbolic integration by Slagle in his 1961 program, SAINT, and by Moses' 1967 improved version called SIN.

MACSYMA is a very powerful problem solving program with the capability of performing over 600 distinct mathematical operations. These include differentiation, integration, vector and matrix algebra, solution of systems of equations, and Taylor's series expansions. It is a very large system consisting of over one half million lines of LISP and MACSYMA programming language code. About half this code has been written by the project staff and about half by various users, and the effort represents over 100 person-years of programming. MACSYMA is used daily by hundreds of researchers from the national laboratories, universities, and industry. It is available both commercially and over the ARPANET.

Some of the features of MACSYMA which contribute to its capability as an expert system are:[8]

- *Non-algorithmic Procedures for Algebraic Simplification* —

Algebra students are all keenly aware of the need for reducing large, unwieldy expressions by simplification to more tractable forms. MACSYMA provides a large set of expression transforming commands to carry out such operations as expansion, factorization, and partial fraction decomposition. It contains a special set of transformation rules, some examples of which are shown below:

$$x \cdot x \cdot x \Rightarrow x^3$$

$$\cos(x-\pi/2) \Rightarrow \sin(x)$$

$$\log(a/b) \Rightarrow \log(a) - \log(b)$$

These non-algorithmic rules improve the efficiency of formula simplification. MACSYMA users may also define their own transformation rules.

- *Semantic Pattern Matching* — The pattern $ax^2 + bx + c$ where a, b, and c are expressions not containing x will match input expression of the form $4x^2 + 4x + 1$ and $(x + 1)^2$ but NOT the expression $4x^2 + 3x + \sin(x)$ since the last term explicitly contains x. Thus, with a relatively small array of input templates, the meaning of a large number of input expressions can unambiguously be determined.

- *Simplification by Hill Climbing* — MACSYMA contains a search-oriented simplifier called SCSIMP which follows a set of rules in simplifying an expression and continues the process as long as the new result is smaller than the previous one. Consider the following expression relating K, L, M, and N:

Given: $$K^2N^2 + K^2M^2N^2 - K^2L^2N^2 - K^2L^2M^2N^2 \quad (11.1)$$

with the additional equations

$$K^2 + L^2 = 1 \quad (11.2)$$
$$N^2 - M^2 = 1 \quad (11.3)$$

Solve for L^2 in (11.2), substitute into (11.1)

$$K^4M^2N^2 + K^4N^2 \quad (11.4)$$

Solve for M^2 in (11.3), substitute into (11.4)

$$K^4 N^4 \quad (11.5)$$

This expression is a great improvement over the original and shows that hill climbing can be an effective simplification heuristic. It suffers from the intrinsic hill climbing disability, however, of not guaranteeing that the final expression is the minimal one. Consider, for example, the following initial expression (with the same constraint equations):

$$K^2N^2 + L^2M^2 \qquad (11.6)$$

Solve for L^2 and substitute

$$K^2N^2 - K^2M^2 + M^2 \qquad (11.7)$$

Solve for N^2 and substitute

$$K^2 + M^2 \qquad (11.8)$$

While (11.8) is obviously the right answer, SCSIMP would fail to find it in its search since the intermediate state (11.7) is larger than the initial state. However, because of the large number of possible expanded intermediate states such as (11.7), SCSIMP does not allow such expansions even though they may be necessary to reach the simplest configuration.

• *Relational Database with Inference* — In many problems in science and engineering, variables or expressions will have ranges or other restrictions associated with them. MACSYMA contains a built-in relational data base for storing such associated information in the format of a semantic network. It then uses a fast inference engine called GPM to perform deductions, property inheritances, set intersections, and other simple inferences. Thus, for instance, if the variable n has the property of restriction to integer values, the expression $\sin((2n+1)\cdot\pi/2)$ could be simplified to ±1.

• *User HELP Program called ADVISOR* — MACSYMA is a prime example of the **POWER × SIMPLICITY ≥ Constant** uncertainty principle. That is, by the very nature of its great power, MACSYMA is complex and often difficult to use. To help resolve this difficulty, an "automated consultant" called ADVISOR has been implemented to assist the user in setting up his or her problem and designing the plan for its solution on MACSYMA. By using the VERBOSE option, the user can instruct MACSYMA to document the progress of its solution as it proceeds. This illustrates the use an expert advisory system to help the user with an expert analysis system.

Current work on MACSYMA includes two areas of improvement. First is the development of an "apprentice" to help with the book-keeping involved in running MACSYMA as a symbolic calculator. Second is the development of a system for attaching range restrictions automatically to variables to correspond to physical reality. For instance, when physicists use the variable MASS it must always be non-negative. This corresponds, in a sense, to adding semantics (meaning) to the existing syntactic structure of MACSYMA.

Work continues on the development of MACSYMA at MIT, and the commercial marketing of the program is now handled by Symbolics, Inc.

11.5 PROSPECTOR — GEOLOGICAL EXPERT SYSTEM

PROSPECTOR is an expert system that was designed for decision making problems in mineral exploration. It uses a structure called an inference network to represent the data base. PROSPECTOR was written in 1978 by Richard O. Duda, then of SRI International.[9] Some of the more important features and contributions of PROSPECTOR include the following:

- The system represents fuzzy input on a range from –5 = *certainly false* to +5 = *certainly true* and produces conclusions with associated uncertainty factors.

- The system's expertise is based on hand-crafted knowledge of twelve major prospect-scale models and 23 smaller regional-scale models.[10] The prospect-scale models describe major ore deposits such as:
    - Massive Sulfide Deposit, Kuroko Type
    - Mississippi-Valley-Type Lead-Zinc
    - Western States Sandstone Uranium

- The system does not *understand* the rules in its knowledge base but *can explain* the steps used in reaching its conclusions.

- The knowledge acquisition system KAS has been developed for easy editing and expansion of the inference network structure in which the knowledge base is stored.

- PROSPECTOR performs at the level of an expert hard-rock geologist and has already proven itself successful at prospecting. It predicted a molybdenum deposit near Mt. Tolman in Washington State which was subsequently confirmed by core drilling as having a value of $100 million.

INFERENCE NETWORK STRUCTURE

The knowledge representation scheme used in PROSPECTOR is called an *inference network,* a form of semantic networks described in Chapter 9 on Knowledge Representation. The main elements in an inference network and their relationship to the corresponding elements of a semantic network may be summarized as follows:

- *Nodes* — Each node corresponds to a propositional assertion rather than a single noun. A typical model contains about 150 nodes. A node might, for instance, contain one of the following assertions:[11]
  - There is pervasively biotized hornblende.
  - There is a cretaceous dike.
  - There is an alteration favorable for the potassic zone of a porphyry copper deposit.

- *Arcs* — In a manner analogous to semantic networks, arcs specify the relationship between nodes. In particular, they represent the inference rules specifying how the probability of one assertion affects the probability of another assertion. A typical model contains about 100 arcs.

- *Inference trees* — The nodes and arcs above may be organized in an inference tree with the following node structure:
  - Top-level hypotheses — no outgoing arcs
  - Intermediate factors — both incoming and outgoing arcs
  - Evidential statements — no incoming arcs.

Thus, the inference network is a "bottom-up" tree structure starting with evidential statements whose arcs lead upwards to intermediate factor nodes implied by the evidential statements. These intermediate factor nodes lead upwards by the antecedent/consequent arcs till the top-level hypothesis is reached. This inference procedure of reasoning from evidence to allowed conclusion is called *forward chaining.* The top-level hypothesis is the "final answer", hopefully of the form:

IT'S GOLD!! DIG HERE ⬇

but generally expressed in the form of a probability distribution of equal probability contours resembling a topographic map.

PROSPECTOR is designed to run in one of three modes: compiled execution, batch processing, or interactive consultation mode. An example of dialog from the interactive consultation mode is shown below (computer regular, user bold print).[12] The user's answers range from –5 (assertion absolutely false) to +5 (assertion absolutely true).

```
The following questions are intended to establish the nature
of the petrotectonic setting.  (These questions will not be
pursued unless a positive answer is given to the next ques-
tion.)

1-  To what degree do you believe that the target area is in
a continental-margin mobile belt?  4

2-  Do you know the age of the continental-margin mobile
belt?  WHY

The vast majority of porphyry copper deposits are younger
than 200 million years.  Major age groups include:
      1. An older group of 200-150 m.y. (million year) por-
      phyries in British Columbia;
      2. An important younger group of 70 to 50 m.y. de-
      posits in the Mid-East, British Columbia (Skeena
      Arch), and Arizona-New Mexico-Sonora (Laramide) copper
      province;
      3. The major belt of 60 to 4 m.y. deposits in the An-
      des of Argentina, Chile, Peru, Ecuador, and Columbia.

Although some major deposits in the western U.S. do not fit
the above groupings, either in terms of age or location,
they are all younger than 250 m.y.  Known porphyry deposits
of Paleozoic age (e.g., in the Appalachians and East Aus-
tralia) constitute a minor fraction of present resources,
Hercynian (late Carboniferous) occurrences in the Kaza-
khstan, USSR, may include some major deposits.

2-  Do you know the age of the continental-margin mobile
belt?  YES

3-  What is the age of the continental-margin mobile belt?
CRETACEOUS

= 136 - 65 million years.  What is your confidence in this
estimate?  4
```

After a number of additional questions by PROSPECTOR are answered by the user, the program announces its conclusions and indicates the evidence in support of the conclusions and the reasoning on which they are based:

```
I suspect that (* there is a Type-A porphyry copper deposit)
(2.65)  There are several favorable factors;  in order of
importance:
      1. the petrotectonic setting is favorable for a type-A
```

```
        porphyry copper deposit  3.626
        2. there is a favorable regional environment for a
        type-A porphyry copper deposit  1.866
        3. there is a favorable intrusive system for a type-A
        porphyry copper deposit  2.607
        ** dominating factor **
There are two positive factors with neutral effect that, if
negative, could have been significant;  in order of impor-
tance:
        4. You were sure that there are granitic, calc-alka-
        line intrusives in the region  5.0
        5. You were sure that the target (or prospect) lies in
        or near an intrusive system  5.0
For which of the above do you wish to see additional infor-
mation? ...
```

Note that at any point in the dialog, the user may ask **WHY** to request the system to explain the basis and rationale for the question. This allows a skilled geologist to follow the line of reasoning PROSPECTOR is following. Other commands provide for tracing inferences, changing previous assertions, and listing the best "current estimate" of the prospect. PROSPECTOR also has graphics capability and, given the geological maps for surface mineralization and rock alteration for the Mt. Tolman area in eastern Washington, it produced a probability distribution map of the same area with the area of high probability of molybdenum deposit highlighted. Subsequent drilling confirmed the presence of ore-grade molybdenum deposits in the area which PROSPECTOR had designated a likely prospect as well as absence of high-grade ore in the area PROSPECTOR identified as low probability.

FUZZY KNOWLEDGE AND BAYES' RULE

Exploration geology provides a classic example of decision making in the face of uncertainty, a process sometimes called reasoning with "fuzzy knowledge." PROSPECTOR works with rules of the form:

IF E THEN H (to degree LS,LN)

where

H = a given hypothesis
E = evidence for the hypothesis
LS = measure of support for hypothesis if E present
LN = measure of discredit to hypothesis if E missing

The values of LS and LN are defined when the model is built and remain constant during the analysis. A small portion of the set of rules might read:

R1:	IF E1 AND E2	THEN	H2(LS1,LN1)
R2:	IF H2	THEN	H1(LS2,LN2)
R3:	IF E3	THEN	H1(LS3,LN3)

The rules comprise the arcs in a large inference net whose nodes consist of hypotheses or assertions of evidence as shown in Figure 11-3.

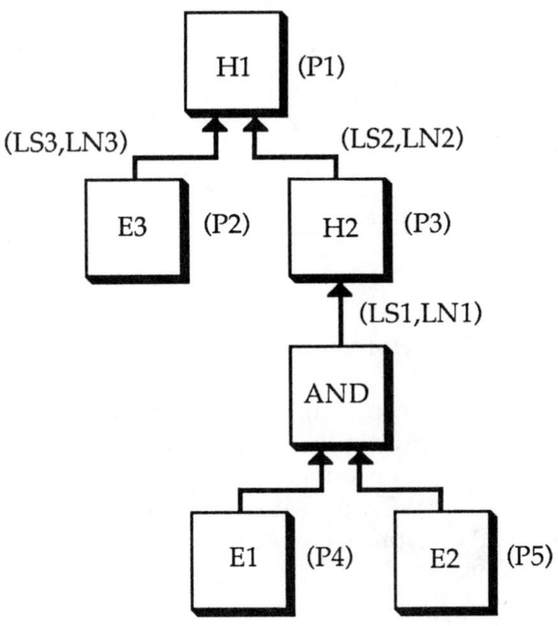

Figure 11-3 Portion of Inference Net from PROSPECTOR This net incorporates the rules R1 — R3 above and indicates how evidence is used in reaching hypotheses. H1 is the top level hypothesis or "conclusion" of this portion of the net.

Each hypothesis H has a probability C(H | E) associated with it, based on evidence E. The probability function is defined as:

$$C(H|E) = \begin{cases} \dfrac{5(P(H|E) - P(H))}{(1 - P(H))} & \text{if } P(H|E) \geq P(H) \quad (11.9) \\[2ex] \dfrac{5(P(H|E) - P(H))}{P(H)} & \text{if } P(H|E) < P(H) \quad (11.10) \end{cases}$$

where

$P(H)$ = *prior probability* of hypothesis H being true in the case of no evidence supporting or discrediting it

$P(H|E)$ = *posterior probability*, the probability of H being true in light of evidence E

So, if H is definitely true (i.e. $P(H|E) = 1$), we get a probability function $C(H|E) = +5$. If hypothesis H is definitely false (i.e. $P(H|E) = 0$), then $C(H|E) = -5$.

PROSPECTOR was the first expert system to incorporate Bayes' rule of evidence for computing $P(H|E)$ and propagating uncertainties through the system. This rule, developed by British mathematician Thomas Bayes states:[13]

$$P(H|E) = \frac{P(E|H) \cdot P(H)}{P(E)} \tag{11.11}$$

where

$$P(E) = P(E|H) \cdot P(H) + P(E|\neg H) \cdot P(\neg H) \tag{11.12}$$

$P(H)$ =*a priori* probability that hypothesis H is true
$P(E|H)$ = probability that hypothesis H being true will result in evidence E
$P(\neg H)$ = *a priori* probability that H is false
$P(E|\neg H)$ = probability of finding evidence E even though H is false

To help interpret Bayes' rule consider the following grim but realistic example:

- H = "Tom is a heavy smoker."
- E = "Tom has lung cancer."

Bayes' rule allows us to compute the probability that Tom is (was?) a heavy smoker based on the evidence that he has lung cancer, in terms of the probability $P(E|H)$ that heavy smokers get lung cancer, the *a priori* probability $P(H)$ that a person is a heavy smoker, and the *a priori* probability $P(E)$ that a person will get lung cancer. Thus, in words, the rule says: the probability that Tom is a heavy smoker based on the evidence that he has lung cancer, is equal to the ratio of the probability that smokers get lung cancer times the likelihood that he was a smoker ($P(E|H) \cdot P(H)$) to the probability of getting lung cancer ($P(E)$). The probability of getting lung cancer is calculated by equation (11.12) as being the sum of the the probability of getting lung cancer if you are a smoker ($P(E|H) \cdot P(H)$) plus the probability of getting lung cancer if you are not a smoker $(P(E \mid \neg H) \cdot P(\neg H))$.

In addition to using Bayes' rule for computing probabilities, PROSPECTOR uses heuristics from the theory of fuzzy sets to propagate probabilities based on logical combinations of assertions. For instance, assertion A may depend on a set of other assertions, $\{A_1, A_2, \ldots, A_k\}$, in either a conjunctive or disjunctive form:

$$\text{Conjunction:} \quad A = A_1 \text{ AND } A_2 \text{ AND } \ldots A_k \tag{11.13}$$

$$\text{Disjunction:} \quad A = A_1 \text{ OR } A_2 \text{ OR } \ldots A_k \tag{11.14}$$

Assume we know the probabilities, $P(A_i \mid E)$, associated with assertions A_i for the case in which evidence E is presented. How can we propagate the probability of A being true in light of this evidence? Lofti Zadeh proposed the following set of heuristic equations which were applied in PROSPECTOR:[14]

$$\text{Conjunction:} \quad P(A \mid E) = \text{MIN}_i\{P(A_i \mid E)\} \tag{11.15}$$

$$\text{Disjunction:} \quad P(A \mid E) = \text{MAX}_i\{P(A_i \mid E)\} \tag{11.16}$$

That is, if A depends in a conjunctive fashion on a set of A_i's being true, then the probability of A being true is approximated by the minimum probability associated with the A_i's. Similarly, if the dependence is disjunctive, then the probability of A being true should go as the probability of the most likely assertion of the set.

In concluding this discussion of PROSPECTOR, it is interesting to note that the generally accepted rule is that a thousand prospects of mineral deposits must be examined before one is found that can be developed into a profitable mine. This means that the typical geologist never makes a "strike" during his or her professional life. In the light of these discouraging statistics, the successful performance of PROSPECTOR is all the more impressive. The PROSPECTOR research project was carried out at Stanford Research Institute (SRI) under funding by the U. S. Geological Survey and the National Science Foundation. Many of the principle researchers of the PROSPECTOR project have since left SRI to form their own company, Syntelligence, with the objective of developing commercial products based on many of the concepts discovered during the PROSPECTOR research.

11.6 MYCIN — MEDICAL DIAGNOSTIC EXPERT SYSTEM

MYCIN is a production rule based expert system for the diagnosis and therapy recommendation for infectious blood diseases. The project started in 1972, and became the Ph.D. thesis work of Edward Shortliffe which was published in 1976.[15] An exhaustive discussion of the MYCIN experiment has appeared more recently.[16] MYCIN shares a number of common characteristics of the PROSPECTOR program, including:

- MYCIN performs at a level equivalent to human experts in the field.

- Reasoning in the face of uncertainty is a crucial part of the MYCIN system. The scale ranges from –1 (certainly wrong) to +1 (certainly right).

- The system's expertise was derived from hand-crafted knowledge in a restricted domain, in this case infectious blood disease.

- A special user interface program, TEIRESIAS, was developed for providing flexible knowledge acquisition and editing.

MYCIN also had some significant differences from PROSPECTOR. These were:

- It used standard production rules rather than inference networks.

- It used *backward chaining* from the diagnostic hypothesis to the data rather than forward chaining as does PROSPECTOR.

- It has been a very influential research program but has never been commercialized.

The purpose of MYCIN is to provide a physician with expert diagnostic and therapeutic advice in a rapid and convenient fashion. The rationale is that doctors must often make quick judgments based on incomplete or ambiguous knowledge in order to save the life of a patient and that any assistance in this process would be helpful. Below we show some sample dialog with MYCIN (human user is bold face):

```
--------------PATIENT-1--------------
1)  Patient's name:  (first-last)
**   Dick H.

2)  Sex:
**  M

3)  Age:
**  52
```

```
4)  Have you been able to obtain positive microbiological
information about a possible infection of Dick H.?
**  Y

5)  What is the infection?
**  ENDARTERITIS
```

[This dialog closely resembles that carried on by a less-specialized physician consulting with expert colleague.]

```
The first significant organism from this blood culture
(CULTURE-1) will be referred to as:

---------------ORGANISM-1-----------------

9)  Enter the identity of ORGANISM-1:
**  Unknown

10)  Is ORGANISM-1 a rod or coccus (etc):
**  ROD

11)  The gram stain of ORGANISM-1:
**  GRAMNEG

12)  Have there been POSITIVE cultures yielding organisms
about which you will NOT be seeking advice?
**  YES
```

[Note that the physician can respond that he or she does not know the answer to certain questions about which the tests are not yet back. After between thirty to ninety such questions, MYCIN produces a diagnosis such as the following:]

```
INFECTION-1 IS ENDARTERITIS  with BACTEREMIA
<Item 1>  E.COLI  [ORGANISM-1]
<Item 2>  SALMONELLA (species unknown) [ORGANISM-1]
<Item 3>  KLEBSIELLA-PNEUMONIAE  [ORGANISM-1]
<Item 4>  PSEUDOMONAS-AERUGINOSA  [ORGANISM-1]
<item 5>  ENTEROBACTER  [ORGANISM-1]
<Item 6>  PROTEUS-NON-MIRABILIS  [ORGANISM-1]
```

This conclusion of MYCIN, as often happens with human experts, is ambiguous. The infection may be caused by any of the six organisms listed.

Rather than recommend a different medicine for each of the six possible organisms (in which case the cure could be worse than the disease), MYCIN recommends an optimal, minimum selection of medications for which there is minimal chance for drug interaction:

```
[Rec 1]  My preferred therapy recommendation is as follows:
     In order to cover for Items <1  2  4  5  6>:
          Give:  GENTAMICIN
          Dose:  119 mg(1.7 mg/kg) q8h IV [or IM]
                 for 10 days
```

```
          Comments:  Modify dose in renal failure
          In order to cover for Item <3>
          Give:  CHLORAMPHENICOL
          Dose:  563 mg (7.5 mg/kg)  q6h for 14 days
          Comments:   Monitor patient's white count

Do you wish to see the next choice therapy?
**  NO
```

So MYCIN's recommendation is for two drugs to cover the six possible organisms. Note that the program only *advises* the physician and that the final responsibility continues to rest with the doctor.

The MYCIN program consists of an inference engine and approximately 500 productions rules of the following sort:

```
IF    1)  the  gram stain of the organism is gram
       negative, and
      2)  the morphology of the organism is rod, and
      3)  the aerobicity of the organism is anaerobic,
THEN
      there is suggestive evidence (.7) that the identity of
      the organism is Bacteroides.
```

The strengths of diagnostic programs as MYCIN demonstrate the real advantages of expert systems. Some of the most obvious are:

- MYCIN does not forget, get tired, or make mistakes as human experts sometimes do.

- Computers can do exhaustive searches, correctly identifying extremely rare diseases which a human expert may never have encountered.

- Computer expert systems can dispense medical advise in the farthest reaches of Alaskan, African, or Australian back country of the quality now available only in major medical centers.

- MYCIN can provide the very latest therapy for use in isolated rural areas where the general practitioner may not have had the opportunity for medical refresher courses in many years.

- MYCIN calculates dosages precisely (based on body weight) which is a refinement that human doctors may not have time to do.

- MYCIN can keep track of a broad range of drugs and possible detrimental synergistic interactions between drugs. This information is so complex that human experts have great difficulty in coping with it.

In view of all these transparent advantages, why is MYCIN not an integral part of every hospital and doctor's office? The reasons are complex and probably more sociological than technical.

1) One technical problem is that MYCIN is restricted to the narrow domain of infectious blood disease. Human diseases often do not always fall into such nicely defined domains. As the range of infections diagnosed by computer expert systems broadens, their usefulness will increase and, one would expect, their acceptance increase along with their capabilities.

2) Its use is not seen as essential by physicians. They have been operating (?) all these years without MYCIN, and relatively successfully. This attitude can be expressed by the cliché "if the system isn't broke, why fix it?"

3) The medical profession is probably the toughest to "crack" by any sort of artificial intelligence system. Physicians take great pride in their intensive training, capability, skill, intuition, and sensitivity to human interactions. If the ordinary layman feels threatened by an "intelligent machine," how much more so will the average physician when he hears of a machine with equal or superior diagnostic skills? Such antagonism was clearly demonstrated in comparative studies, one that was open in which the physicians knew a machine was advising and one that was blind in which the computer's advice was mixed with regular experts. This sociological problem will be the most difficult in winning wide acceptance of medical expert systems.

THE QUESTION OF RESPONSIBILITY

At least two intriguing issues concerning responsibility and medical ethics are raised by medical expert systems. One has to do with responsibility. If, per chance, an error occurs in the medical expert system or in the hardware dispensing it and a prescription is written which results in the death of a patient, who is legally responsible? This question and related issues are beginning to receive serious study.[17]

Secondly, and this may hold the solution to problem 3) raised above, if medical expert systems do become widely accepted, what is the legal responsibility of a physician who makes a "human error" which might have been prevented had he used the standard medical expert system? This kind of legal liability will undoubtedly be the strongest motivation toward widespread acceptance of systems like MYCIN.

11.7 XCON — COMPUTER CONFIGURING EXPERT SYSTEM

John McDermott of Carnegie-Mellon University wrote R1/XCON in collaboration with Digital Equipment Corporation.[18] XCON is the acronym for eXpert CONfigurer and is used to configure the VAX and PDP-11 series of computer systems sold by DEC. XCON is the name used by the Digital Equipment Corporation while the Carnegie-Mellon research team uses R1 which is McDermott's name for the system. He is quoted as saying, "Three years ago I wanted to be a knowledge engineer, and today I are one."

XCON was proposed to DEC management in December of 1978, and a prototype system was demonstrated in May, 1979. The initial system contained about 300 production rules of the standard variety for configuring the 420 possible components of a VAX-11/780 system and detailing its backplane wiring. A completed system containing some 800 production rules was delivered to DEC for acceptance testing in October, 1979. By 1980, DEC personnel had become sufficiently familiar with the operation of XCON to assume full responsibility for its maintenance and development, and they have extended it to contain over 4,000 rules. The growth of the rule base used in XCON over the years is shown in Figure 11-4.

The XCON system was designed to replace human "technical editors". Such editors had been responsible for two operations: checking for completeness of orders, and laying out the physical placement and wiring connections between component modules in the chassis. These tasks are fairly tedious and as a result they attracted engineers with relatively weak engineering backgrounds. Each of the components is specified by eight properties such as voltage, frequency, how many devices it supports, and how many ports it has. In addition to this information, the editors had information indicating which components can or must be associated with other components. This set of rules governing the relationship between components is called "constraint knowledge."

An example of one of the rules from XCON, translated into English, is shown:

```
IF    The current sub-task is assigning devices to unibus-
      modules, and there is an unassigned dual port disk
      drive, and the type of controller it requires is
      known, and there are two such controllers, neither of
      which has any devices assigned to it, and the number
      of devices which these controllers can support is
      known
THEN  Assign the disk drive to each controller and note that
      each controller supports one device.
```

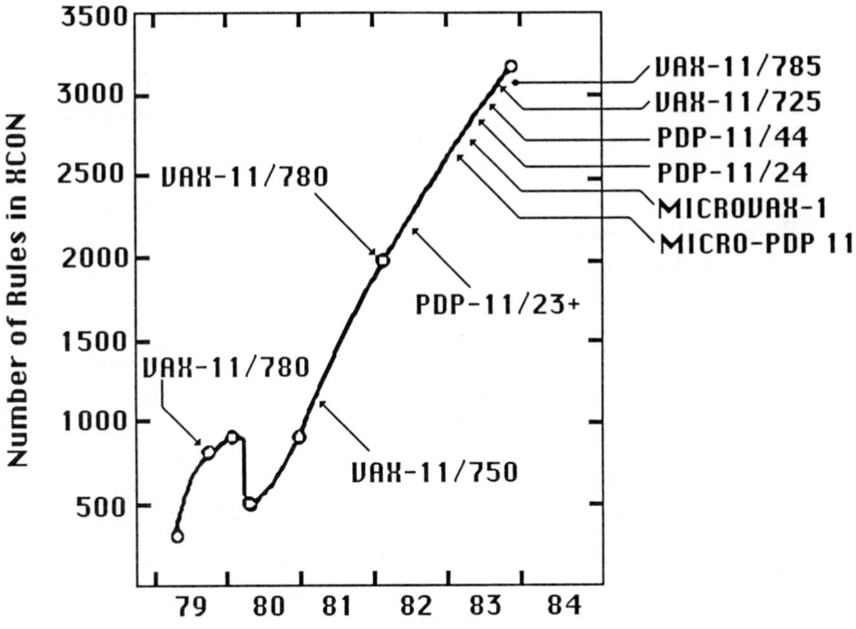

Figure 11-4 The growth of XCON over the years

XCON passed an extensive series of performance tests which were also used to upgrade its performance. A set of ten configurations was submitted to the program and the results were evaluated by a team of twelve people consisting of technical editors, technicians, and engineers. Errors detected were corrected and the cycle repeated until fifty configurations had been produced. This initial testing detected only twelve errors of seven different types. By December, 1979, XCON was judged expert enough to be used for routine configuration of VAX-11/780 systems.

The capabilities of XCON have grown to include configuring the much more complicated PDP-11 family of computer. By 1986 XCON represented an investment of over 50 person-years of human effort.[19] The current R1/XCON system is used to configure over 97 percent of the orders received for VAX-11 systems.

The experience of building XCON yielded a number of lessons which builders of other expert systems have found instructive. These include:[20]

- Since its birth, XCON has grown at a relatively uniform rate as its capabilities expanded from a single line of VAX computers to the complete VAX line and the PDP-11 line as shown in Figure

11-4. This effort has required about four person-years per year.

• The developers of XCON found they did not have to complete the system before putting it to use. This illustrates an important characteristic of expert systems — their incremental growth.

• No matter how much knowledge was added to XCON, it still continued to make occasional mistakes. The developers have concluded that it will never be possible to guarantee 100% error free performance and are resigned to this fact.

• The developers of XCON found that building an expert system is an unending process. An expert system's clientele continue to demand refinement of existing capabilities and extension of the boundaries of the domain of its expertise.

Since 1980, XCON has analyzed over 100,000 unique orders and is presently operating with greater than 99% accuracy. It has become an indispensable and effective business tool. The savings produced by XCON has convinced DEC management that artificial intelligence, particularly its application to expert systems, has a bright future.[21]

11.8 THE RANGE OF EXPERT SYSTEM APPLICATIONS

The five benchmark expert systems described above have proven the feasibility of using knowledge-based systems for solving problems traditionally requiring human experts. In their wake has come a flood of new expert systems, many of which have been published and even more of which are under development as proprietary, "in-house" products for improving industrial productivity. Du Pont, for instance, is reported to have 350 PC-based expert systems presently in operation and expects to be using 2000 expert systems by 1991. The vast majority of proprietary, productivity-enhancing expert systems will never be reported on publicly for obvious reasons relating to competitive advantage.

Donald Waterman has provided an excellent summary of expert systems which have been reported in the literature.[22] To give the reader some feeling for the wide range of application of expert systems we present below a condensed sampling from Waterman's Catalog of Expert Systems.

Agriculture

Expert systems developed at the University of Illinois predict damage to corn caused by the black cutworm and provide consultation on the diagnosis of soybean diseases using knowledge about disease symptoms and plant environment. Another agriculture system helps farmers manage apple orchards by providing advice on how to improve the apple crop. A cotton crop management program determines the best strategy for irrigation and application of fertilizer, defoliants, and cotton ball openers.[23]

Chemistry

Systems have been built to infer the three-dimensional structure of a protein from an electron density map by interpreting X-ray diffraction data, to aid organic chemists in determining the structure of newly isolated, naturally occurring compounds, and to analyze DNA structure from restriction enzyme segmentation data by using the generate-and-test paradigm of DENDRAL. Other systems assist geneticists in planning gene-cloning experiments in molecular genetics, help molecular biologists perform several types of nucleotide sequence analysis, and fine-tune triple-quadrupole mass-spectrometers (TQMS) by interpreting signal data on spectral peak ratios, widths, and shapes.

Computer Systems

Diagnostic expert systems have appeared to help technicians locate the field replaceable units that should be replaced in order to fix faults in PDP 11/03 computers. A programmer's aide helps programmers write microprograms for the Texas Instruments' TI990 VLSI chip using information from manuals and the TI990 control ROM. Another assists in tuning VAX/VMS computer systems in order to reduce performance problems that arise in a constantly changing computer environment. An expert system helps computer operators monitor and control the MVS (multiple virtual storage) operating system for large mainframe IBM computers.

Electronics

ACE identifies trouble spots in telephone networks and recommend appropriate repair and rehabilitative maintenance for the Bell System. Another diagnostic system helps locate faulty modules in a large signal-switching network called a baseband distribution subsystem. Instructional systems simulate an expert demonstrating the operation of the graphical features of a computer-aided design (CAD) subsystem for designing digital logic circuits and teach students how to troubleshoot electrical circuits. Evaluation assistants help circuit design engineers analyze the correctness, timing, robustness, and speed of VLSI circuit designs and assist VLSI designers by performing a hardware allocation from an algorithmic description of a VLSI system.

Engineering

Engineering assistants help engineers determine analysis strategies for structural analysis problems using finite-element analysis techniques and perform structural damage assessment of existing structures which are subjected to earthquake excitation. Nuclear power plant consultants help plant operators determine the cause of abnormal events using models of the reactor, cooling systems, and steam generators and others assist reactor operators in the diagnosis and treatment of nuclear reactor accidents by monitoring instrument readings for deviations from normal operating conditions.

Geology

The DIPMETER ADVISOR infers sub-surface geological structure by interpreting dipmeter logs and measurements of the conductivity of rock as a function of depth around a borehole. Several systems have been built to assist an oil-rig supervisor in resolving problems related to the drilling mechanism sticking inside the borehole and to help engineers maintain optimal drilling fluid properties by diagnosing causes of problems with drilling mud and suggesting treatments. A programmer's assistant helps a hydrologist use HSPF, a computer program that simulates the physical processes by which precipitation is distributed throughout a watershed.

Information Management

A student advisor helps graduate students plan their computer science curriculum from information about the student's academic history and interests. A route-finder helps drivers find routes and navigate in city streets using sophisticated route finding algorithms and a highlighted graphical display of a street map. A toxic material advisor helps information specialists decide which information concerning the manufacture and distribution of toxic chemicals may be released to the public. FOLIO helps portfolio managers determine client investment goals and select portfolios that best meet those goals.

Law

AUDITOR helps a professional auditor evaluate a client's potential for defaulting on a loan from payment history, economic status, and credit standing. Other systems help contractors analyze the legal aspects of differing site condition claims in which the actual site conditions differ from those on the contract. One legal advisor helps lawyers reason about civil law cases by establishing the factual and legal premises of the cause of the action and another assists legal experts in settling product liability cases using defendant liability, case worth, and equitable settlement amounts. Several tax advisors assist attorneys with tax and estate planning for clients with large estates and assist in the investigation of legal reasoning and legal argumentation using the domain of corporate tax law.

Manufacturing

Systems assist managers in a computer system manufacturing environment with paperwork management, capacity planning and inventory management and construct factory job shop schedules needed to complete an order, determine start and end times, and assign resources for each operation. Another spin-off of XCON helps control the manufacture and distribution of DEC computer systems using customer order descriptions and information on plant activity.

Medicine

Diagnostic systems are available to assist the clinician in diagnosing acid-base and electrolyte disorders in patients using a causal model of the disease and patient symptoms, to assist physicians in diagnosing diseases of hemostasis by analyzing and interpreting clinical blood coagulation laboratory tests, and to assist physicians in diagnosing the narrowing of coronary vessels by interpretation of digital angiograms. PUFF diagnoses the presence and severity of lung disease in a patient by interpreting measurements from respiratory tests administered in a pulmonary (lung) function laboratory. Other systems range from monitoring patients in a newborn intensive care unit in an on-line environment to advising physicians on selection of appropriate therapy for a patient complaining of depression.

Meteorology

WILLARD helps meteorologists forecast the likelihood of severe thunderstorms occurring in the central United States.

Military Science

A number of systems have been built to aid battlefield situation assessment analysts by providing tactical interpretations of intelligence sensor reports and to provide weapon allocation recommendations to military commanders in combat situations. Identifiers are available to classify aircraft on the basis of visually observed characteristics such as wing shape, engine configuration, and tail assembly shape and to classify ships by interpreting radar images and comparing them to stored three-dimensional models for each ship.

Physics

GAMMA helps nuclear physicists identify the composition of unknown substances by interpreting gamma-ray activation spectra from neutron bombardment and another system solves problems in mechanics such as pulley systems, moment-of-inertia, and time-rate-distance problems.

Process Control

Diagnostic systems have been developed to identify probable causes of process disturbances in a chemical process plant by interpreting gauge, alarm, and switch data and to diagnoses malfunctions in machine processes by interpreting information from on-line sensors.

Space Technology

An expert controller provides autonomous control of an environmental control/life support subsystem for use aboard a manned space station and another aids in the planning of crew activity on-board the space shuttle orbiter using knowledge on shuttle activities, launch and landing sites, and astronauts' skill qualifications. Diagnostic systems can now troubleshoot spacecraft by monitoring the telemetry stream transmitted to earth, monitor radar station data that estimate the velocity and position of the space shuttle, look for errors, and warn the mission control when errors are detected or predicted.

This survey of expert systems has introduced five significant benchmark expert systems and sampled the proliferation of systems which followed. In the next chapter we consider characteristics common to most expert systems and considerations important for their design.

PROBLEMS AND PROGRAMS

11-1. List at least five categories of knowledge-based systems (automated advisors through true expert systems) from the least competent to the most competent, and indicate the different roles each might play for a given area of application.

11-2. In the Introduction, both the Logic Theorist and the General Problem Solver were referred to as expert systems although one of the programs matches the characteristics of modern expert systems much closer than the other. Discuss which is most typical of modern expert systems and whether it is justifiable to describe the other program as an expert system at all.

11-3. What additional features must be added to conventional production systems to convert them to rule-based expert systems? What advantages of production systems make them the choice for so many expert systems?

11-4. Discuss the economic forces which are at work in driving the expanding market for commercial expert systems and expert system shells. Be sure to include the cost of human and computer resources in your discussion. Make your discussion quantitative (use real numbers from trade magazines and journals).

11-5. The contribution of Feigenbaum's Heuristic DENDRAL to Lederberg's DENDRAL can be interpreted in terms of heuristics to limit the search space. Explain these concepts in a brief essay.

11-6. More than 50 research papers in chemistry have cited the contribution of DENDRAL in solving their research problem. Locate one of these papers and summarize the experiment and the role DENDRAL played in it.

11-7. DENDRAL is now available as a product from a commercial vendor. Who is the vendor, what is the cost of the service, and what are the advertised features of the commercial version of the program?

11-8 An outgrowth of the DENDRAL project was the META-DENDRAL program. What was the objective of META-DENDRAL and what were some of its accomplishments?

11-9. ADVISOR is an "expert advisor" or "automated consultant" to help users of MACSYMA. Discuss the implications of the synthesis of MACSYMA and ADVISOR on the future of expert systems. What features does ADVISOR provide for the user?

11-10. Assume your first job at MIT's Artificial Intelligence Laboratory is to extend the features of MACSYMA to include all of the standard equations of classical physics. Estimate the magnitude of the job, the number of equations involved, and the resources in person-power and computer hardware required.

11-11. Professor Feigenbaum has described DENDRAL as representing a "paradigm shift in AI" from power-based techniques to knowledge-based ones. Write a brief paper on the validity of this paradigm shift.

11-12. Discuss the similarities and differences between semantic nets and the inference networks used in PROSPECTOR. Why was this particular form of knowledge representation selected for this program?

11-13. Describe the molybdenum strike make by PROSPECTOR near Mr. Tolman in Washington State. Did PROSPECTOR make any additional successful prospects since the Mt. Tolman discovery? What commercial programs have emerged from the PROSPECTOR research project?

11-14. MYCIN was extensively tested in both blind and open diagnostic tests against human experts. From your library reading discuss the results of these tests, and why, in light of their success, MYCIN is not a successful commercial product.

11-15. Discuss the implications for programs such as MYCIN for the quality of medical care in remote areas of our own country and for the under-developed nations of the world presently lacking adequate medical care. How might the widespread availability of expert medical systems change the optimum mix of medical doctors, nurses, and medical technicians?

11-16. Discuss the hypothesis: *Legal responsibility to provide state-of-the-art medical diagnosis will provide the strongest pressure for widespread adoption of medical expert systems.* Cite a realistic scenario to justify your argument.

11-17. If XCON continues to grow at the rate it did between 1980 and 1984, how many rules will it contain in 1988, 1992, and 1996? What technological changes may invalidate the extrapolation for the latter dates?

11-18. DEC clearly has a very valuable productivity tool in their XCON program. They also market software. Why do you think they are not marketing XCON or some miniaturized version of it? (Hint: You may wish to distinguish between XCON, the expert system and OPS5, the language in which it is written.)

11-19. Devise a meaningful classifications scheme based on the primary purpose of the program (diagnostician/trouble-shooter; consultant/advisor; etc.) and categorize each of the programs listed in the Section 11.8 according to your scheme. Interpret your results in terms of the directions published expert systems seem to favor.

11-20. Consider an average industrial company with a modest AI program for development of expert systems as in-house productivity-enhancing programs. Discuss the forces favoring a policy of openness, publication, and publicity on the one hand and the forces favoring a policy of proprietary secrecy on the other. Which would you favor?

REFERENCES AND FOOTNOTES

1 Michaelsen, Robert H., Michie, Donald, and Boulanger, Albert "The Technology of Expert Systems," *BYTE* **10**, No. 4, p. 303, April (1985)

2 Feigenbaum, Edward A. and McCorduck, Pamela, *The Fifth Generation — Artificial Intelligence and Japan's Computer Challenge to the World,* Addison-Wesley, Reading, MA (1983)

3 Michie, Donald, "Expert Systems Interview", *Expert Systems* **2**, No.1, p. 21, January (1985)

4 McCorduck, Pamela, *Machines Who Think*, p. 276, W. H. Freeman and Company, San Francisco,CA (1979),

5 McCorduck, *Op Cit*, p. 277

6 McCorduck, *Op Cit*, p. 282

7 Winston, Patrick Henry, *Artificial Intelligence,* Second Edition, Addison-Wesley, Reading, MA (1984)

8 Feigenbaum, Edward A., Barr, Avron, and Cohen, Paul R., (eds), *The Handbook of Artificial Intelligence* Vol.2, p.143–149, HeurisTech Press/William Kaufmann, Inc., Stanford, CA (1981–82),

9 Duda, R. O., *The Prospector system for mineral exploration,* (Final Report, SRI Project 8172). SRI International, Artificial Intelligence Center, Menlo Park, CA., April (1980)

10 Duda, Richard O., and Reboh, René, "AI and Decision Making: The PROSPECTOR Experience," in *Artificial Intelligence Applications for Business,* Reitman, Walter, (ed), p. 136, Ablex Publishing Corp (1984)

11 Harmon, Paul and King, David, *Expert Systems,* pp. 145–150, John Wiley & Sons, New York, NY (1985)

12 Reitman, *Op Cit*, pp. 134–135

13 Tanimoto, Steven L., *The Elements of Artificial Intelligence,* pp. 242 –245, Computer Science Press, Rockville, MD (1987)

14 Zadeh, L. A., "Fuzzy Sets," *Inform. and Control* **8**, pp. 338–353 (1965)

15 Shortliffe, Edward H., *MYCIN: Computer-based Medical Consultations,* Elsevier Press, New York, NY (1976)

16 Buchanan, Bruce G. and Shortliffe, Edward H. (eds), *Rule-Based Expert Systems — The MYCIN Experiments of the Stanford Heuristic Programming Project,* Addison-Wesley Publishing Company, Reading, MA (1984)

17 Brannigan, Vincent M., "Liability for Personal Injury Caused by Defective Medical Computer Programs," in *Ethical Issues in the Use of Computers,* Johnson, Deborah G. and Snapper, John W. (eds), Wadsworth Publishing Company, Belmont, CA (1985)

18 McDermott, J., "R1: A rule-based configurer of computer systems,"

Artificial Intelligence **19,** No. 1, pp. 39–88 (1982)

19 Bobrow, Daniel G., Mittal, Sanjay, and Stefik, Mark J., "Expert Systems: Perils and Promise," *Communications of the ACM* **29,** No. 9, pp. 880–894, September (1986)

20 Waterman, Donald A., *A Guide to Expert Systems,* Addison-Wesley Publishing Company, Reading, MA (1986)

21 Winston, Patrick H. and Prendergast, Karen A., *The AI Business — Commercial Uses of Artificial Intelligence,* pp.41-49, MIT Press, Cambridge, MA (1984)

22 Waterman, *Op Cit,* pp. 244–299

23 Lemmon, Hal, *Science* **233**, pp. 29–33, 4 July (1986)

Chapter 12

ARCHITECTURE OF KNOWLEDGE-BASED SYSTEMS

(PHOTO: COURTESY OF GLORIA WATERMAN)

Donald A. Waterman was a senior computer scientist at The Rand Corporation of Santa Monica until his recent untimely death. He received his B.S. in Electrical Engineering from Iowa State University and his Ph.D. in Computer Science from Stanford University. He has written on both artificial intelligence and cognitive psychology. His research included the design and development of tools for building expert systems, expert systems for the space program, and the development of legal decision systems. He was the author of *Expert Systems: Techniques, Tools and Applications* (with Philip Klahr), *A Guide to Expert Systems*, and co-editor of *Building Expert Systems* (along with Frederick Hays-Roth and Douglas Lenat).

12: ARCHITECTURE OF KNOWLEDGE-BASED SYSTEMS

12.1 INTRODUCTION

The development of any new field of science usually proceeds through three stages: i) *case studies,* ii) *architectural principles,* and iii) *understanding.* In the previous chapter we discussed several important case studies which illustrated many of the features and principles of operation of expert systems. From case studies, certain architectural principles emerge which capture the successful aspects of the case studies and help future system builders avoid their failures. Finally, after many years of developing and using these architectural principles, a true understanding of the science emerges. At present, we are in the midst of stage (ii) both in the science (or art?) of expert systems and in our course of study.

12.2 CHARACTERISTICS OF KNOWLEDGE-BASED SYSTEMS

From case studies of knowledge-based systems, certain characteristics emerge which will guide us in establishing a set of architectural principles.[1] These include:

- Knowledge is the key to the power of expert systems.
- Knowledge is often inexact and incomplete.
- Knowledge is often poorly specified.
- Amateurs become experts incrementally.
- Expert systems must be flexible.
- Expert systems must be transparent.

The history of AI research has shown repeatedly that knowledge is the key ingredient for any intelligent system. Attempts to build intelligent systems based simply on rules of logical operation (such as GPS) have rarely produced useful commercial products.[2] Knowledge about the domain in question simply must be present in some form. The recognition of the importance of knowledge in the performance of expert systems is the basis for the increasing use of the term *knowledge-based system* in place of the older term, *expert system*. The term knowledge-based system also reflects the range of performance level spanned by such systems. Not all knowledge-based systems perform at the expert level.

Knowledge available to the expert system for the particular problem being solved may be inexact or incomplete, particularly for probabilistic sciences such as medicine and geology. Techniques for propagating uncertainties are highly developed, however, and expert computer systems handle such uncertainties much more systematically than human experts usually do. One difficulty encountered in building all expert systems is that human experts often find it impossible initially to clearly state the rules of logic, intuition, and heuristics they use in analyzing the data at hand. The task of the patient, sympathetic, but persistent knowledge engineer is to help the human expert bring these rules to the surface of his consciousness long enough to get them written down on paper.

All "living" expert systems are never finished products but rather, like good human experts, continue to grow in their knowledge and problem solving capability. Experts, both human and artificial, start as amateurs. The history of XCON, starting with 300 rules, expanding to 800 by its acceptance test, and now containing over 4,000 rules, clearly demonstrates this feature of expert systems. To help make this growth as convenient and painless as possible, expert systems must be flexible and transparent. Flexibility is required for easy editing of incorrect data and addition of new knowledge. Transparency is required to reassure hesitant users and to document program operation for all users.

FEATURES OF PROBLEM SOLVERS

Human experts exhibit certain characteristics and techniques which help them perform at a high level in solving problems in their domain. This single distinguishing trait, *performance*, marks an expert. The goal of expert system designers is to duplicate these features as closely as possible in the machine. Human experts do the following:

- *Solve the problem* — This is the *sine qua non* without which neither human nor machine is considered an expert.

• *Explain the result* — To be useful as an advisor to human experts, the artificial expert must be able to explain its chain of reasoning as clearly as would a human expert.

• *Learn* — Responsible human experts continually learn and improve their problem solving capability. In humans, however, learning takes place at many levels. Computers are capable of duplicating the lowest level, that of simply adding more information to their data base or rule set. However, the higher levels of integrating, correlating, and inducing new knowledge is a much more difficult task and has been attempted in only a few programs such as META-DENDRAL and Lenat's AM.

• *Restructure knowledge* — Humans are remarkably adept at reformulating the knowledge at their disposal to fit the needs of a new problem environment. In computer systems this restructuring is equivalent to the transformation from one representation into another. This capability exists in computer systems, but the real problem is in deciding when to use it and the most effective representation to choose.

• *Break rules* — In many of the sciences as well as in other areas of human endeavor, exceptions to the rules are sometimes as common as cases where the rule applies. Remember "*i before e except after c* ..."? Just as the apprentice chemistry student has learned the powerful rules of valence she runs into the exceptions of the rare earths and transuranic elements. The computer simply handles exceptions to the rules as new, more highly qualified rules. In principle it should be easy; in practice the expert system builder must take care to clearly specify all exceptions on the same basis as the rules themselves.

• *Determine relevance* — Human experts can quickly sense when the problem is outside their domain of expertise and refer the inquirer to someone more knowledgeable. In principle this should be a simple task for computer systems; in practice most expert systems do not yet have this ability. Once they get it, interesting possibilities such as "super smart" machines appear. Instead of answers like "I don't know" which must be the response of present systems when asked questions outside of their domain, a super smart system would reply,"Hold on a minute while I refer your problem to system XXX over ARPANET." As monster memories and laser disks appear, such capability won't even require networking; one computer will contain multiple, interacting expert systems.

• *Degrade gracefully* — Meanwhile it is important to build systems which recognize the boundaries of their knowledge and "degrade gracefully" rather then "crash" when reaching the limits of their domain. Competent systems will contain features to respond to questions near the edge or outside of their domain by responses such as:

♦ "In order to answer that I need to know the molecular weight and melting point of Thulium Oxalate. Molecular wt:?"

♦ "I'm sorry, but SOLVER can handle only one equation in one unknown."

12.3 ARCHITECTURAL PRINCIPLES

Some generally accepted principles for constructing expert systems have emerged from analysis of the case study expert systems. The first is:

• **Separate the inference engine and knowledge base** — It is important to make the knowledge as easily accessible, easily identified, and explicit as possible. Once the knowledge begins to become embedded in the inference engine, the operation of the system becomes opaque and much more difficult to correct or expand. Such knowledge then becomes inaccessible to other parts of the program or other programs and thus is lost for further use. A clean separation of inference engine and knowledge base helps avoid duplication and reduced efficiency of the program.

• **Use as uniform a representation as possible** — By using a systematic, uniform representation, the number of rules in the inference engine is minimized and the operation of the system remains relatively simple and transparent. As more representations of knowledge or exceptions to inference rules are added, the combinatorial explosion may obscure the actual operation of the system, making it unmanageable.

• **Keep the inference engine simple** — In addition to helping understand the operation of the system, a simple inference engine makes documentation and explanation simpler. Knowledge acquisition is easier since the information fits a simple pattern required by the inference engine. With a simple inference engine it is easier to know what knowledge to use for improving the performance of the system.

• **Exploit redundancy** — Redundancy can often help overcome problems due to incomplete or inexact knowledge. For instance, a certain diagnosis may be suggested by one set of symptoms with a certain degree of probability. A disjoint set of symptoms may suggest the same diagnosis. By including both sets of symptoms (redundant information) the level of assurance that the diagnosis is correct improves greatly. The general rule, then, is to bring as much information on a particular problem into the program as possible to guarantee as accurate a solution as possible.

12.4 APPLICATION OF ARCHITECTURAL PRINCIPLES — MYCIN REVISITED

To respond to the perceived need of physicians for a tool to assist in the diagnosis and recommended therapy for infectious diseases, Shortliffe defined the following list of prerequisites for the consultation program, MYCIN, which reflects the architectural principles outlined above.[3] Many of these characteristics are shared with other expert systems.

1. *Useful* — The program should respond to a well-documented clinical need and, ideally, should tackle a problem with which physicians have explicitly requested assistance.

2. *Usable* — The program should be fast, accessible, easy to learn, and simple for a novice computer user.

3. *Educational when appropriate* — The program should allow physicians to access its knowledge base and must be capable of conveying pertinent information in a form that they can understand and from which they can learn.

4. *Explain its advice* — The program should provide the user with enough information about its reasoning so that he or she can decide whether to follow the recommendation.

5. *Respond to simple questions* — It should be possible for the physician to request justifications of specific inferences by posing questions, ideally using natural language.

6. *Learn new knowledge* — It should be possible to tell it new facts and have them easily and automatically incorporated for future use, or the system should be able to learn from experience as it is used on multiple cases.

7. *Easily modified* — Adding new knowledge or correcting errors in existing knowledge should be straight forward, ideally accomplished without making explicit changes to the program code itself.

PERFORMANCE OF MYCIN

All evaluations of MYCIN to date indicate that MYCIN is as good or better than most very skilled human experts.[4] In one complex, blind experiment, eight independent evaluators with special expertise in the management of meningitis compared MYCIN's choice of medication with the choices prescribed by nine human diagnosticians for ten difficult cases of meningitis. In the first phase, MYCIN and faculty members from Stanford University Medical School's Division of Infectious Diseases each evaluated ten cases chosen to represent a wide variety of difficult problems. In the second phase, the prominent specialists evaluated each case and reviewed the diagnoses and prescriptions of MYCIN and the faculty members without knowing that a computer was involved.

Two criteria were used for evaluation. First, prescriptions were evaluated to determine if the recommended drugs would be effective against the actual infective agent finally identified. MYCIN and three faculty prescribers consistently prescribed therapy that would have been effective in all ten cases. The second criterion was whether the drugs prescribed adequately covered other plausible pathogens while avoiding over-prescribing. Using this criterion, MYCIN received a higher rating than any of the human prescribers. The evaluators rated MYCIN's prescriptions correct in 65% of the cases. The ratings of the prescriptions of the human specialists ranged from 42.5% to 62.5% correct.

While MYCIN very successfully achieved the objectives for which it was designed and did perform at an expert diagnostic level, it has not become a commercial success. One reason, in addition to the sociological problem discussed in the last chapter, has been the lack of an economical "delivery system". That is, it was written in the days before the widespread availability of powerful microcomputers and work stations. The language used was INTERLISP, a dialect of LISP not available on present microcomputers or other computer facilities available to most physicians. Without an economical delivery system, MYCIN has been unable to make inroads into the average doctor's office.

12.5 KNOWLEDGE ACQUISITION — KNOWLEDGE ENGINEERING

One characteristic of all knowledge-based expert systems is that they must be built from knowledge extracted from human experts. Michie has defined the process of extracting knowledge from human experts and incorporating it into machines as *knowledge engineering*. Several methods by which expert systems may acquire knowledge have been suggested:[5]

- Being told
- Analogy
- Example
- Observation, discovery, and experimentation
- Reasoning from deep structure

Most rule-based systems operate on the first technique, being told explicitly in the form of production rules. However, some systems we discuss in the next chapter, such as SUPER-EXPERT by Professor Michie's group, work by analogy and example. The user provides several sample problems from which the expert system generalizes rules it will use on real problems. This technique has demonstrated the following features:

1. Machine-executable solutions are generated in a fraction of the time a programmer would need to develop a solution by conventional hand coding.

2. The resulting solutions are much more efficient than hand coded solutions.

3. Transparency of the induced rules is lost in the process.

KNOWLEDGE REPRESENTATION

The knowledge representation schemes most widely used in knowledge-based systems fall into the following categories previously discussed:

- Production rules
- Inference networks
- Frames
- Logic-based systems

Examples of the use of production rules include DENDRAL and

MYCIN. Inference networks are used in the PROSPECTOR program, and frames are used in the natural language program, GUS, by Bobrow and Winograd.[6] Some programs use a combination of knowledge representation techniques. One of these is STEAMER, a training aid by Bolt Beranek and Newman for teaching operating procedures for shipboard steam plants.[7]

RESOURCES NEEDED

For developing large systems, a LISP machine or a work station connected to a mainframe or minicomputer with good AI language support has been considered essential. The new generation of 32-bit personal computers has encouraged reconsideration of this criteria. For more modest expert systems or for delivery systems for software developed on larger computers, personal computers with 0.5 – 4 MB are generally adequate. A number of programming tools called expert system "shells" are now available for automating the development of expert systems on a variety of computers. These will be discussed in detail in the next chapter.

12.6 PROBLEM SELECTION CRITERIA

A critical factor in the success of any expert system is in selecting the right problem to solve by a knowledge-based approach. Characteristics of appropriate problems have been identified as:[8]

- There are recognized experts in the area.
- The experts are probably better than amateurs.
- The task takes an expert a few minutes to a few hours.
- The task is primarily cognitive rather than skill-based.
- The skill is routinely taught to neophytes.
- The task domain has high payoff.
- The task requires no common sense.

Most of these criteria simply make good sense. The first three define what expert systems are and set the scale for the effort. Expert systems are appropriate for cognitive fields such as medicine and physics but not for skills such as tennis and bicycle riding. It is essential that the task domain have a high payoff since, in general, a significant effort will be required to write the expert system. Finally, the last criterion emphasizes again that we are much better at teaching computers the intricacies of science, mathematics, and logic than the simple, common sense rules of everyday living. Even the most sophisticated expert system does not possess the common sense of a five-year old child!

A useful, one-sentence test for prime candidates for expert systems can be neatly formulated in the **Phone Call Rule**:

> ***Any problem that can be and frequently is solved by your in-house expert in a 10—30 minute phone call can be automated as an expert system.***

12.7 PHASES OF KNOWLEDGE ACQUISITION

Experience over the past fifteen years of developing expert systems has indicated several phases, not always completely distinct, that characterizes the process of acquiring knowledge. These have been identified as:[9]

• *Identification Phase* — The identification stage involves identifying the key components in the system being developed. These include: the participants, problem characteristics, resources, and goals. The first step is in identifying the participants. The two critical players are the *knowledge engineer* and the *domain expert*. Working together they proceed to identify various aspects of the problem such as the scope of the project, the input data to be used, important terms and their interactions, the form and content of the solution, and possible impediments to building the expert system. Working with the project director, the knowledge engineer and domain expert must identify the resources available for building and testing the expert system. Such resources include expert system shells, knowledge sources, time, computer facilities, and money. Knowledge sources include such resources as data bases, management information systems, textbooks, and prototype problems and examples. In addition to the stated goals of the project proposal, the domain expert will clarify and identify goals and objectives for the expert system in the process of specifying the problem. The relationship between these players and elements of the expert system are shown in Figure 12-1.

• *Conceptualization Phase* — The key concepts and relationships identified in the first phase are made more explicit in the conceptualization stage. The knowledge engineer may formalize the structure of the prototype system using flowcharts and diagrams. In order to reach this stage, the following questions must be resolved: What data are available? What is given and what is to be inferred? How may the task be decomposed into sub-tasks? What processes will be used for the problem solution? What are the constraints and relationships between these processes? What is the information flow?

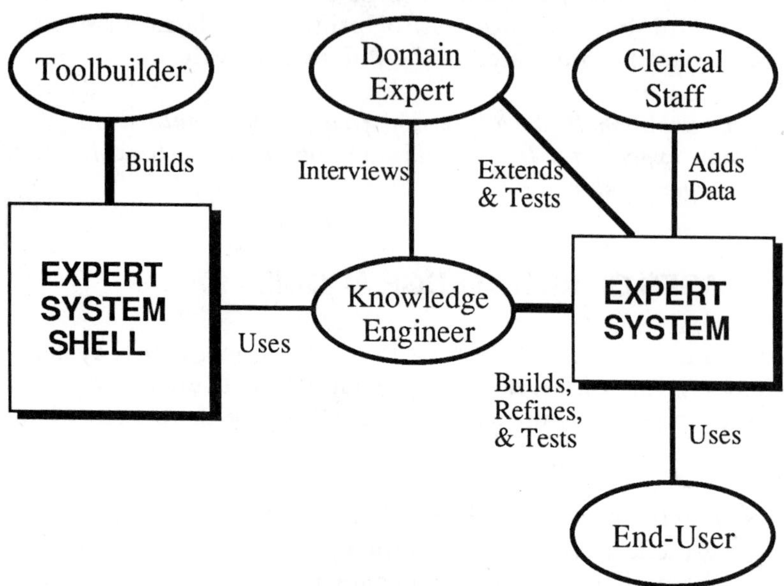

Figure 12-1 Programs and Players in an Expert System[10]

Once the key concepts and relationships are written down, the process of formalizing them and designing an initial implementation is much easier. The knowledge engineer may wish to informally experiment with prototype systems at this point, but it is important that a final selection of representation not be made prematurely.

• *Formalization Phase* — This stage involves mapping the key concepts, sub-problems, and information flow patterns identified in the previous phases into formal representations most appropriate for the problem at hand. Here the knowledge engineer assumes an active role in explaining to the domain expert the capabilities of existing tools, representations, and commercially available system shells. Considerations important in this selection process include the structure of the hypothesis space in which the solution will be sought, the underlying model of the process used to generate solutions, a clear understanding of the nature of the knowledge in the problem domain, and the experience of the system building staff.

• *Implementation Phase* — This stage involves mapping the formalized knowledge of the previous phase into the chosen knowledge representation scheme. In practical terms this means programming the information into production rules, inference networks, or frames. The domain knowledge specifies the *contents* of the resulting data structures. The selection of a representation scheme itself specifies the *form*. This phase of development of the expert system is very critical, because, while little of this prototype program may remain in the final version, this is the crucial test for the adequacy of the representation and the underlying conceptual model.

• *Testing Phase* — After the prototype system developed in the previous phase has successfully handled two or three examples it should undergo a series of rigorous tests using a variety of sample problems. These should include not only the "classical" test examples, but also "hard cases" at the boundary of the knowledge domain and randomly selected cases to statistically sample the performance of the system. Problems typically discovered by such testing usually fall into the following categories:

> **I/O Failures:** Problems frequently appear in the form of awkward data entry or query protocols. The use of subsets of natural language with tolerance for misspellings can alleviate some of this problem. Modern modes of graphical input (mouse driven), pointing, and voice I/O will greatly simplify this common problem.
>
> **Logic Errors**: If errors of reasoning are detected in the testing phase, the problem most likely lies in incorrect, inconsistent, or incomplete inference rules. While we strive to keep production rules independent, it is a difficult goal to achieve. Care must be taken to avoid inferences which are independently valid but which may combine to produce semantic nonsense. Combinations of rules must augment the system to avoid such pitfalls.
>
> **Control Strategy**: Human experts frequently prefer the "natural order" for controlling steps in a solution, particularly for cases involving a hierarchy of tasks and sub-tasks. The proper selection between breadth-first or depth-first search strategies, for instance, may significantly effect the efficiency of the system.

• *Prototype Revision* — An essential element at all stages in the process of knowledge acquisition is the ability to cycle back through previous stages to fine-tune the system for meeting performance specifications. For minor modifications this may mean small changes in the implementation phase; for larger problems it may involve cycling back to the formalization, conceptualization, or even the identification stage for a redesign of the system. If the expert system is viewed as a "living system", such revisions can be interpreted as "life cycles" and "growth pains" essential for the proper development of the product rather than admissions of failure. Since each application tends to be unique with its own hidden quicksand and land mines, the ability to "get it right the first time" comes only with considerable experience. Although sophisticated development environments and expert system shell have gone a long way towards reducing the pain and tedium of building expert systems, the process itself still generally requires careful thought and hand-crafting.

12.8 A SIMPLE DEMONSTRATION PROGRAM — THERMOSTAT

Below we illustrate many of the above ideas using a simple knowledge-based system represented by production rules. The system is designed to advise the janitor on what the thermostat setting should be based on the time of year, day of the week, and time of day. This is one of the tutorial expert systems provided with the EXSYS expert system development package.[11]

PRODUCTION RULES:

```
  ----------------------------------------

RULE NUMBER: 1

IF:
      THE DAY IS MONDAY OR TUESDAY OR WEDNESDAY OR
      THURSDAY OR FRIDAY

THEN:
      IT IS A WORKDAY
  ----------------------------------------

RULE NUMBER: 2

IF:
      THE DAY IS SATURDAY OR SUNDAY

THEN:
      IT IS THE WEEKEND
  ----------------------------------------

RULE NUMBER: 3

IF:
      IT IS A WORKDAY
      THE TIME IS BETWEEN 10 AM AND 5 PM

THEN:
      IT IS DURING BUSINESS HOURS
```

```
----------------------------------------

RULE NUMBER: 4

IF:
      IT IS A WORKDAY
      THE TIME IS BEFORE 10 AM OR AFTER 5 PM

THEN:
      IT IS NOT DURING BUSINESS HOURS
----------------------------------------

RULE NUMBER: 5

IF:
      IT IS THE WEEKEND

THEN:
      IT IS NOT DURING BUSINESS HOURS
----------------------------------------

RULE NUMBER: 6

IF:
      THE MONTH IS JAN OR FEB OR MAR OR DEC

THEN:
      THE SEASON IS WINTER
----------------------------------------

RULE NUMBER: 7

IF:
      THE MONTH IS APR OR MAY

THEN:
      THE SEASON IS SPRING
----------------------------------------

RULE NUMBER: 8

IF:
      THE MONTH IS JUNE OR JULY OR AUG

THEN:
      THE SEASON IS SUMMER
----------------------------------------

RULE NUMBER: 9

IF:
      THE MONTH IS SEPT OR OCT OR NOV

THEN:
      THE SEASON IS FALL
----------------------------------------

RULE NUMBER: 10
```

```
IF:
      THE SEASON IS SPRING
      IT IS DURING BUSINESS HOURS

THEN:
      SET THE THERMOSTAT AT 68 DEGREES -
      Probability=  1
----------------------------------------

RULE NUMBER: 11

IF:
      THE SEASON IS SPRING
      IT IS NOT DURING BUSINESS HOURS

THEN:
      SET THE THERMOSTAT AT 55 DEGREES -
      Probability=  1
----------------------------------------

RULE NUMBER: 12

IF:
      THE SEASON IS SUMMER
      IT IS DURING BUSINESS HOURS

THEN:
      SET THE THERMOSTAT AT 75 DEGREES -
      Probability=  1
----------------------------------------

RULE NUMBER: 13

IF:
      THE SEASON IS SUMMER
      IT IS NOT DURING BUSINESS HOURS

THEN:
      SET THE THERMOSTAT AT 80 DEGREES -
      Probability=  1
----------------------------------------

RULE NUMBER: 14

IF:
      THE SEASON IS FALL
      IT IS DURING BUSINESS HOURS

THEN:
      SET THE THERMOSTAT AT 68 DEGREES -
      Probability=  1
----------------------------------------

RULE NUMBER: 15

IF:
      THE SEASON IS FALL
```

```
        IT IS NOT DURING BUSINESS HOURS

THEN:
        SET THE THERMOSTAT AT 60 DEGREES -
        Probability=  1
------------------------------------------

RULE NUMBER: 16

IF:
        THE SEASON IS WINTER
        IT IS DURING BUSINESS HOURS

THEN:
        SET THE THERMOSTAT AT 65 DEGREES -
        Probability=  1
------------------------------------------

RULE NUMBER: 17

IF:
        THE SEASON IS WINTER
        IT IS NOT DURING BUSINESS HOURS

THEN:
        SET THE THERMOSTAT AT 55 DEGREES -
        Probability=  1
------------------------------------------
```

QUALIFIERS AND VALUES:

A condition used in the rule base is essentially a predicate calculus type predicate composed of two elements, a *qualifier* and one or more *values*. The qualifier is that part of the predicate up to and including the verb. The values are the possible completions of the predicate sentences. The THERMOSTAT system uses six sentences composed of qualifiers and their potential values. These condition predicates and a cross-referenced index of the rules using them are indicated next.

```
1  THE DAY IS

       MONDAY
       TUESDAY
       WEDNESDAY
       THURSDAY
       FRIDAY
       SATURDAY
       SUNDAY

              Used in rule(s):   1   2


2  IT IS
```

```
    A WORKDAY
    THE WEEKEND

          Used in rule(s):  ( 1)  ( 2)   3   4   5

3  THE TIME IS

    BETWEEN 10 AM AND 5 PM
    BEFORE 10 AM
    AFTER 5 PM

          Used in rule(s):   3   4

4  IT IS

    DURING BUSINESS HOURS
    NOT DURING BUSINESS HOURS

          Used in rule(s): ( 3)  ( 4)  ( 5)   10   11   12
          13   14   15   16   17

5  THE MONTH IS

    JAN
    FEB
    MAR
    APR
    MAY
    JUNE
    JULY
    AUG
    SEPT
    OCT
    NOV
    DEC

          Used in rule(s):   6   7   8   9

6  THE SEASON IS

    WINTER
    SPRING
    SUMMER
    FALL

    Used in rule(s):  ( 6)  ( 7)  ( 8)  ( 9)   10   11
    12   13   14   15   16   17
```

CHOICES:

The final goal of the expert system is to produce an answer based on input information. In this example, as in most other expert systems, this answer is a solution consistent with the production rules and input data which the system selects from a finite list of potential solutions. In THERMOSTAT, the solution is a unique temperature selected from the list of six choices shown below. In other systems, there may be multiple allowed solutions, and in some cases each allowed solution may have an associated confidence factor.

```
1  SET THE THERMOSTAT AT 55 DEGREES

      Used in rule(s):   ( 11)   ( 17)


2  SET THE THERMOSTAT AT 60 DEGREES

      Used in rule(s):   ( 15)


3  SET THE THERMOSTAT AT 65 DEGREES

      Used in rule(s):   ( 16)


4  SET THE THERMOSTAT AT 68 DEGREES

      Used in rule(s):   ( 10)   ( 14)


5  SET THE THERMOSTAT AT 75 DEGREES

      Used in rule(s):   ( 12)


6  SET THE THERMOSTAT AT 80 DEGREES

      Used in rule(s):   ( 13)
```

SAMPLE DIALOG

Next we show the operation of the expert system specified above. Note that the rule interpreter and inference engine will ask the user for the minimum information necessary for solving the problem (the month, day of the week, and time). From the three user-supplied answers indicated by arrows below, the expert system can apply rules from its knowledge base to conclude that the season is winter, the day is a working day, and the time is during business hours. Rule 16 then selects one of the allowed choices for solution to the problem.

```
                    Press any key to start:

THE MONTH IS
     1    JAN
     2    FEB
     3    MAR
     4    APR
     5    MAY
     6    JUNE
     7    JULY
     8    AUG
     9    SEPT
     10   OCT
     11   NOV
     12   DEC
→ 2

RULE NUMBER: 6

IF:
     (1)  THE MONTH IS JAN OR FEB OR MAR OR DEC

THEN:
      THE SEASON IS WINTER


THE DAY IS
     1    MONDAY
     2    TUESDAY
     3    WEDNESDAY
     4    THURSDAY
     5    FRIDAY
     6    SATURDAY
     7    SUNDAY
→ 2

RULE NUMBER: 1

IF:
     (1)  THE DAY IS MONDAY OR TUESDAY OR
      WEDNESDAY OR THURSDAY OR FRIDAY

THEN:
      IT IS A WORKDAY


THE TIME IS
     1    BETWEEN 10 AND 5 PM
     2    BEFORE 10 AM
     3    AFTER 5 PM
→ 1

RULE NUMBER: 3

IF:
      (1)  IT IS A WORKDAY, and
```

```
        (2)  THE TIME IS BETWEEN 10 AM AND 5 PM

THEN:
        IT IS DURING BUSINESS HOURS


RULE NUMBER: 16

IF:
        (1)  THE SEASON IS WINTER, and
        (2)  IT IS DURING BUSINESS HOURS

THEN:
        SET THE THERMOSTAT AT 65 DEGREES - Probability=1


PRESS <ENTER> TO GET THE TEMPERATURE SETTING FOR THE THERMO-
STAT


1   SET THE THERMOSTAT AT 65 DEGREES   :1
```

The first, and only, solution to the problem is to set the thermostat to 65 degrees with a probability of 1 that this is the correct solution. Several of the architectural principles presented above are illustrated by this simple expert system:

- The knowledge base and inference engine are cleanly separated.

- The knowledge representation chosen is a very uniform, standard production rule format.

- The inference engine operates in a simple cyclic manner until the conditions for an allowed choice are satisfied or until the backtracking search strategy fails to find a solution.

- The system provides explanation of its reasoning through the option of citing the rules as it applies them. The complete backward chain of rules is reported for solutions based on multiple inference steps.

- The system provides the capability of handling uncertain information through the probability factor which can range from 0 — 100% using one of three author-selected confidence factor schemes.

- The system avoids problems of natural language processing through its use of a menu format for selecting among grammatically correct natural language sentences.

In the next chapter we will illustrate the actual building of expert systems and describe additional features of this and other expert system shells.

12.9 GUIDELINES FOR CONSTRUCTING EXPERT SYSTEMS

At the risk of some redundancy, we summarize this chapter with a list of suggestions and useful maxims for successful expert system development proposed by experts in the field of expert systems.[12,13]

TASK SUITABILITY

It is important to pick the application carefully. Focus on a narrow specialty area that does not involve a lot of common-sense knowledge. Select a task that is neither too easy nor too difficult for human experts. Define the task very clearly. Commitment from an articulate expert is essential. Since knowledge engineering is the task of transferring human expertise into machine-usable form, the commitment from a human expert is essential. Select a task with high potential pay-back to make the project worthwhile. Management commitment of necessary human and material resources is a measure of the task's perceived value to the organization. Be sure that administrative commitment is adequate before proceeding.

BUILDING THE PROTOTYPE SYSTEM (MARK-I)

The system builder is well-advised to become familiar with the problem before beginning extensive interaction with the expert. Clearly identify and characterize the important aspects of the problem. Record a detailed protocol of the expert solving at least one prototypical case. Choose a knowledge-engineering tool or architecture that minimizes the representational mismatch between sub-problems. Start building the prototype version of the expert system as soon as the first example is well understood.

The incremental and modular nature of production systems makes it advisable to work intensively with a core set of representative problems which can augmented later with extensions for more general cases. Identify and separate the parts of the problem that have caused trouble for AI programs in the past and avoid them in Mark-I. Build in mechanisms for indirect reference. Aim at simplicity in the "inference engine" Don't worry about computational time and space efficiency in the beginning. Find or build computerized tools (shells) to assist in the rule-writing process. As in all programming projects, good practice requires careful documentation. Don't wait until the informal rules are perfect before starting to build the system. When testing the system, consider the possibility of errors in input/output characteristics, inference rules, control strategies, and test examples.

EXTENDING THE MARK-I VERSION

If the system does not already provide one, build a friendly interface to the program soon after Mark-I is finished to encourage others to experiment with it. Provide some capabilities for examining the knowledge base and the line of reasoning soon after the Mark-I is finished. Provide a "gripe" facility to obtain user feedback. Keep a library of cases presented to the system for performance validation as the system evolves and grows. This phase of the development lends itself to regular application of a set of standard benchmark programs to monitor the system's behavior as it expands.

FINDING AND WRITING RULES

Don't just talk with the expert; watch her working examples. To assist the dialog between expert and knowledge engineer, use the terms and methods that the experts use. If a rule looks big, it probably is and should be subdivide it into component rules. Look for intermediate level abstractions. If several rules are very similar, look for an underlying domain concept. If tempted to escape from knowledge representation formalism into pure code, resist the temptation for at least a little while.

MAINTAINING YOUR EXPERT'S INTEREST

Engage the expert in the challenge of designing a useful tool. There will be delays and frustrations in the development process. Give the expert something useful on the way to building a large system. Valuable by-products for the expert include formalizing and organizing her thinking as well as providing a preliminary computational tool which may help in her routine analysis. Insulate the expert, as well as the user, from technical problems. Be careful about feeling expert yourself. Becoming an expert requires years of education and practice.

BUILDING THE MARK-II SYSTEM

Throw away the Mark-I System. Its purpose was to explore the appropriate system structure and get a clearer understanding of the task. In the Mark-II and subsequent versions, begin to consider generality. At this point the range of the domain should be carefully defined. Identify the intended users of the final system and select a user/system interface which appears natural and uses the standard syntax of the discipline.

EVALUATING THE SYSTEM

By the MARK II design phase, the management, expert, and knowledge engineer should agree on criteria for evaluating the success of your efforts. This provides system design goals along with enough experience to assure that they are realistic. The user interface is crucial to the ultimate acceptance of the system. A small effort in human engineering can make the difference between success and failure.

GENERAL ADVICE

The system will be more rugged and fool-proof if you exploit redundancy. The more information available, the less chance for error. A conclusion which depends solely on a single rule may be a weak link in the inference process. Be familiar with the architecture of several expert systems. Certain problems are much more naturally adapted to one approach than another. The process of building an expert system is inherently experimental. A useful analogy is the education and training of human experts who do not become experts overnight. You are, in effect, training the computer to become an expert.

In conclusion, we have examined some of the architectural principles which successful expert systems seem to share. From these principles we attempt to specify design criteria and techniques which should be considered in selecting and building knowledge-based systems. Finally we summarized the hard-earned advice of several experts in expert system building. With this background we turn next to examine the tools available for building expert systems and illustrate the process of constructing a small expert system advisor.

PROBLEMS AND PROGRAMS

12-1. Make a list of ten potential expert systems which you think may have commercial value. You may use the summary of expert systems from the previous chapter, but try to select topics from your own everyday experience at the automotive repair shop, doctor's office, IRS office, and college placement office.

12-2. Select the most promising topic from the list developed in 12-1 above after discussing the list with your instructor. Outline the knowledge you will be acquiring, the sources for the knowledge, the knowledge representation scheme you propose using, and the expert system shell you think most appropriate.

12-3. Develop the Mark-I prototype of your expert system. This should include at least 10—20 rules and test results verifying the system operation.

12-4. General problem solving programs such as GPS and AURA are generally dismissed as not being expert systems because of their general rather than narrow domain of interest. Discuss the proposition: *GPS and AURA are expert systems in the restricted domain of effective problem solving techniques.*

12-5. The text refers to expert systems such as XCON as *living systems* to emphasize their continual growth and development. One of the chief motivations of commercial expert system development is to capture, package, and market specific knowledge which implies "freezing" the system at some point. What policies would you suggest to software-houses for marketing *living* systems?

12-6. One perennial problem with expert systems is that they have difficulty recognizing the limits of their knowledge domain. What algorithms and/or heuristics would you suggest for solving this problem?

12-7. A generally accepted architectural principle is that an expert system should have a cleanly separated knowledge base and inference engine. Others have criticized this feature as a weakness of expert systems. What is the basis of this criticism?

12-8. In this chapter the cost of the delivery system was cited as an obstacle to the commercialization of MYCIN. In the previous chapter some of the institutional and emotional obstacles were mentioned. Discuss the potential market you see for a generalized medical advisor similar to the book-format Medical Encyclopedia. What pricing, hardware, and software specifications would you propose?

12-9. One concise definition for potential topics for expert systems is: *Any problem an expert can solve over the phone in 20 minutes.* How does this test meet the problem selection criteria suggested in the text?

12-10. The tools available for developing expert systems range from LISP through Prolog to OPS5 and a host of expert system shells. What are the advantages of writing an expert system in LISP What are the advantages of using a highly structured expert system shell?

12-11. Discuss how a menu-oriented production rule format used for writing THERMOSTAT can use well-structured English sentence production rules without a sophisticated natural language processor.

12-12. Analyze the THERMOSTAT system using the *theory of formal languages* described in the chapter on computational linguistics. List the variables, terminal symbols, and rewrite rules. How many well-formed sentences can the system generate?

12-13. Why would one want to build a MARK-I prototype expert system and then discard it?

12-14. You have studied the *software development life cycle* in introductory level computer science courses. Summarize this life cycle for the task of developing an expert system and indicate what extensions are necessary to accomplish this extended task.

12-15. Many researchers in AI do not consider expert systems a legitimate sub-topic of artificial intelligence. Discuss their objection to classifying expert systems as AI in terms of the distinction between science and engineering.

12-16. While it is possible to dismiss expert system development as a well-understood technology using standard engineering practices, the argument can be made that expert systems may contribute to AI. Discuss how this might happen.

REFERENCES AND FOOTNOTES

[1] Davis, Randall, "Amplifying Expertise with Expert Systems," in *The AI Business — Commercial Uses of Artificial Intelligence,* Patrick H. Winston and Karen A. Prendergast (eds), pp. 17–40, MIT Press,

Cambridge, MA (1984)

2 One outstanding exception to this generalization is the automated reasoning program, AURA, of the Argonne National Laboratory group headed by Dr. Larry Wos. See Wos, L., Overbeek, R., Lusk, E., and Boyle, J., *Automated Reasoning: Introduction and Applications*, Prentice-Hall, Inc., Englewood Cliffs, NJ (1984)

3 Buchanan, B. G. and Shortliffe, E. H., (eds), *Rule-Based Expert Systems: The MYCIN Experiments of the Stanford Heuristic Programming Project*, p. 59, Addison-Wesley, Reading, MA (1984)

4 Harmon, Paul and King, David, *Expert Systems: Artificial Intelligence in Business*, p. 21, John Wiley & Sons, Inc., New York, NY (1985)

5 Michaelsen, Robert H., Michie, Donald and Boulanger, Albert, "The Technology of Expert Systems", *BYTE* **10**, No. 4, p. 310, April (1985)

6 Feigenbaum, Edward A., Barr, Avron , and Cohen, Paul R., (eds), *The Handbook of Artificial Intelligence* Vol.1–3, p. 221, HeurisTech Press/-William Kaufmann, Inc., Stanford, CA (1981–82)

7 Michaelsen, Robert H. et al, *Op Cit.*, p. 310

8 Davis, Randall, *Op Cit*, p. 37

9 Hays-Ross, Frederick, Waterman, Donald A., and Lenat, Douglas B., *Building Expert Systems*, pp. 140–158 Addison-Wesley, Reading, MA (1983)

10 Waterman, Donald A., *A Guide to Expert Systems*, Addison-Wesley Publishing Company, Reading, MA (1986)

11 Huntington, Dustin, *EXSYS User's Manual*, EXSYS, Inc. Albuquerque, NM (1985)

12 Buchanan, Bruce G. *et al*, "Constructing an Expert System," in Hays-Ross, Frederick, *et al*, *Op Cit*, pp. 159–167

13 Bobrow, Daniel G., Mittal, Sanjay, and Stefik, Mark J., "Expert Systems: Perils and Promise," *Communications of the ACM* **29**, No. 9, pp. 880–894, September (1986)

Chapter 13

BUILDING KNOWLEDGE-BASED SYSTEMS

(PHOTO: COURTESY OF THE TURING INSTITUTE)

Donald Michie earned his doctorate in Mammalian Genetics from Oxford University having served during World War II with Alan Turing in the code-breaking center at Bletchley Park. He is founder of the Turing Institute of Glasgow, Scotland, and ITL-Knowlegelink, a commercial firm associated with the Turing Institute. The Institute conducts research on expert systems, machine learning, advanced robotics, and computer vision. He has written *An Introduction to Molecular Biology*, *On Machine Intelligence*, *The Creative Computer: Machine Intelligence and Human Knowledge*, and *The Knowledge Machine*. He is Editor-in-Chief of the ten-volume *Machine Intelligence* series and a Fellow of the Zoological Society of London, the British Computer Society, and the Royal Society of Edinburgh.

13: BUILDING KNOWLEDGE-BASED SYST

13.1 INTRODUCTION

In the preceding chapters we examined some of the early expert systems and studied the systematics and architectural principles which seemed to underlie these systems. Two goals of this chapter are first to summarize the features and capabilities of several existing expert system tools and second to illustrate in detail the construction of an actual expert system. To further illustrate the range of applicability of knowledge-based systems, a number of actual student semester projects are outlined and sample output shown. The chapter closes with a brief discussion of pitfalls to avoid when designing expert systems and potential problems which wide-spread implementation of expert systems may pose.

13.2 CLASSIFICATION OF KNOWLEDGE ENGINEERING TOOLS

A turning point in the history of expert systems occurred when it was realized that generality in design was possible through the appropriate choice of system architecture. That is, by cleanly separating the inference engine from the domain-dependent knowledge base, new expert systems could be constructed by using new knowledge bases with the original control structure/inference engine. The expert system MYCIN had been developed with a clear design objective of keeping the rule base separate from the inference engine. William van Melle used the MYCIN inference engine and a 1975 Pontiac Service Manual to build a fifteen-rule system for diagnosing problems with the car horn circuit.[1] This demonstration provided the basis for the first *expert system shell,* EMYCIN. The acronym was suggested by Joshua Lederberg of the DENDRAL project to represent Essential MYCIN and is also a good mnemonic for MYCIN without rules, i.e. Empty MYCIN.[2]

EMYCIN was the prototype for a series of knowledge engineering tools designed to increase the productivity of expert system builders. As in the case of EMYCIN, several of these expert system shells were closely associated with a particular expert system. In some cases, for example the PROSPECTOR expert system and KAS (Knowledge Acquisition System) tool, the expert system motivated the development of the tool. In others, for example the OPS5 rule-based language and expert systems XCON and MUD, the tool was developed first and facilitated building the expert systems. An excellent discussion and systematic evaluation of the first generation of knowledge engineering tools is presented by Hayes-Roth, Waterman, and Lenat.[3]

THE CHOICE OF SYSTEM

The first question the prospective expert system builder generally asks is: Which language/tool should I select for building my system? The choice must be made from a range of systems which can be illustrated as the spectrum shown in Figure 13-1.

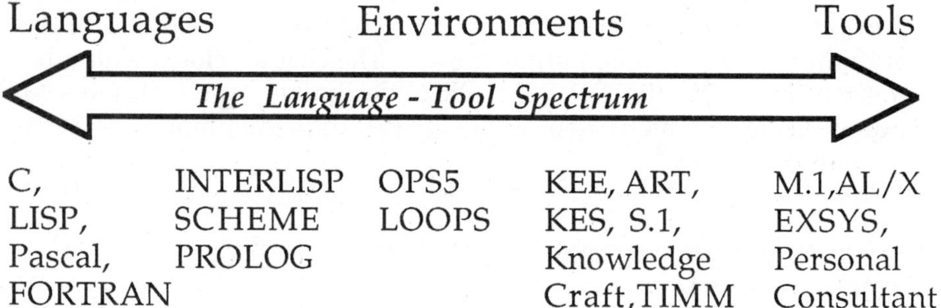

Figure 13-1 Spectrum of Knowledge Engineering Systems Expert system builders must select the system most appropriate for the resources available and the particular task at hand. This figure illustrates some possible choices on the language — tool continuum.[4]

On one end of the spectrum are the standard high-level *languages*. The selection of a high-level programming language provides your expert system with flexibility and computing speed. Problems arise because you must write your own inference engine and maintain the separation of the knowledge base from the inference engine.

At the other end of the spectrum are the commercially available *expert system shells* or tools. The control structure of the expert system already exists and all that the user has to do is add the knowledge base. The price paid for this convenience is the loss of freedom and flexibility imposed by a standard data structure format.

A second dimension of expert system tools is the *environment* provided for the system builder. The environment may be defined as the collection of programming tools available to the system builder to facilitate the production of quality software. It includes (but is not limited to) editors, debuggers, system libraries, file and database managers, and a variety of graphics support routines. The environment that a system provides is as important as the features of the language/tool itself and is a factor in determining the productive capabilities of a system.

The objectives, strength, capabilities, experience, and work load of the expert system development group determine where to settle on the language — tool spectrum. If the objectives of the group includes academic research on expert system development, the choice should be toward the language end of the spectrum to maintain the flexibility and power which languages provide. If the objectives involve getting commercial expert system products "out the door" rapidly, then the highly structured development tools are the best option. If the development group has strong experience in AI programming, then the choice of LISP or Prolog or some combination should most likely be included in the list of available tools for building customized expert systems. If, on the other hand, the group is relatively new in the AI field and has a heavy work load and deadlines to meet, a standard expert system shell provides the optimum strategy.

Some of the best available advice on selecting the most appropriate tool for building expert systems is presented by Waterman.[5] He cites what he calls Davis' Law:

For every tool there is a task perfectly suited to it.

but notes that, unfortunately, the converse is not necessarily true. That is, for a given task there may not be a tool perfectly suited to it. Waterman suggests that users ask themselves the following questions to help select the optimum system:

- Does the tool provide the development team with the power and sophistication they need?
- Are the tool's support facilities adequate considering the time frame for development?
- Is the tool reliable?
- Is the tool maintained?
- Does the tool have the features suggested by the needs of the problem?

In addition, the user should consider the following two questions:

- Is the *price* of the system in line with its projected use?
- Is the system designed for the *mode* in which it will be used?

PRICE

Prices on AI languages range from about $100 on up. Prices for expert system shells range from about $150 to nearly $100,000. A small industry building a diagnostic expert system for a microcomputer-based industrial control system which sells in the $15,000 — $25,000 range cannot afford to add a $20,000 — $50,000 LISP machine to the system to run programs developed with a $65,000 expert system shell. A small expert system built and running on the control system microcomputer is probably most appropriate for this application.

On the other hand, a large corporation which designs and installs heating/ventilating systems worth hundreds of thousands of dollars in large office buildings can afford to buy the best expert system building tools with which to custom design real-time diagnostic and control expert systems. A sophisticated tool is required for building the complex system required for this application, and the high initial cost is rapidly recovered by increased productivity such an environment provides.

MODE

There are at least three easily identified modes of operation for expert system building tools. The choice of operating mode will greatly influence the choice of expert system shell. These modes can be identified as:

- *Research tool* — A large corporation or university with extensive research budgets should select one or more tools to provide for the maximum power and flexibility. No delivery system is required in this mode.

- *Separated Production/Delivery Mode* — In this mode expert systems may be developed on high capacity work stations with sophisticated expert system shells and the expert system products ported down to smaller delivery machines. The production machine is typically a VAX or LISP machine and the delivery vehicle is typically a low-end work station or microcomputer. The advantage of this mode is that the system builders have a powerful development environment with the capabilities of a research tool while the products they generate can be delivered on relatively inexpensive machines.

- *Integrated Production/Delivery Mode* — In this mode the expert system development shell runs on the same machine that is used to deliver the expert system. This is generally a powerful microcomputer or a lower-end work station which may not provide the range of capabilities of more sophisticated systems. The main advantages of this mode are simplicity of use and low cost.

If the objective of the expert system development group is simply to produce and deliver a capable expert system as quickly and cheaply as possible, the choice should be for the most capable expert system tool (shell). Perhaps the strongest argument for this recommendation is illustrated in Figure 13-2.

13.3 SURVEY OF AVAILABLE EXPERT SYSTEM TOOLS

One of the most exciting current developments in artificial intelligence is the trend toward implementation of AI systems on capable work stations and microcomputers. This trend is perhaps illustrated best by the emergence of expert systems and expert system shells for microcomputers with large memories. The pressures behind this trend, indicated below, are fairly obvious, but the consequences have been largely ignored.

TRENDS IN HARDWARE DEVELOPMENT

- Microcomputers are presently available with memories (1–16 Mb) and CPU speeds (8–33 Mhz clock speeds) rivaling those of mainframe computers of a very few years ago.

- Work stations such as the Sun, Apollo, and the TI and MacII series are now available with capabilities similar to dedicated LISP machines. The emerging generation of microcomputers using the Motorola MC68040, Intel 80486, and National Semiconductor NS32532 microprocessor chips will rival the performance of these work stations. These families of 32-bit processors can operate at clock rates of 16–33 Mhz and provide 3–10 MIPS.[6]

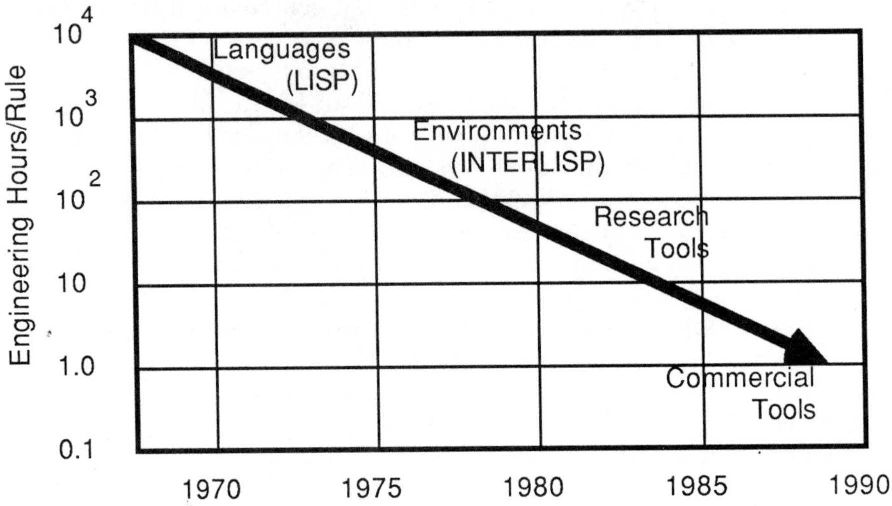

Figure 13-2 Improvement in productivity provided by various Expert System Tools The development of specialized expert system shells has improved the productivity of system developers by more than four orders of magnitude over the original, language-based systems. (Figure from Rick Stephan Hayes, *EXPERTISE* **1**, p. 17, February, 1986)

- These trends toward more capable microcomputers have been realized in the "3M" machine engineered at Carnegie-Mellon University. The 3M machine has 1 megabyte RAM, runs at 1 million floating point operations/sec (1 MFLOP), and has a graphical resolution of 1 million pixels (screen resolution of 1000 × 1000). This is the basis machine referred to as *microcomputer* from here on.

- User-friendly, interactive, graphics-based microcomputer systems provide a far more productive environment for program development than that of the early mainframe batch environment. In fact, the obvious need of AI program development for an interactive programming mode spurred the original development of time-shared mainframes at such institutions as MIT.

- Many of the false starts and unproductive approaches in AI research which were investigated on mainframes can be avoided on microcomputers, shortening the time it takes to implement significant applications.

- Tremendous economic pressures exist for using inexpensive microcomputers as "delivery systems" for applications developed at great expense on larger systems. While this text was in preparation, several of the systems described below evolved from mainframe through minicomputer to personal computer delivery systems.

SURVEY OF EXPERT SYSTEM SOFTWARE

The obvious success of XCON as a productivity-enhancing tool triggered the race for commercially successful expert systems. One of the keys to the rapid and successful development of XCON was the availability of the OPS5, a production rule based programming language. The importance of specialized system–building tools was not lost on the university or private research groups working on expert systems. A number of new companies sprang up to commercialize and market the systems which originated primarily within the university. This phenomenon is discussed and rationalized in some detail by Schank.[7]

The resulting development is a dramatic, text-book example of the dynamics of a responsive free market economy. Several sophisticated expert system building tools soon appeared, and the number continues to grow. This phenomena is very important to the future of AI for several reasons.

- Expert systems represent the debut of AI for the business and industrial communities. As a number of advertisements for expert system shells correctly state: *AI is finally coming out of the laboratory into the market place.* The performance of expert system shells and the products emerging from them will have a great deal to do with the acceptance of AI as a legitimate enterprise by business and industrial leaders.

- The market place will determine the value of AI products such as expert system shells. Interestingly, the expert system shells emerging from university-linked companies were originally priced more than ten times higher than those from small, entrepreneurial companies. To a research group with a $1 million annual budget accustomed to working on multi-million dollar computers, a price tag of $65,000 seems relatively modest, while to a small software house using $5000 PCs for system development, setting the price at $1995 seems a bit daring. The market place is serving a useful purpose in resolving such incongruities.

- The pressure for developing a low-cost delivery vehicle for expert systems is causing the microcomputer to be accepted as a useful AI machine. Concerning the notion that the IBM PC or Apple Macintosh was a serious machine for expert system development, one writer noted, "The reaction in virtually all circles of expert systems development to such a proposal would be derision bordering on hysteria."[8] The same author goes on to say, "The pathway to the success of Apple and IBM in the microcomputer marketplace is strewn with the bodies of scoffers who felt that their own domain of expertise was somehow safe from the penetration of microcomputers because it was simply too complex or too unusual or too unprofitable." The legitimacy of the microcomputer in AI is confirmed by the scramble of virtually all expert system tool developers to re-package their systems for the PC and/or the Macintosh.

Below we summarize in a brief paragraph some of the most important features of a number of commercially available expert system tools. The list of tools is not exhaustive but was chosen to represent a cross section of systems in terms of capabilities and price. More comprehensive lists of tools are given elsewhere.[9] The features listed should be considered a snapshot at one point in time. All the systems are dynamic in nature, with capabilities continually expanding in response to customers' needs and competitive pressures.

While success of any product is not guaranteed in a dynamic marketplace, most of the systems discussed are already several years old and relatively stable. However, the reader should be aware that mergers, acquisitions, and the dynamics of the marketplace may have already significantly altered the list presented here. Also, as these products prove commercially viable one can be certain that the corporate computer giants will move into the field with attractive competing products. A summary of the detailed features of the systems is given in Appendix B.

ART (Automated Reasoning Tool) by Inference Corporation

This system is more than a simple shell. It provides an integrated collection of software tools (i.e. a "toolkit") for building knowledge-based systems, including both production rule and frame knowledge representations, logic, and LISP functional programming. The inference engine supports forward and backward chaining, pattern-matching, and logic programming. Inference rules are used to add facts to the knowledge base and production rules provide the ability to change facts. Data structures called *schemata* allow frame type representation, and *hypothetical worlds* may be studied using a feature called *viewpoints* for defining the context in which facts and rules apply. ART provides a high-speed rule compiler which facilitates real-time analysis. It is written in LISP and runs on Symbolics, LMI, SUN-3, MicroVAX, IBM-PC/RT, Apollo, TI Explorer, and the VAX 780.

KEE (Knowledge Engineering Environment) by IntelliCorp

This is another sophisticated, integrated programming environment. KEE supports a variety of knowledge representation schemes including object-oriented frame language with slots, multiple inheritance, and multiple windows as well as production rules with both object-oriented and data-driven programming. The production system uses backward and forward chaining, and provides a *truth maintenance system* that prevents inconsistent worlds and limits search. There are a variety of control mechanisms available to the programmer. KEE allows integrating several data bases, including a graphics knowledge base, which may be manipulated by commands embedded in the frame slots. The interactive graphics interface provided by KEE is one of the most sophisticated available on expert system-building tools.[10] KEE's open architecture enables the programmer to readily interact with and extend the system. In addition to running on all standard LISP machines, TI Explorer, and VAX 780, the system supports PC-Host, a delivery system in which expert systems may be developed on the VAX and delivered by IBM-PCs.

KES (Knowledge Engineering System) by Software Architecture and Engineering, Inc.

This is a non-integrated knowledge engineering toolkit from which the programmer selects one of the three knowledge representation systems: a production rule system (KES PS), a hypothesize-and-test system (KES HT), or a Bayesian statistical pattern classification system. Each knowledge base has four data types: schema, associations, actions, and free text. All subsystems use the same multiple-choice user-interface format, and the user may interrupt at any time to ask for help or an explanation of the reasoning used. KES PS supports a class hierarchy in which knowledge may be represented by object-attribute-class triplets. KES HT represents knowledge with a frame-like format which is intuitive and easy for novices to master. HT uses abductive reasoning inference engine based on minimal set cover theory. The implementation, originally in LISP, has been rewritten in C and runs on virtually all machines from the IBM-PC to the Cyber 180. The C implementation provides portability which effectively separates the development and delivery system. A unique feature of KES is that it is *embedable*, that is, knowledge-based features and interfaces are easily added to existing C software.

Knowledge Craft by Carnegie Group, Inc.

This hybrid tool uses frame-based "schemata" to represent objects, processes, and control strategies. The schematas contain slots to carry attributes and inheritance information. The system uses an integrated database scheme for storing schemata. Several reasoning methods may be used within one application, including OPS5 rule-based forward-chaining, and logic programming in Prolog. Object-oriented programming supports message passing to schematas, and a feature called *contexts* allows examination of alternative solutions to a problem. Schemata are represented by windows in a mouse-driven, device-independent graphics environment. Carnegie Group has recently integrated Knowledge Craft with their Language Craft program to provide the expert system tool with a natural language interface development tool. Knowledge Craft is implemented in Common LISP and available on the following machines: Symbolics, TI Explorer, and the VAX series including the MicroVAX series. Implementations of Knowledge Craft for the SUN, Apollo, and HP9320 work stations are in progress.

S.1 by Teknowledge, Inc.

This is a rule-based knowledge engineering tool which also supports simple frame-based representation and procedure-oriented programming. Production rules closely resemble those in EMYCIN and carry associated certainty-factors. Frames allow representation of objects with associated inheritance hierarchy. Procedural programming is performed by control blocks which specify the sequence in which objects are created, and attribute values are determined by user queries. The language is strongly typed and all variables refer to a "class" of objects. The knowledge base rules can be modularized into "rule-categories." S.1 provides a multi-window graphics environment with rule consistency checking, help, and explanation facilities. A somewhat simpler tool than ART, KEE, and Knowledge Craft, S.1 is designed primarily for applications in which expertise already exists. Applications have been fielded in diagnosis, engineering design, and planning. Users are expected to be computer professionals with some AI training. S.1 was written originally in LISP but has been converted to C and runs on IBM and VAX mainframes, all LISP machines, AT&T, MicroVAX, Sun, NCR, HP, IBM RT, and Apollo work stations.

DUCK by Smart Systems Technology

This system, developed by Professor Drew McDermott of Yale University, is based on first order predicate calculus. Like Prolog it uses backward chaining, but also provides forward chaining with rule-based knowledge in a LISP environment. Using dependency-directed backtracking and a truth maintenance system, Duck is capable of nonmonotonic reasoning (reasoning under assumptions or inconsistent information). A *data pool* facility supports local databases for representing hypothetical worlds, time sequences, and sets of special purpose information.[11] A program written in DUCK can be run in Duck mode, LISP mode, or a *walk* mode for debugging and explanations. It has been implemented in NISP, a portable dialect of LISP, on Symbolics, Xerox and LMI machines, SUN and Apollo work stations, the TI Explorer, and VAXes.[12]

LOOPS by Xerox Corporation

This is an experimental knowledge programming system developed by Mark Stefik, Daniel Bobrow, and their colleagues at Xerox PARC.[13] LOOPS is essentially a tool kit providing procedure-oriented, object-oriented, access-oriented, and rule-oriented programming in an integrated environment. Procedure-oriented programming is done in INTERLISP-D on which the rest of the system is built. Object-oriented programming consists of objects combining both instructions and data which communicate by sending messages to each other. Access-oriented programming implements the demon paradigm for building programs to monitor other programs. Rule-oriented programming is patterned on the production rule model using a control structure and rule sets. LOOPS provides a powerful and complex programming environment, rather than a simple expert system shell, and is designed primarily as a research tool. It is implemented on only the Xerox 1100 series machines.

OPS5 by the Carnegie-Mellon University Computer Science Department

As the acronym implies, Official Production System, Version 5 (OPS5) is a production system based programming language.[14] It was written by Charles L. Forgy of Carnegie-Mellon University. It contains a powerful pattern matching feature and an efficient forward chaining interpreter which provide for a very general programming capability. This generality places no constraints on the type of problem solving strategy which can be written, but it also requires the programmer to explicitly design both data representation structures and control of flow in terms of rules. The OPS5 environment provides a highly optimized rule interpreter and modest debugging and tracing features. OPS5e is an enhanced version for LISP machines which provides for graphics windows. OPS83 is a compiled version which runs considerably faster than OPS5 and includes procedural programming features. OPS5 is built on the LISP language and runs on a great variety of machines from the Macintosh to the VAX. It is available from a number of distributors including Digital Equipment Corporation.

M.1 by Teknowledge, Inc.

This is a production rule-based system with an inference engine which uses a backward chaining inference scheme. The knowledge base is a distinct file of production rules created by any standard word processor. In the construction, testing, and debugging phase, the user must switch back and forth between the **M.1** operating system and the word processor being used to edit the rules. **M.1** itself is compiled and contains compiler-like features which check the syntax of the knowledge base as it is loaded. Probabilistic information is introduced and propagated by means of an assigned certainty factor. A useful feature of **M.1** is the instrument panel mode of operation in which the screen is partitioned into four windows labeled EVENTS, CONCLUSIONS, REASONING, and OPTIONS. It is written in C and the developer can link to C routines. The present version can handle up to 2000 rules in memory, and the knowledge base can be overlaid, allowing an unlimited size knowledge base. The system runs on the IBM-PC.

Personal Consultant Series by Texas Instruments

This series of expert system shells is modeled after the EMYCIN rule-based system developed at Stanford University. The introductory level program is called Personal Consultant Easy and is designed to acquaint the user with expert system design through self-paced, example-based tutorial sessions. The more advanced program, Personal Consultant Plus has additional features for more difficult problems. It is the system described here. It has been upgraded to provide frames which may contain rules, slots for relevant values, and meta-rules to control the use of knowledge. It is written in LISP and provides a full LISP programming environment, including access to procedures written in the PC-Scheme dialect of LISP. PC-Plus provides an interface to databases and spreadsheet programs for data on which the expert system operates. The system also provides meta-rules which specify which rules are most effective for solving particular problems. The user interface is based on menu-driven pop-up windows with help facilities. Graphics images created by other programs may be embedded and displayed at the appropriate time in the expert systems created by Personal Consultant Plus. The system includes a compiler and can run knowledge bases of up to 2000 rules. The original Personal Consultant which uses only production rules is available at a reduced price. Both systems run on the TI Business Pro, the TI Explorer LISP machine, and the IBM-PC and AT series.

SUPER-EXPERT by Intelligent Terminals Ltd.

Super-Expert is the next generation of **Expert-Ease,** a popular expert system tool sometimes identified as the benchmark program for microcomputer systems.[15] The program was developed by Donald Michie's company Intelligent Terminals Ltd. in Scotland, UK. Its popularity stems from its simple, user-friendly interface to the knowledge base which uses the familiar spreadsheet format. This system allows the user to short circuit the knowledge engineer's role by turning it over to the computer. The secret is an inductive logic algorithm by which the program can generalize (i.e. infer rules) from a set of particular examples. The system designer must structure the material in such a way that the program can infer the logic tree from input examples. It has been shown that letting the computer derive the rules by inference is more efficient than coding the production rules by hand.[16] The system requires a consistent set of examples for deriving its rule base. The program will issue a warning if two identical examples are specified as leading to different conclusions. Help screens are available at almost all levels of operation, and the explanations are prompt and useful. The program provides the capability for the system builder to annotate entries to make the final product well-documented, understandable, and pleasant to use. After the examples have been entered in spread sheet format, the system compiles them into the logic tree it will use for solving particular problems. Such logic tree solutions may be linked in forward chaining style. In a problem session, the program asks the user short, multiple-choice questions. Based on the answers, the program searches the possible "conclusion space" and presents the appropriate answer. The user can get an explanation of the logic used in reaching the conclusion by requesting that the logic tree be displayed. Disadvantages of the system include lack of a system for handling probabilistic information, and no provision for experienced users to short-cut the spreadsheet format and access the logic trees directly. Super-Expert has been implemented on the Macintosh and the IBM-PC.

ESP Advisor by Expert Systems International

This is one of the most powerful and flexible expert system shells available for microcomputers. It is written in Prolog-2 and allows linking of the expert system to Prolog-2 programs. Prolog-2 is a superset of Clocksin and Mellish Prolog which provides an excellent window-based development environment. ESP Advisor uses the Knowledge Representation Language (KRL) for representing facts, parameters, and rules. A useful feature of the KRL is *text animation*, a simple method for embedding text to guide the user during a consultation session. The text animation feature makes this system particularly suitable for designing on-line manuals and advisory systems for providing the user with step by step help through a complex procedure. After the knowledge base has been generated by ES/P Advisor, it is compiled into optimized Prolog-2 for most efficient execution. ESP Advisor does, however,require experienced programmers to master the complexity of the KRL. This system has recently been introduced into the United States and is in widespread use throughout Europe. It has been implemented on the IBM-PC series, the Data General/One, and the VAX and MicroVAX series.

EXSYS by EXSYS, Inc.

This system is a classical production-rule-based expert system shell and is the system chosen for building the examples in this text. The knowledge base is constructed by using a well-designed rule editor to encode the knowledge in IF-THEN-ELSE rules. The rules may be stated in terms of English text or numeric qualifiers. The inference engine provides for either forward or backward chaining or both as user controlled options. Probabilistic information is handled by user selection of one of three types of confidence factors. If different rules assign different confidence factors to the same choice of final solution, the factors are averaged. Explanation of its reasoning is handled by the program reciting the current rule upon a request of "WHY" by the user at any point during the consultation. The system can access any external program which then writes data to disk files which EXSYS automatically reads. This permits linking to database and spreadsheet programs such as Lotus 1-2-3. The system comes with detailed examples and a step by step tutorial on writing an expert system. It is exceptionally easy to learn and use and has proven to be an excellent educational tool. For commercial developers there is a low-cost, one-time developers license for unlimited run-time copies. It is written in C to provide for fast execution and has a rule capacity of about 5000 rules on a 640K machine. It has been implemented on the IBM-PC and the VAX.

TIMM by General Research Corporation

This is a frame-like induction system for selecting possible solutions from a user-defined list. It resembles SUPER-EXPERT somewhat in using example cases to infer a set of IF-THEN rules for reaching similar conclusions for similar cases. The sophisticated, partial pattern-matching algorithm used in this process allows TIMM to cope with situations in which important parameters of the problem may be missing. The system uses certainty values to represent probabilistic information, and the solutions are listed with associated probabilities. A helpful, interactive dialog editor assists the user in selecting appropriate program options and creating the knowledge base. Another valuable feature is that expert systems developed with TIMM can be embedded in a user's application program. When the application program needs a decision, control passes to the expert system which in turn can access a user data base, make the decision, and return control to the application program. TIMM also provides a GENERALIZE mode in which the system generates more general rules from the information contained in the knowledge base. The PC version of TIMM has the following limitations: (1) it lacks arithmetic and math operators for processing input numerical values, (2) it limits the number of solution choices to 15, although several expert systems may be linked together in decision networks. TIMM is written in FORTRAN and runs on any system supporting a FORTRAN-77 compiler, including IBM mainframe, Prime, VAX, Symbolics,and the IBM-PC lines of computers.[17]

GURU by Micro Data Base Systems, Inc.

This is an expert system development environment designed for the business community. It supports a wide range of knowledge representation methods and prefabricated object classes. It integrates a standard production rule knowledge representation using forward and backward chaining inference with useful business software such as relational data base management systems, spreadsheets, business graphics, statistical analysis, programmatic modeling, and report generation. It supports four levels of user interface, including procedural programming, direct command language, menu-based interaction, and a fairly impressive natural language processor for querying databases. Certainty measures may be assigned to rules and variables, and the system offers a choice of 16 separate algebras for combining the certainties of variables and rules. There is no software limit on the number of rules contained in the knowledge base. It provides a fairly complete set of numeric and string functions and supports wild-card and character class matches. GURU is written in C and has been implemented on the IBM-PC, XT, AT, and RT and VAX-11 series. It is an interesting counter example of the trend of porting expert system shells developed on mainframes down to personal computers — it was first developed for the IBM-PC and later transferred to the VAX.

AL/X by Intelligent Terminals, Ltd.

Advice Language/X (AL/X) is a rule-based knowledge engineering language which also supports frame-based representation. It was developed under the direction of Professor Donald Michie, now Chief Scientist of the Turing Institute, Scotland. It closely resembles KAS, the semantic network inference system which is essentially PROSPECTOR without its geology knowledge base. The inference engine uses a combination for forward and backward chaining. Uncertainty is handled by assigning a degree of belief (DB) to each rule and hypothesis and by the system user responding to queries with certainty values (CVs). Probabilities are combined using Bayesian methods. AL/X was first used to analyze oil rig shutdowns in the North Sea and holds the distinction of being the first expert system shell implemented on a microcomputer. AL/X does not provide the user-friendly development environment available on several other systems discussed above and requires a trained knowledge engineer familiar with its operation to encode the domain knowledge into the rule structure, weights, and degrees of belief used in the system. It is written in Pascal and has been implemented on many computers ranging from the APPLE II to the CYBER 175.[18]

TRENDS IN SOFTWARE DEVELOPMENT

During the three years this chapter and the Appendix B table have been in preparation, a number of trends in expert system tool software has become apparent. These include:

- *The move to super-micros* — As the chapter began, there were two well delineated groups of expert system tools: the mainframe and LISP machine group running on machines costing $50,000 — $100,000 or more on the one hand, and the Personal Computer group running on $3000 — $6000 machines on the other. Now, almost all systems provide at least delivery if not development systems on PC level machines. Many of the systems introduced on PCs have also been ported upwards, to VAXes in particular. There is good reason to believe that the advent of 80386 and 68020-based machines in the $5000 — $10,000 range will largely replace the more expensive LISP machines.

- *Decline in Software Prices* — With only one exception among the systems discussed here, the trend in pricing has been downward. Either the price on a given system has been reduced or a vastly improved version is being offered at the same price. This effect closely parallels the improved price/performance ratio of hardware discussed above. Paperback Software has released a $99 product, VP-Expert, which challenges the high-end PC products in its breadth, quality, and features.[19]

- *Rules alone are not enough* — While most of the expert system tools began as production rule systems, many of them have added new knowledge representation capabilities as recognition grew that simple rule systems are often inadequate for complex tasks. A number of the systems have added frame-like structures and object oriented programming to their tool kits.

- *The move from LISP to C* — A trend closely related to the shift to personal computers is the shift from LISP to C as the language in which to write the tool. The primary motivations for this trend is the increased performance and portability provided by languages such as C, Pascal, and FORTRAN.

- *The trend towards embedability* — One of the highly desirable side effects of the move from LISP to conventional programming languages is that expert systems may easily be embedded in user applications. That is, the expert system may be considered as just another function or subroutine to be called when needed by the user's main program. Some estimates indicate that the potential for such embedded knowledge-based systems exceeds that for stand-alone expert systems.

13.4 EXAMPLE — BUILDING *SAILING CRAFT IDENTIFIER*

To illustrate the procedure used in building a knowledge-based system we next describe in some detail the use of one of these shells, EXSYS, to build a classifier system called SAILING CRAFT IDENTIFIER. What motivated the choice of this particular expert system shell and topic? EXSYS was selected as the tool for the following reasons:

- It is an extremely effective educational tool. Its classic production rule format illustrates many of the concepts presented previously in this book. Several of the author's AI classes have used it effectively after a single demonstration session with virtually a 100% success rate in developing functional student systems.

- It is inexpensive. The low initial price and very reasonable one-time delivery license make it a cost-effective commercial tool.

• It contains many of the desirable features of competent, general purpose expert system shells. These features are summarized in the EXSYS paragraph above and will be illustrated in the example developed below.

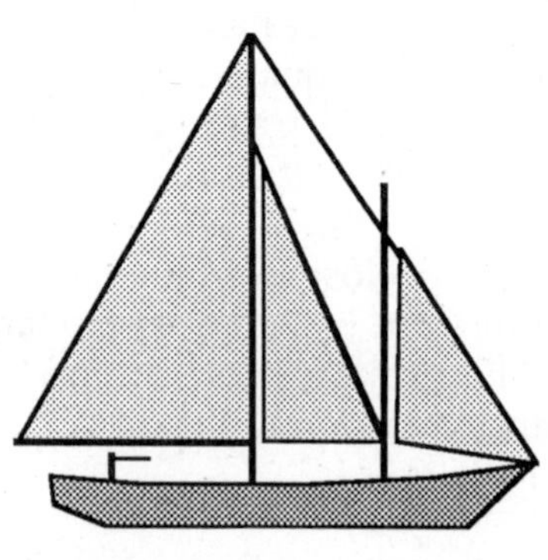

Staysail Schooner

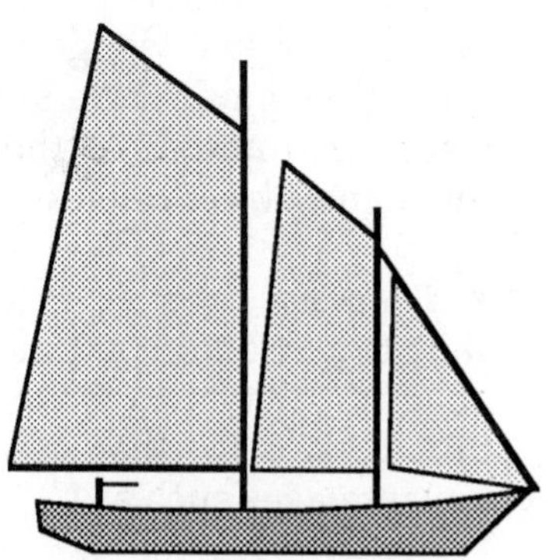

Gaff-Headed Schooner

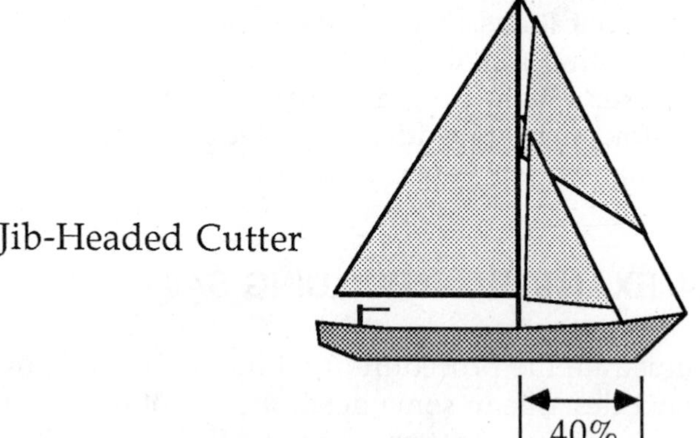

Jib-Headed Cutter

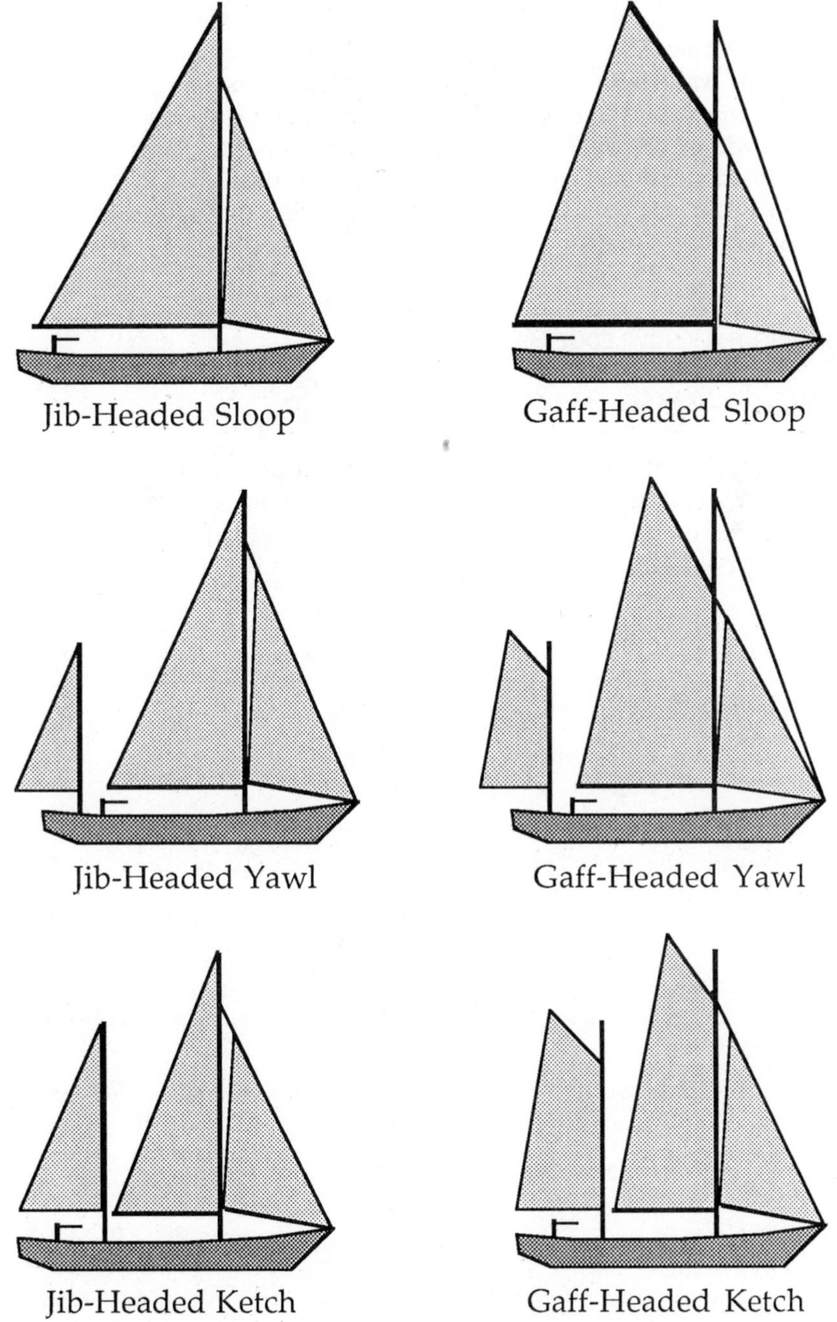

Figure 13-3 Sailing Craft Identified by Expert System These nine vessels with their sail plans are uniquely identified by clues the user provides the expert system in an interactive query system.

The topic *SAILING CRAFT IDENTIFIER* was selected because it is a clean, well-defined, interesting problem illustrating many of the concepts previously introduced. After collecting data on the unknown vessel through three or four queries to the user the classifier is able to uniquely identify each of the nine sailing craft shown in Figure 13-3. With just 17 rules, it also is of manageable size for an introductory AI text book.

BUILDING THE KNOWLEDGE BASE

1. *Setup — User Selected Options*

Upon entering the editor the system developer configures the environment by selecting various options from menu choices. The essential features of this dialog are shown below with the developer's response in bold face and our comments in italics:

Subject of knowledge base:

<<<SAILING CRAFT IDENTIFIER>>>

Author:
--> MORRIS W. FIREBAUGH

How do you wish the data on the available choices structured:

1 - Simple yes or no

2 - A range of 0-10 where 0 indicates absolutely not and 10 indicates absolutely certain. 1-9 indicate degrees of certainty.

3 - A range of -100 to +100 indicating the degree of certainty

Input number of selection or <H> for help:
2

Choices will only be displayed in the conclusions if their final value is greater than or equal to 1

Do you wish to change this lower threshold limit? (Y/N) (Default=N):
N

Number of rules to use in data derivation:

```
      1. Attempt to apply all possible rules
      2. Stop after first successful rule

      Select 1 or 2 (Default = 1):
1
```

Input the text you wish to use to explain how to run this file. This text will be displayed at the start of EXSYS

The SAILING CRAFT IDENTIFIER helps you identify various classes of sail boats from a brief description of their mast structure and sail plan. Please answer the following questions on the number and position of masts and shape of sails:

Input the text you wish to use at the end of the EXSYS run. This will be displayed when the rules are done but before the choices and their calculated values are displayed.

From the information you have given me, I conclude that the sail boat you describe is a:

```
      Do you wish the user running this expert system to
      have the rules displayed as the default condition?
      (The user will have the option of overriding this
      option)  (Y/N)  (Default = N):
N

      Do you wish to have an external program called
      at the start of a run to pass data back for
      multiple variables or qualifiers? (Other external
      programs may also be used to get data for
      single variables or qualifiers)  (Y/N) (Default=N):
N
```

Input the choices to select among. Input just <ENTER> when done. Additional choices can be added later

1 **Jib-Headed SLOOP**
2 **Jib-Headed YAWL**
3 **Jib-Headed KETCH**
4 **Staysail SCHOONER**
5 **Gaff-Headed SLOOP**
6 **Gaff-Headed YAWL**
7 **Gaff-Headed KETCH**
8 **Gaff-Headed SCHOONER**
9 **Jib-Headed CUTTER**
10 **<CR>**

The function that checks new rules against the previous ones does NOT check the validity of mathematical formulas. If you predominantly use formulas, it may be more convenient to switch this option off.

Do you wish new rules checked against the previous rules? Y/N (Default = Y):
Y

2. *Encoding the Rule Base*

At this point the system enters the standard production rule editor. The format of the editor and the available options are shown next:

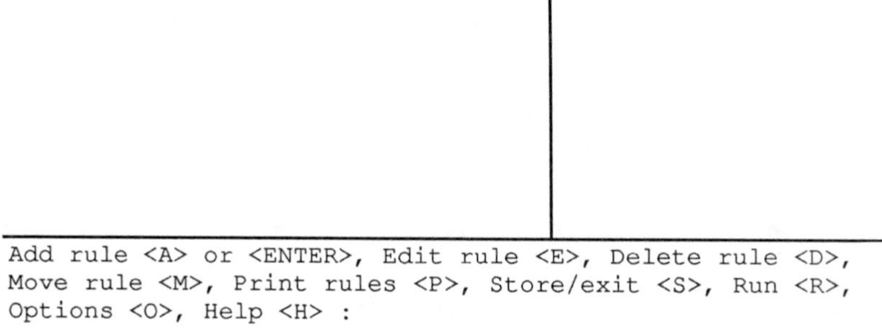

```
Add rule <A> or <ENTER>, Edit rule <E>, Delete rule <D>,
Move rule <M>, Print rules <P>, Store/exit <S>, Run <R>,
Options <O>, Help <H> :
```

Upon typing "A" to add a rule, we get the frame:

RULE NUMBER: 1

IF:

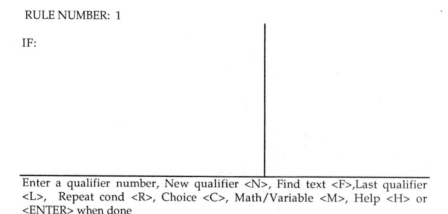

Enter a qualifier number, New qualifier <N>, Find text <F>,Last qualifier <L>, Repeat cond <R>, Choice <C>, Math/Variable <M>, Help <H> or <ENTER> when done

At this point no qualifiers (text variables) have been specified. We then type "N" and get:

RULE NUMBER: 1

IF:

Input Text of qualifier (ending in verb):

So we enter:

RULE NUMBER: 1

The number of masts is

IF:

Input Text of qualifier (ending in verb):

and then hit a CR to indicate that the predicate is finished. The system then responds with numbers requesting possible values which we supply as follows:

RULE NUMBER: 1

IF:

The number of masts is

1 one
2 two

Input acceptable values. Input just <ENTER> when done.

After 2 CRs, the qualifier with its associated values is completed and we get the prompt:

RULE NUMBER: 1

IF:

Qualifier # 1
The number of masts is

1 one
2 two

```
Enter number(s), NOT + number(s), New value (N), Type
correction (T), Delete (D), ≠ or Ø to scroll, Help (H) or
just <ENTER> to cancel.
```

We now have established Qualifier # 1 with two values which will be the basis for the first five rules. To complete the first half of the conjunctive"IF" portion of the first rule we type "1" and see:

RULE NUMBER: 1

IF:

The number of masts is one

Enter a qualifier number, New qualifier <N>, Find text <F>,Last qualifier <L>, Repeat cond <R>, Choice <C>, Math/Variable <M>, Help <H> or <ENTER> when done

Since we want the first five rules to identify the basic craft type which is a function of the number and relative positions of the masts only, we need to create two more quantifiers specifying these quantities. So we type N for new qualifiers and soon have the frame:

RULE NUMBER: 1

IF:

The number of masts is one

Qualifier # 2

The type of vessel is a

1 sloop
2 yaul
3 ketch
4 schooner
5 cutter

```
Enter number(s), NOT + number(s), New value (N), Type
correction (T), Delete (D), ≠ or Ø to scroll, Help (H) or
just <ENTER> to cancel.
```

and

```
RULE NUMBER: 1                              Qualifier # 3
                                        | The position of the mainmast
IF:                                     | is
        The number of masts is one      | 1 forward of the shorter mast
                                        |   (mizzenmast)
                                        | 2 aft the shorter mast
                                        |   (foremast)
                                        | 3 about 40% aft of the bow
                                        | 4 about 25–30% aft the bow
-----------------------------------------------------------------------
Enter number(s), NOT + number(s), New value (N), Type
correction (T), Delete (D), ≠ or Ø to scroll, Help (H) or
just <ENTER> to cancel.
```

Now all qualifiers are ready for completing the first rule. We complete the second half of the conjunctive IF portion by typing 4 to give:

```
RULE NUMBER: 1
                                        |
IF:                                     |
        The number of masts is one      |
and                                     |
        The position of the Mainmast is |
        about 25–30% aft the bow        |
-----------------------------------------------------------------------
Enter a qualifier number, New qualifier <N>, Find text <F>,Last qualifier
<L>, Repeat cond <R>, Choice <C>, Math/Variable <M>, Help <H> or
<ENTER> when done
```

At this point we define what the action part of the rule will be. We can define a new qualifier and set one or more of its values, set one or more values of an already defined qualifier, select and weight one or more of our final choices, or any combination of these actions. Our objective in Rule 1 is to identify the basic vessel type listed in qualifier 2. By typing a second CR, we get to the THEN part of the production rule:

RULE NUMBER: 1

IF:

The number of masts is one

and

The position of the Mainmast is about 25–30% aft the bow

THEN:

Enter a qualifier number, New qualifier <N>, Find text <F>,Last qualifier <L>, Repeat cond <R>, Choice <C>, Math/Variable <M>, Help <H> or <ENTER> when done

Since the basic vessel type is listed in qualifier 2, we type 2 which presents us with the list. By selecting value 1 of this qualifier, we get the completed rule:

RULE NUMBER: 1

IF:

The number of masts is one

AND

The position of the Mainmast is about 25–30% aft the bow

THEN:

The type of vessel is a sloop

Enter a qualifier number, New qualifier <N>, Find text <F>,Last qualifier <L>, Repeat cond <R>, Choice <C>, Math/Variable <M>, Help <H> or <ENTER> when done

Responding with ENTER completes the "THEN" part of the rule. The system then prompts us for the "ELSE" part of the rule which we ignore, then the "Note" part which we fill in, and finally a "Reference" part which we fill in by reference to our domain expert. This completes the rule, and the system lists it one last time for our approval.

In this way, the remaining 16 rules were edited into the SAILING CRAFT IDENTIFIER knowledge base. The listing of these rules is given below.

3. Resulting Rule List

```
RULE NUMBER: 1

IF:
        The number of masts is one
  and   The position of the Mainmast is about 25-30% aft the
        bow

THEN:
        The type of vessel is a sloop

NOTE:
  Sloops have only one mast farther forward than that on a
cutter.

REFERENCE:
  George, M. B., BASIC SAILING, Motor Boating & Sailing
Books, New York (1971) p.5
----------------------------------------


RULE NUMBER: 2

IF:
        The number of masts is two
  and   The position of the Mainmast is  forward of the
        shorter mast (mizzenmast)
  and   The position of the mizzenmast, wrt the helm (rudder
        post), is forward of the helm

THEN:
        The type of vessel is a ketch

NOTE:
  A ketch has a mainmast and a shorter mizzenmast which is
just forward of the helm.
----------------------------------------


RULE NUMBER: 3

IF:
        The number of masts is two
  and   The position of the Mainmast is  forward of the
        shorter mast (mizzenmast)
  and   The position of the mizzenmast, wrt the helm (rudder
        post), is aft the helm

THEN:
        The type of vessel is a yawl

NOTE:
  A yawl is a two-moasted vessel in which the shorter
 mizzenmast is just aft of the helm.
----------------------------------------
```

```
RULE NUMBER: 4

IF:
       The number of masts is two
  and  The position of the Mainmast is  aft the shorter mast
       (foremast)

THEN:
       The type of vessel is a schooner

NOTE:
  A schooner has a shorter foremast ahead of the mainmast.
----------------------------------------


RULE NUMBER: 5

IF:
       The number of masts is one
  and  The position of the Mainmast is  about 40% aft of the
       bow

THEN:
       The type of vessel is a cutter

NOTE:
  A cutter is a single-masted vessel with the mast
 approximately 40% aft of the bow.
----------------------------------------


RULE NUMBER: 6

IF:
       The shape of the mainsail is triangular

THEN:
       The sail plan is jib-headed


NOTE:
  Triangular mainsails are called jib-headed.
----------------------------------------


RULE NUMBER: 7

IF:
       The shape of the mainsail is quadrilateral

THEN:
       The sail plan is gaff-headed

NOTE:
  Gaff-rigged boats have quadrilateral-shaped mainsails.
----------------------------------------
```

```
RULE NUMBER: 8

IF:
        The shape of the mainsail is triangular with 2
        foresails

THEN:
        The sail plan is stay-sail rig

NOTE:
  Staysails fill the gap between maiinsail and jib.
----------------------------------------


RULE NUMBER: 9

IF:
        The type of vessel is a sloop
  and   The sail plan is jib-headed

THEN:
        Jib-Headed SLOOP - Probability=10/10

NOTE:
  A sloop with jib-headed rig is a jib-headed sloop.
----------------------------------------


RULE NUMBER: 10

IF:
        The type of vessel is a yawl
  and   The sail plan is jib-headed

THEN:
        Jib-Headed YAWL - Probability=10/10

NOTE:
  A yawl with jib-headed rig is a jib-headed yawl.
----------------------------------------


RULE NUMBER: 11

IF:
        The type of vessel is a ketch
  and   The sail plan is jib-headed

THEN:
        Jib-Headed KETCH - Probability=10/10

NOTE:
  A ketch with jib-headed rig is a jib-headed ketch.
----------------------------------------


RULE NUMBER: 12
```

```
IF:
       The type of vessel is a schooner
  and  The sail plan is stay-sail rig

THEN:
       Staysail SCHOONER - Probability=10/10

NOTE:
  A schooner with staysail rig is a staysail schooner.
----------------------------------------


RULE NUMBER: 13

IF:
       The type of vessel is a sloop
  and  The sail plan is gaff-headed

THEN:
       Gaff-Headed SLOOP - Probability=10/10
----------------------------------------


RULE NUMBER: 14

IF:
       The type of vessel is a yawl
  and  The sail plan is gaff-headed

THEN:
       Gaff-Headed YAWL - Probability=10/10

NOTE:
  A yawl with gaff-rig is a gaff-headed yawl.
----------------------------------------


RULE NUMBER: 15

IF:
       The type of vessel is a ketch
  and  The sail plan is gaff-headed

THEN:
       Gaff-Headed KETCH - Probability=10/10

NOTE:
  A ketch with gaff-sail is a gaff-headed ketch.
----------------------------------------


RULE NUMBER: 16

IF:
       The type of vessel is a schooner
  and  The sail plan is gaff-headed

THEN:
```

```
        Gaff-Headed SCHOONER - Probability=10/10

NOTE:
  A schooner with gaff-rig is a gaff-headed schooner.
----------------------------------------


RULE NUMBER: 17

IF:
        The type of vessel is a cutter
  and   The sail plan is jib-headed

THEN:
        Jib-Headed CUTTER - Probability=10/10

NOTE:
  A cutter with jib-rig is a jib-headed cutter.
```

4. *The Development Environment*

The development environment in which the expert system is created is at least as important as the more technical details such as knowledge representation scheme or rule capacity. EXSYS, the system shell used to create the SAILING CRAFT IDENTIFIER, provides several simple but extremely useful features for building expert systems. The conceptually simple, menu-driven rule editor has already been described. A second feature which speeds development and debugging of the logic of the system is a cross-reference table which the system developer may request at any point in the editing session. A listing of the cross-reference table is shown below.

QUALIFIERS:

```
 1    The number of masts is

  one
  two

        Used in rule(s):   1   2   3   4   5


 2    The type of vessel is a

  sloop
  yawl
  ketch
  schooner
  cutter

        Used in rule(s):  ( 1)  ( 2)  ( 3)  ( 4)  ( 5)   9
        10   11   12   13   14   15   16   17
```

```
3    The position of the Mainmast is

  forward of the shorter mast (mizzenmast)
  aft the shorter mast (foremast)
  about 40% aft of the bow
  about 25-30% aft the bow

        Used in rule(s):   1   2   3   4   5


4    The position of the mizzenmast, wrt the helm (rudder
post), is

  forward of the helm
  aft the helm

        Used in rule(s):   2   3


5    The shape of the mainsail is

  triangular
  quadrilateral
  triangular with 2 foresails

        Used in rule(s):   6   7   8


6    The sail plan is

  jib-headed
  gaff-headed
  stay-sail rig

        Used in rule(s):  ( 6)  ( 7)  ( 8)   9   10   11
        12   13   14   15   16   17
```

Similarly, a cross-reference table is built for the problem solution choices indicating which rules are involved in each choice.

SYSTEM OPERATION

Another nice feature EXSYS provides the developer is the capability of running the system directly from the editor at any point in the system-building process without having to exit and use the run-time program. This allows incremental testing of the system as it is being built. The independent nature of production rules makes this a particularly valuable tool for building expert systems. We illustrate below a typical session for validating the behavior of the SAILING CRAFT IDENTIFIER. Let's see if the system will properly identify a *gaff-headed ketch* (see Figure 13-3).

From the rule editor line, we simply type "R" for run and see, after a few option setting prompts (User response in bold):

Do you wish to have the rules displayed as
they are used? (Y/N) (Default=N):
<CR>

Recover previously saved input Y/N (Default=N):
<CR>

<<SAILING CRAFT IDENTIFIER>>

by: --> MORRIS W. FIREBAUGH

Press any key to start:
<CR>

```
  The SAILING CRAFT IDENTIFIER helps you identify various
classes of sail boats from a brief description of their mast
structure and sail plan.  Please answer the following ques-
tions on the number and position of masts and shape of
sails:
```

Press any key to start:
<CR>

```
The number of masts is
      1  one
      2  two
```
2

```
The position of the Mainmast is
      1  forward of the shorter mast (mizzenmast)
      2  aft the shorter mast (foremast)
      3  about 40% aft the bow
      4  about 25-30% aft the bow
```
1

```
The position of the mizzenmast, wrt the helm (rudder post),
is
      1  forward of the helm
      2  aft the helm
```
1

```
The shape of the mainsail is
      1  triangular
      2  quadrilateral
      3  triangular with two foresails
```
2

```
From the information you have given me, I conclude that the
```

```
sail boat you describe is a:

      Values based on 0 - 10 system                    VALUE

1  Gaff-Headed KETCH                                      10
```

Yes, from the four answers we provided, the SAILING CRAFT IDENTIFIER correctly classified the vessel we described. Note that it asked only for the relevant information to create the short term memory information from which it could make the appropriate choice.

At this point the system offers us the following useful options:

```
<A>  All choices
<G>  only if value > 1
<P>  Print
<C>  Change and rerun
<line number>  rules used
<Q>  Quit/save
<H>  Help
<D>  Done
```

Suppose we hade mistakenly told the system that the mizzenmast was ahead of the tiller. In fact, the tiller is ahead of the rear mast, making the boat in question a gaff-headed yawl. How difficult is it to change our input to get a correct identification?

EXPLORING ALTERNATIVE SOLUTIONS

Upon typing "C", the system queries us with another useful option:

```
Do you wish to store the current results for comparison with
the new results you will be calculating? (Y/N)  (Default=N):
<CR>
```

We are then presented with the contents of short term memory and invited to change any of the qualifiers and rerun the system. This very conveniently bypasses the necessity for answering the whole list of menu-driven queries necessary for collecting the information required by the production rules. We can change a single condition and rerun the system. The global database after the first run contains the following:

```
1  The number of masts is two
2  The position of the Mainmast is forward of the shorter
mast (mizzenmast)
3  The position of the mizzenmast, wrt the helm (rudder
post), is forward of the helm
4  The shape of the mainsail is quadrilateral
```

Since our error was in the qualifier shown in line 3, we type a 3 and get:

```
The position of the mizzenmast, wrt the helm (tiller post)
is
       1  forward of the helm
       2  aft the helm
```

We enter our change in identification by a "2" and the system lists the short term memory again, with the correction included. Then, choosing the run option, the system concludes:

```
       Values based on 0 - 10 system                 VALUE  PREV.

1  Gaff-Headed YAWL                                     10   NONE
2  Gaff-Headed KETCH                                  NONE     10
```

So EXSYS provides the easiest possible format for debugging the expert system and exploring alternatives during the development process.

This simple 17-rule SAILING CRAFT IDENTIFIER has been discussed in some detail because it illustrates most of the steps of building an expert system and the features that very modestly priced commercial shells provide. To further indicate the usefulness of such expert system shells, we next examine the application of EXSYS in the classroom environment.

13.5 EXAMPLES — BUILDING INSTRUCTIONAL SYSTEMS

Next we summarize several expert systems our students have developed as the final class project in their undergraduate AI course. This list illustrates the range of application which is readily adapted to the production rule format used by many expert system shells. The paragraph summary is the *Starting Text* written by each student to introduce his/her system.

Applied Computer Science Curriculum Advisor by Rick Albright

```
THIS APPLIED COMPUTER SCIENCE ADVISOR EXPERT SYSTEM SERVES
AS AN ADVISOR TO STUDENTS MAJORING IN APPLIED COMPUTER SCI-
ENCE. THE ADVISOR ASKS THE STUDENT A SERIES OF QUESTIONS TO
DETERMINE WHICH COURSES ARE NEEDED FOR DEGREE COMPLETION.
THE STUDENT SHOULD HAVE A CURRENT COPY OF HIS/HER TRANSCRIPT
AVAILABLE FOR REFERENCE. SOME ASSUMPTIONS HAVE BEEN MADE
WHICH MAY CAUSE THE RESULTS TO BE SLIGHTLY INACCURATE.
THEREFORE, INTERPRET THE RESULTS WITH CAUTION!!
```

Heinlein Novel Selector by David Datta

THIS EXPERT SYSTEM WILL AID YOU IN DECIDING WHICH BOOKS BY ROBERT A. HEINLEIN YOU WOULD BE MOST INTERESTED IN READING. IT WILL ASK YOU QUESTIONS ABOUT WHAT TYPE AND SUBJECTS YOU LIKE IN STORIES AND BOOKS. NEXT, IT WILL RANK THE BOOKS BY ROBERT HEINLEIN ON A SCALE OF 1 TO 9 WHERE 1 IS THE LOWEST AND 9 IS THE HIGHEST.

City Street Commissioner Advisor by John D. Elmer

THIS EXPERT SYSTEM PROVIDES A RECORD OF THE CONDITION OF EACH STREET IN KENOSHA FOR THE PURPOSE OF DETERMINING REQUIRED MAINTENANCE. THE PROGRAM WILL ASK THE USER TO PROVIDE THE VALUE OF EACH SECTION IN THE RATING SYSTEM MANUAL. NOTE: ALL CALCULATIONS MUST BE DONE AHEAD OF TIME E.G. SEVERITY + FREQUENCY/2.

Organismal Biology Identifier by David Kanecki

THIS PROGRAM WILL ATTEMPT TO DETERMINE IF A SAMPLE OBTAINED FROM A BIOLOGICAL PROBE IS LIVING. IF IT IS LIVING IT WILL DETERMINE THE GENERA OF THE SAMPLE.

Boy Scout Merit Badge Advisor by Michael V. Krenzke

SCOUTMASTER WILL ADVISE A BOY SCOUT ON THE CURRENT RANK HE PRESENTLY HOLDS. THE SCOUTMASTER WILL ALSO ADVISE THE SCOUT OF WHAT IS NEEDED FOR HIS NEXT ADVANCEMENT.

HELLO YOUNG SCOUT, THANK YOU FOR QUESTIONING ME ABOUT WHAT YOU NEED FOR ADVANCEMENTS. NOW, ALL YOU NEED TO DO IS ANSWER THE QUESTIONS THAT ARE TO FOLLOW AFTER THIS AND THEN I WILL FIGURE OUT WHAT YOU NEED.

Magnetic Disk Duplication Program Advisor by James Morton

WELCOME TO THE EXPERT SYSTEM ON HOW TO COPY A DISK THAT YOU OWN. THIS SYSTEM WILL DO THE FOLLOWING DETERMINATIONS ON HOW TO MAKE A LEGAL BACK-UP: (1) PROMPT FOR THE TYPE OF COMPUTER. (2) PROMPT IF THE PROGRAM IS PROTECTED OR NOT. (3) DETERMINE WHAT PROGRAM AND / OR TECHNIQUE SHOULD BE USED. THIS TECHNIQUE WILL WORK FOR MOST OF THE PRESENTLY PROTECTED DISKS, BUT MAY NOT WORK FOR FUTURE PROTECTION SCHEMES THAT ARE ALWAYS ON THE WAY. IT TAKES FOR GRANTED THAT YOU OWN OR ARE ABLE TO "OBTAIN" USE OF CERTAIN SPECIFIC PROGRAMS AND SOME BASIC KNOWLEDGE OF DISKS AND THEIR FORMAT.

Turf Grass Diseases by Debby L. Mulvihill

```
YOU WILL BE ASKED A SERIES OF MULTIPLE CHOICE QUESTIONS RE-
GARDING THE WEATHER CONDITIONS, TYPE OF TURF GRASS AFFECTED
AND DESCRIPTION OF THE DISEASED GRASS.  THE CHEMICAL/EN-
VIRONMENTAL APPLICATION TO BE APPLIED TO THE DISEASED GRASS
WILL BE DISPLAYED WHEN THE RULES ARE ALSO DISPLAYED.  THIS
EXPERT SYSTEM IS LIMITED TO THE FOLLOWING TURF DISEASES
AND/OR PROBLEMS:
      DOLLAR SPOT, PYTHIUM, GRAY OR PINK SNOW MOLD,
      WILT,CHEMICAL/FERTILIZER BURNS,  DAMAGE DUE TO
      HYDRAULIC FLUID LEAKS OR INSECTS.
```

Hazardous Materials Identifier and Advisor by Susan Schultz

```
THIS EXPERT SYSTEM IS DESIGNED TO IDENTIFY HAZARDOUS MATERI-
ALS USING THE NATIONAL FIRE PROTECTION ASSOCIATIONS' (NFPA)
HAZARD ID CODE:
      BLUE = 0,1,2,3,4
      RED = 0,1,2,3,4
      YELLOW = 0,1,2,3,4
      COLORLESS = W,&,OXY

PRESENTLY,THE FOLLOWING FLAMMABLE MATERIALS ARE RECOGNIZED:
      ACROLEIN
      ALUMINUM CHLORIDE
      BROMOPROPYNE
      CHLORINE TRIFLOURIDE
      DIETHYLZINC
      ETHYLENIMINE
```

Servo-Loop Test Procedure by David Siegler

```
THIS EXPERT SYSTEM WILL HELP THE USER FIND THE FAULT IN  A
SIMPLE SERVO-LOOP CONTROL SYSTEM.  IT WILL TEST THE AMPLI-
FIERS IN A "FALSE MOTOR ON" PROCEDURE AND ALSO TEST THE MO-
TOR IN AN OPEN LOOP MODE.  IN THE OPEN LOOP MODE THE LOOP IS
OPENED AT THE INPUT TO THE FIRING CIRCUIT.
```

Choosing a Micro or Small MiniComputer System by Thomas Wrensch

```
YOU WILL BE ASKED QUESTIONS ABOUT THE SYSTEM YOU WISH TO IM-
PLEMENT.  AFTER YOU ARE DONE, A LIST OF SYSTEMS WILL BE
DISPLAYED.  THE LIST OF SYSTEMS WILL BE  RANKED BY HOW WELL
THEY FIT YOUR NEEDS.
```

Students in an undergraduate AI class can master the expert system shell syntax and successfully complete their projects during the final three weeks of the course. The systems they have produced range from 10 to 160 rules with an average of 40. The details of this experience in using a commercial expert system shell for instruction have been presented to illustrate the functionality of presently available expert system development tools. Many of these tools are very easy to learn, easy to use, and provide powerful and sophisticated features for building knowledge-based systems.

13.6 A CAUTIONARY NOTE

The reader should not conclude from the above discussion that one can simply buy a $400 expert system shell and begin cranking out an expert system every three weeks. The investment required to produce a significant, tested, commercial expert system is still significant in terms of both human and financial resources. MYCIN took over five years to build at a cost of more than 100 person-years of effort and the largest expert system ever built, R1/XCON required 180 person-years. However, the common wisdom of the AI community that building a commercial expert system requires 2 — 30 person years at a cost of $100,000 — $3,000,000[20,21] is in a state of radical revision as new productivity tools come on the market and expertise in building systems develops. Evidence of this increased productivity is apparent in British Petroleum's GASOIL, the second largest expert system ever built. Through the use of modern knowledge-based tools, this 2,500 rule system was built in just one person year.[22]

The cost of building knowledge-based systems is based on the cost of knowledge engineers which will continue to increase as the demand for new systems increases and on the cost of hardware and software tools which will continue to fall rapidly. The net effect is that the overall cost should steadily decline. This trend is apparent in Figure 13-2. Our own experience in which it took about 15 hours to create a 17 rule system confirms the prediction in this figure. In addition, it should be noted that there is a considerable range in the size, content, and sophistication of knowledge-based systems. This spectrum ranges from massive expert systems costing in the $million range to useful knowledge-based advisors which can be built for between $5,000 and $50,000. This reduced cost for production of useful knowledge-based systems will result in increased demand for this type of AI program.

The increased demand and resulting availability of both expert system shells and the knowledge-based products raises a number of questions and issues which we have not had to face previously. We classify these issues in the broad categories of *production pitfalls* and *social issues*.

PRODUCTION PITFALLS

Waterman devotes three chapters to the discussion of potential pitfalls in the production of knowledge-based systems.[23] Some of the most important pitfalls to avoid in building expert systems include:

• *Mismatch between problem difficulty and available resources* — It is easy to be over-optimistic and to underestimate the complexity of the problem and overestimate the resources which will be available for solving it. Suggestions for minimizing the risks of this trap include:

> 1. A clear understanding of the nature of expert systems and a solid commitment of support by management or the project funders. This must include a clear policy of making domain experts available to the knowledge engineers.
>
> 2. A prototype system to test the feasibility of the project. Such a prototype will help measure the problem complexity, the range of available resources, and the appropriateness of the problem and tools selected.
>
> 3. Avoidance of rigid timetables and production deadlines. This is particularly important on the the first expert system project on which considerable training and learning must occur.

• *Inappropriate choice of knowledge-base system building tool* — There is a great temptation, once one becomes familiar with a particular tool, to continue to try to apply it to all problems. This can lead to great inefficiency when the characteristics of the problem don't match the features of the tool. Suggestions for avoiding this problem include:

> 1. Use the highest level, specialized expert system language possible. This means staying as far right on the language/tool continuum of Figure 13-1 as possible. In particular, this means avoiding standard languages such as C, Pascal, and FORTRAN even through your development group will probably contain talented programmers in these languages. The expert system shells have been designed specifically to handle efficiently the knowledge representation structures most useful in building expert systems.
>
> 2. Choose a stable, well-supported tool. It it better to select a proven, well-reviewed expert system tool than a brand new one even though the new one may boast of more powerful features. The reason is that new systems are inherently full of bugs. Even proven systems newly ported to smaller delivery machines gen-

erally have bugs related to system implementation.

3. Switch systems if problems develop. If, during the development of the system, it becomes apparent that the original choice of knowledge representation is seriously hampering development of the system, it is better to switch to a more appropriate representation and the associated tool than to try to continue to "force" the present tool to do a job for which it is not suited. This advice also applies if the present tool contains too many bugs or is not well supported by its distributor.

• *Communication problems between domain expert and knowledge engineer* — A number of problems may develop involving the communication between the domain expert (who presumably is not expert in computer systems) and the knowledge engineer (who presumably is not expert in the domain). One of the most serious is lack of time and incentive on the part of the domain expert to work effectively with the knowledge engineer. Several ways of alleviating such problems include:

1. Before the project starts, get a firm commitment from the domain expert that s/he will be available on a regular basis. Waterman suggests an involvement of at least one half time. A clearly stated company or institutional policy in support of the project is helpful in obtaining this commitment.

2. Knowledge engineers initially unfamiliar with the domain should make a serious effort to master the fundamental concepts, techniques, and jargon of the domain of expertise. This not only helps avoid the "Tower of Babel" syndrome, but it also can prove interesting and stimulating.

3. Domain experts should become involved in hands-on system testing and validation. This is particularly important for domain experts who have little computer experience. The experience helps the expert develop an appreciation of the performance and limitations of the system tools and can be particularly useful in detecting simple conceptual errors introduced by the knowledge engineer.

• *The system implementation is slow and/or unfriendly* — It is not uncommon for poor design to result in initial versions of systems which have flawed performance. This may involve a large rule-based system with key concepts still missing, a rigid system lacking explanation features, a large system with so many highly specific rules that it runs slowly, or a poorly designed human interface that discourages users. Some design concepts which help avoid such difficulties include:

1. *Test and validate your system incrementally as it is being built.* This is a far more effective approach than the two phase approach of building the complete system and then testing it. The incremental technique is particularly easy for rule-based knowledge representations because of the stand-alone nature of production rules.

2. *As the system evolves, design and record a standard test protocol which the finished product must pass.* This will assure the performance tests passed during the development of the system will continue to be met as more rules are added. Otherwise you run the risk of the "tar baby" syndrome — the more you try fixing the system, the more you foul it up.

3. *Try to condense sets of special purpose rules into general categorical rules and variables.* This will not only reduce the number of rules required and speed up the final, run-time version of the system, but it will also make the operation of the system more transparent. The task of the knowledge engineer is to organize and classify the many specific rules provided by the domain expert in order to allow this generalization.

4. *The knowledge engineer should maintain high standards of human engineering in designing the user interface to the expert system.* Clear, concise natural language dialog should be used where ever possible, with a minimum of abbreviation. During time consuming searches or backward chaining, the system should inform the user of what is happening with a blinking message such as "Please stand by while I . . . ."

SOCIAL ISSUES

The risks of the production pitfalls discussed above may be minimized or avoided altogether by careful design and good programming style. Some more philosophical issues are related to the underlying assumptions of the wisdom of trying to capture and use human knowledge in machines. Our basic assumption to this point is clearly that knowledge-based systems are "good things" which will contribute positively to the general welfare of society. However, many of the obvious advantages of expert systems — their cumulative nature, their consistency, their inability to forget, their ease of duplication and distribution, their codification of knowledge, and their cheapness — all contain seeds of serious social problems which are worth considering. The problems they raise are far more serious than the rather trivial criticism raised by the Dreyfus brothers that expert systems do not really exhibit expertise.[24] The Dreyfus brothers argue that in every domain where "know-how" is required to make a judgement and brute force cannot substitute for understanding, rule-based computers cannot deliver expert performance, and it is highly unlikely that they ever will. If their analysis is correct, expert systems pose little threat to society — the real danger is that they are wrong.

A much sharper criticism has been voiced by Joseph Weizenbaum, the author of ELIZA.[25] He states:

> *"What could be more obvious than the fact that, whatever intelligence a computer can muster, however it may be acquired, it must always and necessarily be absolutely alien to any and all authentic human concerns. The very asking of the question, "What does a judge (or a psychiatrist) know that we cannot tell a computer?" is a monstrous obscenity. That it has to be put into print at all, even for the purpose of exposing its morbidity, is a sign of the madness of our times."*

The essence of the problem can be captured by answers to the question:

> **What happens to society as the computer takes over more and more functions formerly requiring human insight, judgement, and intelligence?**

As one possible answer to this question, consider the following scenario. The success of XCON and PROSPECTOR in the early 1980's led to a rapid growth in the availability of high quality, powerful expert system shells in the mid 1980's. By the late 1980's expert systems emerging from these shells were providing aggressive organizations with a very clear and much publicized productivity advantage over conventional operations. In response, by the early 1990's essentially all major industries and institutions had established expert system development groups and were beginning to utilize the product systems in routine operations.

The startling discovery revealed by this movement was the enormous range of middle management and professional personnel which could be effectively replaced by lower level personnel working with sophisticated expert systems. Top management of industrial and high-tech firms found that a $25,000/year technician using a diagnostic expert system could trouble shoot and maintain complex equipment just as effectively as a $50,000 engineer. Although the expert system cost $100,000 to build and customize, the cost could be pro-rated over the company's 25 technicians (formerly engineers) at a tremendous savings. Banks found that most of the analyses of prospective loans formerly requiring a vice president or chief loan officer could be done more consistently and profitably by tellers using standardized expert systems with access to databases containing the borrower's credit records. Hospitals, human service organizations, and local governments found that many of the middle management positions involved evaluation and decision making based on clearly specified policies and rules which were easily codified by commercially available expert systems.

The response of other social institutions was even more diverse and interesting. The Pentagon, as one of the earliest supporters of expert systems, soon became completely reliant on "battlefield manager" systems. The total amount of data available from the battle scene was so overwhelming that only a machine could digest it and make reasonable tactical decisions in a finite amount of time. The most dramatic impact of expert systems on the military, however, was the President's 1995 decision to automate the mid-echelons of the armed services. The Blue Ribbon Commission on Military Effectiveness had determined that 80 percent of the military command structure, particularly in the logistics and supply branch, was performing routine decision making which could be done more efficiently by draftees using expert systems. When the 1994 budgetary crunch required a choice between mid-phase testing of the Strategic Defense Initiative and the middle management career officer, the President chose SDI and expert systems.

The integration of expert systems into the professions also followed some interesting twists and turns. Early court decisions determined that the doctor was legally responsible for problems arising from mis-diagnosis by medical expert systems under his/her control. This was followed shortly by several successful suits by doctors claiming that defects in the medical expert systems had caused them damage. By this time, however, the medical profession was so reliant on expert systems that a select panel of the American Medical Association was established to set criteria and guidelines for certification of medical expert systems. The panel worked diligently from 1992 to 1996 and produced the Standard Code of Accepted Medical Practice (SCAMP) which was to become the benchmark against which medical diagnosticians, both human and artificial, were measured. All existing diagnostic systems were revised to bring them into conformity with SCAMP, and all new systems entering the market were certified by the SCAMP Evaluation and Review committee as meeting SCAMP code. Since expert systems with SCAMP certification essentially defined good medical practice, the number of law suits launched against medical expert systems dropped abruptly to zero and the number of malpractice suits against physicians using expert systems declined sharply.

The case of law followed a somewhat different path. Lawyers themselves soon learned the advantages of legal expert systems in saving them time in legal research and automating many of the tedious tasks of the law office. However, as commercial products, these legal expert systems soon fell into the hands of a brash new breed of *legal advisors*, typically an organization of recent college graduates in business and the humanities with one or two computer hackers thrown in. By advertising legal services at 20—50 percent of the standard rates, legal advisors soon found themselves in one of the fastest growing professions. The key to their success was the Legal Shield Guarantee (LSG) under which they guaranteed their legal advice and services 100 percent against all monetary damages arising from trials in court. Since the expert systems on which they relied incorporated all existing law and all important major precedents, damages rarely occurred.

The response of society to the widespread introduction of knowledge-based systems was interesting and, in retrospect, quite understandable. Initial doubts and suspicion as to their effectiveness soon gave way to more relaxed attitudes and passive acceptance by the general public. In fact, those studying social organization and institutional behavior detected a distinct improvement in the operations of organizations which correlated directly with the extent to which expert systems were implemented. The codification of knowledge and the automation of routine decision making provided a new environment of efficient, smooth, dependable, predictable social intercourse. The competition, disagreements, arguments, and *ad hominem* attacks which marked the earlier period of human decision making gradually disappeared in this new age in which the computer generally "knew best."

Serious questions raised by this scenarios include the following:

- *What happens to all the displaced middle managers?* While this is the perennial Luddite concern of unemployment due to automation, the target group of experts threatened by expert systems is better educated and capable of being more vocal than victims of previous "employment shifts."

- *Will the number of real human experts decline?* The advantages of an artificial expert over a human expert have been discussed *ad nauseam* and virtually assures us that the answer will be "yes". The real question is: What will be the impact of society of this loss of human expertise?

- *How will new knowledge be generated if human experts disappear?* Machines may provide excellent delivery systems for existing knowledge, but they cannot do (or at least to date, have not done) the research which generated the knowledge. Human experts, particularly within the university, typically both generate and disseminate knowledge.

• *Will expert systems promote social conformity and rigidity?* After a company has invested $1 million in a new marketing and pricing expert system and it has performed flawlessly for five years, how willing will top management be to modify it in the face of changing market conditions? If local, county, and state government develop a network of expert systems for allocating resources for human services, how flexible will be its response to a human or natural disaster? Would Einstein have flunked an expert-system-administered exam for his patent office position based on his mediocre elementary school performance?

• *Will expert systems promote social and scientific stagnation?* DENDRAL has already proven itself capable of analyzing mass spectrometer data at the level of a Ph.D. chemist. If DENDRAL is extended to encompass all standard chemical analysis techniques and heuristics, is it not possible that a B.S. chemist skillful in the use of DENDRAL could fill the position presently occupied by a Ph.D. chemist? Will such a combination be as productive and creative as the present research-oriented Ph. D.? What becomes of the proven "critical mass of colleagues" concept for stimulating productive research when some of the colleagues are machines? What happens to interdisciplinary research when knowledge becomes embedded in "brittle" expert systems (brittle systems are those unable to detect the limits of their knowledge)? Can expert systems with their non-expert human servants replace the rambunctious, spasmodic, error-prone, but sometimes brilliant performance of human beings? Will the "good enough" and "functional" ethics which evolve from machine codification of knowledge replace the traditional ethic of the "search for excellence"?

One's answer to these questions depends very much on one's philosophical outlook. Social pessimists will continue to discover these problems, shout the alarm, and claim credit for saving humankind when their predictions do not materialize. Social optimists will point out that we've been through it all before in the industrial revolution, the information revolution, and now the knowledge revolution, so why worry? Humankind does have a genius for developing and mastering new tools and coping with their side effects. Its experience with expert systems should provide another fascinating case study.

PROBLEMS AND PROGRAM

13-1. Discuss MYCIN/EMYCIN as a case study in the separating the knowledge base from the inference engine in a system.

13-2. In some cases, the expert system shell evolved from a pre-existing expert system and in other cases a rule based language was used to write subsequent expert systems. Cite an example of each type of development, and suggest a hypothesis based on your readings to explain the different development paths.

13-3. Various languages, editors, and operating systems offer a variety of *environments* in which to write programs. List three languages with which you are familiar and discuss the environment provided by each, clearly identifying the machine and system under which each runs. Which provides the most features? Which is easiest to use?

13-4. Davis' Law states: *For every tool there is a task perfectly suited to it.* Suggest a task (expert system problem) perfectly suited to EXSYS. Suggest another task for which EXSYS would be quite unsuitable.

13-5. One mode for configuring the development/delivery hardware system is to use a large central computer as the inference engine in a network of personal computers as the delivery system. Compare the advantages and disadvantages of such a system with the three other modes of operation discussed in the text.

13-6. Figure 13-2 shows no signs of an asymptotic limit on the "Engineering Hours/Rule" axis although human response times must provide one. What limit would you suggest for Engineering Hours/-Rule(min) for human designed rules? What automated procedures might make it possible to break through this limit?

13-7. Several new microcomputers presently available from IBM, Apple, Commodore, and Atari have capabilities equivalent to or exceeding those of the Carnegie-Mellon University "3M" machine (1 Megabyte RAM, 1 MFLOPS, 1 Million pixel graphics). Describe three such machines and compare their features to those of the 3M machine.

13-8. Discuss and compare the capabilities of the two microcomputer-based expert system shells, M.1 and EXSYS. How do you explain the difference in pricing policy?

13-9. Which of the systems discussed in the Survey of Expert System Software are direct descendents of the original expert systems described in the Survey of Expert Systems chapter?

13-10. Schank has written extensively on the phenomenon of the spin-off company started by university faculty to market systems developed through university research. Discuss the rationale for such ventures and the benefits they provide. What problems and conflict of interest situations might arise from these ventures?

13-11. From the examples given, discuss how the menu-driven qualifier/value conditions of EXSYS can provide a very impressive natural language dialog without sophisticated natural language parsing of the user's input.

13-12. In what fundamental aspects does the SAILING CRAFT IDENTIFIER resemble the MYCIN expert system? How do they differ?

13-13. Consider the problem of writing a Computer Science Advisor (or a Discipline X Advisor where Discipline X is your major). Using the list of degree requirements and course descriptions from your college catalog, outline the structure of the Advisor, indicate the variables required, estimate the number of rules it would require, and write down five example rules in standard production rule format.

13-14. Many of the adventure games available for computers lend themselves to a production rule based expert system format. Write a brief scenario of a portion of one of these games in terms of a set of production rules.

13-15. One of the most essential requirements for a successful expert system building project is commitment on the part of management. Discuss several pitfalls which such commitment will help avoid.

13-16. The text advises that one stay as far to the right on the language/tool spectrum shown in Figure 13-1 as possible. What special circumstances or problem can you think of which might require at least portions of the expert system to be written in a language such as C, LISP or Prolog?

13-17. A good, user-friendly interface helps avoid problems of user acceptance of new expert systems. What Macintosh-like or MS-Windows features would you suggest for improving the EXSYS editor and run-time programs?

13-18. Write a critique of the scenario for social acceptance of expert systems presented in the text. What additional social reactions or episodes would you predict?

13-19. What additional beneficial social effects would you expect from the wide-spread introduction of knowledge-based systems?

13-20. A number of socially detrimental side-effects were mentioned specifically or implied in the text. Rank the top three problems in order of the risk you see them posing to society and briefly justify your answer. What additional problems do you see associated with the massive introduction of expert systems?

13-21. Any technology that threatens significant changes in the way society operates generates vocal and sometimes violent opposition. How would you answer the criticism that has already been made of expert systems by the Dreyfus brothers and by Weizenbaum? From what quarters and on what basis do you expect the strongest criticism to come in the future?

13-22. What technical and market forces do you think are behind the steady shift of implementation language from LISP to C and other conventional languages?

13-23. Write a critical evaluation of the proposition (pro or con): *By 1995 every major technical device will come equipped with a diagnostic expert system.*

FOOTNOTES AND REFERENCES

1 Buchanan, Bruce G. and Shortliffe, Edward H., *Rule-Based Expert Systems*, pp. 295–328, Addison-Wesley Publishing Company, Reading, MA (1984)

2 van Melle, W., Scott, A. C., Bennett, J. S., and Peairs, M., *The EMYCIN Manual.* Report No. HPP-81-16, Computer Science Department, Stanford University (1981)

3 Hayes-Roth, Frederick, Waterman, Donald A., and Lenat, Douglas B. (eds), *Building Expert Systems*, pp. 169–215, Addison-Wesley, Reading, MA (1983)

[4] Harmon, Paul and King, David, *Expert Systems — Artificial Intelligence in Business*, John Wiley & Sons, Inc. New York, NY (1985)

[5] Waterman, Donald A., *A Guide to Expert Systems,* Addison-Wesley Publishing Company, Reading, MA (1986)

[6] Voelcker, John, "Microprocessors," *IEEE Spectrum* **23**, pp. 46–48, January (1986)

[7] Schank, Roger C., *The Cognitive Computer,* pp. 248–264, Addison-Wesley Publishing Company, Inc., Reading, MA (1984)

[8] Shafer, Daniel G., "Microcomputer-based expert systems: where we are, where we are headed," *Expert Systems* **2**, No. 4, pp. 188–195, October (1985)

[9] Walker, Terri C., and Miller, Richard K., *EXPERT SYSTEMS 1986 — An Assessment of Technology and Applications,* SEAI Technical Publications, Madison, GA (1986)

[10] Richer, Mark H., "An Evaluation of Expert System Development Tools," *Expert Systems* **3**, pp. 166–183, Summer (1986)

[11] Brownston, Lee, Farrell, Robert, Kant, Elaine, and Martin, Nancy, *Programming Expert systems in OPS5,* Addison-Wesley Publishing Company, Inc. Reading, MA (1985)

[12] Product News, *Expert Systems* **2**, No. 3, pp. 172–173, July (1985)

[13] Stefic, Mark, Bobrow, Daniel G., Mittal, Sanjay, and Conway, Lynn, "Knowledge Programming in LOOPS: Report on an Experimental Course," *AI Magazine,* pp. 3–13, Fall (1983)

[14] Brownston, Lee et al, *Op Cit,* pp. 35–37

[15] *PC Magazine,* Vol. 4, Number 8, pp. 108–189, April 16 (1985)

[16] Michaelsen, Robert H., Michie, Donald, and Boulanger, Albert, "The Technology of Expert Systems," *BYTE* **10**, No. 4, p. 303, April (1985)

[17] Lehner, Paul E. and Barth, Stephen W., "Expert Systems on Microcomputers," *Expert Systems* **2**, No. 4., pp. 198–208, October (1985)

18 Dungan, Chris W. and Chandler, John S., "Auditor: A micro-computer-based expert system to support auditors in the field," *Expert Systems* **2**, No. 4., pp. 210–221, October (1985)

19 Stone, Jeffrey, "The AAAI-86 Conference Exhibits: New Directions for Commercial AI," *AI Magazine* **8**, No. 1, pp. 49–54, Spring (1987)

20 Waterman, Donald A., *Op Cit*, p. 180

21 Hayes, Rick Stephan, "Expert Systems — A Summary," *Expertise* **1**, No. 2, pp. 13–17, February (1986)

22 Applications Section, "Ten Minutes to Lay the Foundations," *Expert Systems User*, pp. 16–19, August (1986)

23 Waterman, Donald A., *Op Cit*, p. 186–199

24 Dreyfus, Hubert and Dreyfus, Stuart, "Why Expert Systems Do Not Exhibit Expertise," *IEEE Expert* **1**, No. 2, pp. 86–90, Summer (1986)

25 Weizenbaum, Joseph, *Computer Power and Ruman Reason*, pp. 226–227, W. H. Freeman and Company, San Francisco, CA (1976)

Chapter 14

PATTERN RECOGNITION

(PHOTO: COURTESY OF RANDALL DAVIS)

Dr. Randall Davis is Associate Professor of Computer Science in the Sloan School of Management at MIT. He received the B.A. from Dartmouth College and the Ph.D. in Artificial Intelligence from Stanford University. While at Stanford he contributed to the MYCIN project and developed TEIRESIAS, a tool for knowledge acquisition. His research focuses on systems that work from descriptions of structure and function and that are capable of reasoning from first principles. He is coauthor of *Knowledge-Based Systems in Artificial Intelligence* and serves on the editorial board of the journal *Artificial Intelligence*. He serves as consultant to several organizations and is a founding consultant of Teknowledge, Inc.

14: PATTERN RECOGNITION

14.1 INTRODUCTION

Many of the AI applications presented up to this point may be interpreted in pattern recognition terms. Several early successes in natural language processing were based on matching input sentence patterns with standard pre-defined patterns of sentence structure. In game theory, certain board positions can be interpreted and recognized most efficiently as patterns. An essential element of Prolog interpreters, semantic networks, and production rule systems is the pattern matcher which searches the knowledge base for a match with the input command, network segment, or rule.

Another pattern matching application which many readers have probably used frequently is the *search* or *change* commands available on most word processors. All file handling commands also involve a pattern matching search of the file directory for the requested file. Because pattern matching is such an important technique in computer science, a whole language and literature has evolved in the area. A good introduction to the subject of pattern classification is presented in Duda and Hart,[1] a good discussion of useful mathematical tools provided in Sedgewick,[2] and a formal grammar approach to pattern recognition is presented by Fu.[3]

As we will see in the next chapter, the interpretation of 3-D scenes can, under controlled circumstances, be performed by matching the pattern from a 2-D image with the pattern generated by projecting a real 3-D object onto a 2-D screen. The emerging fields of voice input and scene analysis rely heavily on pattern matching. Finally, the commercially important area of robotics provides a huge potential application area for pattern matching concepts and algorithms as robots acquire the senses of hearing and sight.

14.2 APPLICATIONS OF PATTERN RECOGNITION

The range of pattern recognition applications is broad indeed. Some of the more interesting areas include:

- *Voice recognition* — Some government agencies use voice recognition as the employee's "key" to restricted areas.

• *Fingerprint identification* — Computerized fingerprint systems have reduced the search time from days to minutes.

• *Face identification* — Law enforcement agencies are particularly interested in such systems for scanning large files of "wanted" posters.

• *Handwriting identification* — Foolproof systems would be of great benefit to the banking community.

• *Optical Character Recognition* — OCR is now used widely throughout food chain and other retail stores to increase productivity at the check-out counter.

• *Biological slide analysis* — Chromosome and blood cell counting can be done faster and more accurately using automated counting systems.

• *High energy physics analysis* — The automatic scanning of spark chamber and bubble chamber film has relieved humans of extremely tedious and error-prone analysis.

• *Meteorological data analysis* — Earth satellites can produce weather system photographs faster than humans can scan them.

• *Surveillance satellite data reduction* — The computer can help scan for telltale patterns indicating new weapons deployment or troop buildup.

• *Robot vision* — Many robotics applications in highly constrained environments use pattern recognition with computer vision for unique identification of objects on the assembly line.

14.3 STRUCTURE OF PATTERN RECOGNITION SYSTEMS

Pattern recognition systems tend to share a characteristic system structure. The elements of a pattern recognition system is usually composed of:

1) **Input Transducer** — The input transducer converts the pattern being analyzed into an electronic signal. Commonly used devices include video cameras, image digitizers, flying spot scanners, and microphones. An excellent discussion of the role of transducers in spanning the gap between physical quantities and their symbolic repre-

sentation is given by Pylyshyn.[4]

2) **Preprocessor** — Preprocessors perform additional conditioning of the signal and may include such functions as amplification, spatial filtering, spectrum analysis, and analog-to-digital conversion.

3) **Feature Extractor** — Feature extractors, sometimes called discriminators, perform functions such as template matching, spatial coincidence, and application of "decision surfaces."

4) **Response Selector** — Response selectors are algorithms for selecting the stored pattern which best matches the input pattern. Techniques involve searches, sorts, and least-squares analysis.

5) **Output Systems** — Output systems may be voice generators, graphics, or standard video terminal output. The application of interest will determine the most effective output medium.

In this chapter we will look in more detail at three areas in which pattern matching has proven particularly successful. These areas include:

- Letter recognition algorithm (2-D pattern recognition)
- Spatial reconstruction (pattern recognition in 3-D)
- Voice recognition

These three applications of pattern recognition share the following features, even though they are drawn from widely different areas:

- They each involve the recognition of significant information in the presence of a large "noise" background.

- They each represent applications of pattern recognition techniques to "real world" problems.

- They provide new channels (similar to our senses) through which computers may gain knowledge about their environment more efficiently with a resulting increase in the apparent intelligence of the computers.

Through sophisticated algorithms and hard work, successful pattern recognition systems have been developed in each of the problem areas.

14.4 CHARACTER RECOGNITION — PATTERNS IN 2-D

Character recognition has proven to be an excellent test bed for many of the ideas proposed for pattern recognition. Since the "meaning" of a character is determined by simple identification, character recognizers perform the AI function of extracting meaning from a representation. Oliver Selfridge and his co-workers described the difficulty in identifying input characters by pattern matching and proposed a demon-oriented, parallel processing algorithm they called Pandemonium.[5] The first problem encountered in matching an unknown input character with an inventory of template patterns of the same font involves the three transformations of translation, scaling, and rotation as indicated in Figure 14-1.

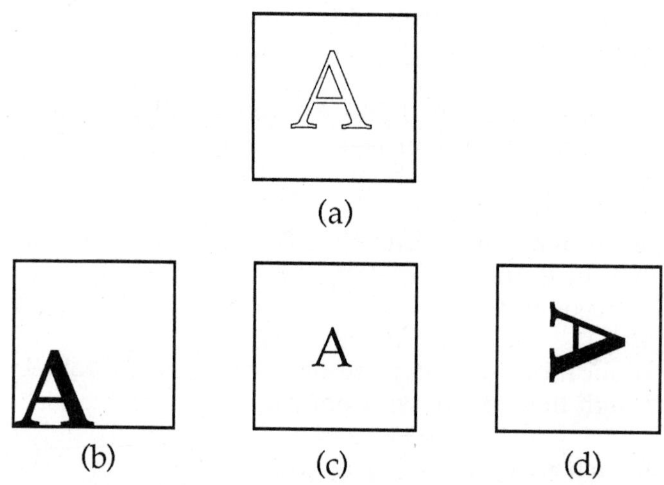

Figure 14-1 Transformations required for template matching In order to match stored template (a) with the input characters shown in the second line requires: (b) translation, (c) scaling, and (d) rotation. An actual template matching for the general case will require some combination of all three transformations.

Once the transformation problem is solved, one can generalize to the problem of transforming between fonts. The difficulties are illustrated in Figure 14-2 and can be summarized by the question: What is an "A"? Humans have an amazing ability to detect the "A-ness" of an object which far exceeds that of any machine recognition program built to date. The solution to this difficult problem is generally of the form of some kind of machine learning. By training the machine by a large collection of identified "A"s of various fonts, it can memorize the variety and range of characteristic features for use in character recognition. One of the first machine learning programs was developed by Leonard Uhr and his colleagues for the purpose of recognizing hand-printed characters.[6] Character recognition from various viewpoints using connectionist models (discussed in the last chapter) continues to be a topic of active research.[7]

An area of character recognition involving even greater difficulty and great practical benefit is the recognition of hand-written characters. Because of the variability of hand writing, the recognition of hand-drawn characters is significantly more difficult than the recognition of standard type fonts. The interpretation of standard fonts is now considered a fairly straightforward exercise in pattern recognition. Programs capable of letter recognition are now available on machines ranging from microcomputers to mainframes.

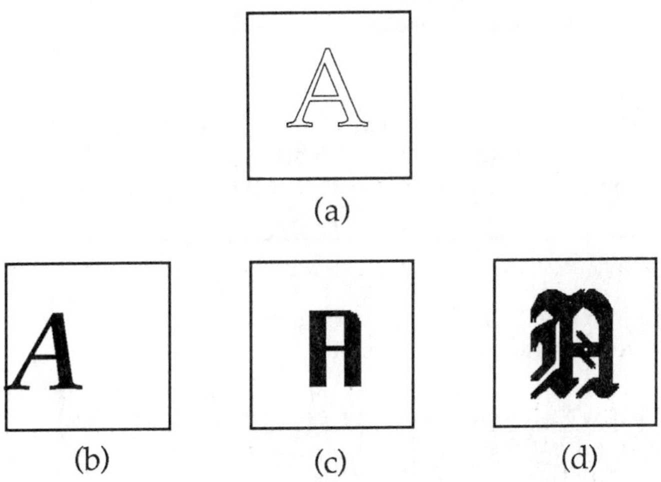

Figure 14-2 Variations on the A Theme The variety of fonts make a generic definition of characters difficult. The overlap between stored template (a) and input characters (b), (c), and (d) would all be poor. The optimum solution for recognizing variety of this type involves machine learning.

TEITELMAN'S RECOGNIZER OF HAND-WRITTEN CHARACTERS

Important early work on hand-written character recognition was done by Teitelman.[8] The Ledeen version of Teitelman's recognizer program is presented here.[9] As in so many other problems of AI, the essential concept of the character recognizer lies in the appropriate representation of input information for efficient subsequent search. The task is to capture the essential information required for a unique identification in the presence of an infinite range of variation.

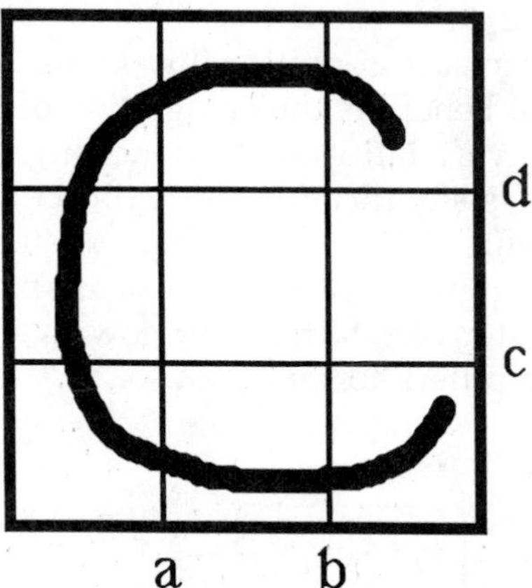

Figure 14-3 The hand-written letter "C" Teitelman's recognizer uses a grid to classify each stroke by a 16-bit representation based on the starting location of the stroke and the number of crossings of each grid line.

Consider the letter "C" as shown in Figure 14-3. The Ledeen-Teitelman algorithm involves the following steps:

1) Draw a rectangle bounding each stroke of the letter. Clearly a "C" is a one stroke letter.

2) Divide the rectangular region into nine equal sub-regions by the "tic-tac-toe" grid as shown.

3) Represent the stroke with a 16-bit encoding system as shown.

The first bit of each 4-bit sub-code indicates the starting location for the stroke, and the next three bits indicate the number of line crossings. Horizontal lines, vertical lines, and dots present special problems for this scheme and are represented as follows:

Horizontal line, left → right	9-9-0-8
Horizontal line, right → left	1-1-0-8
Vertical line, downward	0-8-1-1
Vertical line, upward	0-8-9-9
Dot	0-8-0-8

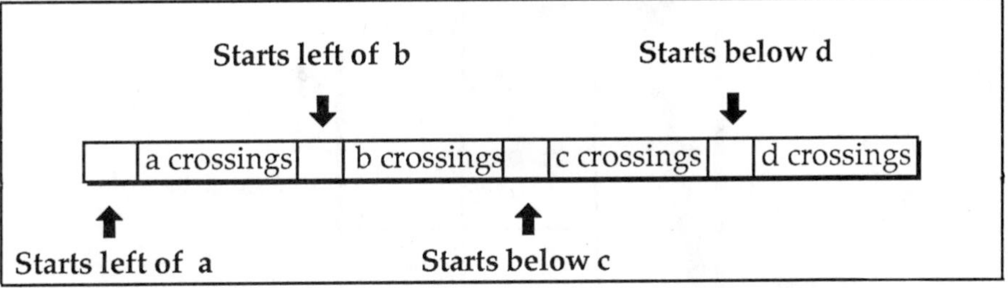

Figure 14-4 Encoding system for Teitelman's recognizer The 16-bit word is divided into 4 four-bit parts, with 1 bit representing starting information and 3 bits for the number of crossings of the region lines. Using this code, the letter "C" may be encoded as 2-2-1-1.

The remarkable result of this work is that any stroke one may use in writing (printed) letters may be uniquely represented by this code. Examples of the code for two more letters are shown in Figure 14-5:

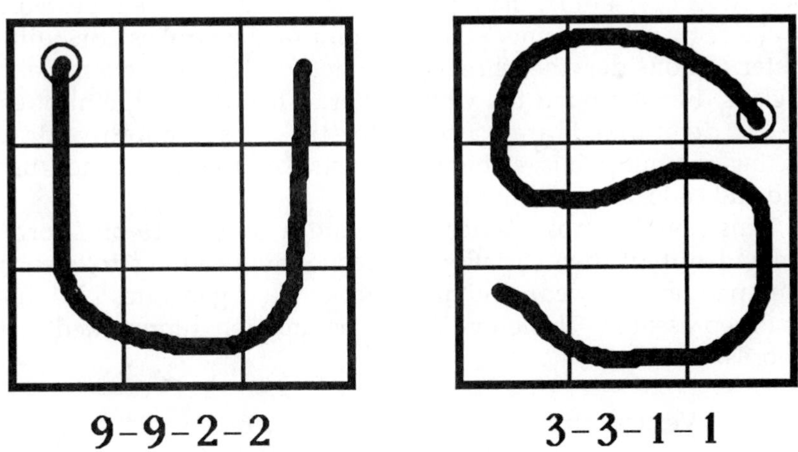

Figure 14-5 Teitelman algorithm Examples of coding of single stroke letters using the encoding scheme described above. Circle indicates starting point of stroke.

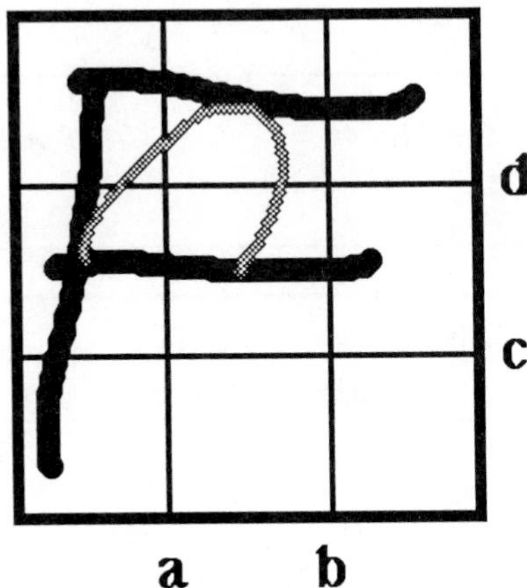

Figure 14-6 The letter "F" set up for Teitelman's recognizer Note the pseudo-stroke connection of the mid-points of three letter strokes. The pseudo- stroke is encoded using the same system as regular strokes.

4) To encode the relative positions of strokes in multi-stroke letters such as *E*, *F*, and *H*, the representation used in (3) is repeated for the stroke required to connect the midpoint of the strokes constituting the letter. Consider the three-stroke letter "*F*", for example. A rectangle is drawn around the whole letter. Then the midpoint of each stroke is determined and a pseudo-stroke is smoothly drawn connecting the midpoints. This pseudo-stroke is then encoded using the grid and code described in (3).

Thus, single stroke letters generate a single, 16-bit word to uniquely identify it (two variations corresponding to the stroke and its reversed path are allowed), and an N-stroke letter generates N+1 16-bit words to represent it. The letter "*F*" can be uniquely represented by the four words:

Vertical stroke	0-8-1-1
Top horizontal stroke	9-9-0-8
Center horizontal stroke	9-9-0-8
Relative position pseudo stroke	9-8-0-10

5) The final phase of the recognizer is the table-look-up routine. In order to standardize the representation, a transpose is performed on this array, generating the following representation of an "*F*":

First component	0-9-9-9
Second component	8-9-9-8

Third component	1-0-0-0
Fourth component	1-8-8-10

Note that every letter has four components according to this scheme. The four entry code is extended to 5 entries to accommodate 4 stroke characters such as *E*. The look-up table or dictionary is then stored in four sections, portions of which are shown:

Section 1

9-9-0-0-0	(A,3), (F,3)
0-12-9-0-0-0	(B,3)
2-0-0-0-0	(C,3)
0-10-9-0-0	(D,3)
0-9-9-9-9	(E,3)
0-9-9-9-0	(E,4),(F,4)
etc.	

Section 2

9-9-8-0-0	(A,3),(F,3)
8-12-8-0-0	(B,3)
2-0-0-0-0	(C,3)
8-10-8-0-0	(D,3)
8-9-9-9-8	(E,3)
etc.	

Section 3

10-0-0-0-0	(A,3)
2-0-0-0-0	(F,3),(G,3)
1-1-0-0-0	(B,3),(D,3),(H,3),(J,3)
1-0-0-0-0	(C,3),(F,4),(I,3)
1-0-0-0-1	(E,3)
etc.	

Section 4

10-8-8-0-0	(A,3)
1-1-8-0-0	(B,3),(D,3)
1-0-0-0-0	(C,3)
1-8-8-8-10	(E,3)
2-8-8-8-0	(E,4)
etc.	

The pattern recognizer should find the letter it has just encoded represented in the table, with each of the four parts appearing in each section of the table one or more times. Since certain letters may be drawn various ways, they will appear a number of times in each section . To help resolve ambiguities between nearly identical letters, the weighting system shown next to the letter is used. The interpretation with the highest weight is considered the correct one. If matching entries are found in fewer than two of the four sections, the recognizer reports failure to recognize the character.

An interesting variation of pattern recognition in hand writing analysis has been reported which indicates the uniqueness of signature identification. By extending the representation system to include the time and pressure profile of hand-written signatures, it was found that the personal signature is a completely unique identification of the individual. Professional forgers could duplicate a given signature with considerable prompting by the computer, but after a few minutes break, the forgers' ability was lost. The rate at which we sign our names and the pressure we exert is at least as unique as the actual pattern the pen traces on the paper. As soon as our signature is complete, the time and pressure information disappears which means, in effect, that we have "thrown away the key". This scheme promises one of the most foolproof systems of personal identification ever developed.

Computer recognition of text, both hand and machine written, continues to be an exciting and productive area of research. One original motivation of the research was to develop a practical reader for hand-coded FORTRAN programs. An excellent summary of the work in this area has been prepared by the IEEE.[10]

14.5 PATTERN RECOGNITION IN 3-D

One of the most productive research tools for the study of elementary particles and the forces between them has been the bubble chamber, a device invented by the Nobel laureate Donald Glaser. Bubble chamber photographs consist of pictures of the tracks of the elementary particles of nature. These form characteristic patterns of tree, kink, and "V" structure which may be classified by a "grammar of particle interactions." The objective of an AI system for analysis of this data is to extract the meaning of a given event by the correct identification of each particle and measurement of its momentum.

The basic principle of the bubble chamber transducer uses the property that charged particles will leave a clearly marked trail of bubbles when passing through a superheated, transparent liquid such as liquid hydrogen. By synchronizing a sharp decompression of the chamber with a burst of beam particles, the liquid-filled chamber becomes sensitive to boiling at exactly the time during which beam particles pass through. There is a finite probability, in fact about 1 in 10 for a typical chamber, that one of the beam particles will strike a hydrogen atom nucleus (a proton) in a cataclysmic collision in which the energy of the beam particle is transformed into creation of new, massive particles. A small subset of these particles have quantum numbers which

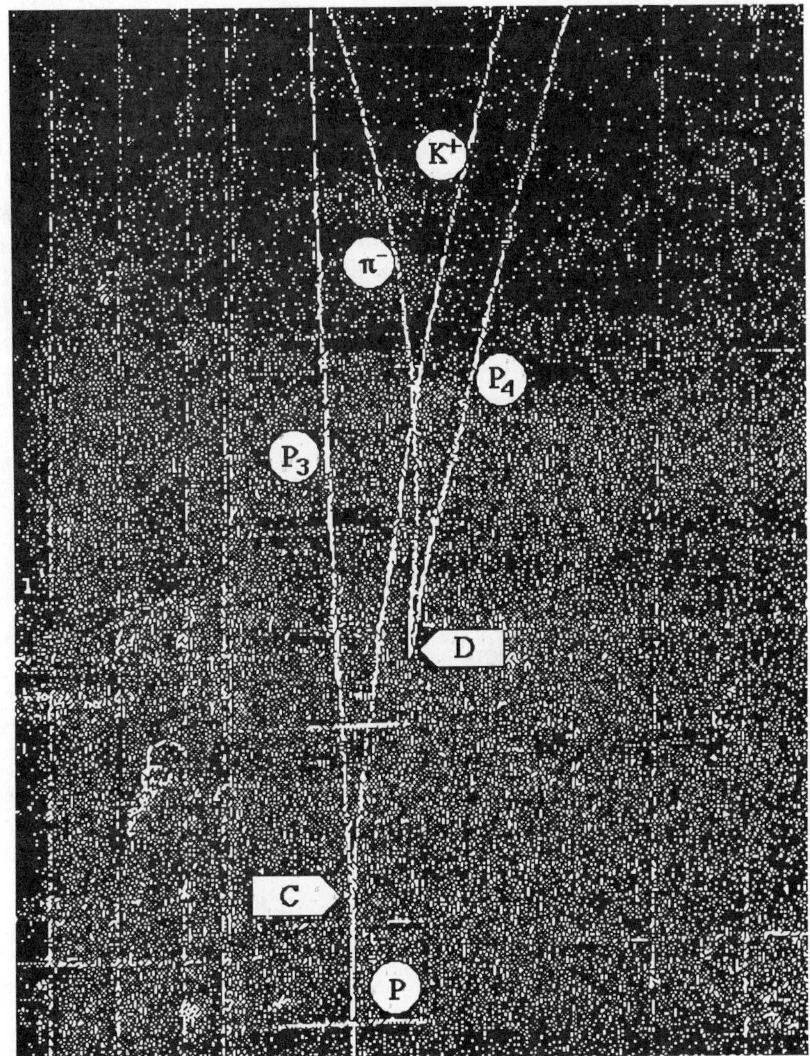

Figure 14-7 Creation of a strange Λ° particle in proton-proton collisions One of the protons strikes a hydrogen nucleus and in the process is converted into a (K^+, Λ°) pair of new elementary particles. The Λ° particle created at **C** flies through the chamber (invisibly) to point **D** where it decays into a proton and a negative pion. This "V" signature identifies it uniquely as the decay of a strange particle.

characterize them as "strange." The object of the experiment discussed here was to study the production of such particles. Photographs of such collisions provide information on the particle identities and angular distributions which tell physicists a great deal about the basic constituents of matter and what forces bind them in the proton.

The physical process which enables physicists to "see" the particles emerging from collisions in the bubble chamber is the boiling of the temporarily superheated hydrogen about the ion pairs created by energetic charged particles passing through the hydrogen target. The strings of tiny bubbles along the paths of charged particles are photographed by a system of three cameras located so as to obtain optimum stereoscopic views of the chamber. Thus, the transducer for this particular pattern recognition task is the system composed of bubble chamber plus associated synchronized cameras. A typical bubble chamber photo produced by this system is shown in Figure 14-7.[11]

The interpretation of this collision may be expressed in the form of a chemical reaction as shown.

$$P + P \rightarrow P_3 + K^+ + \Lambda^\circ$$

where

P = beam proton and target proton
P_3 = final state proton
K^+ = a "K" meson, a strange particle of positive charge
Λ° = a lambda particle, a strange particle with zero charge

The Λ°, being neutral, leaves no visible track in the chamber as it flies from its point of creation **C** to its point of radioactive decay **D** about 1/3 nanosecond later. The decay process may be written as:

$$\Lambda^\circ \rightarrow P_4 + \pi^-$$

where

π^- = a negative pion
P_4 = a decay product proton

The decay products of the Λ° particle appear as the positive proton and negative pion whose tracks form a characteristic "V".

A second example of a characteristic pattern which indicates the nature of the elementary particles produced in high energy collisions is the decay "kink" shown in Figure 14-8. Here a positive pi meson decays at the kink point into a visible positive muon (whose path is about 1 centimeter long) and an invisible neutrino.

How is it possible to unambiguously identify the particles emerging from these violent collisions in a bubble chamber? The analysis of such events represents a classical example of pattern recognition. Most bubble chamber analysis systems may be classified on a

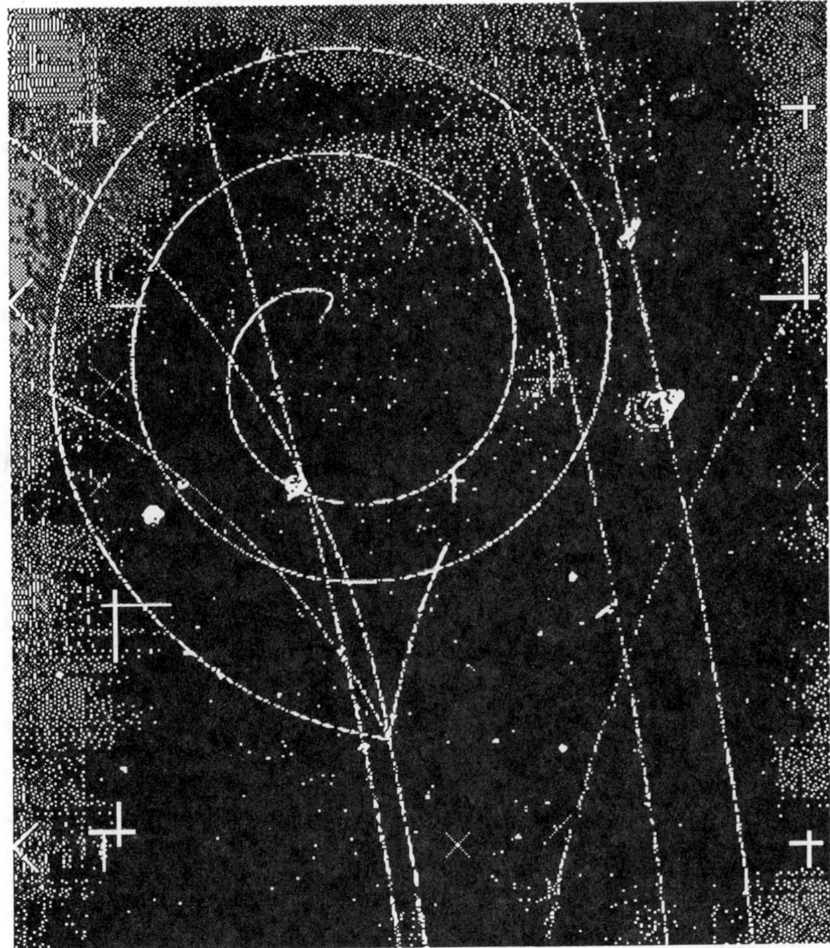

Figure 14-8 Production of four charged elementary particles In this bubble chamber photograph, an incident negative pion strikes a proton and in the collision process, four new elementary particles are created from the energy of the beam pion. One of these is a positive pion which spirals to rest and decays into a positive muon. The + and × symbols are fiducial marks etched on the front and back windows of the chamber for establishing the coordinate system.

spectrum ranging from completely manual systems to totally automated systems.

MANUAL BUBBLE CHAMBER FILM ANALYSIS SYSTEM

In the experiment from which the sample photographs were taken, 37,000 photographs of the Brookhaven National Laboratory 80-inch hydrogen bubble chamber were analyzed by a team of physicists, student scanners, and professional measuring machine operators. The process of identifying the physical reactions occurring on the film involved the following steps:

1) All film was scanned on three-projector scanning tables by humans searching for violent reactions called "multi-pronged" events. Such events signal the creation of new particles from the energy of the beam particle.

2) When an event was found it was examined in detail to see if there was evidence of the decay of strange particles. Evidence included the characteristic "V" decay of neutral strange particles and characteristic "kinks" of charged particle decays.

3) When a strange particle event was identified, the frame number of the event was noted and the picture was sent to a precision measuring machine. A human operator, using a cross-hair on a magnified image, measured 4 to 10 points on each track of the event in each of two or three stereoscopic views.

4) The measurements served as input data for a geometric reconstruction program which used the known magnetic field and camera and fiducial mark positions to reconstruct the particle paths as circular arcs in 3-D space.

5) Using the momentum obtained from the measured radius of the track, various particle identity hypotheses, constrained by the four conservation laws of energy and momentum, were examined. This use of physical laws provides a beautiful example of the addition of knowledge in the form of constraints imposed by the laws of nature for extracting information from a scene analysis.

6) As events were classified by final state, they were stored for later analysis of the kinematics of the reaction. From such kinematic analysis, the physics of the creation process could be studied.

AUTOMATED SYSTEMS — THOMPSON'S SPATIAL COHERENCE ALGORITHM

The problem with such manual experimental methods is that they are very tedious and labor intensive. The experiment cited here was a relatively small one. Larger experiments often require hundreds of thousands of pictures. The manual analysis of just one experiment frequently involves between 10 and 100 person-years of careful, detailed human pattern recognition analysis.

The solution to this experimental bottleneck is to automate as much of the analysis as possible. A number of experimental groups recognized that by careful control of the optics and lighting conditions, high quality photographs could be obtained which would be measured by automatic "flying spot" digitizers. These digitizers use a highly focused beam of light to scan across the photograph. An electronic photo-detector behind the film detects the presence of bubbles by a spike in the light intensity passing through the film. The question then becomes: How can the 3-D track coordinates be extracted from two or more digitized 2-D images?

One ingenious solution to this problem was proposed by Professor Murray A. Thompson, Director of the Physical Sciences Laboratory of the University of Wisconsin-Madison. The Thompson algorithm can be summarized as follows:

1) A segment of computer RAM is designated as a logical 3-D array of 4-bit registers corresponding in their arrangement to a small segment of real 3-D space.

2) As the scanned image for a single track is reconstructed using the geometry of the camera/film position, the track is interpreted as lying on a conical surface with the lens at its vertex. One bit of each memory register which lies along this cone is set to 1 as shown in Figure 14-9.

3) Now a second view is scanned, and the track in question generates a different conical section through real space and the corresponding segment of RAM memory. A second bit is set in registers corresponding to all points along this new, stereoscopic cone.

4) The line of coincidence (intersection) between these two cones must represent the actual path of the charged particle through 3-D space. To double check the result, a third view can be scanned and checked for three-way coincidence.

5) Since the scanning and the 3-D filtering occur simultaneously, the results of the reconstruction are available to guide the scanning process. This corresponds to a form of "planning" to guide the search for a coherent 3-D representation of the 3-D track images. Once a 3-D track is located and the parameters of the corresponding curve

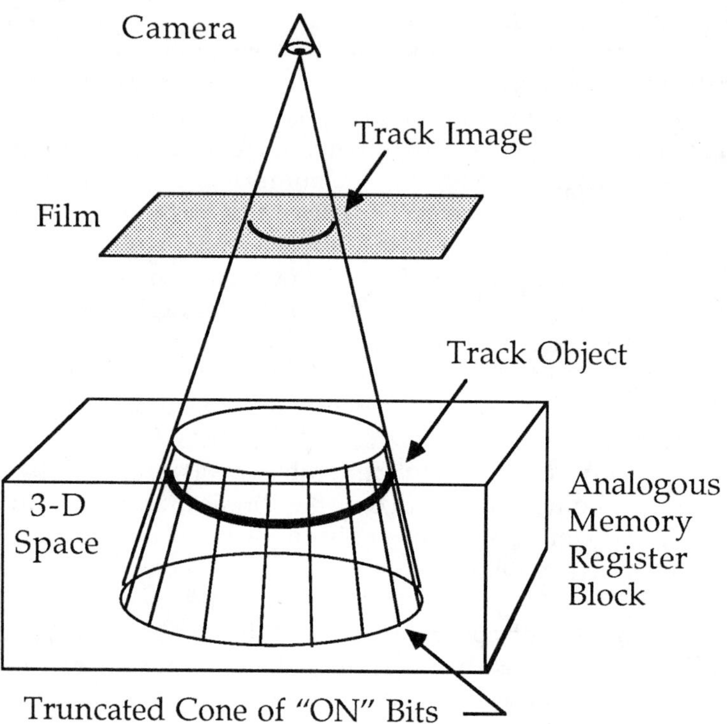

Figure 14-9 Schematic representation of Thompson's Algorithm The 2-D image of a circular track segment maps onto a conical surface with the camera lens at the vertex in 3-D space. The conical surface in 3-D space is represented in the corresponding RAM space by setting the appropriate bit in memory register to "1".

determined, its expected path is projected on a "brick" (rectangular box) through the RAM. If confirming scan information does not appear, this is considered an indication that a collision event has occurred.

The Thompson algorithm has been implemented on a special purpose computer and used for the routine analysis of bubble chamber photographs.

The challenge of the analysis of bubble chamber and spark chamber photographs has inspired considerable work in pattern recognition. Fu describes a special pattern grammar approach for characterizing bubble chamber photographs.[12] One major effort in this area which also introduced many of the concepts of parallel processing was ILLIAC–III, the Illinois Pattern Recognition Computer.[13]

14.6 SPEECH RECOGNITION

A continuing goal of AI research is to teach computers to understand spoken communication. Speech recognition by machine inspires interest for several reasons. There is the intrinsic appeal of simulating one of the most effective channels of human communication. A second attraction is the practical advantage of more efficient human/machine interaction. The average person can speak at about twice the rate that proficient typists can type. Finally, a speech recognizing computer would remove the keyboard as an obstacle in human/machine dialog. This would encourage less technically oriented persons to make more extensive use of machines.

There is a very close parallel between the problems, approaches, and accomplishments of computer vision which we consider in the next chapter and speech recognition systems. In both cases, in a highly constrained environment containing a limited number of objects (shapes or words), the problem has been solved with a high degree of accuracy, and implementations are now available for microcomputers. For both vision and speech, the more general case using a deeper level of understanding (but still constraining the size of the domain) has been solved to a reasonable degree of accuracy through a great deal of effort and considerable expense. And in both cases we can say that the completely general problem remains unsolved with little hope of solution in the near future.

At this point it is useful to distinguish three levels of speech understanding:

- Isolated word recognition
- Continuous speech understanding in a limited domain
- Continuous speech understanding — the general case.

It is also helpful in understanding speech recognition literature to define several new terms. In addition to the definition of *syntax, semantics,* and *pragmatics* from our discussion of natural language processing, speech analysis and understanding study involves concepts of:[14]

1) *Phonemes* — The basic element or atom of human speech from which syllables and words are composed. Most systems use about 40 phonemes composed of 16 vowel and 24 consonant sounds.

2) *Phonotactics* — The syntax of phonemes.

3) *Allophones* — The representation of sounds as they actually occur in words. The use of a phoneme in the context of a word or phrase determines its allophones.

4) *Phonetics* — Representations of the physical characteristics of the sounds in all the words of the vocabulary.

5) *Phonemics* — Rules describing variations in pronunciation due to co-articulation across word boundaries.that appear when words are spoken together in sentences

6) *Morphemics* — Rules describing how morphemes (atoms of meaning) are combined to form words (formation of plurals, conjugations of verbs, and so on).

7) *Prosodics* — Rules describing fluctuation in stress, rhythms, inflections, and intonation across a sentence which help us say what we mean.

ISOLATED WORD RECOGNITION — IWR

One of the first isolated word recognition systems was the "watermelon box" invented by J. C. R. Licklider of Harvard University in the early 1950's.[15] The watermelon box consisted of a microphone connected to resonant circuits tuned to detect the vowels a, e, e, and o in the word "watermelon". When anyone within range of the microphone said "watermelon," a light on top of the watermelon box would flash in recognition. While it was an expert on the word *watermelon*, its vocabulary for word recognition was limited to this one word.

Isolated word recognition is an expanded vocabulary extension of the watermelon box concept in which machine algorithms for pattern matching replace the resonant circuits. This lowest level of speech recognition has proven to be a relatively easy task because it followed the proven maxim of AI: *to enhance the likelihood of success, restrict the problem domain.* This is accomplished by restricting discourse to a relatively limited vocabulary (typically 100 — 1000 words), requiring training by the individual who is to use the recognizer (typically by repeating the vocabulary words several times each), and requiring a clear pause between words.

The training process produces a digital representation (template) of each word in the vocabulary by rapidly sampling the microphone output. The resulting time domain function is then analyzed by fast Fourier transform techniques to produce a frequency spectrum used for subsequent analysis. When the speaker enters a word in actual use, the system digitizes the input and compares the resulting Fourier spectrum to the dictionary patterns. Using some criterion such as least squares analysis, the best match is selected and the computer thereby "understands" the word uttered by the speaker. Note that this pattern matching approach is concerned only with allophones and phonetics and not the more complex problems of phonemics or prosodics.

Such systems can be useful in certain situations and are being marketed by a number of commercial vendors. Applicable situations include use by the physically handicapped, programming applications in which the vocabulary is automatically restricted, and the processing of recorded data taken in difficult situations (recording of part numbers in a poorly lit warehouse, for instance). Isolated word recognizers which perform with an accuracy in the range of 97—100% are available on personal computers for prices in the range of $200 — $1000 (see Appendix B).

Continuous Speech Recognition — CSR

The task of continuous speech understanding is quite analogous to that of general scene analysis in computer vision. And for similar reasons, the problem is far from a solution in the most general case, although significant progress has been made by restricting the domain of the problem. The first reaction by students is often, "Well, if the isolated word recognition problem has been solved on microcomputers why can't we just use the same techniques, add more words to the vocabulary, and use a mainframe computer to solve the continuous speech problem?"

It turns out that the problem is not that simple. One of the key sources of difficulty is that *continuous speech is not just the concatenation of isolated words.* For instance, the sound of a phoneme, syllable, or word depends very strongly on the context in which it appears in speech (its phonemics and prosodics). The phonemic problem is illustrated by the similarity in sound of the two phrases "This guy" and "The sky." Any doubters of the effect of prosodics on speech understanding have only to recite and then sing the popular jingle, "Mares eat oats, and does eat oats, and little lambs eat ivy" to realize the problem faced by continuous speech understanding programs.

A second source of difficulty in training a machine to understand continuous speech in the manner of humans is that humans interpret speech in the context of a broad knowledge of the world. This common sense knowledge allows humans to "read between the lines," fill in the blanks, interpret the speaker's body language, and filter out noise in the environment. All of these human capabilities give humans a tremendous advantage over the most sophisticated computer in interpreting and understanding speech.

THE ARPA SUR PROJECT

In 1971, Allen Newell chaired a study group for the Advanced Research Projects Agency of the Department of Defense (ARPA) which established the guidelines and goals for a 5-year, $15 million effort in *speech understanding research* (SUR). Five major projects were funded and some impressive results obtained. In addition to proving that continuous speech understanding is possible under the proper conditions, the project provided a model for what carefully planned, goal-directed applied research can achieve.

The specifications and goals for the project included:[16]

- The system should accept continuous speech from many speakers.
- The system should recognize a 1000-word standard American vocabulary.
- A high-quality microphone could be used as transducer.
- An artificial syntax was allowed.
- A constrained semantic task domain was allowed.
- The system should perform at less than a 10% semantic error rate.
- The delay from spoken input to computer interpretation could not exceed several times real-time on a computer capable of 100 million instructions per second (100 MIPS).

Several of the systems funded under the project performed as well as or better than the specifications. Three of the most successful were HARPY, HEARSAY-II, (both of Carnegie-Mellon University), and HWIM (Hear What I Mean) of Bolt Beranek Newman (BBN). Some of the details are summarized in Table 14-I.

As is apparent from Table 14-I, the goals of the SUR project were substantially met by the Carnegie-Mellon University group under the direction of Raj Reddy and Bruce Lowerre.[17] Any direct comparison between the programs is difficult since the constraining task for the HWIM program presented a significantly more difficult environment than the other two. Each system used a radically different approach to speech understanding, and the HEARSAY-II project made several contributions of particular significance which have been used in other pattern recognition applications. Next we summarize these approaches and the contributions each made.

Table 14-I
COMPARISON OF ARPA SUR SYSTEMS[18]

GOAL, November 1971	HARPY	HEARSAY-II	HWIM
Accept connected speech	Yes	Yes	Yes
From many speakers	3 male 2 female	1 male	3 male
In a quiet room with good microphone	Yes	Computer room, close talking mike	Yes
With a few training sentences for each speaker	20–30	60	No training
Accepting 1000 words	1,011	1,011	1,097
Using artificial syntax	Finite state language	Finite state language	Restricted ATN
In a constraining task	Document retrieval	Document retrieval	Travel Management
Yielding < 10% error	5%	9%, 26%	56%
In a few times real time	Yes (~80)	Yes, but slower	Not quite (~2000)
Average branching ratio in sentence structure	33	33	196

HARPY

The HARPY project was a late-comer to the SUR project, begun about half way through the five year program by Bruce Lowerre and Raj Reddy. The basic algorithm used in HARPY resembled somewhat a huge and sophisticated watermelon box. That is, it stored every possible pronunciation of every possible sentence that could be spoken using the artificially restricted syntax allowed by the SUR program guidelines. The first step in HARPY was to generate every possible sentence.

Next each word in each sentence was replaced by a smaller network of phonemes representing all possible ways the word could be pronounced. This network of phoneme nodes represented the allophone structure of all possible sentences and was compiled and stored for use in sentence understanding. It provided the allophonic templates against which incoming voice signals were matched.

Given a sentence, HARPY resolved it into a list of candidate phonemes. Then it searched its way through the phoneme network in a left-to-right *beam search* similar to that used in the finite state transition diagram discussed in Chapter 8. If it succeeded in finding a path through the 15,000 node finite state network which matched the words from the input sentence it had deciphered the sentence.

While HARPY won the competition for performance in the SUR program, it is generally conceded that its contribution were more in the area of effective data representation and search pruning rather than significant new insights into the science of speech understanding. Its success depended critically on the limited vocabulary and restricted domain of the problem it solved. To compile the 15,000 allophonic templates for its 1,011 word vocabulary required 13 hours of PDP-10 time. The addition of a single word or phoneme required a complete recompilation of the allophonic database. In terms of the average number of words which could possible appear at any one place in a sentence (called the "average branching ratio") HARPY rated a 33. The average branching ratio for HWIM was 196 in comparison.

HEARSAY-II

HEARSAY-II is considered to be one of the most influential AI programs ever written. The concepts and architecture introduced in this program have spread to numerous applications outside the area of speech recognition. A summary of these contributions and the novel approach used in HEARSAY-II includes:

- The concept of *knowledge sources* each of which independently processes data available to it. The knowledge sources (KS's) act as autonomous production systems or experts in such areas as phonetics, syllables, words, and phrases. Each KS is modular and anonymous, operating on information which it finds in the global data base. Names and functions of various KS's included:

  - SEG — Segments the input acoustic signal into a string of allophones

  - POM — Assigns the allophone strings to syllable classes

♦ MOW — Hypothesizes words from the syllable classes

♦ WORD-CTL — Controls the number of hypotheses by MOW

♦ WOSEQ — Organized words into "islands" of one or more words based on phonetics, syntax, and information theory

♦ VERIFY — Double-checked hypothesized word islands against lower-level acoustic information

♦ PARSE — Checked the syntax of the word islands

♦ CONCAT — Concatenated word islands to form longer phrases

♦ PREDICT — Generated all words that could precede or follow a word sequence

♦ SEMANT — Generated code to execute the intended input command (responded to the meaning of the user's query)

The modular structure of the KS experts facilitated the incremental development of the system. HEARSAY-II started with eight generic KS experts and grew to more than fifteen.[19]

• The concept of a *blackboard* which served as a globally accessible, passive data base for the knowledge sources from which to read and to which to write. The blackboard architecture closely resembles that of production systems discussed in Chapter 10 in which the KS experts act as production rules. The KS's continually examine the information posted on the blackboard. Whenever the information satisfies the precondition for a production, the KS executes its function. Thus the blackboard/KS architecture functions as an asynchronous set of demons which process the incoming acoustic signal into a meaningful command. A blackboard handler module controls the various read/-write requests from the KS experts to prevent conflicts in processing the data.

The blackboard data structure with its associated independent, asynchronous knowledge sources is a natural candidate for machines using parallel architecture. The modular nature of the KS's suggests using independent hardware processors for each expert. As long as the analysis task can be divided equally among N experts a parallel machine should, in principle, operate approximately N times as fast as a more traditional sequential von Neumann machine.

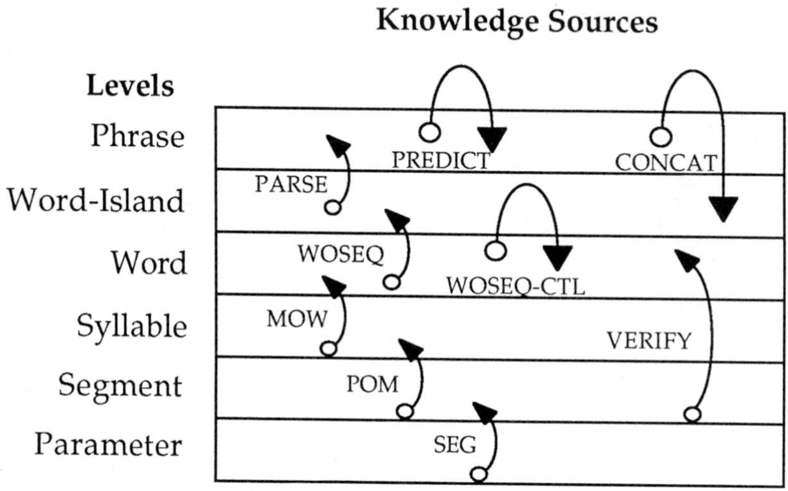

Figure 14-10 Blackboard Architecture of HEARSAY-II The blackboard is shown arranged by level of information from the lowest parameterized acoustic level to the highest level of completely interpreted phrases. Several KS experts are shown performing bottom-up (upward pointing arrows) and top-down (downward pointing arrows) processing.

- Integration of *bottom-up* and *top-down asynchronous, parallel processing*. The raw phoneme information extracted from the microphone signal gradually percolated upward on the blackboard towards higher levels of integration and meaning, while inferences made at the higher levels of the blackboard percolated downward for use of lower level knowledge sources. This integration can be illustrated by a diagram of the blackboard according to level structure as shown in Figure 14-10. Note the function of the knowledge sources in transforming information using bottom-up and top-down strategies.

- The concept of *expectation-driven processing*. Using posted hypotheses on what words would be expected by the syntactic and semantic knowledge sources, a high level of performance was obtained even in the presence of noisy input information. The lower processing level KS's were not capable of a high level of discrimination and would typically generate, for instance, twenty candidate words for each word of a sentence. This leads to a combinatorial explosion of candidate sentences which must be tested for validity if some control strategy is not employed.

The key concept is that syntax and semantics provide severe constraints on acceptable word combinations. Applying rules of syntax and semantics is equivalent to saying that we "expect" certain words to be associated with other words. This provides the essential tool for pruning the search for candidate sentences.

A related concept to reduce the search space introduced by HEARSAY-II was the use of information theoretic constraints in the word sequence generator, WOSEQ. That is, certain combinations of words contain more information than others. As WOSEQ added another word to the word island, it selected the word from the candidate list which resulted in the greatest increase in the information content of the word sequence. This information theoretic approach provided one of the key elements to the success of HEARSAY-II in meeting the SUR goals.

In conclusion, the HEARSAY-II project introduced some extremely valuable concepts which have applicability to a number of areas of AI research. A final comment on the experimental design for HEARSAY-II is in order. The modular structure, with emphasis on independent knowledge sources, was an intentional design consideration. This allowed rapid experimentation with the effect of a given KS on system performance while the other experts remained fixed. The WOSEQ expert was introduced late in the project, for example, and greatly improved system performance. The blackboard architecture provided a flexible environment essential for research.

HWIM

The *Hear What I Mean* project (pronounced "whim") was under the direction of William Woods of BBN. Woods selected an expanded version of his doctoral thesis project as the test bed for HWIM. This was a database query system called Trip which integrated an official airline guide with the travel plans and budgets of Wood's group at BBN. The system understood and responded to requests like "Plan a trip for three people for two days in San Francisco in July."

HWIM used many of the successful features of Wood's LUNAR project, including the Augmented Transition Network. It resembled HEARSAY-II in using knowledge sources as processors at the parametric signal, phoneme, segment, and word level. It differed significantly, however, in its structure. HWIM treated the knowledge sources as subroutines called sequentially by the main control program. It differed from HEARSAY-II and HARPY in two other significant ways. First, it attempted to understand a general grammar based on its complete lexicon rather than the restricted syntax recognized by the

Carnegie-Mellon projects. Secondly, HEARSAY-II made little use of semantics and none of pragmatics or prosodics whereas the WHIM project attempted to use all three. These features made HWIM the most ambitious of the three SUR projects discussed.

A particularly interesting feature of the HWIM research project was the cognitive science strategy employed for system design. In the early stages of the project, human experts were assigned to perform the various functions of speech understanding such as conversion of acoustic signals to phonemes, assembling phonemes into words, syntactic analysis, and semantic analysis. As each expert gained an understanding of the task, s/he attempted to automate it by writing code to perform the same functions by machine. Thus as the project developed, the human experts gradually phased themselves out of the system by substituting equivalent machine code to perform their functions.

Because of the more ambitious goals and more fundamental approach to the speech understanding problem, WHIM did not perform as well in the final evaluation of SUR projects as the well-engineered Carnegie-Mellon projects. All three projects, however, contributed significant new understanding of the problem and useful techniques, many of which have proven valuable in other areas of computer science.

14.7 THE IBM "INTELLIGENT TYPEWRITER"

Following the tremendous progress during the 1971—1976 period of the ARPA project the pace of speech understanding research waned until federal funding was resumed in 1983. However, one of the more productive private efforts underway at present is the "intelligent typewriter" project under the direction of Frederick Jelinek of IBM. The goal of the project is to develop a speech-driven typewriter system.

The system samples incoming microphone waveforms at the rate of 100 Hz and sends the output to a spectrum analyzer. The information then flows through several stages of comparison and pattern matching at the prototype sound, phoneme, and word level. It uses an interesting heuristic of an *a priori* probability factor to select the most common word in cases of ambiguities.

The system has performed at a 95% recognition rate for IBM's 5,000-word office task vocabulary. Furthermore, the system interprets standard English with no restrictions on the type of sentence used. While this is an impressive performance, serious problems remain to be overcome. These include:

- Conversion to *continuous speech mode.* The 95% figure applies for sentences read with pauses between words. Until improvements to overcome this restriction are made, it is unlikely that the system will be widely accepted.

• Conversion to a *speaker-independent mode*. At present it works with only one speaker at a time who must spend considerable time training the system to recognize his or her individual voice.

• *Improvement in the speed*. At present the system runs rather slowly, but this should improve as more capable machines become available.

14.8 CONCLUSION

Pattern recognition tasks are gradually yielding to new understanding, improved algorithms, and more capable computers. Success ranges from complete for the new wave of laser scanners for recognizing printed characters to only partial for the task of continuous speech recognition. Frederick Hayes-Roth, one of the key researchers on the HEARSAY-II project, estimates that it would require an effort the size of a small Apollo project to produce a system capable of general understanding of the 1,000 word Basic English system which has been proposed as an international language. The reason for this pessimistic analysis is the computational problem posed by the combinatorial explosion involved in unrestricted speech analysis.

Speech understanding is a natural candidate for application of new computer architectures which are under development. These architectures range from the massively parallel digital machines using the order of a million microprocessors to the analog connectionist machines built from artificial neural networks. In the last chapter we will return to this subject and examine the architecture of these machines and their accomplishments in detail.

PROBLEMS AND PROGRAMS

14-1. Scan the previous chapters of the text for AI applications which use the technique of pattern matching. List each applications and clearly explain the role pattern matching plays.

14-2. Discuss the role of common sense knowledge in providing the context for human understanding of speech and contrast this human capability with computer systems for understanding human speech.

What does this suggest as an effective route for improving the performance of speech recognition systems?

14-3. Oliver Selfridge devised a pattern recognition system capable of learning called Pandemonium.[20] From library sources describe the principle of operation of Pandemonium and the role demons played.

14-4. Make a list of potential application areas for pattern matching distinct from that presented in section 14.2.

14-5. Draw a functional block diagram of the important elements of a general pattern matching system outlined in section 14.3. Then carefully specify each element of the diagram for the particular application of speech recognition.

14-6. Each of the three major applications of pattern matching presented in this chapter must contend with the problem of the *signal to noise ratio.* Discuss the most important sources of noise for each of the three applications and suggest strategies for minimizing the noise in each case.

14-7. The "signatures" of strange particle events in high energy physics resembles in many aspects the patterns of written characters. Use library sources or an interview with a physics faculty member to list those features which particle signatures have in common with alphabetical characters and in what important ways they differ.

14-8. The laws of mass/energy conservation, charge conservation, baryon number conservation, and strangeness conservation provide the syntax (rules of grammar) which govern what final states (sentences) may be generated in high energy physics. Use a modern physics text to specify the grammar of high energy physics and interpret the allowed final states in terms of all possible sentences.

14-9. Classify the Thompson algorithm according to the elements of a pattern matching system outlined in section 14.3. Interpret the Thompson algorithm as a pattern matching algorithm for performing 3-D space reconstruction from multiple 2-D images.

14-10. Inquire at your local post office as to whether it has facilities for automatic sorting of mail by Zip Code. If it does, try to determine as much as you can about what letter recognizing algorithm is used.

14-11. Teitelman's recognizer may seem a bit arbitrary at first glance. Think about the problem of recognizing handwriting for a while and propose an alternate algorithm to Teitelman's.

14-12. Use the Teitelman recognizer algorithm to represent the letters "J", "D", "X", and "M". Select one of the letters and investigate how much variability in drawing the letter is permitted for a given numeric code. Interpret your results in terms of the uniqueness and generality of the representation.

14-13. Assume your first job assignment is to develop an automated signature guarantee system. Describe what parameters you would plan to use, what hardware you would propose to measure them, and outline the program you would propose for signature verification.

14-14. Who do you see as the largest potential customers for the automatic signature verifier developed in problem 14-13, and what would you suggest as an optimum price?

14-15. Describe applications for which isolated word recognition (IWR) would be useful and applications for which it would be inadequate. What applications have provided the biggest markets for IWR?

14-16. HARPY was able to achieve an error rate for continuous speech interpretation of less than 5%. Discuss for what applications this error rate would be acceptable and for what applications it would be totally unacceptable.

14-17. Discuss the role the *blackboard* plays in the HEARSAY-II program for continuous speech recognition. How might the blackboard architecture be employed for scene analysis in computer vision?

14-18. Several expert system shells have adopted a blackboard architecture for their main database. Discuss what advantages this structure would provide for expert systems and what additional applications might make use of the blackboard concept.

14-19. Many new special-purpose computer chips (ASICs) are becoming available to perform specific applications such as graphics and speech synthesis. Discuss how these hardware devices could be integrated as knowledge sources in the design of computer architectures.

14-20. Make an estimate of the number of sentences possible with a Basic English language of 1,000 words. Assume an average sentence of length 10 words and make reasonable assumptions of the number of nouns, verbs, and so on in the language. Would you recommend a HARPY-like or WHIM-like approach to the problem?

14-21. The text mentions Claude Shannon's information-theoretic approach used by the knowledge source WOSEQ in HEARSAY-II. The information content of an "island" of words is inversely related to the entropy (randomness) of the word sequence. Discuss what criteria WOSEQ would likely use to apply information theory is selecting likely word sequences?

14-22. Discuss one of the following two propositions:

a) One of the most important developments in AI is the availability of capable microcomputers. Important AI techniques can be researched using presently available microcomputers with megabyte memories. The bottlenecks in AI research are due to the shortage of good people with good ideas, not the unavailability of computing power.

b) To date, all significant breakthroughs in AI research have been made on mainframe computers and it is likely to remain that way. Progress on all significant areas as vision, pattern recognition, and game theory search has been limited by the availability of adequate computing resources. Advances will occur only as new super computers come on line to provide the necessary computing power.

REFERENCES AND FOOTNOTES

[1] Duda, Richard O. and Part, Peter E., *Pattern Classification and Scene Analysis*, John Wiley & Sons, New York, NY (1973)

[2] Sedgewick, Robert, *Algorithms,* pp. 257–267, Addison-Wesley Publishing Company, Reading, MA (1983)

[3] Fu, K. S., *Syntactic Pattern Recognition and Applications*, Prentice-Hall, Inc. Englewood Cliffs, NJ (1982)

[4] Pylyshyn, Zenon W., *Computation and Cognition — Toward a Foundation for Cognitive Science*, pp. 147–191, MIT Press, Cambridge, MA (1985)

[5] Selfridge, O. G., "Pattern Recognition and Modern Computers" in *Proceedings of the 1955 Western Joint Computer Conference,* Session on Learning Machines, pp. 91–93, Mar. 1–3, (1955). See also: Selfridge,

Oliver G. and Neisser, Ulric, "Pattern Recognition by Machine" in *Computers and Thought,* Edward A. Feigenbaum and Julian Feldman (eds), pp. 237–250, McGraw-Hill Book Company, New York, NY (1963)

6 Uhr, Leonard and Vossler, Charles, "A Pattern-Recognition Program that Generates, Evaluates, and Adjusts its own Operators," in *Computers and Thought,* Edward A. Feigenbaum and Julian Feldman (eds), pp. 251–268, McGraw-Hill Book Company, New York, NY (1963)

7 Sandon, Peter, "Vision and Learning in Connectionist Networks," *Proceedings of the First Annual Meeting of the Midwest Artificial Intelligence and Cognitive Science Society,* The University of Chicago Department of Computer Science, pp. 145–146, April 24–25 (1987)

8 Teitelman, W., "Real Time Recognition of Hand-drawn Characters," FJCC 1964, p. 559, Spartan Books, Baltimore, MD

9 Newman, William M. and Sproull, Robert F., *Principles of Interactive Computer Graphics,* McGraw-Hill Book Company, New York, NY (1979)

10 Srihari, Sargur N. (ed), *Computer Text Recognition and Error Correction,* IEEE Computer Society Press, Piscataway, NJ (1985)

11 Firebaugh, Morris W., *Strange Particle Production in 8 BeV/c Proton-Proton Interactions,* Ph.D. Thesis, University of Illinois-Urbana, Urbana, IL (1966). See also Firebaugh, Morris W., "Strange Particle Production in 8 BeV/c Proton-Proton Interactions", *Phys. Rev.* **172**, pp.1354–1370, (1968)

12 Fu, K. S., *Op Cit,* pp. 101–105

13 McCormick, Bruce H., "The Illinois Pattern Recognition Computer — ILLIAC III," IEEE Trans. Electron. Comput., **EC-12**, No. 5, (1963). Reprinted in Sklansky, Jack, (ed), *Pattern Recognition: Introduction and Foundations,* Dowden, Hutchinson, & Ross, Inc. Stroudsburg, PA (1973)

14 Feigenbaum, Edward A., Barr, Avron and Cohen, Paul R. (eds), *The Handbook of Artificial Intelligence,* Vol.1-3, HeurisTech Press/-William Kaufmann, Inc., Stanford, CA (1981–82)

15 Johnson, George, *Machinery of the Mind,* p. 124, Times Books

Division of Random House, Inc., New York, NY (1986)

16 Reddy, Raj and Zue, Victor, "Tomorrow's Computers — The Challenges: Speech Understanding," *IEEE Spectrum*, pp. 84–87, November (1983)

17 Reddy, R., Erman, L., Fennell, R., and Neely, R., "The HEARSAY Speech Understanding System: An Example of the Recognition Process," *IEEE Transactions on Computers* C-25, pp. 427–431 (1976)

18 Feigenbaum, Barr, and Cohen, *Op Cit*, p. 330

19 Fennell, Richard D. and Lesser, Victor R., "Parallelism in Artificial Intelligence Problem Solving: A Case Study of Hearsay-II," *Tutorial on Parallel Processing*, pp. 185–198, IEEE Computer Society, New York, NY (1981)

20 Andrew, A. M., *Artificial Intelligence*, pp. 90–94, Abacus Press, Cambridge, MA (1983)

Chapter 15

COMPUTER VISION

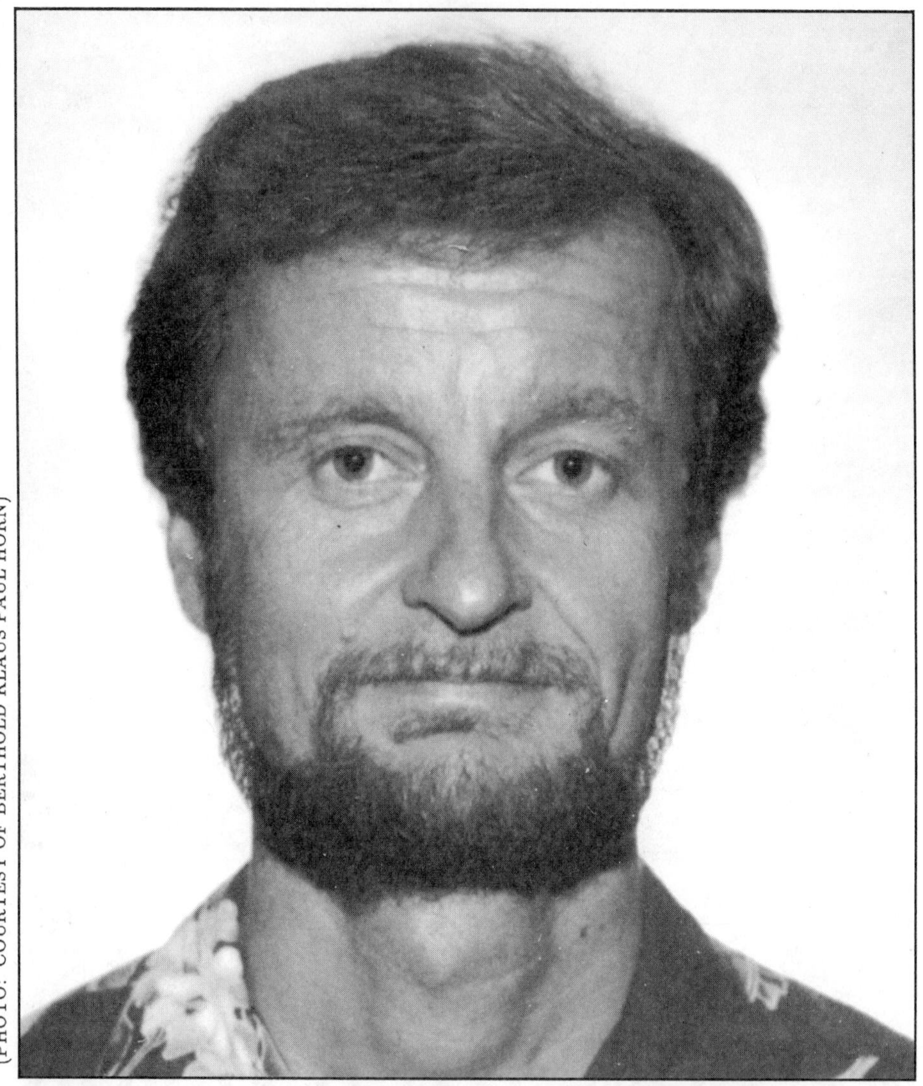

(PHOTO: COURTESY OF BERTHOLD KLAUS PAUL HORN)

Dr. Berthold Klaus Paul Horn is Professor of Electrical Engineering and Computer Science at MIT. Professor Horn's interests focus on robotics with particular emphasis on computer vision. He has published work on extracting the shape of an object from observed shading and on visual motion analysis. Dr. Horn has pioneered an approach to machine vision based on thorough analysis of the image-forming process. He is coauthor with his MIT colleague, Patrick Winston, of the popular book, *LISP*. His latest book, *Robot Vision*, is an outgrowth of his MIT course in machine vision.

15: COMPUTER VISION

15.1 INTRODUCTION

One interesting approach for building more intelligent machines is to augment or expand the senses through which the computer can communicate with the outside world. During the early period of computer development, the only input channel was through the deck of "IBM cards" submitted in the batch mode. How exciting it was when time-sharing systems were introduced and we could actually program the computer interactively! The system suddenly became much more responsive and productivity increased. Another step was to increase I/O capacity by the addition of a pointing device such as light pen, data tablet, and more recently, the mouse. Again, another significant improvement in responsiveness and ease of use occurred as knowledge embedded in the computer enabled the user to escape from the constraints of the keyboard and simply point to what she wanted to do.

Two communication channels of tremendous carrying capacity in humans are those of sight and hearing. The success and power of these modes of communication in humans has inspired research on emulating them by machine. We have already discussed research in understanding human speech in the chapter on pattern recognition. This chapter examines the progress that has been made in teaching the computer to see and understand what it sees — the topic of computer vision. There are strong incentives for productive research in this area, particularly because of the need to provide robots with proper feedback to carry out their tasks. Success in this area also has implications for the area of AI itself. Once computers can see well enough to read rapidly and recognize complex scenes, the task of knowledge acquisition should be greatly simplified and the machine's performance should improve rapidly as the knowledge base grows. It is estimated that 75% of the information received by humans is visual.[1] The human vision system has been fine-tuned for processing and interpreting vast amounts of raw data rapidly and accurately. Computer vision promises an effective approach for solving the problem of the knowledge acquisition bottleneck.

15.2 NATURE'S PROOF OF PRINCIPLE — THE HUMAN EYE/MIND

While great progress has been made in the field of computer vision, the eye/mind vision system sets such a high performance standard that it will probably never be completely emulated by machine. Consider, for instance, the following properties of the human eye:

- The eye contains over 100 million receptors consisting of about 100 million rods and 7 million cones.

- The eye can resolve two objects separated by 0.1 mm at a distance of 25 cm which is equivalent to an angular resolution of .0004 radians.

- The eye has the adaptive characteristic of accommodation or "automatic focussing".

- The eye has an acute color sensitivity which can distinguish over 150 hues.

- The eye can see in light intensities ranging over a factor 10^9.

- The eye can detect an intensity change of as little as 2% over a considerable portion of this range.

- The eye sends its output to the brain, a parallel processor made up of over 10 billion neurons for interpretation.

While certain optical instruments can duplicate many of these characteristics individually, no instrument can duplicate all of them simultaneously. So, just as the brain itself has successfully avoided simulation by machine, the human eye/mind system will continue to out-perform computer vision systems for a long time to come. The eye/mind system is an important "proof of principle" showing that massively parallel neural networks are capable of processing vast quantities of input data rapidly and efficiently.

15.3 ELEMENTS OF COMPUTER VISION

The objectives for computer vision systems range from simple pattern recognition tasks to more complex goals of scene analysis. We consider the following three elements of computer vision suggested by Horn:[2]

- Image Processing

- Pattern Classification
- Scene Analysis.

Before we examine examples of each of these aspects of machine vision, it is useful to study the structure of machine vision systems.

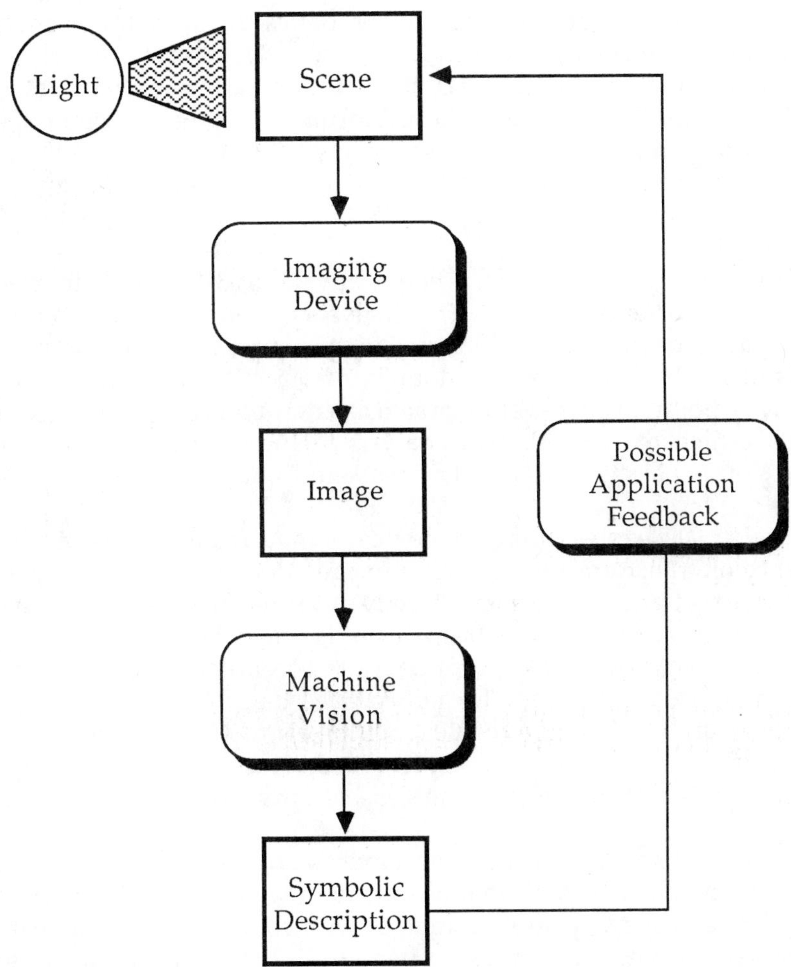

Figure 15-1 Basic Components of Machine Vision System The task of computer vision is to represent a physical scene by the appropriate symbolic description. For specific applications, such as robotics, the system may include a feedback loop for manipulating the scene it is analyzing.

STRUCTURE OF MACHINE VISION SYSTEMS

The basic structure of machine vision systems is illustrated in Figure 15-1.

• *Light Sources* — In analyzing scenes from nature or unposed photographs the light source is generally some combination of the sun and diffuse background light. However, for special applications such as optical character recognition (OCR) and robotics the system designer has much more control over the light source. By careful control of the light source and background it is possible to greatly simplify the task of machine vision and improve the performance of the system. Special application sources include laser beams and intense, pencil beams which scan the field of view of the vision system and can be correlated with the observed objects.

• *Scenes* — The most general scene is any set of 3-D objects in an arbitrary setting or environment. The analysis of general scenes is beyond the capacity of present machine vision systems. However, as in other fields of AI, by restricting the domain of objects and/or their orientation it is possible to develop practical computer vision applications. Scenes which have yielded to analysis include letters on the printed page, simple objects on assembly lines, and human faces.

• *Imaging Devices* — Imaging devices range from processors which enhance or transform photographic images to special purpose imaging tools which transform scenes directly into machine readable images. One form of direct image transducer is the vidicon camera which produces composite video output. More recently, solid state cameras have appeared which used charged coupled devices (CCD) with resolution typically in the range of 500 × 500 pixels. CCD cameras are small (commercially available as a 1.25 × 1.25 × 1.25 inch cube), rugged, lightweight, and provide excellent sensors for robotics applications.

• *Images* — Images from imaging devices are typically represented in computer memory by a bit-mapped array in which each bit corresponds to a picture element (pixel). In images with color or gray-scale features, each picture element has an associated attribute register (typically 4 — 8 bits) for encoding color and gray-scale information. This digitized image provides the raw data for subsequent processing.

• *Machine Vision* — This is the system which interprets the image in terms of features, patterns, and objects which may be recognized by the analysis system and provide the basis for intelligent decisions. Vision analysis systems may be sequential, algorithmic programs for interpreting the pixel data or special purpose hardware using massively parallel architectures for comparing the incoming image with previously stored images. These architectures are examined in detail in Chapter 18.

• *Symbolic Descriptions* — The object of the machine vision system is to produce symbolic representations of the scene of the form: *the letter E*, or *a small red block on top of a large blue block*, or *part # E145379 at an angle of 63°*, or *Donald Michie at a cocktail party*. Such a symbolic description of the scene corresponds to computer understanding of the objects depicted in the image.

• *Possible Applications Feedback* — Feedback provides for actions in response to the visual recognition of the vision system. In the case of a character recognition system, feedback might control the appropriate zip-code slot into which the postal letter is directed. In a "pick and place" application in robotics, knowledge of the part number and angle guides the robot arm in picking up the part and stacking it in the appropriate shipping carton.

IMAGE PROCESSING

The basic function in image processing is to convert an external image into a representation internal to the computer or to process an image already represented internally. This phase of analysis is represented schematically in Figure 15-2:

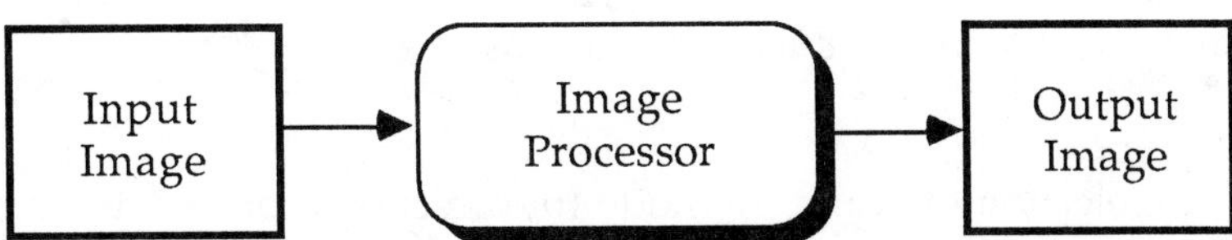

Figure 15-2 Image Processing This phase of machine vision involves converting an external image into an internal representation for subsequent analysis or the refinement of an already existing internal image into an output image. The output image may be designed for human viewing or for subsequent machine analysis.

To illustrate how improved technology has made this lowest level of vision feasible at a very low cost, consider the performance of the Thunderscan high-resolution image digitizer for the Macintosh computer. This two hundred dollar system uses an infra-red laser scanning head mounted in a printer-ribbon-shaped unit which replaces the printer ribbon cartridge in the Imagewriter as shown in Figure 15-3.

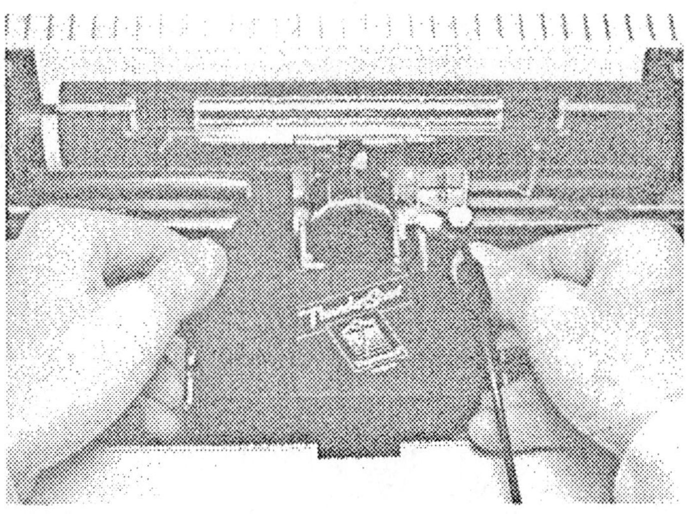

Figure 15-3 Thunderscan laser scanning head The device replaces the regular ribbon cartridge on the Imagewriter dot matrix printer. The image shown is a result of scanning one of the figures from the Thunderscan manual.

The image to be scanned may be any photograph, drawing, or photocopy which can be inserted in the printer. A scanning control program is loaded which controls such functions as:

- Focussing
- Selection of scanning mode (bi-directional or uni-directional)
- Selection of area to be scanned
- Selection of magnification of internal image (25% → 400%)
- Setting of "light intensity"
- Setting of "contrast"
- Selection of gray-scale or high-contrast option

The scan then takes place with the document digitized with a resolution of 576 × 720 pixels over an 8" × 10" source document at 100% magnification. At each pixel, 32 levels of gray-scale information is saved for later half-toning. The image may be saved to disk for subsequent image processing by either the Thunderscan software or such graphics programs as MacPaint. It may be printed out on the Imagewriter dot matrix printer in either a full-sized normal resolution mode or a compressed high resolution mode or on the Laserwriter as a halftone. It also may be embedded in word processed documents, regular data base systems such as Microsoft-FILE, or special graphics oriented data base systems.

In the following example we present a series of figures illustrating the performance of the system. Figure 15-4 is the original image in photocopy form.

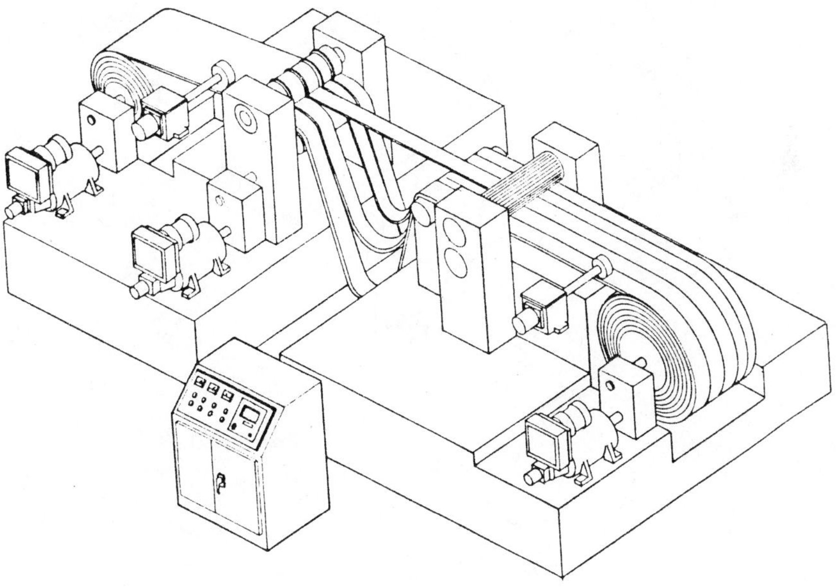

Figure 15-4 Original Object The object to be scanned is an image of a Sheet Metal Slitter System manufactured by UNICO, Inc. of Franksville, Wisconsin.

Figure 15-5 shows the un-retouched output of the scan in which no attempt has been made to optimize the performance of the system. This is what the computer "sees". Two flaws are immediately apparent: a slight shading appears (the light intensity variable was not set high enough) and an anomaly related to the scanner crossing the edge of the image is apparent at the top of the picture.

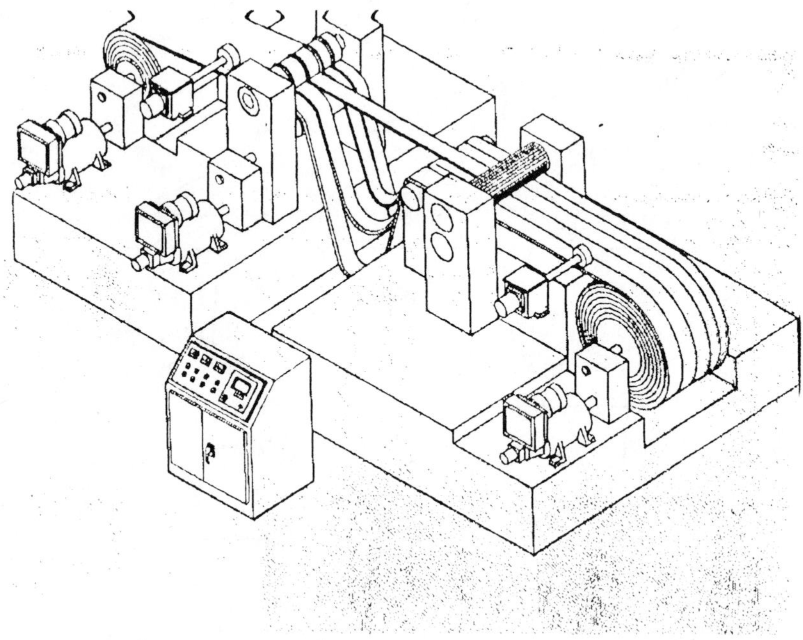

Figure 15-5 Un-retouched output image of digital laser scan of Figure 15-4. Note the problems of light intensity and edge-effect anomaly in the upper part of image.

Now, working with the recorded image off-line we can turn up the contrast and suppress most of the shading problem. We can also edit the resulting image using either the built-in editor of the scanning program or converting the image to a graphics editor document. The results of turning up the brightness, adjusting the contrast, editing the edge-effect anomaly, and adding shading with MacPaint is shown in Figure 15-6.

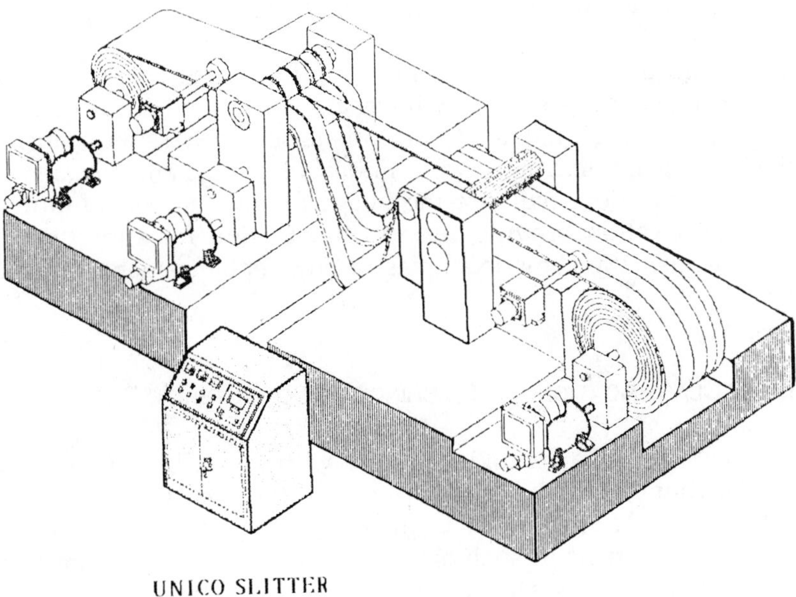

Figure 15-6 Results after processing the image from Figure 15-5 The three editing functions applied were: 1) adjustment of contrast to minimize unwanted shading, 2) point and line editing to correct the scanning anomaly and enhance some lines, and 3) fill editing to shade certain parts of the drawing.

It should be noted that the computer understands nothing about the images produced by Thunderscan or by more sophisticated video and CCD cameras which can transform 3-D scenes into 2-D representations. The analogy would be photographs in an album — the album knows nothing about the contents of the pictures enclosed. If, however, the images are categorized by content and filed in a graphics-oriented database, the first glimmerings of intelligence begin to appear. That is, the computer can be asked to display all states bordering on a certain foreign country, for example, and the graphical database program will flash out the pictures satisfying such criteria, assuming this attribute has been used in the filing process. Note that, by adding knowledge to the raw graphical knowledge base, the intelligence of the system is raised.

In addition to the conversion application of image processing described above, there are many internal applications of image processing. These include digital filtering for noise suppression, transformations for reducing blurring, and techniques for edge enhancement. The first two applications enhance the image for human consumption and the last application provides useful information for subsequent machine analysis. We show examples of edge enhancement later in this chapter.

PATTERN CLASSIFICATION — TEACHING THE COMPUTER TO READ

Analogous to children who, being born with the ability to see, then develop the ability to read, computers have developed the ability to read. This has been a classic problem in pattern recognition with considerable potential benefit in such areas as robotics and the postal service. The task of pattern classification is represented by the operation described in Figure 15-7.

Once the input image has been seen (i.e. registered in memory), algorithms are available for the transformation, filtering, and pattern recognition processes necessary to interpret segments of the graphical image as actual letters, particle track signatures, or assembly-line part silhouettes. We discussed one of these algorithms called Teitelman's recognizer in the previous chapter.

Expensive optical scanners for printed material have been available for many years for mainframe computers. This capability has recently become available for microcomputers. A number of commercial full-page scanners are now available for personal computers. These typically read a full page of text into a word processor text file in 15 seconds or less. In addition, they can also scan convert images into internal pictorial representations, typically at 300 pixels/inch, in the same fashion as the Thunderscan digitizer discussed above.

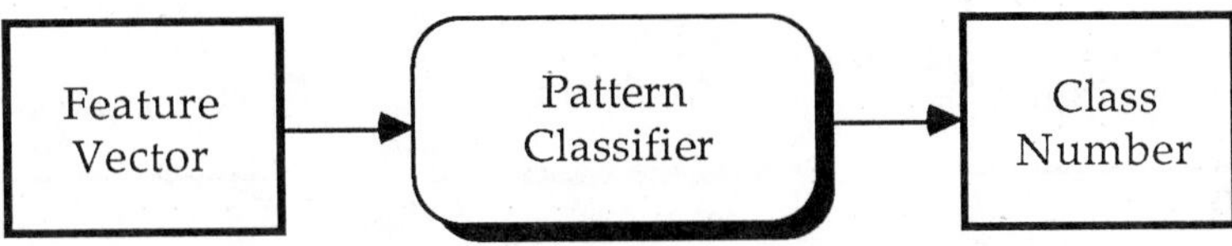

Figure 15-7 Pattern Classification The task of the pattern classifier is to examine the vector (list) of features associated with the image and select the appropriate class corresponding to those features. In the simplest form this task may involve template matching of the input image with stored patterns.

It should be emphasized that once the computer recognizes the graphical image of the letter "A" as the letter A, it "knows" everything there is to know about that symbol. With letter recognition, the letter reading problem is solved. The much more difficult problem of extracting meaning from the written material then becomes a matter of natural language processing as discussed in Chapter 8. The essential fact is that computers can not only see, but also read. This capability is now available on personal computers at a very reasonable cost. However, pattern classification capability has been successfully achieved by limiting the domain in which pattern recognition occurs to the very limited space of letter, track, or part shapes.

15.3 SCENE ANALYSIS — EXTRACTING KNOWLEDGE FROM IMAGES

The most difficult task in computer vision is in extracting knowledge from the information contained in an image. We next review several early efforts to accomplish this task, efforts which proved successful primarily because they restricted the domain of shape interpretation to simple geometries such as Winograd's block world. While these experiments were not founded on a complete theory of machine vision which we consider later, they did illustrate the inference of symbolic scene descriptions from graphical image representations. This task is illustrated in the following figure:

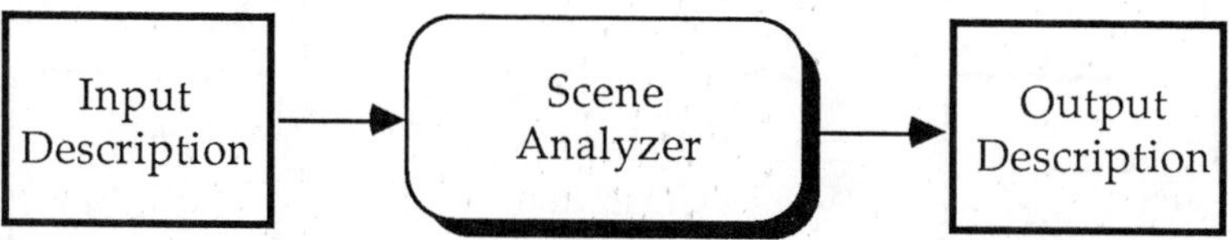

Figure 15-8 Scene Analysis The task of scene analysis involves using knowledge of the task domain (such as physical and geometrical constraints) to infer a more complete, high-level symbolic description of a scene from lower-level graphical or symbolic descriptions. Thus, for instance, geometrical constraints on corners and edges may be used to infer the structure of an object.

ROBERT'S BLOCK-WORLD 3-D PATTERN MATCHER

The first significant program for interpreting 3-D scenes from their 2-D images was written by Larry Roberts of MIT.[3] Pioneering the technique which Winograd was to use subsequently, Roberts restricted the domain of his computer vision system to a photograph of a block world populated by cubes, rectangular solids, wedges, and hexagonal prisms. His program could successfully analyze and identify all the visible objects and determine their location in 3-D space.

The Roberts program used the following steps in its analysis:

1) The system scanned the photograph and produced a digitized input image, much in the style of the Thunderscan image.

2) Edge elements were identified and fused to produce lines that corresponded to the edges of the polyhedrals.

3) The resulting line and polygon data structures were then matched against models stored for primitive blocks (cube, wedge, and hexagonal prism). The match involved application of the standard graphics transformations of scaling, rotation, and translation to the model in order to achieve an optimum fit to the image.

4) By using perspective information (vanishing point concepts) and the *support hypothesis* (objects must sit on each other or on the floor), the program could determine the depth of the object, that is, its distance from the picture plane.

5) The program then generated the resulting interpretation in

the form of a line drawing of the scene as it understood it. This again involved the use of standard graphics transformations, including hidden line removal. Since it understood both the shape and location of all visible objects, it could, upon request, re-draw the scene as it would be observed from a different point of view.

6) By combining primitive objects, the program could also identify more complex objects made up of combinations of such primitive objects.

By using the depth cuing available from the perspective information, Robert's program was able to both identify and locate blocks in 3-D space. This was the first program to perform at that level of understanding.

GUZMAN'S SEE CLASSIFIER[4]

Winston[5] has pointed out that the geometry of objects provides natural constraints which are useful in interpreting the shape and relationships of simple geometric objects. Several AI researchers have made significant contributions to the science of using geometric constraints for understanding scenes composed of simple geometric objects. One of the first programs to use purely geometric principles for inferring the structure of complex geometric objects was Guzman's SEE.

Guzman defined a junction as a point where two or more lines meet. With the eight junction types shown in Figure 15-9 he was able to classify a great variety of scenes containing polyhedral objects. He derived a set of heuristics for interpreting the solid objects which generated each of the junction types shown. On the ARROW junction, for instance, the surface between the top prong and the shaft can be linked to the surface between the shaft and the bottom prong. That is, the two surfaces must belong to the same object. By classifying all junctions of a complex line-drawing image and applying his heuristic rules, Guzman was able to interpret complex scenes such as that shown in Figure 15-10.

While Guzman's program SEE was more capable of recognizing irregularly shaped objects than was Robert's pattern matching program, in some ways it was less sophisticated. The approach used in the SEE program was heuristic and symbolic and did not use physics concepts such as the support hypothesis. It was also unable to locate the objects

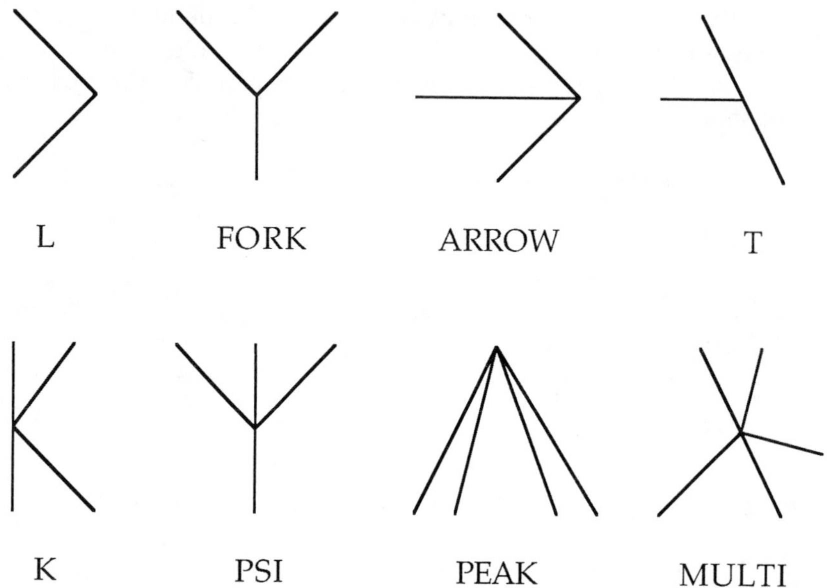

Figure 15-9 Guzman's Junction Classification Scheme With these 8 simple junctions and a set of heuristics representing the relationships of the surfaces they connect, Guzman was able to interpret line drawings in terms of the complex object scenes.

in 3-D space. However, SEE was unrestricted by the trihedral constraint discussed in the next section. Guzman's work used definitions of the allowed junction types and their allowed mapping into real space of vertices.

HUFFMAN AND CLOWES TRIHEDRAL BLOCK WORLD

D. A. Huffman and M. B. Clowes extended the work of Guzman by putting it on a more rigorous geometric basis of allowed configurations of trihedral vertices. The restrictions necessary for analysis of their block world included:

- There are no shadows or cracks.
- All vertices are the intersection of exactly three object faces, that is, we restrict the objects to those exhibiting only trihedral vertices.

• The viewpoint is chosen so that the geometry remains stationary with respect to small motion of the eye.

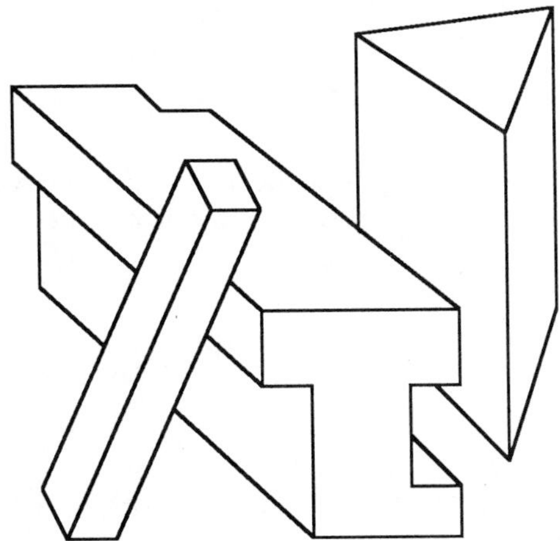

Figure 15-10 Scene analyzed by Guzman's SEE program SEE could interpret fairly complex scenes in terms of the constituent objects but had no ability to locate them in 3-D space.

The investigations of Huffman and Clowes (H & C) were done independently and published at the same time but using different representations. Their work distinguished more clearly between the *image domain* and the *scene domain* and put polyhedral scene analysis on a more systematic basis. Specifically, it is necessary to distinguish the following attributes of each domain:

- Scene domain features
  - ♦ Vertex
  - ♦ Edge
  - ♦ Surface
- Image domain features
  - ♦ Junction
  - ♦ Line
  - ♦ Region

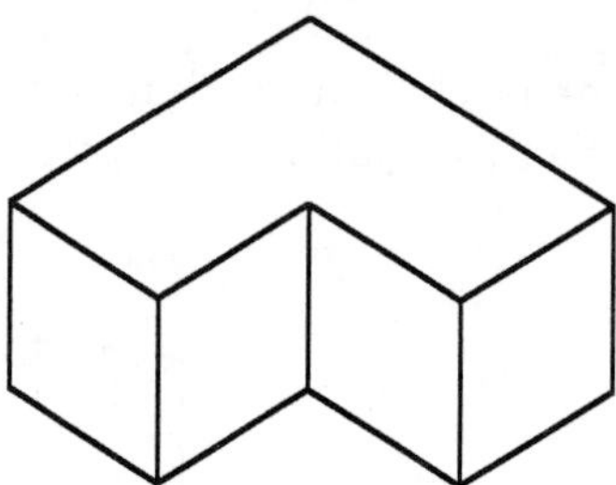

Figure 15-11 Solid object containing only trihedral vertices Trihedral vertices are produced by 3 planes meeting at any point on the object.

Consider the solid object shown in Figure 15-11. We are able to label the lines using the H & C classification scheme according to the three classes:

- Boundary line using an arrow, $\rightarrow$ or $\leftarrow$, with object always on the right.
- Concave interior edge (surfaces meet with an angle ø < 180°), labeled with (–).
- Convex interior edge (surfaces meet with an angle ø > 180°), labeled with (+).

Using this labeling system, we can classify all the lines on the object as shown in Figure 15-12:

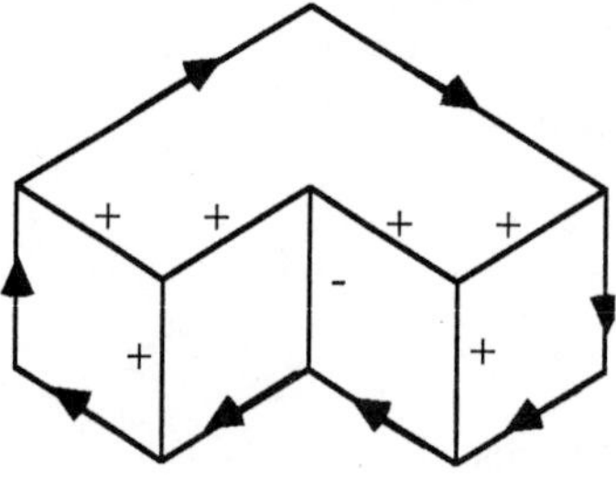

Figure 15-12 Previous solid with edges labeled by Huffman and Clowes (H & C) classification scheme

Huffman and Clowes noted that there are, in fact, only 18 possible junction configurations allowed by the geometry of real space, with the orientations as indicated in Figure 15-13.

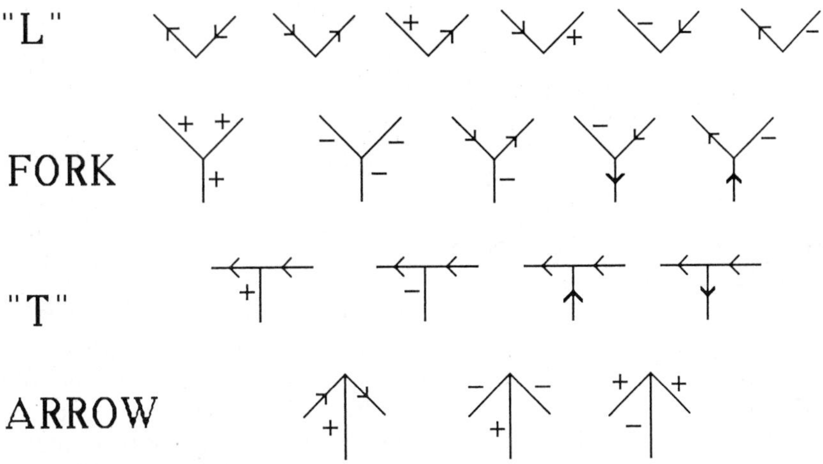

Figure 15-13 Huffman and Clowes classification of vertex types The trihedral vertex constraint reduced the eight vertex signatures introduced by Guzman to these four.

From an examination of Figure 15-13, certain useful rules for labeling images emerge. These include:

1) All edges separating a collection of objects from the background must be labeled by an "→" in clockwise fashion.

2) The only ARROW with "→" labeling its barbs must have a shaft labeled "+".

3) Any FORK with a "+" edge must have 3 "+" edges.

Now let's apply these rules for the identification of a well known object, the cube.

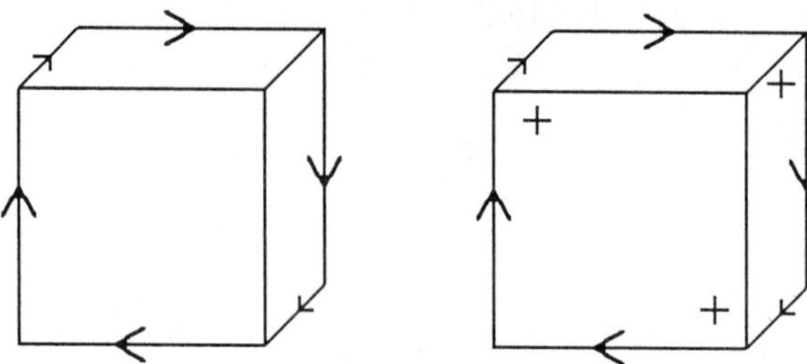

Figure 15-14 Use of constraint reduction for identification of a cube Apply rules 1, 2, and 3 in that order.

Note that the application of the rules listed uniquely identifies the configuration of edges and vertices of the cube's image as a 3-D cube. First we apply rule 1 and label all bounding edges with the right-hand arrow. Next, rule 2 indicates that the only possible edge type for the three ARROW type vertices is the (+) edge type. This is consistent with the FORK type of vertex (only internal vertex) required for the object to be a cube. Note how the constraint information was propagated inward along edges until the configuration of all edges and vertices was identified.

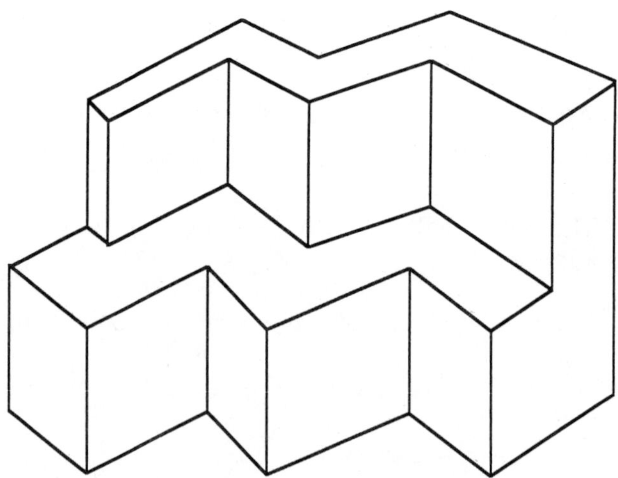

Figure 15-15 The H & C line labeling system can easily analyze complex objects such as this

By restricting their analysis to trihedral polyhedra and using the line labeling convention: convex edge = (+), concave edge = (–), and boundary edge = (→), Huffman and Clowes could identify complex objects such as shown in Figure 15-15:

By first tracing the object using arrow line labeling and the right hand rule, the arrow, corner vertices are identified as (→,+,→). The + boundary is propagated to the forks which makes all fork boundaries +. Next the label table indicates that an arrow with one + barb has a second + barb and a – shaft. Similarly, an arrow with a – barb has a second – barb and a + shaft. This information allows completion of the labeling process. The structure of the object is thus completely determined.

One interesting feature of the Huffman and Clowes algorithm is that it can identify physically "unrealizable" objects.[6] Consider the impossible object shown in Figure 15-16:

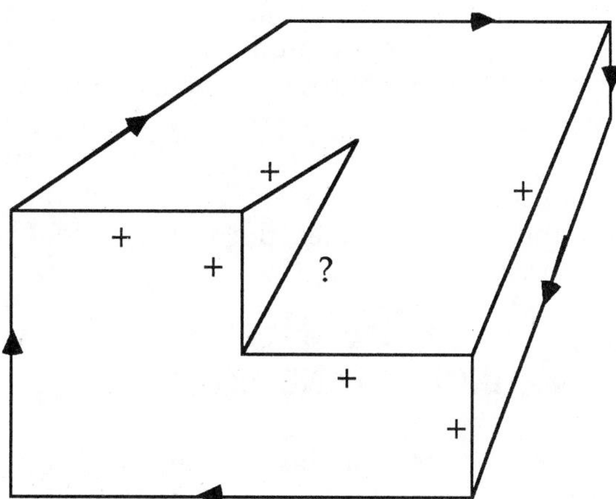

Figure 15-16 Physically impossible object. Physically the top surface cannot be planar and still satisfy the edge geometry shown. Huffman and Clowes' model identifies the object as unreal by failing to reach an unambiguous conclusion about the (?) edge.

Their algorithm indicates that the edge marked (?) must be a concave edge by the ARROW at the left end, but the "L" configurations identify it as a boundary edge. It is therefore ambiguous, indicating a non-unique physical solution and thus a physically impossible object.

WALTZ CONSTRAINT PROPAGATION ALGORITHM

David Waltz of Thinking Machines, Inc. discovered during his thesis work at MIT that by keeping a list of vertex types at each junction and propagating the allowed edge type outward from the vertex, an iterative process developed which rapidly converged to a unique geometric configuration. Consider the internal vertices consisting of two ARROWs, a FORK, and two "Ls" as shown in Figure 15-17.

Assume that no other information is available and that we start at ARROW A1. From the table of allowed geometries, Figure 15-13, we are allowed the three configurations shown. We next propagate this information to vertex "L" along the edge connecting them and this information carried into this vertex eliminates all but two of the original six possible "L" orientations. Propagating the information from these two configurations on to ARROW vertex A2, we make two more important reductions: i) only the upward-pointing "L" configuration matches a possible ARROW configuration, so the downward-pointing hypothesis is discarded, and ii) of the three possible ARROW types, only the double boundary/convex edge configuration matches the incoming information. So vertices "L" and A2 are now uniquely determined. We next propagate the information from vertex A2 on to vertex F. Since the (+) edge connecting them uniquely determines F, this vertex and its outgoing edges are now fixed. The downward-leading (+) edge from F is now propagated back to the starting node, A1. This new information reaching A1 selects one of the three original possibilities and thereby completes the unique identification of the geometry of this portion of the object.

15.5 VISION AND UNDERSTANDING

We have crept up on a much tougher problem which, while trivial for humans, remains fundamentally unsolved by artificial systems. The problem may be phrased in terms of Schank's Explanation Game:

> *"Here is a picture of some scene from the universe. Tell me all about it."*

That is, the ultimate goal of computer vision is the ability to identify the contents of an image and draw logical inferences based on this knowledge. This is the level of visual cognition in which the computer understands the scene it is viewing and can answer questions or take the appropriate action based on this knowledge.

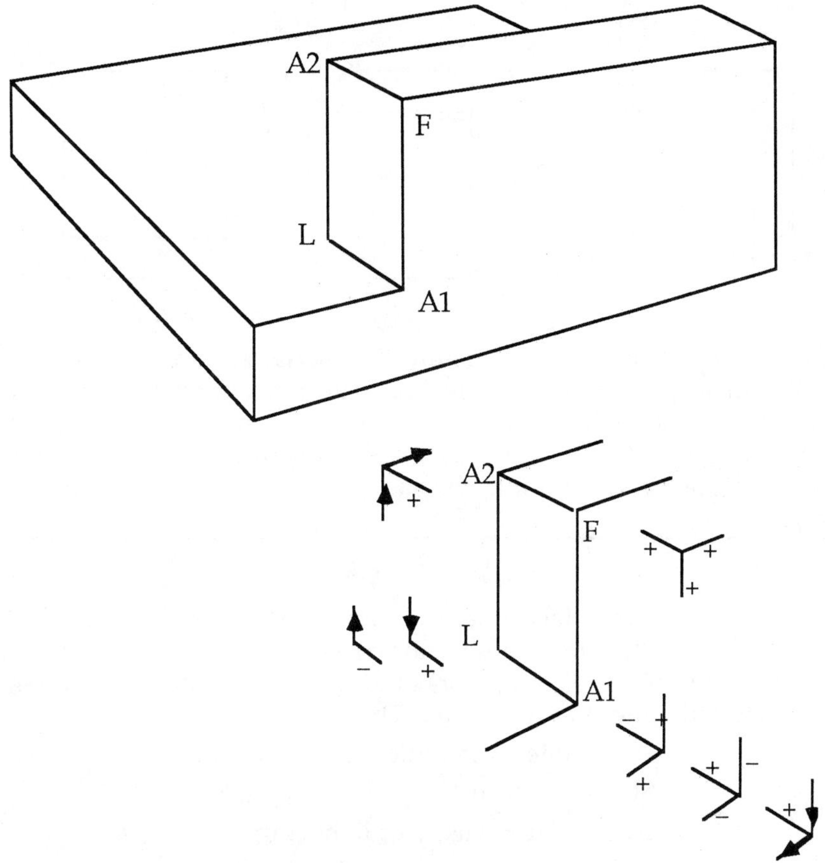

Figure 15-17 The Waltz Algorithm for constraint reduction The vertices are visited in the order: A1 → L → A2 → F → A1 to derive the unique, correct geometry.

Consider the following difficult problems which a computer vision system must solve in order to understand what it is seeing.

- A single image "under-constrains" a scene. That is, although there is a one-to-one mapping of the scene to the image, there is no unique inverse mapping from a single image to a scene. Another way of saying this is that a given image may be generated from an infinite number of scenes. The truth of this observation is evident in the impressive art of stage design both in film and the theater. A simple illustration of how an image under-constrains a scene is shown in the next figure in which the image of the cubical wire-frame can be generated by two significantly different scenes of the cube.

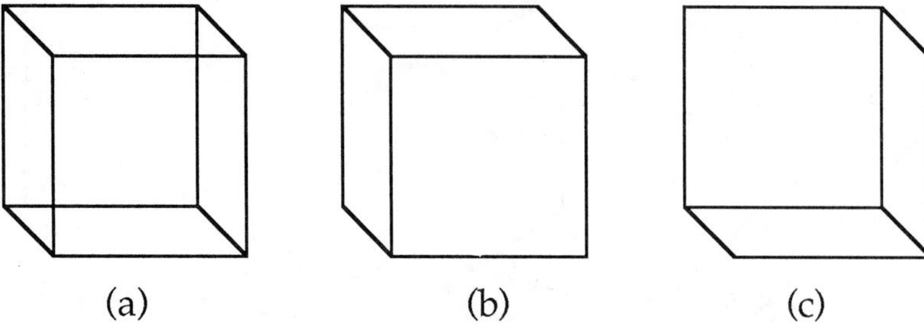

Figure 15-18 The Necker Illusion The Swiss naturalist L. A. Necker developed this figure in 1832 to illustrate perception illusions. Note how image (a) may be interpreted as representing configuration (b) or configuration (c). This illusion also demonstrates how two different physical scenes may map into the same image. (From *Vision* by David Marr)

- Many other factors are involved in mapping a scene into a particular image. These may conspire to confound the system interpreting the image, or, alternatively, to clue the system to correctly interpret the scene. They include:
  - ♦ Atmospheric conditions
  - ♦ Surface texture
  - ♦ Angle and intensity of light source
  - ♦ Ambient light intensity
  - ♦ Depth of field
  - ♦ Camera angle (point of view)

In the most general problem of image interpretation, none of these variables are under the control of the computer vision system. Practical computer vision systems, particularly those used in robotics applications, have succeeded primarily by the careful control of as many variables as possible. Consider the following aspects of the general problem of scene interpretation:

- Images of practical concern involve enormous quantities of data. One aerial photo, for instance, is represented by a 3000 × 3000 pixel array, each one of which contains 8 bits of gray-scale and/or color information. This would require almost a full 10 Mb of disk or RAM. If the processing required 10 operations per pixel it would take 90 million operations to analyze just one photograph.

• Human beings are almost all "experts" in the task of vision, but the expert → expert system bottleneck more nearly resembles a brick wall than merely a difficult knowledge engineering task. That is, when someone interprets photographs with such comments as:

- "That's a picture of a ball, and a pyramid on a box."
- "That's Grandpa Maier and cousin Michelle."
- "That's the Sears Tower of Chicago."
- "That's the Cathedral Group of the Grand Tetons."

and you ask, "How do you know?", the answer is almost always, "I just know, that's all!" This makes the job of the knowledge engineer building an expert system for computer vision extremely difficult.

• Understanding requires *a priori* knowledge of the task domain. That is, without a knowledge of mountains in general and experience in Grand Teton National Park (or pictures of it), you would be at a loss in identifying this splendid configuration of mountains.

• *What we see* is heavily dependent on what we have been trained to see and the context in which we see it. What, for instance, would a native of a recently discovered tribe from the Borneo jungle see if he suddenly arrived on a street corner on Fifth Avenue in New York? Or what would Aristotle see if he viewed a cyclonic storm over the Caribbean from an orbiting earth space station? Many of us have experienced the embarrassment of forgetting the name of a good friend from one social setting when we meet her in a different setting. Context is extremely important for providing the knowledge base for tasks such as understanding images.

• Efficient pattern recognition such as that performed by the brain is organized in a *parallel processing* fashion. Although the neuron has a response time on the order of milliseconds, the brain can perform exceedingly complex pattern recognition processes by bringing the order of 10^{10} neurons to bear on the problem simultaneously. Significant efforts are underway to simulate the operation of the brain by networks of artificial neurons and large parallel arrays of powerful microprocessors. The COSMIC CUBE concept of Geoffrey Fox and Chuck Seitz of the Jet Propulsion Laboratory of California Institute of Technology is one such effort.[7] This machine is designed to use an array of

1024 Motorola 68020 32-bit microprocessors and contain several Gb of memory. Its specifications provide for 10^{10} floating point operations per second (i.e., 10 GFLOPS). This is equivalent to the performance of 100 CRAY-1 super-computers. In the final chapter we consider new computer architectures for simulating the operation of the brain in greater detail.

15.6 THE VISION THEORY OF DAVID MARR

It is clear that block world research projects, while producing systems which worked, are extremely limited in their scope for interpreting realistic scenes from the physical world. There are many other features of life-like scenes which provide information which is useful in the interpretation of images. These include:

- Illumination and shadows
- Transparency and translucency
- Surface texture
- Spatial continuity
- Stereopsis
- Biological specialization and the purpose of vision
- Physics (gravity and material properties)

David Marr has integrated many of these important features into a unified theory which he presents in his book, *Vision*.[8] In *Vision*, Marr presents a synthesis of research done previously along with many of his own contributions to the field. This book represents one of the best current interpretation of this very complex subject.

PROBLEMS WITH EARLIER APPROACHES

The problems defeating earlier approaches to automating the process of visual cognition have been well summarized by Steven Pinker.[9] Pinker classifies traditional theories of shape recognition into the following categories, several of which we have already discussed:

Template Matching

This technique has been presented in the discussion of letter recognition and provided the basis for Roberts' block world analyzer. One of the problems with template matching is that variability in the object (erratic letters or curved lines on objects) defeat the match or lead to false identifications. Secondly, although Roberts successfully solved the transformation from 2-D image to 3-D scene for simple geometric objects, this problem becomes exponentially more difficult for the range and variability of naturally occurring objects. Finally, complex scenes containing a number of objects occluding each other require a figure-ground segregation process for isolating surfaces into parts which then could be matched against stored templates. This difficulty further compounds the first two problems.

Feature Extraction

Feature extraction algorithms attempt to refine template matching methods by extracting certain features present in an image and performing the best match of this set of features with features stored for the original object. For instance, a capital Z letter would generate large weights for the features: (1) one horizontal line, (2) one right-leaning vertical line, and (3) a second horizontal line. Note that feature extraction effectively solves the problems associated with scale and translation transformations in much the same manner as did the Teitelman letter recognizer.

By providing a higher level of abstraction than pattern matching, feature extraction has proven successful for certain applications such as character recognition. However, feature extraction suffers from several of the same problems as template matching. What, for instance, is the *natural* shape for a dog? A dog's logical features would include head, body, legs, and tail. Simply visualizing the variation between a poodle and a bulldog indicates the difficulty of specifying features to identify even a dog's head. Further complications due to 2-D $\rightarrow$ 3-D transformations, shadows, and occlusion eliminate feature extraction as a realistic algorithm for general visual cognition.

Fourier Analysis

There is evidence from physiological research that low-level human vision involves filtering the image by a number of channels sensitive to various spatial frequencies. This idea has been extended to machine vision analysis by transforming the spatial image, I(x,y), into its 2-D Fourier transform, F(u,v), according to the equation:[10]

$$F(u,v) = \int_{-\infty}^{+\infty}\int_{-\infty}^{+\infty} I(x,y)\, e^{-2\pi i(ux+vy)}\, dx\, dy \qquad (15.1)$$

The Fourier transform F(u,v) will, in general, be complex and contains all the information present in the original image, I(x,y). To recover the original image from its Fourier transform requires the inverse transformation:

$$I(x,y) = \int_{-\infty}^{+\infty} \int_{-\infty}^{+\infty} F(u,v)\, e^{+2\pi i(ux+vy)}\, du\, dv \tag{15.2}$$

In actual practice, the Fourier transform reduces to a Fourier series defined by sampling the image I(j,k) at the $(j,k)_{th}$ pixel of an $N \times N$ image.

$$F(u,v) = \frac{1}{N} \sum_{j=0}^{N-1} \sum_{k=0}^{N-1} I(j,k) \exp\left[\frac{-2\pi i}{N}(ju+kv)\right] \tag{15.3}$$

The inverse transformation for recovering the image from the series is:

$$I(j,k) = \frac{1}{N} \sum_{u=0}^{N-1} \sum_{v=0}^{N-1} F(u,v) \exp\left[\frac{2\pi i}{N}(ju+kv)\right] \tag{15.4}$$

The problem of object recognition is then transformed from matching space domain patterns to matching frequency domain patterns. The frequency spectra for all possible objects are stored and compared to the frequency spectra of the unknown object. What possible advantages does this additional level of analysis provide?

First, if phase information is ignored, Fourier analysis will recognize the object independently of where it appears in the image — that is, it provides translational invariant recognition. Secondly, the object and its mirror image have the same amplitude spectrum so Fourier analysis will recognize reflected objects. Finally, by segregating information about sharp edges (high spatial frequencies) from that about overall shape (low frequencies), Fourier analysis provides advantages in recognizing objects with partially blurred boundaries or objects encrusted with junk by comparing selective portions of the spectrum.

Many of these advantages of Fourier analysis apply only to isolated objects. If an object appears in a complex scene, it will produce a radically different Fourier spectrum from the same object appearing at a new position in the scene. Furthermore, from the amplitude information alone it is impossible to reconstruct the image of the scene — that is, one cannot locate the object in the image even if it is correctly identified. So, although spatial filtering provides useful information on object recognition, the Fourier transform algorithm does not provide adequate power for a general vision system.

Structural Descriptions

Structural descriptions are symbolic descriptions of objects, their component parts, and the relationships between them. Data structures for representing the object includes frames and semantic networks. The characteristics of the object and the relationships between its parts may be written in terms of propositional and predicate logic.

The choice of structural description of the objects appeals to many AI researchers for a number of reasons. First, it provides data abstraction without significant loss of information. Thus, the shape of an object may be defined by one set of propositions independent from propositions on its orientation, size, and relationship to other objects in the image. Secondly, the graphical network representation lends itself nicely to a hierarchical system in which an object is composed of parts which themselves can have various arrangements. The structural description combines logical relationships (dog has_part head, tail, etc.) with spatial descriptions (dog is chasing car) in order to answer functional questions which might be posed to the visual recognition system. It also has the advantage of drawing on the large body of machinery compiled by the AI research community.

With all these advantages, why has structural description not provided the solution to the problem of visual machine cognition? The main problem is that the structural description theory is not really a full theory of shape recognition. It may be particularly useful in representing objects and relationships once they have been recognized, but it does not address the fundamental problems of geometry, optics, physics, and pattern recognition which must be resolved before the components of the image are identified. One of the main contributions of David Marr and his colleagues was in stepping back and examining the problem of computer vision as a whole. In doing so Marr drew heavily on the psychophysics of human vision and clearly specified the research program required for successful computer vision.

THE ELEMENTS OF VISION

While *Vision* contains many seminal concepts, only some of the most important will be discussed here. The first major contribution that Marr emphasized is that ***any successful theory of vision must be a computational theory based on an information-processing approach.*** His criticism of previous approaches to scene analysis is that "... these ideas based on Fourier theory are *like* what is wanted, but they are not *what* is wanted; ... ." He points out that extreme care is required in the formulation of theories of vision because nature seems to have been very careful and exact in evolving our visual systems. Evidence for such evolution includes the specialized functions reflecting the *purpose of vision* present in many animals. Certain jumping spiders are sensitive to a red "V" whose presence distinguishes a potential mate from a potential meal. Frogs have special bug detectors built into their retinae, and the rabbit retina has a pattern detector for hovering hawks.

The second major contribution of Marr's vision theory is in recognizing that ***any machine carrying out an information-processing task must be understood at three levels of abstractions***. These are:

- *Computational theory* — What is the goal of the computation? Why is it appropriate? What is the logic of the strategy by which it can be carried out?

- *Representation and algorithm* — How can this computational theory be implemented? What representation should be used for the input, output, and the transformation relating the two?

- *Hardware implementation* — How can the representation and algorithm be realized physically?

Next Marr proposed a ***representational framework for vision*** in which he stressed the importance of the correct representation for deriving shape information from images. Noting that it is probably impossible to derive shape information from an image in one step, he proposed the following sequence of representations for interpreting images:

1) **Image** — Represented by intensity (gray-scale) values, I(x,y), at each point (pixel).

2) **Primal Sketch** — The purpose of the primal sketch is to make certain features of the image such as intensity changes and geometrical organization more explicit.

3) **The 21/2-D Sketch** — The purpose of this sketch is to make explicit the orientation and rough depth of the visible surfaces and the contours of discontinuities in these quantities in a viewer-centered coordinate frame.

4) **The 3-D Model Representation** — This model describes shapes and their spatial organization in an object-centered coordinate frame and contains information on object volumes as well as surface primitives.

Let us consider each of these stages in somewhat more detail.

1) **Image**

Marr made some observations about images which must be considered before any vision system can successfully interpret them. Many of these observations stem directly from the laws of nature and pose problems of such a complexity that previous researchers had simply ignored them.

The primary factors determining the intensity values in an image are:

- the geometry
- the illumination of the scene
- the viewpoint
- the reflectances of the visible surfaces.

How can one distinguish, for example, between a scene containing several objects and one containing a textured surface (e.g. woven fabric, the bark of a tree, or the surface of a river with rapids)? Marr noted that *the items generated on a given surface by a reflectance-generating process acting at a given scale tend to be more similar to one another in their size, local contrast, color, and spatial organization than to other items on that surface.*

Marr also made the fundamental observation that the cohesiveness of matter leads to a continuity in the discontinuities in depth or surface orientation. That is, the physical shape of a solid object provides the basis for the assumption that the loci of discontinuities in depth or in surface orientation are smooth almost everywhere.

2) **Primal Sketch**

The primal sketch is the lowest level symbolic representation of the intensity image. It is still a 2-D representation consisting of a pattern of edge segments, corners, bars, and blobs corresponding to the structure of the original image. A key concept for transforming the image into a primal sketch is the zero-crossing edge detector. Marr and Hildreth have suggested the operator $\nabla^2 G$ as an appropriate filter for edge detection.[11] This operator is a function produced when the Laplacian operator ∇^2 acts on the two-dimensional Gaussian distribution, G(x,y). The Laplacian operator ∇^2 is given by:

$$\nabla^2 = \frac{\partial^2}{\partial x^2} + \frac{\partial^2}{\partial y^2} \qquad (15.5)$$

and the Gaussian distribution is given by:

$$G(x,y) = e^{-\frac{x^2+y^2}{2\pi\sigma^2}} \qquad (15.6)$$

where

σ = standard deviation (proportional to the width of the Gaussian)

The shape of the $\nabla^2 G$ operator is shown in one dimension in Figure 15-19.

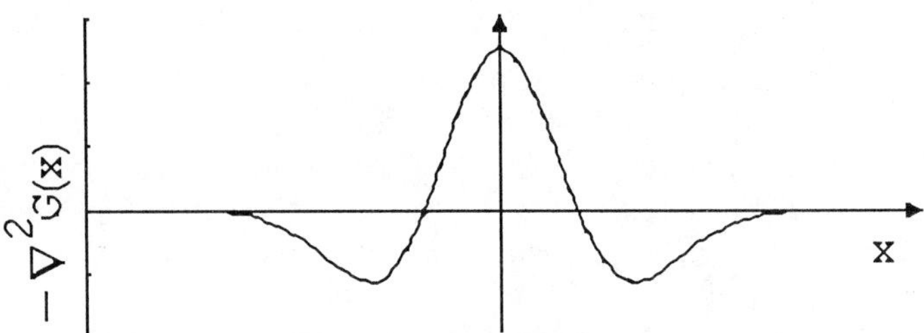

Figure 15-19 Shape of the $\nabla^2 G$ operator This curve is generated by letting the ∇^2 operator operate on the G(x,y) function for the case of y = 0. That is, the curve is a slice through the 2-D function.

The $\nabla^2 G$ operator satisfies two essential features which any good edge-detecting filter should have, namely:

- The filter should be a differential operator taking either the first or second derivative of the I(x,y) image. That is, it senses *intensity changes*.

- The filter should be adjustable so that it can detect edges over a range of spatial scales.

The Laplacian operator satisfies the first criterion and σ in the Gaussian function provides the control knob for tuning the spatial scale. An additional strong motivation for choosing the $\nabla^2 G$ operator is that it nearly identical to the "difference of Gaussians" (DOG) behavior known to apply to mammalian visual response.

The operation of Marr's $\nabla^2 G$ edge detector may be understood conceptually by segmenting it into the following three steps:

1. *Blur the image* — The first step is to set σ to the appropriate scale and apply the Gaussian G as a "point-spreading function" to blur the image. A large σ produces massive blurring for the purpose of detecting the gross features of the image. A small σ produces a slight blurring for detecting the finer features. The formal process of applying G(x,y) to the image I(x,y) is called the "convolution" of G with I and is written $G \otimes I$. The effect of the $G \otimes I$ convolution is to transform a given pixel I(j,k) into a pixel I'(j,k) which is obtained by averaging other pixels within a region of order of σ of the (j,k)th pixel weighted by the Gaussian function. Both Horn and Levine have excellent discussion on spatial filtering and the convolution process.

2. *Apply the Laplacian Operator* — As shown in Figure 15-20, the smoothed edge is most accurately detected by noting where the second derivative goes through zero. In order to determine this the second derivative must be generated. The Laplacian operator performs this function. This may be written formally as generating the transformed image $\nabla^2(G \otimes I)$. It may be shown that $\nabla^2(G \otimes I)$ is mathematically identical to $(\nabla^2 G) \otimes I$. That is, in practice, the Mexican-hat shaped function $\nabla^2 G$ is convolved with the image I to produce the transformed field.

3. *Trace out the zero crossings* — Once the $\nabla^2 G$ transformed field is generated the best estimate of the edge contours are determined by following the contours corresponding to the value of zero of the field. This constitutes an essential element of the primal sketch at that particular scale. The set of zero crossings for a range of scale factors σ_i constitutes what Marr call the raw primal sketch. He also makes the interesting observation that the set of zero-crossings contains virtually all the information of the original I(x,y) image.

The principle of operation of a zero-crossing detector as an edge detector is illustrated in Figure 15-20. Here a slice along x of the blurred edge is shown as the changing intensity pattern in the top curve, the first derivative of this pattern is shown in the middle curve, and the second derivative in the bottom curve. The well-defined zero-crossing point indicated by the arrow marks the edge between the light and dark regions.

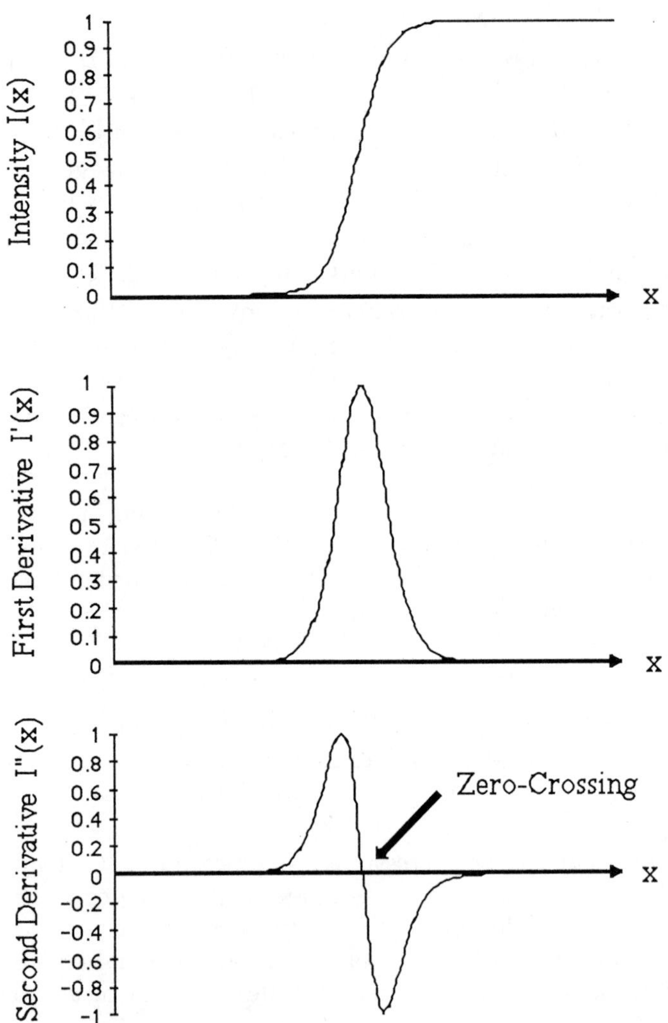

Figure 15-20 Principle of Zero-Crossing Edge Detector The top curve shows a slice through the intensity pattern I(x,y) as we hold y = constant and move along x from a dark region into a bright region through a blurred edge. The point at which the second derivative crosses zero provides a very sharp and reproducible definition of the edge between the light and dark regions.

The effect of applying the $\nabla^2 G$ edge detector can be seen in Figure 15-21. Figure (a) is the original image, I(x,y), Figure (b) is the result of convolving $\nabla^2 G$ with I(x,y) (steps 1 and 2 of the algorithm), and Figure (c) is obtained by tracing out the zero-crossings according to step 3.

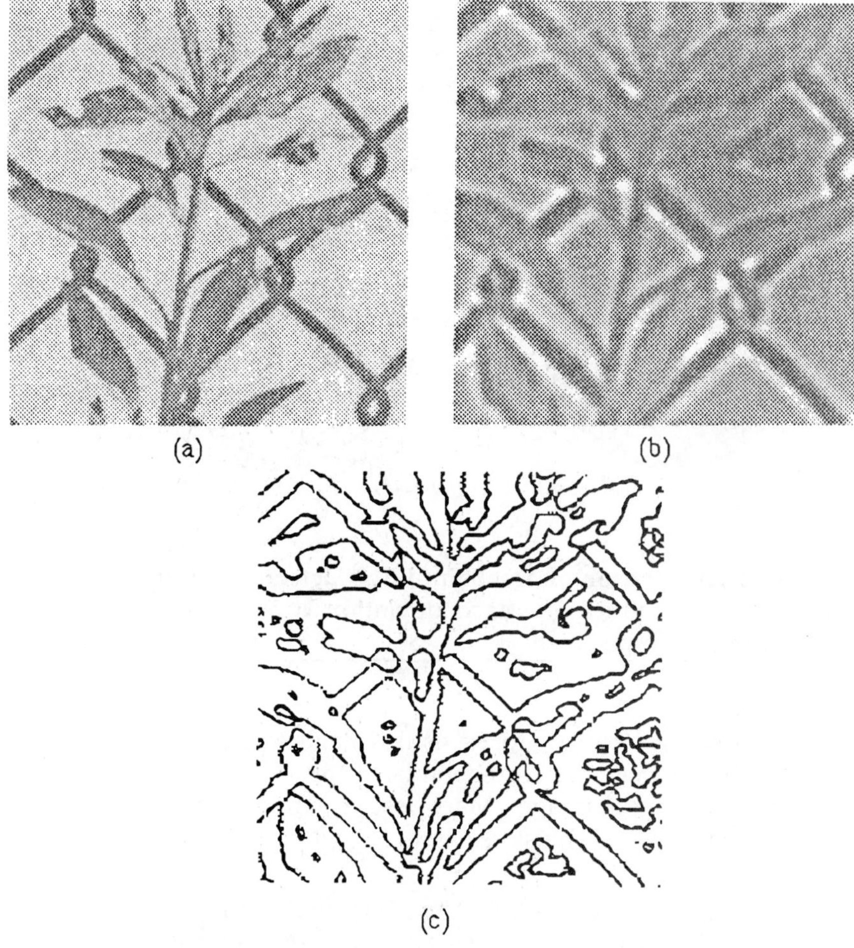

Figure 15-21 Application of $\nabla^2 G$ as Zero-Crossing Edge Detector (a) shows the original image, (b) shows the convolution of the image with a point-spread $\nabla^2 G$ function with $\sigma = 8$ pixels, and (c) shows the results of tracing out the zero-crossings. (From D. Marr and E. Hildreth, "Theory of edge detection," *Proc. R. Soc. Lond.* **B207**, pp. 187–217)

A number of personal computer programs provide effective edge detection using a scale parameter σ of one pixel. Figure 15-22 shows the application of the MacPaint edge detector to some simple images.

Figure 15-22 Application of MacPaint Edge Detector Applying the zero crossing detector with a standard deviation of 1 pixel to (a) and (c) yields (b) and (d), respectively.

If the zero-crossings coincide for several scale factors of the spatial filter, it is highly likely that this corresponds to the location of the physical edge of an object in the image. Marr describes this as the spatial coincidence assumption which he states as:

> *"If a zero-crossing is present in a set of independent* $\nabla^2 G$ *channels over a contiguous range of sizes, and the segment has the same position and orientation in each channel, then the set of such zero-crossing segments indicates the presence of an intensity change in the image that is due to a single physical phenomenon (a change in reflectance, illumination, depth, or surface orientation)."*

3) **The 21/2-D Sketch**

The 21/2-D sketch consists of a matrix of cells in which each cell corresponds to a particular line of sight from the viewer to the scene. Each cell contains symbolic information concerning the element of surface lying along its line of sight. This information includes:

- Orientation of the element with respect to the viewer's coordinate system
- Distance between the element and the viewer
- Presence of a discontinuity in orientation within the cell (if it exists)
- Presence of a discontinuity in depth within the cell, i.e. an edge (if it exists)

The whole range of 3-D spatial reconstruction arsenal is brought to bear on the task of generating the surface information in the 21/2-D sketch. Some of the most powerful tools in this arsenal have been developed by the evolution of the human visual processing system and include:

- *Stereopsis* — Stereopsis is the psychological process by which we determine the relative distance between an object and the viewer by the angular discrepancy in position of the object observed in the stereoscopic binocular views of the eyes.

- *Apparent Motion* — Apparent motion of objects can be readily observed by moving the head slightly while viewing a scene. The set of images produced in such motion is equivalent to a series of stereoscopic images and contains a great deal of 3-D information. A closely related concept is that of *optical flow,* the apparent motion of objects as we move through our environment.

- *Shape Contours* — The image of equipotential lines or slices through 3-D surfaces have a remarkable ability to convey information to human viewers.

- *Surface Texture and Shading* — Both the surface texture and shading convey much 3-D information. Professor Horn has developed a method for extracting shape from shading and can successfully predict the image which a given mountain scene will produce, given the topographic map and time of day.[12]

Note that the 21/2-D sketch has some elements of a 3-D representation without yet being a complete 3-D representation. That is, since the 21/2-D sketch is the result of purely "bottom-up" processing, it contains no information on the back side of opaque objects which could only be obtained by "top-down" techniques such as pattern matching with known objects. It is also still viewpoint dependent — that is, the representation will change as the viewer's position changes.

4) **The 3-D Model Representation**

The final phase in the representational framework for vision involves transforming the 21/2-D sketch into a true 3-D structural description of the objects in a scene. This is the least complete and most problematic aspect of Marr's theory of vision, but Marr and Nishihara have made a number of observations which are proving valuable to vision research.[13] Several of these observations include:

- *Many natural shapes can be reasonably represented by a generalized cone.* — A generalized cone or generalized cylinder is the surface generated by moving a cross section of arbitrary shape along an axis. The axis itself may be curved and the cross section may vary in size but not in shape. So, for instance, a football and a pyramid are ideal generalized cones, while an arm, a tree trunk, a stalagmite, and a snake all approximate generalized cones. These shaped are relatively easy to represent computationally and were chosen as the primitives for the 3-D representations. Marr has shown that it is possible to recover the parameters of a generalized cone from silhouette information alone. Figure 15-23 shows a horn-shaped generalized cone.

- *An object-centered coordinate system simplifies the representation.* — One of the main problems in shape recognition is the great range of variability among objects within a class. A horse, for instance, may have a virtually infinite number of representations corresponding to the range of possible orientations of head, neck, legs, and tail. The solution to this problem of *stability of representation* proposed by Marr and Nishihara is to align the object's primary coordinate system along the axis of the main generalized cone — the torso of the horse in this case. Secondary coordinate systems may then be aligned with the axes of the component parts such as neck, head, and legs. Any axis may be related to any other axis in the system by three cylindrical and three polar coordinates. Thus the problem of an infinite number of representations of a complex objects is reduced to representation of the position and orientation of a relatively small number of invariant parts.

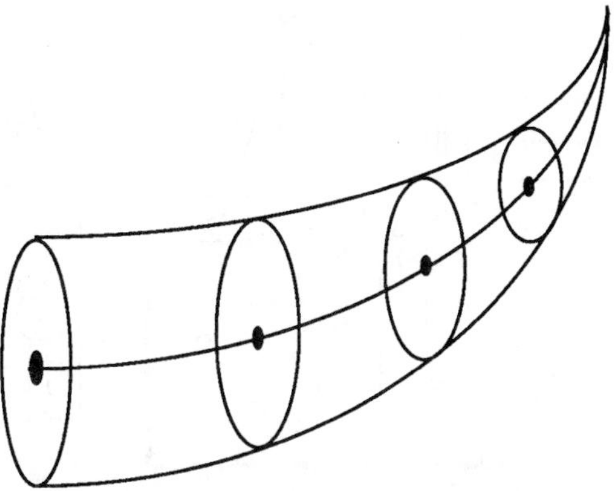

Figure 15-23 Generalized cone in the shape of a horn Generalized cones are generated by moving a closed planar figure (here a circle) along a (possibly curved) axis. The shape may vary in size as it moves. Many of the shapes in nature may be represented approximately by generalized cones.

- *A hierarchical structural description simplifies the analysis.* — Marr and Nishihara noted the tendency of objects to cluster around well-defined "plans" such as primates, quadrupeds, and birds. Thus, the primary coordinate axis for erect primates such as humans would be vertical whereas that of a quadruped such as a horse would be horizontal. By detecting a primarily vertical orientation of an object at an early stage of analysis, all quadrupeds could be eliminated from the search for a matching pattern. Once the class of primates was determined, the need to attempt matches to guppies, parakeets, and beetles would also be eliminated. The hierarchical structural description of candidate objects constrains the search in both the top-down direction (illustrated above) and in the bottom-up direction. If, for instance, the top-level match was ambiguous, but a lower-level match had clearly identified a wing as part of the object, all primates and quadrupeds could be immediately eliminated from the search and interest focussed on the bird and insect kingdoms.

In Figure 15-24 we show the 3-D model of a human in which several of these ideas are illustrated.

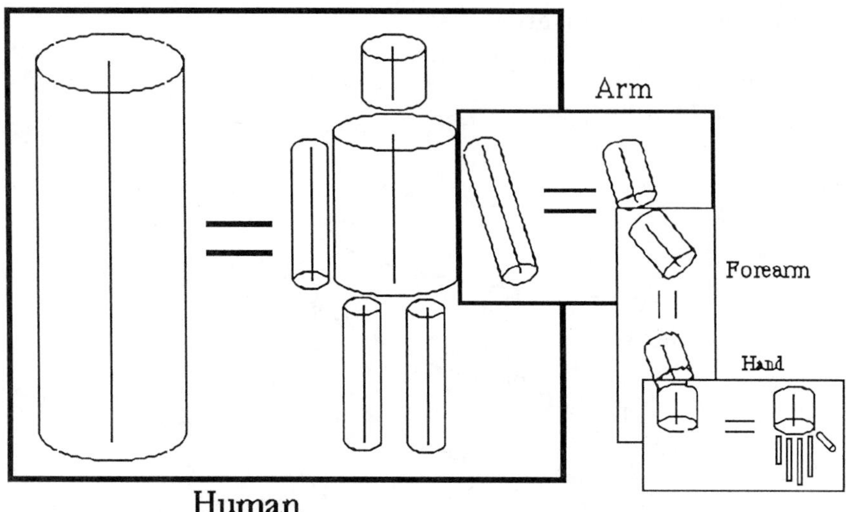

Figure 15-24 Hierarchical 3-D Model of a Human Note the generalized cone structure of each part (in this case, a circular cylinder) and the hierarchical structural description in which each level of description is refined into a description of its parts. The arm, for instance, may be represented by the upper arm, the forearm, and the relative orientation of the two. A complete symbolic description of the human at the second level from the top is defined by 36 symbols: six coordinates each for the torso, head, arm_1, arm_2, leg_1, and leg_2.

Based on these observations and concepts, the Marr/Nishihara algorithm for constructing a 3-D model representation from a 21/2-D sketch can be summarized in the following three steps:

1. Define a primary coordinate system centered in the object being analyzed.

2. Specify the spatial structure of the component parts of the object with respect to the primary coordinate system.

3. Compare this structural description with the set of canonical descriptions stored in the database of possible objects. Select the one most closely matching.

Problems with the Marr/Nishihara Theory

The first three phases of Marr's theory of vision is built on a reasonably secure foundation of analogy with animal and human vision. The final phase of building 3-D representations from the 21/2-D sketch is on a less secure footing although it remains the most important contemporary model of shape recognition. Some of the problems unresolved by the theory include:

- Some geometries defeat the first step of determining the axis of the primary coordinate system. How does one determine the coordinate system for a horse from a head-on image or a human seen from above?

- Many object in nature are not well characterized by generalized cones. Consider, for example, faces, orchids, clouds, and mountain streams. Many natural objects such as mountains, clouds, and coastlines are much more naturally described by fractal geometry than the cylindrical geometry described here.[14]

- The problem of carving an object into its component parts remains difficult for the general case. This corresponds to the "figure from ground" problem in psychology and becomes particularly difficult for the case of complex scenes in which objects are partially occluded by other objects.

- Image understanding may require massively parallel architectures. Much of the success in Marr's research resulted from careful study of the proof of principle — human vision. The top-level of human visual understanding is performed by billions of neurons connected in a network of incredible complexity. Success in machine vision may depend on emerging machines using similar massively parallel architectures. We consider such architectures in the final chapter.

15.7 CONCLUSION

David Marr's contributions have laid the scientific foundation for future development in the area of computer vision. While some of his specific ideas have been criticized,[15] the general consensus was well stated in Science magazine:

> "*Vision* will be seen as a milestone in the history of the subject. Even if no single one of Marr's detailed hypotheses ultimately

survives, which is unlikely, the questions he raises can no longer be ignored and the methodology he proposed seems to be the only one that has any hope of illuminating the bewildering circuitry of the central nervous system. David Marr's lifework will have been vindicated when neuro-scientists cannot understand how it was ever possible to doubt the validity of his theoretical maxims."

PROBLEMS AND PROGRAMS

15-1. Write a program to recognize the capital vowel letters by the technique of pattern matching. Represent each letter on a 8 × 8 matrix as a stored pattern of 1's and 0's. Read in the character by writing it out using mouse strokes and sampling the mouse coordinates and digitizing them on an appropriate 8 × 8 grid.

15-2. Are there any features of the human eye listed in section 15.2 which have been surpassed by machine vision? Which do you believe will be the last to be matched by computer vision? (You may want to use the performance of surveillance satellites as the benchmark for comparison.)

15-3. List at least four levels of computer vision in increasing order of sophistication and indicate the success in reaching each level to date.

15-4. Compare the performance of commercially available image digitizers with the resolution typical of newspaper photographs, magazine color photographs, and typeset book-quality print and photographs.

15-5. Describe in some detail the algorithm you would use to teach a computer equipped with a commercial image scanning device to read.

15-6. How many bytes of memory are required to store a digital image of 640 × 480 pixels with a 32-level gray-scale? How many are required for 1,024 × 768 pixels with 256 colors?

15-7. Several new programs have appeared recently for handling graphical images as standard data file items. Describe five potential applications for such programs. How will the availability of low-cost digital scanners effect the market for such graphical file systems?

15-8. Discuss the potential interactions between graphical file systems and AI applications. In what ways can AI techniques improve the performance of graphical file systems? In what ways can graphical file systems contribute to AI application systems?

15-9. The text indicates that there are many 3-D scenes which can map into a given 2-D image. Sketch a 2-D image and three different 3-D scenes which would produce the 2-D image when photographed.

15-10. Several factors mentioned in the text (atmospheric conditions, surface texture, etc.) were cited as causing possible confusion in the correct interpretation of a 2-D image in terms of the original 3-D scene. Discuss the mechanism by which each factor can confound the interpretation.

15-11. The same factors referred to in problem 15-10 can often aid in interpreting 2-D images as 3-D scenes. Discuss the mechanism (if any) by which each feature may help interpret the original scene.

15-12. The text's assertion "What we see is heavily dependent on what we have been trained to see and the context in which we see it" helps explain why many significant discoveries have been overlooked by very reputable scientists because "The time was not yet right for discovery." Cite several such discoveries which may be interpreted in these terms.

15-13. Re-interpret the Waltz algorithm in recursive language terms.

15-14. Sketch Figure 15-15 and use the Huffman and Clowes reduction techniques to label each edge appropriately.

15-15. Describe in detail how the Huffman and Clowes reduction technique leads to the conclusion that the object shown in Figure 15-16 is impossible.

15-16. Discuss four examples from the animal kingdom in which the *purpose of vision* has led to the evolution of special-purpose retinal "gadgets" which improve the animal's survival. (David Marr's *Vision* is a good reference.)

15-17. Describe in what important aspects Marr's computational vision theory differed from its predecessors.

15-18. What was the experimental basis for Marr's selection of the zero-crossing detector and the Laplacian function as the basis for generating the *raw primal sketch*?

15-19. A popular image analysis technique has been 2-D Fourier transform analysis. Discuss the advantages and disadvantages of this analysis procedure.

15-20. Although the four "earlier approaches" to visual understanding (template matching — structural description) are not as complete theories as that presented in *Vision*, each has had some success in practical applications. Describe an application for each of the four approaches.

15-21. Use Equation 15.1 to compute and plot the 1-D Fourier transform, F(u), for I(x) = $\nabla^2 G(x)$ (assume y and v = 0).

15-22. Verify graphically that the $\nabla^2 G$ function may be closely approximated by the difference between two Gaussians, $G_1 - G_2$, with $\sigma_2 = 1.6\ \sigma_1$.

15-23. "Bottom-up" processes are characterized as *knowledge-free*, while "top-down" processes can be considered *knowledge-rich*. Categorize each of the three representations primal sketch, 21/2-D sketch, and 3-D model according to this scheme and justify your assignment.

15-24. Alex Pentland has developed a very powerful, intuitive model for vision in which the scene structure is composed of parts reflecting a possible formative history of the object.[16] Discuss Pentland's theory and the role fractal geometry plays in it.

15-25. The cornerstone of Marr's theory of vision is that any successful theory must be a computational theory based on an information-processing approach leading to a symbolic representation of the scene. What aspects of the theory may have to be revised if massively parallel architectures prove successful for machine vision?

REFERENCES AND FOOTNOTES

1 Hall, Ernest L., *Computer Image Processing and Recognition,* Academic Press, New York, NY (1979)

2 Horn, Berthold K. P., *Robot Vision,* MIT Press, Cambridge, MA (1986)

3 Roberts, L., "Machine Perception of Three-Dimensional Solids," in *Optical and Electro-Optical Information Processing,* Tippett, J., (ed), MIT Press, Cambridge, MA (1965)

4 Guzman, Aldolfo, "Computer Recognition of Three Dimensional Objects in a Visual Scene," Ph.D. Thesis, AI-TR-228, Artificial Intelligence Laboratory, MIT, Cambridge, MA (1968)

5 Winston, Patrick Henry, *Artificial Intelligence,* First Edition, Addison-Wesley Publishing Company, Reading, MA (1977)

6 Huffman, D. A., "Impossible Objects as Nonsense Sentences," in *Machine Intelligence* **8**, Meltzer, R. and Michie, D., (eds), Elsevier, New York, NY (1971)

7 Fox, Geoffrey, "The Cosmic Cube as a Prototype of the Future General Purpose SuperComputer," Paper CB-3, Spring Meeting of the American Physical Society, April 24–27, 1985. See also: Seitz, C. L., "The Cosmic Cube," CACM, January (1985)

8 Marr, D. C., *Vision,* W. H. Freeman, San Francisco, CA (1982)

9 Pinker, Steven (ed), *Visual Cognition,* A Bradford Book, MIT Press, Cambridge, MA (1985)

10 Levine, Martin D., *Vision in Man and Machine,* McGraw-Hill Book Company, p. 262, New York, NY (1985)

11 Marr, D., and Hildreth, E., "Theory of Edge Detection," *Proc. R. Soc. Lond* **B** 204, pp. 301–328 (1980)

12 Horn, B. K. P., "Obtaining shape from shading information," *The Psychology of Computer Vision,* P. H. Winston (ed), pp. 115–155, McGraw Hill Book Company, New York, NY (1975)

13 Marr, D. and Nishihara, H. K., "Representation and recognition of

the spatial organization of three-dimensional shapes," *Proc. R. Soc. Lond.* **200**, pp. 269–294 (1978)

14 Pentland, A. P., "Perceptual Organization and the Representation of Natural Form," *Artificial Intelligence* **28**, pp. 293–331, (1986)

15 Mayhew, John and Frisby, John, "Computer Vision" in *Artificial Intelligence — Tools, Techniques, and Applications,* O'Shea, T. and Eisenstadt, M., (eds), Harper and Row Publishers, Inc., New York, NY (1984)

16 Pentland, A., "Local analysis of the image," *IEEE Transactions on Pattern Analysis and Machine Recognition* **6**, pp. 170–187 (1984). See also Pentland, A., *From Pixels to Predicates,* Ablex Publishing Co., Norwood, NJ (1986)

Chapter 16

ROBOTICS

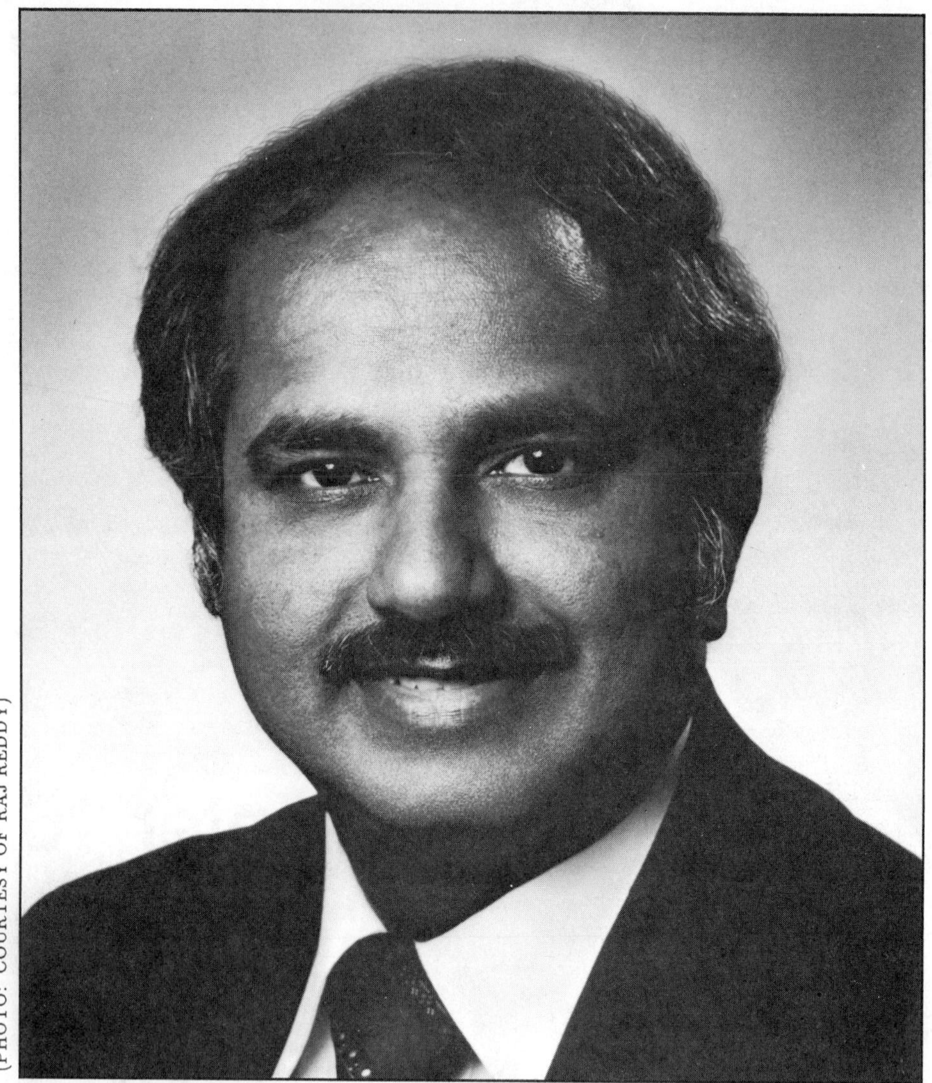

(PHOTO: COURTESY OF RAJ REDDY)

Dr. Raj Reddy is University Professor of Computer Science and Robotics and Director of the Robotics Institute at Carnegie-Mellon University. He received his B.S. degree in Civil Engineering from the University of Madras, India, and his Ph.D. in Computer Science from Stanford University. His current AI research activities involve the study of speech, vision, robotics, and applications specific architectures. Dr. Reddy serves on the board of directors of several corporations, including the Carnegie Group Inc. and Telxon Corp., and is a consultant to many companies and government agencies. He is a Fellow of the IEEE and the Acoustical Society of America, and former President of the American Association for Artificial Intelligence.

16: ROBOTICS

16.1 INTRODUCTION

Robotics is an application area which integrates many of the concepts we have studied in artificial intelligence. A question that immediately comes to mind is: Is robotics really a branch of AI? Or should AI be considered a branch of robotics in light of the much longer history of automata development. Some would even argue that artificial intelligence, as the science of cognitive processes in minds and machines, can never involve applied areas such as expert systems and robotics. Proponents of this argument hold that once an area of AI becomes well enough understood so that it spawns applications it then becomes engineering or technology and no longer qualifies for the label artificial intelligence.

Our position is that there is enough common ground between AI and robotics to warrant at least a survey of this exciting area of application. The critical role of AI in the field of robotics is well summarized in the statement, "Artificial Intelligence is the technological area which needs most to be developed and mastered to accelerate robot evolution."[1] The obvious areas of overlap in which AI has already contributed fundamental understanding and techniques useful to robotics include:

- Scene recognition and understanding through computer vision
- Means-ends analysis as a tool for cybernetics
- Natural language processing for robot programming and control
- Pattern recognition of input sensor data
- Use of models for interpreting and controlling an operating environment
- Models, algorithms, and heuristics for machine learning
- Self awareness and on-line monitoring of system operation

To focus on the trend toward the flexibility provided by intelligent robotics, consider the definition suggested by the Robotics Industries Association:

> *A robot is a re-programmable, multi-functional, manipulator designed to move material, parts, tools, or other specialized devices through various programmed motions for the performance of a variety of tasks.*[2]

This definition fits most industrial applications of robots with the exception of those used for inspection. It also does not include the interesting areas of self-locomotive robots or the so-called "personal robot." While there are useful classes of robots with no intelligence or decision-making ability at all, most robots are now closely integrated with computers. We suggest the following definition of robots of interest to students of AI:

> ***A robot is a computer with the purpose and capability of motion.***

16.2 HISTORY OF ROBOT DEVELOPMENT

The term "robot" itself was introduced by the Czechoslovakian playwright Karel Capek in his play *R.U.R.* whose title is an acronym for Rossum's Universal Robots. In the Slavic languages robot means *worker* or *serf*. In the play, the mechanical servants increased in sophistication and finally revolted and took over the world.

The concept of humanoid automatons actually predates Capek's robots by several hundred years. In the 1700s Jacques de Vaucanson built life-size musician robots which could actually play music. His invention of punched-cards for controlling the Jacquard loom survived until recently in the form of "IBM cards". In the 1770s, the Swiss craftsmen Pierre and Henri-Louis Jaquet-Droz created three marvelous automata, the Scribe, the Draughtsman, and the Musician. The Scribe was an elegantly dressed school boy who could write with a quill pen which he dipped in ink and moved over the paper with graceful strokes. All three Jaquet-Droz androids were powered by a spring-driven clock escapement and controlled by a set of precision cams.[3] Another very impressive series of automata was constructed by Henri Maillardet in the early 1800s. His automata also used cams as read-only memory and could produce very impressive handwriting and art sketches. Finally, from the fields of literature and art we have the tales of E. T. A. Hoffman with the beautiful puppet Olympia with whom

Hoffman falls in love in Offenbach's opera, and the pitiful monster created by Dr. Frankenstein in Mary Shelley's novel.

Later writers such as Isaac Asimov have painted a much less gloomy portrait of robots than those of Shelly and Capek. As robots gradually assume more intelligence we may even find Asimov's three laws of robotics useful for integrating them into human society:[4]

> **First Law** — A robot must never harm a human being, or, through inaction, allow a human being to come to harm.
>
> **Second Law** — A robot must always obey a human being, unless this is in conflict with the first law.
>
> **Third Law** — A robot must protect itself from harm, unless this is in conflict with either of the first two laws.

The helpful robots R2D2 and C3P0 from *Star Wars* tried to live up to the letter of the law, but HAL in Arthur Clark's *2001* fatally violates the first and second laws because of inconsistent instructions. A troublesome ethical issue which many newly graduating students in science and technology must face as they enter their new careers is: Will the robots developed under military auspices obey Asimov's three laws of robotics?

ORIGINS OF MODERN INDUSTRIAL ROBOTS

Two important developments served as precursors to the first generation of modern industrial robots. The first grew out of the need to handle dangerous, radioactive materials at a distance and has evolved into the highly refined branch of engineering known as *remote-control engineering*.[5] Much of the research and development in remote-control engineering was performed at Argonne National Laboratory in Illinois. This involved the remote handling of materials such as plutonium, a radioactive, toxic, and pyrophoric material. Early versions of the Argonne manipulator consisted of two mechanical, two-fingered hands which reproduced the motion of the operator's hands in great detail. The operator viewed the operation of the manipulators through a thick lead-glass window in the wall separating the radioactive materials from human workers. The manipulators were mechanically coupled over the wall by a pulley and cable boom system. In subsequent versions of the Argonne manipulator, truly remote operation was achieved by the use of servo motors with video camera observation. The names *telecheric* or *teleoperator* are now used for these remote-controlled manipulators.

Two problems encountered and solved by the remote-control engineers involved mechanical gain and tactile feedback. For handling heavy objects it is useful to have mechanical gain built into the system so that the human operator does not tire so easily. Secondly, many of the experiments performed by remote control involved chemical laboratory glassware. It was essential that the remote manipulator hand provide a feedback response to the human operator in order to avoid crushing the glassware. The human hand/mind system is amazingly sophisticated in automatically adjusting to this complicated task — we automatically grasp a glass firmly enough so as not to let it slip but not so tightly that we crush it.

These pioneering efforts in remote-control engineering have proven valuable in many applications. Among them are:

- The handling of dangerous and explosive materials.
- Deep sea, ocean floor exploration as demonstrated on the Titanic.
- Space shuttle experiment applications.
- Unmanned exploration of planets, moons, and asteroids.

The second development which made robots feasible was in the field of *numerically controlled machinery.* Numerical control (NC) machines are machine tools such as lathes and milling machines to which digitally-controlled servo motors have been added. In early versions, the operator punched out a paper tape with the proper sequence of control operations and dimensions which served as a "program" for controlling the machine. On more recent machines, a computer is coupled directly to the machine for what is known as direct numerical control (DNC).

By 1954 George Devol realized that these two technologies could be combined to produce an industrial robot. He patented some of the basic concepts of industrial robot design, and by 1956 Unimation, the first company to manufacture industrial robots, was established. Unimation controlled approximately 45% of the United States market.in 1981, and its purchase in 1983 by Westinghouse formally confirmed the involvement of "big business" with robotics. The issues leading to the hiatus in the robotics industry symbolized by Westinghouse's sale of the Unimation Division in 1987 are discussed in the last section of this chapter. Japan has the distinction of being the number one user of industrial robots. They have installed over fifty percent of the robots in operation and account for about 30% of the sales of robots in the United States.

16.3 CLASSIFICATIONS OF ROBOTICS

Classification schemes are useful for conveying aspects of the truth about a certain subject. Robotics lends itself readily to classifications based on a number of different characteristics:

- Purpose and function
- Coordinate system employed
- Number of degrees of freedom of end effector (hand)
- Generation of control system

For a more detailed discussion, the reader is referred to an excellent text on industrial robots by Wesley Snyder.[6]

PURPOSE AND FUNCTION

The broadest classification scheme delineates robots according to their *intended purpose.* This parameter cleanly splits all present day robots into the three categories:

1. *Industrial Robots* — This is the category of "big league" robots capable of performing industrial production processes. Such processes include: welding, material handling, assembly, machine loading and unloading, casting, and painting. Industrial robots typically cost between $25,000 – $200,000.

2. *Personal/Educational Robots* — This is strictly the "little league" class of robotics, but interesting nonetheless. Many personal robots have a range of capabilities surpassing those of industrial robots. Personal robots tend to be general purpose machines (as opposed to highly specialized industrial robots) and cost in the range of $1000 – $15,000. In structure and capability many personal robots resemble Shakey, the robot developed at Stanford Research Institute as a tool for artificial intelligence research.[7] The primary function of personal robots is educational rather than household servant.

3. *Military Robots* — These often go under the name *autonomous vehicles* and include such devices as smart munitions, cruise missiles, and land rovers. They generally have sensing capabilities designed to interpret their environment. Some include the ability to communicate with human or other systems.

The architecture of the first two types of robots usually includes the following structures:

- **End effectors**: Grasping fingers, suction grippers, magnetic devices, or specialized tools.

- **Manipulator arms**: These may include elbows and wrist.

- **Controller**: Generally a capable microcomputer.

- **Sensors**: For providing feedback on performance and the environment.

COORDINATE SYSTEM AND DEGREES OF FREEDOM

There are four basic manipulator geometries as shown in Figure 16-1. These are:

- **Cartesian Coordinates** — This is the familiar (x,y,z) coordinates of the first year geometry class and the simplest to understand. One realization of this geometry is the *gantry crane* for moving equipment on the industrial floor or scientific laboratory.

- **Cylindrical Coordinates** — This is the slightly less familiar (r,θ,z) or (r, θ, h) system for r (reach), θ (rotation), and h (height). The relationship with Cartesian coordinates is given by:

$$x = r\cos(\theta) \qquad y = r\sin(\theta) \qquad z = h.$$

- **Spherical Coordinates** — This is the familiar (r,θ,ϕ) system for the variables r (radius), θ (rotation from the z axis), and ϕ (rotation from the X axis of the projection onto the X-Y plane. The relationship between these coordinates and Cartesian coordinates is given by:

$$x = r\sin(\theta)\cos(\phi) \quad y = r\sin(\theta)\sin(\phi) \quad z = r\cos(\theta)$$

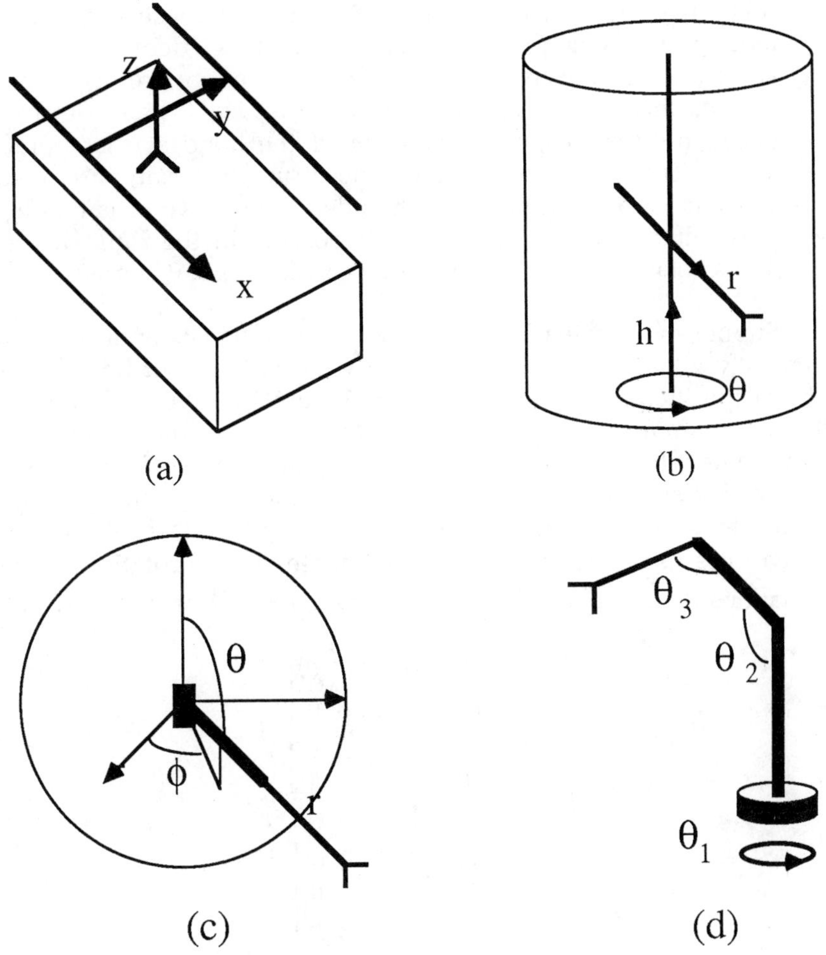

Figure 16-1 Four Standard Geometries for Robots
a) Cartesian coordinate system — "Gantry crane Robot"
b) Cylindrical coordinate system
c) Spherical coordinate system
d) Articulated geometry

- **Articulated Geometry** — This geometry becomes possible as soon as we introduce additional joints into the system. Each additional joint provides one or more additional degrees of freedom for the system. In general, the more degrees of freedom (DOF) a system has, the more capable it is. Consider the articulated robot shown in Figure 16-2, for instance. The rotating base provides one DOF, the hinged shoulder and elbow each provide one DOF, and the flexible wrist provides three DOF through the roll, pitch, and yaw motions. The sum of these independent motions is six degrees of freedom which is adequate for most applications. The first three degrees of freedom are necessary to *position* the hand at any point in (x,y,z) space. The last three are necessary for proper *orientation* of the hand at that point in space. The proper orientation is necessary, for example, for such tasks as inserting a bolt in a threaded hole. Two orientation angles (pitch and yaw) get the bolt pointed in the right direction and a rotation angle (roll) must be correct to get it started.

Suppose we have a *key* (or bolt or screw) with its own coordinate system (x',y',z') and we want to align it with the *lock* coordinate system (or hole) specified as (x,y,z) as shown in Figure 16-3. A well known result from computer graphics says that we can bring these two coordinate systems into alignment by a series of translations and rotations of the primed system located at (X,Y,Z) about the axes of the un-primed system. This can be most conveniently accomplished by transformation matrices using homogeneous coordinates.[8] The rotation matrices for rotations (α,β,γ) about the x, y, and z axis, respectively, are given by:

$$R_x(\alpha) = \begin{bmatrix} 1 & 0 & 0 & 0 \\ 0 & \cos\alpha & -\sin\alpha & 0 \\ 0 & \sin\alpha & \cos\alpha & 0 \\ 0 & 0 & 0 & 1 \end{bmatrix} \tag{16.1}$$

$$R_y(\beta) = \begin{bmatrix} \cos\beta & 0 & \sin\beta & 0 \\ 0 & 1 & 0 & 0 \\ -\sin\beta & 0 & \cos\beta & 0 \\ 0 & 0 & 0 & 1 \end{bmatrix} \tag{16.2}$$

$$R_z(\gamma) = \begin{bmatrix} \cos\gamma & -\sin\gamma & 0 & 0 \\ \sin\gamma & \cos\gamma & 0 & 0 \\ 0 & 0 & 1 & 0 \\ 0 & 0 & 0 & 1 \end{bmatrix} \tag{16.3}$$

and the translation matrices are given by:

$$T(-X,-Y,-Z) = \begin{bmatrix} 1 & 0 & 0 & 0 \\ 0 & 1 & 0 & 0 \\ 0 & 0 & 1 & 0 \\ -X & -Y & -Z & 1 \end{bmatrix} \tag{16.4}$$

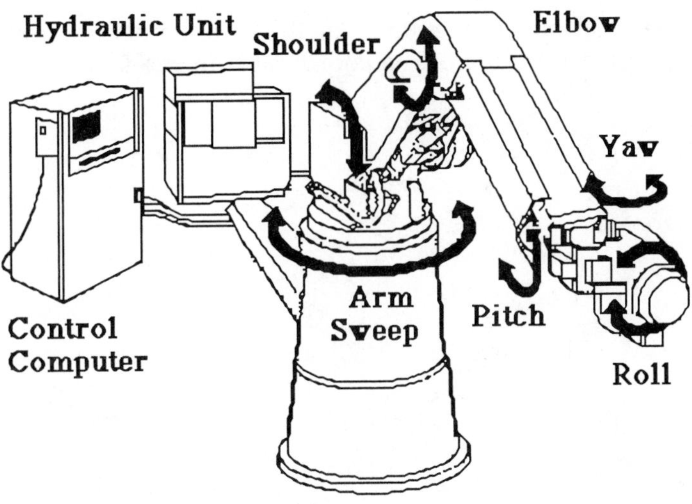

Figure 16-2 T3 — An articulated robot with 6 Degrees of Freedom Note that 6 degrees of freedom are required for completely generalized motion. Three degrees are required for position and three for orientation. (Courtesy of Cincinnati Milacron)

$$T(X_k,Y_k,Z_k) = \begin{bmatrix} 1 & 0 & 0 & 0 \\ 0 & 1 & 0 & 0 \\ 0 & 0 & 1 & 0 \\ X_k & Y_k & Z_k & 1 \end{bmatrix} \tag{16.5}$$

If the top of the keyhole is located at (X_k,Y_k,Z_k) then the key may be lined up with the keyhole by the transformation M where:

$$M = T(-X,-Y,-Z)\ R_y(\beta)\ R_x(\alpha)\ R_z(\gamma)\ T(X_k,Y_k,Z_k) \tag{16.6}$$

where

$T(-X,-Y,-Z)$ = translation to take origin of key to origin of lock

$R_y(\beta)$ = rotation about y axis to put z' axis in yz plane

$R_x(\alpha)$ = rotation about x axis to bring z' axis parallel to z axis

$R_z(\gamma)$ = rotation about z axis to bring x' parallel to x

$T(X_k,Y_k,Z_k)$ = translation to take oriented key to keyhole

Now the the coordinates of a point in the transformed key system V' may be expressed in terms of the coordinates in the lock V system by the matrix expression:

$$V' = V M \tag{16.7}$$

where

$$V = [x \; y \; z \; 1]$$

$$V' = [x' \; y' \; z' \; 1]$$

The details of specifying the correct rotation angles are presented in any graphics text.[9]

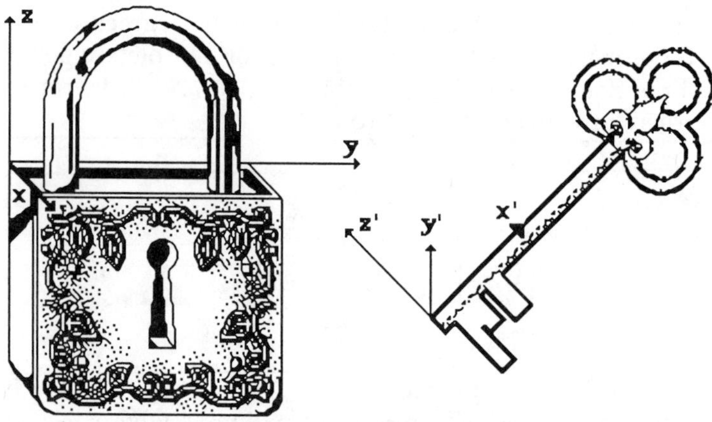

Figure 16-3 Typical Robotic Alignment Problem The problem is to align the key (or screw, bolt, etc.) with the lock (or hole, nut, etc.). Two translations and three standard rotations are required to align the general case.

The nice feature of the matrix representation of transformations is that successive transformations may be described by an operator generated by the matrix multiplication of the corresponding transformations. It should also be noted that in general a relative coordinate system is used to describe the motion at a joint rather than some absolute coordinate system attached to the base. The matrix formalism makes it a fairly straightforward task to transform from the 6-tuple of hinge and joint rotations to the 3-D orientation of the manipulator in the laboratory. Richard Paul presents a very thorough discussion of the mathematics of the coordinate transformations, kinematics, and dynamics of robot manipulators.[10]

GENERATIONS OF CONTROL SYSTEMS

The strategy used in the control system of industrial robots serves as another useful basis for categorization. We can specify these categories in terms of generations:[11]

First Generation — The control system used in first generation robots is based on fixed mechanical stops. The strategy is known as *open-loop* control as illustrated in Figure 16-4 and sometimes referred to as "bang-bang" control. Such open loop systems have much in common with ordinary fixed-cycle washing machines and dishwashers and are equivalent in principle (and less impressive in practice) than the handwriting automata of Henri Maillardet. They are useful for industrial applications such as "pick-and-place" but are generally limited to a small number of moves. They also constitute the largest class of United States industrial robots.

Second Generation — The second generation is also open loop in its control structure, but instead of mechanical switches and buttons it uses a numerical control sequence of motions stored on magnetic tape or disk. This control program may be entered by selecting a sequence of motions on a button box or, in more sophisticated versions, by the use of *teaching pendants* for "walking through" the desired sequence of motions. The major applications of this generation of robots are in spot welding and spray painting, primarily in the automobile industry.

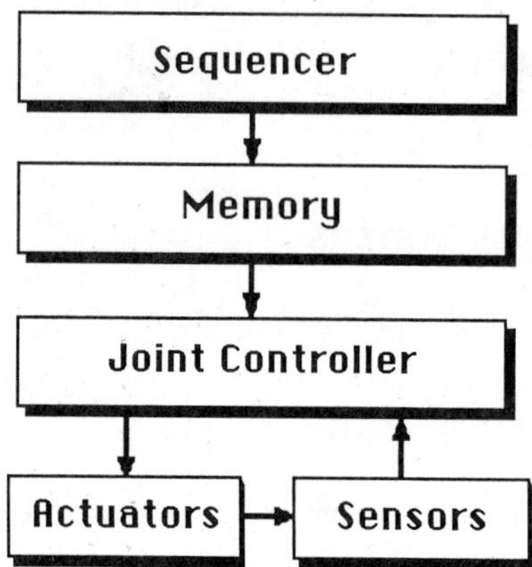

Figure 16-4 Open-loop controller Sequencer and memory may be mechanical (First Generation) or electronic (Second Generation).

Third Generation — Third generation robots use computers for their control strategy and have some knowledge of the local environment through the use of sensors. Thus, they qualify as "intelligent robots", and programming languages such as Unimation's VAL, IBM's AML, and Automatix's RAIL have been developed for writing the control programs. The control strategy is known as *closed-loop* in the language of control theory, and is illustrated in Figure 16-5. By the use of vision, sonar ranging, or tactile sensors, the robot now begins to have an awareness of the local environment and thereby can respond more intelligently. Sensor information allows the robot to be integrated with conveyers and/or other robots in a factory environment.

Fourth Generation — This generation robot qualifies as truly intelligent with more and better sensory extensions for understanding its own actions and the world around it. It also incorporates important AI concepts such as a *world model* of its own behavior and the environment in which it operates. This feature makes possible the intelligent use of fuzzy knowledge and expectation-driven processing which may greatly enhance the performance of the system. Control theory representation of the fourth generation strategy is shown in Figure 16-6. Very few robots presently can be classified in this generation, and the field offers great opportunity for clever and resourceful control algorithms.

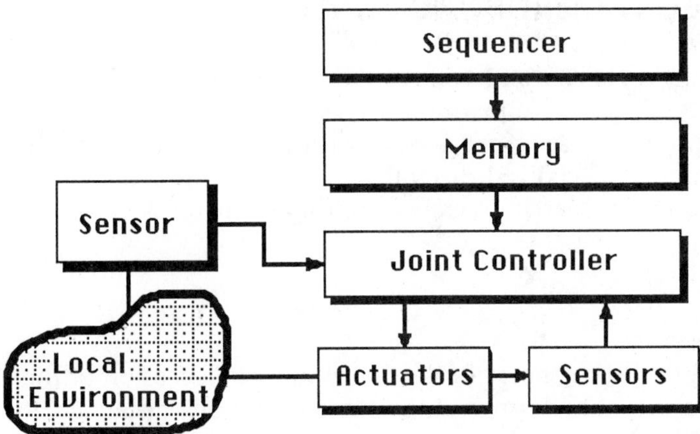

Figure 16-5 Closed-loop controller Third generations systems provide sensors to measure the local environment and modify the control strategy.

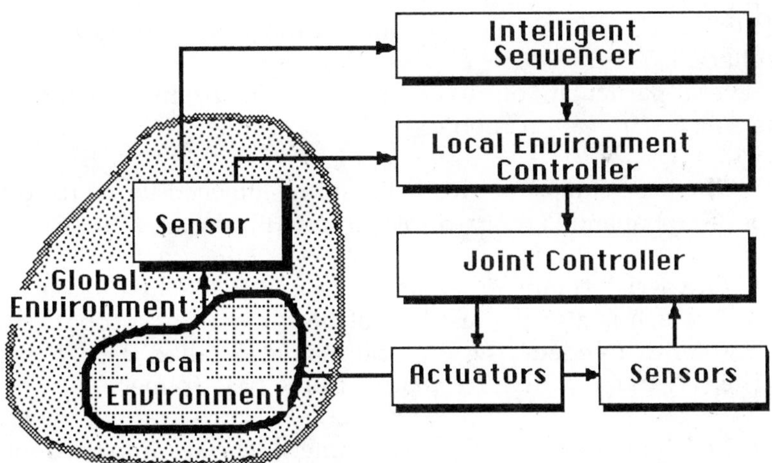

Figure 16-6 Forth Generation Controller This system extends sensor monitoring to the global environment and contains a world model for recording the effects of its actions and helping to determine tasks and goals.

For more details on available sensors and control strategies for use in robot programming the interested reader should see the introduction to robotics by James Rehg.[12]

16.4 THEORY OF ROBOTIC CONTROL

To adequately specify and control the motion of robots, it is necessary to integrate all of the following aspects, each of which requires one or more chapters in a standard robotics textbook. In practice, since each area is a highly specialized discipline of its own, specialists in each field are required for research on extending robot capabilities.

GEOMETRY

We introduced the concept of geometry in our discussion of the degrees of freedom of a robot arm and the transformations necessary to line up a bolt with a hole. In order to treat rotations and translations in an equivalent fashion, homogeneous transformations (4-vectors) are customarily used. An important concept in the geometry of robots is the *work envelope* or *work-space.* The work envelope is the volume to which the end effector has access for a particular robot. For a 3 degree of freedom Cartesian robot the work envelope is a rectangular parallelopiped (box); for a cylindrical robot it is a cylinder (can); and for an articulated robot such as the Cincinnati Milacron T3 it approaches a semi-sphere.

Several particular coordinate frames are so useful that they have become *standard frames* in robotics. These include:

- **The base frame** — This is the frame attached to the fixed base of the robot and is referred to as frame {B} or frame {0}.

- **The wrist frame** — This is the frame attached to the wrist, {W}, which is also the last link of the robot. For a robot with N degrees of freedom, the {W} frame is also called the {N} frame. The {W} frame is defined relative to the base frame.

- **The tool frame** — The tool frame, {T}, takes into account the geometry of end effectors such as tools, suction cups, magnetic graspers, and the pieces they may be holding. The {T} frame is defined with respect to the wrist frame.

- **The station frame** — The {S} frame is defined in terms of the task to be accomplished. It is specified with respect to the base frame and is also known as the *universe frame* or the *world frame*.

- **The goal frame** — The goal frame {G} is the frame into which the robot tries to transform the tool frame. That is, when the robot has moved the tool frame so that it is identical to the goal frame, the task is finished. The {G} frame is specified in terms of the station frame.

KINEMATICS

Kinematics is the study of motion in terms of geometry and time without regard for the forces required to cause the motion. The kinematics of robots describes the position, velocity, acceleration, and possible higher derivatives of these quantities for all movable segments of the robot. Of particular interest are all possible positions and orientations of the *end effector* which define the work-space. A more restricted space called the *dextrous work-space* is that volume of the work envelope within which the end effector can achieve all possible orientations. Given the orientation and length of each arm or link of the robot, it is a relatively straightforward process using *forward kinematics* to calculate the position and orientation of the end effector which is attached to the free end of the chain of links. A much more difficult task, using *inverse kinematics,* is to calculate what set of orientations of intermediate links results in a particular orientation of the end effector. The primary problem of inverse kinematics is that there may exist zero, one, or an infinite number of solutions. If more than one set of joint variables can lead to the same tool configuration, the system is said to be *degenerate.* An *infinitely degenerate* system is one with an infinite number of solutions.

It is apparent that small changes in the arm, shoulder, elbow, roll, pitch, and yaw rotations in Figure 16-2 will result in corresponding small changes in the position and orientation of the end effector. The *Jacobian matrix*, **J(X)**, provides us with a particularly useful and intuitive tool for mapping between different coordinate systems. In terms of the link coordinates x_i (arm rotation, ...) it is possible to derive functions which map out the final tool coordinates, y_i:

$$\begin{aligned} y_1 &= f_1(x_1,x_2,x_3,x_4,x_5,x_6) \\ y_2 &= f_2(x_1,x_2,x_3,x_4,x_5,x_6) \\ &\ldots \\ &\ldots \\ y_6 &= f_6(x_1,x_2,x_3,x_4,x_5,x_6) \end{aligned} \qquad (16.8)$$

which can be rewritten in vector form as:

$$\mathbf{Y} = \mathbf{F}(\mathbf{X}) \qquad (16.9)$$

where

Y = six element vector, end effector position/orientation
F = six element vector of functions $f_1 \ldots f_6$

$\mathbf{X}$ = six element vector of input rotations.

Now small changes in x_i, called Δx_i, result in small changes in y_i, Δy_i, according to the chain rule of differentiation:

$$\begin{aligned}
\Delta y_1 &= \frac{\partial f_1}{\partial x_1}\Delta x_1 + \frac{\partial f_1}{\partial x_2}\Delta x_2 + \ldots + \frac{\partial f_1}{\partial x_6}\Delta x_6 \\
\Delta y_2 &= \frac{\partial f_2}{\partial x_1}\Delta x_1 + \frac{\partial f_2}{\partial x_2}\Delta x_2 + \ldots + \frac{\partial f_2}{\partial x_6}\Delta x_6 \\
&\cdots \\
&\cdots \\
\Delta y_6 &= \frac{\partial f_6}{\partial x_1}\Delta x_1 + \frac{\partial f_6}{\partial x_2}\Delta x_2 + \ldots + \frac{\partial f_6}{\partial x_6}\Delta x_6
\end{aligned} \tag{16.10}$$

or, in vector notation,

$$\Delta \mathbf{Y} = \frac{\partial \mathbf{F}}{\partial \mathbf{X}}\Delta \mathbf{X} \tag{16.11}$$

where

$\Delta \mathbf{Y}$ = six element vector with elements $\Delta y_1 \ldots \Delta y_6$
$\Delta \mathbf{X}$ = six element vector with elements $\Delta x_1 \ldots \Delta x_6$
$\frac{\partial \mathbf{F}}{\partial \mathbf{X}}$ = six by six matrix with (i,j) element $= \frac{\partial f_i}{\partial x_j}$

The Jacobian matrix, $\mathbf{J}(\mathbf{X})$, is defined as:

$$\mathbf{J}(\mathbf{X}) = \frac{\partial \mathbf{F}}{\partial \mathbf{X}} \tag{16.12}$$

Two of the most important quantities in robotics are the velocity and acceleration profiles of the various links and end effector. The higher the velocities and the more rapidly the higher velocities can be reached, the more efficient the robot will become. On the other hand, reaching high velocities rapidly requires large accelerations with corresponding large forces which ultimately limit the performance of the robot.

The propagation of velocities through the robotics system is handled very naturally through the Jacobian matrix. Since we are interested in the vector velocity of the end effector, $\mathbf{Y}' = \frac{\partial \mathbf{Y}}{\partial t}$, in terms of the angular rotation velocities at the various joints, $\mathbf{X}' = \frac{\partial \mathbf{X}}{\partial t}$, we can use the Jacobian matrix to write:

$$\mathbf{Y}' = \mathbf{J}(\mathbf{X})\,\mathbf{X}' \tag{16.13}$$

There are several interesting properties of the "Jacobian", $\mathbf{J}(\mathbf{X})$. One of the most important is that it is not a constant matrix, but rather, as the symbol indicates, a function of the joint parameters, $\mathbf{X}$. Thus, as the sensors report new positions for each link in the robot arm, new Jacobians must be computed.

A second useful feature of the Jacobian matrix is the application of its inverse, $\mathbf{J}^{-1}$ (if $\mathbf{J}$ is not singular). The inverse Jacobian allows us to specify the tool velocity vector, $\mathbf{Y}'$, and compute the corresponding joint velocities, $\mathbf{X}'$ by the equation:

$$\mathbf{X}' = \mathbf{J}^{-1}\,\mathbf{Y}' \tag{16.14}$$

The efficiency of computing the inverse Jacobian is improved by computing the Jacobian numerically for a certain $\mathbf{X}$ and then inverting the numerical matrix rather than computing the inverse matrix symbolically and then evaluating it.

A final application of the Jacobian is in mapping between the torques acting on each joint and the force applied by the tool in static cases (forces in balance). The principle of virtual work states that the work performed in the incremental vector displacements, ΔX and ΔY, is given by the dot products:

$$F \cdot \Delta \mathbf{Y} = \tau \cdot \Delta \mathbf{X} \tag{16.15}$$

where

F = Generalized force vector in tool frame

τ = Generalized torque vector at joints

From 16.11 and 16.12 we know that

$$\Delta \mathbf{Y} = \mathbf{J}(\mathbf{X})\,\Delta \mathbf{X} \tag{16.16}$$

Substituting 16.16 into 16.15 gives an equation which must be true for all ΔX, leading to the result:

$$F^{\mathrm{T}}\,\mathbf{J}(\mathbf{X}) = \tau^{\mathrm{T}} \tag{16.17}$$

where the transposed vectors are required for conformal matrix multiplication.

DYNAMICS

Dynamics is the study of the relationship between the kinematics of an object and the forces and torques applied to it. There are two classes of dynamics problems in the field of robotics. The first class involves specifying the *trajectory* of the end effector and computing the torques required on each joint to produce this trajectory. The trajectory is defined as the path in position, velocity, and acceleration space required to accomplish the task. The second class of problems involves specifying the time-dependent torque at each joint and computing the resulting trajectory.

The simplest dynamics equations are those for a point particle and may be written:

Newton's Second Law:

$$\mathbf{F} = m\mathbf{a} \tag{16.18}$$

Newton's Second Law — Rotational (also called Euler's Equation):

$$\tau = I\,\alpha \tag{16.19}$$

Definition of weight:

$$W = mg \tag{16.20}$$

where

$\mathbf{F}$ = Force vector
m = particle mass
$\mathbf{a}$ = acceleration vector
$= \dfrac{d^2\mathbf{r}}{dt^2} = \mathbf{r}''$
$\mathbf{r}$ = position vector
τ = torque vector
$= \mathbf{r} \times \mathbf{F}$
I = moment of inertia
$= m\,r^2$
α = angular acceleration vector
$|\alpha| = \dfrac{d^2\theta}{dt^2} = \theta''$
g = 9.8 m/sec^2 [acceleration due to gravity]

The simplicity of single particle dynamics is rapidly lost in the complexity of a real robot arm motion, although the three basic laws (16.18) — (16.20) remain deeply embedded in the more complex representations required to describe the dynamics of a robot arm. There are two sources of the complexity:

1. The links of a robot arm are extended, massive objects, not particles.

2. The segments of a robot arm are not free objects, but are constrained by the joints to other links.

This increased complexity is handled by more complex mathematical techniques, including the introduction of a moment of inertia tensor[13] and the Lagrangian formalism.[14] Because of the rotary motion of jointed links, rotational effects such as centrifugal and Coriolis forces now appear. The revised dynamic equation corresponding to the torque and weight equations (16.19) and (16.20) now becomes:

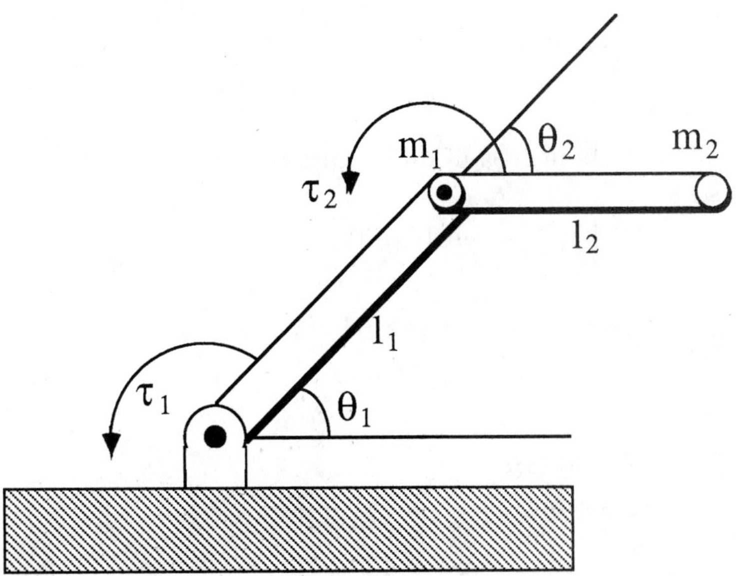

Figure 16-7 Two-link, two-joint robot arm To simplify the analysis, it is assumed that all the mass of each arm is concentrated in points at the end of each arm.

$$\tau = \mathbf{M}(\theta)\,\theta'' + \mathbf{V}(\theta,\theta') + \mathbf{G}(\theta) \qquad (16.21)$$

where

τ = n-vector of the torques at each of n joints

$\mathbf{M}(\theta)$ = n × n mass matrix which includes inertia tensor
$\theta'' = \alpha$ = angular acceleration vector
$\mathbf{V}(\theta,\theta')$ = velocity dependent vector including centrifugal and Coriolis forces
$\mathbf{G}(\theta)$ = gravity term which depends on angle only.

To illustrate the complexity of even a relatively simple robot arm, we consider the two-link system shown in Figure 16-7.

For this configuration, it has been shown that the dynamic variables $\mathbf{M}(\theta)$, $\mathbf{V}(\theta,\theta')$, and $\mathbf{G}(\theta)$ are given by:[15]

$$\mathbf{M}(\theta) = \begin{bmatrix} l_2^2 m_2 + 2l_1 l_2 m_2 c_2 + l_1^2(m_1+m_2) & l_2^2 m_2 + l_1 l_2 m_2 c_2 \\ l_2^2 m_2 + l_1 l_2 m_2 c_2 & l_2^2 m_2 \end{bmatrix} \quad (16.22)$$

$$\mathbf{V}(\theta,\theta') = \begin{bmatrix} -m_2 l_1 l_2 s_2 \theta'^2_2 - 2m_2 l_1 l_2 s_2 \theta'_1 \theta'_2 \\ m_2 l_1 l_2 s_2 \theta'^2_1 \end{bmatrix} \quad (16.23)$$

$$\mathbf{G}(\theta) = \begin{bmatrix} m_2 l_2 g c_{12} + (m_1+m_2) l_1 g c_1 \\ m_2 l_2 g c_{12} \end{bmatrix} \quad (16.24)$$

where

$c_2 = \cos(\theta_2)$
$s_2 = \sin(\theta_2)$
$c_1 = \cos(\theta_1)$
$c_{12} = \cos(\theta_1 + \theta_2)$

Note that this is the solution to the first class of dynamics problem — by simply multiplying out these matrices according to Equation (16.21) we get the two unknown torques in terms of the known masses, link lengths, and specified θ trajectories.

The closed, analytical form of the solution is not particularly difficult for the two-link example shown. However, the closed form solution for the fully articulated, six degree of freedom arm is very complex.[16] Working out the details of the analytic form for a particular configuration requires a considerable human effort. A mathematically simpler but computationally less efficient algorithm involves a two-step iterative technique:[17]

1. Starting with link 1 which is fixed to the base, compute the force and torque about the center of mass of the link required to give the ($\theta, \theta', \theta''$) trajectory for that link. Iterate the solution out to the last link, n.

2. Using the force and torque results from step (1), use the joint constraints, force, and torque balance equations to compute the torque about each joint, starting from link n and iterating in to link 1.

The dynamics of robot manipulators is a rich field for research. Open questions include the choice of representation and computational strategy to optimize the analysis in order to enable real-time control.

CONTROL

In the section on Generations of Control Systems we surveyed the general categories of control strategies used in robotics. Here we look in more detail at the considerations and techniques of feedback control theory.

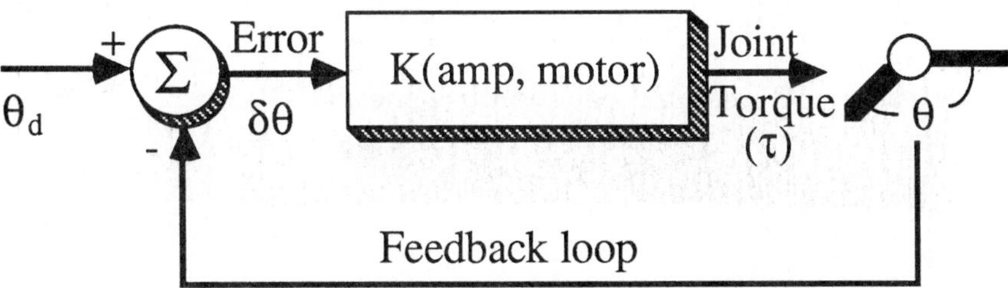

Figure 16-8 Position control feedback system The desired angular position, θ_d, is sent to the system from the left and the actual position, θ, is sensed on the right. The summing circuit, S, calculates the difference between the desired and actual angle $\delta\theta$. This error signal is amplified and drives an actuator (motor or pneumatic piston) to produce a torque which moves the arm in the direction so as to minimize the error signal.

One of the simplest and most direct control algorithms for guiding a rotary joint along a desired position trajectory, $\theta_d(t)$, is the proportional error position control system shown in Figure 16-8. The desired or demand signal, θ_d, is compared to the actual measured position, θ, by the summing circuit, S, which generates an error signal, $\delta\theta = \theta_d - \theta$. This error signal is amplified and drives an actuator to produce a torque on the joint which reduces the error signal.

The mathematics of this control strategy are those of the simple harmonic oscillator (generally damped), familiar to all students in physics and engineering. For the case in which gravity is ignored but friction included, Equation (16-21) reduces to the single differential equation:

$$\tau_m = J_t \theta'' + F_f \theta' \qquad (16.25)$$

where

τ_m = motor torque
J_t = $J_m + J_l$
= moment of inertia of the motor plus reflected moment of inertial of the load
F_f = friction factor

Assuming that the motor torque is proportional to the angular position error, we can write:

$$\tau_m = K(\theta_d - \theta) \qquad (16.26)$$

and the resulting differential equation becomes:

$$K(\theta_d - \theta) = J_t \theta'' + F_f \theta' \qquad (16.27)$$

whose solution is:

$$\theta(t) = \exp\left(\frac{-F_f}{2 J_t} t\right)\left[C_1 \exp\left(\frac{\omega t}{2}\right) + C_2 \exp\left(\frac{-\omega t}{2}\right)\right] \qquad (16.28)$$

where

C_1, C_2 = constants of integration

$$\omega = \sqrt{\left[\frac{F_f}{J_t}\right]^2 - \frac{4K}{J_t}} \tag{16.29}$$

Depending on the values of friction, F_f, and amplifier/motor gain, K, we get the three well known solutions:

1. **Under-damped case** → $\left(\frac{F_f}{J_t}\right)^2 < \frac{4K}{J_t}$
   The arm oscillates as a damped harmonic oscillator ($F_f \neq 0$) or sinusoidally ($F_f = 0$).

2. **Critically-damped case** → $\left(\frac{F_f}{J_t}\right)^2 = \frac{4K}{J_t}$
   The arm approaches the goal, θ_d, as rapidly as possible without overshoot.

3. **Over-damped case** → $\left(\frac{F_f}{J_t}\right)^2 > \frac{4K}{J_t}$
   The arm exponentially approaches θ_d with no oscillation or overshoot.

The position control algorithm leads to problems which require more sophistication of the control system. These problems and the standard solutions include:

- *Gravity (steady-state error) problem* — Because of the torque τ_g exerted by gravity, the final position θ_g using the position control algorithm will be given by:

$$\tau_g = K(\theta_d - \theta_g) \tag{16.30}$$

The solution to this problem is to generate another signal proportional to the time integral of the error signal and of the proper sign to minimize the error signal, $\delta\theta$, and sum the time integral signal into the motor drive signal.

- *Overshoot and oscillation problem* — The position control algorithm always results in some combination of the following undesirable features: oscillation, overshoot, and exponential position, velocity and acceleration trajectories. In general, better performance may be achieved by using a velocity or acceleration control algorithm to generate an "S" shaped or logistic position curve. The constant acceleration/deceleration profile shown in Figure 16-9 can be shown to produce the quickest response of the end effector while minimizing the peak torque stresses at the joint.

The field of control theory is rich in the possible variations of control strategies. In addition to the position and acceleration (torque) control discussed above, the *controlled variable* may be the velocity, θ', of the joint's angular motion or some linear combination of $\theta, \theta', \theta''$. In multiple-link robot arms, the control strategy may involve *feed-forward* signals from link n+1, $(\theta, \theta', \theta'')_{n+1}$, to link n in order to generate the required torque at link n. Another area of active research in robotics control involves integrating models of the robot into the control strategy in order to improve computational efficiency.

SENSORS

The development and refinement of sensors is a key area of robotics research. Since knowledge is the basis for intelligent action, one of the goals of robotics is to increase the knowledge available to the robot. The knowledge necessary for intelligent robot operation is more than sophisticated control algorithms for smooth positioning of the end effector. Without knowledge of the environment in which it is operating, the robot is essentially "flying blindly" and is incapable of responding to a dynamic work environment. Sensors provide the robot with efficient channels for gathering information on the changing situation in which it is operating.

The two most important human senses which robotics researchers try to emulate are touch and vision. The corresponding robot sensors can be classified broadly into two functional categories: *contact sensors* and *remote sensors.*

Contact Sensors

Contact sensors range from simple limit switches to sophisticated *artificial skin.* Contact sensors provide robots with a rudimentary sense of touch. Touch is even more important than vision for many applications of robot manipulators. Consider the general problem of *compliance* in parts assembly. The problem is illustrated in the key and lock Figure 16-3. Rarely will bolts and their holes or tightly connected parts line up perfectly. If the robot blindly went through the process of forcing the key into the lock, a slight misalignment would cause serious damage to the key, the lock, the robot and possibly all three. The problem of compliance is most effectively solved by building force sensitive wrists for grasping the part to be inserted. A number of compliant wrist systems are described by Snyder.[18]

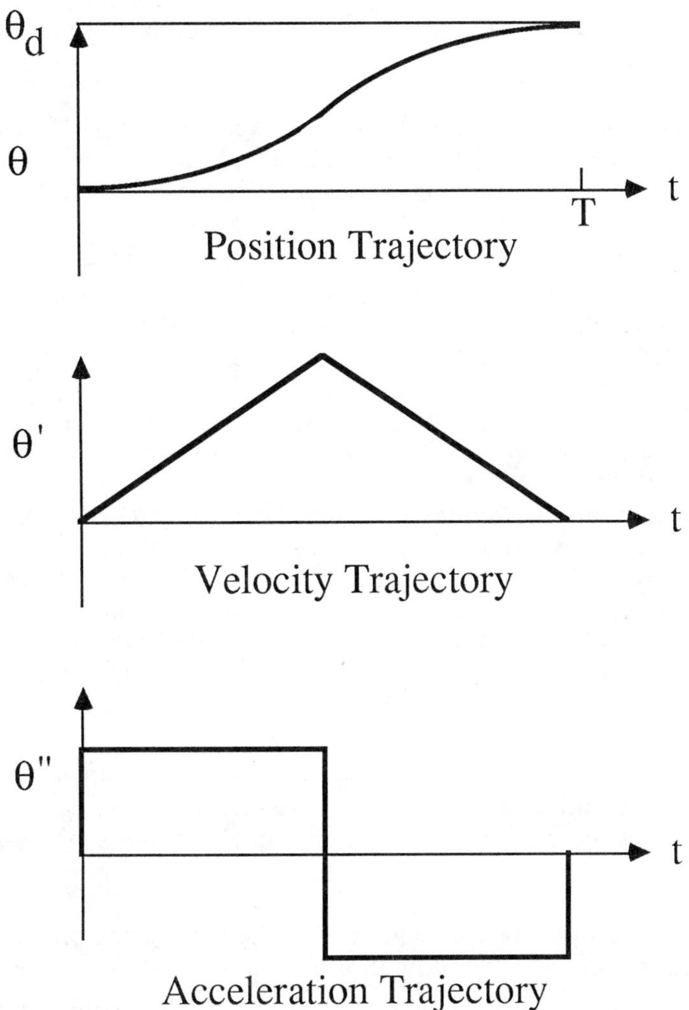

Figure 16-9 Acceleration control strategy Using constant acceleration for T/2 seconds and the same deceleration for T/2 seconds, the maximum average velocity is obtained for a given maximum joint stress. This smoothly positions the end effector in the shortest possible time.

There is a huge range of robotics applications for which tactile sensing is important. Without tactile feedback, the gripper could easily drop the part, scratch it, or crush it. This application has motivated the development of some complex and capable systems. Several features are useful in characterizing tactile sensors. These include:

- *Spatial Resolution* — The spatial resolution of the most sensitive human sensor, the fingertip, is between 1 and 3 mm. This goal has been achieved and even surpassed by several artificial sensor systems.

- *Bandwidth* — The sensor's frequency bandwidth should range from 0 hz to between 100 and 1000 hz for applications requiring vibration sensing.

- *Force sensitivity* — The force sensitivity required will depend on the particular application. However, the goal which several systems have approached is a sensitivity of ±0.01 newtons over a range of 0—10 newtons.

- *Function* — Human tactile perception serves two distinct functions, both of which are goals for implementation on artificial sensors. The first is the *cutaneous* response which conveys information on the texture, temperature, and details of the shape of the sensed object. The second function of the sensor is to provide *kinesthetic* information on the larger features of the shape of an object and its response to applied forces. Both functions are objects of active research programs, but the important goal of integrating both functions has yet to enter the research stage.

An excellent discussion of features of tactile sensors commercially available and under development is given by Pennywitt.[19] Examples from three classes of the more capable tactile sensors are described next.

- **Electro-optic tactile sensors** — The basic principle of electro-optic tactile sensors is the modulation of a light beam by the mechanical deformation of a flexible material. In one implementation an elastic membrane is stretched across an array of cylinders with flexible material protruding from the front of the pistons. On the back end of each piston an LED shines light across the piston where it is detected by a phototransistor. When pressure is exerted on the membrane the flexible material is depressed into the light beam, diminishing the intensity and corresponding photocurrent. The array consists of 10 × 16 sites with a spacing of 1.8 mm. The approximately linear response ranges from 0—6.7 newtons, and the entire array may be read 333 times/-second.

• **Piezoresistive tactile sensors** — The basic principle of this broad category of devices is based on the pressure dependent electrical conductivity of certain materials. Piezoresistive devices range from the proven technology of metal and solid-state silicon strain gauges to recent innovations of conductive elastomers and foams. One commercial device is based on anisotropically conductive silicone rubber (ACS) which is conductive along only one axis of the sheet. The ACS sheet is mated with a flexible printed circuit board with fine conductive lines etched perpendicular to the conductive direction of the ACS sheet. This provides a device with 16 × 16 sensing sites with a spatial resolution of 0.6 mm and a sensitivity of ±0.05 newtons per square millimeter over a range of 0.05 — 0.5 newtons per square millimeter.

• **Piezoelectric tactile sensors** — While piezoresistive materials are passive, piezoelectric materials are active. The later generate an electric voltage in response to changes in pressure. Quartz crystals are the classic piezoelectric material and are used as the clock oscillator for most electronic applications including computers and digital watches. However, conventional piezoelectric materials tend to be brittle, a characteristic making them poorly suited for tactile sensor applications. This problem has been overcome by a new type of piezoelectric polymer which is rugged, inexpensive, and available in flexible thin sheets. One of the most promising of this new class of materials is polyvinylidene fluoride (PVDF).

A University of Pisa research team has developed an "artificial skin," using PVDF, which has remarkable capabilities.[20] This device is based on two layers of PVDF (*epidermal* and *dermal* layers) bonded to a flexible printed circuit board with an array of 8 × 16 electrodes on a 3 mm grid. Also bonded in the multi-layer device is layer of resistive metal paint through which current is driven to maintain a sensor temperature of approximately 37°C. The sensor can detect the rate at which heat flows out of the device, thus enabling it to distinguish metallic (heat conducting) from insulating objects in the same way humans do. By rubbing the sensor across the surface of an unknown material, the PVDF epidermal layer generates a signal, analogous to that from a phonograph needle, which can be used to distinguish various grades of fabric. The same principle can be used to detect slip. The object being held generates micro-vibrations when it begins to slip, and these are readily detected. The sensor has a sensitivity of ±0.01 newtons over a range of 40 newtons.

Remote Sensors

Remote sensors may be defined as non-contact sensors and in general fall into one of the following two classes:

- **Proximity sensors** — Proximity sensors provide two useful functions in robotics. The first is collision avoidance, a function very important for the health and safety of both robots and humans. The second function is to monitor conditions as the end effector approaches the object to be grasped, painted, or welded. Proximity sensors may use light as the communication medium in a wide variety of configurations of source, detector, and wavelength up to infra-red. Sound is the second major communication medium. Ultrasonic ranging, such as that used by the Polaroid transducer, is capable of better than 1 percent accuracy. An object 3 feet away can be located to within 1/2 inch. Several personal robots provide ultrasonic ranging.

- **Computer vision** — We have already discussed this sensor channel in the chapter on *Computer Vision*. The only observation to be added at this point is that computer vision is important to robotics because it has been shown that the only two senses that robots need to behave intelligently are vision and touch. The direct application of vision to robotics is treated exhaustively by Horn.[21]

ROBOT PROGRAMMING

The evolution of robot programming has close parallels to the history of conventional computer programming. This analogous development is shown in terms of generations of languages in Table 16-I.

- **Generation 0: Open Loop** — Open loop or non-servo systems may be based on mechanical drum and cam mechanism (player piano), pneumatic logic, or computer-based programmable controllers. Open loop systems comprise over fifty percent of United States robotic control and approximately 65 percent of foreign robots. Their advantages include low cost, simpler mechanical and electrical systems, a well-established technology, and a large cadre of engineers and technicians familiar with such systems. Although this level of robot programming cannot claim any intelligence, its advantages make it highly unlikely that the 0th generation of robotic programming will soon suffer the same fate as did its mechanical counterpart in the data processing world.

Table 16-I

	Conventional Programming		Robot Programming	
Generation	Description	Examples	Description	Examples
0	Mechanical Open loop	Card sorters, collators	Mechanical Open Loop	Drum program on Seiko 700
1	Machine language	6502, 8088, 68000 µP	Joint control language	ArmBASIC RASP
2	Assembly language	BAL, Assembler	Primitive motion language	T3, FUNKY, VAL,RPL,Rail
3	High level language	Pascal, ADA PL/1,Modula 2	Structured programming language	AML, Maple, PAL,MCL
4	Object, logic oriented language	SMALLTALK, Prolog	Task oriented language	AUTOPASS, RAPT,LAMA

- **Generation 1: Joint control language** — A number of the educational and personal robots support languages for the control of rotations of individual joints. Examples of joint control languages include *ArmBASIC* for robots made by Microbot and the *RASP* language for the Rhino XR robot.

- **Generation 2: Primitive Motion Language** — This mode of robot programming generally involves teaching the robot the desired trajectories using a teaching pendant to guide the end effector through a *point-to-point* path. The teaching pendant is a portable, calculator-like keyboard with controls enabling the user to steer the robot arm along any desired trajectory. At key points along the path, a button is pressed and the programming language records those points for later playback in actual operation. Cincinnati Milacron developed the point-to-point language *T3* to drive the robot shown in Figure 16-2. IBM developed the motion-control language *FUNKY* for its series of industrial robots. Unimation wrote *VAL*, a BASIC-like language. Most of the primitive motion languages allow teaching in Cartesian, cylindrical, or hand coordinate modes.

- **Generation 3: Structured programming language** — The third generation robotics language development paralleled the development of structured languages for conventional programming. They closely resemble Pascal in their syntax and structure, supporting such constructs as FOR and WHILE loops, branching, subroutines, and complex data structures with vectors, frames, and transforms as their basic elements. In addition, they support extensive coordinate transformations between reference frames and improved sensor commands. Examples of structured robotics languages include *AML* and *Maple* by IBM, *MCL* by McDonnell-Douglas, and *PAL* by Sheinman.

• **Generation 4: Task oriented language** — The goal of the as–yet–unsuccessful task oriented languages is similar to that of the successful object and logic oriented conventional languages: to reach a higher level of abstraction in which the computer automatically generates intermediate steps to accomplish high-level goals. Task oriented languages provide high-level commands such as:

```
PLACE OBJECT1 ON OBJECT2
```

which requires a large number of sub-tasks such as locating and identifying OBJECT1 and OBJECT2, calculating a pickup point and approach vector for OBJECT1, moving to pick up OBJECT1, deciding where on OBJECT2 to place OBJECT1, placing OBJECT1 on OBJECT2, and updating the world model to note the new relationship between OBJECT1 and OBJECT2.

Several task oriented languages such as *AUTOPASS*, *RAPT*, and *LAMA* are under development at IBM. However, many of the difficulties first encountered in AI research, such as ambiguities between intent and interpretation, have slowed the entry of task oriented robotics languages into the market place.

DIFFERENCES BETWEEN COMPUTER PROGRAMMING AND ROBOT PROGRAMMING

There are a number of differences between the robot programming environment and a conventional programming environment which make robot programming more difficult. An understanding of these difficulties helps explain why robots have not, in fact, taken over the work place from skilled industrial workers.

• *Need for highly parallel, synchronous programming* — Robot programming must be executed in a *work-cell environment* which almost always involves more than a single autonomous robot. That is, the industrial robot must be integrated with an assembly line and possibly other robots. This involves critical real-time requirements an order of magnitude more difficult than the "whenever" strategy with which most conventional programming works.

- *Need for highly-interactive, real-time integration of sensors* — Intelligent robots must continually monitor an array of sensors, analyze their output in real-time, and act on the basis of this analysis. To effectively use information obtained from their sensors, robots must have the knowledge provided by world models of the environment on which it is operating. This involves a level of sophistication and integration not generally required by conventional programming.

- *Non-standardization between languages* — Because of the commercial nature of robotics enterprises, most robotics programming languages are proprietary and often tailored to a particular model or line of robots. Thus, the tremendous advantages in education and dissemination provided by the standardization of conventional languages such as FORTRAN, BASIC, Pascal, and Common LISP have not been available to robot developers.

16.5 PERSONAL ROBOTS: THE HERO LINE

From an AI viewpoint, the personal robot is considerably more interesting than technically advanced industrial robots. The main difference between the two is that personal robots, by their very design, are much more humanoid in shape and ability than most industrial robots. Several personal robots come with an impressive array of sensors rivaling and in some cases surpassing those of humans. In Figure 16-10 we show HERO-1, the low-cost model of the Heathkit/-Zenith line of educational robots.

To get an idea of the capabilities of such educational, personal robots, consider the following specifications for the HERO 2000, the "big brother" of HERO-1:

- A 16-bit master processor with eleven 8-bit slave processors for simultaneous operation of sensory and manipulative functions. ROM contains 64K and RAM is expandable to 576K.

- Eight closed-loop DC servo-motors with a pulling force of up to 26 pounds and an arm lifting capacity of one pound.

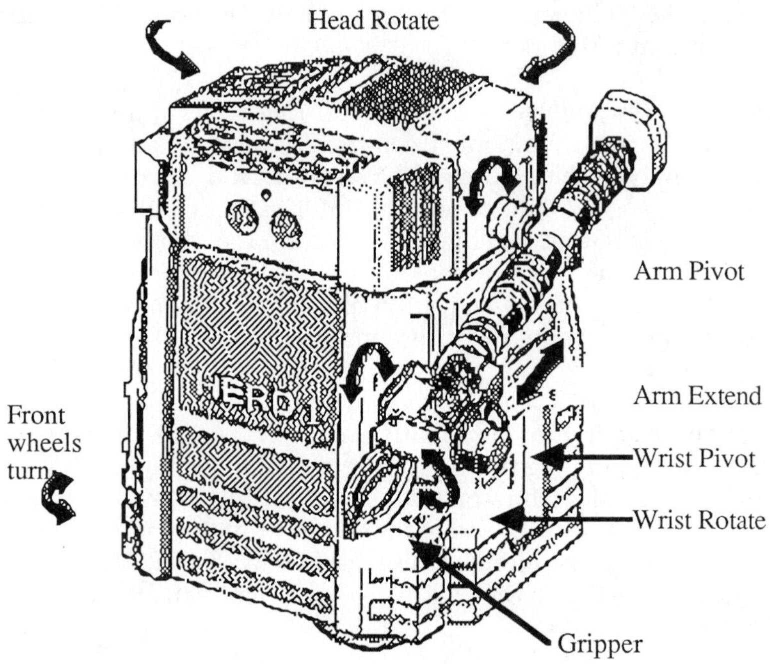

Figure 16-10 HERO-1 Personal Robot This commercially available robot has an arm with 7-degrees of freedom (including the x-y motion provided by the wheels) and a remarkable number of sensors including ultrasonic ranging transmitter/receiver, infrared motion detector, light sensor, and sound sensor. It also includes a phoneme-based voice synthesizer and a teaching pendant.

- Sound is sensed and discriminated at a resolution of 255 levels.

- Temperature is measured over a range of +60°F to +90°F.

- Light is sensed to a resolution of 255 levels at 24 bearings, i.e. with an angular resolution of 15°.

- Sonar ranging using two transducers measures objects from 4.5 inches to 10.5 feet in front of the robot to an accuracy of ±0.5 inches.

- Voice synthesizer which converts text to speech using a 64-phoneme based generator.

- Remote console operation of up to 100 feet is provided using an RF link.

• Optional auto-docking system provides automatic recharging and autonomous operation.

Personal robots were introduced with great fanfare in the early 1980's but have not generated the same enthusiastic reception as did personal computers. They have frequently been oversold as being capable of useful household tasks such as vacuuming or serving drinks. While none are yet capable of any but the most trivial tasks (several can serve as burglar alarms using their ultrasonic motion detectors), all have interesting capabilities which make them valuable as educational tools with research possibilities.

The reason for the difference in public acceptance of personal computers and personal robots can be understood by noting the difference in difficulty between programming a computer to play tic-tac-toe and programming a robot to tie your shoelaces. It is simply much easier to develop algorithms for simple intellectual tasks than for simple tasks requiring manual dexterity. Perhaps one valuable educational role served by personal and educational robots will be to demonstrate the difficulty in automating tasks which three-year-old humans can perform with ease.[22] A detailed description and evaluation of ten commercially available personal robots is given by Higgens.[23]

16.6 ISSUES IN ROBOTICS AND AI

There are some important issues of both a technical and organizational nature which must be carefully considered and resolved before robotics can live up to its promise. Artificial intelligence will provide the strategy for solution to many of the problems which limit the wide-scale application of robotics. There are several paradigms for both robot and industrial plant operations which need serious revision before robots can be effectively integrated into the manufacturing process. We present these issues, paradigms, and revisions by posing three questions and suggesting how AI may help in answering them.

1. What should robots do?

The first paradigm that needs serious revision is that of the R2D2 model, a sort of Super-HERO with anthropomorphic limbs, senses, and intelligence, which a company will buy and train to replace individual workers. As in the early days of AI itself, the unstated assumption of those holding this view is that the more humanoid in appearance and operation a robot can be made, the more effective it will be in performing its robotic tasks. The assumption of this model is that humans are optimally designed to perform manufacturing tasks and therefore deserve to be emulated. As Warren Seering of MIT points out:[24]

> *"This is not true. Humans are designed to throw stones, pick berries, and climb trees. The ability to place a bearing on a shaft has played almost no role in the evolutionary process."*

Shifting the paradigm from *robot-as-humanoid* to *robot-as-machine* helps us answer the question, *What should robots do?* Three characteristics of machines which give them an advantage over humans include:

- **Machines do not breathe** — This fact makes robots well suited for operation in a contaminated, poisonous, dangerous, or extreme environments where one (human) would not want to work or could work only with difficulty. Examples include the extreme conditions of space, nuclear reactors, and sea-bed exploration. The industrial application of spray-painting is an example in which robots have a competitive edge over humans.

- **Machines are strong** — The mechanical forces available from hydraulic, pneumatic, and electrical motors give machines an enormous mechanical advantage over humans. This advantage is the basis of conveyor belts, cranes, and forklifts many of which presently require human operators but which could in many cases be converted to operate robotically. Large industrial spot welders weighing over 100 pounds are an illustration of such an application which is yielding rapidly to robotics.

- **Machines are precise, repetitive, and tireless** — These features which provide the basis for automated assembly lines also provide the basis for successful robot applications. A prime example of a task that is tiresome, repetitive (boring), and requires high precision is that of "board stuffing" or inserting integrated circuits on printed circuit boards. Circuit boards assembled by robots have a much lower defect rejection ratio than those assembled by humans. This increased productivity has made board assembly a rapid growth area for robotics.

Tasks which require one or more of these features of machines are ideal candidates for conversion to robotics. This discussion also suggests that lack of sophisticated sensors and 4th generation robotics languages may be less serious obstacles to robotics than issues of system design and management policy.

2. How should robots do it?

How will robots contribute to the automation of the manufacturing process? Here again the fallacy is the *robot-as-worker* model rather than *robotics-as-intelligent-system-integration*. The misleading scenario is that board assembler Mary Smith gets a pink slip Friday afternoon, and on Monday morning Hubot or Super-HERO wheels in with artificial skin and state-of-the-art vision and begins stuffing boards.

The problems with android robots arise from their *android-like* features rather than their *machine-like* properties. Consider the two contrasting approaches to robotics, the first taken by the Japanese with their simple, *machine-like* SCARA arm and Mitsubishi Melfa arms and the second being the sophisticated *android-like* arms of Cincinnati Milicron's T3 and General Electric's PUMA. The differences can be summarized as:

- *Machine-like* — Resembles jointed milling machine, with typically 3 or 4 degrees of freedom and a single-purpose, fixed tool end effector. Advantages: higher speed, higher precision, higher torque or force to weight ratio, less vibration problems. Disadvantages: less flexibility.

- *Android-like* — Resembles human arm with pivoting shoulder, elbow, and flexible wrist, with 6 degrees of freedom and multiple end effectors. Advantages: more flexibility. Disadvantages: less speed, less precision, less torque or force per unit weight, more vibration.

Certainly the android-like arms are more flexible in function and more consistent with the *robot-as-worker* paradigm of robotics. However, the machine-like Japanese robots have proven enormously successful as evident from the superior quality of Japanese products and the successful sales of Japanese robots in European and United States markets.

Another useful distinction in robotics is based on its goal: Is it worker automation or plant automation? Again, the Japanese experience indicates that robotics is most effective in accomplishing the goal of plant automation. There are several key AI concepts which are essential for implementing robotics for plant automation.[25]

- **Knowledge-Based Approach** — The emphasis on computerized automation is shifting manufacturing from a materials-based to a knowledge-based activity. The goal of a modern, progressive corporation is to use a knowledge-based approach to every aspect of corporate management from design through engineering to production and distribution. The knowledge-based approach allows increased efficiencies in areas such as inventory control through strategies such as "just-in-time-delivery." The highly automated Saturn Corporation division of General Motors will provide a useful case study for the knowledge based approach. The chairman of the G.M. board is quoted as saying "The plan is to run the corporation without paperwork."

• **System Integration** — The advantage of a knowledge-based approach is that it facilitates the system integration essential for plant automation. System integration involves the computerized coordination of the complete manufacturing production cycle from design through distribution. It is particularly important in coordinating the processes of a robotic work-cell or work station. While system integration is important but somewhat fault tolerant on human assembly lines, it is absolutely critical for robot assembly. This elusive goal of complete system integration has been called Computer Integrated Manufacturing (CIM).

• **Distributed Intelligence** — Distributed intelligence will play important roles at two distinct levels of a knowledge-based, automated factory. At the lower, individual robot level, microprocessors will monitor and control every joint in the robotic system. By using knowledge of the joint characteristics as well as knowledge of adjacent elements, it should be possible to overcome many of the mechanical limitations of complex robots. At the higher, plant integration level, networked processors will link every element in the production chain. AI is providing the natural language and expert system tools which will allow management to control the manufacturing process at every level.

• **Representation** — AI can contribute insight on the appropriate choice of representation of knowledge in an effort to achieve computer integrated manufacturing. Rule and object oriented programming are natural structures for application to robotics. A physical object (part) can have an associated object program which it passes to each robot along the assembly line to instruct in its own creation. The knowledge representation and pattern matching algorithms developed for computer vision will apply immediately to robotics. AI work on the transformations between knowledge representations will assist in translating between incompatible robotics languages. The choice of appropriate knowledge representation will undoubtedly play the same key role in enabling progress in robotics as it has in AI.

3. *What management policies are required?*

One might expect that the movement towards robotics would be strongly opposed, particularly by those unions representing the human laborers scheduled to be replaced. Interestingly, unions have generally been supportive of robotics for two reasons: (1) Robots often replace workers in dangerous, dirty, or unattractive jobs, and (2) Most unions recognize the need for productivity increases which robots can help achieve.

Another common misconception is that the transformation to a CIM robotics factory will sweep away the manual laborers but leave management untouched — managers will simply switch from managing people to managing machines. Nothing could be further from the truth. The introduction of robots and knowledge based systems will create a smooth, orderly production environment which will require fewer managers. The more knowledge available to machines, the fewer human judgments must be made. Expert systems in a robotics factory may eventually make decisions now being made by corporate vice presidents.

How should management deal with the resistance which such changes will generate? Neal Clapp, an industrial consultant who General Electric hired to deal with such problems, has proposed what we could call "Clapp's Three Laws of Robotization:"[26]

> 1. *Organizations may not install robots to the economic, social, and physical detriment of workers or management.*
>
> 2. *Organizations may not install robots through devious or closed strategies which reflect distrust or disregard for the work force. For surely they will fulfill their own prophecy.*
>
> 3. *Organizations may only install robots on those tasks which, while currently performed by man, are tasks where the man is like a robot, not the robot like a man.*

While these laws are easier to state than practice, they would certainly create an environment of trust which would ease the transition to robotics. Two other management policies which would help promote an effective transition include:

- **Education as the key** — It is much easier to retrain existing personnel who understand the production process than it is to bring in outside experts. As Rajaram has noted:[27]

> *"...it is good for employee morale, since anyone going through such an experience will have acquired a new and valuable skill. Education is the single most important tool."*

and later:

> *"The effectiveness of an organization will depend upon the education of individuals at all levels, so that they understand the underlying reasons for structural changes."*

- **Flow-of-knowledge principle** — The organization should emphasize *function* rather than *form* or *structure* in any reorganization to incorporate robotics. The guiding principle of the function should be to optimize the flow, exchange, and sharing of knowledge within the organization. Such a policy will help establish a truly knowledge-based organization.

For additional reading in this fascinating area see Ayres and Miller.[28] Several additional general references on robotics are given at the end of the References and Footnotes section.[29]

PROBLEMS AND PROGRAMS

16-1. The relationship between AI and robotics is not immediately obvious. Four possible relationships (among a host of others) can be summarized by the following statements:

a. Robotics is a branch (sub-field) of AI.
b. AI is a branch (sub-field) of robotics.
c. Robotics provides useful tools and techniques for AI research.
d. AI provides useful tools and techniques for robotics research.

Select one of these hypothesis (or a better one if you can) and write a brief justification for your selection.

16-2. Write your own definition of *robotics* (different from the definition of robots given in the Introduction) which captures the concept of a knowledge-based, integrated systems emphasized in the last section.

16-3. What incidents can you foresee which could cause Azimov's three laws of robotics to become part of the legal system? What modifications would be required to these laws to govern the operations of military robots?

16-4. Discuss how *telecherics* might be used as prosthetic devices?

16-5. How does a *numeric control machine* differ from a robot?

16-6. Consider the following three tasks:

a. Spray-painting a flat automotive surface
b. "Pick-and-place" board stuffing of integrated circuits
c. Arc welding an irregular auto chassis

Which of the four geometries of robot design shown in Figure 16-1 is most appropriate for each of these tasks and why?

16-7. In Figure 16-3, assume the key is originally at (X,Y,Z) = (500, 200, 100), and that keyhole position is (X_k, Y_k, Z_k) = (1.5, 2, –1). Assume the key is hanging on a nail such that the x' axis is parallel to the z axis, the z' axis is anti-parallel to the y axis, and the y' axis is anti-parallel to the x axis.

a. What translation matrix is required to move the origin of the key coordinate system to the origin of the lock system?

b. What two rotation matrices are required to align the coordinate systems?

c. What translation matrix is required to move the key system to the keyhole?

d. What single matrix will accomplish these four tasks?

16-8. Almost every home contains a robot which uses the open loop control strategy shown in Figure 16-4. By a change of the function "Joint Controller" to "Water Weight Controller" this figure describes precisely a washing machine. Investigate the control elements of an actual washing machine and fill in as many of the details of the block diagram as you can figure out.

16-9. What tasks could a robot equipped with a 4th generation control system (Figure 16-6) perform which would be impossible for a 3rd generation system? What role do *world models* play in your answer?

16-10. Write a program to plot a cross section of the work envelope of a three joint articulated arm with length of links (1,2,3) in the ratio of (2,

1.5, 1) where link 1 is attached to the base. Would Monte Carlo techniques be useful for this application?

16-11. Write down the Jacobian matrix, **J**(r), to transform a point from a spherical (r,θ,ϕ) coordinate system to a Cartesian (x,y,z) coordinate system.

16-12. If **J**(r) is the Jacobian which transforms a point in cylindrical coordinates into Cartesian coordinates, what is the inverse Jacobian, $\mathbf{J}^{-1}$?

16-13. A standard approximation in computing the kinematics and dynamics of robot arm motion is that, for small angles θ, the trigonometric functions may be approximated by:

$$\sin(\theta) \cong \theta \qquad\qquad \cos(\theta) \cong 1$$

where θ is measured in radians. At what angle θ does this approximation introduce a 0.1% error? How large can θ become before the error gets to 5%?

16-14. In the two-arm robot shown in Figure 16-7, assume $l_1 = 0.5$ m, $l_2 = 0.4$ m, $m_1 = 4.0$ kg, and $m_2 = 3.0$ kg. What is the torque vector, τ, at the trajectory points:

a) $(\theta_1, \dot{\theta}_1, \ddot{\theta}_1) = (0.7854, 1.0, 0.5)$

b) $(\theta_2, \dot{\theta}_2, \ddot{\theta}_2) = (-0.7854, 1.0, 1.0)$?

16-15. Consider a single-joint arm under position control as shown in Figure 16-8. Assume that the moment of inertia is $J_t = 1.0$ kg·m^2, the torque constant K = 100 newton·m/rad. For the initial conditions $(\theta,\theta') = (0,0)$ and $\theta_d = 1.0$, calculate, plot, and interpret the resulting $\theta(t)$ trajectories for the three frictional cases:

a) F_f = 0 newton·m·sec/rad
b) F_f = 20.0 newton·m·sec/rad
c) F_f = 50.0 newton·m·sec/rad

16-16. Prove the statement: The acceleration trajectory shown in Figure 16-9 yields the the most rapid trajectory between any two angular positions for a given maximum torque.

16-17. Working with a friend and using toothpicks or paper clips for probes, measure experimentally the spatial resolution of your finger tips, your fore-arm, and the center of your back. In addition to your experimental results, discuss the experimental procedure, controls, and estimate of error on your results.

16-18. In Table 16-I we cite parallels between 5 generations of conventional programming language and 5 generations or robot programming languages. Give additional features which either confirm or disagree with this classifications system.

16-19. What do you consider the most significant difference between conventional and robot programming languages?

16-20. What research applications do you think would be interesting for personal robots such as the HERO line of educational robots?

16-21. List three tasks you have done either on a paid job or as household duties which you consider the easiest to convert to robotics. What three tasks you have done would be the most difficult? Discuss the reasons for your answers.

16-22. The text presents several strong arguments for building robots in the image of machines. Write a short essay arguing for the hypothesis: *The more anthropomorphic (human-like) a robot is, the more useful it is.*

16-23. What arguments in addition to those presented in the text can you give for building machine-like robots?

16-24. What features of a knowledge representation scheme do you think would prove to be particularly effective to incorporate into a robot programming language?

16-25. Write a short essay on the hypothesis: *A strong education program is the key to acceptance of robotics by both labor and management.*

REFERENCES AND FOOTNOTES

1 Plantier, M., et al, "Teleoperation and Automation: A Survey of European Expertise Applicable to Docking and Assembly in Space,"

ESTEC Contract 4401/80/NL/AK(SC),EUROSTAT, S.A., Geneva, May (1981)

[2] Brady, J. Michael, "Intelligent Robots: Connecting Perception to Action," in *THE AI BUSINESS — Commercial Uses of Artificial Intelligence,* Patrick H. Winston and Karen A. Prendergast, (eds), MIT Press, Cambridge, MA (1984)

[3] Albus, James S., *Brains, Behavior, & Robotics*, BYTE Books (McGraw-Hill), Peterborough, NH (1981)

[4] Glorioso, Robert M., and Osorio, F. C. Colon, *Engineering Intelligent Systems: Concepts, Theory, and Applications*, p. 418, Digital Press, Bedford, MA (1980)

[5] Goertz, R. C., "Manipulators Used for Handling Radioactive Materials," in *Human Factors in Technology*, Bennett, E. M. (ed), McGraw-Hill Book Company, New York, NY (1963)

[6] Snyder, Wesley E., *Industrial Robots: Computer Interfacing and Control*, Prentice-Hall Industrial Robots Series, Englewood Cliffs, NJ (1985)

[7] Raphael, Bertram, *The Thinking Computer — Mind Inside Matter*, pp. 275–283, W. H. Freeman and Company, San Francisco, CA (1976)

[8] Homogeneous coordinates are chosen so as to more naturally incorporate the translation matrix into the transformation matrix formalism. For details on homogeneous coordinates, see: Roberts, L. G., *Homogeneous Matrix Representation and Manipulation of N-Dimensional Constructs*, Document No. MS1045, Lincoln Laboratory, MIT, Cambridge, MA (1965)

[9] See for instance: Newman, William M. and Sproull, Robert F., *Principles of Interactive Computer Graphics*, Second Edition, pp. 346–348, McGraw-Hill Book Company, New York, NY (1979). See also: Foley, James D. and Van Dam, Andries, *Fundamentals of Interactive Computer Graphics*, pp. 258–261, Addison-Wesley Publishing Company, Reading, MA (1982)

[10] Paul, Richard P., *Robot Manipulators: Mathematics, Programming, and Control*, MIT Press, Cambridge MA (1981)

11 Glorioso, Robert M., and Osorio, F. C. Colon, *Op Cit*, pp. 430–431

12 Rehg, James A., *Introduction to Robotics — A systems Approach*, Prentice-Hall, Inc., Englewood Cliffs, NJ (1985)

13 Craig, John J., *Introduction to Robotics: Mechanics and Control*, pp. 162–166, Addison-Wesley Publishing Company, Reading MA (1986)

14 Paul, Richard P., *Op Cit*, pp. 157–195

15 Craig, John J., *Op Cit*, p. 177

16 Coiffet, P., *Robot Technology: Modelling and Control*, Vol. 1, Prentice-Hall, Inc., Englewood Cliffs, NJ (1983)

17 Craig, John J., *Op Cit*, p. 168–173

18 Snyder, Wesley E., *Op Cit*, pp. 216–233

19 Pennywitt, Kirk E., "Robotic Tactile Sensing," *BYTE* **11**, pp. 177–200, January (1986)

20 Dario, Paolo and De Rossi, Danilo, "Tactile Sensors and the Gripping Challenge," *IEEE Spectrum* **22**, August (1985)

21 Horn, Berthold Klaus Paul, *Robot Vision*, MIT Press, Cambridge, MA (1986)

22 Bell, Trudy E., "Robots in the home: Promises, Promises," *IEEE Spectrum* **22**, No. 5, pp. 51–55, May (1985)

23 Higgens, Mike, *A Robot in Every Home*, Kensington Publishing Company, Oakland, CA (1985)

24 Seering, Warren P., "Who Said Robots Should Work Like People," *Technology Review*, pp. 58–67, April (1985)

25 Rajaram, N. S., "Artificial Intelligence — The Achilles Heel of Robotics and Manufacturing", *Robotics Engineering* **8**, pp. 10–15, January (1986)

26 Rehg, James, *Op Cit*, p. 196

[27] Rajaram, N. S., *Op Cit*, p. 15

[28] Ayres, R. U. and Miller, S. M., *Robotics: Applications and Social Implications*, Ballinger Publishing Company, Cambridge, MA (1983)

[29] **Additional References**

Stonecipher, Ken, *Industrial Robotics: A Handbook of Automated Systems Design*, Hayden Book Co., Hasbrouck Heights, NJ (1985)

Blume, C. and Jakob, W., *Pasro: Pascal for Robots*, Springer-Verlag, New York, NY (1985)

Hanafusa, Hideo and Inoue, Hirochika (eds), *Robotics Research*, Proceedings of 2nd International Symposium, Kyoto, Aug. 1984, MIT Press, Cambridge, MA (1985)

Ayres, Robert U. et al, *Robotics and Flexible Manufacturing Technologies — Assessment, Impacts and Forecast*, Noyes Publications, Park Ridge, NJ (1985)

Toepperwein, L. L., Blackmon, M. T., Park, W. T., Tanner, W. R., and Adolfson, W. F., *Robotics Applications for Industry — A Practical Guide*, Noyes Data Corporation, Park Ridge, NJ (1983

Higgins, Mike, "The Future of Personal Robots," *The Futurist*, pp. 43–46, May-June (1986)

Zorpete, Glenn, "Robots for Fun and Profit," *IEEE Spectrum*, pp. 71–75, March (1986)

Robillard, Mark J., *Microprocessor-Based Robotics*, Howard W. Sams, Indianapolis, IN (1983)

Weinstein, Martin, *Android Design*, Hayden Book Company, Hasbrouck Heights, NJ (1981)

Chapter 17

MACHINE LEARNING

(PHOTO: COURTESY OF UNIVERSITY OF WISCONSIN, PARKSIDE)

Ryszard S. Michalski is Professor of Computer Science and Information Technology and Director of the Artificial Intelligence Center at George Mason University. He received his M.S. from the Leningrad Polytechnic Institute and his Ph.D. from the University of Silesia in Poland. He served as Research Scientist at the Polish Academy of Sciences in Warsaw prior to coming to the United States. His research has included machine learning, inductive inference, and the application of expert systems in medicine and agriculture. He has authored over one hundred and thirty papers and is coeditor of two volumes of *Machine Learning: An Artificial Intelligence Approach*.

17: Machine Learning

17.1 INTRODUCTION

It must have occurred frequently to the reader during this course of study that the key to the solution of many of the unsolved problems of AI is *machine learning*. The immediate practical effect of true machine learning would be to enable AI programs to improve their performance automatically in each of the application areas we have studied. At a more fundamental philosophical level, a machine with a clearly demonstrated ability to learn would answer once and for all the question "Can machines think?" since thinking is so strongly intertwined with learning. It is difficult to imagine a thinking being without the ability to learn, or, conversely, a system which can learn from its environment which does not display evidence of thinking. In fact, there is a close parallel between the goals of AI and university education - teaching our subjects to "learn to think."

Jean Piaget, the influential child psychologist, has classified stages of learning in children as *concrete* which is well advanced by the time a child is six years old and *formal* which begins to develop by age 12 in most children.[1] Concrete learning deals with questions of *How to ...?* which are readily resolved by trial and error, while formal learning is more concerned with more abstract questions of *What ...?* relating to bodies of knowledge and frequently requiring symbolic representations. These stages of learning closely parallel the *skill enhancement* and *knowledge acquisition* distinctions discussed below and have close analogs to the stages through which machine learning is progressing.

MACHINE AS MIND

The machine learning analog to skill enhancement is performance improvement. That is, a computer system which can play better chess after several games against a particular player demonstrates machine learning by most any definition. If a vision system can improve its ability to identify faces in a crowd photograph after scanning fuzzy ID card images we would say it is learning to recognize people. If a voice input system improves its understanding of continuous speech by listening to recordings it is fair to say it is learning.

The striking fact is that many of these skills which come so quickly and easily to humans are either impossible or extremely challenging for machines, at least for sequential architecture machines. Although the computing elements of machines operate approximately a million times faster than those of the brain, the massively parallel structure of the brain gives it an enormous computational advantage over the fastest machine for tasks requiring complex pattern recognition. This discrepancy between the performance of the human mind and sequential machines to date provides the first clue to successful AI machine architectures for the future:

Improved performance in complex pattern recognition tasks requires *massive parallel processing.*

The theme of this text has been that successful AI ventures require a knowledge-based approach. The "knowledge bottleneck" was identified in our discussion of knowledge-based systems as the primary obstacle to the wide scale implementation of expert systems. The naive reaction is to assume that since we can have a whole encyclopedia on a single compact disk (and soon, perhaps, access to the whole Library of Congress) the knowledge acquisition problem has been solved.

However, the knowledge acquisition aspect of machine learning requires far more than simple access to a collection of data. Knowledge acquisition involves the integration, organization, representation, and abstraction of data and information in such a way that it can be used for problem solving, decision making, and other cognitive functions we associate with learning and thinking. The incredible difficulty in emulating common sense reasoning illustrates the nature of the problem. And yet the human brain was able to resolve such complexity millennia ago by evolving a complex network of interconnected processing cells. The existence proof of the brain provides the second hint as to the optimal direction for future machine architectures:

The efficient acquisition of knowledge requires a *high degree of interconnectedness* of the knowledge processing system.

In physics, the behavior of two particles before and after they collide is described precisely by the equations of kinematics and the laws of energy and momentum conservation. However, as the number of interacting particles increases, the computational difficulty of specifying the state of all particles at any given time increases rapidly and soon becomes intractable. The solution to the problem of describing the behavior of a large ensemble of particles is found in the statistical laws of thermodynamics. Thermodynamics relates new concepts such as pressure and temperature which emerge as a result of the collective behavior of a large number of gas molecules. In addition, new concepts such as *entropy* emerge as a collective property of a large number of molecules even though the entropy of a single molecule is undefined.

A great deal of research has centered on the behavior of individual neurons, the basic processing element of the brain. Through millions of years of evolution, the ensemble of neurons composing the brain have developed the capacity for intelligence. In analogy with the emergent collective behavior in particle dynamics, the brain exhibits collective features such as memory and learning which are undefined for single neurons. This leads us to the final speculation on the direction which successful new computer architectures for artificial intelligence will take:

> **The optimal path for machine emulation of mental functions such as pattern matching, memory, and learning is through the *emergent collective computational capability of artificial neural networks.*[2]**

MIND AS MACHINE

In addition to the crucial role machine learning will play in developing intelligent machines, it is also of great intrinsic interest to cognitive scientists in their study of "mind as machine", i. e. as a tool for modeling mechanisms through which the human mind learns. The human mind, with its incredibly complex network of neural interconnections, is again proving to be the model for new machine architectures with exciting behavior and great promise.

The *mind as machine* paradigm suggests another novel concept which may prove of great significance to the evolution of human intelligence. The history of technology abounds with cases of the synergistic effects of combining machines to produce more powerful and flexible final products. Combining the self-starter and the automatic clutch with existing machines produced a more "user-friendly" automobile. Combining graphics, windows, and the mouse with existing machines has produced more powerful, interactive computer hardware. Combining knowledge-based routines with existing software (i.e., "embedding" expert systems) enhances the intelligence and performance of the resulting software system. This suggests the possibility of combining high-performance expert systems with human thought processes to enhance the performance of the human machine. Professor Donald Michie's research group is working on experiments in this area, and Michie says "I do think we may be building the foundation on which people can become mental giants in the next generation."[3] An even greater challenge is the integration of massively parallel architectures such as those provided by neural networks within the framework of sequential, symbol-based machines.

The goals of this chapter are to survey the history and present status of machine learning, discuss some of the most interesting new machine architectures, and speculate briefly on the implications of such new approaches for the future of AI.

17.2 DEFINITION AND CLASSIFICATIONS OF LEARNING

Because of the great variety of human experience which is described as learning, the term *machine learning* is nearly as difficult to define as the term artificial intelligence itself. As in other areas of AI, Marvin Minsky offers a brief and comprehensive definition of human learning:

> ***"Learning is making useful changes in our minds."***

A somewhat more focused definition suggested by Herbert Simon captures the essence of human learning which is of particular importance to machine learning:[4]

> ***"Learning denotes changes in the system that are adaptive in the sense that they enable the system to do the same task or tasks drawn from the same population more efficiently and more effectively the next time."***

Finally, Michalski reminds us of the important role representation plays in any cognitive process by his definition:

> ***"Learning is constructing or modifying representations of what is being experienced."***

Several of our intuitive ideas about the nature of human learning are equally valid in describing machine learning. Learning can generally be classified as either *enhancing the skills* of the learner or in *acquiring knowledge* for the learner. Skill enhancement applies to simple motor skills such as learning to walk, hold a glass of milk without spilling it, and hit a tennis ball correctly, as well as to more cognitive skills such as learning to type, speak a foreign language, or solve physics problems.

One feature of skill enhancement which distinguishes it from knowledge acquisition is the role which repetition and practice plays. Skill enhancement involves repeated cycles through the performance loop containing negative feedback which tends to damp out the difference between actual performance and desired performance. Skill enhancement can be interpreted physiologically as establishing and reinforcing a pattern of neural connections for performing the desired function. For young learners, skill enhancement is usually a subconscious activity while more mature learners often find it a painfully conscious activity (as persons struggling to improve their tennis game can attest).

Knowledge acquisition involves the collection, classification, organization, integration, and abstraction of knowledge. In terms of increasing levels of abstraction, knowledge includes *data* (facts and measurements made on the environment), *information* (rules and relationships governing the data and the environment), and *meta-knowledge* (knowledge about the knowledge already acquired). By classifying the data and organizing it within a framework specified by the relationship information the learner creates a model of the system s/he is studying.

This model is further refined by integration of additional data and information. For reasons of economy and generality, the rules, relationships, and models are represented symbolically. The most abstract level of knowledge is that of meta-knowledge. Meta-knowledge involves the ability to evaluate the knowledge available, what additional knowledge may be required, and systematics implied by the present rules. Thus, a machine with meta-knowledge would demonstrate behavior resembling what we refer to in humans as "consciousness" and "inductive reasoning."

CHARACTERISTICS OF HUMAN LEARNING

While one of the main theses of this chapter is that the structure of the human mind provides useful insight on optimal architectures for machine learning, there are some limitations of human learning that we should recall. These will help us keep the proper perspective as we survey the experiments in machine learning which, to date, have not yielded useful, general-purpose learning systems. With the exception of rare child prodigies such as Mozart, human learning is generally characterized as:

- **Slow** — Humans take 5-6 years to master the basic motor skills of eating, dressing themselves, and manipulating their environment. In addition, during these years they develop an operational use of language and interaction with other humans. During the next 12-20 years they learn more abstract concepts of human history, art, and symbol manipulation which prepares them to function in and contribute to society. Thus, the first one third of most people's lives is devoted primarily to learning, and for many individuals, particularly in dynamic, technological societies, the process often never stops.

• **Inefficient** — Progress in the cognitive sciences and theory of human learning continues at a steady pace, and yet new insights from this research seem to have little impact on the formal educational system. One senses that little has changed in the teacher/learner relationship since the days of Socrates. Although new technologies such as computer aided instruction (CAI) and interactive compact disks (CDI) have been shown to be effective and efficient learning tools, they have had little practical effect on the process of formal learning. The cycle of educational innovation is as predictable and perennial as the flowers which bloom in the spring and about as enduring. This is due primarily to the inertia and conservatism of educational institutions which are exceeded only by those of the church. This is not meant to disparage either institution, since this conservatism is a reflection of the high value society places on educational and religious institutions.

• **Expensive** — If we put the cost of primary and secondary education at a conservative estimate of \$5,000/year and that of higher education at \$15,000/year, the cost of formal learning ranges from \$60,000 to \$120,000 per student.[5] This is a direct result of the previous two attributes of human learning — it is slow and inefficient. Any progress made in improving the efficiency of human learning, either by learning the same knowledge faster or learning more knowledge in the same period, would yield tremendous benefits. As the above cost estimates indicate, the savings would be considerable.

• **No copy process** — Human learning, as opposed to machine learning, permits no easy duplication of the learning process. When a computer program demonstrates an ability to learn, that program is easily copied and becomes available on all similar computer systems. Unfortunately, this is not the case with human learning. Human learning is the ultimate individual experience. Although the particular skill or knowledge may have been learned by all previous humanity, the learning experience still remains unique for each person. Much as our overworked students might wish to the contrary, there is no pill they can take to learn French or calculus.

• **No internal representation** — At the root of the difficulty in understanding human learning (and subsequently emulating it with machine learning) is our almost total lack of understanding of the internal representation of knowledge and the learning process taking place in the brain. The lack of knowledge of how knowledge is acquired and represented in the brain impedes both the teacher and the learner in achieving an optimal learning strategy. To overcome this lack of an internal representation, good teachers use their intuition, creativity, and imagination in concocting models with which to deal with their students (e.g., "Joe's a left brain type" or "Jane's sharp — all I have to do is tell her once" or "Eric needs lots of drill and practice"). Recent neural network research is providing glimpses of how the brain may store information, but we are a long way from using such insights to improve human learning.

• **Learning strategy is a function of knowledge** — It has been clearly demonstrated that the learning strategies of children differ from those of adults. The primary difference is the amount of knowledge available to the learner — adults generally have much more knowledge to guide the learning process than do children. The situation is further complicated by the fact that the amount of knowledge available determines the optimal mix of learning strategies used by a particular individual. Since no two individuals have precisely the same knowledge, no two individuals will use the same learning strategies.

The human mind continues to serve as the paradigm for machine learning. However, in spite of its amazing capabilities, the mind has its limitations, not the least of which is our understanding of its operation.

CLASSIFICATION OF LEARNING STRATEGIES

An important parameter in the classification of learning strategies is the degree of inference required on the part of the learner. Inference or inductive reasoning involves the generation of rules or generalizations from a set of particular examples. A widely accepted classification scheme spanning the spectrum from no inference required to a great deal is summarized as follows:[6]

1. ***Rote Learning*** — This is the lowest level of both human and machine learning. In human learning it corresponds to memorization of facts with no need to draw inferences from them. In machine learning it corresponds to knowledge being represented directly in the system by programming or simple data base systems. No further processing or transformations on the data are required in order to use it. The performance of systems employing rote learning may be

enhanced by *selectively forgetting* knowledge which is rarely used or proves to be incorrect.

2. ***Learning by Instruction*** — This level of learning is also known as *learning by being told* or *learning by taking advice.* Knowledge acquired from a teacher or textbook is transformed by the learning system into an internal representation applicable to the problem at hand. This learning mode closely parallels the formal student/teacher relationship in a typical classroom situation. The primary responsibility of structuring and representing knowledge remains with the teacher, but now the learner must perform some inference in order to transform the knowledge into a readily usable representation. The learner's role in this mode of learning may be considered to be that of performing a *syntactic reformulation* of the knowledge provided by the primary source (teacher, textbook, encyclopedia, and so on).

3. ***Learning by Deduction*** — This level of learning shifts even more responsibility for transforming knowledge into a usable form from the teacher to the learner. The constraints on knowledge representation from the source are relaxed. The learner draws deductive inferences from the knowledge and reformulates it in the form of useful conclusions which preserve the information content of the original data. Deductive learning includes knowledge reformulation, compilation, and organizational procedures such as *chunking* which preserve the truth of the original formulation.

4. ***Learning by Analogy*** — This mode of learning combines deductive and inductive learning. The first step is the inductive inference required to find the common substructure between the problem domain and one of the analogous domains stored in the learner's existing knowledge base. The next step after generalizing to a common substructure is to map the solution from the selected analogous domain to the problem domain. This analogical mapping is performed by deductive logic. Schank has proposed a variation of learning by analogy which he calls *learning by being reminded*.[7]

5. ***Learning by Induction*** — This is the learning mode requiring the greatest degree of inductive reasoning and includes the sub-categories of:

- Learning by example
- Learning by experimentation
- Learning by observation
- Learning by discovery.

Learning by example involves the process of *concept acquisition* in which general concept descriptions are inferred from a set of examples provided by a teacher, the environment, or the knowledge base of the learner itself. The acquired concept should be general enough to explain all of the positive examples provided but restricted enough to exclude any counter-examples. If the source of examples is the environment, the learner may have the option of performing experiments from which it receives feedback. This form of learning by experimentation also goes under the name *stimulus-response learning.*

Learning by observation and learning by discovery both take place without aid of a teacher. They are both a form of *descriptive generalization* in which the learner infers general rules and regularities which explain the observations. Inference techniques employed in these modes of learning may include curve fitting of data, classification of observations and objects, and *conceptual clustering* in which simple concepts are classified. The observations may take place in a *passive mode* in which the learner does not interact with the environment or in an *active mode* in which the learner may experiment on the environment to perform stimulus-response learning. The objective of both modes is the discovery of economical theories to account for the observations.

A MODEL OF MACHINE LEARNING

A useful model for machine learning is shown schematically in Figure 17-1. The essential elements of the system include the following four components:

1. A set of rules or data structures in which the **knowledge base** is represented. This is a dynamic structure which will be revised and expand as more knowledge is accumulated. The correct choice of knowledge representation is critical to the success of the learning system.

2. A **task module** or performance algorithm which uses input and rules stored in the knowledge base for solving the problem at hand. The task module must produce a quantifiable output for use in measuring system performance and comparison with ideal systems.

3. A **feedback module** or critic which compares the output of the performance module with that of an idealized system. The feedback information is a type of error signal to guide the learner in revising the knowledge base.

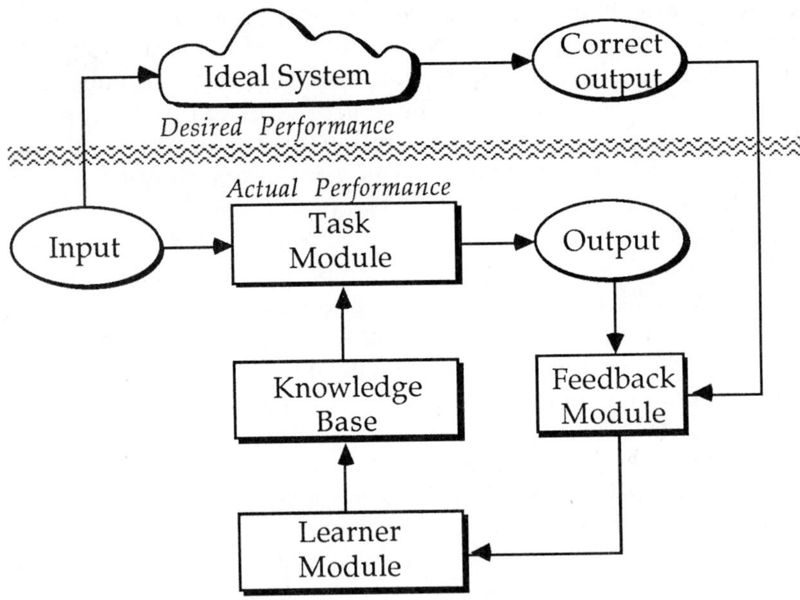

Figure 17-1 Feedback Model of Machine Learning The feedback module generates an error signal which the learner module uses to restructure or augment the knowledge base in order to improve the performance of the task module. Subsequent actual performance should be more in line with the desired performance of an ideal system. (Model based on Richard Forsyth's "paradigm for learning."[8])

4. A **learner module** which uses the error signal to upgrade and augment the rules in the knowledge base to minimize the discrepancy between the actual output the correct output from the ideal system.

The logic and simplicity of this paradigm for machine learning may be a bit deceptive. The key to success of any such feedback system is the power and flexibility of the representation system chosen for the knowledge base. The issue of appropriate representation in machine learning has been one of the most difficult problems in other areas of AI research as well. Knowledge representation is particularly difficult in machine learning because, in addition to representing knowledge correctly, the scheme chosen must support the dynamic modification of the knowledge base under program control.

17.3 MACHINE LEARNING AS THE HOLY GRAIL

Machine learning has been the holy grail of artificial intelligence from the earliest days. Alan Turing estimated that it would take sixty programmers working steadily for fifty years and making no mistakes to program a conventional machine to play the imitation game successfully.[9] He recognized that a more efficient technique for reaching this goal was by *learning machines* which he proposed should learn in the manner of children. Turing stated "I have done some experiments with one such child machine, and succeeded in teaching it a few things, but the teaching method was too unorthodox for the experiment to be considered really successful."

This record of only limited success has continued to be a characteristic in the quest for a general learning system. One of the pioneers in machine learning, Arthur Samuel, in reviewing twenty years of research on the field, commented, "The situation with respect to machine learning is particularly distressing."[10] Within restricted domains, however, there have been some outstanding successes in machine learning, one of the first of which was Samuel's own checkers playing program.

17.4 SAMUEL'S CHECKERS PLAYER

The first program to clearly demonstrate the capacity for learning was Samuel's checkers player.[11] Samuel's interest in checkers started in 1946 as he was searching for a demonstration project to stimulate additional funding for a computer he was building at the University of Illinois. After learning that Claude Shannon was working on a chess program, he chose checkers and states:[12]

> *"Checkers was my next choice. It happened that a world champion checker match was to be held in the neighboring town, Kankakee, the next spring and it seemed quite reasonable at the time for us to put together some sort of computer in a few months and for me to write a checker program during this same period of time that could challenge and beat the new world checker champion at the conclusion of this match. This would give us the publicity that we needed. How naive can one be?"*

The project was, in fact, to take a great deal of Samuel's spare time over the next twenty years. His move to IBM in 1949 provided him with the machines on which to implement his checkers playing program.

The characteristics of checkers which made it an ideal test bed for the first learning program include:

1) The activity must not be deterministic in the practical sense. Samuel computed the number of choices of moves to explore every complete path in checkers as 10^{40}. At 3 choices per nanosecond this would require 10^{21} centuries of computer time.

2) A definite goal must exist and at least one measure for determining progress towards the goal must exist. The goal is to win and an obvious measure of progress is the number of pieces of each color on the board.

3) The rules of the activity must be definite and they should be known.

4) There should be a background of knowledge concerning the activity against which the learning progress can be tested.

5) The activity should be one that is familiar to a substantial body of people so that the behavior of the program can be made understandable.

The first task was to incorporate the *rules of the game*. Next, Samuel generated possible moves down the game tree a minimum number of ply and evaluated each of the resulting board positions with a "scoring polynomial" (static evaluation function). His original evaluation function was a linear polynomial of four terms: (1) piece advantage, (2) denial of occupancy, (3) mobility, and (4) a hybrid term which combined control of the center and piece advancement.

The most effective look-ahead strategy was based on a quiescent heuristic and can be summarized as follows. The minimum look-ahead distance was generally set at three. Unless one of the following three conditions was satisfied, the evaluation function was applied and the optimum move was selected using an alpha-beta minimax procedure. The three conditions causing exceptions to this rule were: (1) the next move is a jump, (2) the last move was a jump, or (3) an exchange offer is possible. If any of these exceptions apply, look-ahead continued to four ply. At ply 4 the evaluation function was applied if conditions (1) and (3) were not met. At a ply of five or greater, the program stopped the look-ahead whenever the next ply level did not offer a jump. At a ply of eleven or greater, the program terminated the look-ahead, even if the next move was to be a jump, if one side was ahead by more than two kings. The program stopped at 20 plies regardless of all conditions.

This strategy proved effective for exploring promising paths to a greater depth (to incorporate the horizon effect) and for accommodating the restriction on branching imposed by a jump situation.

The actual choice of ply cut-offs was restricted by the memory limitations of the IBM 704 on which the program was implemented.

ROTE LEARNING IN CHECKERS PLAYER

The first of three learning modes Samuel incorporated in his checkers player is what he called *rote learning*. By rote learning he means that the computationally expensive results of evaluating a particular board position can be indexed and saved for future reference. This is equivalent to memorizing the value to the machine of that board position and greatly increases the *look-ahead power* of the system. If, for instance, board position X has been evaluated to a depth of *three* ply in a given game and is encountered in a later game at the end of a *three* ply search from board position Y, the effect is to provide Y with a *six* ply search through the path containing X. Board position Y might be generated in a later search from position Z and provide a 9-ply search along the X-Y path and so on.

Rote learning provided another advantage for improving the performance of the checkers player. Samuel discovered that it was necessary to impart a sense of direction to his program to press it toward a win. For instance, from a given board position a large number of paths on the game tree may all lead to a win but with a considerable range on the number of plies required to reach the winning state. Optimum play from this position requires the shortest path to the win. By storing the ply value for each board position it has evaluated Samuel used rote learning to direct the program to push for a win, or, if behind, to adopt delaying tactics.

A final feature which rote learning provided was the mechanism for *forgetting*. Each new board position was arbitrarily assigned an age. When a board position was referenced to update its score or use it in the look-ahead process, the age recorded for this position was divided by two. This process was called *refreshing* the memory. Approximately every twenty moves each board position was automatically aged by one unit. When the age of a given position reached an arbitrary maximum value the position was deleted from memory (i.e. *forgotten*). Forgetting was particularly important for the limited capacity machine Samuel used for the checkers player. Even with machines of virtually unlimited memory capacity, forgetting is a valuable concept for increasing the efficiency of computation.

Samuel used several techniques for training the program in the rote learning mode. These included play against itself, play against many different humans including master players, and use of published play by masters (book games). In his own evaluation of the success of the rote learning mode, Samuel states:

> *"The program learned to play a very good opening game and to recognize most winning and losing end positions many moves in advance, although its midgame play was not greatly improved. This program now qualifies as a rather better-than-average novice, but definitely not as an expert."*

This performance was based on a memory tape containing approximately 53,000 board positions. Samuel estimated that significant improvement of the midgame play would require storing at least twenty times that many board positions. Although it was infeasible to devote the expensive computers of the day to this task, Samuel noted that the computer would require less time to become a master through rote learning than a human master player would.

Learning by Generalization — Linear Evaluation Function

An obvious way to improve the efficiency of a learning program is to generalize on the basis of experience and save only the generalizations. This corresponds to a higher level of abstraction in representing the inference process. Samuel chose modification of the coefficients of the evaluation polynomial as the representation for this generalization.

$$f_j = \sum_{i=1}^{16} c_{ji}\, y_{ij} \qquad (17.1)$$

where

f_j = static evaluation function for node j
c_{ji} = weight coefficient for parameter i
y_{ij} = parameter i for node j

The evaluation function included the piece-advantage terms as before and was revised to include a subset consisting of 16 variable coefficients drawn from a reserve inventory of 38 parameters. The central idea of the learning process was to determine the highest point in the multi-dimensional scoring space as a function of the 16 coefficients.

In order to generalize on the basis of self-play, the program was structured to act as two different players called Alpha and Beta. Alpha generalized after each move by adjusting the coefficients of its linear evaluation function and replacing terms which seems to have little importance by new parameters drawn from the reserve inventory. Beta used the same evaluation function for the duration of a game.

After each game, the relative playing ability of Alpha and Beta were compared by a neutral evaluation function. If Alpha won or was ahead when play terminated, Alpha's evaluation function was transferred to Beta. If Beta won or was ahead, Alpha was given a black mark. After three black marks, Alpha was assumed to be on the wrong track and its scoring polynomial was drastically revised, usually by reducing the coefficient of the leading term to zero. The three black marks by Alpha indicated that it had reached a secondary maximum in the hill-climbing process in coefficient space (i.e., a false summit). The drastic revision of the scoring function effectively jumps to a new region in coefficient space in an attempt to continue improving Alpha's performance.

To determine how much each coefficient should be changed after each move, an "error function" Δ is computed for each position. The function Δ is the difference between a performance standard and Alpha's estimate of the value of the present board position. The performance standard is computed by a deeper, minimax search from the present position using the present Alpha evaluation function. If Δ is negative, Alpha's polynomial is overestimating the position value. It Δ is positive, Alpha is underestimating it. By careful tabulation of the features of the present position, a *correlation coefficient* may be computed which predicts the dependence of Δ on a given feature. Learning is achieved when the existing Alpha polynomial yields the same position value as the performance standard would give, that is, when Δ is minimized. A large positive correlation coefficient occurs for features which, if not weighted heavily enough, would lead to a large positive Δ value. If the correlation coefficient turns out to be negative, the term is contributing with the wrong sign and a reversal of sign is indicated.

The correlation coefficient also provides a useful tool for identifying terms of little significance or importance in their predictive value. After each move, the term with the lowest correlation coefficient is identified and a "low-term tally" is incremented for this term. When the low-term tally reaches some arbitrary number (from 8 — 32) the term is replaced by the top term from the reserve list and added to the bottom of the reserve list. In this way, the least significant terms are eliminated from the evaluation function. The effect of the process is to select the most significant terms from the inventory of parameters.

Samuel concluded that the experiment to learn by generalization of the evaluation function did prove that learning took place. He says:

> *"The program appeared to be approaching the quality of play which caused it to be described as a 'better-than-average player.' A detailed analysis of these results indicated that the learning procedure did work and that the rate of learning was surprisingly high, but that the learning was quite erratic and none too stable."*

At the heart of the problem is the fact that the evaluation function used was *linear* in the terms evaluated. That is, the errors in Alpha's estimation were attributed to errors in the assigned values of the term coefficients *independently*. Such a linear evaluation function ignores the very real correlations between parameters. For instance, the coefficient multiplying the number of kings on the board must depend very strongly on their board position, mobility, number of men on the board and so on. The final learning strategy is an attempt to solve this flaw by introducing correlations between parameters.

LEARNING BY GENERALIZATION — CORRELATED EVALUATION FUNCTION

The correlations between n parameters of the evaluation function may be represented by an n-dimensional array which Samuel called a *signature table.* The axis of each dimension is subdivided into cells, typically three corresponding to +1 (position good for the program), 0 (position neutral for the program), –1 (position bad for the program). If, for instance, the evaluation function was based on just three parameters, each of which could have three values, the evaluation space would resemble the structure of a Rubik's cube with a total of 27 cells.

The concept is that each board position may be characterized by assignment to one of these cells. The contents of the cell represent the static evaluation function value for that particular combination of features. To train the system as to what the contents of each cell should be, Samuel used book games recorded between master checkers players to present 250,000 board situations to the system. Each cell j of the signature table has two registers associated with it: A_j for agree and D_j for disagree. For each of the book value moves there is one cell which represents the book value move and a number of other alternatives which were not selected by the master players. If a particular cell was an allowed cell which was not the cell chosen, the D_j counter was incremented by one. The A_j counter for the cell selected by the master players was incremented by n, the number of non-selected, allowed moves. The associated correlation coefficient, C_j, for cell j is then computed by:

$$C_j = \frac{(A_j - D_j)}{(A_j + D_j)} \tag{17.2}$$

One can consider this type of learning as "learning by example" or "book learning" in which the book values are statistically averaged to provide instruction to the computer on the optimum move for each category of board positions.

Since the number of dimensions in parameter space was 24, Samuel found it necessary to develop a hierarchy of signature tables to provide data compression (otherwise the 24-dimensional table would have required 6×10^{12} cells). Through the inclusion of correlations between evaluation function parameters, the signature table system provided a considerable improvement over both the rote learning technique and the linear evaluation function generalization. Although this final version of Samuel's checkers player played at a championship level, it lost to the 1965 world champion by a score of 0–4.

17.5 QUINLAN'S ID3

We are well aware of the great power of classification schemes as aids to learning. As the student may have noticed, we have begun almost every chapter with one or more systems for categorizing the concepts under consideration. The representation which Samuel found most effective for teaching his checkers player was essentially a classification scheme for categorizing each board position on an n-dimensional feature matrix. The basic idea behind J. R. Quinlan's "Interactive Dichotomizer 3" (ID3) is to use classification to learn the essential features of a set of examples.[13] The effective algorithm used in ID3 is the Concept Learning System (CLS) developed by Hunt, Marin, and Stone as a psychological model of the process people use when given simple concept-forming tasks.[14]

The CLS algorithm involves determining the feature (attribute or variable) which is most discriminatory and then dichotomizing (splitting) the data (or training instances) into classes categorized by this feature. Next a significant feature of each of the subsets is used to further partition them, and the process is repeated recursively until each subset contains data of one kind only. The resulting set structure is called a discrimination tree, each node of which is feature discrimination test and each branch of which is the subclass of training examples satisfying the test.

Quinlan proposed an entropy function for selecting the feature which best discriminated among the training examples. The appropriate feature was the one which led to the minimization of the entropy function. Since increasing entropy of a system corresponds to increasing randomness or loss of order, the function that minimizes the entropy of the system is that which provides the highest degree of order for the system. Information theory indicates that this corresponds to the maximum information content of the system.

The algorithm Quinlan used for sampling very large sets of training examples goes as follows:

1) Select a random subset of size W (called the "window") from the training set.

2) Apply the CLS algorithm to form a rule for the current window.

3) Scan the entire training set for exceptions to the current rule.

4) If exceptions are found, insert some of them into W and repeat from step 2. The insertion may be done either by replacement of some of the existing examples of the set or by augmenting the existing set with the new exceptions.

ACCOMPLISHMENTS OF ID3

Two of the accomplishments of the ID3 program have been in the areas of learning new strategies for the end-game in chess and as a rule generator for expert systems. Donald Michie describes the experience of master-level chess player Ivan Bratko in using ID3 to analyze a set of chess-master formulations of rules for playing king and rook against king. Describing the rules ID3 produced, he says:[15]

> *"... Bratko translated the rules back into English, expecting to find something like the original textbook formulation. Instead, something startlingly different appeared. Bratko discovered that the six rules obtained were more complete, concise, and understandable by far than the chess-master formulations to be found in the books. In place of pages of diffuse text and diagrams was a set of rules so simple and clear-cut that anyone could grasp and even memorize them. A child could learn the rules and use them to play this end game as skillfully as a master."*

ID3 has provided the basic inference algorithm for a number of commercial expert systems, including Super-Expert (described in Chapter 13) and RuleMaster™.[16]

17.6 MICHALSKI'S INDUCE

Michalski and his colleagues have extended the generality of the classification approach with their research on *learning by observation*.[17] We refer to this research by the name of one of their systems, INDUCE. In this approach the basic classification is by *concept* rather than the simpler feature or attribute classification approach used in

ID3. Concepts are defined as logical products of relations on selected attributes. The approach uses *conceptual clustering* to arrange events into a hierarchy of classes described by conjunctive concepts (concepts related by AND). Michalski describes one version of this method, called Attribute-based Conjunctive Conceptual Clustering, as follows:

> **Given:**
> — a set of events (physical objects or abstract entities)
> — a set of attributes to be used to characterize events, and
> — a body of background knowledge, which includes the problem constraints, properties of attributes, inference rules for generating new attributes, and a criterion for evaluating the quality of candidate classifications.
>
> **Find:**
> A hierarchy of event classes, in which each class is described by a single conjunctive concept. Subclasses that are descendants of any parent class should have logically disjoint descriptions and optimize a *clustering quality criterion.*

Objects and classes are described by structural representation expressed in Annotated Predicate Calculus, a typed predicate calculus with additional operators. The system uses background knowledge in the form of inference rules for deriving high-level descriptive concepts from the low-level concepts initially provided. The goal of INDUCE is to find a few concepts in the rule space, each of which cover all the training events while remaining as specific as possible.

ACCOMPLISHMENTS OF INDUCE

Consider the following classification problem of structured objects proposed by Michalski and Larson.[18] The problem is: given a series of trains with various attributes find the simplest rule which distinguishes the east-bound trains from the west-bound trains. The problem was posed to human subjects and to a descendant of INDUCE. The first and simplest rule generated by the program was, in predicate calculus language:

> ∃ car_1 [length(car_1) = short] [car-shape(car_1) = closed top]
> ::> [class = Eastbound]

which may be rephrased in English as:

1) *If a train contains a car that is short and has a closed top, then it is eastbound, else it is westbound.*

Two more rules which INDUCE generated are:

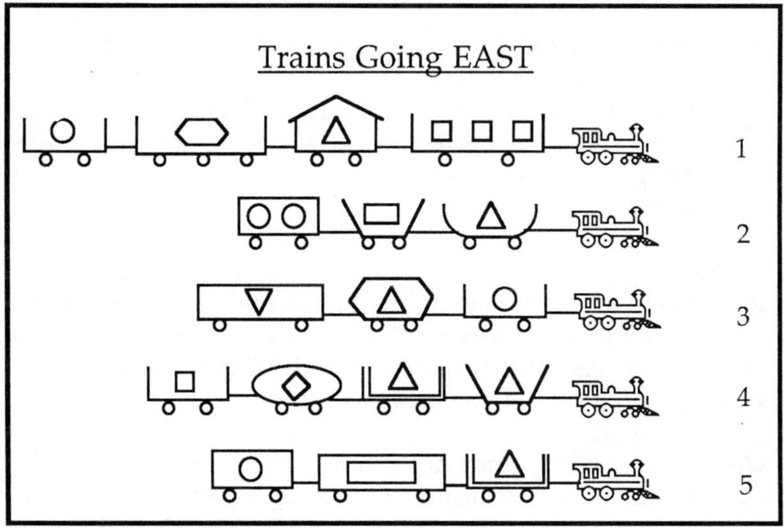

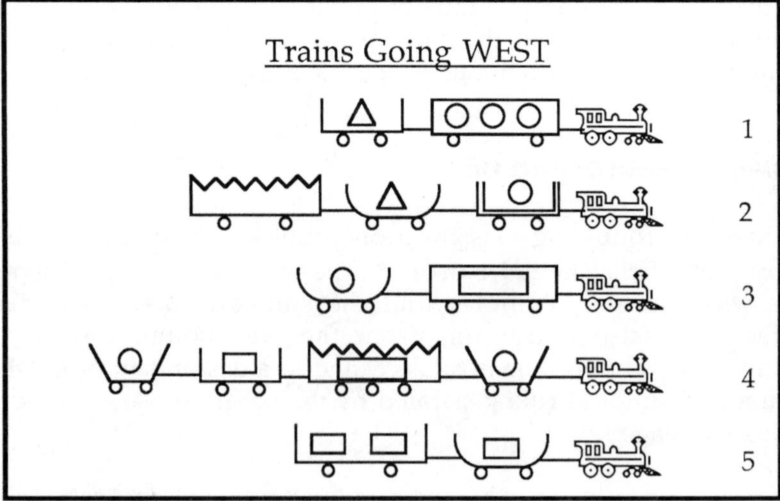

Figure 17-2 A Problem for INDUCE Find the simplest rule to distinguish "trains going east" from "trains going west." *(Copyright © 1980 IEEE)*

2) If a train contains a car whose load is a triangle, and the load of the car behind is a polygon, then it is eastbound, else it is westbound.

3) If there are two cars, or if there is a jagged-top car, then westbound, else eastbound.

Of the 72 attempts by humans, 44 discovered rule (3) and six others suggested a variation based on counting axles. Only three people discovered rule (1) and no one found rule (2). Two humans did discover the concise rule: *If there are more than two kinds of freight, then eastbound, else westbound.*

Michie discusses two other interesting sidelights of Michalski's experiment. One is that the CDC Cyber 175 computer which ran the Pascal program required about 10 seconds of computing time corresponding to approximately 10^9 binary discriminations. If this approach were followed by humans operating at a maximum of twenty binary discriminations per second, it would take three years of uninterrupted mental effort. Secondly, Michie notes that the first two rules involved no counting. Counting seems to be a human invention of very recent origin on the evolutionary time scale.

A more practical application of Michalski's classification approach to learning is his soybean disease expert system.[19] After 45 hours of consultation with an expert plant pathologist, Michalski and Chilausky extracted a set of rules for identifying nineteen soybean diseases based on 35 descriptors such as leaf spots, seed shriveling, time of the year, and so on. To train the computer system, data on 307 diseased plants was collected and tabulated along with a value for each of the 35 descriptors. These training examples were used by AQ11, the predecessor of INDUCE, to generate a new set of rules which differed from those of the original expert pathologist. To test the rules induced by the program against those of the human pathologist, 376 new disease cases were submitted to both. The set of rules produced by the human pathologist correctly identified 83 percent of the cases. The rules generated by AQ11 correctly identified 374 of the 376 cases (99.5% accuracy). The University's plant pathologists are now using the machine-induced rules for their routine diagnoses.

17.7 LENAT'S AM/EURISKO

The final case study in machine learning illustrates one of the highest levels of inductive learning — *learning by discovery*. The first program discussed is AM (Automated Mathematician), the Ph. D. thesis project of Douglas Lenat.[20] AM was able to discover many elementary mathematics concepts of arithmetic and set theory from an initial set of set theory concepts and search heuristics. Eurisko, an acronym for *eureka heuristic,* is a descendent of AM in which heuristics themselves are considered concepts which can be discovered and evolved. The AM/Eurisko series of programs is more than a highly successful set of programs for machine learning. It is a research program built on the assumption:

> ***Heuristic, rule-guided search is an operational model of human intelligence.***

Lenat summarizes his theory of human intelligence as follows:[21]

1. Human cognitive tasks can be described as searches, i.e., as explorations wandering toward some goal.

2. We are guided in these searches by a large collection of informal rules of thumb called heuristics.

3. We access relevant heuristics in each situation, and follow their advice.

Lenat then set himself the task of attempting to represent discovery heuristics and a knowledge base internally in a machine, turning the system loose, and observing what the machine would discover.

This approach is significant for several reasons. First, it is based firmly on the central AI hypothesis that humans are symbol-manipulating information processors. Secondly, it acknowledges the importance of knowledge as the basis for intelligent behavior. Knowledge is incorporated explicitly in the knowledge base of initial concepts and implicitly in the set of search heuristics. Finally, rather than the specific, goal-oriented research of many earlier AI projects, Lenat's approach mostly closely resembled the open-ended explorations of human inventors and scientists.

AM — The Automated Mathematician

Since Lenat's pre-Ph.D. degrees had been in physics and mathematics, it is not surprising that the subject he chose to explore was mathematics. The specific area was *set theory* and the program used a LISP-based frame structure to represent 115 core concepts. The concept of primes, for instance, was represented by a frame with slots and slot-values as shown in Figure 17-3.

At the beginning of a run of AM most of the slots of the concept frames are empty. As the run proceeds, a set of 243 heuristics were used to fill the slots for existing concepts, propose plausible new concepts, and evaluate the degree of significance of concepts (indicated as WORTH in Figure 17-3).

What sort of heuristics would one use to guide a machine in its search for significant mathematical discoveries? Humans define significant mathematical concepts as those which are *interesting*. The key concept Lenat defined to guide the heuristic search was what he called *interestingness*. The interestingness of a concept was an attempted measure of its mathematical significance from an intuitive and aesthetic point of view. Interestingness is determined by such factors as *coincidence*, behavior in *extreme cases*, the *frequency* of examples of a given concept, and the behavior of examples of concepts when interesting functions and their *inverse functions* are applied. The interestingness of each concept was estimated in the slot called WORTH on a scale of 0—1000.

The AM heuristics were represented in the form of production rules. Two examples of heuristic rules are shown below.

IF all examples of a concept C turn out to be examples of another concept D as well, and C was not previously known to be a specialization of D,
THEN conjecture that C is a specialization of D, and raise the interestingness value of both concepts.

IF F: A → B is an interesting function,
and there's some interesting or extremal in subset X of B,
THEN it's worth defining, naming, and studying $F^{-1}(X)$.

During execution, AM performs the actions specified by the applicable production rules. The control strategy is governed by an agenda of jobs ordered by priority. A typical job might be "Fill-in examples of primes." In operation, AM acts as if it were in the following endless loop:[22]

Repeat:

Step 1. Select a concept to evaluate and generate examples of it.

Step 2. Check these examples looking for regularities. Based on the regularities,
  a) update the assessment of the interestingness of the concept,
  b) create new concepts,

c) create new conjectures.

Step 3. Propagate the knowledge gained (especially from new conjectures) to other concepts in the system.

```
NAME: Primes
DEFINITIONS:
        English: Numbers with two divisors
        Predicate Calculus:
              Prime(x) ≡ (∀z)(z|x) → z=1 XOR z=x)
        Iterative: (for x>1): for i from 2 to x—1,¬(i|x)
SPECIALIZATIONS: Odd-primes, Small-primes,
 Pair-primes
GENERALIZATIONS: Positive-natural-numbers
IS-A:         Set
EXAMPLES:
        Extreme-exs: 2,3
        Extreme-non-exs: 0,1
        Typical-exs: 5,7,11,13,17,19
        Typical-non-exs: 34,100
CONJECTURES:
        Good-conjecs:
              Unique-factorization, Formula-for-d(n)
        Good-conjec-units: Times, Divisors-of,
              Exponentiate, Nos-with-3-divis, squaring
ANALOGIES: Simple Groups
WORTH: 800
ORIGIN: Divisors-of-1 (Doubletons)
        Defined-using: Divisors-of
        Creation-date: 3/19/76 18:45
HISTORY:
        N-good-examples: 840
        N-bad-examples: 5000
        N-good-conjectures: 3
        N-bad-conjectures: 7)
```

Figure 17-3 Frame Representation of the Primes Concept Initially, most slots of the concept frames are blank. As the heuristic-guided search continues, examples are generated and slots are filled in according to the heuristic rules.

ACCOMPLISHMENTS OF AM

AM did indeed perform as a powerful discovery system. It quickly found obvious set-theoretic concepts such as De Morgan's theorems but failed to discover any sophisticated concepts from set theory such as diagonalization. Instead, AM became interested in the concept of *equality* and generalized that to the relationship *same-size-as*. This led to the discovery of the natural numbers and the whole field of arithmetic. During a two-hour run AM defined several hundred concepts, about half of which were reasonable, and noticed hundreds of relationships between them, most of which were trivial. Most of the invalid or uninteresting concepts (which Lenat calls "losers") were detected as such and discarded by AM itself.

Among the interesting arithmetic concepts discovered by AM were addition, subtraction, multiplication, division, exponentiation, perfect squares, pairs of perfect squares whose sum is also a perfect square, and prime numbers. AM was surprised to discover that addition and multiplication are related (e.g., $N + N = 2 \times N$) and, in fact discovered multiplication by three other routes besides repeated addition. From the discovery of multiplication came the concept of *divisors-of* (using the "IF f looks interesting, THEN try f^{-1}" heuristic). While investigating the divisors-of concept, AM stumbled onto the concept of prime numbers by applying the extreme cases heuristic (examples of the set of numbers with 0, 1, or 2 divisors). AM reported its discovery of primes with the following dialog:[23]

```
*** Task 66 ***:  Considering numbers which have very small
sets of Divisors-of

2 Reasons:
(1)  Worthwhile to look for extreme cases.
(2)  Focus of attention :  AM recently worked on Divisors-of

Filling in examples of numbers with 0 divisors.
0 examples found, in 4.0 seconds.
Conjecture:  no numbers have 0 divisors.

Filling in examples of numbers with 1 divisor.
1 examples found, in 4.0 seconds.  e.g.:  Divisors-of(1) =
{1}.
Conjecture:  1 is the only number with 1 divisor.

Filling in examples of numbers with 2 divisors.
24 examples found, in 4.0 seconds.  e.g.:Divisors-of(13) =
{1  13}.
No obvious conjecture.  This kind of number merits more
study.
Create a new concept:  Numbers-with-2-divisors.
```

At this point Lenat intervened and suggested that the name of the concept be changed to "Primes."

While AM was investigating the properties of primes it discovered additional interesting mathematical relationships. These included Goldbach's conjecture that every even number greater than 2 is the sum of two primes and the Fundamental Theorem of Arithmetic which states that any number can be factored into a unique set of primes.

ISSUES AND PROBLEMS WITH AM

One natural question about this remarkable record of automated mathematical discovery is whether Lenat had somehow "stacked the deck" with his selection of the knowledge-base of concept frames and heuristics so that all of these discoveries were merely a regurgitation of the input information. Lenat's answer to this criticism is an adamant "No!". He points out that the goal of the project was to show that a relatively small set of general heuristics can guide a nontrivial discovery process. Each task was proposed by a heuristics that was used many times during the runs, and no heuristics was "cooked up" to handle only a single situation. While AM discovered no new mathematics, many of its discoveries were previously unknown to Lenat and were made through unique arguments. AM's interest in maximally factorable numbers has stimulated additional human research in this area.

Key arithmetic concepts which AM failed to discover include the concept of infinity, "closure", rational or irrational numbers, remainders, and greatest common denominators. Also, after the first two hundred concepts were discovered, the "hit rate" of interesting concepts dropped from greater than 50% to less than 10%. Lenat interprets this decline in productivity of AM as due to an inadequate set of discovery heuristics.

EURISKO

The failures of AM's heuristics prompted Lenat to consider the question of how heuristics themselves are discovered. The answer which Lenat proposed is the key concept of Eurisko and can be stated:

Discovery heuristics may themselves be represented as concepts.

Eurisko is based on the idea that a program can contain heuristics for discovering and developing heuristics. The same operators which AM used to create new mathematical concepts can be used to create new heuristics. The new heuristics can be evaluated by observing them in action and collecting empirical data on their performance. Heuristics which perform well should have their interestingness or worth raised while those which prove ineffective should have theirs lowered. As the task domain shifts certain heuristics will prove more effective while some of those effective in the previous domain may lose their efficacy.

A THEORY OF HEURISTICS

The rationale for the concept that heuristics may be represented and manipulated as mathematical concepts is made in what Lenat calls his Theory of Heuristics.[24] The central line of argument rests on the following five assumptions:

1. **New domains of knowledge δ can be developed by using heuristics.** New concepts and relationships between them can be discovered by using heuristics to suggest plausible actions and to prune implausible ones. This requires heuristics of varying degrees of generality, an adequate knowledge representation scheme, some initial hypotheses about the domain δ, and the ability to collect data and test conjectures about that domain.

2. **As new domains of knowledge emerge and evolve, new heuristics are needed.** The introduction of new devices, theories, and techniques continually change the nature of a given domain. To adapt to such changes, the applicable heuristics must also change. Consider, for instance, the changes in heuristics for effective writing which were brought about by the introduction of word processors.

3. **New heuristics can be developed by using heuristics.** Points 1 and 2 above imply that it is necessary to discover new heuristics. The key to this process is to let δ = *heuristics* in point 1, that is, to recognize that *heuristics* itself is a domain of knowledge. This requires an appropriate representation of heuristics and some hypotheses about their nature.

4. **As new domains of knowledge emerge and evolve, new representations are needed.** Just as new heuristics are needed for dealing with changing domains, so new representations are essential. Representations must evolve as domain knowledge is accumulated.

5. **New representations can be developed by using heuristics.** Points 1 and 4 indicate that new representations must be developed as the domain changes. By recognizing that representation of knowledge is a domain just like mathematics or heuristics, point 1 indicates that we should set δ = *representation* somehow.

Note that this theory of heuristics comprises a complete research program for machine learning through discovery, although much research is required for effectively implementing points 3 and 5.

ACCOMPLISHMENTS OF EURISKO

Eurisko has a number of impressive accomplishments to its credit. One of these, described in considerable detail by George Johnson[25], was its repeated victories in the enormously complex war game called Traveller. In Traveller, each player has a defense budget of one trillion credits and must build a fleet consisting of less than one hundred ships within the specifications provided by an extremely complex set of rules. The design of just one ship involves specifying over fifty factors such as the amount of fuel to carry, armor thickness, types and sizes of weapons, and choice of computer guidance system.

Lenat provided Eurisko with 146 Traveller concepts ranging from specific items such as Beam-Laser, Meson-Gun, and Computer-Radiation-Damage to general concepts such as Acceleration, Weapon, and Game. Each night Eurisko fought simulated battles, collecting data which it used to evaluate its design heuristics. After some 10,000 battles, Eurisko arrived at its fleet description of ninety-six small, slow, heavily-armored ships, each armed with many small weapons. Since most other entries consisted of fleets of about twenty lightly armored, heavily armed fast ships, Eurisko's strange fleet was a source of considerable amusement — until play began.

Eurisko handily won every battle and became the the top-ranked Traveller player in the United States. To avoid a recurrence of a machine champion, the tournament directors changed the rules substantially for the following year and did not announce the new set of rules until about a week before the tournament. But by this time Eurisko had learned heuristics that were general and powerful enough that they could be applied to new versions of the game. So Eurisko won the second tournament as well. After the directors threatened to discontinue the tournaments if Eurisko entered again, it retired undefeated.

A second, somewhat more practical application of Eurisko is in the field of VLSI design. Eurisko generalized a 2-D integrated circuit junction design to three dimensions, using a symmetry heuristic. The new design allowed the structure to serve as either a NAND gate or an OR gate. As Donald Michie describes this discovery, "It had not occurred to the human designers that this could be done, partly because the complexities of VLSI had compelled them to simplify the design space in their minds and rule out the possibility of an element acting as a gate and a channel simultaneously."[26]

A final application of Eurisko is in modeling the mechanisms by which DNA molecules store their information and perform mutations. Classical Darwinian evolutionary theory holds that changes in the species come about through random mutations. Lenat has speculated that DNA molecules may contain heuristic knowledge for *plausible* mutations rather than completely *random* ones. He conjectures that natural selection began with primitive organisms and a random mutation scheme for improving them. By this weak method of random generation followed by stringent testing the first primitive heuristics accidentally came into being. By generating plausible, beneficial mutations, these DNA-encoded heuristics immediately over–shadowed the less efficient random mutation mechanism. This Eurisko-like model of natural selection may help explain the extraordinary effectiveness of evolution.

17.8 CONCLUSION

The importance of machine learning to AI and to society at large is difficult to overemphasize. As we have stressed throughout the book, the performance of intelligent systems is most directly related to their knowledge content and representation. Most AI programs written to date have achieved their knowledge through careful "hand crafted" programming. With the exception of those programs described in this chapter, most AI systems have been purely deductive in nature and have not involved learning or self improvement through experience.

There are at least three reasons for pursuing research on true machine learning:

- It will shed light on the cognitive processes taking place in the human mind. This is goal has motivated many AI researchers such as Schank and Simon. Interesting problems in both human and machine learning involve analogical reasoning, processes of theory formation, and the optimum combination of learning strategies as a function of accumulated knowledge.

- Successful machine learning systems will solve the "knowledge bottleneck" which is seriously handicapping the development of truly capable expert systems. Inductive learning systems such as Michalski's INDUCE and Michie's Super-Expert make possible the automatic generation of rules from example databases and avoid the tedious hand crafting of rules required by other systems.

• User friendly learning systems will greatly simplify our lives by helping us cope with the explosion of knowledge and information. A learning system which could sort, sift, and organize the information which continually bombards us would free us from the tedium of doing this job "by hand."

There is a final issue which should be introduced at this point. Throughout the book we have stressed the importance of knowledge and the appropriate representation of knowledge for building intelligent systems. While we have been concerned with the structure (architecture) of knowledge, we have completely ignored the *architecture of the machines* processing the knowledge. We have also implicitly accepted the premise that a *physical symbol system was the optimal path* to artificial intelligence. The "hidden agenda" underlying virtually all traditional AI research is that, since both minds and machines process symbols, they are somehow equivalent and therefore it should be possible to construct a machine to exhibit intelligence.

The fact remains, however, that the structure of a machine does effect its performance. The architecture of our hydro-carbon-based minds is profoundly different from that of silicon-based computers. Could it be that the limitations encountered in silicon-based systems are somehow related to these differences in architecture? Would a rewiring of silicon-based systems to better emulate our hydro-carbon-based system result in improved performance? In the final chapter we examine in considerable detail such questions and the implications of machine architectures for AI.

PROBLEMS AND PROGRAMS

17-1. Combine the principle ideas contained in the three definitions of *learning* presented earlier in the chapter into your own definition. Present both an abstract definition and a concrete example illustrating the effect of learning.

17-2. In addition to the characteristics of human learning listed in the text, there are others in which humans performance is inferior to that of a machine. Two that immediately come to mind are: fallibility and forgetfulness. Discuss these two characteristics and any others (not in the text) that you can think of, and comment briefly why, with all these flaws, the human mind works so wonderfully.

17-3. What does the statement mean: *"The optimum learning strategy is a function of accumulated knowledge"*? Give examples.

17-4. Give specific examples of each of Michalski's five classes of learning from *Rote Learning* to *Learning by Induction.*

17-5. The text indicates that Samuel's checkers player used both *rote learning* and *forgetting* in its early version. In what sense was rote learning used, how did it improve the performance of play, and why was forgetting important?

17-6. When Samuel revised his checkers player to include learning by generalization, he tried two strategies: (i) hill climbing with a linear evaluation function, and (ii) a correlated evaluation function. Which of these was most successful and why?

17-7. Entropy plays an important role in both Ross Quinlan's ID3 program and in John Hopfield's neural network (see Chapter 18). In Quinlan's program entropy is minimized by classification to create maximum order and learning is achieved in the process. In neural networks, a solution is obtained by letting the circuit loose to seek an energy minimum and hence a maximum entropy state. How can this be? (Hint: thermodynamics provides the clue — compare systems on which one does work to those which do work on the environment.)

17-8. How does a classification scheme such as Quinlan's ID3 provide a power tool for learning through example?

17-9. In what ways does Michalski's learning program differ from Quinlan's?

17-10. Before looking at the solution on the following page, study Figure 17-2 and try to derive a rule which distinguishes the east-bound from the west-bound trains. What variables are evident for use in classification? How might one encode these efficiently in a computer language?

17-11. Assume you were going to write AP (Automated Physicist), a program to learn physics by discovery in the manner of Lenat's AM. What heuristics would you suggest for guiding the machine in its discovery of new concepts?

17-12. In addition to the the heuristics you provided AP, what type and form of data would you provide? (Remember: Physical law is a description of *natural phenomena.*)

17-13. In what ways did *Eurisko* differ from *AM*? Discuss Eurisko as a *meta-AM* in terms of levels of abstraction. Is there the danger of an infinite regress in programs such as Eurisko? Give an example.

REFERENCES AND FOOTNOTES

1 Boden, M., *Piaget*, Harvester Press, London (1979) See also Gruber, H. E. and Voneche, J. J. (eds), *The Essential Piaget: An Interpretive Reference and Guide*, Basic Books, New York, NY (1977)

2 Hopfield, J. J., "Neural networks and physical systems with emergent collective computational abilities," *Proc. Natl. Scad. Sci. USA* **79**, pp. 2554–2558, April (1982)

3 Michie, Donald, "Expert Systems Interview," *Expert Systems* **2**, No. 1, pp. 20–23, January (1985)

4 Simon, Herbert A., "Why should machines learn?," in *Machine Learning — An Artificial Intelligence Approach*, Michalski, Ryszard S., Carbonell, Jaime G., and Mitchell, Tom M. (eds), Tioga Publishing Company, Palo Alto, CA (1983)

5 U. S. Department of Education report gave the cost as $4,538 for public elementary and secondary schools and $14,294 for full time college and university students as of August, 1987.

6 Michalski, Ryszard S. , "Understanding the Nature of Learning: Issues and Research Directions," in *Machine Learning — An Artificial Intelligence Approach*, Vol. II, Michalski, Ryszard S., Carbonell, Jaime G., and Mitchell, Tom M. (eds), pp. 3–25, Morgan Kaufmann Publishers, Inc., Los Altos, CA (1986)

7 Schank, R. C., *Dynamic Memory: A Theory of Reminding and Learning in Computers and People*, Cambridge University Press, Cambridge, UK (1982)

[8] Forsyth, Richard, "Machine Learning," in *Artificial Intelligence — Principles and Applications*, Yazdani, Masoud (ed), Chapman and Hall, New York, NY (1986)

[9] Turing, A. M., "Computing Machinery and Intelligence," in *Computers and Thought*, Feigenbaum, Edward. A. and Feldman, Julian, (eds), McGraw-Hill Book Company, New York, NY (1963)

[10] Samuel, Arthur L., "AI, Where it has been and where it it going," *Proceedings of the Eighth International Joint Conference on Artificial Intelligence*, Karlsruhe, West Germany, IJCAI–83, p. 1155, 8–12 August (1983)

[11] Samuel, A. L., "Some Studies in Machine Learning Using the Game of Checkers," *IBM Journal of Research and Development* **3**, pp. 211–232 (1959) and "Some Studies in Machine Learning Using the Game of Checkers II — Recent Progress," *IBM Journal of Research and Development* **11**, pp. 601–617 (1967). See also Samuel's paper of the same title as the 1959 paper in *Computers and Thought*, pp. 71–105, Edward A. Feigenbaum and Julian Feldman (eds), McGraw-Hill Book Company, New York, NY (1963)

[12] Samuel, Arthur L., 1983, *Op Cit*, p. 1153

[13] Quinlan, J. R., "Semi-autonomous acquisition of pattern-based knowledge," in *Introductory Readings in Expert Systems*, Donald Michie (ed), Gordon and Breach, New York, NY (1982)

[14] Hunt, E. B., Marin, J. and Stone, P., *Experiments in Induction*, Academic Press, New York, NY (1966)

[15] Michie, Donald and Johnston, Rory, *The Knowledge Machine — Artificial Intelligence and the Future of Man*, p. 136, William Morrow and Company, Inc., New York, NY (1985)

[16] Michie, D., Muggleton, S. H., Riese, C. E. and Zubrick, S. M., "RuleMaster: A Second Generation Knowledge Engineering Facility," *IEEE and AAAI First Conference on Artificial Intelligence Applications*, Denver, CO, December (1984)

[17] Dietterich, T. G., and Michalski, R. S., "Inductive Learning of Structural Descriptions: Evaluation Criteria and Comparative Review of Selected Methods," *Artificial Intelligence* **16**, pp. 257–294 (1981). See

also: Stepp, Robert E. and Michalski, Ryszard S., "Conceptual Clustering of Structured Objects: A Goal-Oriented Approach," *Artificial Intelligence* **28**, pp.43–69, February (1986)

18 Michalski, Ryszard "Pattern Recognition as Rule-Guided Inductive Inference," *IEEE Transactions on Pattern Analysis and Machine Intelligence*, Vol. PAMI-2, No. 4, pp. 349–361, July (1980)

19 Michalski, R. S. and Chilausky, R. L., "Learning by Being Told and Learning from Examples: An Experimental Comparison of the Two Methods of Knowledge Acquisition in the Context of Developing an Expert System for Soybean Disease Diagnosis," *International Journal of Policy Analysis and Information Systems* **4**, No. 2, pp. 125–161 (1980)

20 Lenat, D. B. "AM: An artificial intelligence approach to discovery in mathematics as heuristic search," reprinted in *Knowledge-Based Systems in Artificial Intelligence*, Davis, R. and Lenat, D. (eds), McGraw-Hill Book Company, New York, NY (1981)

21 Lenat, Douglas B., "The ubiquity of discovery," in *Artificial Intelligence*, Vol. VI from the NCC, O. Firschein (ed), AFIPS Press, Reston, VA (1984)

22 Cohen, Paul R. and Feigenbaum, Edward A., *The Handbook of Artificial Intelligence*, Vol. 3, pp. 441–442, HeurisTech Press, Stanford, CA (1982)

23 Lenat, Douglas B., "The Role of Heuristics in Learning by Discovery: Three Case Studies," in *Machine Learning — An Artificial Intelligence Approach*, Michalski, Ryszard S., Carbonell, Jaime G., and Mitchell, Tom M. (eds), pp. 259–260, Tioga Publishing Company, Palo Alto, CA (1983)

24 Lenat, Douglas B., "The Role of Heuristics in Learning by Discovery: Three Case Studies," pp. 263–302, *Op Cit*

25 Johnson, George, *Machinery of the Mind — Inside the New Science of Artificial Intelligence*, Times Books, New York, NY (1986)

26 Michie, Donald and Johnston, Rory, pp. 121–123, *Op Cit*

Chapter 18

NEW ARCHITECTURES FOR AI

(PHOTO: COURTESY OF JOHN HOPFIELD)

John Hopfield is Professor of Chemistry and Biology at the California Institute of Technology. Prior to his Cal Tech appointment he served as Professor of Physics at Princeton University and on the technical staff of Bell Telephone Laboratories. He earned his A.B. from Swarthmore College and his Ph.D. from Cornell University. He began his research in the field of electron transfer processes and photosynthesis and more recently has examined the emergent computational properties of large neural networks. He and his Bell Labs colleague David Tank have demonstrated the use of neural networks for solving complex AI problems. Hopfield is a recipient of a MacArthur Fellowship and the Oliver Buckley Prize of the American Physical Society.

18: NEW ARCHITECTURES FOR AI

18.1 INTRODUCTION

The final topic we consider in this book is the subject of new architectures for the next generation of AI computers. The recurrent pattern in AI applications, from games to machine learning, has been that the shift from "toy programs" to significant systems has involved an exponential growth in the amount of computing required. In certain areas, notably expert systems, significant problems may be represented and solved on machines of traditional architectures. In many other areas, notably machine vision, pattern recognition, and learning, the computational requirements for useful, real-time systems exceed the capabilities of even large supercomputers.

The limitations which traditional, serial computer architectures and our present techniques for encoding knowledge place on AI computing may be identified in terms of three "bottlenecks."

18.2 BOTTLENECKS IN AI COMPUTING

These three limitations can be summarized as:

- **Physical Limits** — Signal propagation in a machine cannot exceed about 2/3 the speed of light, *c*. This limit, which we call the *Einstein Bottleneck*, is illustrated schematically in Figure 18-1. Note that this is not simply a limit set by state-of-the-art VLSI (very large scale integration) technology, but rather a fundamental limit set by the laws of physics. As one wag said, "186,000 miles/sec is not just a good idea. — It's the law!"

The one contribution VLSI can make to postponing the point at which Einstein's bottleneck limits computer speed is through continued miniaturization of circuits in order to reduce the distance factor, x. The present 0.1 micron technology is already within a factor of 10 – 100 of the conceivable lower limit set by molecular structure. It is extremely difficulty to conceive of computing elements much smaller than single molecules!

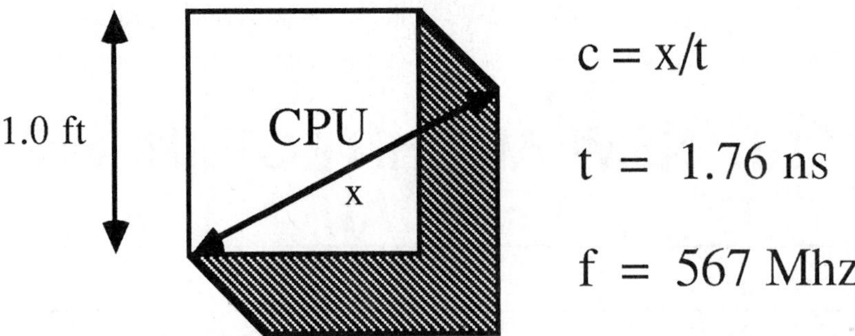

Figure 18-1 The Einstein Bottleneck The speed of light in vacuum, $c = 3 \times 10^8$ m/sec = 186,000 miles/sec, is the upper limit on the speed of any object, including information. This speed limit implies an upper limit on the clock rate for traditional, synchronous machines. A mainframe of dimensions on the order of 1 foot could not run faster than about 500 Mhz, even using light as the communication medium. Signals on wires or PC boards run even slower.

• **Structural Limits** — The traditional serial (sequential) Babbage/von Neumann, two-component architecture results in inefficient utilization of computing resources. The first aspect of this problem we call the *Babbage Bottleneck* which results from the separation of the CPU (Babbage's "Mill") from the main memory (Babbage's "Store") as shown in Figure 18-2.

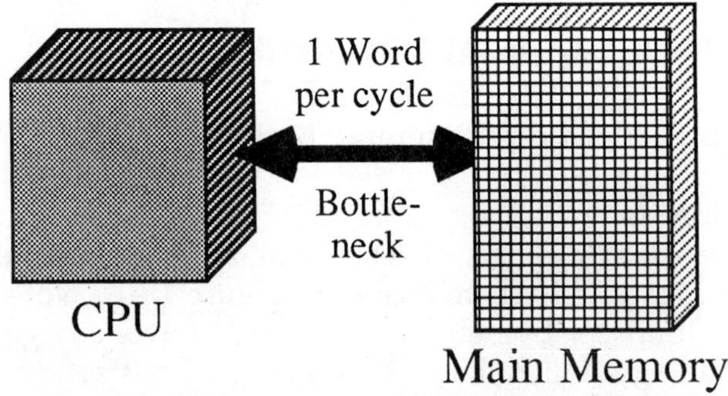

Figure 18-2 The Babbage Bottleneck Information (either data or instructions) is transferred to the the CPU one element at a time, the computation performed, and the result typically stored back in memory. The vast majority of memory and even CPU is idle during most of this process, resulting in under-utilization of computing resources.

The other aspect of the Babbage/von Neumann limit is related to the sequential control structure defining von Neumann architectures. This is illustrated in Figure 18-3. This problem is particularly severe for many AI applications which tend to use iterative and recursive algorithms for tree-structured and array-structured problems. There is evidence that both Babbage and von Neumann recognized the limitations which sequential, two-part architectures set on computation and had considered performing certain operations in parallel on their machines.

Note that both the Babbage and von Neumann bottlenecks become even worse as the size of computer memories and programs increases. In an early typical 64K personal computer each memory location had a duty factor of 0.0015 %. In a large, 4 Gb mainframe, this factor falls to 2.3×10^{-8} %. That is, the fraction of time a typical memory cell of a 64K serial personal computer is "working" is 65,536 as large as that is a typical memory cell in a 4 Gb serial machine.

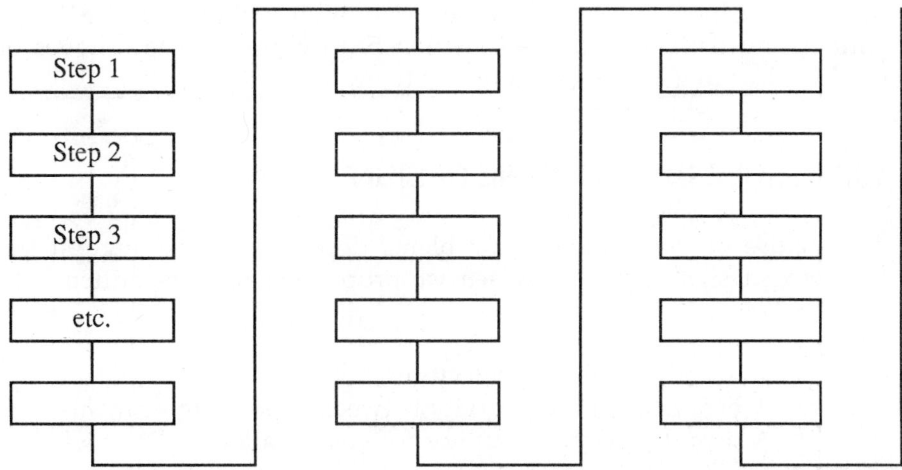

Figure 18-3 The von Neumann Bottleneck The sequential structure specified by the stored programs in von Neumann machines means that only one operation is being performed at any one time. Such a serial architecture is poorly suited to typical knowledge-based AI problems .

• **Knowledge Acquisition Limits** — The *Feigenbaum bottleneck* describes the problem of transferring knowledge from experts and the outside world into a useful internal representation in the machine. This is essentially the problem of *machine learning* discussed in the last chapter. With the exception of a few expert system shells which can learn by carefully structured examples, most typical AI applications involve careful and detailed "hand-crafting" of knowledge into a representation useful to the machine. As Feigenbaum repeatedly reminds us, "In the knowledge lies the power." Truly powerful AI systems will be knowledge-based, and building them easily will require automating the process of knowledge acquisition.

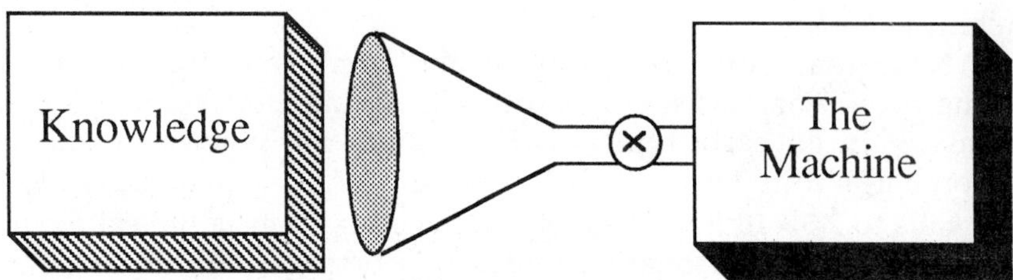

Figure 18-4 The Feigenbaum Bottleneck — Knowledge acquisition and learning The tedious hand-crafting required by many AI systems limits their power and the ease with which they can be built. Automating the knowledge acquisition process through techniques of machine learning would solve this bottleneck.

18.3 ISSUES IN AI MACHINE DESIGN

The nature of the bottleneck problems described above suggest the following design principles which we proposed in the introduction to Chapter 17:

- Massively parallel architecture
- A high level of connectivity between processing elements
- A neural network metaphor for computation

The first two principles are widely accepted as valid and provide the basis for the architectures for virtually all of the next generation machines. The third principle is much more controversial but is rapidly gaining adherents as neural network devices demonstrate the capability of solving difficult AI problems. Neural networks also provide easy learning procedures for resolving the knowledge acquisition bottleneck.

Before we look in detail at some of the architectures which are being investigated for overcoming these bottlenecks, it is important to note that there are serious differences of opinion on several issues in the design of a new generation of machines for AI. We can focus on these issues by stating them in the form of questions.

1. *Do we need new machines or new ideas and algorithms?*
While the general wisdom holds that new machines are necessary for solving the next generation of AI problems, not all AI researchers share this view. This issue was well summarized by Randall Davis:[1]

> *"Imagine that someone has hooked up a million processors in an N-cube; what would you — or anyone — do with it? ... I find it almost vacuous to hear claims of constructing massive parallelism without any good idea of how to use that to do something."*

2. *Should problem structure dictate machine design?*
Some researchers, like Guy L. Steele, argue that the structure of the problems should determine the design of new machines;[2]

> *"We need to identify standard paradigms of parallelism that have widespread utility and only then build hardware specifically to support these paradigms."*

Others, such as Nobel Laureate physicist Ken Wilson of Cornell University and Jack Schwartz of New York University, believe the first priority should be to build powerful parallel machines and get them into the hands of application-oriented groups. This is necessary, they point out, in order to understand the machines and accumulate experience in using them.

3. *What is the optimum configuration of massively parallel systems?*
Granted that it is important to construct new machines with massively parallel architecture, it is then necessary to determine the optimum configuration of number of processors, size of memory segments, and so on. Specific issues in machine architecture involve the *granularity* (size and number of processors), *topology* (network by which processors are connected), and *synchrony* (control mode of executing parallel instructions).

4. *Does the physical symbol system hypothesis provide the optimal metaphor for solving real AI problems?*
The disappointing progress in emulating human neural network (brain) performance by the traditional, symbolic, digital approach in such pattern recognition tasks as vision, speech understanding, and machine learning raises serious questions as to whether the physical symbol system hypothesis is adequate for solving this class of AI problems. These tasks which are intrinsically analog in nature may be much better suited to analog, artificial neural network solutions than to the traditional, digital, symbolic solutions.

It is difficult to overemphasize the importance of this last issue. If, in fact, analog, non-symbolic neural network systems are more appropriate and effective in demonstrating artificial intelligence than physical symbol systems, the cornerstone of traditional AI research will have proven inadequate. The Universal Turing Machine hypothesis says that all machines are in principle equivalent. So one cannot prove, for instance, that the general machine vision problem cannot be solved on a digital machine. However, to do so may be equivalent to "cutting butter with a chain saw" — it may be technically feasible but not too smart.[3] The explicit acknowledgment that the human brain provides the best model for an architecture for displaying intelligence may be the key to progress in artificial intelligence research.

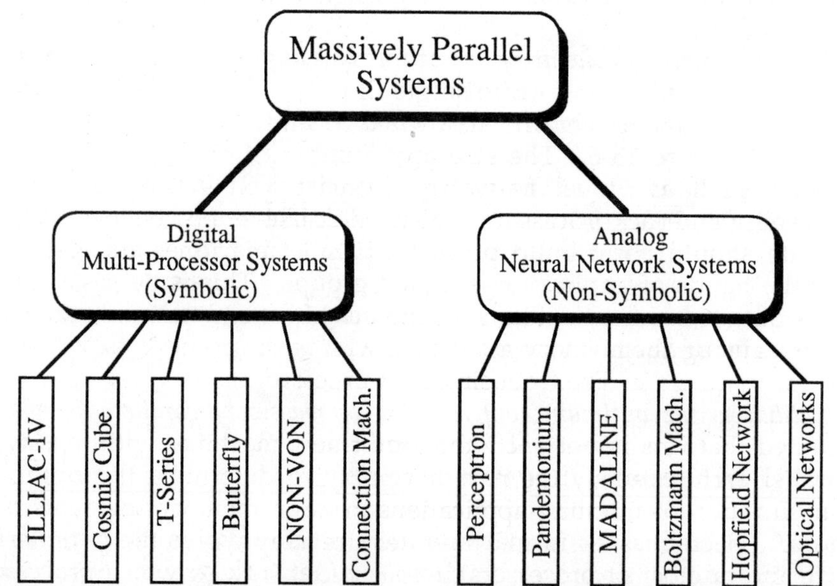

Figure 18-5 Categories of Massively Parallel Systems Most experiments in massively parallel computers can be classified as either digital or analog in design. Digital machines can, of course, emulate analog processes, and several of the analog machines have been modeled on digital machines.

This digital/analog distinction provides the basis for classifying massively parallel computer architectures into two general categories shown in Figure 18-5. In the next two sections we consider each of these two categories of architecture in greater detail.

18.4 DESIGN OF PARALLEL DIGITAL ARCHITECTURES

Now let us examine some of the factors in the architecture of the next generation digital AI machines in more detail. An excellent discussion of multi-processor system architectures is presented in considerably more depth by Leonard Uhr.[4]

GRANULARITY

A general rule in computer architecture design is that the cost of a machine is, to a first approximation, proportional to the area of the integrated circuitry (the silicon "real estate"). For a machine with a given silicon area, one of the first design problems becomes: how should the integrated circuitry of a serial, von Neumann machine be restructured to provide parallel processing? One may visualize this process as "dissolving" a large single CPU with its associated memory into smaller units, each with its own CPU and associated memory as shown in Figure 18-6. The size and number of the basic processors define the *granularity* of the system. Systems with tens to hundreds of relatively powerful processors are called *coarse-grained,* while systems with tens of thousands to millions of simple processors are *fine-grained*.

Not only must the size and number of processors be determined, but the amount of memory associated with each processor must be set. Processors range in size from single bit processors to processors capable of handling 64 bits.

As one might expect, the optimum choice of granularity is strongly influenced by the nature of the problems to be solved. For typical number crunching applications in traditional languages such as FORTRAN, a coarse-grained architecture may be most appropriate while for vision applications a fine-grained system would permit each pixel to be assigned its own processor. A fine-grained system provides a higher degree of parallelism but at the price of a much greater overhead in communications between the increased number of processors. In addition, the constraint of a fixed amount of silicon real estate implies that if the number of processors increases, their power and flexibility will decrease. As indicated in Table 18-I, the granularity of massively parallel machines built to date ranges from 16 powerful 32-bit processors to 65,536 simple, 1-bit processors.

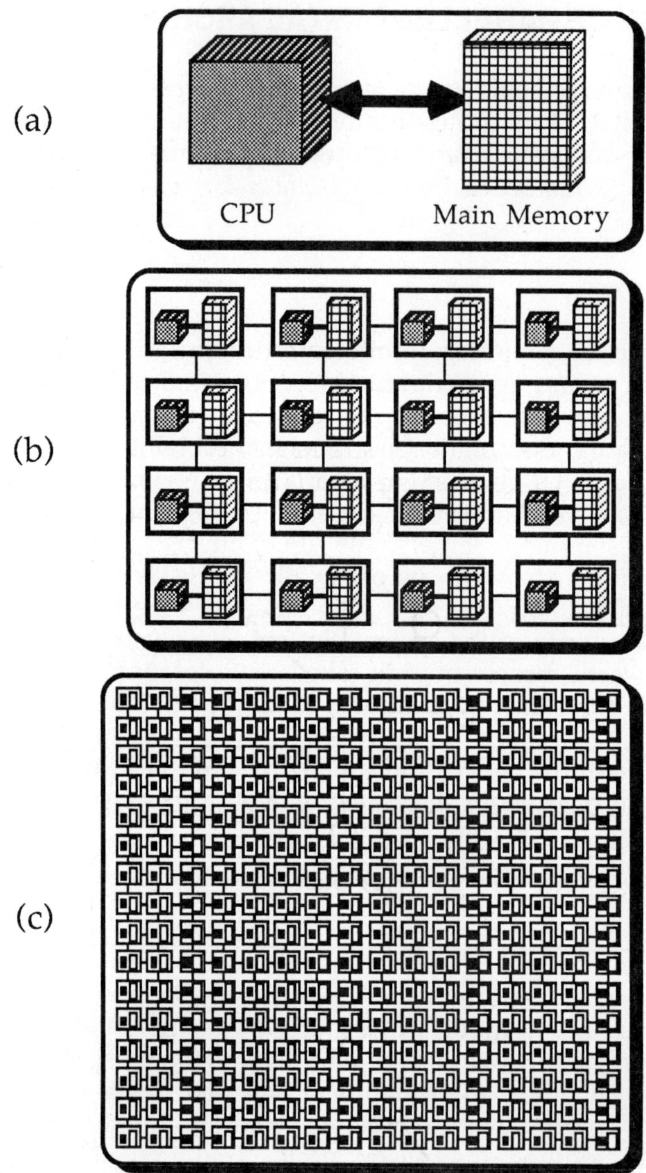

Figure 18-9 The Concept of Granularity To build a digital parallel architecture machine, the area of integrated circuitry traditionally allotted to a single CPU and associated memory, (a), must be reconfigured into smaller structures such as the coarse-grained 16-processor system shown in (b) or the finer-grained 256-processor system shown in (c).

TOPOLOGY

Of equal importance to the granularity of the system is the physical topology of the communication network between processors and between processors and associated memory. An exhaustive survey on research on various connection topologies is presented in an IEEE tutorial edited by Wu and Feng.[5]

An important class of topology consists of a 1-D linear array of processors widely used in "pipeline" architectures. The concept is that data will pass through the pipeline with each processor performing a particular calculation or transformation on the data. If each of the N processors completes its computation in M clock cycles, a new data value enters the pipeline and a final answer emerges each M cycles. Since a serial machine would require M × N cycles to carry out the N computations, a pipeline machine with N processors is theoretically N times as fast as the serial machine.

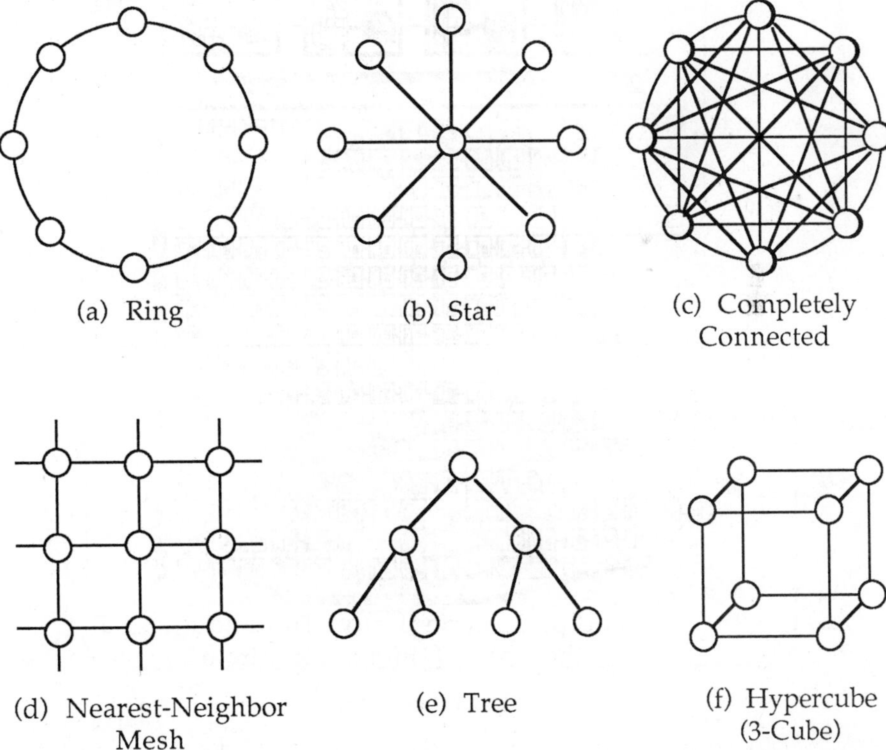

Figure 18-7 Connection Topologies for Parallel Processor Networks Each circular node represents a processor with varying amounts of associated memory. Each topology offers particular advantages and suffers from certain limitations.

Other important architectural topologies under investigation are shown in Figure 18-7. They range from the lightly connected ring, star, and nearest-neighbor topologies, through binary tree and hypercube connections, to the expensive, completely connected networks.

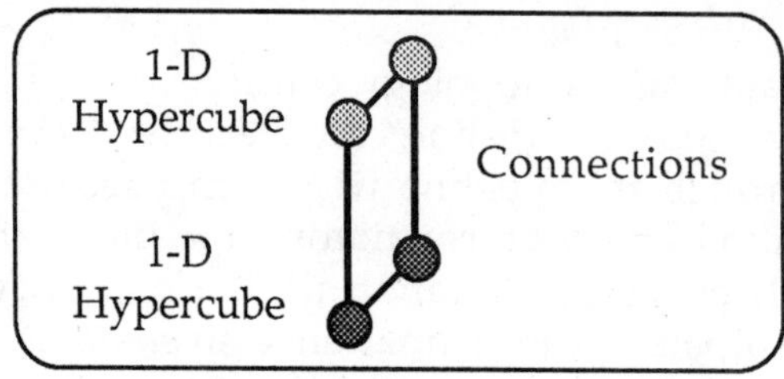

(a) 2-D Hypercube

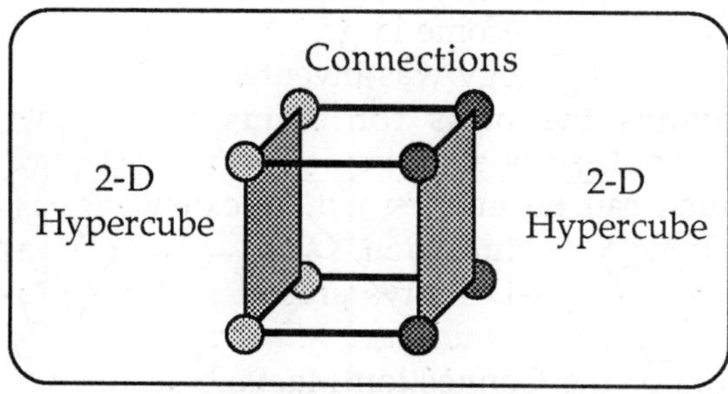

(b) 3-D Hypercube

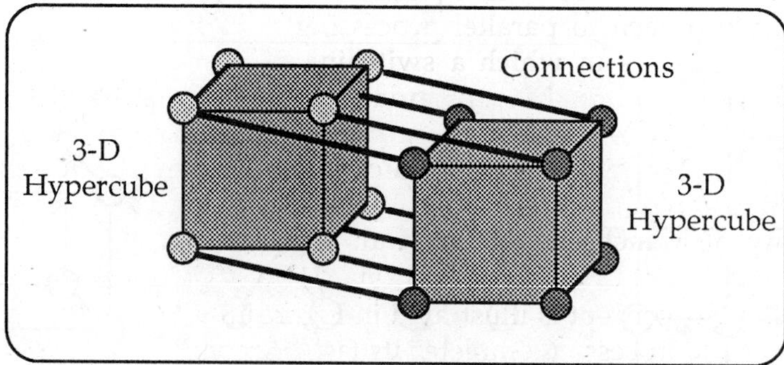

(c) 4-D Hypercube

Figure 18-8 Concept of Hypercube Connection Topology Note that each processor in a 2-D hypercube (a square) requires, at most, two communications lines to reach any other processor. The 3-D hypercube requires three and the 4-D hypercube requires four connections.

For a system with coarse granularity (a small number of large processors), the ring and star topology offers simple and fast communication. For a large range of physical problems in fields such as hydrodynamics, aerodynamics, image processing, and graphics, the nearest neighbor mesh provides a simple topology which is well matched to the problem. For longer range communication, however, it becomes inefficient.

For both the tree and hypercube topologies it can be shown that the number of connections, n, which a given processor must traverse to talk to any other processor is at most n = log N where N is the number of processors in the system.

Thus, these topologies become increasingly efficient, relative to many other topologies, as the number of processor increases. The direct connection of all processors to all other processors (called a crossbar network) requires N^2 switches. This becomes prohibitive as the number of processors become large.

The hypercube topology was invented at Cal Tech as the Cosmic Cube and provides the basis for a number of new commercial machines. The topology is a particularly interesting configuration of connections which can be understood by extending simple 1-D, 2-D, and 3-D connections to n-dimensional space. The concept is illustrated in Figure 18-8 in which 1-D arrays are connected to form 2-D arrays which are, in turn, connected to form 3-D arrays, and so on. The 65,536 simple processors of the Connection Machine are connected through a 16-D hypercube topology.

All of the topologies described above are "static" in the sense that the connections are provided by hardwiring of the circuits. Another important approach to parallel processing is provided by "dynamic" network topologies in which a switching network allows data to be dynamically routed to the appropriate processors. Dynamic network topologies allow a particular data item to flow through the system according to the address tag which accompanies the data. This approach was developed by Ian Watson and his colleagues at the University of Manchester in England. Professor Arvind of MIT has used this data-driven topology to build the Tagged Token Dataflow Machine.[6] The concept is illustrated in Figure 18-9.

As each processor completes its task, it repackages the data it has just processed with a tag indicating which processor the packet should go to next. The tag controls the switching network which routes it to the appropriate processor. As the packet reaches the next processor, the processor checks that all required information is available and then proceeds with its processing. Thus, the dataflow architecture resembles an asynchronous, object-oriented, pipeline architecture. Its great advantage is that the duty cycle for all processors is relatively high.

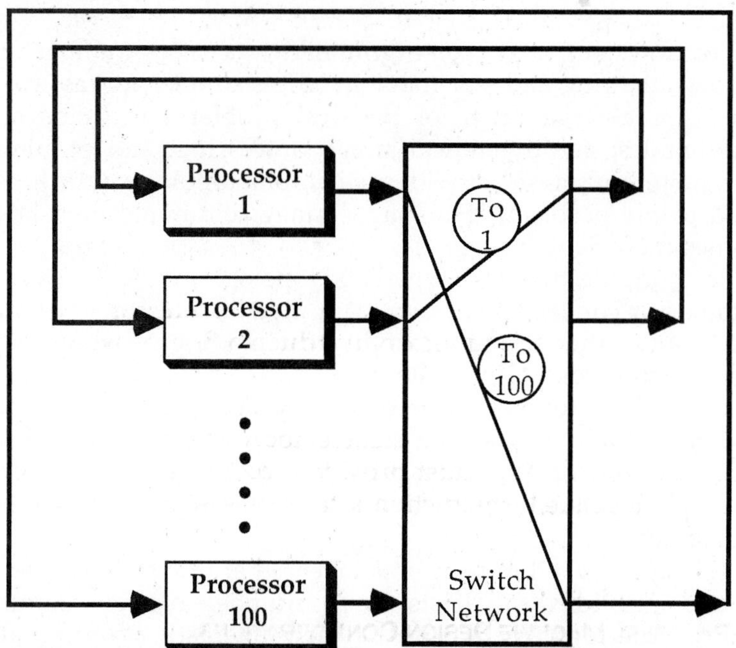

Figure 18-9 The Data-flow Architecture This architecture consists of N processors connected by a N × N packet-switching network. Each processor recognizes tokens addressed to it and carries out its assigned operations when it has the necessary information.[7]

Networks for performing the switching are known by such names as *shuffle-exchange, Petri, Benes, Clos, Banyon, omega, delta,* and *crossbar* networks.

SYNCHRONY AND CONTROL

The third dimension along which massively parallel systems must be classified is *mode of control and synchronization* of the processors. The possibilities range from a totally synchronous mode in which all processors operate in "lock-step", performing identical instructions on different data streams, to a totally asynchronous, autonomous mode in which each processor functions as an independent computer and communication between processors occurs infrequently as the need arises.

The general classification given these two different modes is:

- SIMD — Single-instruction, multiple-data mode

- MIMD — Multiple instruction, multiple-data mode.

Of the two modes, the SIMD is the more easily implemented but less flexible. It is well suited, however, to many applications involving data which can be represented as dense arrays such as matrix manipulations and image processing. In the SIMD mode, a single instruction stream is broadcast to all processors. Each processor may choose to execute the instruction or ignore it depending on tests it makes on its existing data.

While it might appear that the MIMD architecture would offer greater speed, power, and flexibility due to its greater generality, practical considerations limit its actual performance. In order for each processor to perform an independent set of instructions, for example, it must be supplied with either sizable local memory to hold these instructions or the system must provide a complex switching network to transfer independent instruction sets from some central memory to each processor.

OTHER PARALLEL MACHINE DESIGN CONSIDERATIONS

In addition to the granularity, topology, and control mode, several other problems must be faced and solved by massively parallel machine designers. These include:

1. *Allocation of memory resources* — Assuming that the system must provide a certain amount of memory, what is the optimal allocation of that memory? Should it divided equally and assigned to each of the multiprocessors (as indicated in Figure 18-6) or should it be a single, large central memory accessible by all processors or some compromise between these two extremes?

2. *Intrinsic flexibility in granularity, topology, and control* — The designer must decide how much flexibility s/he wishes to build into the machine. That is, by clever switching and connection schemes it is possible to dynamically alter each of these three dimensions of parallel systems. However, it can only be done at the price of much more complex hardware and adds considerably to the cost of the machine.

3. *Division of labor between serial and parallel components* — Most parallel processors systems require a host serial computer for tasks such as reading in the programs, down-loading program microcode to various parallel processors and merging and printing the final results. The system designer must specify which tasks to assign to the serial component, which to assign to the parallel component, and precise protocol for communication between the two components.

4. *Scalability and extendability* — An important aspect of parallel architectures, particularly to customers of commercial systems, is the ease with which the system can be expanded. As indicated in Table 18-I, most systems are scalable, that is, expandable by adding more processors at a relatively constant cost per processor. By the nature of the tree and hypercube topologies the scalability is generally by factors of two. Systems with incremental scalability are called *extendable* and the process of expanding them resembles adding more memory cards to serial machines.

5. *The problem of language* — The single most serious problem in applying massively parallel systems is that of language. A little thought makes it apparent that each architecture requires its own language or at least a customized implementation of some standard concurrent language. A number of languages, including FORTRAN, LISP, PL/1, Algol, C, and Pascal have been extended with at least a minimal instruction set to specify which processes should run concurrently. Some of these, such as PL/1, provide provide instructions such as FORK, JOIN, CALL, and WAIT to explicitly exploit parallelism of the processors. The extended languages are known as Pardo (parallel do) Fortran, MultiLisp, Concurrent C, and Concurrent Pascal. Some languages, such as Inmos's OCCAM have been written explicitly for its powerful transputer parallel processor.

In Table 18-I we summarize some of the most important features of a number of massively parallel digital systems. Most of them started as academic research machines several of which have subsequently been commercialized.

18.5 THE CONNECTION MACHINE

As an example of an interesting machine which perhaps best represents the concepts and implementation of massively parallel digital architecture, let us examine the Connection Machine in more detail. This machine grew out of the Ph.D. thesis work of Daniel Hillis of MIT. His thesis has been published as a book, *The Connection Machine*, in which he provides a very clear rationale for parallel architectures in general and for the design considerations which led to the Connection Machine in particular.[8] This book provides an excellent introduction to the design of parallel-architecture machines.

The two primary design requirement for the Connection Machines were:

Table 18-I (a)

Characteristics of Parallel Digital Machines								
Machine	Institution (Inventor)	Date	Architecture (Granularity)	Connection Network	Number of Proc.	Processor	Bits/ Proc.	Memory/ Processor
MC-68020	Motorola		SISD	—	1	—	32	16
ILLIAC-IV	Univ. of ILL. (D. Slotnick)	1966	8X8 Array (Large scale)	Mesh	64	Custom	8,32, 64	
Cray-XMP Cray-2	Cray Research (Seymour Cray)		MIMD (Large grained)	Pipeline	2 2 - 16	Cray-1 Cray-1	64 64	
Matrix-1	Saxpy Computer Corporation	1987	SIMD (Large scale)	Ring-connected systolic array	32	Proprietary 32-ns ECL	32	128 Mword (Common)
MPP	Goodyear Aerospace Corporation	1979 1983	SIMD (Fine grained)	Mesh	16,384	Custom NMOS	1	1024
Cosmic Cube	Caltech (Chuck Seitz)	1985	SIMD (Large grained)	Hypercube	32, 64, 128 - 1024	8086→ 80286→ proprietary	8-32 in iPSC	512 K
Butterfly	BBN	1984	Common bus (Large Scale)	Butterfly multiple-path switch	16,32, 64,128, 256	68020 (68881)	32	4 Mbyte
T-Series	Floating Point Systems, Inc.	1986	SIMD-MIMD (Large grained)	Hypercube (Transputer)	16	Inmos Transputer	32-64	1 Mb
The Connection Machine	MIT (Danny Hillis)	1981	SIMD (Fine grained)	Hypercube, mesh, and direct address	16384, 65536 $\rightarrow 10^6$	Custom designed VLSI	1	4096 bits
DADO	Columbia Univ. (Salvatore Stolfo)	1982	MIMD (Large grained)	H-Tree binary tree	8, 16 1024	68020	32	
NON-VON	Columbia Univ. (David Shaw)	1982	SIMD,MIMD MSIMD (fine grained)	Binary Tree	32 LPEs + 16K SPEs	Off-the-shelf	8	

Table 18-I (b)

Characteristics of Parallel Digital Machines

Machine	M FLOPS	MIPS	Language Support	Scaling?	Host Computer	Commer-cialized	Comments
MC-68020		1–4	All	—	—	Yes	This is a representative processor used as the PE in parallel systems
ILLIAC-IV				Yes 6500	Burroughs	No	This $60,000,000 computer was the world's most powerful computer during the late 1970s.
Cray-XMP Cray-2	630 1300		All		None	Yes Yes	These machines are representative of commercial supercomputers
Matrix-1	900-1000		Fortran, C, VAX standard	Up to 32 proc.	VAX	Yes	This is the first general-purpose commercially available systolic computer.
MPP	~ 500X VAX	216-430	MPP Pascal, Forth	Yes	VAX 11/780	Yes	The MPP (Massive Parallel Processor) uses 1 processor per pixel for image processing.
Cosmic Cube	8-10	100	Fortran,C ASM286 XENIX	Yes	Intel System 310	Intel NCube Ametek	The CalTech Cosmic Cube has been commercialized by 4 companies. Data shown for 128 node Intel iPSC.
Butterfly		230		Yes	VAX-11/750	Yes	Shared memory machine scales to at least 256 processors.
T-Series	4000	160	Occam *C,*LISP Fortran	Yes	Micro-VAX II	Yes 1986	"Industrial strength, commercial processor"
The Connection Machine	2500	2000 ↓ 10000	CMLISP C		VAX, Symbolics 3600	Yes	Highly academic machine at an extreme point on fine grained scale, sold by Thinking Machines, Inc.
DADO	240× VAX 750			Yes to 8 K Proc.	Sun work-station	Yes	This Columbia University research prototype with 1024 CPUs is now marketed in 8-processor boards
NON-VON	~100X VAX 780		OPS5			No	A research machine designed to study architectural principles in the design of a general AI machine

- Many Processors
- Programmable Connections

The first condition provides enough processors to be allocated as necessary to match the problem requirements. The second requirement provides maximal flexibility for connecting the processors by software in configurations appropriate to the problem. This flexibility in matching the topology of the machine to the topology of the problem is the basis for the name *Connection Machine.*

The schematic block diagram for the prototype CM-1 Connection machine is shown in Figure 18-10. In this design, there are 65,536 cells, each containing a 1-bit processor and 4K of memory. The details of the cell design is shown in Figure 18-11.

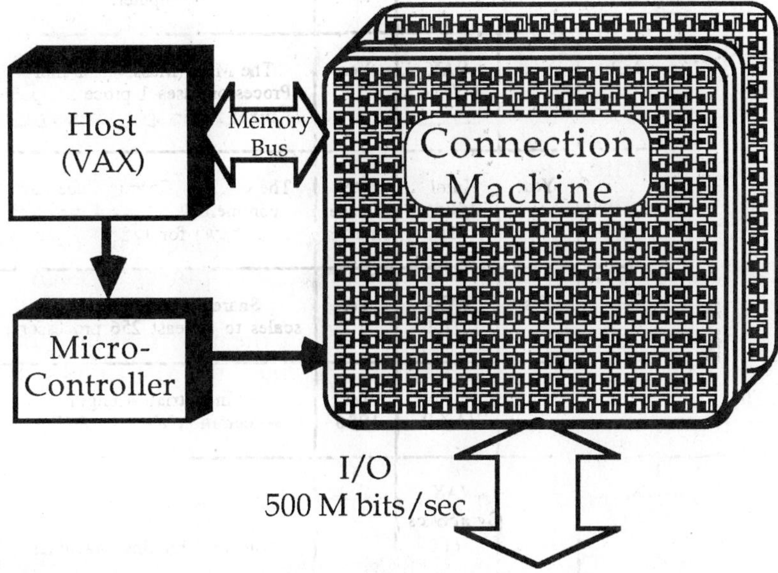

Figure 18-10 Block diagram of the CM-1 prototype Connection Machine Each board of the Connection Machine contains 512 1-bit processors, each of which has 4096 bits of associated memory. The total machine has 65,536 processors and 32 Mb of memory and has a top speed of 10,000 MIPS. From *The Connection Machine* by Daniel Hillis.

Note that the Connection Machine is not a stand-alone system, but rather relies on a host computer for program control. It should also be apparent that each of the 1-bit processors has little computing power of its own. Computing occurs through the orchestrated interaction of thousands of cells. In fact, an operational mental picture of the Connection Machine is that it consists of a massive memory, each cell of which has an embedded processor of very modest capability. That is, it acts as an *intelligent memory*.

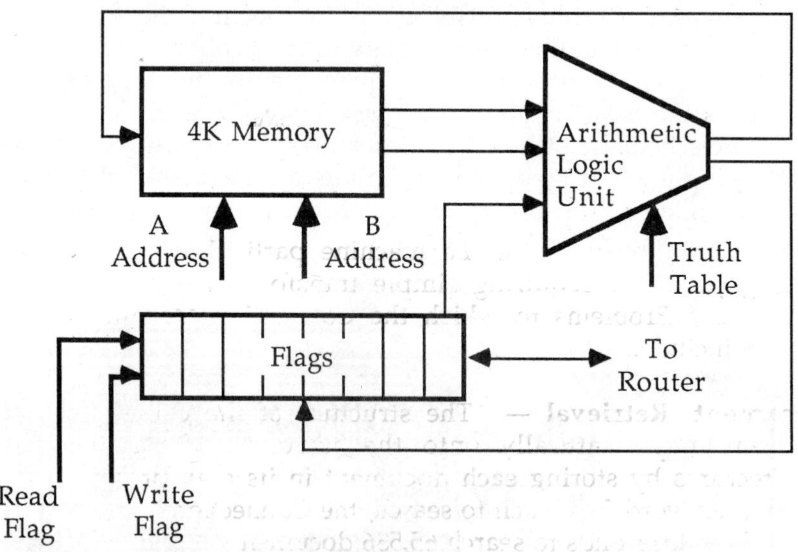

Figure 18-11 Architecture of the 1-bit processing element used in the Connection Machine Although the processing power of each single cell is small, massive computing power is achieved by the collective action of thousands of processors acting on the information stored in the flags and local memory. From *The Connection Machine* by Daniel Hillis.

SUMMARY OF FEATURES OF THE CONNECTION MACHINE

Granularity — The Connection Machine lies at the extreme fine-grained end of the granularity spectrum. It contains 65,536 1-bit RISC processors, each of which has an associated 4K bits of memory and an 8-bit flag register.

Topology — Three connection topologies are employed in the Connection Machine. These include a 16-D hypercube topology by which each processor can communicate with each other processor, a nearest neighbor mesh through which each processor can communicate with processors on its North, South, East, and West, and a slower broadcast network which links each processor with the host computer.

Synchronization and Control — All processors execute the same instruction at the same time (except those disabled by their control flags). Thus the Connection Machine is a purely SIMD machine. The microcontroller (see Figure 18-10) accepts macroinstructions from the host computer and issues "nanoinstructions" to each of the parallel processors at a rate of 3 million per second. Details of the control strategy are available elsewhere.[9]

ACCOMPLISHMENTS OF THE CONNECTION MACHINE

Depending on the problem application area, the Connection Machine executes between 2,000 and 10,000 MIPS.[10] This speed and its fine-grained parallelism make the machine particularly well suited for solving problems requiring simple transformation of massive data structures. Problems to which the Connection Machine have been applied include:

Document Retrieval — The structure of the document retrieval problem maps naturally onto the structure of massive parallel architectures by storing each document in its own processor. When given a keyword for which to search, the Connection Machine required about 50 milliseconds to search 65,536 documents.

Image Processing — Digitized images typically contain a million or more pixels and stereo images require twice as many. Again, a natural mapping of this problem into the Connection Machine involves storing each pixel (or small group of pixels) in it own processor. From two stereo images of mountainous country, the machine can produce a detailed contour map of the area in less than ten seconds.

Fluid Dynamics — A standard approach to solving many problems in mechanics, electromagnetism, and heat transfer is that of finite element analysis. The basic idea is that the region of interest is subdivided into numerous small regions in each of which the physical parameters of interest can be considered constant or smoothly varying. This approach is used in fluid dynamics in which a finite number of particles is distributed among a finite number of cells. The equations of fluid dynamics then predicts how the particles move from cell to cell. In one application, the Connection Machine simulated the motion of 32 million particles moving on a 4000×4000 grid. Computing at the rate of one billion cell updates per second, the machine computed 100,000 time steps in less than thirty minutes.

The development of the Connection Machine was specifically motivated by the desire to build a machine for solving AI problems.

The system can handle semantic networks, for example, by mapping nodes (concepts) onto processors and arcs (relationships) into connections between the nodes. Production rules could, for instance, map onto processors and instructions relating them, and the system cycled until an equilibrium solution is reached. The Connection Machine appears to be a thoughtful and well designed logical extension of parallel architecture for implementing the traditional symbol processing metaphor of artificial intelligence research.

One final observation should be made at this point. That is that knowledge in the Connection Machine is stored in the pattern of connections between processing elements. This characteristic, along with its massive, fine-grained parallelism, are features which the Connection Machine shares with neural network architectures described below.

18.6 DESIGN OF NEURAL NETWORK COMPUTERS

As the final topic of the book we introduce neural network computers and discuss their structure, characteristics, and advantages for AI applications. Before we examine neural networks in detail, it is helpful to outline some design principles which provide the foundation for neural network research. These include:

- *Artificial neural networks are inspired by biological neural networks* — A nearly universal belief of neural network researchers is that nature, working through evolution, has provided us with optimized models of information processors in the neural network structure of organs such as the eye and the brain. The corollary to this assumption is that to the extent that artificial systems can mimic natural processes they will succeed.

- *Neural networks employ distributed, parallel processing to perform computation* — The storage, processing, and communication of information in neural networks occurs throughout the whole network rather that at specific sites or memory locations. Thus, both memory and processing in neural networks are *global* rather then *local* in nature.

- *Computation by neural networks emerges spontaneously from fundamental physical principles* — John Hopfield of the California Institute of Technology has shown that collective computational properties arise spontaneously from a network of elementary neurons.[11] He has described this computational behavior in terms of the motion of individual neurons in a phase space of computational energy and interprets the resulting collective behavior in terms of the entropy of an isolated system. A neural network may be considered a *relaxation system* which *settles into a solution.*

• *Neural networks are self-organizing systems* — When presented with an image, pattern, or example, a neural network computer adjusts its internal state automatically to store the information in a form which the user neither needs to know nor could interpret if s/he did know it. This information may be recalled whole and accurately by presenting the network with only a partial image or an noisy image. This property which is very difficult to achieve with conventional architectures is called *content addressable memory.*

• *Knowledge is stored by the strengths of the interconnections between neurons* — Connections between neurons which lead to the "right answer" are strengthened while those leading to "wrong answers" are decreased by repeated exposure to sample problems. Thus, neural networks have the ability to learn in a manner closely parallel to human learning. This process is described as Hebbian learning.[12]

• *Neural networks compute significant results in a small number of steps* — Since neurons in the brain operate in times of the order of tens of milliseconds and collectively can make intelligent decisions (recognize a face, etc.) in the order of a second, they must be performing this sophisticated pattern recognition task in 100 or less serial steps. This is the basis for the *100-step program constraint.*

• *Learning is a fundamental, essential aspect of neural networks* — One of the most striking and impressive characteristic of neural networks is ease and naturalness with which they can learn. This is the fundamental reason for considering new architectures as potential solutions to the machine learning problem.

A Brief History of Neural Network Computers

It is essential for understanding the present state of development of neural network computers to have at least an inkling of the history of their development. This history is enormously fascinating and reveals a level of controversy and personality conflict unusual even for the rambunctious field of AI.

The Early Years — Promises

As we indicated earlier in the book, the work of McCulloch and Pitts in 1943 had shown that a network of neurons with binary response functions was capable of computation. Donald Hebb proposed in 1949 a model for learning in neural networks through the strengthening of connections between elements connecting the input stimulus neurons and the correct output pattern neurons. Dean Edmonds and Marvin Minsky built an electromechanical learning machine in 1951 which incorporated these ideas in a motor-driven memory of 40 control knobs. This work led to Minsky's Ph.D. thesis at MIT on *Neural Nets and the Brain-Model Problem.*

In the late 1950s and early 1960s, Frank Rosenblatt of Cornell University and a high school classmate of Minsky's invented a type of neural network which he called the *perceptron.* Rosenblatt made some very strong claims for the capabilities of the perceptron, and one of the most significant results of his work was the *Perceptron Learning Theorem*:

> *"Given an elementary α-perceptron, a stimulus world W, and any classification C(W) for which a solution exists; let all stimuli in W occur in any sequence, provided that each stimulus must reoccur in finite time; then beginning from an arbitrary initial state, an error correction procedure will always yield a solution to C(W) in finite time, ..."*[13]

Marvin Minsky and his MIT colleague Seymour Papert felt that claims for perceptron performance were exaggerated and misleading, and stated:

> *"Perceptrons have been widely publicized as 'pattern recognition' or 'learning machines' and as such have been discussed in a large number of books, journal articles, and voluminous 'reports'. Most of this writing ... is without scientific value and we will not usually refer by name to the works we criticize."*

And later:

> *"Appalled at the persistent influence of perceptrons (and similar ways of thinking) on practical pattern recognition, we determined to set out our work as a book."*[14]

In their book *Perceptrons* Minsky and Papert proved mathematically the capabilities and limitations of the single-layered, linear perceptron of the type promoted by Rosenblatt. They correctly pointed out that hundreds of experiments using the learning, adaptive, or self-organizing features of perceptron-like devices usually worked quite well on very simple problems but that their performance deteriorated very rapidly as the tasks assigned to them got harder.

The Dark Ages — Disillusionment

The failure of perceptrons to live up to their expectations and the publications of *Perceptrons* dampened the enthusiasm for research on this type of device and brought research on neural networks to a virtual halt during the 1970s. While many researchers abandoned neural networks to reorient their work along traditional symbol processing approaches, a few workers pursued the path suggested by the early perceptron work.

Among these were the experimentalist Dr. Bernard Widrow of Stanford University. Professor Widrow was a participant in the 1956 Dartmouth Conference at which AI as a discipline was born. He and his students at Stanford first built Adeline, an adaptive linear neuron computer, in the early 1960s. Adeline used negative feedback to overcome some of the problems of the perceptron. This work was extended to the multiple-neuron Madeline which demonstrated the capability of recognizing spoken words and visual patterns independent of translation. Widrow and his student Hoff invented one of the simpler learning rules which is still widely used in training neural networks.[15]

On the theoretical side, Stephen Grossberg of Boston University published extensive mathematical analyses from the late 1960s up to the present which established the foundation for associative learning in neural networks.[16] James Anderson developed a simple linear associator model in 1977 which he called Brain State in a Box (BSB).[17] The BSB model demonstrated learning by incorporating a positive feedback loop within the pattern of interconnections.

A number of Japanese researchers persisted in both theoretical and applied work on neural networks through this period. These workers include Professor Shun-ichi Amari of the University of Tokyo who has investigated the cooperative/competitive approach for learning first proposed by Grossberg. Kuniko Fukushima of the NHK Laboratories has developed the *neocognitron*, a multi-layer extension of the perceptron which is capable of speech recognition and written pattern recognition independent of position and distortion.[18] In Finland, Teuvo Kohonen contributed important theoretical work on associative memory and continues to apply neural networks to solve problems such as the analysis of grammar.[19]

Rebirth of Connectionism

In the 1980s, several events occurred which reestablished neural network research as a credible endeavor and culminated in the IEEE First Annual International Conference on Neural Networks (ICNN) in San Diego in June, 1987. The San Diego ICNN marked the official beginning of the discipline of neural networks and is the neural network equivalent of the 1956 Dartmouth Conference in establishing AI as a discipline. Among the most significant events which revived the study of neural networks were:

- The publication by physicist John Hopfield in 1982 of *Neural networks and physical systems with emergent collective computational abilities.* In this and subsequent papers, Hopfield presented a simple analog circuit model of a neural network and used it to solve practical problems such as the design of an analog-to-binary converter and the traveling salesman problem.[20] Hopfield showed that collective computational abilities arise spontaneously from networks of neurons with elementary properties and proposed a thermodynamic theory of computational energy for explaining this behavior.

- The establishment of the PDP (Parallel Distributed Processing) Study Group by James McClelland of Carnegie-Mellon and David Rumelhart of UCSD and the subsequent publication of their three volume series, *Parallel Distributed Processing.*[21] This study group grew out of the UCSD Institute for Cognitive Science, and Rumelhart and McClelland's three volume series is the bible for connectionists. The study group is composed of distinguished neural network scientists including Nobel prize winner Francis Crick.

- The emergence of commercial neural network products. At the first ICNN, at least six commercial neural network systems were demonstrated. These include products by the Hecht-Nielsen Neurocomputer Corporation, Nestor, Inc., and Neuronics, Inc. The HNC was established by Dr. Robert Hecht-Nielsen with Stephen Grossberg as a consultant and markets a neural network system called ANZA. Nestor was founded by two Brown University researchers, Nobel prizewinning physicist Leon Cooper and Charles Elbaum. Their first product recognizes handwritten information on checks and documents. Neuronics was established by Matthew Jensen, a recent graduate of the University of Chicago. The first product of Neuronics is MacBrain, an remarkably clever neural network simulation program which was introduced and attracted considerable attention at the ICNN.

• The American Physical Society's conferences on Neural Networks for Computing. The first of these was held at Santa Barbara in 1985 at had 60 participants. The second was held at Snowbird, Utah, in 1986 and included 160 participants. This conference resulted in an important proceedings, *Neural Networks in Computing*.[22] These conferences established neural network research as respectable activity with a firm basis in physical law and cognitive psychology theory. A year later, the first IEEE ICNN attracted nearly 2000 participants.

The Neuron Model

Artificial neural networks are patterned after real neural networks. The basic computational element of real networks is the neuron, a stylized model of which is shown in Figure 18-12.

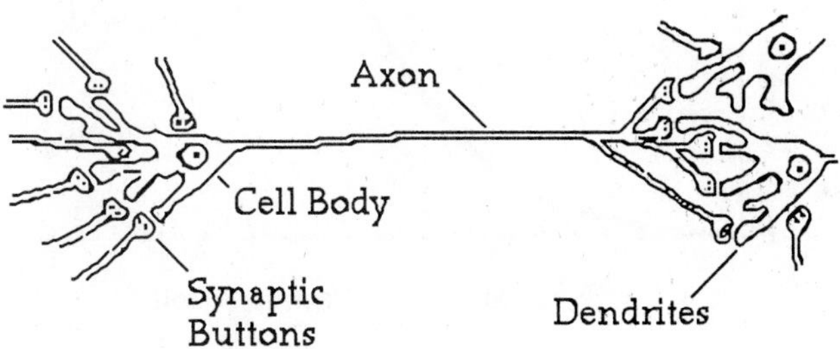

Figure 18-12 A Typical Biological Neuron The four basic parts of a real neuron such as those found in the brain are: (1) Synaptic buttons or synapses which serve as output devices, (2) the cell body which sums the membrane potentials provided by the synapses and fires at a rate which is a non-linear function of the total voltage, (3) the axon which carries the electrical signal from the cell body to subsequent synapses, and (4) dendrites, branch-like structures which provide sensory input to the cell body. (Figure abstracted from *Parallel Distributed Processing*, Rumelhart and McClelland)

The cell body sums the membrane potentials between the synaptic buttons and the dendrites and "fires" voltage spikes down its output axon at a rate which depends on the sum of the input voltages. This dependence has been found to be sigmoid in shape, resembling the function shown in Figure 18-13.

It has been found experimentally that synaptic connections can produce either excitatory or inhibitory effects. Excitatory neurons (Type I) greatly outnumber inhibitory neurons (Type II) and tend to respond more rapidly to changes of input. Inhibitory neurons provide a type of delayed negative feedback and help explain phenomena such as numbness and visual acuity. The central neurons in the visual field of interest provide an excitatory signal while the off-axis neurons produce an inhibitory signal. Thus a point excitation of the visual retina will result in "Mexican hat" spatial distribution of excitation/inhibition of the type proposed by David Marr in the vision chapter.

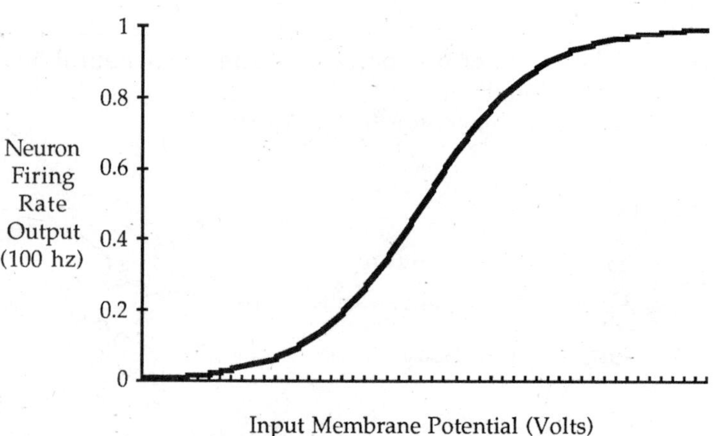

Figure 18-13 Neuron Activation Function The neuron sums the input potentials and fires at a rate shown in this sigmoid function. The maximum firing rate may be several hundred spikes/sec. The membrane potential ranges from about –0.1 volts for 0 firing rates to about 0 volts for the maximum firing rate.

DESIGN CONSIDERATIONS IN ARTIFICIAL NEURAL NETWORKS

There are a number of considerations which enter the design of an artificial neural network system. The transition from biological neural network to artificial neural network is illustrated in Figure 18-14.

The most general neural network models assume a complete interconnection between all neurons and resolve the cases of non-connected neurons (i,j) by setting the connection strength $T_{i,j} = 0$. There are, however, a number of system design parameters which must be specified for any neural network model. These include:

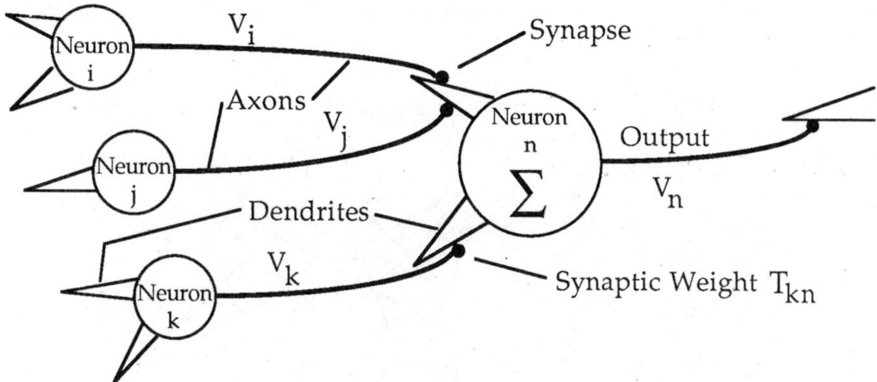

Figure 18-14 Model of Neural Network The output of neuron n is generated by multiplying the sum of the input voltages weighted by the synaptic weight or connection strengths $T_{i,j}$ between neuron i and neuron j by the non-linear transfer function.

- The structure of the system, i.e. the number of "layers"
- The synchrony of the system
- Symmetry of the interconnections
- Feedback structure employed
- The transfer or activation function relating input to output
- The formulation of a learning strategy

Structure of Neural Networks

The original perceptron is considered to be a single-layered network as indicated in Figure 18-15. That is, given an input pattern, the perceptron could be trained to produce the correct output pattern by varying the weights connecting input neurons to output neurons.

Synchrony, Symmetry, and Feedback

The two possible classes of synchronous operation of neural networks are:

- Synchronous — Controlled by sequential clock cycle
- Asynchronous — Instantaneously response constrained only by an RC "settling time"

Perceptrons and the majority of neural networks simulated on digital machines are synchronous by the very nature of sequential machines.

Natural neural networks and the class of neural networks represented by Hopfield analog circuits are naturally asynchronous.

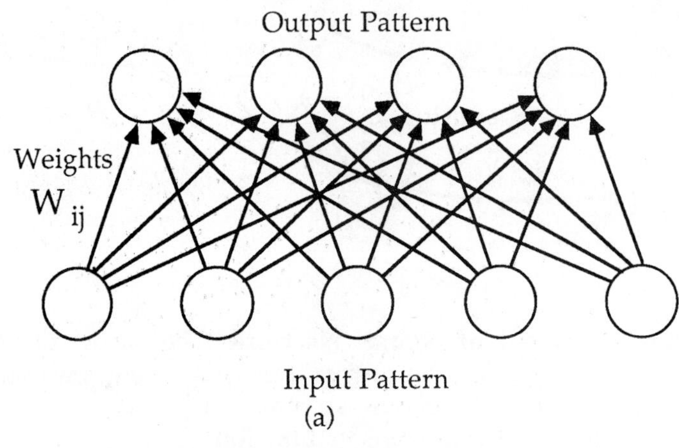

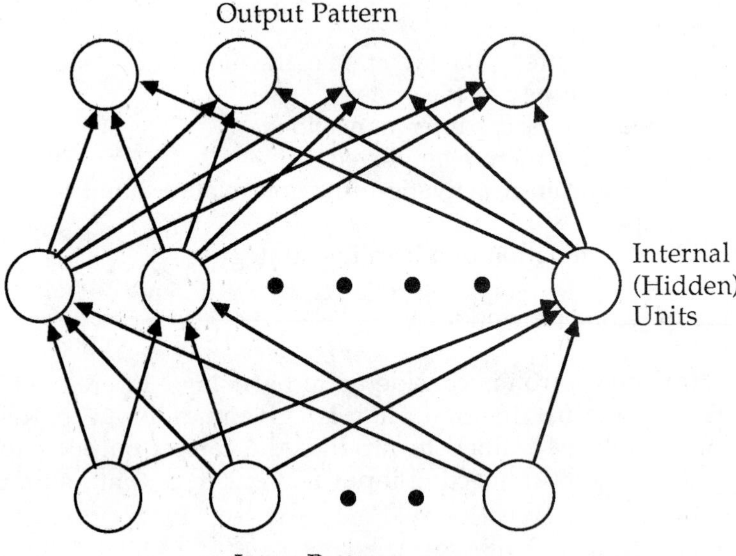

Figure 18-15 Structure of Neural Networks (a) shows the single-layered structure used in the perceptron. (b) shows multi-layered structures used in modern neural networks. The two-layered network shown in (b) may be extended to an N-layered network. This structure overcomes many of the weaknesses of the perceptron.

The symmetry of connections is illustrated graphically in Figure

18-16. Three logical possibilities for connections between neuron i and neuron j are: $i \rightarrow j$, $j \rightarrow i$, and $i \leftrightarrow j$. For the case of symmetric connection $i \leftrightarrow j$, two subclasses are possible: $W_{ij} \neq W_{ji}$ (asymmetric strengths) and $W_{ij} = W_{ji}$ (symmetric strengths).

Figure 18-16 can also be used to characterize feedback mechanisms within neural network circuits. Figure (a) illustrates a feed-forward mechanism in which the state of the input (at bottom) propagates forward to produce an output (which may serve as input to subsequent layers). Figure (b) illustrates feedback in which the state of a neuron several layers deep in the network is returned to a preceding layer by "back propagation". Figure (c) indicates a total interconnection configuration which provides a natural and complete feed back.

Note that synchrony, symmetry, and feedback are very closely related concepts. For example, in layered, synchronous circuits, feedback corresponds to connections between subsequent and preceding layers of the activation. Bi-directional connections between all neurons provide complete feedback.

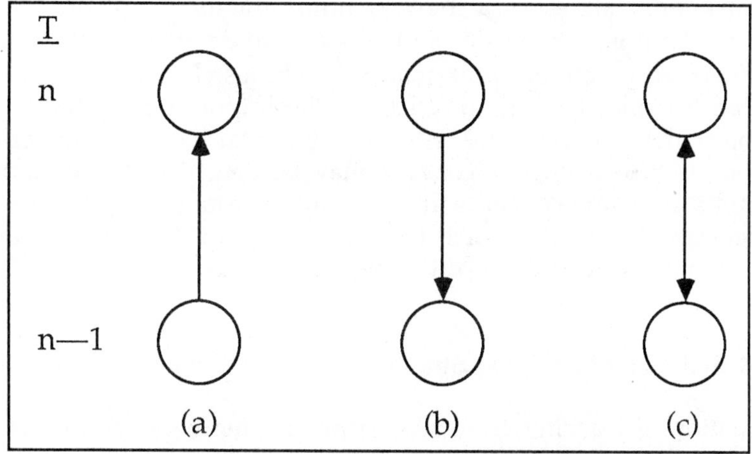

Figure 18-16 Interconnection structures In (a) the bottom neuron sends its information to the top neuron but is unaffected by the state of the top neuron. That is, for synchronous operation, the state of the top neuron at time n is determined by the state of the bottom neuron at time n–1. In (b), the state of the bottom neuron at time n is determined by that of the top neuron at time n-1. In (c) the state of each neuron at time n is determined by the state of the other at time n–1. For asynchronous operation each neuron reacts with the other with the response time governed by the RC time constants of the neurons or circuits emulating them.

Structure of the Transfer Function

Hopfield has emphasized the importance of a non-linear transfer function for emergent collective computational behavior of neural network circuits. Several non-linear transfer functions have been investigated, and four of these are summarized in Figure 18-17. The first of these functions is the sigmoid, shown earlier as Figure 18-13, which is generated by the Boltzmann distribution familiar to physicists and chemists. This distribution function, $P(\Delta E)$, describes the probability that a given state is populated in terms of the temperature, T, and the gap, ΔE, between the energy of the state and the Fermi energy.

$$P(\Delta E) = \frac{1}{(1+e^{-\Delta E/T})} \tag{18.1}$$

Hopfield interpreted the total activation of the circuit in terms of the circuit's "computational energy" and proved that an symmetrically-connected asynchronous neural network will automatically adjust its internal energy states to achieve a minimum in the overall energy function. Hinton, Sejnowski, and Ackley have extended this concept with their research on Boltzmann Machines.[23] This research has provided a firmer basis in physics for the importance of the sigmoid function which had been suggested by empirical biological experiment. The computational energy concept may be considered a variation of Shannon's entropy concepts in communication theory. The minimum energy states into which Hopfield's circuits settle correspond to states of maximum entropy of the neural network.

The Formulation of Learning Strategies

Formulation of learning strategies for neural networks continues to be one of the most active and productive areas of research in the field. One of the first strategies proposed was the *perceptron learning rule* for adjusting the weight, W_{ij}, between input unit j and output unit i when presented with the "true value", t_i, for unit i. This learning rule may be stated in terms of the learning rate, η, and activations a_i and a_j as:

$$\Delta W_{ij} = \eta\,(t_i - a_i)\,a_j \tag{18.2}$$

This rule is equivalent to the set of rules:

1. Change weights only on those connections to neurons

with activation $a_j = 1$.

2. If the present value, a_i, of neuron i is the true value, t_i, make no change in the weight connecting it to neuron j.

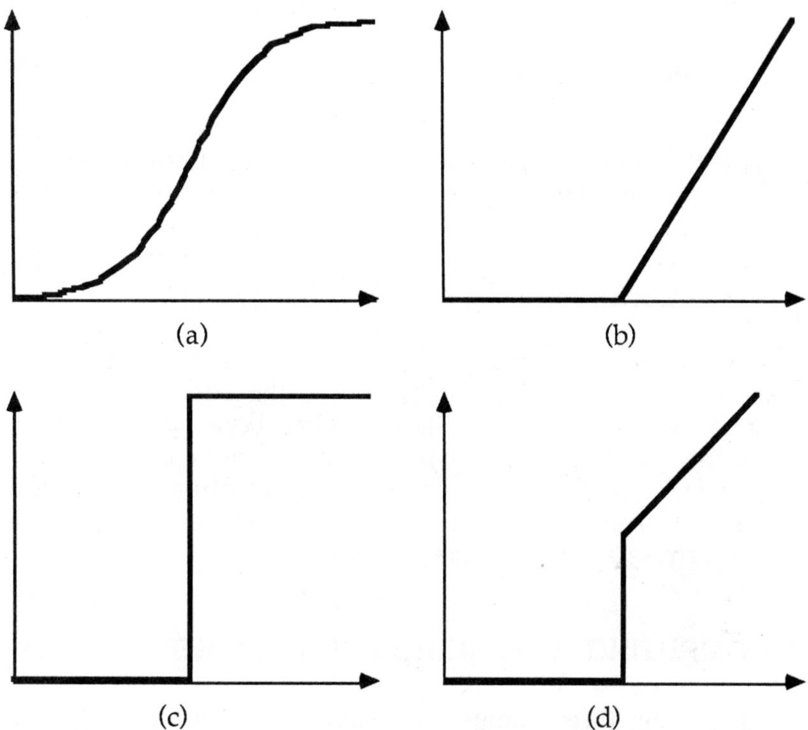

Figure 18-17 Non-Linear Transfer Functions The x-axis in each case is the weighted sum of synaptic inputs from other neurons and the y-axis is the resulting activation of the neuron in question. Function (a) is the sigmoid corresponding to the Boltzmann distribution, (b) and (d) are variations on linear-threshold behavior which resemble a sigmoid, and (c) is a step function equivalent to a Boltzmann distribution with $\Delta E = 0$. Both the perceptron and Hopfield circuits use the step function (c).

3. If unit i has an activation $a_i = 0$ when the true value $t_i = 1$, then increase the weights on all active connections by amount η.

4. If unit i has an activation $a_i = 1$ when the true value

$t_i = 0$, then decrease the weights on all active connections by amount η.

Rumelhart, Hinton, and Williams have proposed a variation of this rule which they call the *generalized delta rule.* Using pair *p* of input and desired output patterns as data, the generalized delta rule generates a correction to the (i,j) weight, $\Delta_p W_{ij}$, given by:

$$\Delta_p W_{ij} = \eta \, (t_{pj} - o_{pj}) \, i_{pi} \qquad (18.3)$$

where

t_{pj} = target input for *j*th element of output pattern p
o_{pj} = *j*th element of the actual output pattern from input pattern p
i_{pi} = value of the *i*th element of the input pattern
η = fractional change in weight (learning rate)

These simple learning strategies produce excellent results in simple systems. But as system complexity grows, the effectiveness of many learning strategies decreases. Stephen Grossberg has written extensively on the theory of learning in neural networks, and his *theory of cooperative/competitive learning* appears to offer great promise. Research in learning in neural networks offers many of the same challenges as research in learning in traditional AI.

18.7 COMPUTING WITH NEURAL NETWORKS

We next consider three examples of computing with neural networks or systems which emulate them. The first is a mathematical model for an associative memory, second are results from a digital program which emulates the behavior of a neural network, and finally a discussion of the Hopfield circuit and its accomplishments.

CONTENT ADDRESSABLE MEMORIES

One of the most impressive and attractive features of neural networks is the ease with which they can be programmed as *content addressable* or *associative memories.* Content addressable memories are extremely interesting from a computer science point of view because of the following characteristics:

- Informations is defined and retrieved from memory by specifying *what* is stored rather than *where* it is stored.

- Content addressable memories are *distributed over the network* (i.e., global rather than local)

- Pattern recognition by associative memories is effective using *noisy input*, incomplete input, and even erroneous input.

- Associative memories are extremely *fault tolerant*. Their performance degrades gracefully as one or more neurons are destroyed.

Bart Kosko, Chairman of the first ICNN, has developed a very simple and elegant mathematical description of a bidirectional associated memory (BAM).[24] Consider the two-group neural network shown in Figure 18-18. The purpose of a BAM is two-fold: (1) Given pattern A (or some noisy portion of it), recall B, and (2) given pattern B (or some noisy portion of it), recall A.

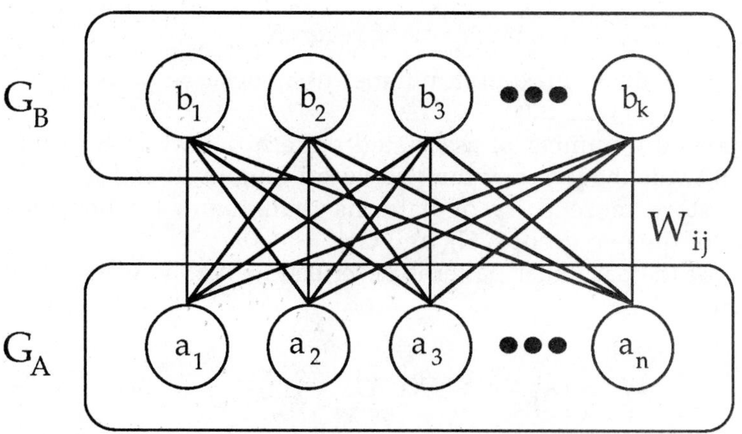

Figure 18-18 Bidirectional Associative Memory Two groups of neurons, G_A and G_B, are completely connected with each other (but not among themselves) with a connection weight matrix, W_{ij}. Multiple pattern pairs (A_1,B_1), (A_2,B_2), ... (A_m,B_m) may be encoded by the matrix, W. The number of pairs stored is limited to $m \leq \min(k,n)$.

Assume, following Kosko, that we have two pairs of patterns, (A_1,B_1) and (A_2,B_2) defined as:

$A_1 = (1\ 0\ 1\ 0\ 1\ 0) \qquad B_1 = (1\ 1\ 0\ 0)$

A_2 = (1 1 1 0 0 0) B_2 = (1 0 1 0)

The first step in encoding these vectors into a connection matrix, W, is to transform them into a bipolar representation using the algorithm 1 → 1; 0 → –1:

A_1 = (1 0 1 0 1 0) → X_1 = (1 –1 1 –1 1 –1)
B_1 = (1 1 0 0) → Y_1 = (1 1 –1 –1)
A_2 = (1 1 1 0 0 0) → X_2 = (1 1 1 –1 –1 –1)
B_2 = (1 0 1 0) → Y_2 = (1 –1 1 –1)

Next the weight matrix is generated by the operation:

$$W = \sum_{i=1}^{m} X_i^T Y_i \tag{18.4}$$

where

X_i^T = the transpose of vector X_i
m = maximum number of associative pairs

The maximum number of associated pattern pairs which can be stored in the BAM is the lesser of the two vector lengths, k and n. That is, one cannot store more pairs of patterns than there are neurons in the smaller of the two groups, G_A and G_B.

For the particular patterns described above the weight matrix can be calculated as:

$$W = X_1^T Y_1 + X_2^T Y_2 \tag{18.5}$$

$$= \begin{pmatrix} 1 & 1 & -1 & -1 \\ -1 & -1 & 1 & 1 \\ 1 & 1 & -1 & -1 \\ -1 & -1 & 1 & 1 \\ 1 & 1 & -1 & -1 \\ -1 & -1 & 1 & 1 \end{pmatrix} + \begin{pmatrix} 1 & -1 & 1 & -1 \\ 1 & -1 & 1 & -1 \\ 1 & -1 & 1 & -1 \\ -1 & 1 & -1 & 1 \\ -1 & 1 & -1 & 1 \\ -1 & 1 & -1 & 1 \end{pmatrix} \tag{18.6}$$

$$= \begin{pmatrix} 2 & 0 & 0 & -2 \\ 0 & -2 & 2 & 0 \\ 2 & 0 & 0 & -2 \\ -2 & 0 & 0 & 2 \\ 0 & 2 & -2 & 0 \\ -2 & 0 & 0 & 2 \end{pmatrix} \qquad (18.7)$$

Two characteristics of neural networks are immediately apparent from this simple two-neuron-group system:

1. Knowledge of patterns within the system is encoded in the connections.

2. Knowledge is distributed rather than localized within the system.

Now that we have encoded the two patterns in the W matrix, how can we recover pattern B, given pattern A (or some noisy portion of it)? The following iterative algorithm provides the solution:

1. Read vector A
2. Compute vector B by the matrix product $B' = A \cdot W$
   $B = S(B')$
3. Compute vector A by the matrix product $A' = B \cdot W^T$
   $A = S(A')$
4. Repeat steps 2 and 3 until a stable (A,B) solution is reached.

Since the elements of the A' and B' vectors will not, in general, be binary, it is necessary to apply a threshold function S to each element. S is the sigmoid or step function defined in terms of a threshold value, X_{th}, by:

$$\begin{aligned} S(x) &= 0 \text{ if } x < X_{th} \\ S(x) &= 1 \text{ if } x > X_{th} \\ S(x) &= x \text{ if } x = X_{th} \end{aligned} \qquad (18.8)$$

Selecting $X_{th} = 0$ assures a binary output pattern, and it is easily shown that, given $A = A_1$, this procedure generates B_1 in a single iteration. If one or two bits of the original A_1 are flipped (to simulate noisy or erroneous input data) several iterations of the algorithm may be required to reach a stable solution. It has been shown that such a BAM will always converge rapidly.

This example may readily be extended to illustrate several more features of neural networks.

1. Associative memories work effectively despite incomplete information.

2. Associative memories work effectively despite noisy or erroneous information.

3. Associative memories are fault tolerant of the circuit itself. That is, several of the connections in W could be damaged or cut and the memory would still function correctly. As the damage is increased, the systems suffers a "graceful degradation" rather than abrupt failure.

Next we illustrate these features of content addressable memories with a digital neural network emulation program.

EMULATION OF NEURAL NETWORKS ON DIGITAL SYSTEMS

A number of commercial neural network emulation systems are now available which run on personal computers. We show next some examples illustrating the ease with which simple neural networks may be emulated with such systems.[25]

Example: Parity Operation — XOR

One of the most devastating results from the book *Perceptrons* was the fact that single-layer perceptrons were not capable of the parity operation. The parity operation is a single output bit which is 1 if the number of 1's in the input pattern is odd and 0 if the number of input 1's is even. For a two-bit input, the parity operation is identical to the XOR function.

As a result of this history, one of the first mandatory exercises for any neural network system is to demonstrate that it is capable of computing the XOR function. The solution, of course, is to use a more generalized neural network (e.g., a multi-layered system) rather than the limited, single-layered perceptron. The following example illustrates such a two-layered system with one neuron in the hidden layer.

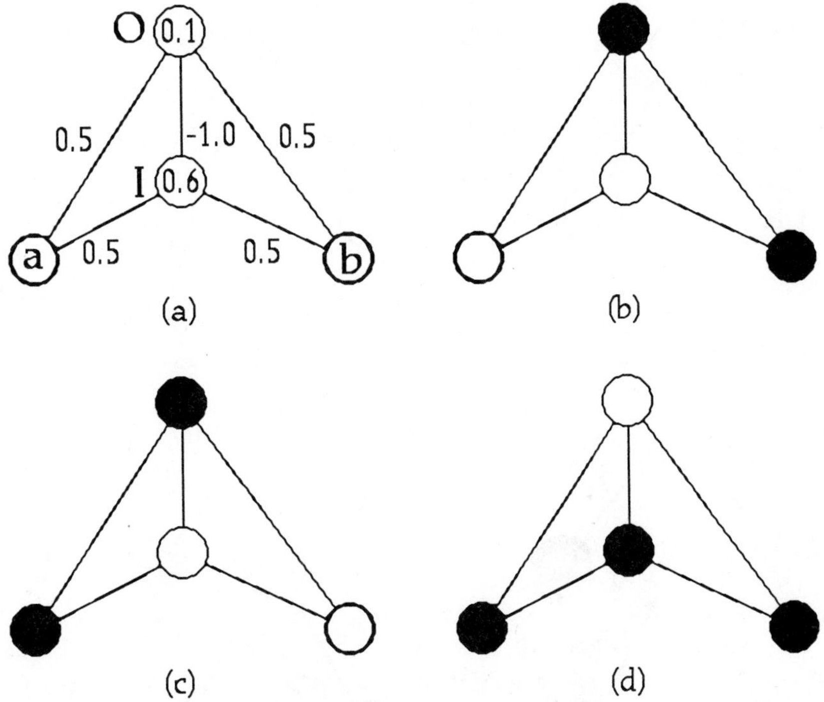

Figure 18-19 Exclusive OR (XOR) Neural Network The connection weights are shown beside the connections, and the threshold for a step-function sigmoid are shown inside the neurons. The two input neurons are **a** and **b** which are clamped to 0 or 1. The XOR function appears on the output neuron, O, and the inner or hidden neuron is labeled I. The four possible values of the XOR truth table computed by the emulation program are shown in a, b, c, and d.

This example shows that neural networks are capable of computing the XOR function. How difficult would it be to program other elementary logical functions with neural networks? The answer is: It is trivial! Figure 18-20 shows four primitive logic gates designed on the neural network emulator.

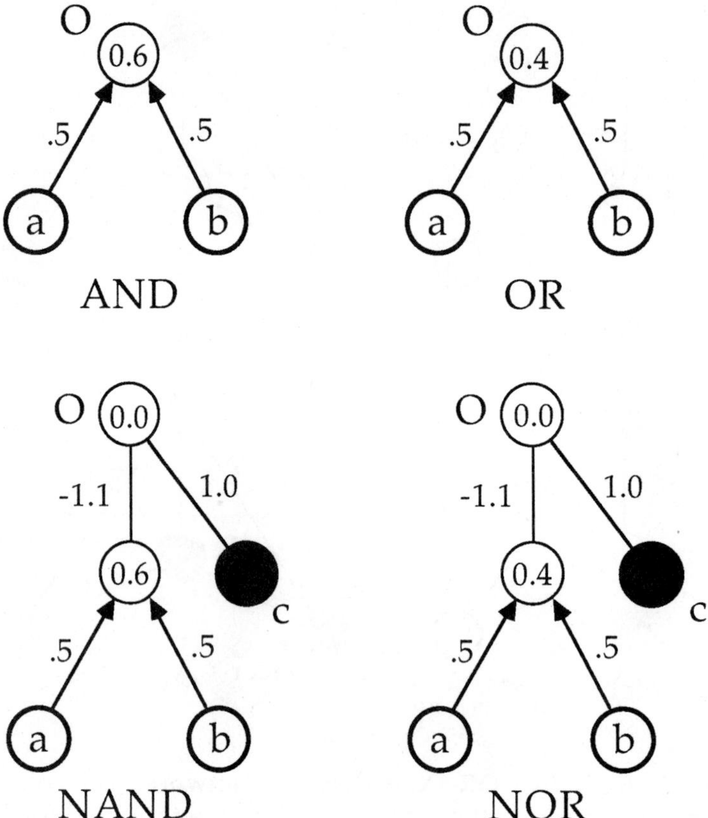

Figure 18-20 Neural Network Implementation of Logic Gates Note that the structure of AND and OR gates is identical with only the threshold of the output unit differing. NAND and NOR gates require an additional fixed input provided by neuron **c** clamped to 1 in this implementation.

From a theoretical point of view the results shown in Figure 18-20 are interesting because they prove that neural networks are in principle capable of any computation of which a traditional von Neumann machine is capable.

Example: Content Addressable Memory

Next we present an example of the design of a content addressable memory in which are stored two different associated patterns. The two arbitrarily selected patterns are the symbol pairs (**T,1**) and (**F,0**) as shown in the two panels of Figure 18-21. This example is particularly important because it illustrates another feature of neural networks — their ability to learn and organize themselves.

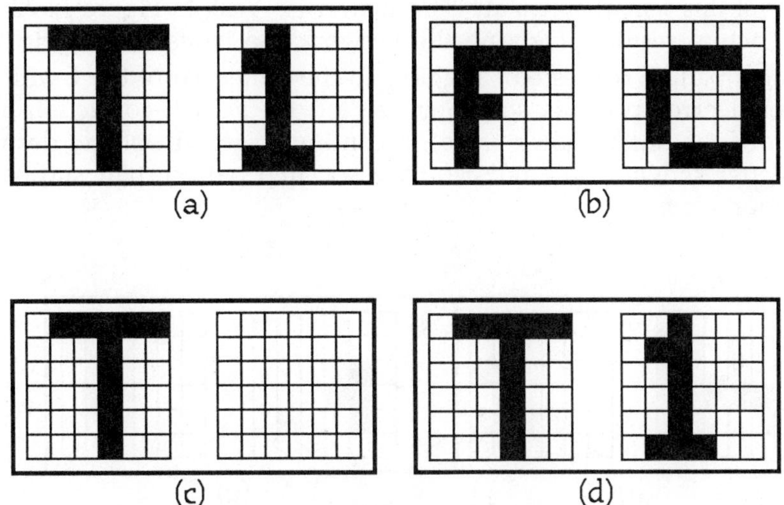

Figure 18-21 Bidirectional Associative Memory Each panel illustrates a network of 72 neurons arranged in two completely connected 6 × 6 groups. The pattern (**T,1**) was toggled in (a) and the command LEARN issued. Then the pattern (**F,0**) was entered as shown in (b) and the network told to LEARN. When the pattern **T** was entered as in (c), the content addressable memory returned pattern (d) in the next cycle.

The network was constructed by arranging two groups of neurons in a square array of 6 × 6 neurons each. No connections were explicitly established between neurons. Next the pattern (**T,1**) was toggled in by clicking on the indicated neurons. The program was then told to "Learn" this pattern by clicking on the LEARN icon. The program automatically connected all "ON" neurons with positive connection weights. The next step in programming the associative memory was to clear all neurons to 0 and toggle in the (**F,0**) pattern. When the learning command was issued for this pattern the appropriate connections weights were established or modified.[26]

After the network learned these two pattern pairs, the input of a **T** generated the associated **1** in a single cycle. Similarly, entering a **1** in the right block of neurons generated a **T** in the left block. Likewise, an input **F** generated an associated **0** and a **0** recalled an **F**. The whole process of entering the patterns and training the system required less than a minute (once the tedious CAD task of building the neural arrays was complete).

Now the claim was made in the previous section that a BAM such as we describe here is capable of remembering associated patterns in the presence of incomplete or noisy data. Are the networks shown capable of this remarkable feat? The answer is: Yes! In Figure 18-22 we shown actual results of giving the network the barest clue as to the associated pattern requested. Toggling in the center bar of the **F** with an additional error pixel as shown in (a) led to the self-correction and growth of the letter shown in (b), a continued growth of the desired input letter shown in (c) and a fully associated pattern pair shown in (d) in four successive cycles.

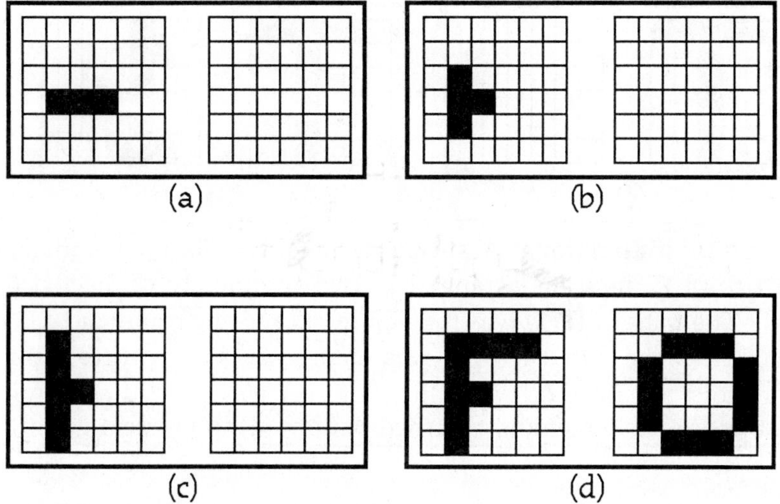

Figure 18-22 Recall of Pattern Pair in a BAM Given the clue shown in (a), the neural network emulator corrects an error and begins growing the letter in (b), continues the growth in (c), and fully recalls the associated memory in (d).

It should be noted that this network does not distinguish between the two blocks of neurons as did the Kosko circuit discussed in the previous section. That is, the learning process builds connections between the ON neurons composing the **F** itself as well as between neurons of the **F** and the **O**.

A logical question in light of this impressive performance would be, "Just how noisy could the input signal be and the associative memory still reach the correct solution?" To investigate this question we entered the **(T,1)** pattern and then began to mutilate it and add extraneous information until the pattern (a) shown in Figure 18-23 was all that remained. Certainly very little of the original pattern was available to assist the network in recalling the desired memory. The subsequent panels of the figure shown the behavior of the network in correctly recalling the full association from very fragmentary and noisy input data.

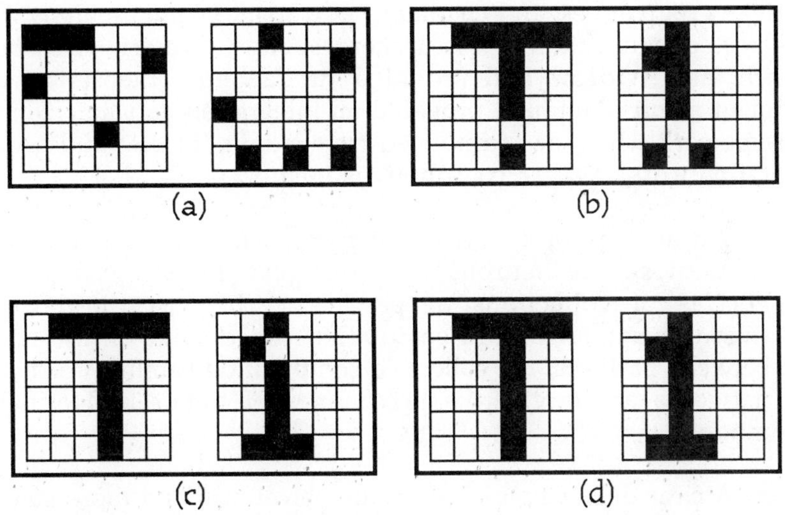

Figure 18-23 Extraction of Signal from Noisy Data From the fragmentary data and erroneous information in (a) the same neural network as in Figures 18-21 and 18-22 was able to correctly recall the association shown in (d).

There are two more attractive characteristics of neural networks which the above example of an associative memory illustrate. First is the self-organization of the circuit. That is, at no time in the programming or use of the associative memory is it necessary to explicitly "wire" or program the network. The details of the learning process and associated weight pattern in which the knowledge resides are invisible and unnecessary for the user to know in order to use the system effectively. Secondly, while increasing the knowledge stored in conventional, sequential memories increases the search time to find an item, the search time to recall an item from content addressable memory is independent of the amount of stored information, at least to a first order. This is, of course, how human memory works — more information allows us to make decisions faster rather than slower as on traditional sequential machines.

HOPFIELD'S NEURAL NETWORKS

The seminal papers of John Hopfield and his associates mark the turning point in the fortunes of the connectionist school of AI. The publication of *Perceptrons* had largely discredited the neural network approach, and symbol-oriented AI researchers dismissed connectionists as a fringe group at best and charlatans at worst. While previous work by respected connectionist researchers such as Amari, Grossberg, Kohonen, and Widrow had provided fundamental theoretical and experiment results, Hopfield provided an integration and new conceptual framework which has stimulated tremendous interest and growth in neural networks. These contributions include:

- An analogy of *emergent computational properties* of collections of simple neurons with *emergent thermodynamic properties* of collections of particles. Just as the laws of thermodynamics are insensitive to the details of the forces between particles, the collective computations abilities of neural networks are insensitive to changes of detail in Hopfield's model.

- A clear delineation between the perceptron and more general, biologically-inspired neural networks. Perceptrons were connected strictly as "feed forward" devices while Hopfield's circuit incorporates strong back-coupling. Perceptrons used two-state neurons while general neural networks use nonlinear, graded response functions such as the sigmoid. Perceptrons used clocked synchrony while real neural networks operate asynchronously.

- A systematic study of a content addressable memory using a simulated network of model neurons with simple properties. The study determined the storage capacity of an N-neuron system, the nature of errors encountered, and an interpretation of the behavior of the system in terms of a phase space of the neurons states. The study proved that even simple McCulloch-Pitts binary neuron networks were capable of computing using strong feedback.

- A proposed linear electrical circuit (Hopfield circuit) for solving the differential equations of classical neurodynamics. The Hopfield circuit provided the prototype for subsequent implementation of neural networks in VLSI circuits.

- A computational energy argument which proved that a neural network using symmetric connections between neurons will always go "down hill" in phase space and reach an energy minimum corresponding to a problem solution. Thus, Hopfield circuits will always reach a solution (although it may not be an optimum solution) and avoid problems of oscillations.

- The solution of two nonbiological, "hard" problems having combinatorial complexity. These problems included an analog to binary converter and the traveling salesman problem (TSP).

The Hopfield Model

In his 1982 paper, Hopfield used McCulloch-Pitts neurons with two states: $V_i = 0$ ("not firing") and $V_i = 1$ ("firing at maximum rate"). Neuron *i* was connected to neuron *j* by a connection strength T_{ij}, and non-connected neuron pairs had $T_{ij} = 0$. Each neuron i used a step-like transfer function with threshold U_i defined as:

$$\left.\begin{matrix} V_i \rightarrow 1 \\ V_i \rightarrow 0 \end{matrix}\right\} \text{ if } \sum_{j \neq i} T_{ij} V_j \left\{\begin{matrix} > U_i \\ < U_i \end{matrix}\right. \qquad (18.9)$$

The behavior of neural networks consisting of N = 30 neurons and of N = 100 neurons was studied by Monte Carlo techniques. Hopfield found that about 0.15N states can be simultaneously remembered before error in recall becomes severe. When the constraint of $T_{ij} = T_{ji}$ was relaxed, three types of behavior was observed:

- Settling into a minimum energy state in about 4 cycle times
- Limit cycle was occasionally observed: $A \rightarrow B \rightarrow A \rightarrow B\ldots$
- Chaotic wandering in a small region of state space.

In their 1984 neural network model, Hopfield and Tank extend the original work to include nonlinear, graded response neurons with a sigmoid transfer function, f(u), giving the firing rate as a function of the effective input potential u. The electrical characteristics of a given neuron cell i is determined by the cell capacitance, C_i, and the membrane resistance, R_i. The state of the whole neural network of N neurons is described at any one time by the state vector $(u_1, u_2, u_3, \ldots u_N)$. The dynamic behavior of the system is described by a set of coupled, nonlinear differential equations which may be written as:

$$C_i \frac{du_i}{dt} = \sum_{j=1}^{N} T_{ij}\, f_j(u_j) - \frac{u_i}{R_i} + I_i \qquad (i = 1,\ldots,N) \tag{18.10}$$

These are considered the equations of classical neurodynamics and correspond to current balance conditions. They state that the current charging the cell capacitance to voltage u_i is the sum of the synaptic currents from neurons j, minus the leakage current from the i_{th} neuron, plus any input currents I_i from external neurons.

The basic neuron of the Hopfield-Tank circuit is shown in Figure 18-27. This is an operational amplifier which sums the voltage signals form inputs j to produce the current which charges (and discharges) the RC circuit.

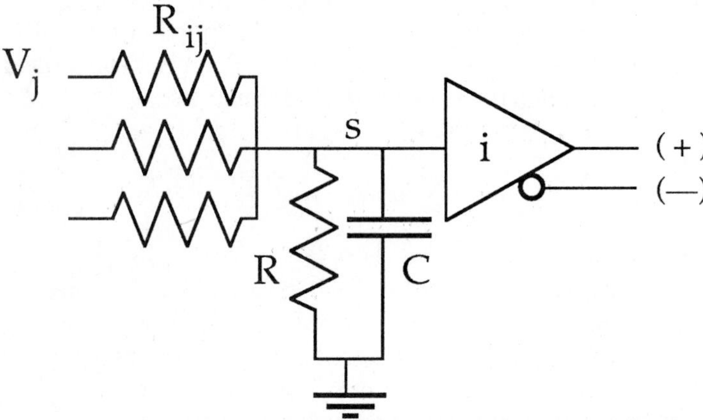

Figure 18-24 Circuit Model for a Hopfield Neuron The weighting resistors R_{ij} link the output of neuron j to the input of neuron i. As long as the voltage at the summing point, $V_s << V_j$, the circuit performs the linear summation of input signals, V_j. The time constant of the circuit is determined by the product of the membrane resistance, R, and the cell capacitance, C. Note the (+) and (–) outputs which provide excitatory and inhibitory signals for feedback to other neurons in the circuit.

These neuron are networked in the "cross-bar" configuration shown in Figure 18-25. Note that the output of each neuron may, in principle, be connected to the input of each other neuron. The excitation may be excitatory (using + output) or inhibitory (using the inverted, – output). The connection from neuron i to neuron j is made through a resistive element of $R_{ij} = 1/T_{ij}$ which sets the weight connecting these two elements. Thus, strong connections (T_{ij} = large) are provided by small resistors and weak connection (T_{ij} = small) by resistors of large value. Note also that most operational amplifiers provide a linear response function between a lower and upper power supply voltage limit, giving in effect a sigmoid transfer function.

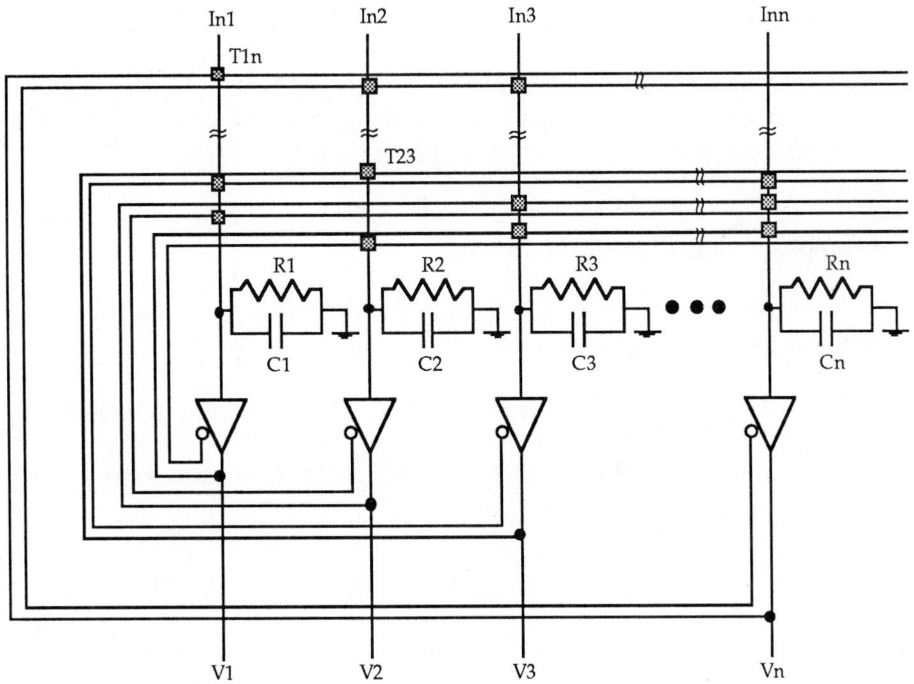

Figure 18-25 Hopfield-Tank Neural Network Circuit Model This model provides a network with powerful computational abilities. The RC network provides integration of the incoming signal, summing the inputs from each network, the weights are determined by fixed resistors linking the output of each neuron with the input of each other, the bipolar output of the amplifier provides excitatory and inhibitory inputs for other neurons, and linear operation of op amps with saturation at ± 15 volts simulates a sigmoid transfer function.

This network of artificial neurons incorporates many of the important features we know about real neurons.

- The input to neuron *i* is the weighted sum of outputs from all other neurons *j*. This provides the maximum possible feedback.

- The transfer function relating the output, $f_i(u_i)$, to the input potential, u_i, for neuron i is approximately sigmoid in shape.

- The frequency response of the neuron is determined by a cell capacitance, C_i, and membrane resistance, R_i. All excitations/-inhibitions are instantaneous in the asynchronous mode of operation.

- The symmetry condition, $T_{ij} \equiv T_{ji}$ may be applied by proper choice of connecting resistors, assuring that the circuit will reach an energy minimum without oscillation.

Accomplishments of Hopfield Circuits

The general approach which Hopfield proposes for solving hard problems by neural networks is outlined as:

1. Construct an energy function, E, for which a minimum corresponds to the solution of the problem. For high gain amplifiers (in which the sigmoid function reduces to a step function), the energy function may be written:

$$E = -\frac{1}{2} \sum_{i;j} T_{ij} V_i V_j - \sum_{j} I_j V_j \qquad (18.11)$$

2. For states of the system representing possible solutions, E should correspond to a cost function to be minimized.

3. Let the system loose, and it will settle into an energy minimum corresponding to an optimal solution.

To illustrate the use of neural networks in solving problems, Hopfield and Tank describe their solution to two interesting problems.

Example: Analog to Binary Converter

The first is an analog to binary (one-to-four-line) converter using seven neurons. Given an analog signal, X, the circuit computes a binary output voltage vector (V_3 V_2 V_1 V_0) which correspond to the analog signal over the decimal range of 0 — 15v. The energy function for this application is given as:

$$E = \frac{1}{2}(X - \sum_{j=0}^{3} 2^j V_j)^2 + \sum_{j=0}^{3} (2^{2j-1}) [V_j(1 - V_j)] \tag{18.12}$$

The first term on the RHS is minimized in a least-squares sense when $X = 8V_3+4V_2+2V_1+V_0$. For instance, a vector $(V_3\ V_2\ V_1\ V_0) = (1\ 1\ 1\ 1)$ corresponds to $X = 15$ in which case the term within parentheses vanishes. The second term constrains the syntax to a set of V_js corresponding to 1 or 0. That is, the second term will vanish when $V_j = 0$ or 1. The result of the analysis yields a connection strength given by:

$$T_{ij} = -2^{(i + j)} \tag{18.13}$$

and an input weight vector, I_i, given by:

$$I_i = (-2^{(2i - 1)} + 2^i X) \tag{18.14}$$

Inserting the proper resistors, R_{ij}, corresponding to the inverse of the weights and setting the input weight vector according to Eqn. 18.14 produces a circuit that accurately converts the analog signal, X, to the correct 4-bit digital vector.

Example: The Traveling Salesman Problem

The traveling salesman problem (TSP) for a small number of cities is readily solved on symbol processing machines by exhaustive search. However, the combinatorial explosion defeats even supercomputers for problems with a large number of cities. For instance, a 30 city problem allows about 3×10^{29} possible solutions. A Connection Machine running at 10 GIPS would take about 10^{12} years to search all these possibilities for the optimum solution using pure exhaustive search. In actual practice, of course, elegant digital algorithms can solve the TSP, obtaining in a reasonable amount of time a better solution than that obtained by neural networks.

The neural network solution to the N-city TSP is simple in both concept and execution. The network structure is best represented by a square $N \times N$ matrix of neurons in which each row correspond to a city and each column corresponds to the relative position (stop) in the TSP tour. The completely connected weight matrix, T_{ij}, requires two types of weights:

1. Inhibitory weights between a given neuron and all others neurons in the same row and column. This will inhibit states corresponding to two "ON" neurons in the same row (a given

city being visited twice) or two "ON" neurons in the same column (the n_{th} stop in the tour assigned to two different cities).

2. Excitatory weights connecting every city with all other cities on all other tour stops. A simple choice of connection resistor connecting city i to city j, R_{ij}, equal to the mileage between cities guarantees an energy function E proportional to the total mileage of the TSP tour. Minimizing this energy function automatically minimizes the total tour length.

With this simple 900 neuron neural network program, Hopfield and Tank were able to find one of the best 10^7 solutions for the 30-city problem in a few time constants of the circuit (about 0.1 second). That is, their circuit can select good solutions and reject bad ones by a factor of greater than 10^{22}.

This performance illustrates two other interesting properties of neural networks.

- Artificial neural networks seem to resemble real neural networks in providing "good enough" solutions rather than "the best" solution. Natural selection provided for the survival of those who could see "well enough" to spot the sabre-toothed tiger and run "fast enough" to escape it. There was no particular survival value in running the four minute mile.

- Noise and statistical fluctuations, generally considered as troublesome and detrimental to the performance of traditional systems, actually improve the performance of neural network computers. The reason is that the Hopfield energy function may have local minima which do not correspond to the global minimum. This is equivalent to the "foothills" problem of the hill-climbing heuristic. A noisy signal or stochastic perturbations of the system can carry the state vector over the lip of the local energy minimum into a more optimal solution.

OTHER APPLICATIONS OF NEURAL NETWORKS

Constraint satisfaction optimization problems such as the two applications above are naturally suited to neural network solution. The range of application, however, is much broader than this class. A scan of recent neural network conference proceeding reveals, among others, the following applications.

- *String parsing in context-free grammar* — A simple algorithm has been developed to convert any context-free grammar into a connectionist network which parses strings in the language defined by that grammar. The system can parse strings of arbitrary but fixed maximum length, n. The network is fast, O(n), and deterministic. It consists of binary units which compute a simple function of their input. When the grammar is expressed in Chomsky normal form, $O(n^3)$ units are needed to parse inputs of length n.[27]

• *Vowel and consonant discrimination* — A Hopfield model of 120 neurons has been applied to the study of problems in automatic discrimination of vowels and consonants. A fast Fourier transform was used to represent the vowel sounds in single syllable words by 120 frequency values. This data was used to generate the connection matrix, T_{ij}. The resulting system performed perfectly on 51 of 64 test runs and came close to the correct state on the remaining 13.[28]

A sampling of papers from the First ICNN proceedings include:[29]

- *Neural Network Solution of the Four Color Problem*
- *A Crew Scheduling Problem*
- *The Airline Marketing Tactician (AMT): An Application of Adaptive Network*
- *RHO-Space: A Neural Network for the Detection and Representation of Oriented Edges*
- *A Connectionist Model for Stereo Vision*
- *Neuromorphic Architecture for Fast Adaptive Robot Control*

One of the most fascinating demonstrations of the capability of neural networks is the work of Terrence Sejnowski (a former student of Hopfield) and Charles Rosenberg on a program that can learn to speak by reading English text.[30] Their neural network simulation program, NETtalk, consists of 203 input units (neurons), 80 hidden units, and 26 output units. The system used a Boltzmann distribution as transfer function and a modified Widrow-Hoff learning algorithm for training the hidden units.

The training data was a phonetic transcription of 1024 words from informal, continuous speech of a first grade child. In the second phase of the experiment, 1000 of the most common words from *Miriam Webster's Pocket Dictionary* were use as training data. The input letters from the transcription were aligned with the desired output phonemes for purposes of training the network. The only "fine tuning" was to insert a "—" for silent letters. Input consisted of a 7-letter window with 29 dedicated neurons representing the 26 letters of the alphabet and three units for encoding punctuation and word boundaries. The 80 hidden units (neurons) formed their own internal representation for mapping input letters to output phonemes by repetitive learning during the training session. The 26 output units consisted of 21 articulatory phonemes and five units for encoding stress and syllable boundaries. Training sessions consisted of repeated reading of the input transcription at the rate of about 2 letters/second on a VAX 11/780 FPA.

The results of the training sessions were played through an amplifier and speaker. In the authors' words:

> *"The distinction between vowels and consonants was made early; however, the network predicted the same vowel for all vowels and the same consonant for all consonants, which resulted in a babbling sound. A second stage occurred when word boundaries are recognized, and the output then resembled pseudowords. After just a few passes through the network many of the words were intelligible, and by 10 passes the text was understandable."*

After 50 training passes using the child's data, the system achieved a 95% accuracy for mapping English text into speech. In the experiment with words from Webster's Dictionary, a 98% accuracy was obtained through the use of 120 hidden units. Skeptics might argue that the system just "memorizing" the training words rather than "truly learning to speak English". To test the generalization of the machine learning process taking place in NETtalk, the researchers submitted a 439 word continuation of text from the same speaker. The performance was 78%, indicating that much of the learning was transferred to novel words even after a small sample of English words.

18.8 ISSUES IN NEURAL NETWORKS AND AI

The student may ask: If neural networks have all these wonderful features such as self-organization and learning, why aren't researchers in traditional symbol-oriented AI all switching to the network paradigm? One answer is: Many are! The first ICNN attracted nearly 2000 participants, and the second is expected to attract 4,000—5,000, the same number as the national AAAI conference on traditional AI.

A more realistic answer is that neural network research, just as traditional symbol-oriented research, faces extremely difficult problems and challenges. Below we discuss some of these problems, and make some suggestions for resolving the differences between the two research communities.

• *Programming neural networks is difficult* — The Hopfield circuit provides feedback from the output of one neuron to the input of all other connected neurons through resistors. Each constraint satisfaction problem must be "hand wired" just as early AI applications were often *ad hoc* in nature. In order to implement the Hopfield circuit as a general purpose VLSI chip, it is necessary to include some type of programmable resistor for varying connection strengths. This is essential for most learning algorithms and also in order to use the same chip for different problems. Even with a convenient, well-engineered neural network simulation program, it was necessary to make $O(N^2)$ lateral inhibitory connections and $O(N^3)$ diagonal excitatory connections by hand to solve the N-city TSP.

• *Learning in neural networks is hard* — Just as in traditional, symbol-oriented AI, the dramatic success of neural networks on the smaller problems such as associative memories has been difficult or impossible to scale to larger, "real-world" problems. One of the most difficult problems is the design of effective learning algorithms. At the heart of the problem is the choice of knowledge representation to use in the hidden units connecting input to output neurons. Just as success in representing knowledge in symbols has proven the key to useful applications in traditional AI, successfully representing knowledge in circuits is the key to problem solving with neural networks.

• *For many applications, symbol-based knowledge provides superior performance to circuit-based knowledge* — Expert systems are an obvious example of a highly successful application of symbol-based knowledge, although James Anderson of Brown University has successfully implemented MYCIN in a neural network. Even for pattern detection tasks, traditional methods may be best. A direct comparison of matched filter processing and neural networks for detecting lines in images proved the matched filter superior to a Hopfield associative memory in computational efficiency.[31]

• *Neural networks may have been oversold* — As impressive as are some of the recent neural network experiments, they have not greatly surpassed the accomplishments of Professor Widrow's MADALINE of more than 25 years ago. Again, neural networks are not immune from many of the problems relating to the combinatorial explosion of solutions which continue to plague symbol-based approaches.

SOME OBSERVATIONS AND SUGGESTIONS

1. Neural networks have proven valuable in performing what is often called "low level" cognitive processing, particularly in such areas as pattern recognition and content addressable memory. These are areas which have proven particularly difficult for "high level" symbol-oriented approaches. Our suggestion is that the optimum architecture for future intelligent machines will involve the integration of low-level circuit-based pattern recognition modules with high level symbol-based control and inference engines. Research has not even begun on what design considerations are required for such an integration.

2. If, indeed, the optimum path to the design of intelligent machines is to create them "in the image of Man" (integrating circuit-based detectors with symbol-based reasoning), a tremendous research effort is required to determine which approach is most applicable for which problems. Digital circuits compute and neural networks compute, as we have shown, but some tasks are most naturally suited for one mode of computing and some for the other. As the capabilities of neural networks become manifest, serious attention should be given to the task of mapping the unresolved tasks of AI into one of the three categories of knowledge representation:

- Symbol-based Knowledge
- Circuit-based Knowledge
- Hybrid Symbol/Circuit-based Knowledge

3. Neural network and symbol-based AI researchers should "bury the hatchet." While there are serious differences within both the symbol sect of AI and the connectionist sect of AI, the disagreements between the two sects is particularly virulent. Marvin Minsky, whose recent book *Society of Mind*[32] is one of the most poetic and elegant expositions of many fundamental neural network concepts, refuses to use the term "neural network" even once in the book. In fact, referring to both perceptrons and present commercial neural network programs, Minsky recently stated, "They couldn't do an exclusive-OR then and they can't do one now."[33]

Such comments are not well taken by the neural network community but help one understand hyperbole such as that from Bart Kosko, Chairman of ICNN-87, "Artificial intelligence is dead — Long live neural networks!"

If such exchanges inspire the *competitive* spirit of researchers to work harder to understand their systems and harness them for intelligent behavior, perhaps they serve a useful purpose. However, we suspect that the problems of AI are so difficult that they will require the best *cooperative* efforts of both schools of thought to realize the goals of AI. Neural network researchers need critical analyses of their systems such as Minsky and Papert offered in 1969 for the Perceptron of the early 1960s. Symbol-oriented researchers need to appreciate the elegance, simplicity, and speed with which neural networks can solve many of the low level cognition tasks which have stymied workers in the fields of vision, speech analysis, and pattern recognition. And certainly the integration of low level neural network modules in high level symbol-based machines will require the cooperation of scientists in both areas.

4. Finally, the Physical Symbol System Hypothesis should be reexamined in light of recent results of neural network research. Questions which neural network research raise include: Should learning of the form demonstrated by Sejnowski's NETtalk be classified as intelligent behavior? Can distributed patterns such as the memories stored in a BAM be considered symbols? Can knowledge be stored in an analog content addressable memory?

Symbol systems, by their very nature, require discrete tokens for representation. That is, the token is the symbol which represents some object, quantity, action, or concept. By no stretch of the imagination or abuse of the language can the memory of the face of a childhood friend be considered a symbol, although, of course, a name could be associated with the face. The name then becomes the symbol, but the faint image of the face remains a very weak pattern of neural activations within the brain. The manipulation, processing, and recall of this memory, we would claim, is intelligent behavior which involves symbol processing only in assignment of a name token (if at all).

Research on artificial neural networks indicates that these systems share, by design, many of the characteristics of the brain. To the extent that artificial neural networks exhibit behavior such as recall, association, classification, and learning which we consider intelligent in humans, it would seem reasonable to conclude that non-symbolic intelligent processes exist.

Once the artificial intelligence community acknowledges that intelligence can be achieved through both symbol manipulation and non-symbolic processes, much of the controversy will die away. Many of the knotty problems of AI will yield more rapidly if the two schools of thought cooperate in sharing their perspectives, understanding, and techniques.

PROBLEMS AND PROGRAMS

18-1. Compare the speed of operation of the basic human computing element, the neuron, with that of the basic computing machine. Carefully indicate the measure of time you use for the neuron. For the measure of computing speed, should you use the clock rate, MIPS, MFLOPS, or logical inferences per second? Indicate the source of your information for both numbers.

18-2. Compare the size of the basic human computing element, the neuron with the corresponding machine computing element. Assume that there are 10^{10} neurons in the human brain. What is the corresponding digital machine element? Justify your answer and indicate the source of your information.

18-3. Compare the duty cycle of a typical memory location of a Commodore-64 (64K memory) with that of a typical Apollo work station with 5 Mb memory.

18-4. Compare the performance of memory recall from the database of a typical digital machine with that from human memory as additional information is stored in each. What conclusions can you draw from this comparison?

18-5. The central principle of the connectionist school is that intelligence can emerge from the collective action of a large number of non-intelligent neurons. Compare this concept with the emergence of thermodynamic laws from the mass action of millions of molecules. Clearly distinguish thermodynamic variables from individual particle variables.

18-6. Compute the speed advantage of communicating with optical fibers with index of refraction $n = 1.4$ compared to communicating with a coaxial copper cable on which the signal propagation velocity is $0.67\,c$. Will using light communication with optical fibers lift the limitations imposed by the Einstein bottleneck?

18-7. The structural limits to the speed of computer were described in the text as the *Babbage bottleneck* and the *von Neumann bottleneck*. In what ways do these bottlenecks differ and in what ways are they connected?

18-8. Is the *Feigenbaum bottleneck* a limitation imposed by machine hardware or by our ability to represent data? How might machine learning solve or relieve this bottleneck?

18-9. Randall Davis and Ken Wilson take diametrically opposite views on the issue of the value of massively parallel machines for solving AI (or, for that matter, *any*) problems. Summarize their positions and your own and give reasons for your choice.

18-10. The text classifies all massively parallel computers into the two categories summarized by: (i) digital and (ii) analog. Qualify this distinction, and list other characteristics for these two classes of machine.

18-11. How might the nature of the problem affect the choice of the optimal granularity of a parallel digital system? Give an example illustrating your arguments.

18-12. Discuss the advantages and disadvantages of the three classes of topology for digital architectures: ring, nearest neighbor mesh, and hypercube.

18-13. Compare and contrast the Arvind Data-flow Machine architecture shown in Figure 18-9 with that of the Hopfield network shown in Figure 18-25. What advantages do such dynamic, re-entrant networks have over static networks?

18-14. What are the basic differences between SIMD and MIMD control modes for parallel machines? Which is a subset of the other, which is most flexible, and what limits the performance of MIMD machines?

18-15. Discuss the design criteria and basic features of The Connection Machine. For what applications are they being used?

18-16. Which of the design principles of neural network computers is most at odds with the Physical Symbol System hypothesis of AI?

18-17. What is the empirical evidence for the *100-step program constraint* for neural network systems?

18-18. Write a brief history of neural networks and discuss the parallel with the history of traditional AI. What role did the book, *Perceptrons*, play in this history? How does the present state of neural network research reflect this history?

18-19. What events rescued neural networks from the doldrums of the 1970s? In what order of importance would you list these events?

18-20. List the basic design parameters for a neural network system and indicate what choice of parameter was selected for the Hopfield network.

18-21. What role do hidden units play in neural networks? Does the Hopfield circuit employ hidden units?

18-22. The text indicates that *synchrony, symmetry,* and *feedback* are closely related concepts for neural networks. Discuss these relationships and illustrate your discussion graphically.

18-23. Hopfield has said that the essential ingredient for computational abilities in neural networks is the non-linear transfer function (sigmoid distribution). What is the basis for this statement?

18-24. Interpret the perceptron learning rule as a hill-climbing algorithm.

18-25. Given the two (A,B) patterns:

$$A_1 = (1\ 1\ 1\ 0\ 0) \qquad B_1 = (0\ 1\ 0\ 1\ 0)$$
$$A_2 = (1\ 0\ 1\ 0\ 1) \qquad B_2 = (0\ 1\ 1\ 1\ 0)$$

calculate the BAM connection matrix, W, for encoding these two pattern pairs.

18-26. Using the weight matrix, W, from exercise 18-38, verify the error tolerance of the associated memory by the following three experiments: (1) flip one bit of A_1 selected at random and observe what B pattern is recalled; (2) flip two bits of A_1 and repeat; (3) flip 3 bits of A_1 and repeat. What are your conclusions on fault tolerance of the system?

18-27. Verify the "truth table" for the XOR circuit shown in Figure 18-22 and the four elementary logic gates shown in Figure 18-23 for each of two transfer functions: (i) step function with threshold at 0.5, and (ii) graded linear function with threshold at 0.5 and a slope of 1.

REFERENCES AND FOOTNOTES

1 Torrero, Edward A. (ed), *Next-Generation Computers*, p. 81, IEEE Spectrum Series, New York, NY (1985)

2 Torrero, Edward A. (ed), *Op cit*, p. 81

3 The author is indebted to British environmental activist, Amory Lovins for this analogy drawn from the nuclear energy controversy. Lovins compared the use of high-grade electricity for such mundane tasks as space heating to cutting butter with a chainsaw, an analogy with which the author does not agree.

4 Uhr, Leonard, *Multi-Computer Architectures for Artificial Intelligence: Toward Fast, Robust, Parallel Systems*, 358 pp., John Wiley & Sons, New York, NY (1987)

5 Wu, Chuan-lin and Feng, Tse-yun (eds), *Interconnection Networks for Parallel and Distributed Processing*, 647 pp., IEEE Computer Society Press, Silver Spring, MD (1984)

6 Dertouzos, Michael L., "Harnessing Computers Together," *Technology Review*, pp. 44–57, February/March (1986)

7 Backus, John, "Function-level Computing," in *Computers for Artificial Intelligence Applications*, Benjamin Wah and G.-J. Li (eds), pp. 62–67, IEEE Computer Society Press, Washington D.C., (1986)

8 Hillis, W. Daniel, *The Connection Machine*, MIT Press, Cambridge, MA (1985)

9 Gabriel, Richard P., "Massively Parallel Computers: The Connection Machine and NON-VON," *Science* **231**, pp. 975–978 (1986)

10 Hillis, W. Daniel, "The Connection Machine," *Scientific American* **256**, pp. 108–115, June (1987)

11 Hopfield, J. J., *Op Cit* (1982)

12 Hebb, D. O., *The Organization of Behavior*, John Wiley and Sons, New York, NY (1949)

13 Rosenblatt, F., *Principles of Neurodynamics*, p. 596, Spartan Books,

New York, NY (1962)

14 Minsky, Marvin and Papert, Seymour, *Perceptrons — An Introduction to Computational Geometry*, p. 242, The MIT Press, Cambridge, MA (1969) See also, *Perceptrons — Expanded Edition* (1988)

15 Widrow, B. and Hoff, M. E. "Adaptive Switching Circuits," *Institute of Radio Engineers, Western Electronic Show and Convention, Convention Record, Part* **4**, pp. 96–104 (1960)

16 Grossberg, Stephen, *Studies of mind and brain: Neural principles of learning, perception, development, cognition, and motor control*, Reidel Press, Boston, MA (1982) and *The Adaptive Brain*, Vols. I and II, North Holland, Amsterdam, (1987)

17 Anderson, J. A. and Hinton, G. E. (eds), *Parallel models of associative memory*, Lawrence Erlbaum and Associates, Hillsdale, NJ (1981)

18 Fukushima, K. "Cognitron: A Self-organizing multilayered neural network," *Biological Cybernetics* **20**, pp. 121–136 (1975)

19 Kohonen, T., *Associative Memory: A system theoretical approach*, Springer-Verlag, New York, NY 1977) and *Self-organization and associative memory*, Springer-Verlag, Berlin (1984)

20 Hopfield, John J. and Tank, David W., "Computing with Neural Circuits: A Model," *Science* **233**, pp. 625–633, (1986)

21 Rumelhart, David E. and McClelland, James L. (eds), *Parallel Distributed Processing — Explorations in the Microstructure of Cognition*, Volume 1 – 3, MIT Press, Cambridge, MA (1986)

22 Denker, John S. (ed), *Neural Networks for Computing, AIP Conference Proceedings* **151**, American Institute of Physics, New York, NY (1986)

23 Hinton, Goeffrey E., Sejnowski, Terrence J., and Ackley, David H., "Boltzmann Machines: Constraint Satisfaction Networks that Learn," Technical Report CMU-CS-84-119, Carnegie Mellon University, Pittsburgh, PA (1984)

24 Kosko, Bart, "Constructing an Associative Memory," *BYTE* **12**, pp. 137–144, September (1987)

25 The program use here was MacBrain™ which is available from Neuronics, Inc., Box 738, Cambridge, MA 02142

26 The learning algorithm in the early version of MacBrain used here also connected ON neurons to nearby OFF neurons with non-zero weights. These weights were surgically removed by a lobotomy, i.e. by manually setting all ON-OFF neuron connections to zero.

27 Fanty, M. A., "Context-free Parsing with Connectionist Networks," *AIP Conference Proceedings* **151**, *Op Cit*

28 Gold, Bernard, "Hopfield Model Applied to Vowel and Consonant Discrimination," *AIP Conference Proceedings* **151**, *op cit*

29 Caudill, Maureen, and Butler, Charles (eds), *Proceedings of the First International Conference on Neural Networks*, 2670 pp., IEEE, San Diego, CA (1987)

30 Sejnowski, Terrence J. and Rosenberg, Charles, R., "Parallel Networks that Learn to Pronounce English Text," *Complex Systems* **1**, pp. 145–168 (1987)

31 Grant, P. M., and Sage, J. P., "A comparison of neural network and matched filter processing for detecting lines in images," *AIP Conference Proceedings* **151**, *Op Cit*

32 Minsky, Marvin, *The Society of Mind*, Simon and Schuster, New York, NY (1986)

33 Minsky, Marvin, as quoted by R. Colin Johnson, "Neural Networks Naive, Says Minsky," *Electronic Engineering Times*, p. 41, August 3, (1987)

Appendices

Appendix A:

INTRODUCTION TO PROGRAMMING IN LISP

by

Yong Y. Auh[§]

A.1 Getting Started

LISP is a language which has been used in artificial intelligence and other areas of computer science for symbolic processing and the study of computational models. It was invented in the late fifties and has been evolving ever since. During its evolution, many "dialects" have been created. Just like dialects of human languages, some of them are close enough that speakers of those dialects have no problem understanding each other while some of them may occasionally have trouble communicating with each other because of idiosyncratic words and phrases. However, they are still dialects of one language. They all share the same core structure and are essentially based on a small set of primitives. For this reason they are easily inter-translatable. Of course there could be exceptions. For example, hardware dependent features may pose problems for translators. For most cases, however, the differences are marginal. That is why we can still talk about "the LISP language."

This article is intended to provide a basic introduction to programming in LISP while covering important features of the language at the same time. Since there are many dialects and many implementations on a variety of computer systems ranging from 8-bit machines to supercomputers, selection of a dialect suitable for everyone's needs is almost impossible. In this article, we choose a dialect called Scheme, originally developed by G. Steele and G. Sussman of MIT in the mid seventies. Because it is clean, small, yet powerful, it is now being used in many educational institutions. Also excellent implementations are available for a variety of computers including personal computers such as the Macintosh and IBM PC. They are quite affordable, too.

Most of the examples in this article can run on other dialects with little or no modification.

This article is not a survey of common language features. Rather we are trying to motivate the necessity of new constructs with an emphasis on a functional style of programming.

Before we get started, a friendly note for experienced programmers may be in order. People who have extensive programming experience with conventional programming languages such as Pascal, C, Fortran, or Basic could have some difficulty understanding the LISP way of programming. Since LISP is a rather different kind of language, imposing preconceived notions from conventional programming languages may not be helpful for proper understanding of LISP. Good programmers of conventional languages can become good LISP programmers too, but it will require a somewhat different mental framework. Good advice for experienced programmers would be that they should try to be as naive and open-minded as possible. Pretend that you know nothing about programming languages, at least for a while. Your expertise in other languages will come in handy later. Until then you are just a student with a bright eager mind.

If you have never done any programming before, and have no idea what "loop" means, and what "integer variable", etc., mean, no need to worry. LISP is great as one's first programming language. In fact, it is highly recommended that one learn LISP before any other language. It provides a very good foundation for understanding of various programming models.

A.2 LISP is Expression-Oriented.

In order to make it easy to understand basic principles underlying the LISP language, we review how we use our ordinary mathematical expressions.

What is the meaning of the symbol "3"? Of course, it is the number three. We could have used the Roman numeral "III" to refer to the same number. We call the symbols for numbers *numerals*. That is, numerals refer to their corresponding numbers. Surely we all know that. It's so self-evident that nobody bothers to say it.

Now consider "2 + 1". Is it a symbol? "2" is a symbol, and so are "+" and "1". "2 + 1" is a meaningful composition of symbols. Let's call symbols and meaningful compositions of them "expressions." So an expression is either a simple symbol or a meaningful composition of symbols and expressions. While "2 + 1" is an expression, "2 +" is not.

There must be some rules for constructing meaningful expressions.

Different languages have different rules for composition of meaningful expressions. For now, we focus on the informal expressions our ordinary mathematical discourse. Although we could formally describe the rules for mathematical expressions, that's not of our immediate concern. We are more interested in how to get the meanings of complex expressions. Getting back to the example "2 + 1", what does this expression mean? Probably most of you would answer that it is three. If you write the answer on paper, you may write "3". What is the relationship between the expressions "2 + 1" and "3"? Does the expression "2 + 1" mean the expression "3"? No, surely not. They are just two different ways of referring to the same number.

According to the normal meanings of the expressions "2", "+" and "1", the complex expression "2 + 1" means the number three. And the expression "3" also means the number three. In fact, there are infinitely many expressions which mean the number three: 4 – 1, 5 – 2, etc. However, the symbol "3" seems to have some sort of advantage over other expressions which mean the same number in that it is the simplest expression among them. For each number, there are infinitely many expressions referring to it. But there is one simple symbol referring to it. One of the things LISP systems do is, given an expression, find a simplest expression which has the same meaning as the given one. In essence, LISP is a system which tries to find the meaning of an expression and print an expression which has the same meaning. The process of finding an expression's meaning is called ***evaluation***. So "2 + 1" is evaluated to "3", or $2 + 1 \to 3$, in symbols.

Now let's consider a different type of mathematical expression. How do we understand the phrase "add2(x) = x + 2"? It is a definition of a function named "add2", which adds 2 to its argument. So the meaning of the expression "add2" is a mathematical function. Then what is the meaning of "add2(2)"? According to the definition of "add2", add2(2) will be equal to "2 + 2", i.e., 4.

If we provide definitions of functions to the system, and use the functions together with arguments, we get complex expressions. Evaluation of complex expressions will produce their meanings. LISP systems are typically interactive systems which accept users' new definitions, and use them when evaluating complex expressions by first evaluating the arguments and then applying the definition (or meaning) of the function to the results.

However complicated an expression might be, the same principle of functional application applies. For example, in order to evaluate "add2(add2(2))", we first evaluate "add2(2)", which is 4. And then we evaluate "add2(4)", which is 6. Since we gave the definition of "add2" to the LISP system, it can figure out the meaning of complex expressions such as "add2(add2(add2(0)))", and so on. The system just figures out the meaning of the argument, "add2(add2(0))" first, and then uses that to get the meaning of the whole expression.

The essence of programming in LISP is in defining new functions as needed. Since there is no function designated as the "main" function, they can be reused in many different ways. In order to write a "program", we define new functions and collect some pre-defined ones, and then apply some "top-level" function to a list of initial arguments.

A.3 Syntax of LISP is Simple and Consistent

In ordinary mathematical locutions, some function symbols are put between their arguments: e.g., "3 + 2". But most new definitions such as "add2" come before the argument(s). The notation of putting a function symbol between its arguments is called *infix notation*, and that of putting a function symbol before its arguments is called *prefix notation*. Ordinarily, we use both infix and prefix notations. However, every infix notation can be replaced by a prefix version: e.g., +(3, 2) instead of 3 + 2. We can thus use prefix notation exclusively. Almost all LISP systems use a variation of this prefix notation. But, instead of writing +(3, 2), we can write (+ 3 2). This notation is called *Cambridge Polish* notation. In this notational system, a function application expression is a list of a function expression and its arguments enclosed by a pair of matching parentheses. The function expression and its arguments are separated by spaces instead of commas. This notation is simple and consistent. In any complex expression, the first item refers to a function. (*Note: This statement is not exactly correct when macros and special forms are considered. After all macro expansions are done, the first item will be either a special form such as if or a function expression.*)

A.4 LISP Systems are Interactive

LISP systems wait for the user to type an expression, evaluate it, and print the result for the user to see. And then this process is continuously repeated. Typically, there is a special marker indicating that the system is waiting for the user to type in some expression. This marker is called a *prompt*. (Most computer operating systems have such a process. For example, MS-DOS prints its system prompt, say A>, and executes what the user types in, and then prints the prompt again.)

Now you should try some simple examples on your system of

choice. Start your system, and when you see the prompt, type "(+ 1 2)" and hit the carriage return or some specified key to tell the system to start evaluating it. (">>>" is assumed to be the prompt.)

```
>>> (+ 1 2)
3
>>> 3
3
>>> (* 456 789)
359784
>>>
```

As you can see from the example, the system finds the meaning of the expression "(+ 1 2)" and writes the result using the simple symbol "3", and then prints the prompt again. This process of printing a prompt, reading an expression, evaluating it, and printing the result is the so-called ***read-eval-print*** loop.

Exercise: Try the following examples:

```
(* 3 4), (* 3 (* 2 2)), (+ (* 4 5) (- 7 1))
```

In order to define new functions, we do as follows:

```
>>> (define (add2  x) (+ x 2))
add2
>>> (add2  4)
6
```

Exercise: Translate the following function definitions in LISP syntax and try some examples on your system.

square(x) = x * x
average(x, y) = (x + y) / 2

A.5 LISP Provides Predicates and Conditional Expressions.

In order to define more varieties of functions, we need some constructs other than simple function application. Take, for example, the following function:

max(x, y) = x	if x > y
= y	otherwise

In order to express this function we need a conditional expression and predicates which indicate true or false conditions. LISP provides such constructs. In fact, they are quite similar in form to those

Most Scheme implementations provide a rich set of mathematical functions. The following is just a representative set of mathematical predicates and functions. Refer to your system's manual for more detail.

<u>Predicates</u>

(number? obj) →	#!t if obj is a number, #!f otherwise
(< n1 n2) →	#!t if n1 is less than n2, #!f otherwise
(<= n1 n2) →	#!t if n1 is less than or equal to n2, #!f otherwise
(= n1 n2) →	#!t if n1 is equal to n2, #!f otherwise
(<> n1 n2) →	#!t if n1 is not the same as n2, #!f otherwise
(>= n1 n2) →	#!t if n1 is greater than or equal to n2, #!f otherwise

<u>Functions</u>

+	–	*
/	1+ (or add1)	1– (or sub1)
max	min	quotient
remainder	modulo	ceiling
floor	round	truncate
gcd	lcm	acos
asin	atan	cos
exp	expt	log
sin	sqrt	tan

above. The "max" example can be translated as follows:

```
(define (max x y)
      (if (> x y) x y))
```

If we are interested in the result of applying a predicate, say, ">", we can just type:

```
>>> (> 3 2)
#!t        ;  #!true, or t can be printed depending
           ;  on systems.
>>> (> 3 2)
()         ; or #!f or #!false
```

Oh, by the way, anything typed after a semicolon like these lines is understood as comments. Comments are ignored by programming language processors. Almost all programming languages provide some way of inserting comments into program texts. LISP is no exception.

A.6 LISP Provides Good Numerical Processing Facilities

The *if-expression* combined with predicates allows us to define many new functions. We will define some here. Take a look at the factorial function. It is defined as

$$
\begin{aligned}
n! &= 1 & \text{if } n = 0 \\
&= n*(n-1)! & \text{otherwise}
\end{aligned}
$$

In other words, if n is 0, 0! is defined as 1, and for other numbers, factorial of n is n times the factorial of n–1. Notice that the factorial symbol we are defining is used on the right hand side of the definition, too. It looks dangerously like a circular definition. But such definitions are ubiquitous, and they are called recursive function definitions. In LISP, recursive functions are as natural as any other functions. In fact, learning to use recursive functions without fear is the single most important step in good LISP programming. So we will try some more examples. Before we leave the factorial example behind, let's express it in the LISP syntax.

```
(define (factorial n)
    (if (= n 0)
        1
        (* n (factorial (- n 1)))))
```

Let's review some exemplary mathematical functions and express them in the LISP syntax. Some examples may be already present in your system, and you may not be able to redefine them. In that case, try different names, e.g., "my-*" instead of "*".

(1) Exponential function (positive)

n^p = 1	if p = 0
= n*(n^(p–1))	otherwise

```
(define (^ n p)
    (if (= 0 p)
        1
        (* n (^ n (- p 1)))))
```

(2) Recursive definition of * (positive multiplication) in terms of + function

x*n = 0	if n = 0
= x + x*(n–1)	otherwise

```
(define (* x n)
    (if (= 0 n)
        0
        (+ x (* x (- n 1)))))
```

(3) Remainder

remainder(x, y) = x–y	if x–y < x
= remainder(x–y, y)	otherwise

(4) Greatest common divisor

gcd(x, y) = x	if y = 0
= gcd(y, remainder(x, y))	otherwise

(5) Fibonacci sequence

fib(n) = 1	if n = 0 or 1
= fib(n–2) + fib(n–1)	otherwise

```
(define (fib n)
   (if (or (= n 0) (= n 1))
       1
       (+ (fib (- n 2)) (fib (- n 1)))))
```

As we saw above, you can define any mathematical function with LISP. There are some LISP systems which provide numerical processing as good as Fortran. With LISP, we don't worry about numerical overflow. Try 1000!. With most conventional programming languages, we have to specify the size of the result even before the computation! (How are we supposed to know the size of the result before computation?) LISP systems automatically allocate enough space for bigger numbers. Of course, they provide floating point numbers, too. However, we don't specify types of numbers for the function definitions. This brings us to an important point. In LISP, expressions are not typed, but the objects they refer to are of course typed. When we define functions, we don't specify the types of their arguments as in Pascal, C, etc.

> Exercise: How would you express *trib(n)* in the following sequence of numbers?
>
> Tribonacci sequence: 1, 1, 1, 3, 5, 9, 17, ...

A.7 Recursion is a Method of Problem Decomposition

In section A.4, we saw some examples of recursive functions. It is important to realize that recursion can be considered as a method of problem decomposition. For example, in order to compute *n!*, we first compute *(n-1)!* and then multiply the result by *n*. In the case of the Fibonacci sequence, in order to compute the n'th term, we first get the n-2'th and n-1'th terms, and then add them together. Recursion, in other words, can be viewed as just a special case of defining auxiliary functions to handle smaller problems.

A.8 LISP is Well-Suited for Symbol Processing

Although we can use LISP exclusively for number crunching, LISP's fame is primarily due to its symbol processing capability. What is symbol processing any way? In the previous sections, we discussed expressions and their meanings, or the things the expressions refer to. In a very important sense, expressions represent objects. They are symbolic representations of objects. Quite often, by manipulating the representations, we can achieve what's intended. As an example, consider typical computer representations of numbers and numerical operations on them. Numbers are represented as sequences of bits, and by manipulating on the sequences of bits (such as shift, etc.) we can do addition, multiplication, and so on. Since most AI problems are nonnumerical, we can appreciate why symbolic processing is important for AI.

When we try to solve a problem, we first need to express the problem, and design a suitable representation of the problem. And then by manipulating the representation, we can get the desired solution which must be expressed in an understandable form.

As an example, let's consider rational numbers. Each rational number can be represented as a fraction, e.g., 2/3, 1/1, etc. How would we represent them so that we can do operations such as addition and multiplication on them? Note that we are already using symbolic representation of rational numbers, that is, the numerator followed by "/" and the denominator. Given a sequence of a numerator, "/", and a denominator, we understand what rational number it represents. As long as we have a common understanding, we could use some other representation, say a list of the symbol "rational" followed by a numerator and a denominator: e.g., 2/3 is represented as "(rational 2 3)". "(rational 2 3)" is more verbose than 2/3, but we understand what it means. We also can find out, given a representation of a rational number, its numerator and denominator by checking its second and third elements, respectively. In LISP programs, objects are typically represented as *lists*, and functions are defined to manipulate the representations. Thus LISP systems provide various predicates and functions to facilitate list processing.

<u>Basic List Processing Constructs:</u>

(null? <obj>) → #!t if <obj> is a list, #!f otherwise

(car <list-obj>) → the first element of the <list-obj>

(cdr <list-obj>) → the rest of the <list-obj> except the first element

(cons <obj-1> <obj-2>) → a pair <pair> such that (car <pair>) is <obj-1> and (cdr <pair>) is <obj-2>

(list <obj-1> ... <obj-n>) → a list of the objects

( ), nil → constant referring to the empty list.

In order to build a list of numbers, we use *list*. *list* can be used with any number of arguments: e.g., (list 1) → (1), (list 1 2 3) → (1 2 3), etc. Lists can be embedded in other lists: e.g., (list 4 (list 1) (list 2)) → (4 (1) (2)). The empty list is represented naturally by "( )". But because of tradition, *nil* also refers to the empty list. Given a list, we can add a number or list as its first element. *Cons* does this job: (cons 1 (list 2 3)) → (1 2 3), (cons 2 ( )) → (2), etc.

Given a list, we can check if it's empty or not by using the predicate *null?*: "(null? ( ))" is true, while "(null? (list 2 3))" is not.

Given a list, we should be able to get access to its elements. *Car* and *cdr* are for that. *Car* is a function which refers to the first object of a list: (car (list 1 2 3)) → 1, (car (list (list 7 9) 8)) → (7 9), etc. On the other hand, *cdr* of a list refers to the rest of the list excluding its first element: (cdr (list 1 2 3)) → (2 3), (cdr (list (list 7 9) 8)) → (8).

Let's define the function *second* which returns the second element of any list provided it has at least two elements. Note that the second element of any list, *lst*, is the first element of (cdr lst). So we should write: (define (second lst) (car (cdr lst))). How about *third* and *fourth*? We leave these as exercises.

It would be nice to have a more general function which takes a list, *lst*, and a number, *n*, and returns the *n*'th element of *lst*. However, before defining this function, to get more practice, let's try the *length-of* function which computes lengths of lists. Note that (length-of ( )) = 0, and (length-of (list 1)) = 1. If a list doesn't have any element, its length is 0, and the length of a non-null list will be equal to the length of the cdr of the list plus 1. So we can define it as follows:

```
(define (length-of lst)
    (if (null? lst)
        0
        (+ 1 (length-of (cdr lst)))))
```

Since we will be working with lists a lot, and recursion on the structure of lists will be a very important tool for programming, it is very important to understand this example. Now let's try the general *nth-element* function. (nth-element (list 1 2 3) 1) will be 1, (nth-element (list 1 2 3) 2) will be 2, and so on. Note that (nth-element (list 1 2 3) 2) is the same as (nth-element (cdr (list 1 2 3)) 1). So using a very similar idea, we define the function as:

```
(define (nth-element lst n)
   (if (= 1 n)
       (car lst)
       (nth-element (cdr lst) (- n 1))))
```

A.9 How to Name Names

In the previous section, we discussed a way of representing rational numbers, i.e., representing 2/3 as (rational 2 3) for example. The trouble is if you type it as it is after the system prompt, the system will assume that "rational" is a name for a function since it occupies the first position of the expression. For example:

```
>>> (rational 2 3)
Undefined procedure: rational
```

In LISP there is a way to tell the system that what we mean is a list instead of function application. Try the following:

```
>>> (quote (rational 2 3))
(rational 2 3)
```

We can find such constructs in the English language, too. Compare the following sentences:

(a) New York is the largest city in the US.
(b) 'New York' has seven letters in it.

In (a), *New York* refers to the city while in (b), *'New York'* refers to the name of the city. In (b) the name is *quoted*! The notation of quoting is used to form another expression referring to the quoted name. LISP's *quote* has the same meaning. Try:

```
>>> (quote x)
x
```

Since we work with lots of lists in LISP programs, LISP provides a handy way of quoting expressions just like English's single quote.

```
>>> 'x
x
>>> '(1 2 3)
(1 2 3)
>>> '(rational 2 3)
(rational 2 3)
```

Internally, '(1 2) is the same as (quote (1 2)). Therefore, the following two expressions have different meanings.

```
>>> '(1 (2))
(1 (2))
>>> '(1 '(2))
(1 (quote (2)))
```

Thus we can form names of names, names of names of names, and so on.

We know how to define new functions using *define.* The same *define* can be used to define variables to have values:

```
>>> (define lst-1 (list 1 2 3))
lst-1
>>> lst-1
(1 2 3)
>>> (car lst-1)
1
>>> (cdr lst-1)
(2 3)
```

As we have seen, lists are constructed from basic objects like numbers and other lists. Basic objects are called *atoms,* and they are fundamental building blocks of lists. Any number is an atom, any quoted simple expression is an atom. So *rational* is referring to an atom. There is a predicate *atom?* which checks the type of the argument.

```
>>> (atom? 'x)
#!t
>>> (atom? '(1 2))
()
```

Note that the system will say *( )* instead of *false.* In LISP, *( )* plays many roles. It means *false* because it's equivalent to 0, and it means an empty list. So *( )* is both an atom and a list.

Among numbers we can test equality with =, and among atoms in general, *eq?* tests equality.

```
>>> (eq? 1 1)
#!t
>>> (eq? 'a 'a)
#!t
>>> (eq? 'rational (car '(rational 2 3)))
#!t
```

However, this predicate doesn't work for lists. It's just not defined that way. For lists, we can define equality-checking predicate. Two lists are the same if they are structurally equivalent and have the same matching elements. Another way of saying this is:

lst-1 and lst-2 are equal
if either they are both empty
    or if they are both atoms and they are eq?

or (they are both lists and
their car's are equal and their cdr's are equal)

In LISP this is expressed as:

```
(define (equal-list? lst1 lst2)
   (if (and (null? lst1) (null? lst2))
       #!t
       (if (and (atom? lst1) (atom? lst2))
           (eq? lst1 lst2)
           (if (or (atom? lst1) (atom? lst2))
               (and (equal-list? (car lst1) (car lst2))
               (equal-list? (cdr lst1) (cdr lst2)))))))
```

LISP systems already have *equal?* which is more general than our version. This example is meant to show that based on *eq?*, *atom?*, and list processing functions *car*, *cdr*, and *null?*, we can define equality predicates for other types of objects.

Getting back to the representation of rational numbers, given two expressions representing rational numbers, how would you determine if they refer to the same number or not? We know that n1/d1 = n2/d2 when n1 * d2 = n2 * d1. So as long as we know how rational numbers are represented, and how to get the numerator part and the denominator part, we should be able to tell whether two representations are equal:

```
(define (rational= rat1 rat2)
  (= (* (numerator-of rat1) (denominator-of rat2))
     (* (numerator-of rat2) (denominator-of rat1))))

(define (numerator-of rat) (car (cdr rat)))
(define (denominator-of rat) (car (cdr (cdr rat))))
```

Note that when we change the representation, we only need to revise the functions *numerator-of* and *denominator-of*. Now that we know how to access numerator and denominator parts from the representations, we should be able to construct new representations from the components.

```
(define (make-rational numerator-part denominator-part)
   (list 'rational numerator-part denominator-part))
```

When we know how to interpret representations and construct them, we can define operations on rational numbers easily. The following is a direct translation of the equation:

$$\frac{n1}{d1} + \frac{n2}{d2} = \frac{(n1*d2 + n2*d1)}{(d1 * d2)}$$

```
(define (rational+ rat1 rat2)
  (make-rational
     (+ (* (numerator-of rat1) (denominator-of rat2))
        (* (numerator-of rat2) (denominator-of rat1)))
     (* (denominator-of rat1) (denominator-of rat2))))
```

*rational**, *rational—*, and *rational/* can also be defined easily.

A.10 Standard List Processing Functions

All the list processing functions can be built up from the functions *null?*, *car*, *cdr*, *cons* and *list*. But most implementations provide a lot more pre-defined ones for efficiency. Since they are frequently used, they are normally hand-coded to get high efficiency. In this section we are going to define some of the standard list processing functions ourselves. Writing the function definitions is a good way to really understand their meanings.

When you try these, you may want to use different names in order to avoid conflicts with intrinsic functions on your system.

(1) (length lst) returns the length of lst.

```
(define (length lst)
    (if (null? lst)
       0
       (+ 1 (length (cdr lst)))))
```

(2) (append lst1 lst2) returns the appended list.

```
(define (append lst1 lst2)
    (if (null? lst1)
       lst2
       (cons (car lst1) (append (cdr lst1) lst2))))
```

(3) (reverse lst) returns the reversed list.

```
(define (reverse lst)
  (if (null? lst)
       ()
       (append (reverse (cdr lst)) (list (car lst)))))
```

(4) (memq x lst) returns a sublist of *lst* starting with x if x is an atom and it is a member of lst. Otherwise, it returns ( ).

```
(define (memq x lst)
    (if (null? lst)
```

```
            ()
            (if (eq? x (car lst))
                lst
                (memq x (cdr lst)))))
```

(5) (member x lst) same as *memq* except that it checks equality with *equal?* instead of *eq?*.

(6) (assq x alist): when x is an atom and alist is a list of pairs, it returns the first pair whose car is eq to x.

```
(define (assq x alist)
    (if (null? alist)
        ()
        (if (eq? x (car (car alist)))
            (car alist)
            (assq x (cdr alist)))))
```

(7) (assoc x alist) Same as *assq* except it uses *equal?* instead of *eq?* for testing.

There is a salient pattern in these definitions. The functions try to find if a list has some property by first checking special conditions, i.e., if the list is null. If not, they check if the first element has that property; if so, they return desired value. Otherwise, they check the remaining list. In the case of functions trying to build lists with certain property, they check the special conditions, e.g., when one of the argument list is null. If it is not, the function combines the results of operating on the first element and the remaining list. For example, in the definition of *append*, it just puts back the first element of the first list to the result of appending the remaining list to the second list. These patterns reflect the patterns we see in the problems themselves. One of the ways to describe the problem of appending would be:

(append ( ) <list>) → <list>

(append <x> ∧ <rest> <lst>) → <x> ∧ (append <rest> <lst>)

where <x> ∧ <rest> means that the head of the argument is <x> and <rest> is the rest.

We can easily see that the definition corresponds nicely to the description of the problem itself. The following is the pattern for the function *reverse*.

(reverse ( )) → ( )

(reverse <x> ∧ <rest>) → (append (reverse <rest>) (<x>))

Getting the pattern of the problem right is the most crucial step for this kind of definition. For practice, we will define some more functions. Suppose we want to remove the first occurrence of an object from a list. How would we describe the pattern?

(remove <x> ( )) → ( )
(remove <x> <y> ∧ <rest>) → <rest> if <x> = <y>
→ <y> ∧ (remove <x> <rest>)
otherwise.

So the LISP definition would be:

```
(define (remove x lst)
    (if (null? lst)
        ()
        (if (eq? x (car lst))
            (cdr lst)
            (cons (car lst) (remove x (cdr lst))))))
```

Corresponding to the notation ∧, LISP has the so-called dotted pair notation. (x · <list>) means the list we get by applying the function *cons* to x and <list>: In LISP jargon, *consing* x to <list>. Note that '(1 · (2 3)) is equivalent to '(1 2 3). In fact '(1) is equivalent to '(1 · ( )). From now on we will use the dotted pair notation to describe the patterns.

What if we want to remove all the occurrences of x from *lst* if they are immediate members of *lst*? For example, (remove-all 1 '(1 2 1 3 (1))) would be (2 3 (1)). Note that the last occurrence of 1 is still there because it is not a direct member of the list. It is a member of a member of the list. The description of the problem would be:

(remove-all <x> ( )) → ( )
(remove-all <x> (<y> · <rest>))
→ (remove-all <x> <rest>) if <x> = <y>
→ (<y> · (remove-all <x> <rest>)) otherwise.

In LISP form,

```
(define (remove-all x lst)
    (if (null? lst)
        ()
        (if   (eq? x (car lst))
              (remove-all x (cdr lst))
              (cons (car lst) (remove-all x (cdr lst))))))
```

Here is another interesting example. Suppose we want to remove all the occurrences of x in the list whether or not they are immediate members. Let's call this function remove*. So (remove* 1 '(1 2 1 3 (1))) will be (2 3 ( )). Consider a case when the head of the list is a list. Then we will have to get (remove* x (car lst)) first and then cons it to (remove* x (cdr lst)). Actually that is the only difference.

(remove* <x> ( )) → ( )
(remove* <x> (<y> . <rest>))
 → (remove* <x> <rest>) if <x> = <y>
  ((remove* <x> <y>) . (remove* <x> <rest>))if <y> is a list
  (<y> . (remove* <x> <rest>)) otherwise.

In LISP form,

```
(define (remove* x lst)
    (if  (null? lst)
         ()
         (if (eq? x (car lst))
             (remove* x (cdr lst))
             (if (list? (car lst))
                 (cons (remove* x (car lst))
                       (remove* x (cdr lst)))
                 (cons (car lst) (remove* x (cdr lst)))))))
```

In the last definition, there are four levels of if-expressions. It may not be unreadable, but there should be a better way to express multiple condition checking. Fortunately, there is one. The following is a translation of *remove** using the *cond* special form.

```
(define (remove*  x lst)
    (cond
       ((null? lst) ())
       ((eq? x (car lst)) (remove* x (cdr lst)))
       ((list? (car lst)) (cons (remove* x (car lst))
                                 (remove* x (cdr lst))))
       (else (cons (car lst) (remove* x (cdr lst))))))
```

In a sense, this *cond* expression better captures the pattern we described above. The general form of *cond* is

(cond (<condition1> <exp1>) ... (else <exp-n>)),

which is equivalent to:

(if <condition1> <exp1> (if ... <exp-n>)...)

For more practice, let's try substitution functions. These are quite analogous to removal functions except that we substitute the new objects for the old ones instead of removing them. *(subst old new lst)* substitutes the first occurrence of <old> with <new> in the <lst>:

(subst <old> <new> ( )) ⇒ ( )
(subst <old> <new> (<y> · <rest>))
→ (<new> · <rest>) if <y> = <old>
→ (<y> · (subst <old> <new> <rest>)) otherwise

```
(define (subst old new lst)
      (cond
         ((null? lst) ( ))
         ((eq? old (car lst)) (cons new (cdr lst)))
         (else (cons (car lst) (subst old new (cdr lst))))))
```

Exercises:

(1) Define *subst-all,* which replaces all the immediate occurrences, and *subst**, which replaces all the occurrences. Hint: see the patterns we used for *remove-all* and *remove**.

(2) Define *(offset x lst)* which returns the position of *x* in *lst*. If *x* is not in *lst*, it returns 0. e.g.,

(offset 7 ( )) → 0
(offset 7 '(1 7 9)) → 2

(3) Define *(find-group x list-of-lists)* which returns a member list of the *list-of-lists* that has *x* as a member.

(find-group 'x ( )) → ( )
(find-group 'x '((1 y) ( ) (a x v))) → (a x v)

A.11 Boolean Formula Evaluation

In the previous section, we covered many list processing functions. So we should try some more interesting examples. Some of you may know Boolean logic. Even if you think you don't, you really know it. That is, as long as you know how to use the words *and*, *or* and *not*. We know that *(and <sentence-1> <sentence-2>)* is true if both sentences are true, and that *(or <sentence-1> <sentence-2>)* is true if one of the sentences is true, and that *(not <sentence>)* is true if <sentence> is false. Our problem is to determine truth value of complex sentences formed with *and*, *or*, and *not*, when truth values of basic sentences occurring in them are known. For basic sentences we use arbitrary symbols like "p", "q", "p2", and so on. For instance, we want to be able to tell that '(and (or p (not q)) r) is false when p is false, q is true, and r is true. We need to somehow represent the situations in which truth values of basic sentence symbols are specified, and then decide how to determine truth value of a given sentence. For now let's assume that there is a nice representational scheme for the situations, and we also know, given a sentence symbol and a situation, how to tell its truth value. That is, we have:

(value-of <basic-sentence> <situation>)
→ true if the sentence is true in the situation
→ false otherwise

Then we could describe the problem in the following way: (We call the function *boolean-eval*.)

(boolean-eval <basic-sentence> <situation>)
→ (value-of <basic-sentence> <situation>)

(boolean-eval '(not <sentence>) <situation>)
→ true if (boolean-eval <sentence> <situation>) = false
→ false otherwise

(boolean-eval '(and <sentence1> <sentence2>) <situation>)
→ true if (boolean-eval <sentence1> <situation>) = true
and (boolean-eval <sentence2> <situation>) = true
→ false otherwise

(boolean-eval '(or <sentence1> <sentence2>) <situation>)
→ true if (boolean-eval <sentence1> <situation>) = true
or (boolean-eval <sentence2> <situation>) = true
→ false otherwise

Translated into a LISP form:

```
(define (boolean-eval sentence situation)
    (cond
     ((basic-sentence? sentence)
      (value-of sentence situation))
     ((eq? (car sentence) 'not)
      (if (eq? 'true
              (boolean-eval (cadr sentence) situation))
```

```
            'false
            'true))
    ((eq? (car sentence) 'and)
     (and (eq? 'true
                (boolean-eval (cadr sentence) situation))
            (eq? 'true
                (boolean-eval (caddr sentence) situation))))
    ((eq? (car sentence) 'or)
      (or (eq? 'true
            (boolean-eval (cadr sentence) situation))
          (eq? 'true
              (boolean-eval (caddr sentence) situation))))
    (else (error "Unknown type of boolean sentence"))))
```

Here we have some new functions and a new type of object, i.e., strings. Since we use many combinations of car and cdr, LISP systems provide additional functions like *cadr, caddr, cdddr*, etc. You can expand them by inserting the appropriate number of c*r with parentheses. So (cadr lst) becomes (car (cdr lst)), (caddr lst) becomes (car (cdr (cdr lst))) and so on.

basic-sentence? is just a more meaningful name than *atom?* in our problem's context. We define it just as *(define basic-sentence? atom?).*

Remember that we have not decided on the particular representation of situations, therefore we can't define the function *value-of*, yet. Normally, we don't decide on the representation until we know what kind of things we want to do with the representation. In this case, all we want is to find out truth values of basic sentences, but for other purposes we may want to be able to change the situation easily. Another reason we just give a name to the access function and defer the decision until later is that this way we can change the representational scheme without having to modify the other parts of the program (i.e., other functions). At any rate, now we have to make up our mind on the representation. Since we need to be able to find associated values of basic sentence symbols, we might represent the situations as association lists, that is, list of pairs of sentence symbols and their matching values: e.g., ((p false) (q true) (r true)). Then we would define *value-of* as below:

```
(define (value-of sentence situation)
   (cadr (assq sentence situation)))
```

That's it. We just completed a little program to do some meaningful task. Test the following:

```
(boolean-eval '(or (and (not p) (or q r))
      (and (not r) (not q)))
      '((p true) (q true) (r false)))
```

```
(boolean-eval '(and (and (or r p)
        (or q r)) (not q))
        '((p true) (q false) (r false)))

(boolean-eval '(and (and (not p)
        (or q r)) (and (not r) (not q)))
        '((p false) (q true) (r true)))
```

A.12 Graph Search Problem

Here is another problem which has a lot of practical value that we can solve without too much difficulty. We would like to know whether we can find some node in a graph starting from any arbitrary node. A graph is a collection of nodes in which some nodes are connected. Often, arrows indicate connection in graphic representations as follows:

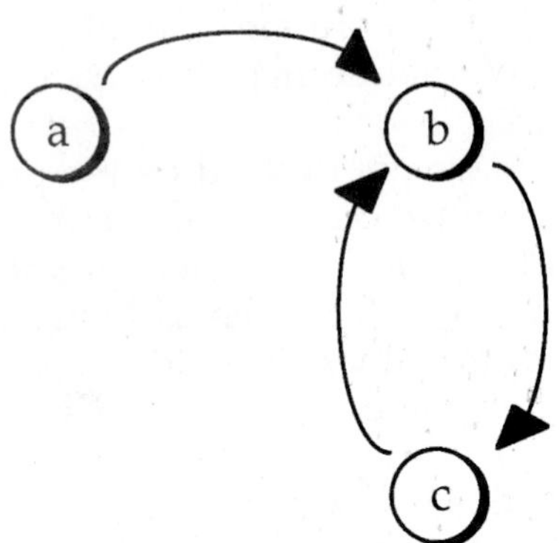

Note that while ***b*** is accessible from ***a, a*** is not necessarily accessible from ***b***. Given a pictorial representation, humans just follow arrows to find out whether some nodes are accessible from a particular node. In order to make the ordinary computer to do the job, we have to represent the graphs in some form and also express the idea of following the arrows in some form. There are many ways to represent graphs depending on our needs. What matters to us is that we should be able to find out what nodes are immediately accessible from a given node. So to make things easy, let's assume that we can find, given a node and a graph representation, the nodes which are immediately accessible, which we call neighbors. The function which does that job is *neighbors-of*.

The function we are trying to define, *graph-search*, takes a target node, a source node and a graph, and determines if the target node is accessible from the source node in the graph. One thing to keep in mind is that a blind search can fall into an infinite loop as below.

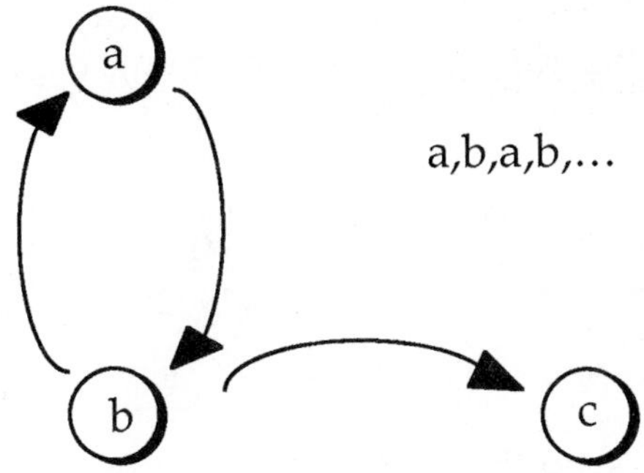

So we need to keep track of which nodes we have traveled through so far, and if there are more nodes to check. Let's define an auxiliary function which keeps track of them like the following. This function will go through the *remaining-nodes* to find a possible path to the *target* node. If we find the *target* node in the *remaining-nodes*, we stop. If *remaining-nodes* is null, that means we can't get to the *target*. So return *( )*. What happens if the node we check is not the target? Then we will add its neighbors to the *remaining-nodes* and add it to the *visited-nodes* list, and continue.

```
(define (search-aux target graph visited-nodes remaining-nodes)
   (if   (null? rem-nodes)
         ()
         (let ((next-node (get-next-node remaining-nodes)))
            (cond
              ((memq next-node visited-nodes)
               (search-aux target graph visited-nodes))
                    (cdr remaining-nodes)
              ((eq? target next-node) #!t)
              (else
                   (search-aux target
                         graph
                         (cons next-node visited-nodes)
                         (add-nodes
                               (neighbors-of next-node graph)
                               (cdr remaining-nodes))))))))
```

let is a new expression which introduces a temporary variable. When we need to refer to some object several times, we can use a temporary name for it. It's just like in ordinary mathematical locution as we can see from the following example: "Let x be a member of *A union B*; then either x is a member of *A* or x is a member of *B*." The syntax of *let* is:

(let ((<variable-1> <exp-1>) ...) <body of the let-expression>)

When we evaluate the <body of the let-expression>, the specified variables have the values of their matching expressions. For example,

```
(let ((x 2) (y 5)) (+ x y)) → 7
(let ((x 2) (y 5))
      (let ((x 3)) (+ x y))) → 8
(let ((x 2) (y 5))
      (let ((x y)) (+ x y))) → 10
```

For now, let's keep things as simple as possible. We define *get-next-node* as just *car*, and *add-nodes* as *append*:

```
(define get-next-node car)
(define add-nodes append)
```

Now we have to decide on the representation. For convenience's sake, let's assume that graphs are represented as a list of pairs of nodes and their neighbors. Then the definition of the function *neighbors-of* will be straightforward. For instance, the following graph will be represented as ((a (b c)) (b (a)) (c (d)) (d ( ))).

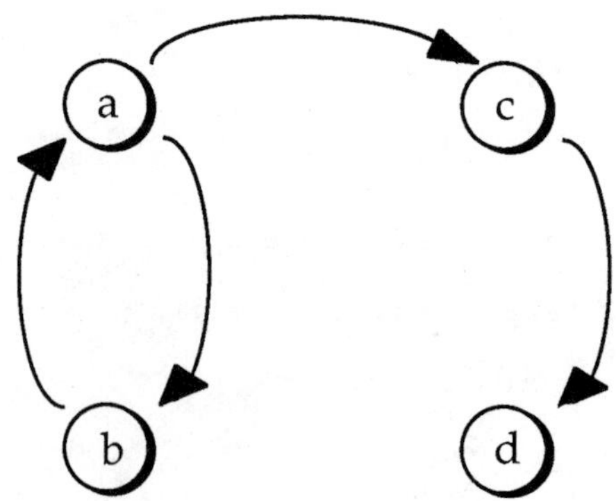

So the definition of *neighbors-of* will be:

```
(define (neighbors-of node graph)
   (cadr (assq node graph)))
```

With the following definition of graph-search, we should be able to test our program:

```
(define (graph-search target source graph)
      (search-aux target
            graph
            ( )
            (neighbors-of source graph)))
```

Exercises:

(1) What happens if we use the following definition of add-nodes instead of *append*? Try to find the order of nodes being compared.

```
(define (add-nodes new-neighbors old-neighbors)
   (append old-neighbors new-neighbors))
```

(2) Define (path-finder target source graph) which returns a path from the source to the target represented as a list of nodes travelled. While searching, we have to collect the nodes along the way. Modify the program to do that. It may not be as difficult as it looks.

(3) Define (find-paths target source graph) which returns all the paths from the source to the target.

A.13 Functions as Objects

Suppose we want to increment all the numbers in a list by 2. One way to define a function doing this, say add-2-to-all, is:

( ) → ( )

(<n> · <rest>) → (<n>+2 · (add-2-to-all <rest>))

```
(define (add-2-to-all lst)
   (if (null? lst)
       ()
       (cons (+ 2 (car lst)) (add-2-to-all (cdr lst)))))
```

What do we do if we need a function which multiplies the elements by 3? Certainly we could define a brand new function *multiply-all-by-3*:

```
(define (multiply-all-by-3 lst)
   (if (null? lst)
       ()
```

```
          (cons (* 3 (car lst))
          (multiply-all-by-3 (cdr lst)))))
```

The trouble is that these functions are not general enough, so whenever we need a function which applies some function to all the elements in a list, we will need another function definition. We are missing some important generalizations here. What we should be saying is something like this:

```
(if (null? lst)
       ()
       (cons (apply the-desired-function-to (car lst))
          (do-recursion-on-the-remaining-list...)))
```

Fortunately, we can have such a general function. In Scheme, functions are treated on equal footing as other objects. (From here on, we should say "Scheme" because Scheme is different from other LISP dialects in handling functional objects. Most of these examples are translatable into COMMON LISP or some other LISP dialects, though.) Thus we can make a list of functions, we can return functions as values of functions, we can pass functions as arguments for other functions, and so on. Try the following:

```
(define (apply-to-all function lst)
   (if (null? lst)
       ()
       (cons (function (car lst))
             (apply-to-all function (cdr lst)))))

(apply-to-all add1 '(1 2 3)) → (2 3 4)

(apply-to-all car '((1 2) (3 4) (5 6))) → (1 3 5)
```

add1 is a one-argument function adding 1 to its argument. We can use any function taking one argument. It would be inconvenient if we can only use named functions as in the examples. In fact we can use any function as long as it takes one argument. In Scheme, we don't have to define functions with specific names to pass them as arguments for other functions. Just like in English, we can refer to functions without giving specific names. Corresponding to the expression "the function which adds 3 to its argument," we have in Scheme "(lambda (n) (+ 3 n))." *lambda* is a special word indicating that the expression led by it refers to a function. Right after *lambda*, we specify the parameter list, and the body of the function follows. In the previous sections, we have defined a lot of functions in the form (define (<function-name> <parameter> ...) <function-body>). They could have been defined in the following form, too:

```
(define <function-name>
   (lambda (<parameter> ...)
        <function-body>)),
```

which means that <function-name> is a name referring to the function expressed as (lambda ...). Armed with this fancy word *lambda* and *apply-to-all*, we can call (apply-to-all (lambda (n) (+ 2 n)) '(1 2 3 4)) to get (3 4 5 6). Without having to come up with new names and bunch of definitions, we can achieve what we want. As an exercise, try this technique to *multiply-all-by-3*.

> Exercise: Define (prefix-to-all x list-of-lists) which *conses* x to all the elements in the list-of-lists. e.g.,
>
> ```
> (prefix-to-all 'rational '((2 3) (4 5) (6 7)))
>      → ((rational 2 3) (rational 4 5) (rational 6 7))
> ```

In Scheme, there is a pre-defined function called *mapcar* which has the same meaning as our *apply-to-all*. Here is another good exercise: Define *mapcar2* which takes a 2-place function and two lists, and returns the result of applying the function to the pairs of elements from the lists: e.g., `(mapcar2 + '(1 2 3) '(4 5 6)) → (5 7 9)`.

Now that we know how to pass functions as parameters, let's try to define a rather useful function. The summation symbol S is defined as:

$$\sum_{k=i}^{n} f(k) = \begin{cases} f(i) & \text{if } n = i \\ f(n) + \sum_{k=i}^{n-1} f(k) & \text{otherwise} \end{cases}$$

We can express this as:

```
(define (summation lower-bound upper-bound function)
   (if   (= lower-bound upper-bound)
         (function lower-bound)
         (+ (function lower-bound)
            (summation  lower-bound (- upper-bound 1)
                                    function))))
```

Try these examples:

```
(summation 1 10 (lambda (n) n))
(summation 1 20 (lambda (n) (* 2 n)))
```

We said in the above that we can return functions as values of functions. How do we do that? Maybe we should first ask ***why*** we do that. Given any arbitrary number, say n, we can construct a function which takes some number and adds n to it. We can define a function which does this sort of construction. For instance, taking any number, it will return a function of one argument that adds that number:

```
(define (make-inc-function n)
    (lambda (m) (+ n m)))
```

Given a number, say 7, `(make-inc-function 7)`, returns the function `(lambda (m) (+ 7 m))`.

> Exercise: When f and g are both 1-place functions, *f o g* (composition of f and g) refers to a function such that (f o g)(x) = f(g(x)). Define this o (name it 'comp'). Test:

```
((comp add1 sub1) 2),
((comp (lambda (n) (* 2 n))
  (lambda (m) (+ 7 n))) 3).
```

A.14 Assignments and Other Imperative Constructs

If you know some other programming language, say Pascal or C, you might be anxious to find out how to say "assign 7 to i" in LISP. Well, it's there. All you have to say is `(set! i 7)`. But before you start translating your favorite programs into LISP using *set!* all over, we should discuss problems of programming with assignments. Suppose you are having a heated discussion with your friend, and your friend uses some terms in many different ways. Then it will be difficult for you to refute his argument because it is a moving target. In order to talk sensibly, you have to always figure out how he is using some terms and in what sense. He seems to change the meanings of those terms arbitrarily. It may not be impossible to figure out how he uses his terms and how and when he changes them, but it would save time for both of you if he used them consistently. Using assignments is like that. You assign some value to a variable at some point of the program, say i := 7, so when I see an expression "i + 3", I assume it means 10. Wrong! Somewhere in the program, before we come across the expression, the value of "i" may have changed. Perhaps when you call some procedure, "i" is assigned another value in the body of the procedure. In most cases, this problem is due to bad design.

When we read and try to understand programs, it puts too much burden on us humans if we have to keep track of changes in the meaning of variables. If a variable has a unique meaning, certainly it will be easier to understand programs. Of course, we can have temporary variables like those introduced by "let". But they are like abbreviations, and we are used to that kind of temporary names. We know that once we get out of the context for those variables, i.e., the body of *let*, they are meaningless. So we can focus on a small segment of a program at a time.

Another point we should make is that, in order to write programs in imperative style, that is using assignments, intermediate variables, and so on, quite frequently we have to do an extra level of translation in order to express the functions (and algorithms) we need. That is, we must think about how the computer will do the job instead of describing what the computer should do. Try to redefine, using assignments, the functions we defined recursively without using any assignment in section A.6. You will have to worry about where to store intermediate values, what to return, and so on. The computer may have to work along a similar line, but program designers don't have to lower themselves to the level of computers. That's the compiler's job. Aren't compilers supposed to translate programs into lower level instructions? Good languages allow programmers to be able to express their ideas easily and clearly. If we see a recursive pattern in our problem, we should be able to express it as it is.

However, there are some legitimate uses for assignments. Suppose we need a program to model a system which changes in time. For example, a person's age changes over time. For such applications, use of assignments seems natural. We don't use assignments just to express algorithms because compilers will do that any way.

If we have assignments, we also need a construct to do them in some sequence. In Scheme, it's called *begin*. *begin* can be followed by any number of expressions.

```
>>> (begin (set! x 1) (set! x 0) x)
0
```

Note that (begin ...) is an expression whose meaning is that of its last expression, i.e., *x*.

Conventional programming languages provide iterative constructs such as *for*, *while*, and *repeat*. In Scheme, they can be defined as macros or provided as special forms. One notable construct in Scheme, *do*, is a rather general iterative construct. If we have an algorithm expressed iteratively, we might use this construct. For example, we might re-express the algorithm for Fibonacci sequence as:

```
(define (fib n)
   (if   (= n 0)
         0
```

```
(do ((i n (- n 1))
    (prevl 1 (+ prevl prev2))
    (prev2 0 prevl))
    ((= i 1) prevl))))
```

The general form of do-expression is:

(do ((<variable> <initial-value-exp> <update-exp>)
  ...)
    (<termination-condition> <ret-expression> ...)
  <body-exp> ...)

It is analogous to the Pascal construction:

```
begin
    <variable> := <initial-value-exp>; ... ;
    while not <termination-condition> do begin
        <body-exp>;
        ... ;
        <variable> := <update-exp>;
        ... ;
    end;
    <ret-expression>;
    ... ;
end
```

A.15 Macros and Language Extension

In Section A.4 we mentioned the *read-eval-print* loop. Like most things in life, things are not as simple as they look. Or there are a lot more things in life than it looks, to put it differently. This "read-eval-print" loop has one more service for you. When we type an expression, before it evaluates the expression, the system transforms the expression into another if there is any special word in it. These words which tell the system to transform the expression before evaluating it are called *macros*. Suppose we define "invert-minus" as a macro with the following transformation:

(invert-minus <n> <m>) ⇒ (– <m> <n>)

When the system sees an expression like (+ 4 (invert-minus 2 3)), it will first transform it into (+ 4 (– 3 2)), and then evaluate it, returning the result 5. When do we use macros? One of the main uses for macros is to extend the language with new special forms. Recall that in function applications, we evaluate the arguments first, and then apply the function to them. Now suppose we want to have a special form (unless <condition> <expression>) which is understood as "if the condition is not met, return the meaning of the <expression>, else return nil." Suppose we define "unless" as a function. Then we have to evaluate the arguments, i.e., <condition> and <expression>. And then if the meaning of <condition> is false, return the meaning of <expression>, else return nil. Well, it may sound OK, but what happens to the expression?

```
(unless (= n 0) (/ 1 n))
```

Suppose n happens to be 0. Then we will try to evaluate (= n 0), which is true, and (/ 1 n) will be tried. But (/ 1 0) will generate an error. The trouble is that (/ 1 n) was not supposed to be evaluated when (= n 0) is true. So, instead we define "unless" as a macro which will be transformed into (if (not <condition>) <expression> nil). The system knows that "if" is special, so it evaluates the condition part first and then decide which part of the if-expression it will evaluate.

We define macros by specifying the transforming function:

```
(macro unless
   (lambda (exp)
      (list 'if
        (list 'not (condition-part exp))
        (exp-part exp) 'nil)))
```

where *condition-part* and *exp-part* are defined as *cadr* and *caddr*, respectively.

The transformer function takes the whole expression whose car is the macro name, and returns a new expression to be evaluated. Note that we can write such macros because programs are represented as lists. Just as we can create new lists by transforming another list, we can transform one program into another.

A.16 Where to Go from Here

Learning a language is not just memorizing words and phrases. Without learning to think and look at things from a new perspective, we can't truly learn a new language. We should experiment with what we learned. Now that we have some basic knowledge of the language, we should try to tackle bigger problems. A short bibliography is provided here for further adventure. Have fun.

BIBLIOGRAPHY

1. Abelson, H. and G. J. Sussman with J. Sussman, *Structure and Interpretation of Computer Programs* , The MIT Press, Cambridge, MA (1985)

This is a must for any aspiring AI programmer. All the examples are in Scheme. This text teaches not only the Scheme language but also good practices of programming by working out extensive programming projects in detail.

2. Brooks, Rodney A., *Programming in COMMON LISP* , John Wiley and Sons, New York, NY (1985)

Nice little book if you have access to a COMMON LISP implementation and want to learn it.

3. Charniak, Eugene, Christopher K. Riesbeck, and Drew V. McDermott (1980) *Artificial Intelligence Programming,* Lawrence Erlbaum Associates, Hillsdale, NJ. See also Second Edition with James R. Meehan (1987)

Rich sources of good artificial intelligence programming projects.

4. Dybvig, Kent, *The Scheme Programming Language* , Prentice-Hall, Inc., Englewood Cliffs, NJ (1987)

Highly recommended to any serious Scheme programmer. Good examples using more advanced features of the language such as continuations and engines.

5. Friedman, Daniel P. and Matthias Felleisen, *The Little Lisper, 2nd Edition,* Science Research Associates, Chicago, IL (1986)

This is one of the most enjoyable little book on programming. If you enjoyed reading this article, you will be delighted with this book.

6. Steele, Guy L., Jr., *COMMON LISP: The Language,* Digital Press, Burlington, MA (1984)

This is a reference manual, not a tutorial. Good to have a copy around if you are interested in COMMON LISP.

§ Yong Y. Auh is Research Scientist at UNICO, Inc. of Franksville, WI. He holds an M.A. in Linguistics from Indiana University and is a candidate for the Ph.D. in Philosophy and Computer Science from Indiana University. His research is in the area of the foundations of AI.

Appendix B:

SUMMARY OF COMMERCIAL AI SYSTEMS

B.1 INTRODUCTION

The computer and information science industries are very responsive to harnessing new technology to perceived needs. A number of new companies have sprung up in the last several years to commercialize AI products born in the universities and research institutes. There are now too many companies to present an exhaustive list here, but the companies and products described in this chapter should give the reader a sketch-map of the industry. Other authors present a more detailed summary of commercial vendors.[1]

The reader is cautioned that the information in this appendix is at best a snapshot of a portion of the AI industry at one point in time (approximately mid-1986). The computer industry in general and the AI segment in particular is dynamic and volatile. It is highly probable that a number of the companies listed below will have vanished in the mists of failed dreams, acquisitions, and Chapter 11 proceedings by now. However, if AI is ever to benefit humankind, the first signals of its success will appear as achievements in the marketplace. The commercialization of AI is well underway, particularly in the area of expert sytems, and this appendix will indicate the nature and details of several typical products.

Another caution to the reader is that author has collected and filtered much of the data below from a variety of sources. While objectivity in the analysis was our goal, we admit to the likelihood of error and subjective judgements. In an attempt to achieve accuracy of the data, all of the companies manufacturing expert system shells listed below were contacted, shown the manuscript and asked for corrections and reactions to the analysis. A number of errors in factual data were

1 William B. Gevarter, *Intelligent Machines*, Prentice-Hall, Inc., Englewood Cliffs, NJ (1985)

corrected in the process. We appreciate the fine cooperation of the expert system industry in this effort.

In additions to the above qualifications, we should note that it is very easy to predict precisely what features of the data below will have been outdated by now. These predictions are based on close observation of the AI industry over the past several years. In particular, with regard to the data on expert system shells:

- The capabilities of the systems will have been expanded.
- The price of the systems will, in many cases, have fallen.
- The range of machines on which the system are delivered will have grown to include most "super-microcomputers."
- The languages in which the systems are written will have shifted from LISP to other high-level languages, particularly C.

With these qualifications in mind, we present the following information in the order presented in the text.

B.2 NATURAL LANGUAGE PROCESSING SYSTEMS

Artificial Intelligence Corporation
Waltham, MA

This company markets a program called *INTELLECT* for mainframe computers. INTELLECT is written in PL-1 and serves as the natural language front-end for large database systems. The company has tried to keep the package standard, rather than customizing it for each customer. The only custom feature is in the dictionary definitions. It takes about two weeks to produce a program for a particular data base application. There are now several hundred programs in the field.

Cognitive Systems, Inc.
New Haven, CT

This company was founded by Roger Schank to provide the opportunity to implement the ideas his group at Yale had developed in the laboratory. The product goes under the general name PEARL and it incorporates many of the features from SAM to CYRUS. It provides a customized natural language front-end to large data bases or applications programs. One of their products is called EXPLORER and can manipulate and answer questions on a data base containing over one million oil wells, each with 175 fields of information. This information includes geological information on depth of certain geological features. The user might request, for example:

> ***Please give me an isopach map from the smackover to the**
> ***eagleford in Hemphill County, Texas with a contour interval**
> ***of 100 feet and a scle of 1" = 2000'.**

to which the system would reply:

> **By SCLE, do you mean SCALE (Y or N)? y**

and then proceed to produce the requested contour map.

Symantec, Inc.
Sunnyvale, CA

This company is marketing a NLP system, *Q & A,* which serves as a front end for data base management systems on microcomputers. If you want to know how many of your customers live in Moscow, Indiana, you simply query the system by "How many of my customers live in Moscow, Indiana?". Q & A is written in Pascal and is designed to be very portable, compact, and efficient. It is designed to be customized by the user.

Excalibur Technologies Corp.
Albuquerque, NM

This company markets a program called *SAVVY* which serves as a system interface for microcomputers. The algorithm used is template matching rather than linguistic, and it is designed to be user customized.

Microrim, Inc.
Bellvue, WA

This company sells a natural language interface to the R:Base data base management system. It uses the transition network approach and some 500 rules to parse input commands. It is capable of handling multi-relation queries and runs on microcomputers.

Texas Instruments Inc.
Austin, TX

TI sells a number of NLP and other AI software which run on a variety of machines. One interesting NLP product is *NLMENU*, a menu oriented data-base/query system in which all possible sentences of the language are generated by menu selection. NLMENU provides the full expressive power available for a given data-base but avoids the ambiguity arising when a query fails. The program also bypasses the requirement for perfectly typed queries imposed by most systems by using a mouse-driven menu selection to generate input queries.

B.3 SPEECH RECOGNITION SYSTEMS

A number of interesting commercial speech recognition systems have appeared on the market. While the marketplace is dynamic and there are no assurances that such products will last, the following four products illustrate the range of capability presently available.

LIS'NER 1000

This is a speaker dependent, unconnected speech system which consists of a hardware card, microphone, and software package for Apple II and Commodore 64 microcomputers. It uses template matching to recognize any word in a 64 word vocabulary. It can also generate speech using either linear predictive coding (LPC) or phoneme synthesizer. The LIS'NER 100 technical specifications include:

- Speaker dependent, unconnected word recognition accuracy of 95-98%
- Recognition time for 8 words: 0.2 seconds
- Recognition time for 64 words: 1.0 second
- Vocabulary: unlimited in groups of 64 words
- Capacity: Hundreds of vocabularies callable from disk
- Operation: transparent, parallel voice entry device
- Ultra lightweight headset-style electret microphone
- One-watt on-board amplifier with volume control.
- Price: under $200
- Distributor:

  A.P.P.L.E.
  21246 68th Avenue S.
  Kent, WA 98032

IntroVoice III

This is an "intelligent voice/keyboard" configuration compatible with the IBM-PC or IBM-XT series of microcomputers. It is a speaker dependent system designed primarily for use as a voice controller for standard software packages such as WordStar® and Lotus 1-2-3®. The technical specifications for IntroVoice III include:

- Discrete word, speaker dependent accuracy of > 98%
- Discrete phrase length ≤ 1.25 seconds
- Vocabulary: up to 160 word/phrases per vocabulary
- Operation: transparent, parallel voice entry device
- Minimum pause between words: 160 ms.
- Response time: 50 + N (ms) where N = active vocabulary size
- Distributor:

  The Voice Connection
  17835 Skypark Circle, Suite C
  Irvine, CA 92714

VoiceScribe 1000

Dragon Systems, Inc. and Cherry Electrical Products Corporation have worked together to produce a low-cost card for Intel 80286 and 80386-based machines. The VoiceScribe 1000 was designed as a speech recognition development tool for personal computers, and the Xerox Corporation has recently placed a mass order. Features of the VoiceScribe 100 include:

- Speaker-independent and speaker-dependent word lists
- 1000 word vocabulary
- Near real-time operation on 80286 and 80386 machines
- Hard disk systems allow multiple vocabularies for different personnel and varied tasks
- Price: $1,195
- Manufacturer:

  Cherry Electrical Products Corporation
  3600 Sunsett Avenue
  Waukegan, IL 60087
  Phone: 312-360-3500

KVS 3000

The Kurzweil Voice System 3000 is a sophisticated automatic speech recognition system which operates in either a speaker dependent or speaker independent mode. It contains on-board storage of 3000 tokens which gives it a vocabulary of 1000 words/phrases. It has the attractive feature of being speaker adaptive which means its performance improves through use. The KVS 3000 may be used in one of two modes:

- Transparent integration in which it pretends to be a workstation keyboard

- RS-232 Connection to host computer

Other technical specifications include:

- Recognition accuracy: 100% on selected vocabularies
- Response time ≤ 250 ms
- Language independent: can be trained to recognize any language
- Expandable: vocabulary size can be increased in 3000 token blocks
- Manufacturer:
  Kurzweil Applied Intelligence, Inc.
  411 Waverly Oaks Road
  Waltham, MA 02154-8465

The next product in the Kurzweil voice recognition line is the Kurzweil Voicewriter which resembles the KVS 3000 but has a vocabulary of 10,000 words.

B.4 SUMMARY OF EXPERT SYSTEM BUILDING SHELLS

To supplement the general discussion presented in Chapter 13, we present additional technical details and analyses of a cross-section of expert system shells in Table B-I.

The table is arranged in a facing-page format so that all sixteen systems appear on each pair of pages.

Table B-I (a)

Name	Vendor	KR Scheme	Environment	Editor
ART™ Automated Reasoning Tool	Inference Corporation 5300 West Century Blvd Los Angeles, CA 90045 (213-417-7997)	Hybrid "toolkit" with frames, goals & production rules	Windows, with automated reasoning, real-time capability	Excellent - Graphics icon editor
KEE™ Knowledge Engineering Environment	IntelliCorp 1975 El Camino Real West Mountain View, CA 94040 (415-965-5500)	Object-oriented-frames w/multiple inheritance, production rules	Comprehensive, interactive,integrated graphical.	Strong for rules, representation, and interface
KES II Knowledge Engineering System II	Software Arch.&Eng.,Inc. 1600 Wilson Blvd. Arlington, VA 22209 (703-276-7910)	Production rules, Baysian hypothesize & test	Uses multiple-choice user interface	Line-oriented
Knowledge Craft™	Carnegie Group Inc 650 Commerce Court Pittsburgh, PA 15219 (412-642-6900)	Frame-based with inheritance & procedural attachment Integrated prod syst	Integrated command interpreter with graphics windows, alternate solution sys	Knowledge-base, frame & rule editors,OPS & Prolog workbn
S.1	Teknowledge, Inc. 1850 Embarcadero Road Palo Alto, CA 94303 (415-424-0400)	Rule-based, frame-based, procedure oriented i	Runs under UNIX, windows compiled C environment, can link in C routines	Knowledge-base editor
DUCK	Smart Systems Technology 7700 Leesburg Pike Falls Church, VA 22043 (703-893-0429)	Logic programming in a LISP environment	Time dependent, non-monotonic reasoning	Varies among LISP environments
LOOPS	Xerox AI Systems 250 N.Halstead St, Box7018 Pasadena, CA 91109 (800-228-5325)	Rule, access, object & procedure oriented programming	Graphics oriented, mouse driven, with useful gauges	Excellent, graphics oriented
OPS5 (and OPS83)	ArtellIgence, Inc. 14902 Preston Rd, Suite 212 Dallas, TX 75240 (214-437-0361)	Rule-based, OPS83 adds imperative programming	Mouse, windows & graphics on all machines	Varies among several dialects

Table B-I (b)

Name	Vendor	KR Scheme	Environment	Editor
M.1	Teknowledge, Inc. 1850 Embarcadero Road Palo Alto, CA 94303 (415-424-0400)	Production Rule system	Compiled C environment, can link to C routines	May use regular word processor
Personal Consultant™ Series	Texas Instruments Box 809063,Dept.DEE02 Dallas, TX 75380-9063 (800-527-3500)	Production Rule with frames, meta-rules and mapping	English-like Abbreviated Rule Language, external program interface	Pop-up menus with integrated graphics
Super-Expert	Softsync, Inc. 162 Madison Avenue New York, NY 10016 (212-685-2080)	Infers decision tree rules from examples with support for hierarchic structure	Spreadsheet format, 255 examples each with 31 decisions	Standard spreadsheet, read ahead
ESP Advisor	Expert Systems International 1700 Walnut Street Philadelphia, PA 19103 (215-735-8510)	Logic-based, KRL (Knowledge Representation Language)	Advice-giving shell in Prolog, can link to Prolog programs	Menu-driven screen, "text animation"
EXSYS	EXSYS, Inc. P. O. Box 75158, Sta.14 Albuquerque, NM 87194 (505-836-6676)	IF-THEN-ELSE Production Rules, math capabilities	Color graphics rule editor	Menu-driven full-screen text editor
TIMM	General Research Corp. 7655 Old Spring House Rd. McLean, VA 22102 (703-893-5900)	Frame-like, multi-dimen. state space; rules inferred from user examples	Inference engine uses similarity match ing, generalizes new rules, checks complet	Query-based dialog to build rules, system checks consist.
GURU	Micro Data Base Systems,Inc. P. O. Box 248 Lafayette, IN 47902 (1-800-323-3629)	Production rules with natural language interface	Integrated AI system, Data-base,word proc spreadsheet,graphics	Windows oriented NL interface
ExTran	ITL-KnowledgeLink 36 George House Glasgow G12AD, UK (44-41-552-1353)	Hierarchies of decision -tree rules	Links to Fortran and C-based DBMS and graphics	Built-in interactive editor

Table B-I (c)

Name	Explanation	Probability	Language	Machines	Graphics
ART	Excellent - Graphics browser	User-defined certainty factors	LISP C	Symbolics, Sun, VAX Lisp Machine, IBM-PC/RT, TI Explorer	Excellent - Includes animation
KEE	Excellent - Graphical and highly interactive	User-defined certainty factors	LISP	Xerox,Lambda, Sun Symbolics, IBM-RT TI Explorer, VAX,HP	Excellent - Object & icon oriented
KES II	Explanation, help justify, and "Why"	Certainty factors, symbolic probability	LISP → C	Cyber 180,Xerox VAX, Apollo, Sun, IBM-PC	Windows & Menus or dialog
Knowledge Craft™	Graphics-oriented trace facility	—	Common LISP CRL+/OPS5/ Prolog	VAX, TI Explorer, Symbolics, Sun, HP 9320, Apollo	Excellent - Window oriented
S.1	English text help and explanation	Certainty factors	LISP LISP → C C → Ada	AT&T, microVAX, Sun, Apollo,VAX, Xerox, Symbolics IBM-maniframes	Menu and mouse driven
DUCK	First-order, predicate calculus	Must program	NISP, Franz LISP, Common LISP	Lambda,VAX, TI Explorer, Xerox, Apollo, Symbolics	Through LISP Environment
LOOPS	Not evident, since this is not an ES shell	Not evident, since this is a research tool	Interlisp-D	Xerox 1100 series	Original Xerox Star inspired windows
OPS5	Must program - more a language than a shell	Must program	C and ExperLISP	Macintosh, Apollo IBM-PC,VAX, microVAX, Xerox	Uses mouse, windows, and menu

Table B-I (d)

Name	Explanation	Probability	Language	Machines	Graphics
M.1	Improved, custom text (How and Why)	Certainty factors (–100 — 100)	Prolog → C	IBM-PC	Windows for tracing and debugging
Personal Consultant Series	Yes, uses "How", "Why" and Review	Certainty factors	PC Scheme	TI Business-Pro, IBM-PC/AT	Incorporates captured pictures
Super-Expert	Help available, shows logic tables used	Not indicated	Forth for PC version, Pascal for Mac version	IBM-PC, Macintosh	Spread sheet screens
ESP Advisor	User interacts through scripts plus Help	Must program in Prolog	Prolog-2 (Knowledge base in KRL)	IBM-PC,/XT,/AT Data General/One VAX, MicroVAX II	LCD Screen or good use of color graphics
EXSYS	User-controlled runtime report generator	Several types, including threshold	C (Can link to data programs)	IBM-PC, VAX NEC 9801 Macintosh (soon)	Color-coded text (no real graphics)
TIMM	Identifies all rules used in consultation	Certainty values reliability (0 - 100)	FORTRAN	IBM-PC, Prime, VAX 11/780, Zenith, IBM Mainframes	Menu-driven text screen only
GURU	Recites notes on rules upon Why or How request	Variety of Certainty factors	C	IBM-PC, VAX 11/780, IBM Mainframes	Menu-driven windows
ExTran	Responds to Why and How queries	Certainty factor when used with CX module	Fortran	IBM MVS/TSO Vas VMS and Ultrix Unix workstations IBM PC	Interface to Sun Tools windowing

Table B-I (e)

Name	Hand-Craft	Delivery	User Sophistication	Price
ART	Very flexible tool-kit for customizing	See Machines	Powerful system integrating frames, rules, and goals. Development tool requires experienced AI programmers	$65K, Copy 1 + Volume discount
KEE	Flexible environment	Uses VAX host with IBM-PC,	A flexible and powerful environment to assist experienced programmers in constructing expert systems.	$65K ($2K)
KES II	May be embedded in other program	See Machines	Knowledge engineer may select one of three KR schemes for building user-friendly expert system.	$25K (Main) $7K (68000) $4K(micro)
Knowledge Craft™	Yes, with OPS5 & Prolog integration	—	Offers experienced programmers a choice of control strategies and knowledge representation techniques	$26K–$50K
S.1	Through links to UNIX sys. languages	See Machines, also, delivery on IBM-PC/AT	Shell for computer professionals to develop and deliver efficient expert systems for diagnosis, design,& planning.	$25K - $80K $3K on IBM-AT (delivery)
DUCK	Through LISP environment	See Machines	Experienced AI programmers have four modes: logic, rule-based, non-monotoic reasoning, and deduction.	$6K ($1,200)
LOOPS	Very flexible tool	Xerox 1185 is a $10K machine	Powerful knowledge engineering language to assist experienced AI programmers in developing systems.	Available for $300 on Xerox 1100s
OPS5	General KR and control structure	Already is on lower end.	Widely used knowledge engineering providing experienced programmers a good environment for building ES.	$325 - $15K

Table B-I (f)

Name	Hand-Craft	Delivery	User Sophistication	Price
M.1	Restricted, rule-based tool	Run-time version	Knowledge-based rules written in English-like language help less experienced programmers write ES.	\$5,000
Personal Consultant Series	Can link to external programs	Run-time copy for \$95, or \$995 for Pkg of 20	Less experienced programmers can use this EMYCIN-like shell for writing ES of up to 2000 rules.	\$2,950 =PC-Plus, \$495 for PC-EASY
Super-Expert	Rigid spread-sheet format	Is own delivery system	Domain experts and less experienced AI programmers may enter examples from which system infers rules	\$200
ESP Advisor	Very good through Prolog Link	Consultation shell+ compiled knowledge base	Power and flexibility of KRL,requires some programming experience, easy for small-scale systems.	\$895 = PC \$2950=μVAX \$4800 = VAX
EXSYS	Fairly rigid rule format	\$600 1-time run-time license	Very easy-to-use with excellent tutorials, user interface and 5000 rule capacity	IBM-PC=\$395 VAX = \$1500 (\$10,000)
TIMM	Fairly rigid example format	EXONLY = run-time module	Easy-to-use shell with good dialog to guide domain experts in linking system into decision networks (embeddable).	TIMM-PC = \$1,900, TIMM = \$19K
GURU	System development tool	Run-time version for \$300	Powerful ES shell integrated with database, word processing, etc. Complexity requires experts only	\$2,995
ExTran	Standard rule format	Run-time "Driver"	Good development and operation environment, but requires knowledge engineer to program.	PC = \$3K work st=\$7.5K minis= \$27K mains = \$44K

Table B-I (g)

Name	References
ART	*AI Magazine*, Spring, 1986, p. 14–15 Harmon & King, *Expert Systems*, p. 132 Waterman, *Guide to Expert Systems*, p. 357 *Expert Systems* **2**,Oct.85,p. 244
KEE	*Expert Systems* **2**,Oct.85,p. 245 Waterman, *Guide to Expert Systems*, p. 348 Harmon & King, *Expert Systems*, p. 133
KES II	*Expert Systems* **2**,Oct.85,p. 247 Harmon & King, *Expert Systems*, p. 131 Waterman, *Guide to Expert Systems*, p. 360
Knowledge Craft™	*Artificial Intelligence Report* **2**, p. 3–11 *Expert Systems* **2**, July, 85, p. 173 *AI Magazine*, Spring, 1986, p. 115
S.1	*Expert Systems* **2**, Oct, 85, p. 243 *Artificial Intelligence Report* **2**, p. 3–11 Harmon & King, *Expert Systems*, p. 132
DUCK	*Expert Systems* **2**, July, 85, p. 173 *Artificial Intelligence Report* **2**, p. 6-7 Waterman, *Guide to Expert Systems*, p. 351
LOOPS	Harmon & King, *Expert Systems*, p. 131 Expert Systems 2, Oct, 85, p. 252 Waterman, Guide to Expert Systems, p. 353
OPS5	*Expert Systems* **2**, Oct, 85, p. 247 Waterman, *Guide to Expert Systems*, p. 362 Hayes-Roth et al, *Building E.S.*, p. 183–186

Table B-I (h)

Name	References
M.1	*Expert Systems* **2**, Oct, 85, p. 243 Harmon & King, *Expert Systems*, p. 131 *PC Magazine*, April 16, 1985, p. 145
Personal Consultant Series	*Expert Systems* **2**, Oct, 85, p. 246 Waterman, *Guide to Expert Systems*,p. 363 Harmon & King, *Expert Systems*, p. 130
Super-Expert	*PC Magazine*, April 16, 1985, p. 119 Harmon & King, *Expert Systems*, p. 129 Waterman, *Guide to Expert Systems*,p. 109 (Reviews of its predecessor, Expert-Ease)
ESP Advisor	*Expert Systems* **2**, July, 85, p. 174 *Expert Systems* **2**, Oct, 85, p. 192 *PC Magazine*, April 16, 1985, p. 131
EXSYS	*Expertise* **1**, The ES Journal, January 86, *Expert Systems* **2**, Oct, 85, p. 192,246 *PC Magazine*, April 16, 1985, p. 113
TIMM	*PC Magazine*, April 16, 1985, p. 113 Harmon & King, *Expert Systems*, p. 119 Waterman, *Guide to Expert Systems*,p. 108
GURU	*PC Magazine*, May 27, 1986, p. 151 *PC Magazine*, April 16, 1985, p. 119 *BYTE*, pp.281-285, August, 1986 *PC-WEEK*, March 18, 25, April 1,8 (1986)
ExTran	D. Asgari and K. L. Modesitt, *Proceedings IEEE*, pp. 65–71 (1986)

fini

INDEX

NUMERIC

A

B

C

D

G

H

I

J

K

L

M

N

O

Q

R

S

T

U

V

W

X

Z